HAUNTED SKIES

Preserving the Social History of UFO Research

HAUNTED SKIES VOLUME 1 Revised 1939-1959

First paperback edition printed 2016 in the United Kingdom.

A catalogue record for this book is available from the British Library.

ISBN 978-0-9956428-0-5

Published by

Haunted Skies Publishing

For more copies of this book, please email: johndawn1@sky.com

Telephone: 0121 445 0340

Designed and typeset by Bob Tibbitts ~ (iSET)

Printed in Great Britain

FOREWORD

By TIMOTHY GOOD (2010)

IN this volume, the first of others relating to sightings of unidentified flying objects reported in the United Kingdom from 1940 to the present day, John Hanson and Dawn Holloway have uncovered much new supportive evidence for the reality of this still largely ridiculed phenomenon. Not content with accepting many published reports at face value, the authors have travelled the length and breadth of the country, tracking down the original witnesses – and sometimes discovering new ones in the process.

A significant number of the reports presented here come from qualified observers such as Royal Air Force and police officers. A UFO report uncorroborated by physical evidence (for example, photos and radar) is only as good as the witnesses' testimony. From my limited involvement in their exhaustive research I know just how conscientiously John and Dawn have double-checked the

reported facts, expending a great deal of time and trouble in what has amounted to **over a decade-long project. *Haunted Skies* is an important addition to the literature and a fascinating read for the layman and researcher alike.

*Timothy Good is internationally regarded as one of the most respected researchers in the field of UFO research, and is a best-selling author of many books on the subject, including *Alien Base, Beyond Top Secret* and *Unearthly Disclosure.*

**Authors – now 15 years!

INTRODUCTION

JOHN Hanson and Dawn Holloway, consultants for the famous *Flying Saucer Review* welcome the reader to the new and revised edition (in colour) of *Haunted Skies*, Volume 1.

We do hope you like the changes. If you have any comment or would like to contribute sightings you may have experienced yourself, we can be contacted on email: johndawn1@sky.com or telephone 0121-445-0340.

Daily Mail Journalist – Michael Hellicar

"We are not alone"

"As a freelance journalist, I've investigated UFO sightings in France, the U.S. (Roswell), Brazil, Suffolk, Devon and Somerset. I've interviewed police and military officers – cool, trained observers, not given to hysteria – who have seen things in the sky and, in some cases, descending from nowhere to land on solid ground, and been impressed by their eye-witness accounts.

Anyone who reads John and Dawn's compelling research into UFO sightings, impartially, unsensationally and straightforwardly reported, will be convinced (as I became, a long time ago) that 'we are not alone'. Their *Haunted Skies* books will have you looking up into the skies for a long time to come.

There have been too many authoritative sightings of UFOs for the whole subject to be dismissed as a flight of fancy, so to speak, by cranks and obsessions about the subject. It is an unfortunate fact that ufology has been given a bad name by a few crackpots. But the evidence turned up by John and Dawn confirm that out there are many, many sane, sensible people, who have witnessed sightings that cannot reasonably be shrugged off as clouds or weather balloons or – a particular favourite by the naysayers – aircraft refuelling in flight."

MYSTERIES

MYSTERIES have always captured the attention of the public over the years, whether it is sightings of the Loch Ness monster, 'flying saucers', or ghostly apparitions. Despite huge changes in science and technology, in an age dominated by the Internet and its worldwide communications, when UFOs, witchcraft, demons, vampires and all manner of other urban myths should now only exist as childhood fantasies or the product of some virtual reality game, it seems incomprehensible to accept that periodically, our skies continue to be the focus of inexplicable phenomena.

Sightings can be traced back many years

Sightings of inexplicable objects can be traced back hundreds of years.

We are all familiar with those images of 'flying saucers' depicted in the old black and white science fiction films of the 1950s, showing man's struggle to vanquish the invading spaceships and their grotesque occupants. Such scenarios illustrating the eternal struggle between man and his alien counterpart now form the foundation of a science fiction culture, which has matured from those grainy, flickering, celluloid images of yesteryear, to Hollywood blockbusters, incorporating the latest in computer graphics.

Ironically, the alien spaceships – now immortalised in many of these fictionalised accounts, along with their occupants – may have far more in common with the real phenomena than one could ever imagine. It is chilling to imagine that these objects which have plagued mankind were, in our opinion, here long before Man made his presence known on this planet!

How did it all begin?

Following reports of a massive saucer-shaped object, seen hovering over a Birmingham suburb in January 1995, by two police officers – one of whom was my (John) son Christopher, and members of the public, we felt unwilling to accept the suggestions made later, in a local newspaper, that this was evidence of any shooting star, particularly after having spoken to the officers concerned. Our curiosity now well and truly aroused, we decided to contact the Birmingham UFO Society, run by Robert and Marilyn Aldworth, anticipating that they would be able to offer us a rational explanation – after all there was no such thing as UFOs or 'flying saucers' were there?

Marlyin and Robert Aldworth

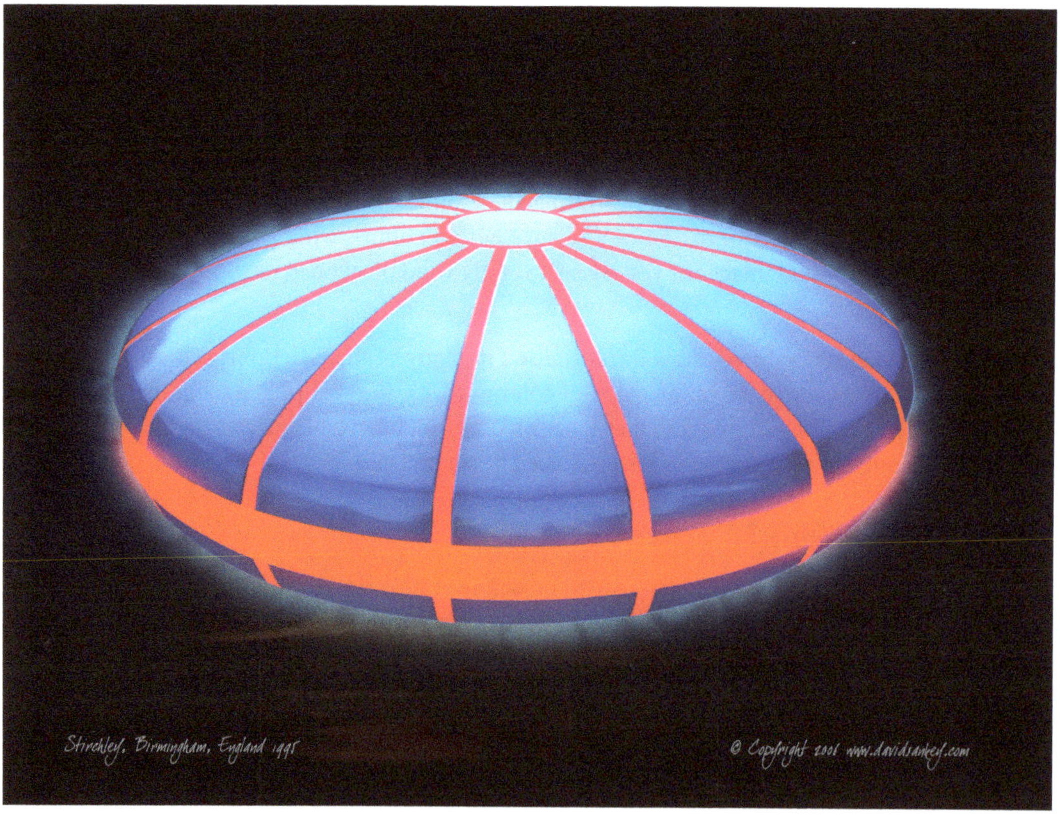

Plastic alien photographed in Area 51

After expressing our interest in finding out further information on UFOs, they gave us all the details concerning the incident. The couple then invited me (John) to a UFO lecture being given at Birmingham University by a speaker who showed slides of Area 51, which included 'photos of alien beings.' When a member of the audience had the temerity to stand up and challenge them on the authenticity of the photos, the lecturer reluctantly admitted to "having made them of plastic and rubber to illustrate what he believed the aliens to look like".

We vowed never to be involved in anything like this ourselves. We decided to conduct our own research into the enigmatic subject, wondering if there was any real substance to many of the bizarre sightings that had attracted newspaper attention over the years. Often accompanying the articles were garish drawings, depicting the sinister presence of 'flying saucers' hovering over towns and cities and projecting beams of destruction downwards onto the hapless populace.

Would we find little evidence of anything?

Would we find little evidence of any real phenomena, or would our research suggest the opposite – that there was more than ample evidence indicating that UFOs (and their occupants) were worthy of further investigation – and should we ignore the glamour and sensationalism attached to the subject? Bear in mind, that even at this stage of our research, we had accepted, without any reservation, the statistics offered by various UFO organisations, and the MOD (who were adamant that 99% of UFO sightings could be explained away).

Tracing the researchers and the witnesses

We then set ourselves the task of tracing many retired UFO investigators, who had been actively involved with researching and documenting UFO activity during the mid-to-late 20th Century. We wanted to obtain accurate accounts of many fascinating incidents, involving a wealth of not only rich UFO imagery but occasionally, the sightings of what appeared to be the occupants. They are the real heroes of this book; without them we would have nothing to publish. Sadly, at the time of revising this book, a number have also passed away.

Although many of the UFO witnesses themselves were now elderly, their memories generally remained undimmed by the passage of time. It was always a pleasure and privilege to share their personal experiences, many of which were often found to have been sensationalised out of all contexts by the media.

Understandably this proved to be a costly, time-consuming exercise. We were not always successful. Time had taken its toll, not only on the witnesses themselves but on material collected by a veritable army of UFO enthusiasts. Unfortunately, on a number of occasions following their demise, important documents pertaining to those investigations had been burnt or thrown away. However, thanks to the assistance of many others, we were able to accumulate a number of personal letters, documents, photographs and UFO memorabilia, collected over decades, relating to now long-forgotten UFO events. Hopefully they are brought back to life in the pages of our books, cataloguing the presence of something inexplicable occasionally seen in our skies, in order to advance our understanding that Planet Earth appears not to be the exclusive domain of human beings.

Generally still the butt of humour by the media

We felt – despite the current demise of UFO books dictated by concerned publishers, who believe investing in new UFO books would yield little return – that the general public still remained intensely interested in UFO events, as can be seen by the sporadic bursts of interest still taking place in the first decade of the 21st Century. Sadly, while outstanding UFO sightings continue to be brought to the public's attention, they continue to be the butt of humour and ridicule by the tabloid newspapers.

Unique series of books written with a passion!

We hope the reader will judge us on the content and the amount of hard work required, involving thousands of hours and also pounds, compiling what we believe to be a unique series of books, based literally on the examination of a colossal number of sightings, rather than judging us on any occasional inadvertent inaccuracies, such as an incorrect date or name, understanding it would now be impossible to trace many of those witnesses.

Some can be explained away rationally

We accept the possibility that some reports of strange lights in the sky contained within these pages could be explained rationally away as misidentification of man-made or celestial objects. However, we should be careful of dismissing sightings like these as having no value, knowing that to many of the witnesses these incidents were judged as falling well outside their everyday occurrences.

For every sighting report of interest involving 'craft, or saucer-shaped objects seen', we rejected out of hand ten or twenty other reports involving 'strange lights in the sky.' At the time we believed them to be of no value, but now realise the importance of their corroboration to other sightings.

Whether such manifestations represent excursions into our plane of existence by an ancient 'alien' race, whose predetermined objectives (if they have any) remain still unknown, is a matter of personal opinion.

It's already here!

The evidence suggests we are dealing with a phenomenon that exists alongside human existence on the planet, but whose purpose and agenda (if, in fact, there is one) may have little to do with the affairs of man.

21st century already under way

As we enter the first quarter of the 21st Century, how many people know or care to remember the huge 'bursts' of worldwide UFO activity that took place during the middle of the 20th Century, when multiple sightings of strange flying craft and their even stranger humanoid occupants took place?

Whilst we accept that in the majority there is no reason to disbelieve such accounts, we should not be influenced by those who seek to propagate the UFO/ET myth by telling us sightings of UFOs are representative of ongoing Alien incursions into Planet Earth!

Have alien artifacts landed during Earth's long history?

This is not to say that on occasion throughout Earth's history, logically, some alien artifacts have found their way onto this planet. Why shouldn't they? After all, we have sent craft containing greetings and physical artifacts out into the depths of space. One wonders how any alien race would react to the discovery of a spacecraft from Earth on their planet?

How might we appear to them?

We were shocked to discover that the majority of reports we examined could not be attributed to flights of fancy, vivid imaginations, mis-identifications, or the perambulations of fantasy-prone, attention-seeking individuals, proving to us personally that unidentified flying objects were not constructed by the hand of any human agency. Even more staggering in its implications is the realisation that if it was humanly possible to catalogue day-by-day reports of UFO activity that have taken place outside the UK, we would see that far from living in a sterile world, our planet is teeming with all manner of strange things and even stranger occupants. No doubt we will appear as strange to the aliens as they to us! What they are and where they come from are questions that still cannot be answered, but we believe in time they will.

As the reader will see primarily this is a book cataloguing British UFO reports presented day by day, in order to show just how prolific UFO activity was then. But we have included some American sightings because of their importance and obvious contrast with sightings occurring over England. Space prevents us from including all of the sightings brought to our attention.

MOD destroyed UFO reports prior to the 1960s

In addition, one should take into consideration that the MOD admitted, some years ago, that they had destroyed UFO sighting reports brought to their attention by the public before the 1960s.

For us the journey from original scepticism to the acquisition of knowledge of the UFO subject, enabling clarity of perception and understanding, has been a long one. However, we believe we have more than adequately proved to ourselves the presence of something, or someone, whose continued existence continues to haunt our planet to this very day.

Special thanks to our much loved dog – Maude, who accompanied us to all of those wonderful places and people we were to meet over the years. Sadly, she passed away on 18th May 2009 – gone but never forgotten.

This is Maude and her owner, Chris Hanson

Dedicated to Gordon Creighton editor of *Flying Saucer Review* and Chief Petty Officer Edward West who served on *HMS Kelly* under Lord Louis Mountbatten –both gone but never forgotten.

Gordon Creighton (left). Chief Petty Officer Edward West (right). King George V boards HMS Kelly

'Ted' piping the King aboard – second left.

During our quest we became influenced by people such as Trevor James Constable (USA) for his research into Etherian Physics, offering us evidence that *"UFOs are either biological organisms, native to the Earth's atmosphere, or intelligently controlled craft"*, and Mr Gordon Creighton (1908-2003), late editor of *Flying Saucer Review* – a journal that has been in publication since 1955 – who continued to raise public awareness about the UFO subject right into his mid-nineties.

Gordon told us about his own sighting of a pulsating 'disc', crossing the sky of China in 1941, while a distinguished diplomat at the British Embassy. He also described his many discussions with Dr. A.J. Hynek – an internationally renowned UFO researcher, who was involved with the official US Air Force investigation into UFOs, and the former Director of the Center for UFO Studies – who expressed the view *"that the UFO problem was very much occult in nature and paranormal in origin, likely to be phenomena of different vibrations, rather than visitations to this planet by Extraterrestrials"*. We believe valid comments such as these, borne from painstaking research into the UFO subject, provide the key to unlocking the UFO secrets and comprehending what lies behind a phenomenon that has baffled mankind for many years.

John Lennon:

"If the masses started to accept UFOs it would profoundly affect their attitudes towards life, politics, everything. It would threaten the status quo. Whenever people come to realise that there are larger considerations than their own petty little lives, they are ripe to radical changes on a personal level which would eventually lead to a political resolution in society as a whole"

20,000 years ago!

The drawing below is a copy of a carving found in Iran, Persia. It is the God Ahura Mazda, driving a winged disc. This engraving, dated as 2,500 years ago, shows God holding a control ring at the left-hand of the winged Sun. Similar picture and carvings have been discovered in Greece, China, and Iraq. Ancient temple records of India and Tibet confirm evidence of flying machines called Vimanas, 15-20,000 years ago!

RT. ©

NUREMBERG PHENOMENA.

A recording in Nuremberg tells us that on the 4th April 1561,large numbers of flying objects were seen flying near the Sun at Sunrise,they were described as blood red and bluish black globes, some of the globes were flying side by side with blood coloured crosses.
Two large tubes were seen to contain smaller discs or globes,their was also a great black object shaped like a spear,it looked as if the objects were fighting each other,after an hour they fell to the ground were they let off a lot of steam.

1561

Drawn by UFO artist and Researcher Derek Samson, of NICAP UK

Derek Samson and family

1901 – Birmingham boy's Close Encounters with occupants of craft?

In Volume 24, No. 5 of *Flying Saucer Review*, there is an interesting account of an early close encounter with mysterious 'beings' at Bournbrook, near Bournville, Birmingham, from Jenny Randles and Philip Barnet. It involved a boy, aged 10, who was returning to his terraced home, when near the garden of his house he encountered a green / blue metallic sheen coloured 'building', which should not have been there. It was about five to six feet wide, four feet high and three feet deep. It had a stack or turret on the top, and a small square door.

Two 'beings' came out of building

The door opened and out stepped two small entities. Their clothing was a tight-fitting coverall of grey-green and they wore helmet/caps of black, with two projections sticking out of the top. The boy thought that they looked sort of military. One 'being' approached, holding its arms wide. The witness interpreted this as a warning to move away, and did so. The 'beings' returned through the door and soon followed a bright flash, and the bottom of the hut glowed in a 'circle of light'. The hut rose up in an audible WHOOSH and streaked away across the rooftop in a curved flight.

The witness (who was interviewed in 1979 by Jenny) was judged as genuine, taking into consideration that this event had taken place over 70 years ago. Obviously this man has passed away by now, but thanks to Jenny it is not unreasonable to suppose that this incident has substance and appears to have taken place. Unfortunately his name was kept confidential, so we are unable to take this matter further – notwithstanding the locality, being only a few miles away from the Bournville Village estate – home to the famous Cadbury Chocolate factory.

Despite publicity by us, some years ago, we were unable to track down any family members who might have been able to corroborate what is, after all, a very strange and interesting account, many years before the term 'flying saucer' or 'UFO' was used.

1904 – White 'body' the size of the moon

Mr J.W. Hobbs, of Ellsmere, was working at the *Three Cocks* in Breconshire, and walking to his lodgings on a bright moonlit night, accompanied by Mr Thomas Pryce – the stationmaster – when they saw a blue -white 'body', about the size of the moon, shooting across the sky in an east to north direction, leaving a trail of sparks in its wake.

> *"Our first impression was that the moon had fallen from the sky. After recovering from the shock, we saw the full moon shining serenely in the southern sky. I have since concluded that it was a large bolide but, though I have seen several, I have never seen one so large or so brilliant. Curiously, about a fortnight later, a signalman at the same railway station reported seeing a similar object pass overhead."*

1906 – 30th October –Atlantic: Ships crew sight three objects

On 30th October, several crew members of the steamer St. Andrew, including Chief Officer V.E. Spencer, saw three objects fall into the sea about eight kilometres away. This was followed by a huge 'meteor' disc-shaped, metal object, 16 feet in diameter, which fell into the sea about 2.5 kilometers away in a rocking motion, leaving a red streak. **(Source: *New York Times*, 5.11.1906)**

1909 – Phantom Zeppelin airships seen over Great Britain

The 'wave' of sightings of phantom Zeppelins over the British Isles, during the spring of 1909, might have remained a peculiar footnote in English social history but for the works of Charles Fort. It appears that while many people suggest these are examples of early UFO sightings, with occasional alien occupants, logic indicates otherwise. Each individual report can only be judged on its own merits, bearing in mind UFO sightings are not a modern-day phenomenon.

We were to come across reports from the end of the Victorian era (1899) of luminous glowing 'balls of light' heading through the sky, changing direction while in flight, and cigar-shaped objects 'like a flying bomb', with square windows, seen crossing the sky in October 1910, as man struggled to master the aerodynamics of flight.

7th May – England: Cylindrical object over cliff top at Clacton

At 10.30pm on 7th May 1909, a long dark cylindrical object was sighted hovering above cliff tops at Clacton-on-Sea, by Mr Egerton Fee. A few minutes later the object, which carried no lights, flew away heading north-east.

Ones first impression from the description is to

speculate whether this was a UFO – unlikely, understanding it was reported that a naval practice bag was found at the scene (convenient).

On 16th May it is disclosed that two men, speaking a foreign tongue, made enquiries about the incident. Interesting as these accounts are, no conclusions can be drawn from what is, after all, very scant information.

12th May – England: Questions in the House

On 12th May 1909, Sir George Doughty, MP for Grimsby, clamed in Parliament that the German War Department had already carried out a secret naval exercise in the North Sea, designed to test the capabilities of the British coastal defenses. The Unionist claimed two steamers had been commandeered at Hamburg and loaded with soldiers, which was sailed into the mouth of the River Humber and back, without the manoeuvres coming to the notice of the British Admiralty.

Doughty claimed his source was a *"German military officer"* and said the operation demonstrated how *"the whole east coast and its rivers are exposed to any surprise visit of this nature."* In reply, Mr McKenna for the Liberal Government said he had no knowledge of these alleged manoeuvres.

16th May – England: Mysterious machine passes overhead

Mrs Wigg from Lowestoft, Suffolk, was awoken, at 1.30am, by a noise similar to a motor car.

She looked out of the widow and saw:

> *". . . a dark bottle-shaped object, heading south-west at low altitude, and what looked like a man steering at the front of the machine".*

Several others also heard engine sounds and saw flashes of light. (**Source:** ***Flying Saucer Review***)

18th May – Wales: Tubular object and two men seen on road

Mr C Lethbridge – a 'Punch and Judy' operator – was driving home from Senghenydd, through the Caerphilly Mountains.

As he drove around the bend he saw a tubular object and two men, wearing heavy fur coats and fur caps. He approached within 70 feet, before the sound of his spring cart alerted them.

The men spoke with a foreign tongue, and appeared to pick something up from the floor before re-entering the machine, which took off in a zigzag movement, accompanied by the loud noise. As it cleared a telegraph pole, two lights shone out.

The grass was found depressed and a variety of debris was recovered from the scene, including a pin and chain with a label on it in French, and typewritten instructions in English.

(Source: *London Daily Mail*, 20th May 1909)

During First World War

England: 'Flying Platform' over Aldeburgh

A spectacular sighting took place during the First World War, over Aldeburgh, Suffolk, when a 'flying platform', containing a number of occupants, was seen to move across the sky in broad daylight. Our research into this matter, including an interview with the daughter of the woman concerned, revealed (contrary to popular belief) that this was no German sub-cloud car, hung down from a Zeppelin passing overhead, or a Zeppelin that crashed at Theberton, during a raid over England in 1916.

A Zeppelin airship

Mrs Agatha Whiteland

It involved Aldeburgh, Suffolk, woman Mrs Agatha Whiteland – then living at 10 Leiston Road (where she lived for 59 years).

This is what she had to say (drawn from interviews):

> *"I had made the beds up and dusted the front bedroom. I happened to look out of the window, but seeing nothing was going on was on the point of going downstairs when I saw something coming along from the marshes on my right, straight along the road 'wobbling' right in front of me. It then turned sharp right and went between the back of the Railway Hotel and the cart shed, with a room above it (about 20ft-25ft between), over the top of the other cart shed mentioned, over the railway, which had on the railings of the station platform a large printed sign about 8ft long.*
>
> *It was one of those things you look at again, hoping just to see someone or something moving. It seemed to be just higher than the telegraph wires, about 30ft off the ground; it then turned and went towards the station yard. I did think it would hit the shed roof or side (this was the cart shed ground floor and first floor, with the top of ridge 25ft or so above road level. The men inside were looking straight out, as all were clustered around the 'platform'. I wondered how it could move without an engine, as no sound was heard. I looked up in the sky to see if anything was holding it up. I couldn't see anyone kneeling between the men to work it, and watched it go for a long while."*

This proved to be (not understandably) a matter that was the subject of considerable curiosity by her son, Mr Alfred E. Whiteland, of Saxmundham, Suffolk, who was aged three-and-a-half at the time.

Wrote to the 'Daily Mirror'

Having felt convinced that his mother had seen something extraordinary, he wrote a letter to the *Daily Mirror* newspaper, which was published on the 8th August 1968, and caught the attention of Charles Bowen – then Editor of *Flying Saucer Review*, who later published a short article covering the sighting.

Alfred:

> *"My mother has often told the following story over the years and, as she is eighty-four, I would like to find out for her who these mystery men were and what they were doing. This is her story. It was about the middle of World War I, and on a weekday she had gone upstairs just before dinner, opened the casement window and looked out to see who might be on the road. Having looked up and down and noticed there was no-one in sight, she was about to step back when something urged her to look again. A little above the level of the house, eight to twelve men appeared on what seemed to be a round platform with a handrail around it. This they were gripping tightly. She could see them so clearly. They were wearing blue uniforms and little round hats, not unlike sailors. She heard no sound from the machine as it came off the marshes. It turned a bit and went over the railway yard to disappear behind some houses. Have you any explanation for this?"*

Agnes:

Further enquiries revealed a sister, Agnes (88), who was living in Suffolk. She very kindly allowed us to visit her at her home address in 2008, where she confirmed knowledge of the story.

> *"It was my mother who told my eldest brother, Alfred, who died in 1989, that she had seen an airship with a big basket hanging underneath. Alfred at the time told Norbert, then me – 'that's I'm afraid all I know'. When Norbert died, I dealt with all his paperwork, but found no photographs or references to it."*

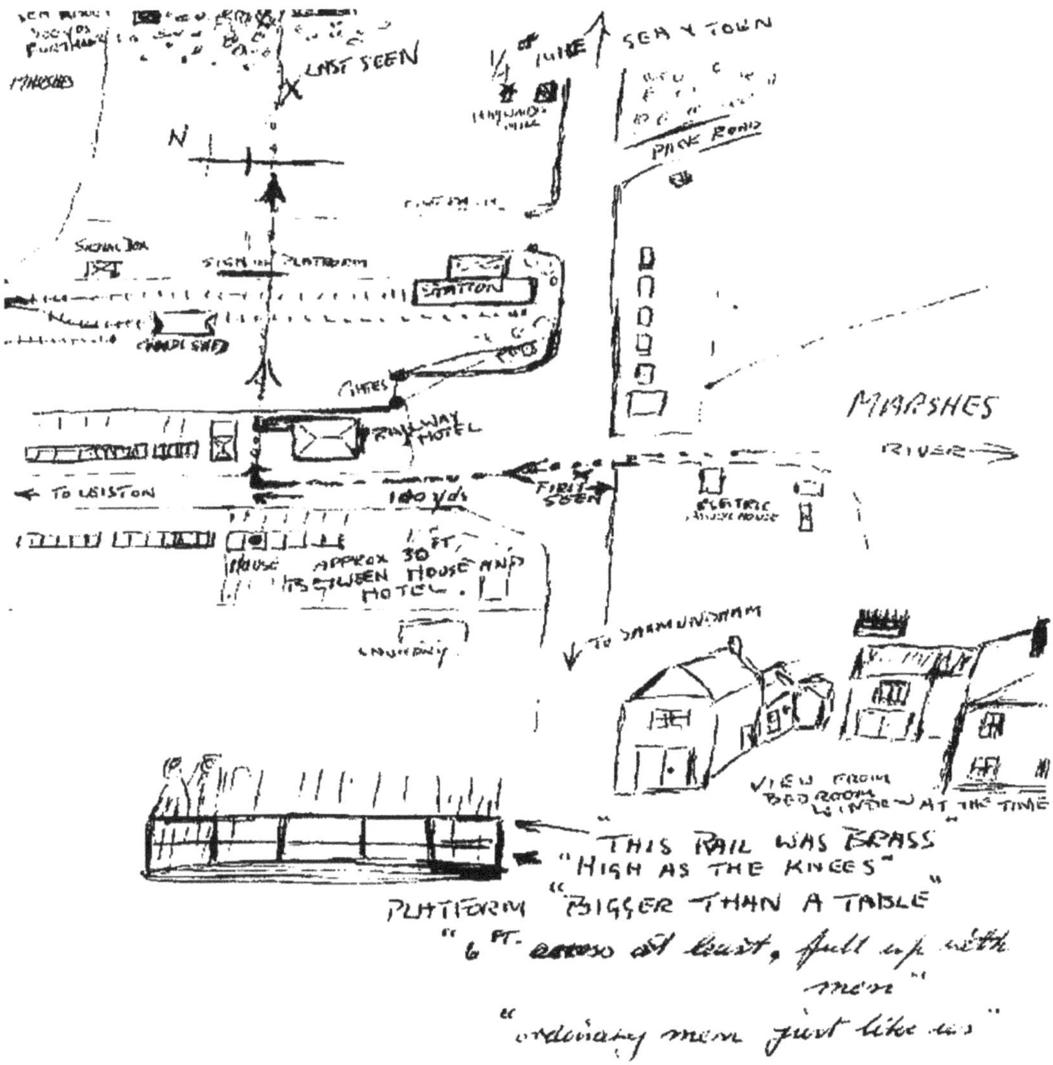

The Whiteland Family, Aldeburgh c 1929 (left) and other family members in Woodbridge, Suffolk,

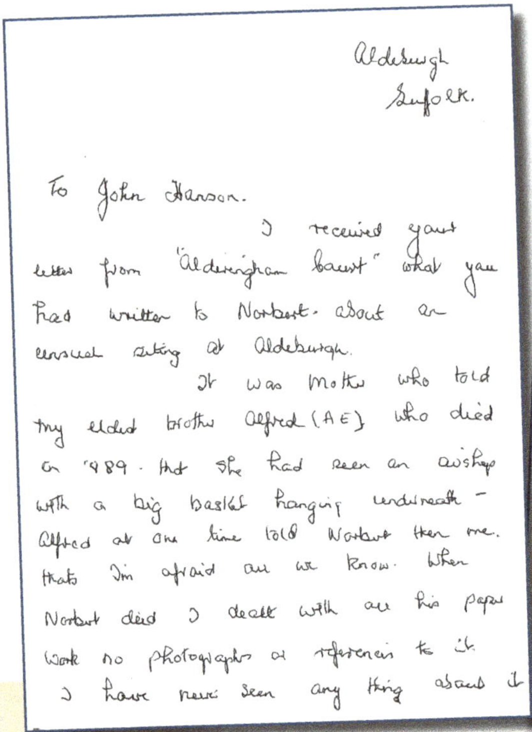

Aldeburgh
Suffolk.

To John Hanson.

I received your letter from 'Aldeingham Court' what you had written to Norbert about an unusual sighting at Aldeburgh.

It was Mother who told my eldest brother Alfred (A E) who died in 1989 – that she had seen an airship with a big basket hanging underneath – Alfred at one time told Norbert then me. that's I'm afraid all we know. When Norbert died I dealt with all his paper work no photographs or references to it. I have never seen any thing about it

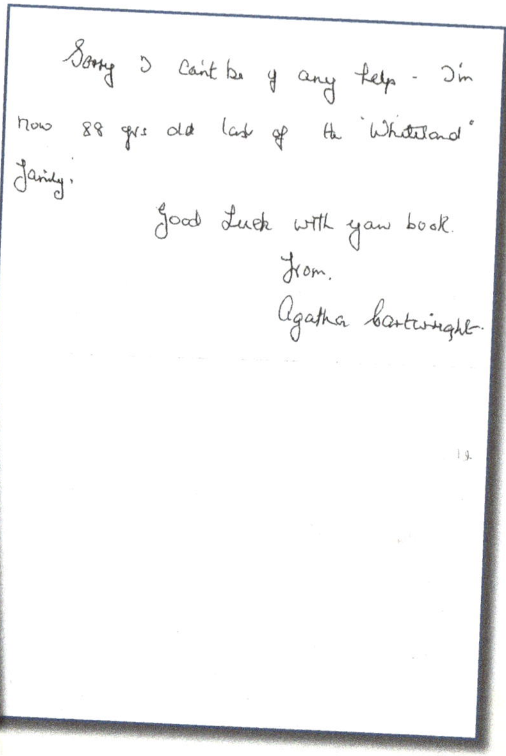

Sorry I can't be of any help – I'm now 88 yrs old last of the 'Whitland' family.

Good Luck with your book.

From.

Agatha Cartwright.

Roy and Agatha

1911 – Will-o'-the-wisp nearly causes disaster

Llanfyllin Doctor Felix Jones whose practice extended over a large area was at his home address when a man called on horseback from the Cowyny Valley to ask him to give aid to a very sick relative. This involved a journey of 9 miles involving some assistance from Mr J. Rees Davies who often accompanied the Doctor on his rounds. After having a hot drink the trap was prepared with four horses to take them on the ride. It was usual for people to shine a lantern or stable lamp at the house where sickness was present. On this particular winter's night they saw a light and Mr Davies guided the horses towards it. They seemed to journey a long way and then in the nick of time they pulled up after the light suddenly extinguished. The looked out and were horrified to see that they were on the brink of a deep drop down the hillside having been mislead by a Will –o- the- Wisp! (Source: Oswestry and Border Counties Advertiser, 16.3.1955)

1912 – Triangular shadows

During this year at Chisbury, Wiltshire, a Mr Charles Tilden Smith reported that he had seen two fan-shaped, or triangular, heavy shadows on the face of clouds towards the west direction overhead. When the clouds passed by, the 'triangles' were still there. In a report sent to the science journal, *Nature*, Mr Smith remarked that from time to time the apparitions varied in size.

1919 – England: Close Encounter with Unidentified Flying Object

An unusual sighting took place on 22nd January 1919, at Shuttlewood, a village situated a few miles from Chesterfield, Derbyshire (later the subject of a thoroughly researched article that appeared in an edition of *Flying Saucer Review* 1975 by Mr Ananda Sirisena following contact with the witness during his later years).

Thomas Hills Harrison

Teenager Thomas Hills Harrison (16) had just stoked the fire in the greenhouse, situated behind his home in Chesterfield Road, and was walking back to the house. He noticed his father staring through the living room window, pointing to a light in the chicken pen about 50 yards down the garden, which was one and-a-half acres in size, containing apple trees along the path - three of them in the pen.

Went to investigate

The son went to investigate, curious as to what could be illuminating the apple trees casting long shadows in all directions.

View from Bolsover Road showing the rear of the property, hawthorn hedges etc.

He opened the chicken coop gate.

> *"As I passed through the gate I saw a 'globe of light' in the pen, halfway along the top side. It was about four and-a-half feet from the ground and completely stationary".*

Thinking that someone was behind the light, maybe their next door neighbour – Charlie Robinson, he shouted out:

> *"You'll be burning your flashlight out, Charlie."*

There was no answer. Thomas walked up to within six feet of the 'light', which he described as being:

> *"...the size of a tennis ball, emitting as much light as a present-day storm mantle lantern. It was a perfect sphere and beautiful to look at – like an oversized pearl. I took a semicircular walk around and back again; there was no one holding it. It did not dazzle in the least, as I stood there looking at it for a full ten minutes."*

Looked for a stick to touch it

> *"Wishing my father would come out and see what the matter was, I decided to look on the ground for a stick to touch it and see what happened. Just then, the 'globe' seemed to sense what I was going to do and started to move away towards the wire netting. At about the speed of a tortoise I received an impression that it was being quite friendly, particularly as it moved so very slowly. I ventured closer, the deg of the light not a distinct line but a cotton wool effect.*
>
> *When it reached the netting the globe fell to the floor, creating an effect not unlike a fireball as it did so. It then regained its normal shape, making a scaring sound, and started to climb up the netting. Mr Harrison decided to go outside the hen cote to follow it, but changed his mind."*

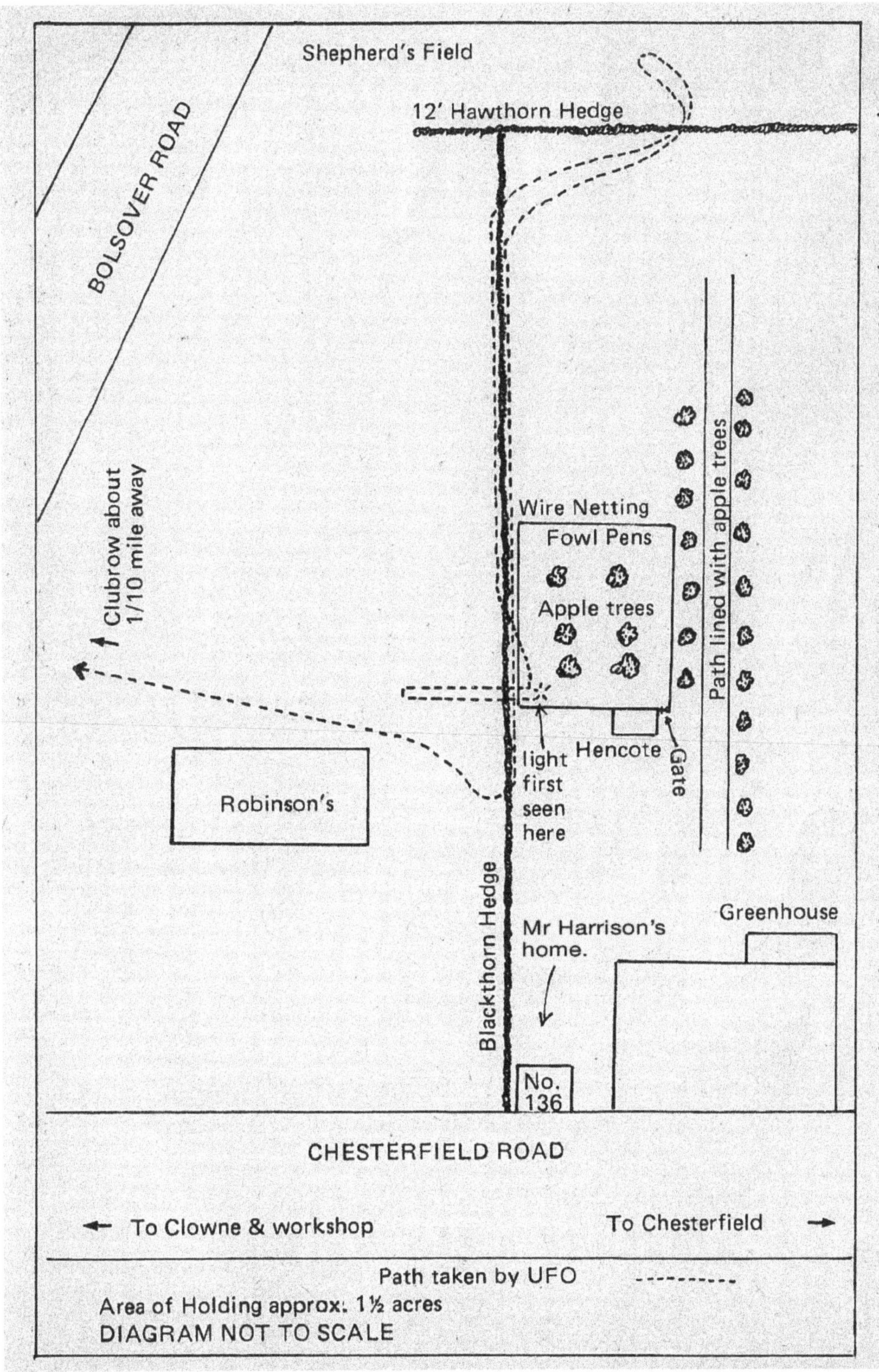

Diagram showing the path taken by the light at Shuttlewood, January 22, 1912 (not to scale)

Thomas Hills Harrison
as a child by one of the apple trees

Thomas Hills Harrison
in later life in his watch shop

Pointless to try and chase it

This was a decision reinforced by the thought that the fence must be broken down and he could not follow it that way, but proved not to be the case, as his sister – Mrs Newman (who was about 20 yards away) – observed the object going through the netting.

Thomas:

> *"The 'light', which had only moved about ten or more yards into the garden, then began to approach my position at a fast rate.*
>
> *I took off my coat to try and ward it off; within seconds it jumped a foot or more, to negotiate the netting in my direction, and turned to the right when only a few feet away.*
>
> *I ran after it, as fast as I could, to the bottom of the pen, where it jumped the netting again. It seemed to want to keep 4-5 feet off the ground. It then maintained a slow but fast walking speed and followed the top of a young three feet high blackthorn hedge at the bottom of the garden, realised it was hopeless to keep chasing it, so I stopped and watched it turn right. When it came to a very high uncut hawthorn hedge, it soared ten feet to a gap in some branches and stayed there for a good few minutes, before passing through and I lost sight of it."*

This was not the end of the story

Believing that this was the end of the matter, Mr Harrison started to make his way back home. He had only gone ten paces, hoping the 'light' would show itself again. Glancing over his shoulder he was stunned to see Farmer Shepherd's field floodlit with a brilliant white light.

> *"The 'light' must have been 200 candle watt powers. I couldn't see the 'ball of light' until a few minutes later, when it came back to the same treetop, where it hovered again for a few minutes. Just as I expected, it came back over the same path towards me.*
>
> *I searched for a stick to defend myself, but could only find a very short one. On its return journey it was only about five candle watt and orange in colour – a change which I noted must have been gradual, as there was no sudden switchover.*
>
> *When it was within a few yards of me I felt my hair standing on end and, as though it knew, it stopped instantaneously and moved three or four yards to the left and into Robinson's garden, where it stayed still.*
>
> *I went through the hedge and knocked on Robinson's door, but there was only an elderly aunt in at the time. We watched the 'light' go past us to the left, in the north-east direction, and follow an old hawthorn hedge – then cross the field towards Bolsover Road, about one tenth of a mile in distance. It circled around the tops of a row of houses (known as Club Row), several times, and then soared into the sky heading due east."*

The entire episode had lasted 35-40minutes for it was nearly 10.50pm when Thomas returned home. Her remembers the exact date because his father said, *"Another two days and it would have come on your birthday."*

Thomas made some enquires over the next few days hoping that someone else would have witnessed it – but he was unsuccessful

Strange vivid dream after sighting

Not unusually in matters such as these, especially where the incident can prey on one's nerves, Thomas told of experiencing a vivid dream where he relived the incident, but with one or two differences. The first was seeing the 'ball' split open to reveal,

> *"...a quarter section on the left, with a patch moving from right to left – something like the map of Spain. I then asked why you are here, or what is your message? To the west of the 'globe' I saw a huge red arch, which filled the sky and registered on my brain that it was the world on fire, or some other world. When I thought 'but the world's surface is mostly water', another arc pushed into it from the left and obliterated the first scene with one of ice, showing rocks and ships stuck in the ice.*
>
> *I was trying to take in all these details, when everything suddenly disappeared and I realised it was a dream."*

Thomas also mentioned something else of interest. An apple tree, planted by his father on the same day as the incident, a few feet away from where the object had been seen, bore fruit in the winter . . .

> *"as if the lights had changed its timing".*

View from outside 136 Chesterfield Rd, looking towards Clowne.

He added:

> *"There was a strange blackout, or halo around the light which I find difficult to explain, because the whole fowl run and trees had plenty of illumination, yet there was a circle of darkness immediately around the light. This 'puzzle' cropped up again in the dream I had during the early hours of the next morning."*

Thomas Hills Harrison ended up as a retired jeweller and antique clock restorer; his memory of the event in the mid 1970s, over 55 years later, was quire clear. A friend brought an electrical device, called a Tesla Coil, around to the house. When it was switched on, it made an identical sound to what the light had made.

According to the Internet 2016, this address is registered as Orchard Cattery, 136 Chesterfield Road, Shuttlewood, Chesterfield, Derbyshire S44 6QN

(Source: *Flying Saucer Review,* Volume 20, No. 5, March 1975 – 'The light at Shuttlewood', *Ananda Sirisena)

Ananda Sirisena

*Ananda was born in Sri Lanka but has been living in England since 1963. He became interested in UFOs as a result of a personal experience on 8th July 1964 and has spent considerable time researching George King and the Aetherius Society since 1966. He is a member of the Society for Planetary SETI Research. Information on this researcher and a list of some of the presentations that he has done at various conferences and venues can be found on http://spsr.utsi.edu

1926 – 17th March – England: Silver-grey UFO over Essex

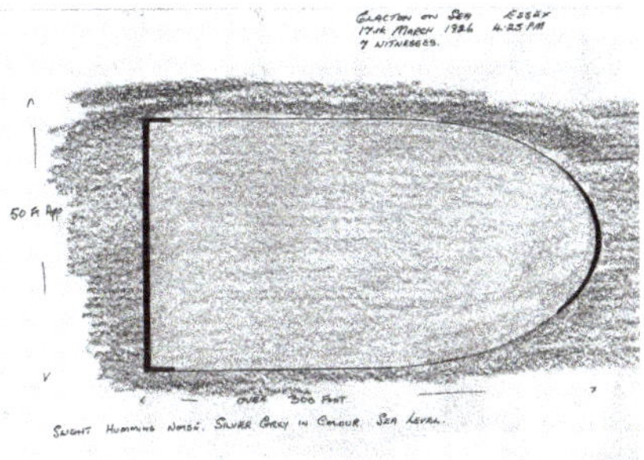

Mr John J. Manser, born in 1910, was 16 years of age at the time, when he saw something very unusual, at 4.25pm, while out fishing with his brother and father, off Clacton Peer in Essex. The peace and tranquility was shattered when his brother shouted: *"Look at that airship!"*

John looked out over the sea and saw:

> *"...a huge silver-grey object. There were no tail fins or cabin, nor any windows or propellers, but we could hear a faint humming noise. It was skimming just above the water, heading towards Brightlingsea. It was moving fast and was about 300 feet long, with depth of 50 feet. I would say it was approximately a mile away. It had a blunt end and rounded front."*

This report was brought to the attention of Ron West, in 1976. John told him that his father and brother had passed away.

Sadly, so would John – fortunately his sighting survives.

1927 – England: Red 'ball of light' halts tram at Leicester

A Leicester woman described a sighting that took place in 1927, when she saw a 'red ball' drop down from the sky and hover in front of a tram, causing it to come to a dramatic halt, while travelling along Humberstone Road, Leicester, before shooting across the sky and disappearing from sight. Was there a natural explanation? Could it have been a fireball? If so, why did it hover for a few minutes?

1928 – England: ghostly dancing couple seen

Mrs Jose Steadman, from Halesowen, West Midlands, wrote to us a number of years ago about a strange event witnessed by her father – David George Hadley (born 13.3.1913), his brother Alfred, and friend Harry Henshaw – while out walking.

Jose:

> *"They were living in the small picturesque village of California, which consisted of Clinton's Farm, Taylor's Farm and Non such Farm (now swallowed up by Birmingham 32) One hot summer's day, the three men were walking over fields to Tom Knockers wood – a place of beauty at that time of the year. After walking for some time, they decided to stop for a rest on a stile. Then all three of them witnessed the amazing sight of a lady in a crinoline dress and a man in tails, slowly waltzing up the field towards them. To the astonishment of the three men, the 'couple' carried on through a hawthorn hedge and continued their dance across the next field."*

In January 2016 I (John) met up with Jose, who is very interested in spiritual matters and possesses an impressive library of books devoted to the subject. She told me that she has the ability to see

Jose Steadman

spirits of the departed and one wonders if her father, David (on the left) shown with Jose's late husband, Jack, may also have had the same 'gift'.

1929 – England: Abduction experience near Strensall, York

Someone who was to experience more than his fair share of UFO sightings was Clacton-on-Sea, retired Merchant Navy Officer – William Anderson (aged 87 in 1990). Although he is no longer with us, he would have been delighted to see his encounters in print. This is the least we can do for someone who was judged very genuine by Essex UFO researcher Ron West – the forgotten man of UFO history, who laboured long and hard to painstakingly preserve the result of his investigations into reported UFO activity around East Anglia.

Why is it not surprising to find people who witness a UFO event to then go on to see other strange things in our skies?

William, to our knowledge, was involved in at least half a dozen sightings throughout his early life that included life aboard a Merchant Navy vessel, which took part in the dangerous Arctic Convoys during World War Two.

So it begins…

*"In a way I feel this was the most important sighting of all, because it was this experience that showed me the 'light' as to what was happening to me. I had been in the Merchant Navy about two years and was on home leave to York. One evening, after having been drinking with some friends, I was walking home to *Strensall, at 10pm. I kept feeling that someone or something was watching me, but put it down to imagination.*

White glowing 'ball of light' seen

At 11.15pm I was passing open farmland, when I noticed 'a white ball of glowing light' just inside a gateway. I heard my name being called and looked around to see who was calling me, but could not see anybody.

I heard my name again and realised this was in my head. I then began to walk towards the 'ball of glowing light'.

Dome-shaped vehicle seen

As I approached closer, I was stunned to see an oval vehicle of some sort with a dome shape on top. There was a doorway with a ramp way leading into it. Although there was nobody about, I knew I had to enter the vehicle – don't forget I didn't even know what UFO or 'flying saucer' was! I didn't feel frightened, but calm and full of confidence.

On entering through the doorway I heard the ramp come up and shut behind me – even that didn't worry me. I made my way into a circular room on my left, where I undressed and sat on a pedestal-type seat, which looked like it was made of clear plastic and warm to the touch.

The next thing I became aware of was lying on a table of the same material. Looking up I saw a small cigar-shaped object, hovering above, projecting a 'beam of light' onto my forehead. I heard a voice saying, 'We will always know where you are and if I needed any help or advice…' I asked how this was going to happen, but didn't receive any answer.

*Strensall is a village and civil parish in the unitary authority of the City of York in North Yorkshire, England, on the River Foss north of York and north-east of Haxby. Before 1996 it had been part of the Ryedale district.

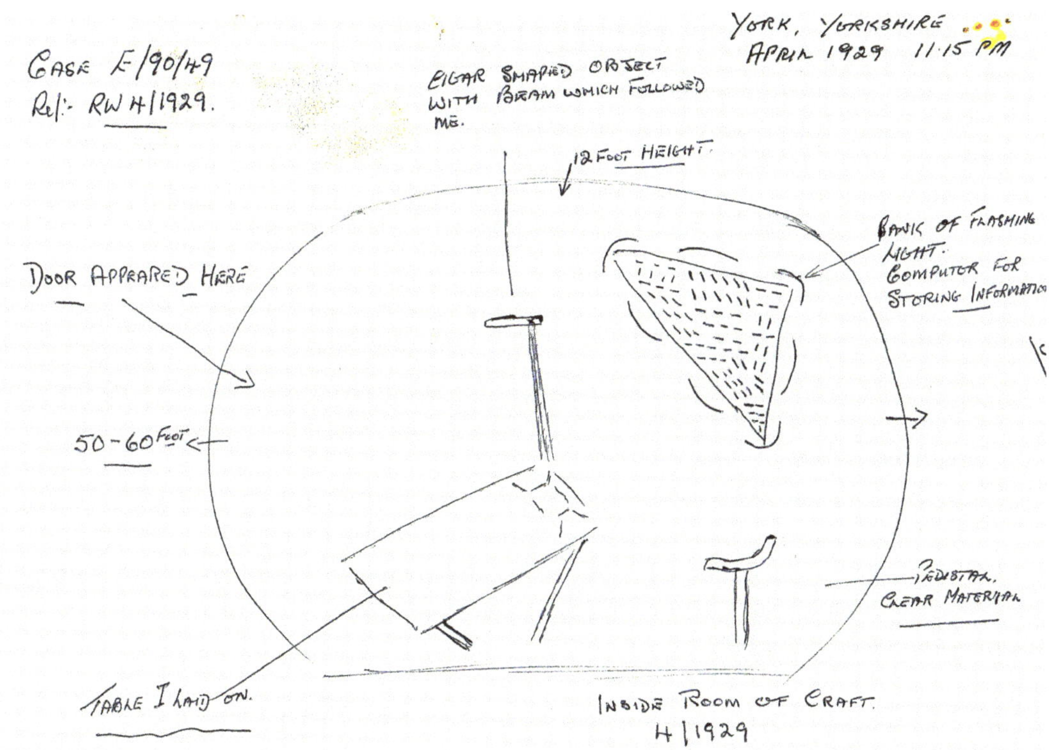

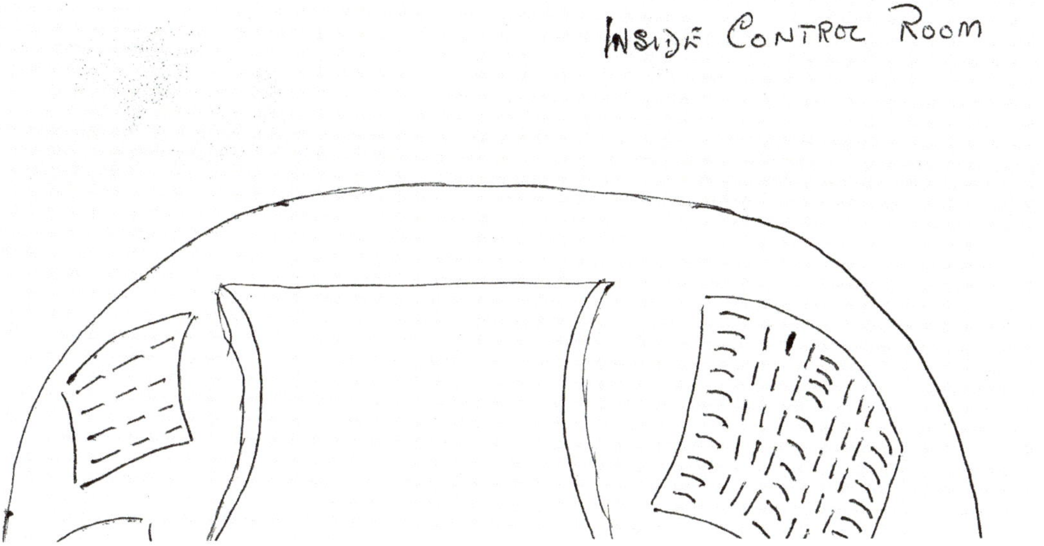

Force field present

I got off the table and walked around the room, lit by a blue white glow; the source of this lighting wasn't apparent. However, there was a bank of lights on the wall – mainly yellow, blue, and green lights – which I understood was a type of computer for storing information.

As I walked around, the cigar-shaped object was overhead and followed me. I then noticed something strange – my feet were six to nine inches above the floor. I was told that a force field was keeping me from touching the floor and that it wouldn't harm me. I tried to touch the wall but was prevented from doing so, presumably by the same force field. I was then asked if I wanted to see the main control room and, after agreeing, I remember going through a wall which suddenly opened in front of me. The control room contained banks of flashing lights and three clear pedestals similar to the one I had sat on."

At this point William wondered why he still hadn't seen anybody, despite communication – albeit telepathically. 'They', or whatever 'they' were, told him his eyes would be able to focus upon their forms, but they showed him a picture in his mind which he describes as . . .

"Six feet, six inches, to seven feet tall, with blonde, page-boy type hair down to his (or her) shoulders, long arms, with six fingers, very pale skin, and deep blue to purple eyes – very beautiful to look at".

The next thing is that he remembers waking up in his own bed, at home, the following morning!

"This caused a problem with my parents. My father had locked the house at 1.30am, and there was no way I could have got into the house. I am unable to explain how this could have happened. In addition, all of my clothes were missing."

(Source: Ron West UFO archives)

1930 – Flaming object seen, then a mysterious 'figure'

Kirby Lonsdale timber merchant Philip Irving (then 80) – a former 'desert rat', who had served under Field Marshall Montgomery in the Second World War (with shrapnel in his knee as a reminder) – contacted the North Lancashire UFO Investigation Group, in 1996, wishing to bring their attention to what he witnessed one summer in 1930, at midnight, while on the sandbanks at Haverigg when a teenager.

Philip:

"A the time, I lived with my parents and sister in a small cluster of houses close to the shore. I was returning home from the cinema, at 9.30pm, when I noticed 20-30 people on the shore, looking up into the sky at this big 'ball of fire' descending through the sky to about 5,000 feet. It had flames coming out of the back and I stayed to watch it, as it sunk lower and lower – until I lost sight of it. Did it land? I can't say.

A couple of days later I was walking back home when I saw what I first thought was the devil, but then realised he didn't have a tail. The figure was about five feet eight inches tall, covered in red-brown hair, with something silver that looked like aluminum wrapped around his waist and boots. He had narrow human like features and sort of hollow cheek bones. I looked at him – he looked at me, and I ran! Was there any connection with what had taken place a couple of days previously?"

(Source: As above/*Westmoreland Gazette*, Kendal, 20.2.1996 – 'Close encounter of the brown and hairy kind')

1939 – England: 'Red light' over the County

A Shropshire man recalls what he and his mother saw in the early 1930s:

> *"We were watching the stars, when suddenly a large 'red light' dropped out of the sky towards the west. It swung backwards and forwards like a pendulum, for a few seconds, and then vanished upwards out of sight. Had it been a meteor, it would have dropped earthwards or streaked across the sky."*

(Source: Gavin Gibbons)

13th November – England: Landed bell-shaped object seen

Described by Jenny Randles as "a superb piece of investigation" was a report submitted by Leicestershire UFO researcher Mark Brown, relating to a report of a bell-shaped object seen at Brockworth, Gloucestershire, on the 13th November 1939 – long before the terminology of 'Flying Saucers' or even UFOs was used in common language.

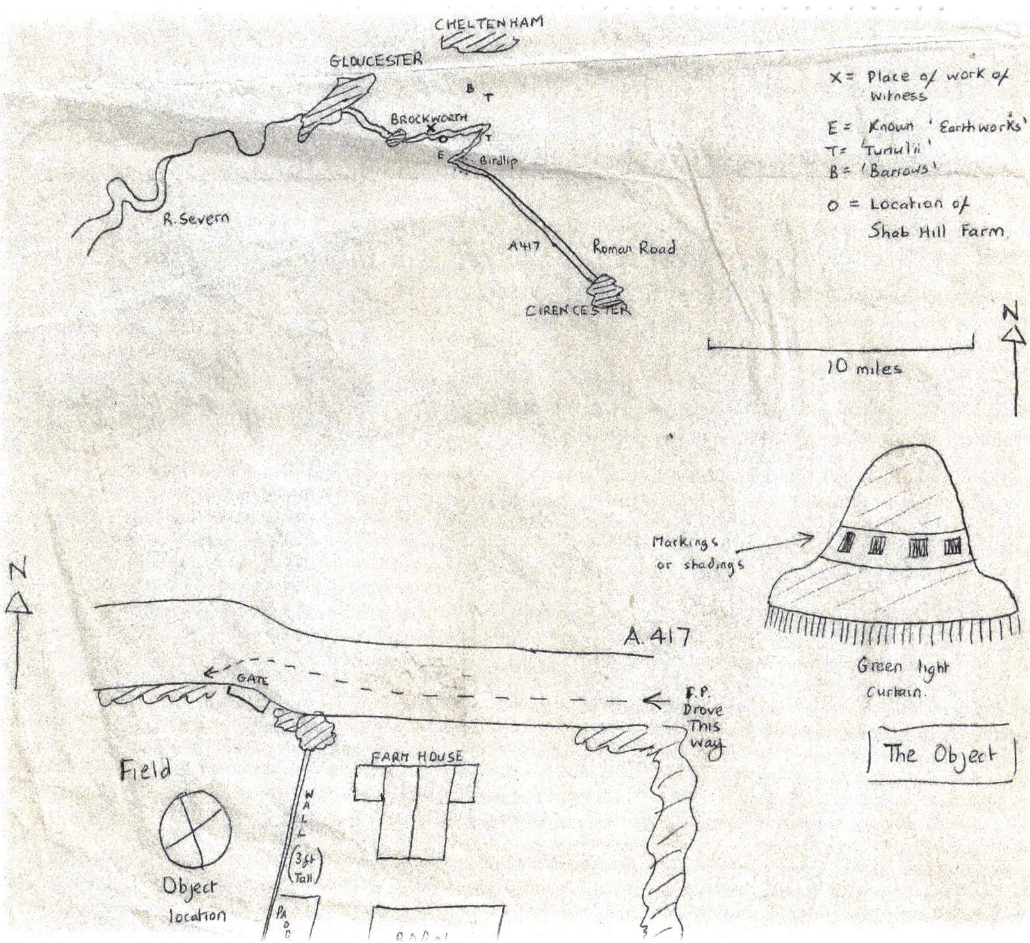

The witness (given the name 'Mr FP') would, in all probability, have passed away by now. He was 72 when interviewed by Mark – then living in the Leicestershire area. Over the years we have tried to trace Mark, in order to establish the real name of the witness and learn more about this fascinating sighting, but have been unsuccessful so far.

Gloster Aircraft Company

At the time, 'Mr FP' was living in London – a city haunted by fears of a German invasion. Being a building contractor he was classified as doing essential work and had been assigned to create an extension to the Gloster Aircraft Company, situated close to the village of Brockworth. In late 1939, this locality, with its green rolling hills, was still relatively untouched by the seething troubles which faced the world, as it still is today.

On the Monday morning of the incident, the witness motored to work passing the beautiful place of Birdlip, at 7am, with its spectacular view over the valley – (well-known to myself and Dawn, especially me with my links to Cheltenham). He then carried on his journey along the A417 from Cirencester, which took him onto the favourite part of his drive over Barrow Wake and Cuckley Hill with its ancient settlements and fine views over the Severn Valley.

John Hanson relaxing at his late-'60s favourite drinking hole.

He went past the *Air Balloon* public house (one of John Hanson's favourite haunts back in the late 1960s, even being stranded there, one night, with his old girlfriend, Barbara Anne May, after his Ford Popular broke down.) [John: My father – the local RSPCA Inspector at Cheltenham – was not happy about coming to sort the car out!]

High-pitched humming noise heard

About two thirds of the way down 'Mr FP' passed a farm, which would normally be the centre of much activity when a dog always came out and barked at the car. On this morning, the farm appeared deserted.

> *"As I drove past the farm buildings, I heard a high-pitched humming noise – like a finely tuned electric motor. Puzzled, I continued on my journey and reached a gate at the back of the farm, offering me views over the hedgerows, when I saw something like nothing else I had ever encountered in my life before."*

Like a child's spinning top

"It looked like a child's spinning top, admiralty grey in colour, with dark shadings inset about one quarter up the side. They looked like windows or apertures of some sort. The bottom of the object had a skirt, giving the whole appearance of a bell. From the bottom emerged a pale green curtain of light, which came equally from the full width of the base. I thought this was well worth looking at, and pulled the car up to a halt on the grass verge. The humming noise appeared to come from the object – which wasn't moving – approximately 20 feet off the field. I estimated it was 25-30 feet wide and 20 feet high. After a couple of minutes, suddenly, the object shifted its position, which began slowly as it tilted to an angle of about 80 degrees, and moved away to one side. Just prior to this action, the green light faded out. At this point I became quite frightened and got back into the car and drove away without looking behind."

'Mr FP' drove back to the village and, after presumably collecting his thoughts and having calmed down, told his manager that he was going back to the farm. His curiosity well and truly aroused, he made a careful search for any traces of where the object had been but found nothing. He then walked over a wall bordering the farm, but there was still no sign of life. Frighteningly, since that date, he never saw any sign of activity at the farm again. One may be inclined to wonder why the man did not go to the farm and ascertain whether they had seen the object, or that at the very least see if they were ok. Clearly the only man that can answer this is probably not even alive.

Did the same UFO return?

After the war, he moved to Loughborough and took up a position as a landlord. In 1958, not unusual for matters such as this, he was subject of a second UFO sighting, which took place when he and his family were awoken by a strange, eerie, familiar noise. His wife, frightened, asked him what he thought it was. Discretion being the better part of valour, they didn't investigate further until the noise began to die away. On looking through the window, they saw a large green glowing light – bright enough to illuminate the room.

According to the witness, the next morning, the *Leicester Mercury* told of local UFO sightings that same night.

Mark Brown

Despite the enormous amount of time that had passed since the original incident, Mark Brown visited the locality and discovered the farm was Shab Hill Farm – home of the Barnfield family. Other enquiries to trace any missing person(s) who may have lived at the farm, and examining newspaper archives to determine whether anything untoward had occurred at the farm following the UFO sighting, proved unsuccessful. **(Source: *Science & The UFOs*, 1985, page 3, Jenny Randles and Peter Warrington)**

In the *Leicester Mercury*, dated 28th April 1982 – Is there anybody out there? – Reporter Shirley Elsby interviewed Mark, (part extract), introducing him as the 24-year-old BUFORA Regional Investigator for the Midlands.

Mark:

"It is the cause of the different phe-nomena which interests me. The majority of members are probably hard headed sceptics when it comes to the theory that Earth is being visited by beings from outer space. I am certain that we are being visited by alien intelligences or by controlled craft from another world. I have never come across a case that has led me to believe it is something totally outside man's capability to design, or outside the possibility of the Earth's forces to manufacture."

1940 - 1949

England: UFO close encounter, Warwickshire

ONE of the earliest encounters with the occupants of a landed UFO took place in the summer of 1940 on the outskirts of Meriden, a small village situated near Coventry, Warwickshire. The almost unbelievable version of strange events told by local girl, Cathie Connelly (aged 18 in 1940) was – thirty years later – the subject of much interest during the mid-1970s, when it came to the attention of UFO researcher – Bob Tibbitts, who took over as Head of CUFORG (Coventry UFO Research Group) from Post Office workers – Donald Speed and Dave Heath. In his new role Bob Tibbitts went on to produce UFO magazine *Syntonic*, costing the princely price of five pence in 1971!

Bob Tibbitts:

> *"At that time the three of us, Donald, Dave and myself, met in Coventry to talk informally about the subject. I suggested we should expand the group to involve other members of the public but Donald and Dave disagreed, so I took over running the group along with Gary Ashby – with Donald's agreement. We had quite a turnout at the meetings, which were held in various pubs!"*

First met Cathie Connelly

> *"It was at one of these meetings in the Albany Pub, Earlsdon, Coventry, that I first met Cathie Connelly, who had an amazing story to tell; we were talking about what 'the operators' of the UFOs may look like, when a woman in the audience stood up and exclaimed words to the effect, 'No, they don't look like that at all'. I asked her a number of questions and she agreed to write out an account of what had taken place."*

It is a case that still intrigues Bob, despite the many years that have elapsed. He believes something extraordinary occurred to Cathie – a Scottish lady, in her late forties/early fifties at that time (1970) living in Canley, Coventry. Sadly Cathie has since passed away.

> *"I have to admit that when I first heard of what Cathie claimed had happened, all those years ago, it seemed too incredible to believe, especially when she revealed a number of journeys made in the 'craft' (UFO) to places like New York and Rhodesia. However, as time went on, I realised I was dealing with a genuine lady, who firmly believed in what she had experienced."*

Without ever having interviewed Cathie Connelly ourselves, we knew it would be impossible to form any judgment as to the genuineness of what was reported, but knowing the quality of Bob s research into the UFO subject, felt parallels could be drawn with other incidents involving similar close encounters of 'alien' abduction.

Bob Tibbitts

Summer of 1940

"I remember her telling me that one of the entities had something in its hands, apparently occupied with some sort of device they pointed towards her. I wondered at the time (if this was an objective rather than subjective experience) whether they had been taking photos of her, or cleaning their hands or cleaning something else at the time. This is purely conjecture on my behalf, but I also wondered if the entities (whoever they were) had used some sort of implement to incapacitate Cathie and had taken her on board, and then released her later from the effects of this device. I believe that much of what she recalled during the years that followed was a slow release of the memories of the event buried within her subconscious memory."

Bob Tibbitts – An update on the Connelly case:

While reviewing material for this updated volume of *Haunted Skies* I would like to offer to it's readers the full account that Cathie presented to me. I had asked her at the time to write out what she remembered of her encounters with the strange 'people' during those years. What she wrote about is very close in many details, to other accounts of interaction with the phenomenon. There are aspects that appear to show that whatever was presenting itself to Cathie, it had the ability to show carefully-selected 'snippets in time' to her. There are also similarities to other cases of this type involving pregnancy testing, possible harvesting of human eggs, testing of the eyes/ears of the abductees and also psychological tests. There is even the 'message' about war and it's effects on the world.

These episodes may have served some purpose that we can only speculate about but seem to act as 'lessons' to her and have a very personal meaning that spans the then war in progress and her obligations to fellow man and her role within her chosen religion.

The case had been covered prior to my involvement by researcher Ken Rogers of Contact UK in the magazine *Awareness*. His observations about the case are also presented in an edition of *Gemini* magazine. It is interesting to note that Ken Rogers had observed certain similarities of Cathie's case, to that of Betty and Barney Hill, who's 1961 contact with 'aliens' is well documented. Norman Oliver also had views on Cathie's encounters, in a previous edition of *Gemini*, the magazine that he edited.

Below is Cathie s account as she related in her own words and handed to me in 1970. You see from the way she describes events that she appeared still to be very mixed up and possibly confused at that time. I am not surprised though, as the events had taken place starting in 1940 and through to 1952, with the phenomenon still interacting with her in later years – the passage of time would have taken a toll on her memories. There may also have been portions of her encounters that had been purposefully held back by whatever intelligences had initiated the contacts. Included will be a full account that was to appear in *The Flying Saucer Revelation*, (1969) – the book I wrote was to remain unpublished. The account also appeared in a special edition of *Syntonic*, CUFORG *Newsletter* and also appeared in the first edition of *Gemini*. I also present scanned images of the hand-written account that Cathie submitted to myself and which were preserved in CUFORG files of the time.

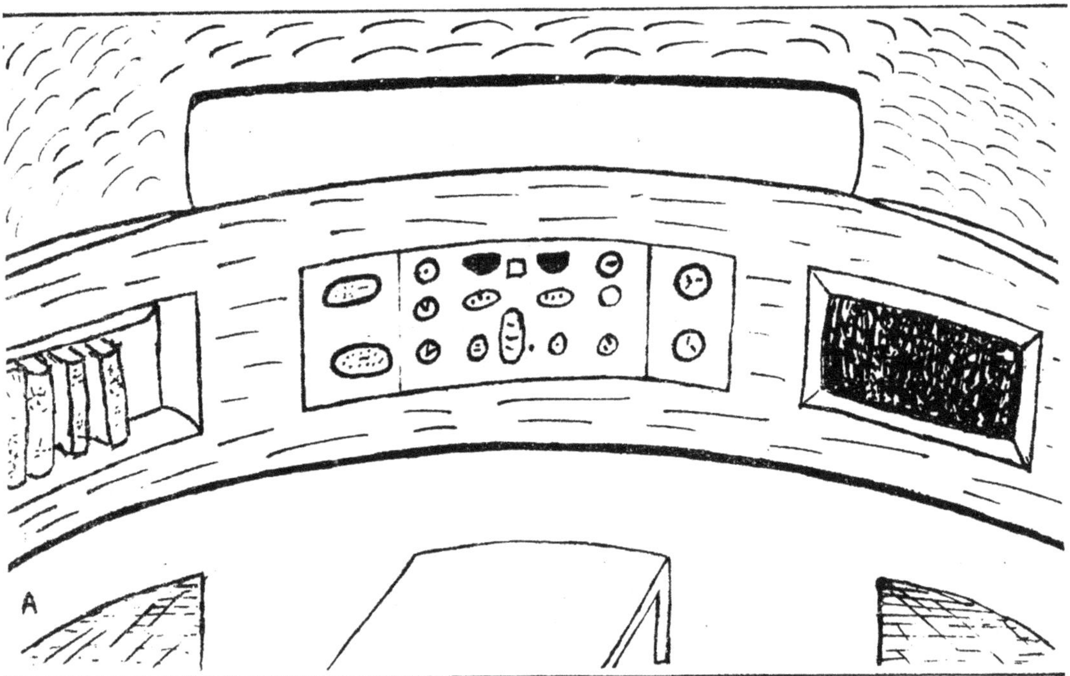

A diagram based on the originals drawn by Cathie that appeared in Syntonic

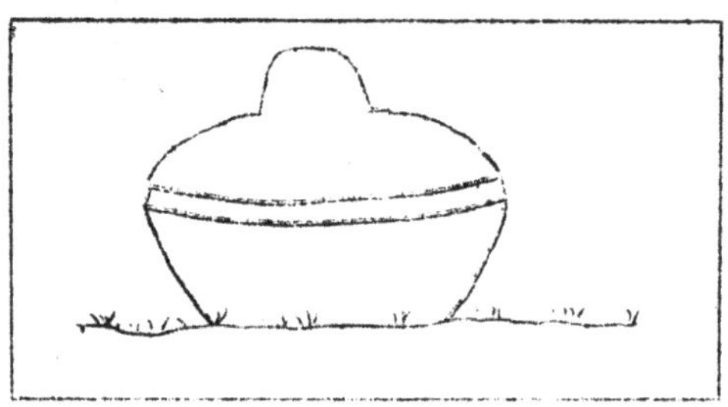

The Craft at Meriden

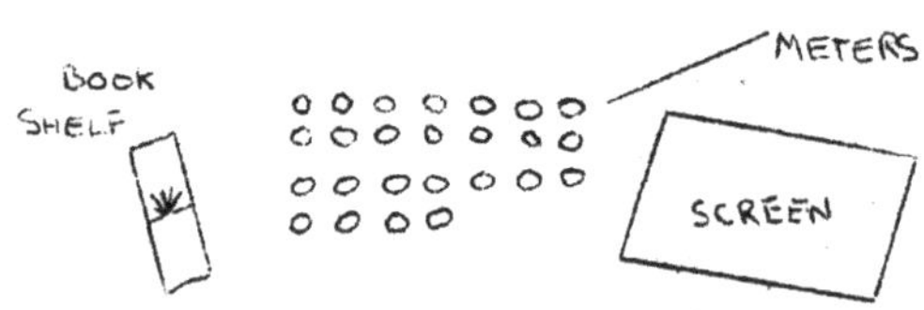

Inside the Craft.
Both sketches by Mrs. Connelly originally.

RETURN PERSONALLY TO: R.W. TIBBITTS., (CUFORG),

AT MEETING.

11/5/70

THE ACCOUNT: One Sunday in the war years, I went out to walk for pleasure. As I walked down a country lane in Merideon. I saw a metal dome shaped struture. I thought it was a pernoment building. Next to it was a line of smoking chimneys poking through the grass. There was tall men all round the structure adjusting something in the centre, and as I walked up to pass them. The man at the centre of the part facing the lane ~~tour~~ turned round raised his hands he appeared to be cleaning them with a duster. He walked closer to me. I smiled to him he did not smile back till he had finished cleaning his hands. Then he gave me a slow smile. He seemed to be weighing me up. At this time I was employed by the Renold Chain Co. I helped an older man in a store room in the centre of the machine shop. We also sharpened tools. One day my colleauge gave me a micomiter & asked me to go in the machine room & inspect some chain links. These dropped out of the machines into oblong metal boxes. Labours moved them into neat piles. While I was inspecting them a man who looked like the men I saw at Meriden spoke to me. He said your war is upsetting my world. I reminded him it was his world to. He replyed I dont come from this world take me to your King & Queen. I told him I could not. He then asked me if I were colour blind. I said no. He enquiered whom he should contact. I said scientists & the Government. He asked me several times to come with him. I refused. He then asked me if I would come on a long journey with him & I would see nice colours I said no. Walking was my greatest pleasure & soon after meeting the man in the factory I found myself in a space-craft surrounded by men Holding me down on the table. One of them said we are not going to hurt you. We only want to see if you are pregnant. I said whats pregnant. He said you dont know. Then I said my mum said if you go out at this time of night old Nick will get you. Why have you come for me I have not hurt anyone. He said who is old Nick I said the Devil I think. Then I said if you are not the devil you cant be god because your skin is Then I stopped short & said no one ever told me the colour of Gods skin. He had slits at the side of his mouth reaching almost to his ears. His ears were long and animal looking they lay flat on his head. His nostrils were straight up & down on his face. His coloured skin was unblemished. His face had a cat like appearance. He had no whites in his eyes. I told him we had good plastic surgeons & I explained what they could do for him. Very jently he said if I had everthing changed I would be alright. Then he said come with me & I will show you something. He took me over to a window he called it the scanner. We travelled a little. Then we watched air warfare all the pandimonium & voices of the airoplane crews were relayed inside the space craft. I said there are too many people in those boats down below. All the time a voice above my head kept saying this is your world. I kept denighing it. I pointed to one of the airoplanes & said this is not my world he is a cockney. The voice said this is your world look they are coming in all directions. Then I looked down below & said what is that wailing o it is not wailing it is music, music in hell. Then the crew of one of the planes spotted us. They started shouting spasmodically. They have got a captive. It is a woman no it is a child dont shoot dont fire I aint hanging arround to find out. Now we seemed to be travelling alongside the airoplane. The crew at one side the airoplaine were looking straight at us. One looked straight at me & done the sign of the cross. My space friend said do you know him I said no. Why did he move his hand at you then. I replyed he must be a catholic He was praying for me I think. I hope he will be alright. I Hope they will all be alright. My space friend said you will be alright. Then we changed course I was looking at the statue of liberty. My space friend said I wont tell you what that is bathie I might embarass you. Then we seemed to be travelling above a street in New York I said what time of day or night is it the news vendors are very busy. Something important must have happened. I cant see any women. Men are buying the newspapers. Some are standing in shop door ways reading. Others are just glancing then folding the news papers and hurrying on. We changed course again. I was alone at the scanner. My space friend was standing in the middle of the room. The others had gone into other compartments. I looked down & saw a man on a stake shaped like an oblong cross. There was a crowd of people running backwards & forwards throwing what appeared to be dirt & stones a small boy at the back was immitating them. I dont think he could see the man on the stake. I said the man is beautiful. He must have been loved as a child to make him look like that why are they doing this to him now. The voice above me said why. Those people dont look like savages They must have been misiformed. The voice above me said this is your world. I was indignant. I replyed this is not my world those people are savages living in the past. Then the voice said are they different where you come from. At this I burst into tears rushed to the man in the centre of the room & said I am sorry I thought you were the devil. It is peacefull in here hell is out there. The next time I was in the craft they showed me a film of me trying to walk accross the traffic lights. I was always told this was the best place to cross. I was frustrated I told them I hated traffic lights finally a policeman with a white coat showed me accross the Road. The policeman said are you colour blind I said no. He then said you are colour blind I used to work at st dunstans. I was crossing the road another time a young woman was standing near by. She had a shopping basket & two children. She said something to the little boy. He walked over to me took my hand & walked back to the lady we crossed the road together. On other occasions the policeman showed me accross. I told the spacemen I got embarrased & came out in a sweat on these occasions because I must be stupid or backward as I was neither very young or very old but a healthy grown-up girl. The spacemen then said how do you know you are not colour blind. I replied because colour blind people only see black and white I can see more than that. What colours can you see then. When I was little my teacher gave me a colour card with the names on the side. Later she gave me a test without the names. They took me back in time to go through the colour test again. Then they said cathie you memorised the names on the side not the colours your teacher never included amber. They were also interested in my hearing. I told them when anyone spoke fast the words got all churned together. I had never been able to comunicate this to any one before although both my colour & hearing had been in question. When I insisted I was not colour blind. They said we only want to help you grinned & one man said. It is the least we can do. You once helped me. I said I did not help you I only told you to go to a plastic surgeon. He replyed you done the best you could. They put me under sedation when I came round I remember saying I cant bare any one to touch my eyes. Then I said your skin must be green I can see the colour very clear on your ears. It is a new shade of green I bet my people would like it. Another time I was on the craft The space men said a bus is coming along the road. Cathie we want you to get on if you can. I said if there is an empty seat I well get on. They repeated get on if you can. The bus stopped. There was confusion they said I could not get on the bus it was not allowed. They were all dark skinned people on the bus. I said there is an empy seat I forced my way on. The passengers said havent you brought Fritz with you I thought they

I ment a dog. I said I havent got a Fritz. I made my way to the empty seat. A young well built man was sitting there. He deliberately oppened his knees to make it difficult for me to sit down. I forced myself on the corner. The driver then asked for my fare. I got some money out he said that is not good I got some more money out he said that is no good. He said where do you come from I said Coventry. He said you will have to get your money changed. I said I wont be here long enough. They wont even let you sit in an empty seat in this place. What is the name of this place Rodesia he replyed. The bus started up. I said bloody. a you lady was sitting near by with a small boy on her knee. She quickly put her hand on her ears she said you swore. I retorted swearing wont do him lasting harm segregation will. The man next to me closed his knees. Then the passengers said where did you come from before you got on the bus I said a flying saucer. The people in the flying saucer told me to get on the bus if I could. The bus stopped there were hands touching my knees saying be quiet you are upsetting the driver he cant consentrate. Where do you want to get off. I said I dont know my space friend said he would meet me. They all went quiet. The bus started up again. The tall space man flagged the bus down soon afterwards. The driver & others stretched out their hands in a friendly jesture to help me off the bus. The space man was grinning. He said did she behave herself. The driver replyed she was alright if they were all like her we would be allright. Another time I was on the craft they took me to Florida. Another time they were asking details about blood transfusions. We were also talking about Resus babys Etc. One of the men said these people know more about jenetics than we do. There was talk about having an exchange of Ideas with us. Another time I was on the craft I was looking through the scanner. I saw myself between the ages of 11 & 13. I saw myself kneeling at the alter in a little wooden salvation army church. The Salvation army baptain was with me. I think he daubed water on me I am not sure. The space men asked me what we were doing. I said the captain was reading out what I was promising to undertake. The space men said. Do you always keep a promise. I said I dont make a promise that is impossible to keep I never break a promise. Then the voice said your back in square one bathie because— I replyed if I am back in square one because— . What square are all the murderers liears theives Ect. in. The voice replyed they are not in any square at all. It is your job to get them in the running. I said you are not asking much are you. Then I saw the little girl kneeling at the alter. The voice said you promised legience to God. Do you know what legience to god means. I said yes legience to God means legience to people of all religions & creeds, Colours. Then I said God knows I never break a promise he will help me to keep it. This story is cut short the odds are against me writing it. Ken Rogers has the rest of the information that is needed to make a complete story. A story that was ment to end with a mirical.

Yours Sincerely

C. Connelly

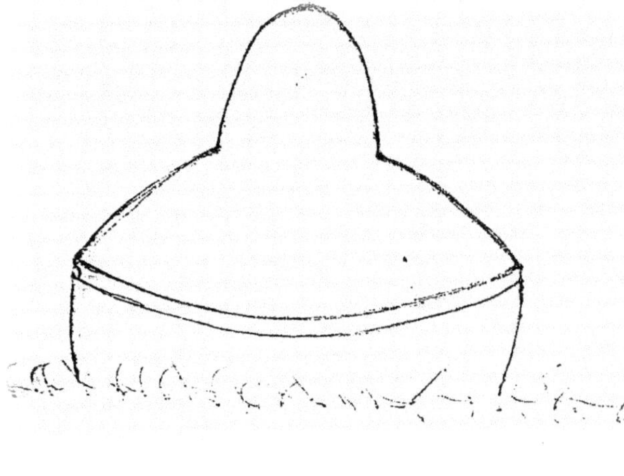

Cathie:

"One Sunday afternoon, during the War years, I went out for a walk down a country lane in Meriden, near Coventry. By sheer accident I came across a metal, dome-shaped structure which I took then to be a permanent building. Next to this structure was a line of smoking 'chimneys', poking up through the grass. There were tall men all around the structure, apparently adjusting something at the centre.

As I walked past them, the man at the centre of the part facing the lane raised his hands to face level and appeared to be cleaning them with a duster. As he walked closer to me, I gave him a smile but he did not smile back until he had finished cleaning his hands. He then gave me a slow smile and he seemed to be weighing me up.

All the men were wearing one-piece garments. They had unusually high foreheads and their skin seemed to be tanned. This was unusual because during the War people tended to be 'pasty-faced'. There was definitely something different about the eyes.

The structure appeared to be quite strong – that is solid – giving off a grey-blue light. I recall walking past and, on re-tracing my footsteps, was surprised to find that it had disappeared.

A few months later I had a second experience. This time it took place at work (the Reynolds Chain Company, in Coventry). On this occasion I was inspecting some chain links in the machine room, with a micrometer which I had been given. As I did this, I noticed a tall, youngish man also engaged in this work. He seemed at complete ease and under no strain, compared with the others. His overalls were also unusually clean. He saw me and came over. I then recognised him to be one of the crew I had seen by the craft at Meriden. He said 'Your war is upsetting my world'. I reminded him that it was his war too, but he replied: 'I don't come from this world – take me to your King and Queen'. I told him that I could not. He then asked me if I was colour blind and I answered saying: 'No'. He then enquired whom he should contact and I told him that he contact the head scientists and leaders at their country homes.

He asked me several times if I would go with him – and once he asked me to go on a long journey with him and see 'nice colours'. I refused. He had no accent and I don't recollect seeing him again at the factory during the whole three years that I worked there.

If I ever got depressed or miserable, I used to think of this unusual person and yearn for a meeting with him.

Then, one day in 1951, I arrived home to find that I had a visitor. He explained that he was a 'messenger' and said that he had asked to sign up for the job. He said that unless I really did want to meet the person who I had met at the factory, I was to refrain from thinking and intruding upon his thoughts. I was completely bewildered and recalled thinking that he must have been mad, as it was impossible for me to have done that.

I was taken several times to the craft, which was usually situated ion some lonely grassland spot. I got the the impression that these people had something for erasing your memory from the time of contact until you were on the craft. I am sure that it had something to do with the unusual 'watch' that they wore upon their wrists.

The centre of Meriden, Nr. Coventry as it appears today.

One time I found myself in a spacecraft, surrounded by men holding me down on a table. One of them said: 'We are not going to hurt you. We only want to see if you are pregnant'. I said: 'What's that?' He answered with a question: 'You don't know?' I then said: 'My mum says that if you go out at this time of night, 'Old Nick' will get you. Why have you come for me, I have not hurt anyone?' He asked who 'Old Nick' was, and I replied that he was the Devil. Then I said that if he was not the Devil, he could not be God because his skin . . . then I stopped short and said that no-one had told me the colour of God's skin.

The man had slits at the side of his mouth, reaching almost to his ears. The ears were long and animal-like, lying flat upon his

head. His nostrils were straight, long holes, disappearing up into his face. His coloured skin was unblemished. Most of the crew looked similar to us, averaging six to seven feet in height with high foreheads and greased black hair cut to just above the shoulders. Others in the craft were very different. They had blue complexions, in fact it was one of these men who talked to me."

Bob Tibbitts:

Mrs Connelly says that she was told that the beings that looked like us were 'prisoners' and that the others were free to come and go from the craft.

The man (interrogator) had a cat-like face with no whites to his eyes – these being set to the side of his face. The men similar to him all wore either brown or blue one-piece overalls.

Cathie:

"I told him that we had very good plastic surgeons and I explained to him what they could do to change his face. Gently he replied: 'If I had everything changed, then I would be alright'.

The craft inside was about the size of four double bedrooms. It was well lit all through but I could not tell where the light came from. One side of the wall was filled with a sort of scanner which I was taken over to. The other wall was filled with row upon row of meters. In the centre was the table, which was made from some sort of fibre-glass; this slid into the floor.

As I looked through the scanner I could see that we were travelling – I saw aeroplanes engaged in combat; all the pandemonium of voices. I could hear the crews of the aircraft speaking. Looking down to some water below, I could see ships and said that there were too many people in them. All of the time a voice above my head kept saying: 'This is your world' – But I kept denying it. I pointed to one of the aircraft and said that this was not my world . . . 'he is a cockney'. The voice again said: 'This is your world – look they are coming in all directions'.

Then the crew of one of the 'planes spotted us. They started shouting spasmodically: 'They have got a captive; it's a woman; no, it's a child; don't shoot; don't fire . . . I aint 'angin' around to find out'.

Now we appeared to be travelling alongside the aircraft and some of the crew were looking straight at us. One of them made the sign of the cross to me. At this my space friend asked if I knew him and I told him that I didn't. He then asked why he had moved his hands at me and I explained that he might have been a catholic and was praying for me. I then said that I hoped that they would be alright. The man said that I would be alright.

Then we changed course and I was looking at the Statue of Liberty. My space friend then said that he wouldn't tell me what I was looking at, as he did not wish to embarrass me. Then we seemed to be flying above a street in New York and I could see news vendors selling lots of papers. Something very important must have happened as many men were buying papers – but I could see no women.

When we changed course again I was standing alone at the scanner and my space friend was standing in the middle of the room; the other men had gone into other compartments. Only on one occasion did I hear them speak in any other language than English and it was completely unintelligible.

I was asked many questions, such as how blood transfusions were carried out and about household gadgets. They wanted to know about everything I had ever done or witnessed and what I believed to be right and wrong. Often they did not understand what I meant and asked me to visualise such things. One time I got rather tired of all the questions and cursed my interrogator. I didn't mean any harm but they insisted I retracted it because: 'we do not understand the power of thought'. If you wish someone ill, it can often bounce back on yourself. They said it wouldn't harm them but may have an adverse effect on my children and me.

While I was at the scanner I looked down and saw a man on a stake, shaped like an oblong cross. There was a crowd of people running backwards and forwards, throwing what appeared to be dirt and stones. A small child at the back was imitating them but I don't think he could see the man on the stake. The man on this stake was beautiful and I wondered why those people were doing that to him. The voice above my head said: 'This is your world'. I was indignant. I replied that it was not my world but that they were savages from the past. Then the voice said: 'Are they any different to that where you come from?' At this, I burst into tears, rushed to the man in the centre of the room and said that I was sorry that I thought of him as the Devil and that it was peaceful in the craft and hell was outside.

I was told that these people were Christian in attitude but were not ceremonious where they come from. They said that we were still immature and had to grow up.

Whatever my space friends say, they will not harm us. They are very kind and patient and always I felt at complete ease with them. The older members of the crew told me that it would do me no good to tell of my encounters as it would be of no benefit to me personally.

I was told that in order to have success (in making contact), a great number of people had to believe that it is true and can be done. One of the crew claimed to be a member of the 'Wildlife Preservation Society', so I was half-jokingly told. By 'wildlife' they meant our human race. They very much wanted to help mankind.

They took away my initial fear of them and the unknown and unfamiliar ways of their lives. I was shown a book in which there was writing very similar to Chinese or shorthand. They also gave me a map of a solar system to look at. When I asked where they came from they told me to look to the east to find their people. The book was fairly thick with a dark embossed cover. Another interesting feature in the craft was a black screen on which white lettering would appear and seemingly self-erase.

I was told that some of the crew has signed up for the mission without knowing really what it entailed. However, the driver, or leader of the craft always knew the purpose. He was responsible for the craft and never left it, unless there was a replacement.

They wanted to exchange ideas with us and wanted to obtain some of our gadgets for trading. They wanted us to grow up but as one of them pointed out, 'it involves a great deal more than you think' but that it will come.

On board the spacecraft were people from different planets. The older ones didn't particularly want to be involved with our planet but the younger ones did express the will to make contact. They asked me whom they should contact. I was bewildered and so were they but they said they would keep trying. There would be a lot of misunderstanding and errors but we will understand in the end.

The next time I was in the craft they showed me a film of me trying to walk across a road by some traffic lights. I had always been told to do this as it was the best place to cross."

Bob: On several occasions Mrs Connelly was taken back in time where she saw herself as a child.

Cathie:

"They were also interested in my hearing. I told them that when anyone spoke to me fast, the words all got churned together. Again they asked me if I was colour blind and said that they only wanted to help me and that it was the least they could do . . . 'You once helped me', the man said. I told him that I did not help him but only told him to go to a plastic surgeon. He said that I had done the best that I could."

Bob: It seems that the beings then operated in some fashion upon Cathie's eyes and apparently cured her difficulty in distinguishing one colour from another.

Cathie:

"They put me under sedation and when I came around I remember saying that I could not bare anyone touching my eyes. Then I said to the man, 'Your skin must be green, I can see the colour very clearly on your ears'."

Bob:

Cathie was told by the beings that before people could live together in harmony on earth, there would be trouble amongst the races. She was told that it could be so bad that people of all races would be too ashamed afterwards to mention it. Keep this in mind while you read her statement about another 'test' which she may have been subjected to.

Cathie:

"Another time when I was in the craft, the spacemen said that there was a bus coming along the road and they wanted me to get on it if I could. I said that if there was an empty seat I would get on. They repeated: 'Get on it if you can'.

When the bus stopped and I tried to get on, there was confusion. The people inside said that I could not get on the bus; it was not allowed. The people on the bus all had dark skins. After seeing an empty seat, I forced my way on. They said: 'Haven't you bought Fritz with you?' I thought they had meant a dog. I said that I hadn't got a dog and made my way to the empty seat. A young, well-built man was sitting next to the seat. He deliberately opened his knees to make it difficult for me to sit down. I forced myself onto the corner of the seat. The driver then asked for my fare and I got some money out but he said that it was no good. I got more money out but he still refused it. He asked me where I came from and I told him I came from Coventry. He then told me that I would have to get the money changed, but I told him that I would not be there long enough. I asked him what the name of the place was and he said that it was Rhodesia.

As the bus started up I swore, using the word 'bloody', as I was so uncomfortable on the corner of the seat. At this, a young lady who was sitting near by with a small child upon her knee, covered the child's ears and said: 'You swore!' I retorted that swearing would not do any lasting harm but segregation would. The man next to me closed his knees. Then one of the passengers asked where I had come from before I had got on the bus. I told them that I had come in a flying saucer. When I told them that the people in the flying saucer had told me to try and get on the bus, it stopped and people told me that I was upsetting the driver and had to be quiet. They asked me where I wanted to get off and I said that I didn't know but my space friends would meet me. They all went quiet as the bus started up once more.

Soon afterwards the bus was flagged down by the tall spaceman. The driver and other passengers stretched out their hands in a friendly gesture to help me off the bus. The spaceman grinned and asked if I had behaved myself. The driver said that I had been alright and wished that all white people were like me.

Another time I was on the craft, they took me to Florida and we had been talking about Rhesus babies and blood transfusions and one of the men said: 'These people know more about genetics than we do.' Then there was some talk about having an exchange of ideas with us.

On another occasion when I was on the craft I was looking through the scanner and I saw myself in the past, between the ages of 11 and 13. I saw myself kneeling at the altar in a little wooden Salvation Army church. The Salvation Army captain was with me. I saw myself being daubed with water by the captain. At this the spaceman asked me what we were doing. I said the captain was reading out what I was then promising to undertake. Then the spaceman said: 'Do you always keep a promise?' I said that I never make a promise that is impossible to keep and that I never break a promise. Then the voice above my head said: 'You're back in square one, Cathie, because …' I replied: 'If I am back in square one because …, what square are all the murderers, liars, thieves, etc., in?' The voice replied: 'They are not in any square at all. It is your job to get them in the running.' I said: 'You are not asking much, are you?' Then I saw myself as the little girl, kneeling at the altar and the voice said: 'You promised allegiance to God. Do you know what allegiance to God means?' I said: 'Yes, allegiance to God means allegiance to people of all religions, creeds and colours.' Then I said that God knows I would never break a promise and that he would help me to keep it.

This story is cut short – the odds are against me writing it. Ken Rogers has the rest of the information that is needed to make a complete story. A story that was meant to end with a miracle."

Bob: Please see Ken's comments in 'Gemini' magazine, Vol. 1 No.2, which follows as plates.

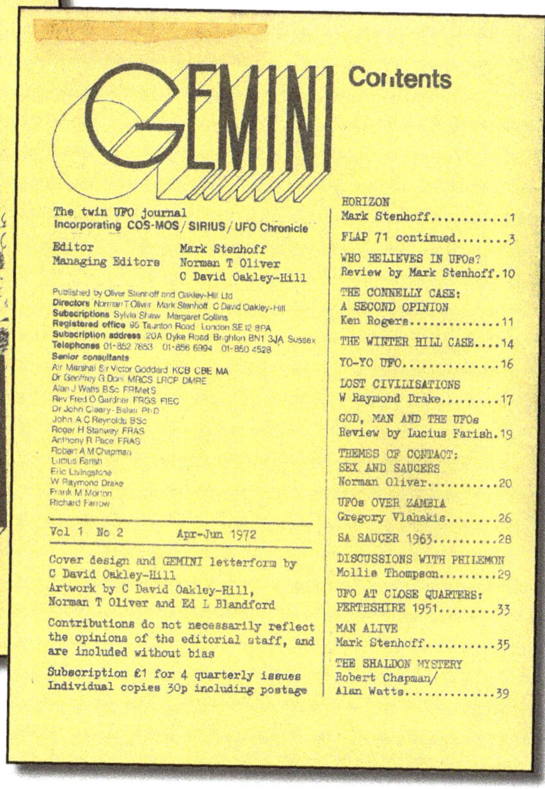

GEMINI

The twin UFO journal
Incorporating COS-MOS / SIRIUS / UFO Chronicle

Editor Mark Stenhoff
Managing Editors Norman T Oliver, C David Oakley-Hill

Published by Oliver Stenhoff and Oakley-Hill Ltd
Directors Norman T Oliver Mark Stenhoff C David Oakley-Hill
Subscriptions Sylvia Shaw Margaret Collins
Registered office 95 Taunton Road London SE12 8PA
Subscription address 20A Dyke Road Brighton BN1 3JA Sussex
Telephones 01-852 7653 01-856 6994 01-850 4528
Senior consultants
Air Marshal Sir Victor Goddard KCB CBE MA
Dr Geoffrey G Doel MRCS LRCP DMRE
Alan J Watts BSc FRMetS
Rev Fred O Gardner FRGS FIEC
Dr John Cleary-Baker PhD
John A C Reynolds BSc
Roger H Stanway FRAS
Anthony R Pace FRAS
Robert A M Chapman
Lucius Farish
Eric Livingstone
W Raymond Drake
Frank M Morton
Richard Farrow

Vol 1 No 2 Apr-Jun 1972

Cover design and GEMINI letterform by C David Oakley-Hill
Artwork by C David Oakley-Hill, Norman T Oliver and Ed L Blandford

Contributions do not necessarily reflect the opinions of the editorial staff, and are included without bias

Subscription £1 for 4 quarterly issues
Individual copies 30p including postage

Contents

My thanks go to the contributors who have allowed me to present their views or experiences in GEMINI 2:

Mollie Thompson for enabling her "Discussions" to have a wider audience.

Reg Chapman for permitting the story of his contact to appear.

Gregory Vlahakis for details of his Zambian experiences.

W Raymond Drake for excerpts from his book SPACEMEN IN THE ANCIENT WEST.

Lucius Farish for his review of GOD, MAN AND THE UFO'S.

Ken Rogers for his "second opinion" on the Connelly case.

Last, but by no means least, Ed Blandford, a former COSMOS editor who I am delighted to welcome to these pages as an illustrator - and a darn good one too!

Norman Oliver

Ken Rogers wrote the following before reading the story of Mrs Connelly by Bob Tibbitts in GEMINI 1. As a consequence I had intended amending his contribution slightly to allow for this: on re-reading it, however, I consider it would detract from the comparison to do so; nothing, therefore, has been altered, but the reader should bear in mind that Bob Tibbitt's report had not been seen by Ken at the time of writing.

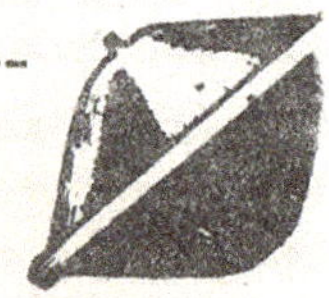

THE CONNELLY CASE

A Second Opinion – Ken Rogers

I have been asked to write-up my impressions of Mrs Connelly. I first heard of her when I was BUFORA's Information Officer. She had completed one of the lengthy sighting report forms with details of the landed craft she saw in 1940.

Subsequently I held a lengthy correspondence with Mrs Connelly and visited her in the presence of her family and alone on numerous occasions, when I taped and noted her descriptions of the events which took place between 1940 - 1950.

I am at a slight disadvantage here because I do not have a copy before me of the detailed investigations that were subsequently made by Bob Tibbitts. However I will say that I

11

was very impressed by the whole of Mrs Connelly's testimony.

She is a simple urban housewife, a Scotswoman, middleaged. I could not fault her on any of the story she related to me. She seemed to have been induced to a form of amnesia and parts of her testimony would often end with "now all is a blank."

At one of the first contacts Mrs Connelly was asked if she would take "them" to the country homes of scientists and leaders as the war was upsetting their world. She believed that they came from somewhere in this galaxy. When asked they would say "Look to the East and you will find us." There was a distinct difference about their eyes: they were patterned like big cats' eyes. "I could not see any pupils or whites. However, on closer examination, I did notice what appeared to be a shadow which went over the eyes, a very faint circle where the white should begin. I recall stating that they didn't have any whites in their eyes."

She did not approve of their method of contact but was drawn to them and came to like them very much. She is under the impression that they must be among us and know about most things that we do. She feels that they are simply observing our progress, but did not wish to get involved until it was safe.

They tried to get her to mind read, but she found she could only do it occasionally.

They wore instruments on their wrists: she believed it was the manipulation of these that gave her the effects of amnesia.

The craft she describes as being small and compact inside: about the size of four double-bedrooms.

They had a tasteless liquid that looked like beer, and pills. Mrs Connelly said she was given a drink "in a beige coloured tumbler, about five inches long with a very comfortable rim." (who would describe a tumbler as such?) It looked as if it was made of fibre glass. The liquid was neither hot nor cold, yellowy coloured, like iodine, although not unpleasant.

Several statements that were made to Mrs Connelly interested me. They seemed to sound right - just what one would expect to hear from an advanced being from another world. For instance, she was told that this (our world) was of highly qualified children. One of the reasons that it did not progress faster on positive lines was because no one lived long enough to give the necessary guidance. When our people grow older

12

they often become senile. Mrs Connelly was asked everything she knew, what she believed to be right and wrong, about bloo transfusions and how they were administered, about household gadgets. They told her that they were interested in an 'exchange of ideas.'

On September 19 1961, the American couple Betty & Barney Hill were allegedly captured by beings from a craft and taken aboard for physical examination, and were later returned suffering from a form of amnesia.

Apart from the similar circumstances of effects of loss of memory and the physical examination to which Mrs Connelly was also subjected, in the heavily detailed account that I obtained from Mrs Connelly, other startling similarities occur. For instance:

1. The Book. Betty Hill under hypnosis described: "On a cabinet there was a fairly big book...and asked if she could have it. It was like Japanese writing, different...it had sharp lines, some very thin, some medium and some heavy. It had some dots. It had straight lines and curved lines. And the leader laughed and he asked me if I could read it. And I told him no...."

A. Mrs Connelly describes: "Someone pointed to a wall on my left hand side. There was an alcove down the middle of the wall with what appeared to be a shelf in it...A book with a dark embossed cover was on it. A man opened it and asked me if I could read it. I said no and asked if it was Chinese. They all laughed and said,'you think it is Chinese?' I then stated it is not, Chinese writing is fancy. This was not writing as I knew it."

2. The Map. Betty Hill under hypnosis: "And he went across the room and pulled out a map, and he asks me had I ever seen a map like this before....There were all these dots on it. Some were little, just pin points. And others were as big as a nickel. And there were lines...going from one dot to another. And there was one big circle, and it had a lot of lines coming out from it."

B. Mrs Connelly describes: "Then he put his right hand to the side of the wall, pulled out a map, asked me if I had ever seen a map like it before...I said no. The world is a bigger place than I thought. Then I pointed to a circle. I said who lives there?"

Did these contacts really take place, or did Mrs Connelly

13

simply read about other contact stories, and together with a fertile imagination dream the whole series of episodes up one evening?

I tend to think that a series of contacts did take place, but perhaps not necessarily physical in nature, although paradoxically her descriptions are in places so definite that on the other hand one would tend to think that the events which are described were in fact very real indeed. Certainly they were very real to Mrs Connelly. The UFO phenomenon, however, is a very complicated subject and the forms in which it manifests itself can be very devious in nature.

Dr Hynek with David Oakley-Hill (left) and Mark Stenhoff at the reception party given in October 1972 by the UK publisher of "The UFO Experience"

Bob: At my last meeting with Cathie Connelly, I posed a few more questions to her. Those questions and her answers follow.

Q Why were you walking down the lane at that particular time?

A **For pleasure.**

Q Did you immediately recognise the dome-shaped structure as what you now know to be a 'UFO'?

A **No.**

Q How tall were the men standing around the object in relation to it?

A **About half it's size.**

Q You mentioned that one man did something with his hands before returning your smile. Could you expand upon this?

A **He, or another man, told me that he photographed me.**

Q What were your impressions when you found that the object had vanished?

A **Mystified.**

Q Exactly how did the watches worn by the beings affect your memory?

A **I know now that it brings my memory back.**

Q What appeared upon the 'scanner'?

A **The outside world and scenes through the walls of buildings.**

Q Which group of beings called themselves prisoners?

A **The people who looked like us.**

Q Were any names mentioned? If so, please give them.

A **Yes. 'Jasiv' or 'Jaskik'.**

Q Describe the facial features of the blue-skinned beings.

A **Cat face.**

Q Did they always talk to you in English?

A **Yes.**

Q Did they communicate to you in any other way?

A **Yes. Telepathy. The people who looked like us also used telepathy.**

Q How did you discern the younger members of the crew from the elder members on the craft?

A **The smoothness of the skin.**

Q Did these beings foretell any future event?

A **Yes. On the scanner.**

Q What made you feel that these men were from space?

A **They showed me a map of a solar system.**

Q What was (is) their purpose in coming to the Earth?

A **To show us our capabilities.**

Q Why did they decide to contact you?

A **I was in an ideal place. It had to be someone.**

Q How is it possible to contact these people?

A **Praying. This is telepathy.**

Q You say that you have had recent contact with these people. How did you recognise them?

A **By past acquaintance and their watches. (They touch them with one finger).**

Q Have you been in one of their craft recently?

A **No.**

Q Did you eve see any of these craft land or take off?

A **No.**

Q Did you ever fly in one?

A **Yes.**

Q Did you ever leave the Earth in one of these craft?

A **Yes.**

Q Did you, or any of the beings have any difficulty in breathing during your contacts?

A **No.**

Q Did you hear any odd sounds near the craft?

A **Yes. Like fast running water.**

Q Were any peculiar smells present during or subsequent to your contacts?

A **No.**

Thank you Cathie.

6th June – England: UFO over Woodbridge Airfield, Suffolk

During the morning of the 6th June, Mr William Green (aged 74 in 1995) living in Grays, Essex, was on night spotting duty, manning a gun site at Woodbridge Airfield, guarding dummy aircraft parked nearby. At about 2.30am, through binoculars, he sighted a grey-white saucer-shaped object in the sky between 10-15,000 feet, and some 30 feet across.

> *"I went to the identification telescope on the gun platform and looked through it at the object, which appeared to be hovering over the dummy airfield. I immediately awoke the Sergeant Major and told him about it. He said, 'It's a weather balloon or meteor'.*
>
> *I then telephoned Headquarters and told them what I had been seeing. They confirmed that no searchlights were in use over our locality, or aircraft or weather balloons. They suggested I was seeing a gas cloud! The object started to move from left to right slowly, for a few minutes, before gathering speed and moving away. I logged it and was made the butt of humor by my colleagues."*

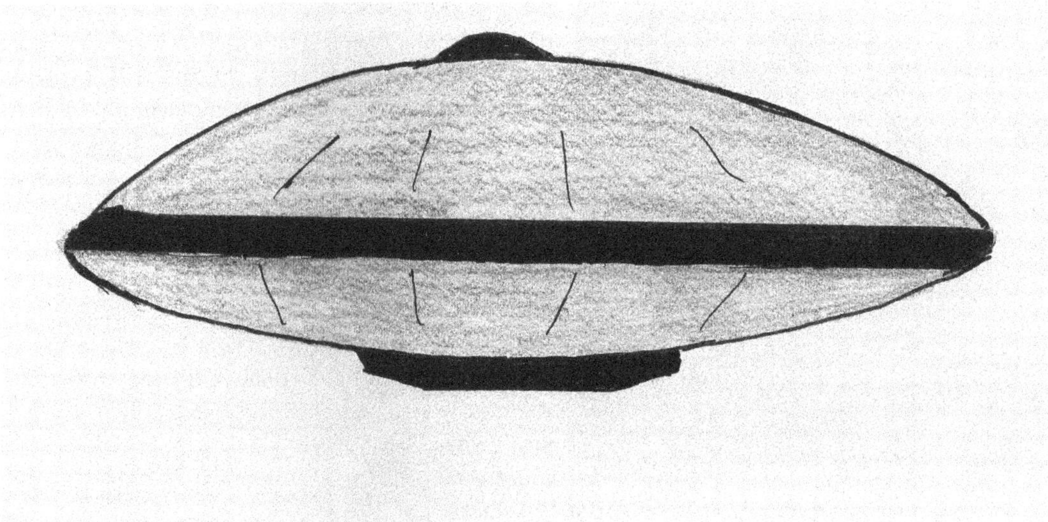

In 1941, during the 'Battle of Britain', a Spitfire was shot down accidently by the Royal Observer Corps at Hellfire Corner. They had arranged a competition for identifying aircraft that day. These were being filmed by the cine section. Somebody behind William asked:

> *" 'What are those aircraft?' He replied, 'Ice cream merchants', and was told off by the Brigadier, who said, 'This is a war, not a game, you idiot.' "*

William:

> *"When the film was developed it was found they were Italian aircraft, but no apologies were given.*
>
> *Sometime after this we were sent to Gloucester Airport, where they manufactured Typhoon and Tornado aircraft. Our gun sight was on top of a hill overlooking the airport. Hostile*

> *aircraft were reported in the area. I identified one of those aircraft with an engine on one wing and greenhouse observation turret on the other wing. I was called an idiot again, and told no aircraft could fly like that. Some time later, I once again proved them wrong. I can't remember the make, but it was a German recognition plane."*

(Source: Ron West Interview 1995)

England: UFO descends over Stansted Army Base, Essex

In the same year, Emily Crewe was twenty-one years of age and a member of the Women's Auxiliary Territorial Service. She was stationed at *Stansted Army Camp, Essex; some six miles from the centre of Bishop's Stortford, where 900 personnel were accommodated (now home to Britain's third airport).

Mopping the kitchen floor, one lunch-time, Emily heard a commotion outside on the parade ground. Looking out of the window she saw a number of running soldiers, clearly panicked, accompanied by shouts of 'take cover!' Thinking the base was under attack by German aircraft, she ducked down but glanced upwards through the open window and saw a huge, glowing, golden 'ball' – the size of a hut – slowly descending through the air above the parade ground, with what looked like sparks coming away from it, which came to rest just above the ground, then slowly moved over and up against the window pane of the kitchen. She locked the kitchen door and stood there, stunned, trying to make sense of what was happening. Her shock turned to curiosity when she saw what appeared to be a skin or outer covering, resembling translucent rubber, with something moving about inside. It then began to shake or wobble like a jelly, while performing a number of strange motions in the air, before moving sideways against the wall of the kitchen – where it stopped dead and then gradually went out of her line of vision.

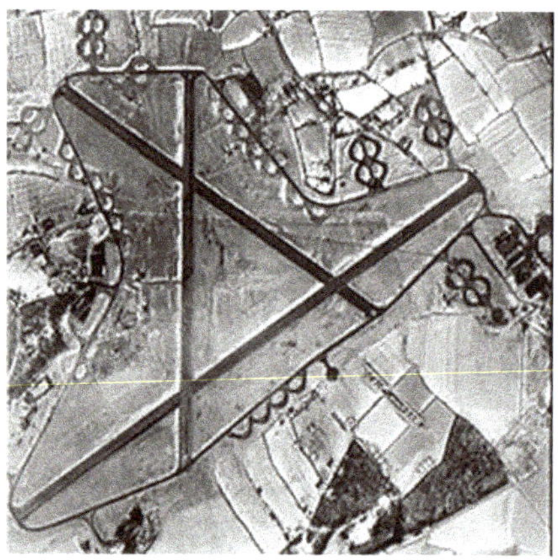

Stansted Mountfitchet

Warned to keep quiet

Later Emily and the other service personnel were assembled on the parade ground and warned not to say

*During Second World War Stansted Mountfitchet was used by the Royal Air Force and the United States Army Air Force as a bomber airfield and as a major maintenance depot. Although the official name was Stansted Mountfitchet, the base was known as simply Stansted in both written and spoken form.

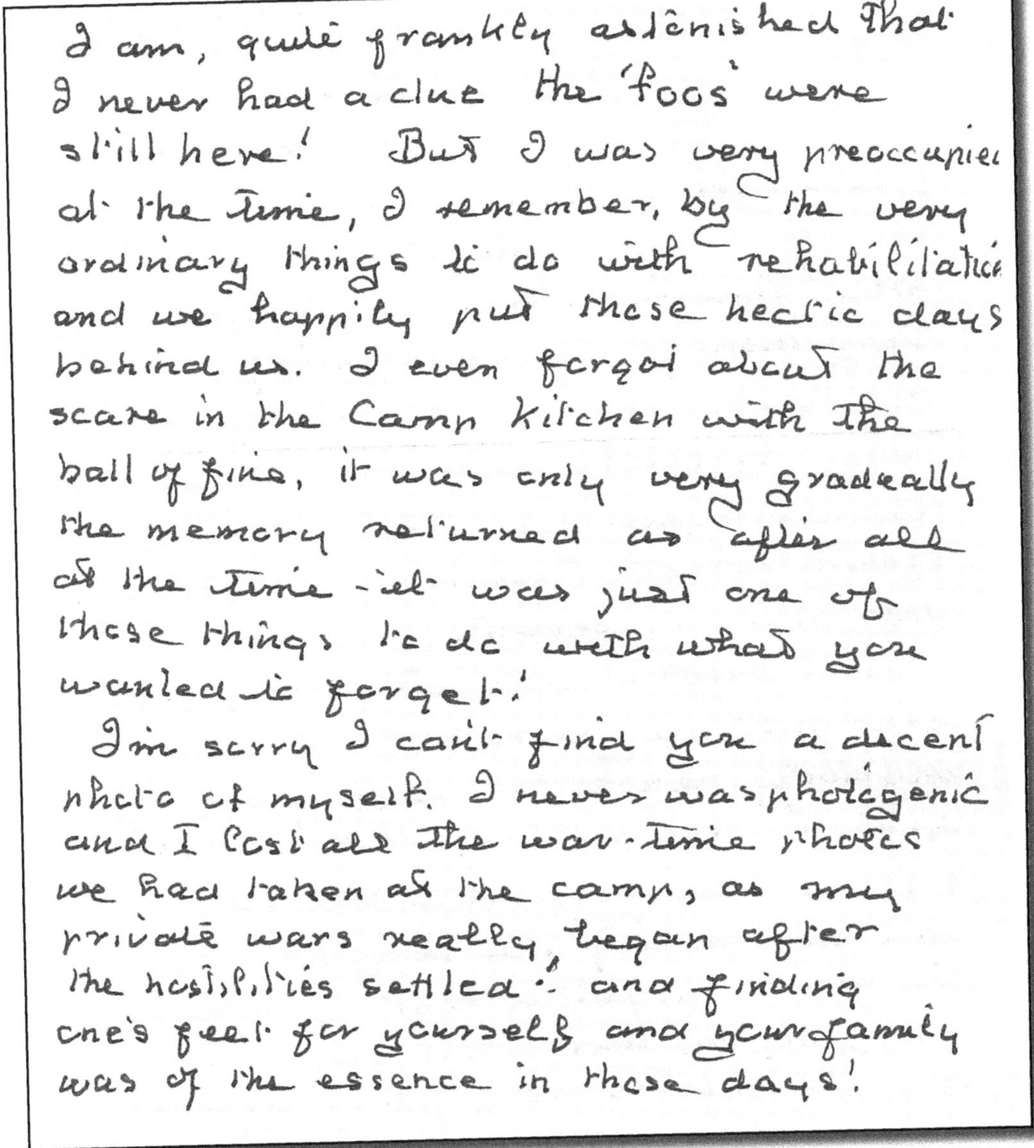

I am, quite frankly astonished that I never had a clue the 'foos' were still here! But I was very preoccupied at the time, I remember, by the very ordinary things to do with rehabilitation and we happily put these hectic days behind us. I even forgot about the scare in the Camp kitchen with the ball of fire, it was only very gradually the memory returned as after all at the time -it was just one of these things to do with what you wanted to forget!

I'm sorry I can't find you a decent photo of myself. I never was photogenic and I lost all the war-time photos we had taken at the camp, as my private wars really began after the hostilities settled! and finding one's feet for yourself and your family was of the essence in these days!

anything about the incident, although she learnt from excited conversations held with others that the object *"was last seen jumping the wire fence surrounding the camp, before disappearing into the nearby forest"*.

The sighting was to provide the trigger of great interest to Emily Crewe – a woman in her 90s, as the original Volume 1 of *Haunted Skies* went to press – who was to become the founder member of BEAMS (British Earth and Aerial Mysteries Society), more than capable of holding an in-depth conversation with the authors on a variety of subjects, interjected with her own brand of unforgettable humour.

Easter – England: Domed object, with beings stood next to it

Arthur Long wrote to the Essex UFO Research Group, in 1992, wishing to bring their attention to something that he had witnessed in 1940, during the Easter school holidays, when aged 10 years old and living in Oldchurch Road, Romford, in Essex.

War had broken out in September, just under a year ago, and this was a period commonly referred to as a 'phony period' because of a lull in any hostile activity.

> *"At the back of the house was a huge gravel pit, about two miles square, inside of which were four lakes. One spring day, at about 3pm, I went down the garden to collect our neighbour's dog to take it for a walk. The weather was fairly bright with a few fluffy clouds about. I walked along with two lakes on my right and two on the left. These lakes were fenced off but, as I was friends with the farmer's son, I was allowed to walk over the land. I climbed over the fence and began looking out for the large grey carthorse, which was often put out to graze on the field. He was a friendly animal and I had, in fact, ridden him and fed him grass. I looked out for him but there was no sign of him; instead, I saw a shiny dome-shaped object – a bit like two saucers stuck together – with what I took to be two 'men' standing at the side of it. I wasn't surprised, to begin with, as there was a conglomeration of other pieces of discarded machinery abandoned there by either the farm or the gravel company."*

Arthur stood there, puzzled by their presence, wondering what they were doing with equipment in an area now grassed over, as excavations had stopped some years ago.

> *"They had shiny overalls on, which reminded me of barrage balloon material."*

Decided to run away

At this stage Arthur was at a height and looking down onto the unfolding scene below, estimated to be about 150 feet away.

At this point the dog barked, causing one of the 'men' to either wave or shake his fist.

> *"I climbed through the fence and ran as fast as I could along the centre path, running away from the direction of my home rather than towards it. Why I did that I have no idea.*
>
> *I must have run a good 500 yards, pulling the dog behind me, and stopped due to being out of breath. The dog barked again and a voice said 'Hello'."*

Extremely frightened, Arthur tuned around to see a lady walking her dog. She was a friendly local woman – a retired schoolteacher for a local girl's school. She asked him what was happening and he told her he had been just playing with the dog.

Object takes off in a burst of light

> *"As we walked back along the path together, heading homewards with the place where I had seen the strange men and machine in front of me, I saw a series of flashing bright lights – like a massive firework – some 6 feet in diameter, about 200 yards away from us. It shot out slightly at an angle and then seemed to pause, before shooting upwards at fantastic speed and disappearing from sight. I tried to talk to the woman about it; she dismissed it as being a thunderbolt or shooting star."*

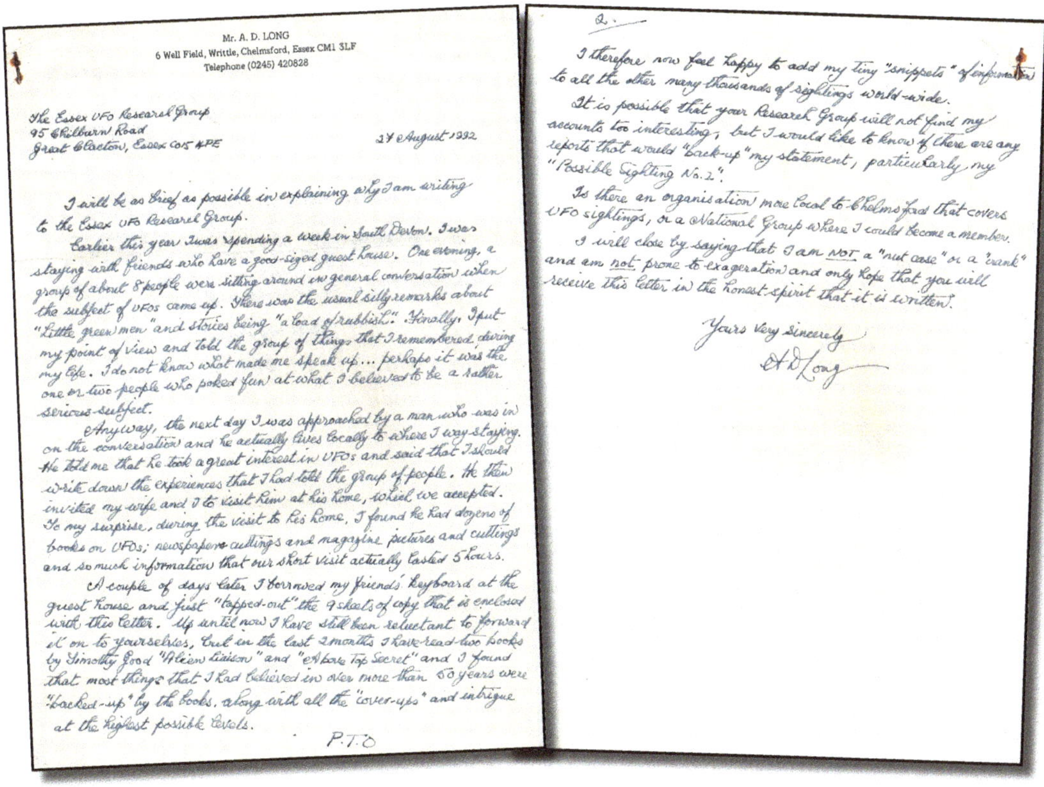

Mr. A. D. LONG
6 Well Field, Writtle, Chelmsford, Essex CM1 3LF
Telephone (0245) 420828

The Essex UFO Research Group
95 Chilburn Road
Great Clacton, Essex CO15 4PE

27 August 1992

I will be as brief as possible in explaining why I am writing to the Essex UFO Research Group.

Earlier this year I was spending a week in South Devon. I was staying with friends who have a good-sized guest house. One evening, a group of about 8 people were sitting around in general conversation when the subject of UFOs came up. There was the usual silly remarks about "Little green men" and stories being "a load of rubbish". Finally, I put my point of view and told the group of things that I remembered during my life. I do not know what made me speak up... perhaps it was the one or two people who poked fun at what I believed to be a rather serious subject.

Anyway, the next day I was approached by a man who was in on the conversation and he actually lives locally to where I was staying. He told me that he took a great interest in UFOs and said that I should write down the experiences that I had told the group of people. He then invited my wife and I to visit him at his home, which we accepted. To my surprise, during the visit to his home, I found he had dozens of books on UFOs; newspapers cuttings and magazine pictures and cuttings and so much information that our short visit actually lasted 5 hours.

A couple of days later I borrowed my friends' keyboard at the guest house and just "tapped-out" the 9 sheets of copy that is enclosed with this letter. Up until now I have still been reluctant to forward it on to yourselves, but in the last 2 months I have read two books by Timothy Good "Alien Liaison" and "Above Top Secret" and I found that most things that I had believed in over more than 50 years were "backed-up" by the books, along with all the "cover-ups" and intrigue at the highest possible levels.

P.T.O

2.

I therefore now feel happy to add my tiny "snippets" of information to all the other many thousands of sightings world-wide.

It is possible that your Research Group will not find my accounts too interesting, but I would like to know if there are any reports that would "back-up" my statement, particularly my "Possible Sighting No. 2".

Is there an organisation more local to Chelmsford that covers UFO sightings, or a National Group where I could become a member.

I will close by saying that I am NOT a "nut case" or a "crank" and am not prone to exageration and only hope that you will receive this letter in the honest spirit that it is written.

Yours Very Sincerely
A D Long

After arriving home Arthur handed the dog back and told his mother what he had seen.

> *"When my father came home, I then repeated the story. He then advised me that I should carry on attending Sunday school and make up my own mind about the incident when I was an adult."*

Somewhat as a rather sad footnote to this incident took place a few days later, during another walk to the location concerned.

> *"I stood there looking down on the original scene and, to my horror, saw workmen loading the poor old grey horse onto the back of a lorry. It had thick yellow mud on its legs and the belly of it had been cut wide open – there was no sign of any blood. Somebody told me they would have cut the belly open to let the water out, after it had been found drowned in the lake. I was more concerned about the horse."*

1941 – England: Child injured during encounters with entities

One such account, involving a rare complaint of actual physical injury, was outlined to us by Alison Richards – a woman in her late 60s – whom we met on a number of occasions at her Kidderminster home. We were accompanied by Phil Hoyle of the Shrewsbury UFO Group – a man who specialises in counselling women claiming to have been the subject of alien abduction experiences.

Alison outlined her early childhood memories, from when she was aged between five and six. These included a series of bizarre, frightening experiences, while living with her badly crippled mother in a tiny cottage, lit by gas and candles, in Kidderminster, Worcestershire.

Father away fighting in the Ninth Army

At the time, her father – a soldier with the Ninth Army – was away fighting in North Africa, during 1941.

> *"When mum went to bed, she had to bandage on a metal splint to her leg, as her only way of getting about was to hop. It was always an unwritten rule that if I needed her, perhaps because of sickness, I would always go to her, except for when I had a visit from what I can only describe as 'horse beings', who always entered the room from out of the linen cupboard, next to a window over the stairs, when I would scream and shout for her. By the time my*

From: "Alison" <akjcj@blueyonder.co.uk>
To: <johndawn@hansonholloway.fsnet.co.uk>
Sent: 28 September 2007 23:51
Subject: From Alison

Hi John and Dawn .... biggest Thank You for all the lovely photo's and e.mail, what a wonderful surprise when I switched on my computer. It felt like Christmas.
I have read your manuscript " How it all Began " and am really impressed with all the topics you have covered. Well Done x x Is it your introduction on your web.site only I haven't been there yet, but I will !

I noticed you said, you were interested in matters that have taken place in the UK during 1940 / 1966 ? You also said that you had found the photo of my ' arm ' but my scars are on my left (shin) leg, John and Dawn.
I was born in 1940. In 1942 / 3 my Father was in the 8th Army and fighting in North Africa / Monte Casino, etc. My Mom was badly crippled by Polio as a child and wore a caliper, built-up shoe and used a walking stick but she was only 25 and so pretty.
We lived in a tiny, two up - two down (one of six) cottage, with a gas mantle in the front room and candles in the kitchen and bedrooms.* Kidderminster Knocked down Oct '10

When Mom went to bed, she had to bandage on a metal splint to her leg and had to hop to get around and it was always an " unspoken " thing, that if I ever needed her (perhaps if I felt sick or woke up with the ' croup ') I would run from my bedroom to hers and she would attend to me .... Except when the "HORSES " WERE IN MY ROOM when I would scream and cry for her and she would have to struggle to get to me.

In my tiny back bedroom, there was a cupboard over the stairs, next to the window (where Mom kept the folded bed linen) and the HORSES would always come from there. By the time Mom got to my bed, they had always gone back through the cupboard or the window.
Of course, Mom never saw them and would spend lots of time, holding me and telling me that " HORSES couldn.t possibly get up our stairs and were too big to get into the bedroom and back downstairs and anyway, how would they get in and out of the doors " ?

Not always but four times, they hurt me, John and Dawn. I would have flesh, gouged out of my left leg (on my shin bone) about the size of a 5 pence piece and I would have to have ointment and a bandage on, until it had scabbed over and got better.

These ' holes ' in my leg would worry Mom so much. She thought at first that I must have caught my leg on some loose wire (on the bed springs ?) but there wasn't any ! Then she and a neighbour, thoroughly checked the mattress ...... nothing to hurt me ? She wondered if I had been bitten (by something Big) but not on the SAME leg, in the SAME place and perhaps months apart ? But, it was always after the HORSES had been in my room.

I was 67 in August and still have the scars on my leg. Two of them have sort of faded (a bit) over the past 62 years but I can see them and know where they are. I am sending you a drawing I did, *mum had reached the bedroom, they had left via either the window or the linen cupboard. I kept telling mum what I had seen. She insisted horses could not physically get into the house, but I knew they were real because, on at least four occasions, they actually hurt me. I would end up with flesh gouged out of my left leg on the shin bone, about the size of a five pence piece. The injuries to my leg (which always happened after the shortest one came into the room) frightened my mother. She thought, to begin with, that I had caught the leg on a loose mattress wire on the bed spring. She and a neighbour thoroughly checked the bed but could find no trace of what was causing these injuries to occur, always in the same place on the shin."*

Sadly, Alison died in August 2008. We pondered if the 'horse entities' she described had parallels with the small alien beings often described as 'greys', whose role in abduction phenomena are well documented.
(Source: Personal interviews)

More to this than meets the eye

We never ceased to be amazed by the variety of inexplicable phenomena brought to our attention by the public. These range from strange unidentified lights in the sky to saucer-shaped structured objects, occasionally seen on the ground, with their 'alien' occupants. These physical 'incursions' into our airspace seem to leave the witness with all sorts of emotions as they grappled to come to terms with having experienced something well outside the parameters of everyday life.

More frightening are the reports released through regression techniques or memory flashbacks, of childhood experiences involving the unwarranted intrusions by 'friendly playmates'; small beings normally invisible to the adult human eye, whose appearances are often dismissed by the parents as being the result of a vivid imagination or bad dreams. Unfortunately, as the child enters puberty, the experiences appear to become more disturbing. If it is unlikely these things are from outer space, then where exactly do they come from? Dr. J. Allen Hynek – prior to his death, the world's leading authority on UFOs – eventually abandoned the 'nuts and bolts' explanation.

England: UFO sighted over Wiltshire

Another early UFO sighting came from ex-WRAF servicewoman Mrs Ena Stevens, known to her friends and family as 'Stevey'.

In 1941, 'Stevey' was a young girl living with her parents. Their worst fears appeared to have come true after church bells began ringing, signifying a possible German invasion.

> *"We rushed out into the street, fearing the worst, but were relieved to discover that the alert had sounded after a barrage balloon had come adrift from its moorings. My mother, who was gazing intently towards the Wills tobacco factory, shouted out for a telescope, as she could see something next to the chimney. My father handed the telescope to her. She looked through it and then asked me to take a look. I was shocked to see a gunmetal grey, saucer-shaped object, hovering at an angle in the sky, halfway down the chimney. Suddenly, it shot off upwards at terrific speed and was gone."*

RAF Neatishead

Ena was a former radar operator, stationed at RAF Neatishead – now living in Swindon, Wiltshire. She provided a fascinating insight into reports of UFOs tracked on radar at the base. Royal Air Force Neatishead was established during World War II.

> *"Its function was to carry out ground controlled interceptions with the aid of plan position radar displays. The first radar (Type 7) at Neatishead was installed in September 1941, with an establishment of two officers and forty airmen and airwomen who were billeted in a local village."*
>
> **(Source: Personal interview)**

Summer – England: UFOs sighted by scouts over Yorkshire

Thomas Austin wrote to us with regard to what he saw one day in the summer of 1941, whilst on a camping trip with the Skipton Christchurch scouts, near Gargrave in the Yorkshire Dales. Early one morning he was talking to another boy, when:

> *"Five 'blobs of light' appeared low down in the sky, glinting as they caught the rays of the sun. Within a short time they were nearly overhead, now almost motionless in the sky, allowing us to see what resembled darkened globes, with these 'shapes' moving about inside and a structure beneath, showing a number of portholes around the body of each craft. Suddenly all objects headed eastward at tremendous speed – gone out of sight in seconds. We told the scout master what we had seen. He suggested they were probably weather balloons, which had broken loose."*

(Source: Personal interview)

IDENTIFICATION CARD Serial No. 190

(For Representatives of Foreign Governments or Missions)

Name Sir Hugh C.T. Dowding Nationality British

Address 1785 Massachusetts Ave., Washington, D. C.

Title or position Technical Advisor

Member or representative of BRITISH AIR COMMISSION

Good until 30th June, 1941.

Authorized to visit only that facility or activity stated in accompanying specific letter of authority

Age 58 Height 5' 11" Weight 150 Eyes blue

Authenticated by

(Signature of bearer) Official title Air Commodore Air Attache

Date issued 15th Jan 1941. Embassy or Legation British

We also discovered that Lord Dowding made a visit to the USA to discuss the problem of 'Flying Saucers' in this year.

Summer – France: UFO landing and entities seen

We attempted to track down other European reports from around that area during this period of time, and came across an account from Madame Madeleine Arnoux, who was riding her cycle in the summer of 1941, (aged 13), along the road towards the village of Le Verger, when she decided to stop and pick some berries from a nearby wood on what was a stormy and overcast day. As she looked along the road, which took a pronounced curve to the right before disappearing into woodland, she saw standing a 'thing' stationary beside some trees, with some 'beings' quite near to it – less than three feet in height, dressed in a sort of brown overall. The 'machine' must have been about the size of a small car of the Volkswagen class – dull grey metallic in colour.

> *"I was rooted to the spot and could only watch them as they stood stock-still. How long this mutual observation went on for I can't say, but I remember the oppressive atmosphere, the stormy state of the weather, and a feeling of being unable to move. I then felt myself free to bend down to retrieve my bicycle. When I looked up towards the strange apparition, there was nothing – except a violent wind blowing the trees about."*

Madeleine was terrified and didn't tell anyone what she had seen for forty years, until talk of 'flying saucers' began, when she realised, without a doubt, this is what she had seen.

(Source: F. Lagarde, *Lumieres Dans la Nuit*, No. 118, June 1972, from translation by Gordon Creighton)

1942

UFO over Malta: aircraft sent up to investigate

In 1942 Major Eddie *Axisa, MBE/MIOM/AMIE, was a second lieutenant in charge of a coastal battery of two 4.5 anti-aircraft guns near the Port of Tewfik Bay, Malta.

One sunny morning, after completing general maintenance on the guns, he was walking away from the command post towards some shade:

> *"The alarm sounded. I ran back and spoke to Gunner Magrin, who told me he had spotted a very bright star-like object on a bearing of 255, at an angle of 75 degrees. Sgt. Profon Tanti, the radar operator, turned his radar towards the direction indicated by the spotter. At this point the whole command post crew was now in position, with the guns fully manned and awaiting orders – the 'object' still stationary in the sky. Our radar failed to pick up the 'object' and I recall Sgt. Tanti complaining vociferously about the shortcomings of his equipment. The height finder, Gunner Grech, reported his Goetz height finder was stuck at infinity.*
>
> *We presumed other gun sights must have also seen the 'object', because a couple of aircraft were sent up to investigate. All of a sudden the target, still bright and stationary in the sky, disappeared from view. In those days none of us had ever heard of the expression 'Flying Saucers' or UFOs."*

(Source: Personal letter/interview)

25th March – England: RAF pilot fires on UFO over Essen

Another UFO incident involving the crew of an RAF Bomber took place at about midnight on March 25th 1942, while flying back from a bombing mission over Essen, according to French UFO Researcher Henri Durrant. Details of this were found in his book, *The Black Book of Flying Saucers* (1970). His report describes the appearance of an 'orange sphere seen following the aircraft, between 1-2,000 yards away. The tail gunner then opened fire, hitting the object several times, without any noticeable effect'.

In view of a number of differing accounts found on the Internet relating to this incident, we tried to trace M. Durrant, without success, but were later informed that he had passed away some years ago.

Gordon Creighton

Gordon Creighton told of having received a report from Miss O.M. Beaton of Vancouver, Canada, who described an encounter with a UFO, told to her by Pilot Officer Roman Sobinski – then living in Richmond, British Columbia.

> *"On March 25th 1942, at midnight, he saw a round disc, or sphere, glowing orange in colour, flying at an estimated speed of 180mph, following his aircraft, about 1,200 yards away over the Zuider Zee, Holland, while returning from a bombing raid on Essen, at 15,000ft, after it was reported to him by his tail gunner. Sobinski, who saw the object was closing in on the aircraft, gave instructions to fire on it. Several rounds appeared to enter the object but made no impression. It then disappeared at an estimated speed of 1,000mph."*

*On September 21, 2007 at St Luke's Hospital, Major EDDIE AXISA, MBE, late RMA of Sliema, aged 87, passed away peacefully, comforted by the rites of Holy Church. Loved and remembered by his wife Carmelina, née Attard, his beloved only daughter Mary, wife of Ray Runza, his grandson Robert, Sue and his great-grandson Nicky, his sister Joyce Abela, family, other relatives and friends. The funeral leaves St Luke's Hospital tomorrow, at 1.30pm, for St. Gregory's parish church, Sliema, where Mass praesente cadavere will be said at 2pm, followed by interment in the family grave at the Santa Maria Addolorata Cemetery. No flowers by request but donations to the Down Syndrome Association, Valletta, will be greatly appreciated. **(Source: Times of Malta.Com)**

Research revealed that the 300th and 301st Polish Bomber Squadrons were stationed at RAF Hemswell, Lincolnshire (302 and 303 being Fighter Squadrons), and that on 26th March 1942 a Vickers Wellington Bomber, serial number Z1262, from 301 Polish Squadron, was shot down by flak soon after unloading on Essen, with the loss of all its crew, which confirms the Squadron was on duty that night. **(Source: Patrick Grasson, 2006)**

April/May – England: Terrifying silver UFO appears overhead

At 12.45am, Joan Coombs (aged 69 in 1988) and her friend – Mrs J Bowman, had been out for the evening and missed the last bus from Wembley Park Station. They began their trudge home and reached Blackbird Cross, when:

> *"This huge dull silver 'thing' appeared; it was elliptical and about 60 feet long. Its base was all lit up; we were terrified. It was accompanied by a weird swishing noise. After a few minutes (it seemed much longer), it disappeared as suddenly as it had arrived."*
>
> **(Source: Ron West)**

Summer 1942 – England: Close encounter with 'being', Northumberland

One evening in the late summer of 1942, serviceman – Albert Lancashire – was stood on guard duty outside a radar site, situated two miles from Newbiggin-on-Sea, Northumberland. Suddenly he noticed a bright yellow light, surrounded by a black cloud, shining down from the sky over the sea, approximately a few hundred feet above him. Believing it to be German in origin he ducked back inside the guard box, not wishing to be seen.

> *"The yellow light rolled back onto itself, its position now much lower but still over the water. I felt impelled to go outside. As I did so, another light appeared about a yard in front of me, a little above my head. I threw my arms in the air and felt myself being drawn to 'it'. I walked along this beam and found myself aboard a spacecraft, containing members of a crew about our own height, the captain wearing goggles with dark hair. I was directed to lie down on a couch, or table, looking upwards at this blue domed ceiling. There was a man leaning over me. He was wearing a skullcap like a surgeon, with thick glasses, and smiled at me as if in welcome. I am sure that some sort of medical examination took place but still cannot remember the details, although I was to later suffer from a rash on my tongue, which I believe was connected."*

Witnessing of other manifestations

Albert Lancashire – who later took up employment as a signalman with British Rail, and deemed genuine in nature by the various UFO researchers with whom he came into contact – was to become the subject of other strange events over the years, involving manifestations of UFOs and paranormal phenomena, sometimes witnessed by others.

(Source: Lionel Beer/Norman Oliver/BUFORA/Eric Richards, Page 5, *BUFORA Journal*, Volume 4, No. 3, Summer, 1974)

July – England: Close encounter at Frome, Somerset

Ronald Evans (9) was a wartime evacuee lodging with a family in Frome, in Somerset. It was a hot day, so he decided to go and collect firewood in a nearby forest.

> *"I saw a green haze, like the sun, streaming through the trees. As I approached closer I saw a strange 'craft' – as big as a house – in a clearing. I heard a 'man's' voice say, 'Don't be afraid' and then a hand stopped me from going forward. I was terrified to begin with, but then felt calm. The 'man' had large eyes, a small nose, and a face that looked as if a 'G' force was dragging it back. He was tall with long hair and wore a matt grey skin suit."*

Called himself ABNEMOS

The 'man' stepped into the green haze and immediately his body transformed like an x-ray. He told Ron that he would never come out if he stepped into the haze.

Ron:

> *"He said his name was Abnemos. In the centre of his chest was a control panel. He touched some buttons and three silver balls emerged from the panel. Two hovered over my shoulder, one over my head."*

The 'man' walked back into the craft; as he did so the bottom of the object opened, showing what looked like 20 more 'beings' – some like small children. Slowly, the four claw-like legs buckled beneath the round 'craft' and it rose upwards, turning bright white with flashing red rim. It spun and then vanished.

Years later, he told a friend what he had experienced.

Ron:

> *"He said I was loony, so I just kept quiet. Call me crank or a nutcase, but what I saw that day was beautiful – the most marvellous thing that ever happened to me."*

(Source: Ron West)

August – Russia: UFO appears over the Tula region

During this month the German Army was involved in a bitterly fought retreat, digging trenches and then having to move back every 7-10 days. At about 2pm in that month, a group of soldiers – one of whom is now living in England – saw what he regarded as the most baffling object he had ever seen in his life:

> *"Out of the cloudy sky slowly appeared a dull, silvery, huge, cigar-shaped object – something like a Zeppelin, but much bulkier and rounder at the front. It remained stationary in the sky for at least a minute. I could not see any visible windows or gondola. What made it amazing was the absence of engine noise. It then shot off upwards, at an angle, and was, within seconds, out of sight – again with no noise or vapour trail. We talked about it afterwards, but in the end shrugged it off as a mirage.*
>
> *I later reported it to the Commanding Officer, because it was thought it could have been a Russian secret weapon.*
>
> *The object was about 300 yards long and 100 yards at its thickest point (twice the size of the ill-fated Hindenberg Airship).*
>
> *It was very smooth and was of an aluminum colour."*

The man's son-in-law, Mr J. Burns, B.Sc. – then a member of BUFORA, living in Lanarkshire, whom we spoke to a few years ago – wrote a letter to *Flying Saucer Review*, which was published in Volume 24, No. 4 (November 1978). Mr Burns – who described his father-in-law as being a very practical man, who did not show any interest in such phenomenon – was able to determine that the height of the object was 3,400 feet and 4,300 feet away from the observers (accepting a margin of error that could be as high as 40%).

October – England: Cigar-shaped object sighted over Cheshire

In October 1942, James Toft – then employed at the Royal Ordnance factory in Radway Green, Cheshire – was on his way to the muster point at the factory, after an air raid warning siren had gone off. He was accompanied by the foreman – Mr W. Harper – and five other men, when they saw a large object, like a double parachute, resting upon a large cigar-shaped object with a light at both ends, floating from side-to-side in a pendulum-like swinging motion.

> *"We thought it was a *German doodlebug and threw ourselves to the floor, waiting for the bang. It never happened. After an interval, one of the men shouted, 'It's going off'. We looked up and saw the cigar-shaped object shoot up into the sky at an incredible speed, heading towards Alsager, quickly out of sight."*

*The Fieseler Fi 103, better known as the V-1 'Buzz Bomb', (German: Vergeltungswaffe 1, retaliation weapon), colloquially known in Britain as the 'doodlebug', was an early, jet-powered cruise missile, used by the Germans during World War II. The V-1 was developed at Peenemünde by the Luftwaffe during the Second World War. Between 13th June 1944 and 29th March 1945, it was fired at population centres, such as London and Antwerp.

According to Mr Toft, all manner of strange explanations were offered by those who heard of the incident

Following a visit to the scene shortly after the event, he and Mr Smith discovered a burnt patch on the ground. Unfortunately, owing to the ongoing conflict, details of this incident were soon forgotten. **(Source: BUFORA, Roger Stanway)**

29th November – Turin: RAF Bomber sights UFO

At 10.40pm on 28th November 1942 the crew of a RAF Bomber, under the command of Captain W.O. Lever, were carrying out a raid over Turin, at a height of 11,000 feet, fifteen to twenty miles south-east of Turin, when they saw at the same height but slightly below the aircraft, on a level course, an object described as being '200 feet in length, with four red lights spaced at equal distance along its body'.

After carrying out their mission, the same luminous object was seen by the crew while approaching the Alps, at 10.45pm, at a height of approximately 14,000ft, heading west-south-west up a valley, below the level of the peaks, before disappearing from view.

The captain also told of seeing a similar object a few months previously, north of Amsterdam, apparently on the ground, but was later seen travelling at high speed at a lower level along the coast, seconds before its lights extinguished.

(Source: Declassified MOD records, AIR 14/2076)

December – England: RAF Hurricane in dogfight with UFO

In December 1942, RAF Pilot B.C. Lumsden was flying a Hurricane Interceptor at 7,000 feet over the mouth of the Somme River, during early evening, when he noticed two steadily climbing orange lights – one slightly above the other. He first thought they might have been tracer flak, but discarded this idea as they were moving too slowly and had, by now, increased in size and brightness, port and astern. At 7,000 feet, they stopped climbing. Now level with the Hurricane, Lumsden then executed a full turn but found the objects still with him. Worried, he put the aircraft into a steep nosedive but was unable to shake them off, now approximately a thousand feet below him.

After straightening up at 4,000 feet, he brought the speed of the aircraft to 260mph and eventually lost sight of them.

> *"I found it hard to make other members of the Squadron believe my story but, the following night, one of the Squadron Flight Commanders in the same area had a similar experience with mysterious green lights." (Source: Declassified Records, MOD)*

1943

England: UFO 'light display' over Surrey

Margaret Gadge from Alfold, near Cranleigh, in Surrey, had originally contacted the Aetherius Society about her sighting which took place in 1943 or 1944. The report was then eventually forwarded on to UFO researcher Ananda Sirisena who then spoke to us in 2016 about the incident.

Margaret, who was aged 12, at the time, had this to say:

> *"It happened at 11.15am; the exact date is unknown. I noticed 'a geometric design' of four or five scintillating stars, linked by straight white lines – as though we were being framed for observation". (Forming a pentagon in the sky)*

The object or objects remained in the sky for several hours. There was a blue sky and bright sun. She also remarked that the pattern in the sky was very large – apparently, many times the size of a full moon – when Ananda spoke with her on the phone about the incident.

In 1987 she had remarked:

> *"Out of the four people who were at the sighting – one is dead, another did not take much interest, and the other two are in Australia. I never forgot this sighting, being exciting and uplifting."*

The fact that it remained stationary in the sky for several hours is remarkable.

Margaret:

> *"They formed beautiful, scintillating pastel colours in the form of stars. After several hours we looked up and the phenomenon had gone."*

Her father explained it away as *"America aircraft stunting!"* Margaret believed it was extraterrestrial. *"None of us had heard of UFOs."*

May – England: 'Orange ball' seen over Channel

Retired RAF/Royal New Zealand officer Gordon Cammell was the skipper of a Lancaster Bomber, returning from a mission over Germany in May 1943.

> *"We were flying over the Channel, when the crew and I spotted what looked like a huge 'orange ball' stationary on, or just above, the sea, 7-8000 feet below us. When we landed at RAF East Wretham, Suffolk, and reported the sighting to the debriefing officer, he was unable to offer any explanation. Whatever the object was, it certainly wasn't an aircraft or ship, because the light given off wasn't reflected in the water below it.*
>
> *On another occasion we were told about a silvery gold cylindrical object, with apparent portholes along its side, seen by the crew of a Halifax Bomber as they prepared to drop their bombs over an armament works at Essen, in the Ruhr Valley."* **(Source: Personal letter)**

26/27th May – Germany: Cylindrical object sighted

On the night of the 26th/27th May 1943, RAF Sgt. Pilot G.N. Cockcroft from Bradford, West Yorkshire – then based at RAF Little Rissington, Gloucestershire (No. 6 (P) AFU Pilots Advanced Flying Unit) – found himself seconded to No. 77 Squadron 4 Group Bomber Commando, stationed at Elvington, near York, taking part in an air marking raid over Essen, Germany, which involved dropping incendiaries on the target by the lead Bombers to illuminate the target.

"The first wave had already bombed the general target area – now well alight. Two or three minutes before our final run-in, at approximately 18,700ft, we saw in front but slightly to port, at about the same height, a long cylindrical object, silver/gold in colour, very sharply defined, hanging in the sky at an angle of approximately 45 degrees, showing a number of evenly spaced portholes along its length."

The first person to sight the object was Sgt. Pilot Ray Smith, of the Royal Canadian Air Force:

"I think the first reaction of most of us was amazement, because the object just had no right to be there. After a very short space of time, about 20-30 seconds, it suddenly began to move and, retaining its altitude, climbed rapidly until it vanished from sight. The speed it attained seemed to us completely incredible, moving at thousands of miles per hour.

As it accelerated, the outline became more blurred and the shape foreshortened. The size is more difficult to judge but it was very large, certainly much bigger that our own aircraft, appearing at least as long as a 'king-sized cigarette', or small cigar, at arm's length.

We then completed our bomb run and returned to base. The intelligence officer debriefing us was given a description of the object, but we were unable to judge what importance was attached to it and, quite frankly, it was just another unusual phenomenon which, since apparently harmless, was of far less importance than other wartime hazards."

Despite investigations made by the authorities on both sides, no satisfactory answer was ever found for the appearance of these curious light flight phenomena, described as looking like 'flying silver balls', 'discs', and 'Christmas trees', often seen pacing the aircraft in precise formations.

(Source: Norman Oliver, BUFORA)

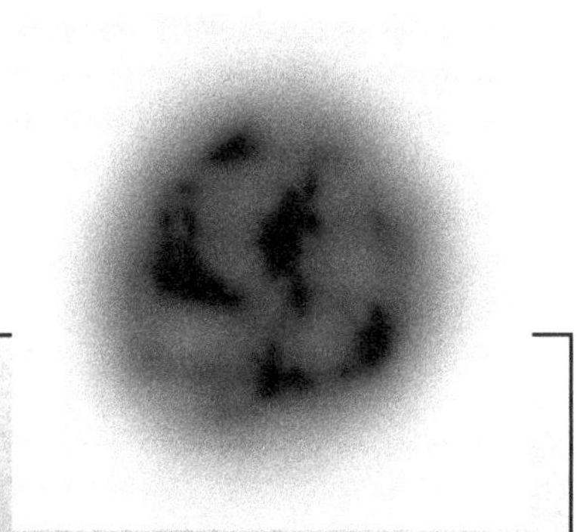

May – England: RAF Serviceman's close encounter with 'alien being'

Another witness, Mr John Warren of Batley – then stationed at RAF Ludham, Norfolk, as an armourer in May 1943, aged 22 – had an even stranger tale to tell. At that time, RAF Ludham was part of 12 Group, RAF, which had been the second most important part of Fighter Command during the Battle of Britain. John Warren was walking back to the camp after having missed the last train.

> *"I had been to North Walsham, a town roughly nine miles from RAF Ludham I then , hitched a lift in a truck to *Catfield, a village about three-and-a-half miles from the camp. Being a little worse for wear, I decided to sleep under a railway signal box. Some time later I awoke and decided to walk back to the base"*

*Catfield is a village and a civil parish in the English county of Norfolk. The village is 19.7 miles south-east of Cromer, 17.3 miles north-east of Norwich and 136 miles north-east of London.

Noticed a 'light' in the field – 'figure' seen

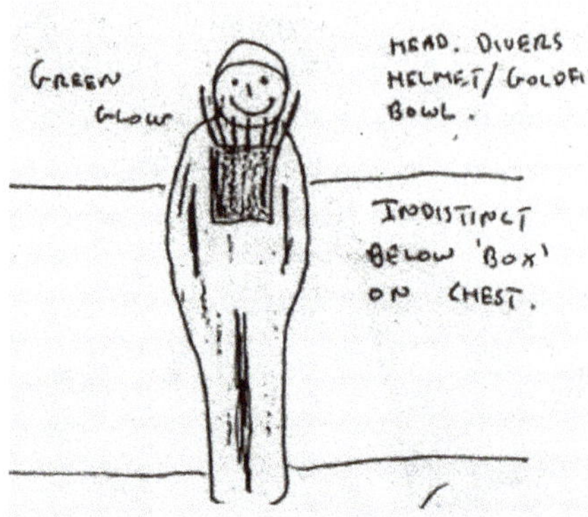

"A little over a mile from the camp, I noticed a 'light' in one of the fields that bordered the narrow country lane and saw a 'figure' standing in the field. Not expecting to encounter anybody that late at night, I became a little nervous and quickened my pace slightly. As he drew closer, I noticed the 'figure' was wearing what appeared to be a greyish-white 'boiler suit'. Attached to the front of the 'suit' was a box that cast a greenish glow onto the face of the 'figure', visible beneath what looked like an old-fashioned diver's helmet. It had a round face, without any noticeable cheekbones or chin. The 'figure' stared at me as I approached, with a smile on its face that terrified me. As I passed the 'figure', standing behind the bushes that bordered the field, about thirty to a hundred yards away, I saw a large, domed object in the field behind this grinning entity. A second 'figure' was moving around, doing something with the ground – as though taking samples."

Domed object seen

The domed object reminded John of a large bell tent. It was stony-grey and gave off no light. John passed their location and walked quickly, terrified, but not running for his life. He glanced back and saw both 'figures' were now doing something in the ground around the bell tent. He looked forward, and kept going until he reached RAF Ludham. He wondered if they were German agents that might have landed on the nearby coast. However, he could not imagine what they were doing in those odd suits with the green, glowing light. Also, a structure the size of the dome he saw would have been awkward to carry over the countryside from the coastline, some seven or eight miles distant.

John arrived back to his camp and the safety of the Nissan huts in which the men were billeted. He settled into bed, wondering about what he had just witnessed, when he was startled by something coming through the window. Fearful that the entities from the field had come for him, John was relieved to discover that it was his friend, 'Taffy', returning from a late night romantic liaison.

John Warren

'Taffy' appeared very agitated when John saw him. John asked 'Taffy' (a cook at the camp) if anything was wrong, but 'Taffy' declined to elaborate.

Another possible witness

Next morning, after breakfast, John asked him what had frightened him so much the previous night. 'Taffy' explained that he had seen something outside of Catfield and had run all the way back to the base.

John said: *"I didn't tell him that I had also seen something. 'Taffy' didn't go into any details beyond 'having seen something'."*

Before the night he saw the 'figures' and their dome-shaped 'craft', John had used that road many times, going to a local swimming spot, but afterwards he never went along the road alone and never went swimming there again. He confined his drinking to either the NAAFI (Navy, Army and Air Force Institutes) or went to the pub in Ludham, which took him along a different road. It being 1943, John had never heard of 'flying saucers' and didn't even equate what he saw as having anything other than an earthly explanation. Since the years have passed, John now believes that what he saw was not of this world.

John Warren and wife

Philip Mantle:

"I pondered if John Warren did see an extraterrestrial craft in that East Anglia field in 1943. What were its occupants doing poking holes in the ground? Why did they simply watch him with a fixed grin as he hurried past? If they were German agents, surely they would have stopped this lone airman from divulging their location. What had happened to 'Taffy'? It seems that he also saw the same thing as John, but it had terrified him so much that he had ran back to the base. If the family of 'Taffy' (John said his real name was Jennings, or Jenkins, and that he was Welsh) are reading this, perhaps he told them of his wartime encounter. This is a fascinating story from a time before 'flying saucers' were the vogue. It demonstrates that the UFO phenomenon did not begin in the United States in 1947."

Sadly John was to be the victim of a non-stop car accident many years later. While walking along the road ironically it was the circumstances of his death that was to lead to much newspaper publicity which culminated in the arrest of the woman concerned following police investigation.

(Sources: BUFORA – Trevor Whittaker/ Philip Mantle/Audrey Church)

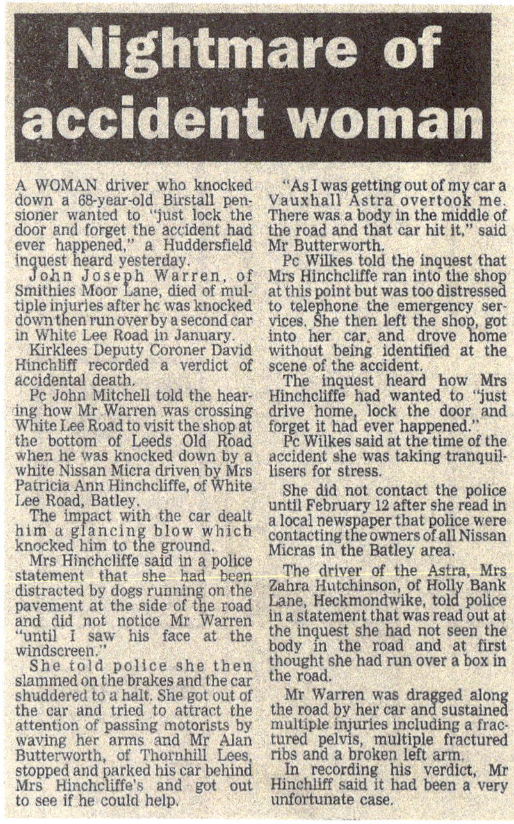

Nightmare of accident woman

A WOMAN driver who knocked down a 68-year-old Birstall pensioner wanted to "just lock the door and forget the accident had ever happened," a Huddersfield inquest heard yesterday.

John Joseph Warren, of Smithies Moor Lane, died of multiple injuries after he was knocked down then run over by a second car in White Lee Road in January.

Kirklees Deputy Coroner David Hinchliff recorded a verdict of accidental death.

Pc John Mitchell told the hearing how Mr Warren was crossing White Lee Road to visit the shop at the bottom of Leeds Old Road when he was knocked down by a white Nissan Micra driven by Mrs Patricia Ann Hinchcliffe, of White Lee Road, Batley.

The impact with the car dealt him a glancing blow which knocked him to the ground.

Mrs Hinchcliffe said in a police statement that she had been distracted by dogs running on the pavement at the side of the road and did not notice Mr Warren "until I saw his face at the windscreen."

She told police she then slammed on the brakes and the car shuddered to a halt. She got out of the car and tried to attract the attention of passing motorists by waving her arms and Mr Alan Butterworth, of Thornhill Lees, stopped and parked his car behind Mrs Hinchcliffe's and got out to see if he could help.

"As I was getting out of my car a Vauxhall Astra overtook me. There was a body in the middle of the road and that car hit it," said Mr Butterworth.

Pc Wilkes told the inquest that Mrs Hinchcliffe ran into the shop at this point but was too distressed to telephone the emergency services. She then left the shop, got into her car and drove home without being identified at the scene of the accident.

The inquest heard how Mrs Hinchcliffe had wanted to "just drive home, lock the door and forget it had ever happened."

Pc Wilkes said at the time of the accident she was taking tranquillisers for stress.

She did not contact the police until February 12 after she read in a local newspaper that police were contacting the owners of all Nissan Micras in the Batley area.

The driver of the Astra, Mrs Zahra Hutchinson, of Holly Bank Lane, Heckmondwike, told police in a statement that was read out at the inquest she had not seen the body in the road and at first thought she had run over a box in the road.

Mr Warren was dragged along the road by her car and sustained multiple injuries including a fractured pelvis, multiple fractured ribs and a broken left arm.

In recording his verdict, Mr Hinchliff said it had been a very unfortunate case.

England – 'Flying saucer' seen at Barkingside

Mr E.R. Bilbrough wrote to us in 2010 about what he saw, in 1943, while walking towards Barkingside Railway Station, one early evening, to collect his workman's railway pass for the next day's travel to work.

> *"The air raid sirens had sounded, but there was no air activity – no searchlights or gunfire – which was very odd. As I walked along Somerby Road, then Salisbury Avenue I saw a 'flying saucer' shaped object over Barking Railway Station, heading towards the direction of Barking Park, estimated to be about 300 feet off the ground, silently rotating, showing various coloured lights around it. Suddenly, it shot off across the sky and was soon out of sight. The whole episode lasted no more than five minutes. I will never forget what I saw and felt inclined to write to the MOD, in May 2008, but was advised they didn't keep records going back that far."*

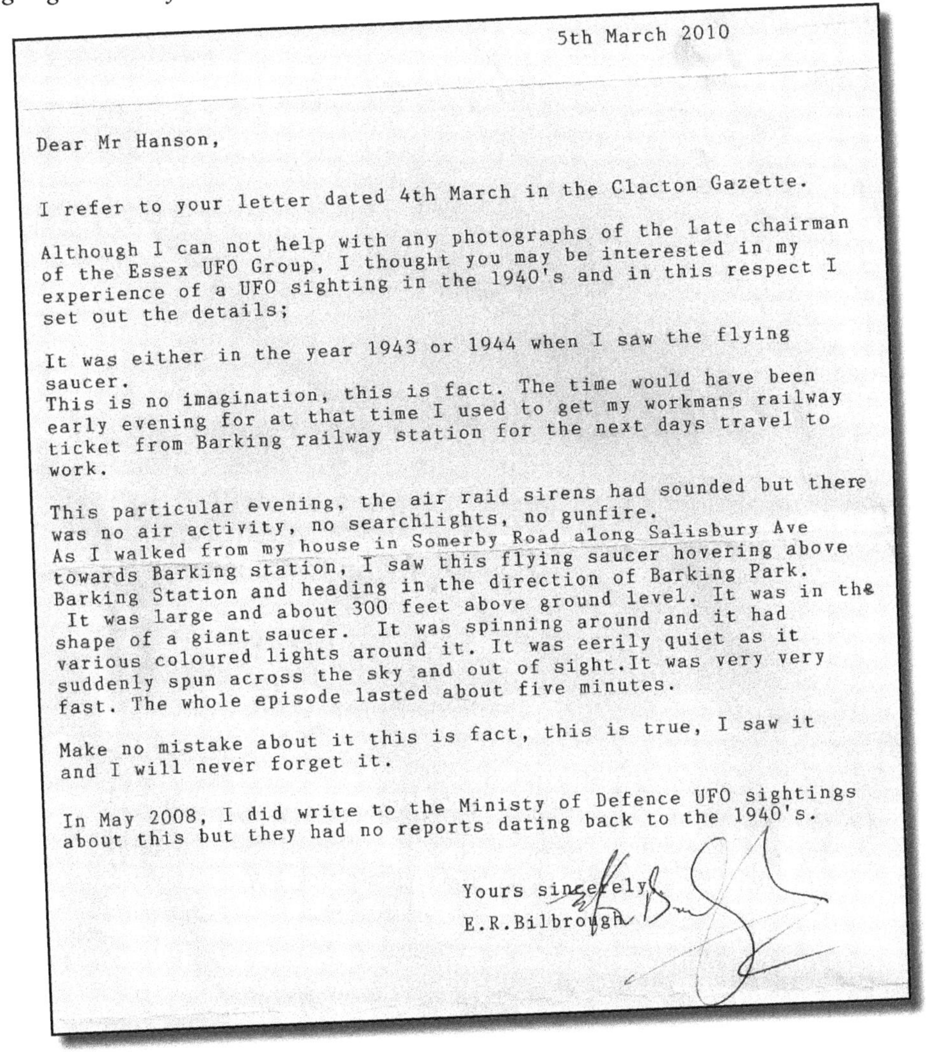

5th March 2010

Dear Mr Hanson,

I refer to your letter dated 4th March in the Clacton Gazette.

Although I can not help with any photographs of the late chairman of the Essex UFO Group, I thought you may be interested in my experience of a UFO sighting in the 1940's and in this respect I set out the details;

It was either in the year 1943 or 1944 when I saw the flying saucer.
This is no imagination, this is fact. The time would have been early evening for at that time I used to get my workmans railway ticket from Barking railway station for the next days travel to work.

This particular evening, the air raid sirens had sounded but there was no air activity, no searchlights, no gunfire.
As I walked from my house in Somerby Road along Salisbury Ave towards Barking station, I saw this flying saucer hovering above Barking Station and heading in the direction of Barking Park.
It was large and about 300 feet above ground level. It was in the shape of a giant saucer. It was spinning around and it had various coloured lights around it. It was eerily quiet as it suddenly spun across the sky and out of sight.It was very very fast. The whole episode lasted about five minutes.

Make no mistake about it this is fact, this is true, I saw it and I will never forget it.

In May 2008, I did write to the Ministy of Defence UFO sightings about this but they had no reports dating back to the 1940's.

Yours sincerely
E.R.Bilbrough

UFO approaches B17 Bomber

In late 1943, while on a daylight mission over Central Germany, Louis Kiss – then a tail gunner on the 'Phyllis Marie' B-17 Bomber of the 390th Bombardment Group, 3rd Division of the 8th Air Force.

> *"We saw an odd looking sphere approach the B-17 from behind and below. It was about the size of a basketball and a shimmery gold colour. The 'ball' reached the aircraft and hovered just above one wing, after slowly moving from the rear. Soon it passed over the top of the aircraft to the other wing, when it hovered. I was tempted to shoot at it with my machine-gun, but considered the proximity of the 'ball' to the gas tank. The 'ball' moved towards the rear again, and was caught in the backwash of the engines and rapidly disappeared from sight."*

(Source: ***Just Cause*****, Number 32, June 1992/Lawrence Fawcett and Barry Greenwood)**

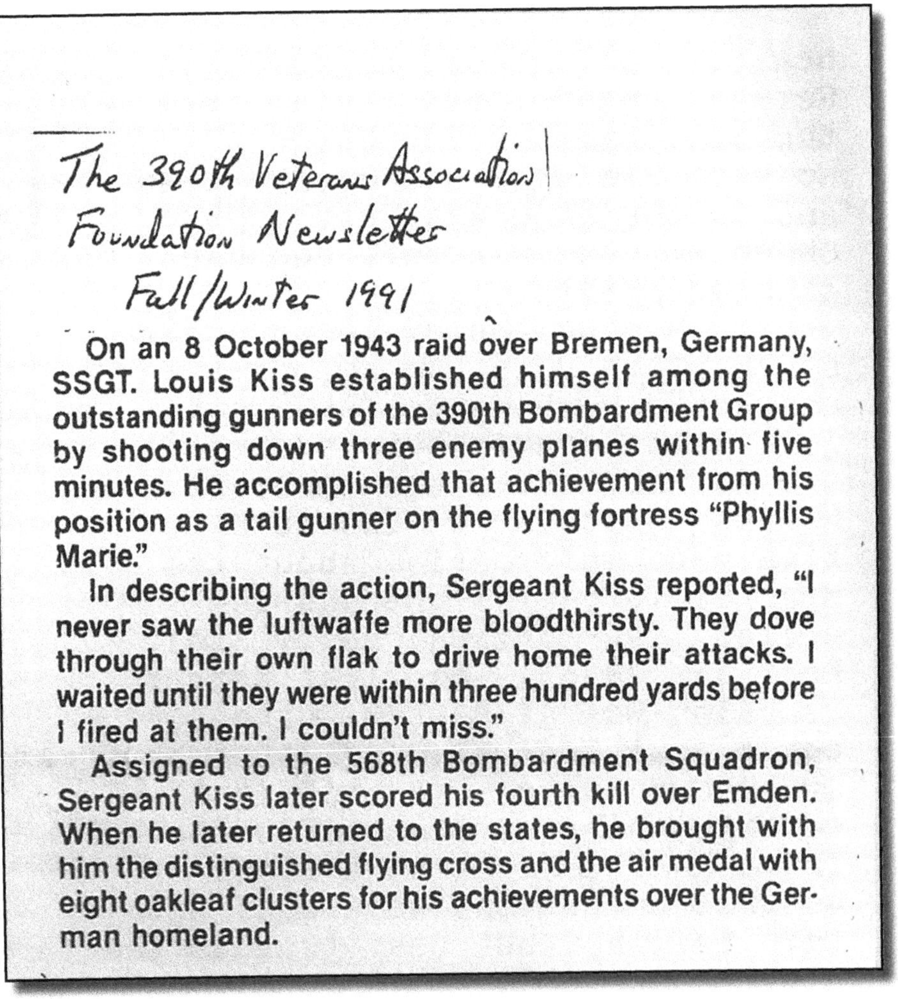

The 390th Veterans Association Foundation Newsletter
Fall/Winter 1991

On an 8 October 1943 raid over Bremen, Germany, SSGT. Louis Kiss established himself among the outstanding gunners of the 390th Bombardment Group by shooting down three enemy planes within five minutes. He accomplished that achievement from his position as a tail gunner on the flying fortress "Phyllis Marie."

In describing the action, Sergeant Kiss reported, "I never saw the luftwaffe more bloodthirsty. They dove through their own flak to drive home their attacks. I waited until they were within three hundred yards before I fired at them. I couldn't miss."

Assigned to the 568th Bombardment Squadron, Sergeant Kiss later scored his fourth kill over Emden. When he later returned to the states, he brought with him the distinguished flying cross and the air medal with eight oakleaf clusters for his achievements over the German homeland.

1944

2nd January – England: Triangular UFOs over Northumberland

On 2nd January 1944, Warrant Officer Able from Number 8 Coastal Operational Training Unit was flying over Alnwick, Northumberland, at 22,000ft, when he saw four 'huge black triangular objects in the sky'. **(Source: Station Operational Book)**

20th February – England: 'Flying disc' over London

On 20th February 1944, Mr J.W. Chambers was staying at his mother-in-law's house in Streatham, London, when the air raid sirens went off.

> *"I sat in the shelter, expecting to hear the sound of anti-aircraft fire and explosions from falling bombs. All I heard was this hollow sound, totally unlike any sounds I had heard before. I ventured outside and saw a metallic 'disc' slowly crossing the sky, caught in the cone of several searchlight beams. It had no wings and wasn't a balloon. I was amazed to see that none of the anti-aircraft guns opened fire on it."* **(Source: Letter to Ivan W. Bunn)**

27th April – Germany: RAF pilots sight UFOs

George Bernard Dye

Over the years, we spoke on a number of occasions to retired RAF Air Gunner, George Bernard Dye and his ex-skipper, Arthur Horton, about what took place whilst they were returning home to England from a bombing mission over Germany in Lancaster Bomber, Serial number 1M4777L, call sign 'Q' for 'Queenie', during the early hours of 27th April 1944. Their story was a truly remarkable one, involving the sighting of what is now commonly referred to as a 'Foo fighter'.

George:

> *"After successfully fending off an ME 110 German fighter, I noticed the appearance of five glowing 'balls of light' heading straight towards the aircraft – which I took to be rockets, to begin with. I radioed the skipper, Arthur Horton, who proceeded to put the aircraft into a number of steep turns in an effort to shake them off, to no avail. After about ten minutes the objects, showing tail-like flames moving in spurts of speed, seemed to burn and fade away. Although I went on to complete 28 operations, I never saw anything like this again."*

Arthur Horton still remembers the incident well.

> *"Following a radio transmission from one of the air gunners, I understood that we were being pursued by several glowing objects, with short stubby wings. Having absolutely no idea what these things were, I rammed the throttles forward in an attempt to outrun the objects, but despite pushing the aircraft at full power, could not shake them off. One of the gunners asked me if they should open fire.*
>
> *I considered my options as the seconds ticked away. Were they magnetic? Were we expected to attack them? I decided to instruct my gunner not to fire. After all, they hadn't made any move to attack us. As we crossed over the French coast, with our engines still screaming at full power, I received a message to tell me they had just faded away."*

Arthur Horton

1 Park Place
Park Rd.
Thackley
Bradford
W. Yorks. BD10 0TG
6.4.2000

☏ 01274 612426.

Dear Mr Hanson.

In answer to your letter of 1.4.2000, I am quite happy to relate for you my version of the phenomenon of the "orange glows" seen by my gunners on the night of 26.4.44.

We were returning from Essen when my gunners reported several "orange glows" coming in toward us from behind - the rear gunner thought that they had a very short stubby wings. I threw the aircraft through all the evasive tactics I knew, only to have the objects follow with apparent ease - it was something entirely new to us - the objects took no offensive action against us, my gunners were asking "shall we fire at them skipper?" my brain - racing - were they magnetic? did they have to touch us? were we expected to fire at them? split second decisions had to be made - I instructed the gunners not to fire - they were not harming us at that point. By now I had the throttles "through the gate" giving excess power to the engines. After crossing the French coast and out to sea, the objects apparently "died out".

The whole episode had lasted some ten minutes, we had lost some fourteen thousand feet, and travelled some fifty miles.

On our return to base (Mildenhall - Suffolk) it was reported in our debriefing report, it was made quite a joke for a while. I have a copy of our debriefing report, obtained from the archives at Kew, in which no mention is made of the event.

My log book just contains the cryptic words - "Chased by rockets".

On that particular night, my own navigator having an eye infection, was replaced by F/Lt. A. Nicholl, the station navigator, a man of great experience and many operations, also witnessed the event.

The other witness (now deceased) was my wireless operator, W. White.

In the nose of the aircraft the bomb aimer, my flight engineer, and myself - pilot - were of course unable to actually see the objects, and had to rely on the continuous commentary at the time.

General Data.

Date 26.4.44
A/C Lancaster III LM477
Duration of Flight 4 hrs 35m

I was born on 18.6.1912
Last occupation (20 years) before retirement :-
Rowntree - York - Production Function - Managerial Status.
UFO Sightings - none.

We - the crew - continued our tour of operations to complete our 30 missions, never again seeing - or hearing of - anything like our experience on 26.4.44.

I hope that the above may be of use to you, and wish you well in your investigations

Yours Sincerely
Arthur Horton

Arthur Horton

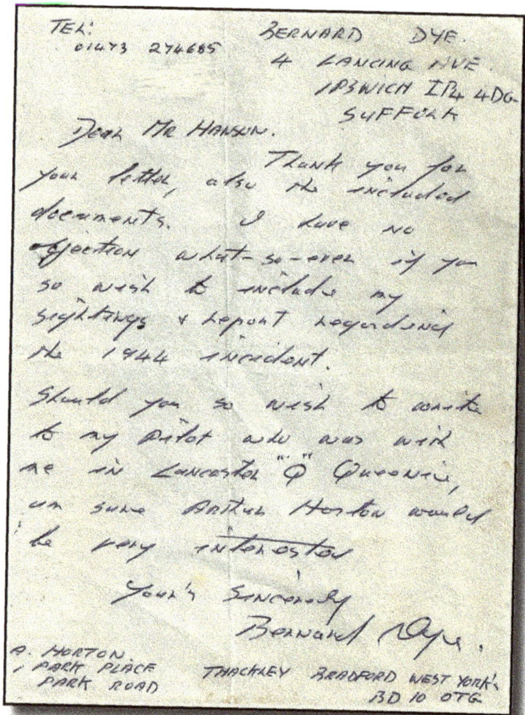

TEL: 01473 274685

BERNARD DYE.
4 LANCING AVE.
IPSWICH IP4 4DG.
SUFFOLK

Dear Mr Hanson.

Thank you for your letter, also the included documents. I have no objection what-so-ever if you so wish to include my sightings & report regarding the 1944 incident.

Should you so wish to write to my pilot who was with me in Lancaster "Q" Queenie, am sure Arthur Horton would be very interested

Your's Sincerely
Bernard Dye.

A. HORTON,
1 PARK PLACE
PARK ROAD
THACKLEY BRADFORD WEST YORK'S
BD 10 OTG

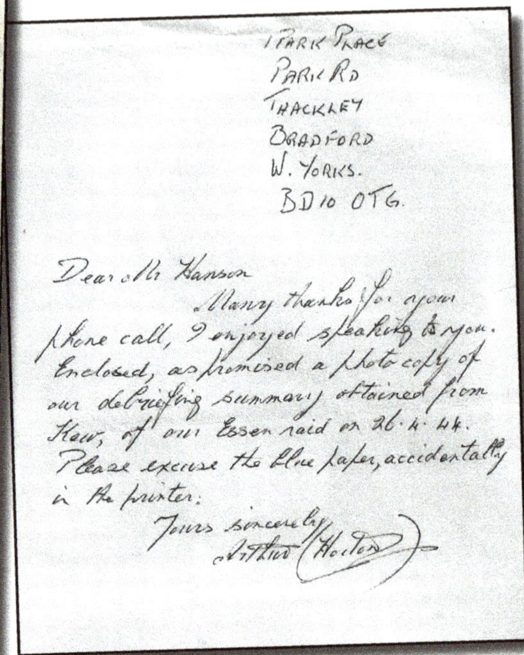

1 Park Place
Park Rd
Thackley
Bradford
W. Yorks.
BD10 0TG.

Dear Mr Hanson

Many thanks for your phone call, I enjoyed speaking to you. Enclosed, as promised a photo copy of our debriefing summary obtained from Kew, of our Essen raid on 26.4.44. Please excuse the blue paper, accidentally in the printer.

Yours sincerely
Arthur Horton

Official explanation: chased by rockets!

George Bernard Dye

On landing at Mildenhall Airbase, Suffolk, the incident was treated with good humour during the debriefing, rather than concern. Many years later, Arthur managed to obtain a copy of his report from the Public Records Office at Kew, in London, and was surprised to see no mention of the incident – just a slight reference contained in the aircraft log book, 'Chased by Rockets', which should come of no surprise, as reports like these were heavily censored in order to prevent knowledge of such matters being brought to the attention of the public. Sadly, time had taken its toll. We never personally met Arthur Horton, although we spoke to him on the telephone about the incident many times. We did, however, meet George at his Ipswich home in June 2006, when he proudly showed his collection of wartime memorabilia. Curiously, we were to discover that a vision of 'Jesus' was seen in the sky over Ipswich, Suffolk, during an air raid alert on 27th April 1944, after which the Church of St. Nicholas, Ipswich, was besieged by witnesses wishing to offer prayers.

Scotland: Beams of green light, Bass Rock

Ex-RAF serviceman Stanley Richardson, who served with Air Sea Rescue, heard of the strange things seen by the servicemen during flying operations, but dismissed them as 'fairy tales' until...

> *"We were searching for a ditched aircrew off Bass Rock, off East Scotland, and using the searchlight in the gathering dusk to illuminate the sea, when suddenly, a bright beam of*

intense green light came down from the cloud above us for two or three seconds, before switching off. I thought I was seeing things and left it at that.

A couple of years later I was with my wife, driving through Tunbridge Wells, one evening, when I saw an identical intense beam of green light reaching from broken cloud to the ground, which lasted a good five seconds. I thought to myself I'm imagining it, until my wife exclaimed to me that she had just seen this beam of green light appear."

UFO sighted over Italy, during battle with German Forces

In 1944, Antonio Szachnowski – a former Polish soldier and veteran researcher from the London area until his death in 2006 – was engaged in a battle with opposing German Forces in Northern Italy, on a sunny day with a blue sky, when suddenly,

"...a silver egg-shaped object appeared, glistening with light in the sky. Immediately, both sides fired their anti-aircraft guns at the object, believing it to be the enemy. A short time later, it tilted and moved rapidly upwards out-of-sight".

Antonio was to become the head of Anglo Polish UFO Research for many years afterwards.

(Source: Personal interview/letters)

24th May – Off the Irish coast: US Bombers followed by Foo fighters

Retired Merchant Navy Officer William Anderson (aged 87 in 1990) from 16, Trafalgar Road, Clacton-on-Sea, Essex, has many memories of the Second World War. They included a number of UFO sightings, which he meticulously recorded. The first took place at 4.20am on the 24th May 1944.

"We were aboard ship off the Irish Coast when we heard the sound of aircraft overhead; action stations weren't sounded, as we had been advised they were B52 Flying Fortresses, allied aircraft. I was stunned to see a total of seven objects behind four of the planes – 'round balls of orange light', at a height of about 1,500 feet.

Each and every movement of the aircraft in formation was duplicated in flight by the orange objects, which appeared to be following them. There were two groups of two and a group of three. I was later told, after the war, that they were called Foo fighters."

(Source: East Anglian UFO & Paranormal Research Association)

Summer – Arnhem: Soldier encounters landed 'flying saucer'

Leslie Grant was a soldier with the British Army, on his way to deliver vital supplies to Arnhem, in summer 1944, with a colleague, when he found his route blocked by a bridge destroyed by Allied bombers. Seeking another way around, he managed to get his lorry stuck down a steep valley and went to look for help.

Advised of something strange at the top of the hill

After coming across a captured German tank, manned by a British crew (it had a yellow triangle on it), he asked them to tow his lorry to the top of the hill. The man agreed, but said a very odd thing:

> *"Don't be surprised when you see something strange at the top."*

Leslie:

> *"I hadn't got a clue what he was on about and continued on the journey. When we reached the top, I saw this huge grey circular 'thing', approximately 100 feet in diameter, just resting above the ground on three tripod legs, with a dome on top and what looked like slatted windows around its circumference."*

Like pushing against rubber

Leslie stood there, trying to work out what it was – bearing in mind he had never heard of UFOs or 'flying saucers' – and decided to walk towards it, but found when about 70ft away, his passage was blocked by what felt like an invisible force stopping him, *"...like pushing against rubber"*.

Frightened, he returned to the lorry and drove away. When he finally reached his destination he went over to the commanding officer and told him what had been seen, but was shocked when the man warned him to keep quiet about it.

Mrs Phyllis Moonie

We contacted Mrs Phyllis Moonie – then a UFO investigator for the well respected Essex UFO Group, run by Dan Goring, editor of *Earth-link* – hoping to glean further information about the incident. Mrs Moonie told us she saw no reason not to accept as other than genuine the version of events given to her by Leslie, who was then employed as a bus driver at the same depot as her husband. Unfortunately we were unable to speak to Leslie himself, as he had passed away.

(Source: Phyllis Moonie)

This was not to be the only occasion when we were to come across reports relating to what appears to be some type of invisible force-field surrounding the perimeter of the UFO. Could this sighting in some way corroborate the highly controversial alleged developments of 'flying saucers' produced by Nazi Germany, during the Second World War, which some people maintain were capable of flight to the moon and beyond, or are the German 'flying saucers' just a myth? Did German fighters attempt to chase UFOs then? They certainly reported the same phenomena as the Allies

July – England: 'Flying discs' sighted passing over London

Mr H. Harris – a Fleet Street journalist with over 40 years' experience, who lived through the London Blitz – was awoken at 2.30am by an air raid alert, in July 1944. On going to the window, he looked out and saw a red object in the sky approaching his position.

Mr Harris shouted for his wife to come and have a look, believing it to be an example of Hitler's secret weapon, after hearing from a classified Government source leaked to the Press (not the public) to expect the launch of new weapons against Britain.

> *"As it approached closer, I was able to see it consisted of a number of small 'red balls', or 'globes of light', that changed into five or six luminous pink discs, plain and flat from an angle, flying silently in a line astern formation. In the darkness it was difficult to estimate height, speed and distance.*

GERMAN UFOS

> *They could have been 30-50 feet in length, travelling between 2-300mph, at a height of 300-500 feet, passing maybe a mile right across my line of vision close to, if not actually over, Wembley Stadium. I watched them until they passed out-of-sight to the north, in the direction of Watford or St. Albans."*

Mr Harris believes that although the objects could have been shot down easily, no searchlights were seen. He speculated that the lack of retaliation may have been fear of widespread devastation should they have been shot down.

(Source: letter to John Dennis Llewellyn)

England: German 'doodlebugs' followed by UFOs

William James Steel from Hastings, Kent – then employed as a diesel plant operator by the local Council, at Fairlight Quarry (now a nature reserve) – was clearing rubbish from a nearby waste tip, one afternoon in 1944, when he happened to look skywards and see:

> *"...two V1 German flying bombs, heading towards London. Imagine my surprise to see they were being apparently followed by two small 'silver discs', making a high-pitched whining noise. I wondered if they were top secret weapons being launched to attack the rockets, or were they taking photographs, because nothing happened?"*

(Source: Gary Steel)

10th August – USA: Pilot sights UFO over Sumatra

Shortly after midnight on the 10th August 1944, Captain Alva M. Reida – then based at Kharagpur, India, with the 468th bomb group 792 Squadron – was on a mission from Ceylon, bombing Palembang, Sumatra, flying a US Army Air Force B-29 Super Fortress, at the tail end of fifty aircraft going in for attack, at two to three minute intervals, flying at a height of 14,000 feet and speed of 210mph.

> *"Our assignment was to bomb the target and drop photo flash bombs attached to a parachute before photographing damage on another fly over. While in the general area we were exposed to flak, but immediately after leaving this area it ceased. About 20-30 minutes later, the right gunner and co-pilot reported a strange object pacing us 500 yards off the starboard wing. At that distance it appeared as a spherical object – probably five or six feet in diameter, very bright and intense, red or orange in colour, showing a halo effect. My gunner reported it coming in from about a 5 o'clock position (right rear) at our level. It seemed to throb, or vibrate, constantly. Assuming it to be some kind of radio controlled object sent to pace us, I went into evasive action, changing direction constantly as much as 90 degrees and altitude of about 2,000 feet, but it followed our every manoeuvre for about 8 minutes, always holding a position about 500 yards out in a 2 o'clock position (right front) in relation to the plane. When it left it made an abrupt 90 degree turn and accelerated rapidly away, before disappearing into the overcast."*

(Source: NICAP, *The UFO Evidence*, 1964, Page 23)

11th August - France: RAF radar operator sights UFO

Ronald Claridge

The following day Ronald Claridge, DFC, AEA – then a radar operator aboard Lancaster Bomber 'F' for Freddie – was returning home on 11th August 1944 from his 68th mission over enemy territory, on their way back from Pellice, flying over France, when he noticed the 'Fishpond' radar screen had gone blank.

> *"I advised the pilot, Brian Frow (who retired as an Air Commodore), what was happening. All of a sudden he shouted out, 'what the hell is that?' I peered out of the astrodome next to my seat and noticed an enormous 'ring of lights', stretching across the sky. As my eyes became more accustomed, I saw the lights formed part of a huge 'disc' flying parallel to the aircraft, at an estimated height of 20,000 feet, at an approximate speed of 280mph. Then a strange sense of calm seemed to envelope the aircraft. Nobody opened fire. It seemed odd no turbulence could be felt from the presence of the object.*
>
> *A few minutes later it moved away at a colossal speed, ruling out any possibility that it was a conventional aircraft.*
>
> *When the bomber landed a full report was submitted to one of the officers, who debriefed the crew. He didn't seem surprised by what the airman had seen, but ordered them not to discuss what had happened. To this day I don't know what it was we saw, but I am convinced it was not constructed by human hands. Don't forget we didn't even know what UFOs or 'flying saucers' were."*

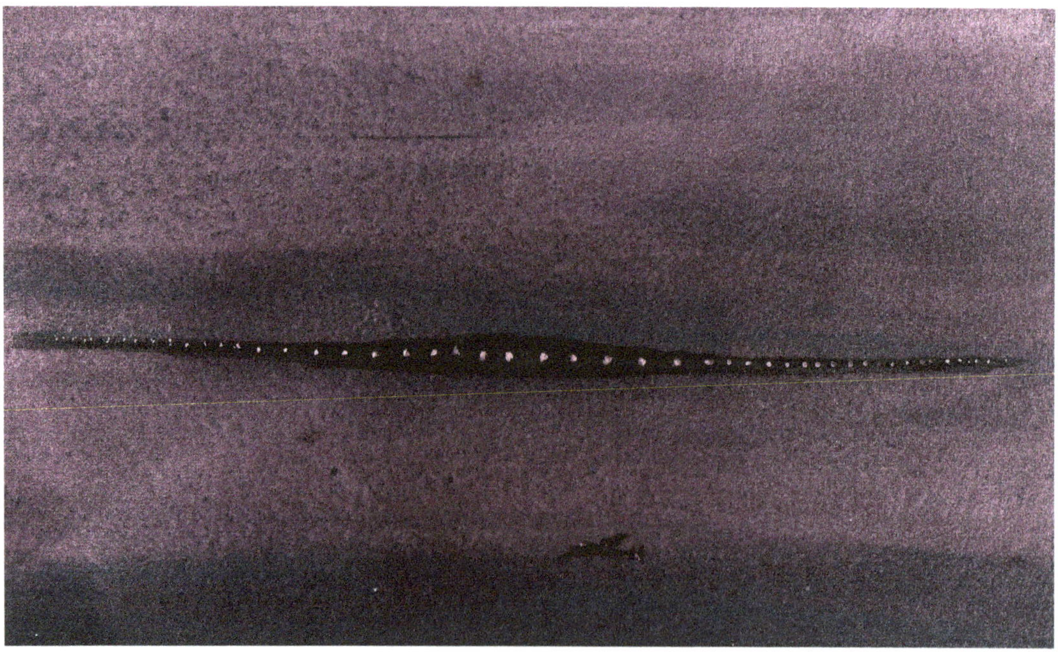

Air Cdre Brian Frow

Master bomber whose crew shot down three German fighters returning from a raid

AIR COMMODORE BRIAN FROW, who has died aged 79, was awarded the DSO, and a DFC and Bar, for sustained operations over the most heavily defended targets in Germany and occupied Europe.

In the New Year of 1944 Frow was posted to No 7 Squadron in the Pathfinder Force. Shortly before his arrival at No 7's Oakington base, the squadron's Short Stirlings had been replaced by Lancasters. At the age of only 21, Frow was a flight commander in the rank of squadron leader, and he was soon given the added responsibility of acting on some raids as master bomber.

Frow: crippled Lancaster riddled with holes

As such, he was provided with an additional navigator who was an expert in map reading and visual bombing at low level; he would help the squadron to identify and mark the target, while Frow's aircraft would endure heavy ground fire as he assessed the accuracy of the markers.

Frow would tell the main force bombers to wait until he called them in to the target. When the first markers had been snuffed out by exploding bombs, he had to call in more aircraft to drop further target indicators. As the bomber stream departed, the master bomber was required to make a final low level run to assess damage, and then to drop delayed fuse 1000 lb bombs to discourage enemy salvage operations. On one such raid Frow was homeward bound over France when his rear gunner spotted a Ju 88 alongside him; it was stalking a fellow Lancaster. Frow reduced speed and, dropping behind the enemy night fighter, shot it down.

The Ju 88s usually operated in pairs, and a second night fighter attacked Frow's Lancaster from astern. It scored direct hits – but fortunately the mid-upper gunner managed to retaliate more effectively, and sent it blazing to the ground.

Even as this happened, Frow's Lancaster suffered a third attack. This enemy night fighter was also destroyed; but, at that moment, Frow's intercom failed and the port aileron did not respond to an urgent attempt to take evasive action.

The aircraft, now over the moonlit sea, turned on its back, became unstable and lost height rapidly. Frow throttled back and continued to heave at the controls – and was much relieved to resume level flight when only 800 ft above the water.

He took stock. Most main systems were not functioning correctly; the undercarriage could be lowered only manually; the brakes were defective; and one or more engines might seize up at any time. Even so, Frow reckoned that a controlled landing was possible, though the chances of fire were great because of fuel leaks in the tanks. He made his approach at Woodbridge, in Suffolk, and got away with it. The "Lanc", riddled with more than 100 bullet and cannon shell holes, was a write off.

Frow, educated at Dulwich College, had been inspired to fly in his boyhood by the displays of Sir Alan Cobham's Flying Circus. During school holidays he revelled in plane spotting at Croydon Airport. Following membership of the Officers' Training Corps, Frow joined the Local Defence Volunteers in 1940 and at the age of 17 he was placed in charge of a section of 20 men.

This object was seen by the eight members of my crew returning from a raid on the oil fields at Pelice. My Fish Pond, Radar Screen went blank and I personally watched this object for at least 3 minutes as did the rest of my crew. I was in the Astra Dome with 360 degree vision.

This object was enormous and we had never seen any thing like it before. We were about 1000 yds from it. There was no turbulence at all. We lost all feelings of aggression and our gunners made no attempt to open fire. We were at 20000 feet and flying at 250 miles an hour.

This object suddenly flew ahead of us at a speed which could not be achieved today.

Please note: The expressions, U.F.Os and Flying Saucers had never been heard of in 1944.

We all had a feeling of euphoria which lasted some hours. All fear and War Like feelings had left us.

All this was reported to our debriefing Officers at 7 Sqdn Oakington and we were told not to discuss what we had experienced even among ourselves.

I swear the Statement I have made is true and would welcome any interrogation that might help to solve this mystery.

Ronald R. Claridge.

2.6.04

Ronald R. Claridge DFC AEA.,

P.O.Box 690,

Kilifi,

Kenya.

Dear John,

Thank you for your package of what I found to be very interesting material. I have no objections to anything I have written or experienced made public.

Personally I think after about sixty years the British Authorities should make their own findings public. I have not read what the Mail has written about U.F.O., sightings.

I will repeat what I have written about my experience on 11:8:44.

We were a Master Bomber Crew. Our Pilot was S/Ldr Brian Frow who remained in the R.A.F., and attained the rank of Air Commodore before he retired some years ago. We remained friends until he died three years ago. The funny thing was that although I knew him well I could never get him to discuss what had happened that night.

I suppose at that time we were the most experienced Bomber Command Crew, none of us had completed less than 60 Operations. I was on my 68th.

On the night in question I was the Radio and Radar operator. The first thing I noticed was that my "Fishpond" screen went blank, I was just informing the Pilot when he yelled over the intercom, "What the hell is that?"

I got into the Astra Dome which was next to my seat. At first all I could see was an enormous string of bright lights which seemed to be travelling along side of our Lancaster. These lights seemed to stretch to infinity. At first that was all I could see but as my sight adjusted the lights became a part of a huge disc.

At a rough estimate this object was flying about a 1000ft from us.
I think the most important thing was that we all felt no fear. We were flying over France where German Fighters hunted in packs and we had been shot up on a previous occasion when our Aeroplane was landed with 182 wholes in it and it never flew again.
Our gunners were very alert and "Gung Ho" and yet they made no attempt to open fire or to give the Pilot any instructions, The feeling of calm seemed to permiate the Lancaster. I think it was at that time I thought that this must be the ultimate weapon, no one wanting to fight anymore! Even today I wonder if this is what the Powers that be are worried about?
I really think that from that experience my War was over. I was a Warrant Officer which made me rather a Law unto Myself. In fact after I had completed 78 Operations I hardly ever reported in to my Signals Office until after the War.
As a Pathfinder Crew we were eight members and we all experienced the same feelings.
At the time we were flying at about 20000ft at 280 mph but we experienced no turbulence from this enormous craft. All of our crew watched this craft for at least three minutes when suddenly at what must have been an enormous speed it was gone ahead of us. This was a speed which could not have been achieved today. Another strange thing was that we never discussed what we experienced on our final leg back to base.
I am still convinced that our experienced was not anything of this World.
I would like to point out that none of uswas religious nor could our feelings be due to mass histeria, remember we had never heard of U.F.Os.

Within an hour we had landed and were being debriefed. Everything we had experienced was written down but I had the feeling that what we were telling the briefing officers did not surprise them. It was strange that they did not seem at all interested in our raid on Pelice.

I expected that the next day we would have another debriefing but what we had experienced was quickly forgotten but I do remember that we were instructed that we were not to discuss anything that had happened on that Operation even among ourselves. A few weeks later we finished operating and split up from the Squadron. "7".

I would be prepared to answer any questions about my experience by any interested party.

Looking forward to your reply.

Youre sincerely,

Roy Claridge

Roy Claridge.

Ronald R. Claridge D.F.C. A.E.A.,
P.O.Box 690,
Kilifi,
Kenya.

29th May 2004.

Dear John and Dawn Holloway,
Thank you for your letter and notes I was most interested to read about people who have experienced "Contact" with U.F.O.s, sometimes having lasting medical complaints. I must say that personally I have never experienced any of those conditions nor did Brian Frow. At the time I experienced the feeling of euphoria and relaxation ~~which~~ that I still have strong memories, which would never have happened while flying over enemy territory.
I do remember telling the de briefing Officer that I considered we had experienced the "Ultimate Weapon", as while this object was flying alongside us all warlike feelings had disappeared. I wonder why we always think of weapons which kill and destroy?
Would Western Countries be fearful of such a weapon? It would certainly change the World. I wonder if this (what) is really worries the "Powers That Be"
PersonallyI have been convinced there has been a cover up since 1944.
I was also interested in Crop Circles. No doubt there has been a lot of fakes and hoaxes but recently some of the intricate and accurate patterns could never have been completed over night by human hand and I say this as a professional artist.
About my crew, I am afraid I must be the only survivor, Brian Frow died last year.
I enclose a photograph of my crew taken on 7 Squadron sometime in 1944. This is the only photograph I think exists. On a Pathfinder Squadron we were not allowed to take photographs of either our aeroplanes or crews. This was an official one which I did not recieve until about ten years ago from Brian Frow. You might wonder about myself and our engineer. We are not wearing brevets. This is because we had had our battledress jackets made reversable in order for us to make a getaway in case we crashlanded. The Engineer spoke some German and I a little French. The Spaniel was mine and has become quite famous as a War Dog. He was awarded a Pathfinder Badge.

The Lancaster was F Freddie which was shot up and we had to land at the R.A.F. Emergency Landing Field at Woodbridge which by coincidence was only a couple of miles from Rendelsham Forest where later a number of sightings were made by the Americans at their base at Bent Waters.
I still remember having an odd feeling after a short sleep after we had landed at Woodbridge, which might have been caused by the shock of having been badly shot up. I had the feeling of being in an area of pine trees and sand dunes I do not think it was a dream but I really had the feeling I had died. There was another odd thing. On our way back to the Squadron by truck,as our Lancaster never flew again we stopped at a roadside cafe. At the entrance there were two Fruit machines which would take sixpences. All the crew had a go and I was last.Of course they won nothing. I had a sixpence left and put it in the first machine I got the Jack Pot. I collected about twenty pounds which was a lot in those days. The owner was not very happy and said that to his knowledge neither machines had never paid out a Jack Pot since the War had started. As a bit of a joke I put in another sixpence in the other fruit machine and the same thing happened, another Jackpot. The cafe owner was furious.
I used to have a cottage at Snape which was only about eight miles from Rendlesham and I used to pass the Forest and Bent Waters every week day on my way to the school I taught in just out side Ipswich but never experienced untoward.feelings.
I suppose from that day onward I became a sort of lucky charm for the rest of the Crew. Perhaps I was lucky as I was convinced that I would survive the War. By the time we had finished operating I had completed 76 Operations.

One of the letters you sent me mentions "Cover Ups". These have happened on a number of occasions.
You might be interested in the following: I have had a cover up for more than sixty years and I have been told by the Royal Air Force Association that the matter is still sensitive. After sixty years?
This concerns a War Crime forced on my crew by one of the highest ranking R.A.F. Officers of the second World War.

Approximate side view outline of UFO seen from the RB-36.

This resulted in the deaths of over 2000 civilians, the murder of two of my crew and others who died convenient deaths. Graves falsified and my own surfival only due to prompt action by a S/Ldr Young who was killed a few months later leading the second Dam Raid on 617 Squadron.
I realise that this may seem a bit like a "James Bond" novel but since I first started research on this matter I have good proof that the Officer must have been working for the Germans.
Apart from this I am minded of an old Intelligence saying " Never Forgive and Never Forget".
Shakespeare had the right idea:"Oh what a tangled web we weave when at first we practice to deceive"

I give here a few details of my own background:
I finished my service in the R.A.F.V.R. in 1952 and joined the Army Teaching Service. Posted to Cyprus in 1953, spent six years before returning to U.K. Taught for a few years in U.K. Took a job as Head in Ghana working for the Italian Consortium of Impregilo running their school for senior staff children. Next a job as Head for the Staff School in Nigeria at the Kainji Dam. Four years later I became head of the senior staff schoolfor Caltex Oil at Yosu in South Korea. Returned to U.K., for a year then took a post of head teacher at Hillcrest Preparatory School Nairobi.Became a Kenyan Citizen 25 years ago. Retired in 1985when I decided to paint professionally.
My service Number was 928434.

I do hope this blurb has not bored you?

Yours sincerely,

Roy Claridge

Ronald R. Claridge.

Sorry for The Scrappy Letter.

We were to come across details of an identical object, seen in 1956, when the crew of a United States Air Force Convair RB-36H aircraft of 78th Squadron, sighted a huge metallic 'disc' with an estimated diameter of 100 feet, hovering just off their left wing, 300 yards away. Although some of the crew took photographs of the UFO, these were later seized along with the flight log. After landing, they were warned not to talk about what they had seen for twelve years. We showed Ron Claridge a copy of the illustration, prepared many years later by the crew. He agreed it was identical to what he and his crew had seen. **(Source: Richard Haines)**

August/September – England: UFO approached V1 Bombs

At 3pm, Mrs Winifred Smith was living on the second floor at 49, Elgin Avenue, Chelmsford, when she heard the sound of the air raid siren going off, and went onto the veranda to have a look before seeking the sanctuary of an air raid shelter.

She looked across the landscape and saw four 'Buzz Bombs' (V1's) all in a line, heading towards the London area.

> *"When they had drawn level, I was surprised to see an enormous delicate blue bubble (like a huge soap bubble) approach from behind the bombs and move up to the second and third missile, before heading towards the first as if inspecting them. Seconds later, the first V1's engine cut out, at which point the 'bubble' flew away across the sky. I fell down onto the floor and covered my ears, waiting for the explosion. There was a huge bang, so I waited for it to subside and looked out just in time to see the 'bubble' rolling away into the distance."*

Dan Goring, from the Essex UFO Study Group, interviewed her during the 1980, when she was living in Park View Crescent, Baddow, in Chelmsford. He said:

> *"I asked her what she thought the object was. She thought it might have been some device sent up by British Intelligence to inspect German bombers."*

Bob Easton, of BUFORA, interviewed her.

> *"Mrs Smith couldn't actually say that she saw the object spinning, but it rolled across the sky like a ball.*
>
> *During the next 20 years or so from the date of the occurrence, the family referred to it as being 'Mum's soap bubble' in a light- hearted way. Many of them had been 'brought up' on this story. It wasn't till the early 1960s that members of the family heard accounts of 'Flying Saucers' and UFOs and made the connection."*

(Source: Douglas Cannin, Bob Easton, BUFORA/Dan Goring, Essex UFO Study Group)

August – Irish Coast: Mysterious UFO seen over the sea

Merchant Navy Officer William Anderson was on duty, at 4.30am, when he and other members of the crew sighted a large object, hovering about 100 feet above the sea off their port bow.

> *"As we approached closer, all of sudden the lights came on – just like Christmas tree lighting up – reds, blues, greens and whites.*

I was able to clearly see a domed-shaped object – like an airship, but much bigger; it had a type of dome on top. Underneath, the lights were spinning in a clockwise direction. I sent for the Captain to come on deck. The strange 'craft' was keeping pace with us; we were doing 15 knots at the time, but it didn't seem to be moving. We asked the radar operative to check his scope, but he said nothing was showing.

By this time the Captain had arrived and couldn't believe his eyes. We continued our observation through binoculars at this fantastic sight. It was a good 1,000 feet long about 800 yards away from us, and had what looked like some openings in the back end. There were windows or portholes – about a dozen of them, projecting blue to white lights. We didn't see anyone on the mysterious object. Our radio operator tried to contact shore but was unsuccessful in relaying any messages, due to the heavy interference. We signalled the object with lights, but failed to attract any response. About an hour later, it inexplicably vanished from view. The incident was reported to the Admiralty when we arrived home; they warned us not to talk about it forever."

September – England: UFO paces V1 'doodlebug'

Whilst there may be a conventional explanation for some of the strange things seen by the crews of allied aircraft during the Second World War, it beggars belief to try and explain away a sighting over Maida Vale, London, in September 1944. A female resident told of seeing:

"...four V1 Flying Bombs, flying astern, heading towards Marble Arch, when a bright spherical object appeared in the sky resembling a soap bubble, which flew towards the bombs – like a rolling ball in the sky. As it approached the leading V1, the rocket began to descend. I took cover, fearing the inevitable explosion. When I looked upwards again, I saw the object climbing at incredible speed towards the north-west, as other V1's began falling over the Pall Mall area." **(Source: BUFORA, Robert Easton)**

28th September – Nova Scotia: Orange 'globes' harass German fighters

William Anderson found himself witnessing the second sighting of what became known as 'Foo fighters', while in a convoy of ships heading to Russia.

"At 6.50am we were off to Nova Scotia, when we heard that German aircraft were attacking the convoy. Incredibly, the German aircraft appeared to halt their attack on us and weave all over the sky, after we saw them being harassed by a number of orange 'balls of light'. It was an amazing sight; some of the German airplanes flew away with some of the bombs still attached."

(Source: Ron West, Essex UFO Study Group)

21st November – Germany: RAF Pilots sights UFO display

On the 21st November 1944, RAF Sgt. L. Bucknell was a wireless operator aboard an RAF Bomber on a mission over Aschaffenburg, Germany, piloted by Flying Officer Markes, when he saw 'weird lights', resembling rockets, dashing about the sky. It was enough to unsettle him; little did he know that over the forthcoming years many similar 'UFO displays' would be sighted in the skies of England.

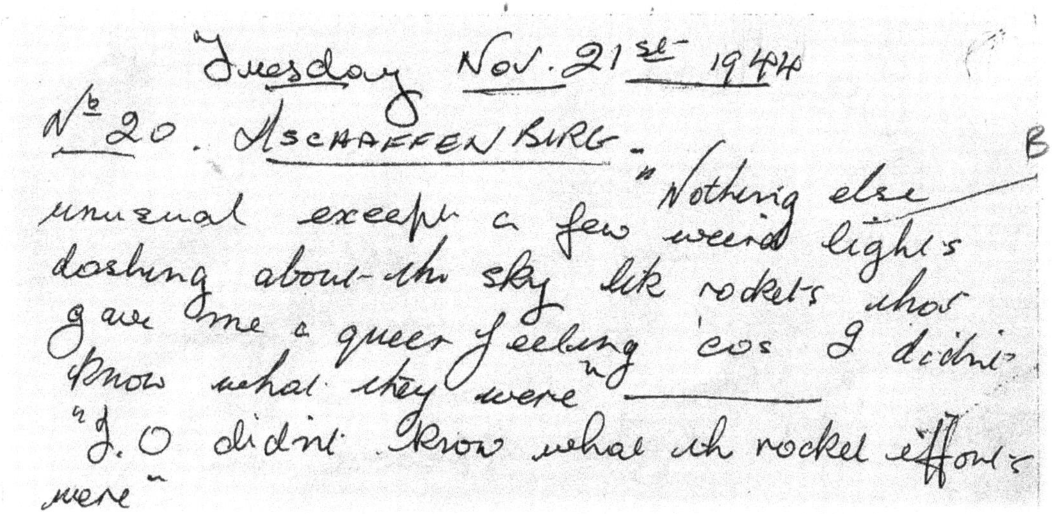
Tuesday Nov. 21st 1944
No 20. ASCHAFFENBURG.
"Nothing else
unusual except a few weird lights
dashing about the sky like rockets which
gave me a queer feeling 'cos I didn't
know what they were"
"I.O didn't know what the rocket effects
were"

27th November – France: American Pilot sights orange 'globes of light'

At 10pm one November evening, Lt. Ed Schlueter from Oshkosh, Wisconsin, took off in his night fighter from Dijon, France on what he thought would be a routine mission for the 415th Night Fighter Squadron. He was accompanied by radar observer Lt. Donald J. Meiers, and Lt. Fred Ringwald, intelligence officer of the 415th.

They began their search pattern on either side of the Rhine River north of *Strasbourg, combing the reasonably clear night skies against a backcloth of some clouds and a quarter moon visible – very much alert, for there were mountains nearby, and the inside of the aircraft darkened for night vision.

Lights seen – then glowing objects

Lt. Ringwald was the first to see some 'lights' over the hills, which he brought to the attention of the pilot who dismissed them as being probably stars. After further conversation, they realised that there weren't any hills, followed by the sighting of eight or ten glowing orange 'balls of fire' moving through the air in a row, at terrific speed.

Schlueter saw them far off his left wing and wondered if they were enemy fighters pursuing him? He immediately checked by radio with Allied ground radar stations, who confirmed this was not the case.

Lt. Schlueter did not know what he was facing – could it have been some new and lethal German

*Strasbourg is the capital city of the Alsace region in north-eastern France. It is the seat of the European Parliament and sits near the German border, with culture and architecture blending German and French influences. It is known for its Gothic Cathédrale Notre-Dame, featuring daily shows from its astronomical clock and sweeping views of the Rhine River from partway up its 142m spire.

weapon? He turned into the 'lights', ready for action. The 'lights' disappeared – then reappeared, far off. Five minutes later, they went into a flat glide and vanished.

Decided to keep quiet

The puzzled airmen continued on their mission, and destroyed seven freight trains behind German lines. When they landed back at Dijon, they decided to do what any other prudent soldier would do – keep quiet for the moment.

If you tried to explain everything strange that happened in a war, you would do nothing else. Further, Schlueter and Meiers had nearly completed their required missions, and did not want to chance being grounded by some sceptical flight surgeon for 'combat fatigue'.

The sighting was also covered in the American Legion Magazine. Mysteriously, there was no mention of a number of glowing objects but states:

> *"Upon returning to base saw a red light flying through area about 35 miles ENE. Came in at about 2,000 feet off starboard and then it disappeared in a long streak."*

One wonders the reason for this?

Few nights later

A few nights later, (given as the end of November 1944) Lt. Henry Giblin, of Santa Rosa, California, pilot, and Lt. Walter Cleary, of Worcester, Massachusetts, radar-observer, were flying at 1,000 feet altitude when they saw a huge red light 1,000 feet above them, moving at 200 miles per hour.

Three lights seen!

Through January, 1945, the pilots of the 415th continued to see the "Foo-fighters," and their conduct became increasingly mysterious. One aircrew observed lights, moving both singly and in pairs. On another occasion, three sets of lights, this time red and white in color, followed a plane, and when the plane suddenly pulled up, the lights continued on in the same direction, as though caught napping, and then sheepishly pulled up to follow. The pilot checked with ground radar – he was alone in the sky. This was true in every instance that Foo-fighters were observed.

10th December – Canada: RAF pilot sights 'pixie' on aircraft

Over the years we were to hear of all manner of strange and almost unbelievable close encounters with UFOs, and occasionally their alien occupants – incidents we would probably once have dismissed as being frivolous and unworthy of serious study. Bearing in mind the often noted association between UFOs and 'paranormal' occurrences that sometimes followed a sighting, we wondered if some of the pilots had experienced close encounters involving the occupants of these 'craft.'

Gremlins, aliens, pixies or unknowns

Was it just a myth that pilots had encountered what became known as 'gremlins' – the mischievous invisible 'beings' blamed by aircrew for causing mechanical problems to aircraft and made famous by Roald Dahl? Was there any substance behind stories of these creatures having allegedly being seen by RAF servicemen, understanding their reluctance to report such matters?

We finally came across somebody who had the courage to tell what he saw, while on a training flight in Manitoba, Canada, based at Gimli RAF Airbase, 18 SFTS – then a training base for the British Commonwealth Air Training Plan, under the guidance of the Royal Canadian Air Force.

Retired RAF Pilot/Navigator Sergeant William Davis, RAF Serial number 1805619, born on 7th May 1923, now a retired head teacher living on the Isle of Wight, witnessed a bizarre incident while flying his Anson V aircraft, West of Lake Winnipegosis on the 10th December 1944, close to the town of Brandon, Canada. Bill was waiting for the lights of Gimli control tower to come up, after having completed a 2 hours and 45 minutes journey as part of his pilot's course to earn his 'wings.' He checked his map and kept a good lookout, his eyes sweeping the horizon and continually checking the instruments in the cockpit.

Two bumps seen on the nose of the aircraft

"I noticed what looked like two curious bumps, one either side of the nose of the aircraft, like tiny exhaust pipes, although the nose itself was empty. I decided to carry out a proper check when I landed and dismissed it from my mind. Suddenly, my eyes flashed back again to the nose. The 'exhausts' had begun to move. They now looked like hands. I thought this cannot be happening and checked to see if this wasn't some kind of reflection.

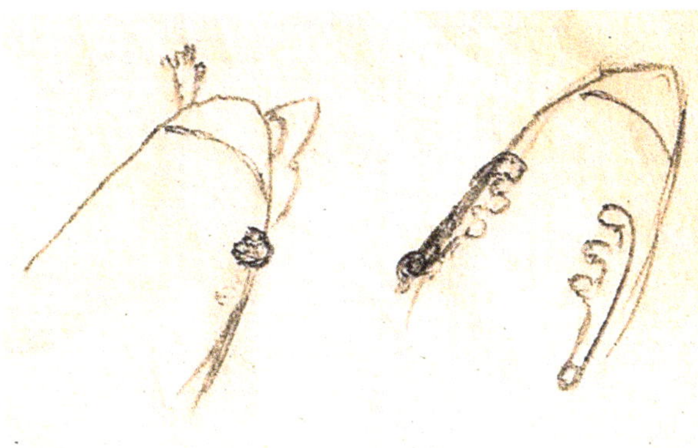

Sergeant William Davis

Entity appears

Then a small entity, resembling a pixie, or elf – the ones associated with folklore – appeared outside the aircraft, a few feet away from where I was sat. I thought this cannot be happening and pinched my thigh hard and tried to think what checks I could carry out inside the aircraft. I will never forget its pinkish face – European in nature, with a thick, short trimmed beard, close cut, covering its features, reminding me of an old English naval seaman, dressed in some sort of green garb, height approximately 18 inches tall, apparently watching something in the sky to my left, moving slowly in a nonchalant manner as if walking around the estate. I was close enough to see that instead of fingers, he had what looked like little exhaust stubs, no thumbs, and pointed shoes made of velvet or some such material, rather than leather. He began to stroll towards me and was no more than 12-15 inches away, when something appeared to catch his eye. By this time I was shouting and gesticulating through the window, trying to attract his attention, but then realised he was unlikely to hear me because of the sound of the aircraft engines. I had the impression he could not see me at all and was probably unaware of my existence. After about 30 seconds he sat down, looked below, gave a slight lift with his hand on the side and pushed himself off the nose, before disappearing from view."

He had not been suffering from delusions – others had seen it too

Bill continued on his journey. Exhilarated by the experience, after landing he mentioned to some of the ground crew what he had seen and wasn't surprised when they burst out laughing. Fearing reports of such nature could have prevented him from gaining his 'wings', he decided to keep quiet but received a visit in his barracks, the next day, by a senior flying instructor, who reassured him he hadn't been suffering from delusions, as he wasn't the only pilot to have reported seeing the small being!

Having spoken to Bill and his son, who has no reason whatsoever to disbelieve his father's account, strange as it may be, one wonders if there is any connection with the eerie reputation of the area, still steeped in reports to this present day of strange sightings of 'creatures' seen swimming in the Lakes Manitoba and Winnipegosis.

Bill:

"It seemed so bloody real. I was not drinking, or flying at great height. I was fully awake and alert. I know what I saw and will never forget. I gained my 'wings' in January 1945 and was told I was now a Commissioned Pilot Officer. Sadly, the MOD has refused to recognise my rank."

In a letter sent to us in October 2009, Bill had this to say:

"I still think we will eventually get to the bottom of these sightings and what's behind them, to [sic] many people suffer being ridiculed and still stick to their stories; there seems to be a pattern behind them which links them."

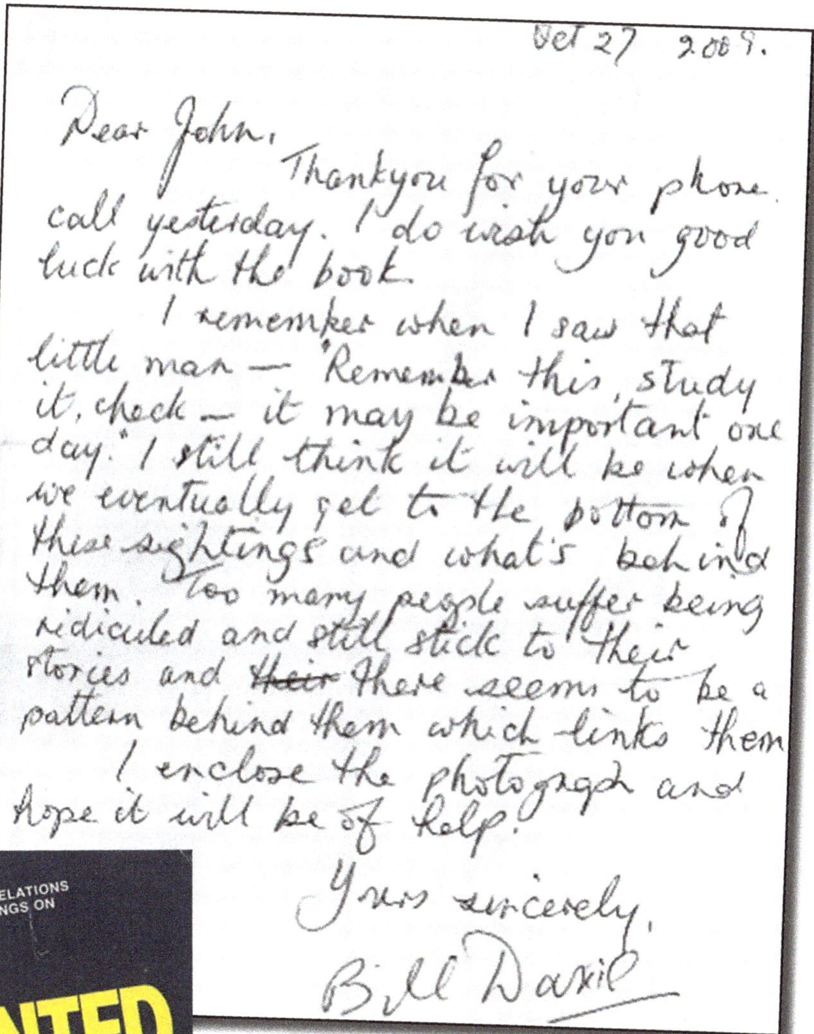

Oct 27 2009.

Dear John,

Thankyou for your phone call yesterday. I do wish you good luck with the book.

I remember when I saw that little man — 'Remember this, study it, check — it may be important one day.' I still think it will be when we eventually get to the bottom of these sightings and what's behind them. Too many people suffer being ridiculed and still stick to their stories and ~~their~~ there seems to be a pattern behind them which links them.

I enclose the photograph and hope it will be of help!

Yours sincerely,

Bill Davis

Book: *Our Haunted Planet*

In his book, *Our Haunted Planet*, John Keel tells us that Bomber crews often reported seeing 'little green men' that invaded the aircraft and caused all sorts of mischief.

The Press labelled them as gremlins; others suggested the crews were hallucinating, due to the high altitude.

22nd December – Germany: UFO over Koblenz, during bombing raid

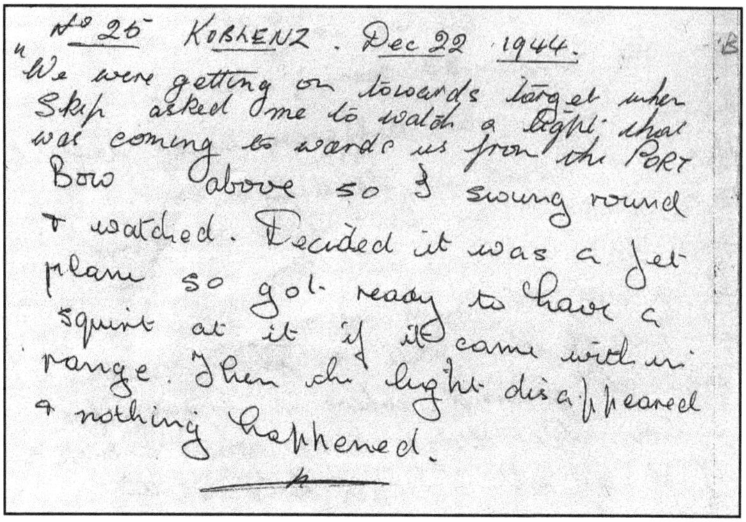
No 25 KOBLENZ. Dec 22 1944.
"We were getting on towards target when Skip asked me to watch a light that was coming towards us from the PORT Bow above so I swung round & watched. Decided it was a jet plane so got ready to have a squirt at it if it came within range. Then the light disappeared & nothing happened.

On 22nd December 1944, RAF Sgt. L. Bucknell was once again taking part in a bombing raid over Germany and heading towards the target of Koblenz, when the skipper warned him of a 'light' approaching from above. Thinking it was probably a jet aircraft heading towards them, he prepared to open fire when it suddenly disappeared.

22/23rd December – France: Pilot sights two 'lights'

Another 415th night fighter squadron pilot and radar observer was flying at 10,000 feet altitude near Hagenau.

> *"At 0600 hours we saw two 'lights' climbing toward us from the ground. Upon reaching our altitude, they levelled off and stayed on my tail. The 'lights' appeared to be large orange glows. After staying with the plane for two minutes, they peeled off and turned away, flying under perfect control, and then went out."*

24th December – USA: Pilot sights glowing red object

The next night the same two men, flying at 10,000 feet, observed a single red flame. Lt. David L. McFalls of Cliffside, N.C., pilot, and Lt. Ned Baker of Hemat, California, radar-observer, also saw:

> *"...a glowing, red object, shooting straight up, which suddenly changed to a view of an aircraft doing a wing-over, going into a dive and disappearing."*

This was the first and only suggestion of a controlled flying device.

Golden 'ball', with metallic finish, seen in daylight

What the 415th saw at night was borne out in part by day. West of Neustadt, a P-47 pilot saw:

> *"...a gold-colored 'ball', with a metallic finish, which appeared to be moving slowly through the air. As the sun was low, it was impossible to tell whether the sun reflected off it, or the light came from within."*

Another P-47 pilot reported "a phosphorescent golden sphere, 3 to 5 feet in diameter, flying at 2,000 feet."

St. Elmo's fire was the explanation!

Various explanations were offered by scientists for what the airmen were seeing. They included St. Elmo's light – a well-known electrical phenomenon appearing like light or flame, during stormy weather, at the tips of church steeples, ships' masts, and tall trees.

1945

2nd January – Germany: RAF Bomber opens fire on UFO

RAF Flt. Lt. Vernon Wilkes, DFC, was based at RAF Hemswell, Lincolnshire, with 150 Squadron and formed part of the crew aboard RAF Lancaster Bomber NG264 IQB, piloted by Flying Officer G. Markes. On the night of 2nd January 1945, they were flying over Nuremberg, Germany.

> *"Visibility was clear. There were bags of the usual queer lights and flares all over the deck. A light appeared on the starboard quarter and began to follow us. I had seen plenty of these before at different times, but this one closed in steadily – almost going out at times, and then blazing up again. It came close enough to light up my turret and the rest of the aircraft before diving into the ground, where it burned for a time. The skipper told us to open fire if we saw another one. A short time later, another one appeared and acted in the same manner as the other, so I told Danny (Sgt. Danny Driscoll, rear gunner) to 'have a squirt at it' with his guns. I saw the tracer appear to go pretty close to the object. I cannot say if it hit it or not, but it dove straight down and hit the ground."*

The crew wondered if the flaming objects could have been what were rumoured to be a new type of flak shell or device, supposedly simulating a fully laden bomber exploding, followed by blazing debris falling to earth, nicknamed

Vernon (shown in Rendlesham Forest, some years ago)

'Scarecrows'. The RAF did nothing to discourage the story that the Germans fired such shells to demoralize their opponents. Why bother when conventional shells were doing the real thing? 'Scarecrows' became accepted in Bomber Command reports, but post-war research has so far failed to find any evidence of the German use of such a device. It is more likely that some crews may have seen the effect of another German weapon (SCHRAGE MUSIK) 'slanted music' – the name for an arrangement of guns mounted in a firing upwards position, installed on German night jet fighters.

(Source: Personal interviews in 2006 with Joan and Vernon)

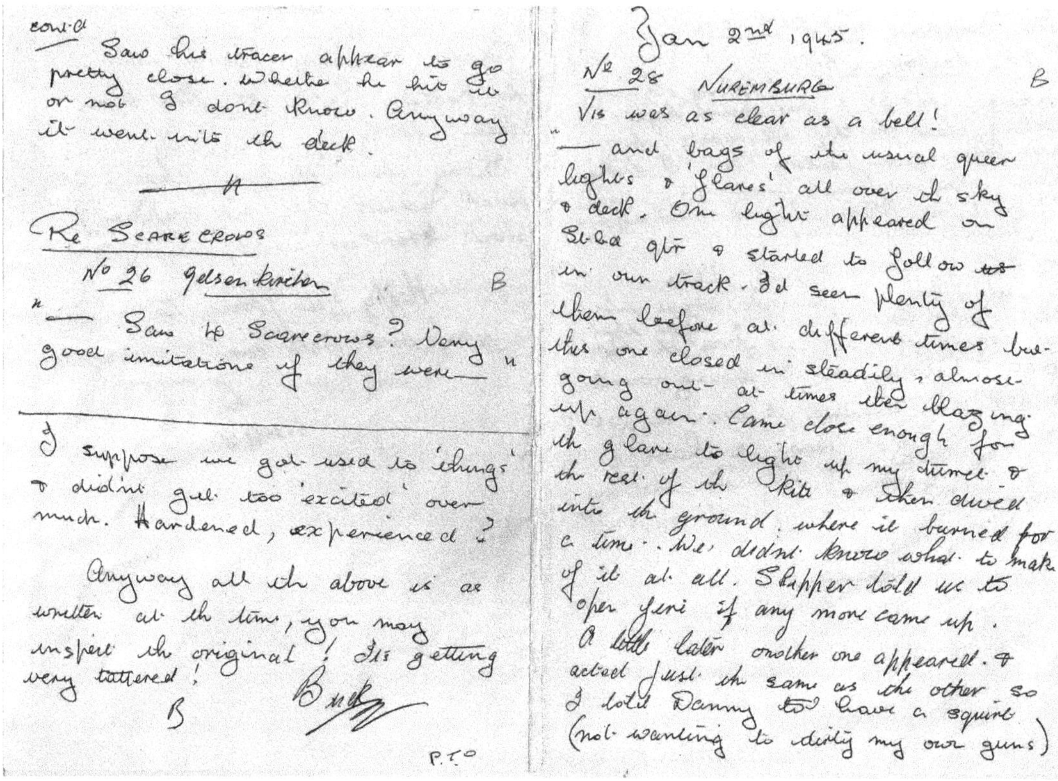

cont'd

— Saw his tracer appear to go pretty close. Whether he hit us or not I don't know. Anyway it went into the deck.

—— H ——

Re Scarecrows

No 26 Gelsenkirchen B

" — Saw the Scarecrows? Very good imitations of they were — "

I suppose we got used to 'things' & didn't get too 'excited' over much. Hardened, experienced?

Anyway all the above is as written at the time, you may inspect the original! It's getting very tattered!

B

Buck

P.T.O

Jan 2nd 1945.

No 28 Nuremburg B

Vis was as clear as a bell!

" — and bags of the usual queer lights & 'flares' all over the sky & deck. One light appeared on Stbd qtr & started to follow us in our track. I'd seen plenty of them before at different times but this one closed in steadily, almost going out at times then blazing up again. Came close enough for the glare to light up my turret & the rest of the kite & then dived into the ground where it burned for a time. We didn't know what to make of it at all. Skipper told us to open fire if any more came up. A little later another one appeared & acted just the same as the other so I told Danny to have a squirt (not wanting to dirty my own guns)

26th March – Germany: RAF pilot sights 'glowing ball' over Berlin

Another serviceman to sight something odd during the closing stages of World War Two was a former RAF Pilot, operational with 541 Squadron. His logbook entry for 26th March 1945 reads:

> *"I was flying at about 17,000 feet towards Berlin, cruising at 360mph. When over the Ruhr, I spotted a pink light ahead and thought the Germans were using some form of new defence, as they would be tracking me by radar. However, as I approached and went past it at about 20-30mph, approximately 50 yards away on my starboard side, I saw what appeared to be a 'ball of light', 5-6ft in diameter. I calculated that as I was flying at 360mph in an easterly direction, it was travelling at a speed of over 300mph. I last saw it as I turned my head to the right and looked through the Perspex cockpit cover."*

August – off the Irish Coast: Saucer-shaped object seen by ship's crew

Seaman William Anderson was on watch at the time, at 4.30am. The ship was off the Irish Coast and they were heading home from America.

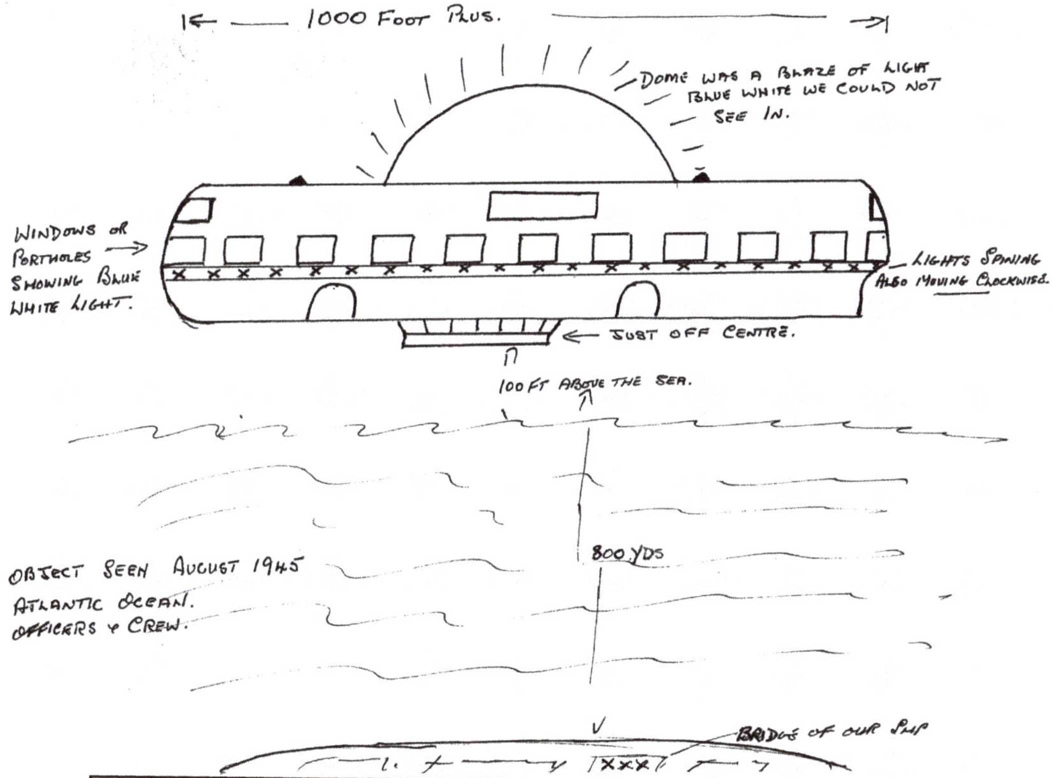

UFO SIGHTING ACCOUNT FORM

SECTION A

Please write an account of your sighting, make a drawing of what you saw and then answer the questions in section B overleaf as fully as possible. Write in **BLOCK CAPITALS** using a ball point pen.

I was an officer in the Merchant Navy during the war, I remember it was August 1945, we were on our way back from America just off the Irish Coast, I was on watch at the time, it was 4·30 am, when suddenly we saw this very big oblong/Oval shape off our port bow, I thought at first it was another ship, but it was stationary about two foot above the waves, its lights suddenly came on, it was like a christmas tree all coloured lights, Reds, Greens, blues, Whites and Yellows, When the lights came on we could see that it was an oval shape, like an airship but much bigger, it had a type of dome on the top also one underneath, the lights were spining, also going in a clockwise direction,

Please continue on a separate sheet if necessary.

I sent down for the Captain

1946

6th May – England: 'Flying saucer' lands in London

On the 6th May 1946, an elderly couple – Mr Davison and his sister, then living at Burrows Court, off Pear tree Croft, Fulham, London – heard a commotion outside their flat. They went outside to have a look and were shocked to see a dove-grey coloured 'flying saucer' object, lying on the communal garden. They telephoned the *Chelsea News* and a reporter arrived. This is as much as Margaret Fry knows about the case, but is satisfied, from her enquiries, that it was a genuine account.

We asked the local library if they could check the Chelsea News for this date, but found nothing of consequence. We even made an appeal in the local newspaper, asking if anyone remembered the couple, but were unsuccessful.

(Source: Dan Goring)

1947

January-April – England: UFOs tracked on radar over East Coast

During the period between January and April 1947, UFOs were plotted by radar, on a number of occasions, crossing the East Anglia coast near Norwich, at estimated speeds of 400 mph. Thanks to declassified operational records, previously kept by Eastern RAF Fighter Sector, we learnt of the RAF response behind a number of operations implemented in a bid to identify an 'unidentified flying aircraft', officially designated as X306 but nicknamed by the pilots as 'C' for 'Charlie'. 16147 Army commitments were met by 595 Squadron and Meteors of 245 Squadron, operated under Neatishead Control on intercept practice. An unidentified aircraft had been plotted on WC 9585, at 30,000 feet, and eastern Sector Operations were requested by Group to scramble a Mosquito of 23 Squadron to intercept. However, as there were no aircraft available with oxygen, an aircraft of 11 Group – which was already airborne on a 'Bull's-eye' Exercise – would try to intercept under Trimley Heath Control. The interception was unsuccessful, owing to engine trouble and the A1 going under.

RAF pilot scrambled to intercept target

One Mosquito of 23 Squadron, piloted by Flight Lieutenant Kent, was at readiness at RAF Wittering to attempt interception on the unidentified aircraft, which had been plotted several times lately, at 2040 hours. The 'bogey' was plotted in WN6038. The plot was at one time heading south. The Mosquito, which had been brought to standby, was returned to readiness but when the plot again headed into Eastern sector Area, the Mosquito was scrambled at 2327 hours, although getting within one or two miles, several times, no interception was made of the target, which took violent evasive action. The plot faded at 1.15am and, after patrolling on a north-south line for some time, the aircraft returned to base.

We contacted Mr William Kent – the pilot of the aircraft (now a retired Group Captain) – who had this to say:

"I remember the incident well. At no time, at any height, did I sight anything visual, but one had to understand the extreme care needed to avoid collision by steering a few degrees off centre, when closing on a target at a speed of 10-20 knots (11-23 miles per hour). The following day, I discussed what had happened with the Neatishead Flight Controller and a report was later sent to the Commanding Officer of the Group, who decided the unidentified aircraft was most probably a leaking meteorological balloon – a conclusion assisted by a suggestion made by myself that a burst meteorological balloon was a distinct possibility, deduced from its behaviour. After all the term 'flying saucers' was unheard of and not taken seriously."

Although the date of the incident is not known, the operational record book kept at RAF Wittering, in the entry for the 17th January 1947, contained the following information: quote:

'One Meteor of 245 Squadron was at standby from 1300-1600. One Mosquito of 23 Squadron was at standby from 1900 hours. This Aircraft was scrambled just before midnight to intercept an unidentified high-flying object. An interception was made when the aircraft was at 18,000 feet, a contact being obtained at 1500 yards, but the observer was unable to hold it as the target was jerking violently. Further contact was obtained whilst the target lost height to 200 feet when both target and fighter faded going out to sea. The watch was stood down at 0130 hours.'

According to the operational record book kept at RAF Coltishall:

"An unidentified aircraft [was] sighted at 11.15pm, January 23rd 1947, at 28,000 feet, and the readiness aircraft scrambled under Barrington, control handed over to Langtoft and Neatishead in turn; the plot faded and the aircraft returned to base after an uneventful flight."

England: Domed object, showing three spheres, seen over Bristol

Mr Geoffrey Bird – an investigator for 'Probe' – told of a number of interviews held with a resident of Withywood, Bristol (known as Mr 'P') who was out fishing with a friend, Jim, on Portishead docks, one afternoon in 1947, when they noticed what appeared to be an aircraft on fire. As it got closer, they saw:

"...a circular angled object, aluminum in colour, showing a 'pimple' or dome on its top, with three 'balls' or spheres set into its underside, forming a triangle."

When at a distance of some 300 yards, a Mosquito Bomber appeared, at which stage the 'craft' flipped onto its side and shot off at speed, vanishing from view. Five minutes later, two police officers and a Customs official arrived and, after a short conversation, escorted the men to the police station, where they were interviewed separately for over five-and-a-half hours, followed by another interview by two other officials. By this time the two witnesses were fed up and decided to leave, refusing to sign any declaration to keep quiet about the matter. Three weeks later they were visited by a Group Captain and Flight Lieutenant, who showed them identification and apologised for the way in which they had been treated. **(Source: *'Probe'* Case Reference P16-81/E)**

10th May – England: Two UFOs sighted over Chester

On 10th May 1947, Mr Fortt and his companion were exercising their dogs in a field at Chester, at 11pm, when they sighted a red, metallic, oval object, descending through the air – *'like two soup bowls, one on top of the other, with a row of bright lights in the middle, making a feint humming noise.'* Mr Fortt called out in alarm to his companion, following which the object shot away at terrific speed. **(Source: DIGAP)**

June – England: Spinning 'silver ball' sighted over Lancashire

Stanley Roberts from Heydock, St. Helens, Lancashire, was out walking with friends in the vicinity of the Black Horse public house, near RAF Burtonwood, Warrington, in June 1947.

> *"It was a warm, sunny morning. Suddenly, a coal lorry travelling along the road stopped abruptly. The driver got out and pointed up into the sky. Another lorry pulled up. Wondering what they were seeing, we looked up and saw this spinning silver grey 'ball of light' in the sky, just hovering there, about a thousand feet up in the air. Other witnesses were Mr and Mrs Wardman. He was an ex-Naval Commander. Unfortunately, they both died some years ago. A USAF Jet Fighter then flew over. I can't say whether he saw the UFO or not. One thing is certain, we did. You couldn't miss it. A few seconds later, it shot away across the sky and vanished from view."*

Summer – England: Silver cigar-shaped UFO seen over Birmingham

Some years ago we met NICAP (National Investigations Committee on Aerial Phenomena) Investigator, Derek Samson – formerly of Shirley, Solihull, West Midlands – to talk about his personal interviews with a number of UFO witnesses, over the years.

Derek Samson

Derek showed us some finely hand-painted illustrations, prepared from his own UFO sighting in 1947, while living with his parents in Wellington Road, Perry Barr. This was to trigger-off a lifetime's interest in UFO research.

> *"We had a small garden, which, because of its size, did not take much upkeep. My father liked to tend his roses, while I often experimented with the growing of different species of privet hedging certain small trees. One mid-afternoon in summer, just after a rainstorm had left everything sparkling wet as the hot sun shone down, I happened to look up into the sky, when I saw a large silver object, shaped like an airship or zeppelin, with rows of what looked like portholes along its side, before it disappeared behind a large storm cloud. At the time I knew very little about 'flying saucers'. Had I observed an airship or UFO?"*

Summer – England: 'V'-shaped formation seen over Birmingham

Another strikingly similar incident of what could well have been the same object took place in the same district of Birmingham, at around the same time. Mr Peter Corden was on his way home, after watching a film at the Mayfair Cinema, Perry Barr, Birmingham, at 10.30pm, one summer evening in 1947:

> *"I was staggered to see a formation of luminous 'discs', flying across the sky in a 'V'-shaped formation. When I read about the incident in the following day's Birmingham Evening Mail, I was amused when they explained it away as being the reflection of tram lights!"*

(Source: Carole Corden, 2005)

June – England: Mysterious ring-shaped UFO seen over Dorset

Illustrating the way in which a diversity of strange phenomenon were being seen then (as they are still are now, over 50 years later) was a sighting from a Dorset housewife – Sylvia Clarke – who was walking to school in June 1947, when she noticed a grey ring-shaped object, with a peculiar 'bump' on one side of the 'ring', completely motionless in the sky.

> *"My first reaction was to wonder if it could have been a smoke ring, ejected from a steam locomotive at the nearby Weymouth Railway station, but then I realised that this explanation could not fit, as the smoke ring was at quite a height with its 'bump' now very distinctive on its outer edge, rather than fading swiftly as one would have expected."*

We were to come across other similar reports. They included a dark grey smoky ring, rotating across the sky over Sandwich, Kent, in 1947, and a grey smoky ring floating just above the waters of the Kennet and Avon canal, some years later.

(Source: Personal interview)

14th June –USA:-Lincoln County ranchers find wreckage

Harassed' Rancher who Located 'Saucer' Sorry He Told About It

W. W. Brazel, 48, Lincoln county rancher living 30 miles south east of Corona, today told his story of finding what the army at first described as a flying disk, but the publicity which attended his find caused him to add that if he ever found anything else short of a bomb he sure wasn't going to say anything about it.

Brazel was brought here late yesterday by W. E. Whitmore, of radio station KGFL, had his picture taken and gave an interview to the Record and Jason Kellahin, sent here from the Albuquerque bureau of the Associated Press to cover the story. The picture he posed for was sent out over AP telephoto wire sending machine specially set up in the Record office by R. D. Adair, AP wire chief sent here from Albuquerque for the sole purpose of getting out his picture and that of sheriff George Wilcox, to whom Brazel originally gave the information of his find.

Brazel related that on June 14 he and an 8-year old son, Vernon were about 7 or 8 miles from the ranch house of the J. B. Foster ranch, which he operates, when they came upon a large area of bright wreckage made up on rubber strips, tinfoil, a rather tough paper and sticks.

At the time Brazel was in a hurry to get his round made and he did not pay much attention to it. But he did remark about what he had seen and on July 4 he, his wife, Vernon and a daughter Betty, age 14, went back to the spot and gathered up quite a bit of the debris.

The next day he first heard about the flying disks, and he wondered if what he had found might be the remnants of one of these.

Monday he came to town to sell some wool and while here he went to see sheriff George Wilcox and "whispered kinda confidential like" that he might have found a flying disk.

Wilcox got in touch with the Roswell Army Air Field and Maj. Jesse A. Marcel and a man in plain clothes accompanied him home, where they picked up the rest of the pieces of the "disk" and went to his home to try to reconstruct it.

According to Brazel they simply could not reconstruct it at all. They tried to make a kite out of it, but could not do that and could not find any way to put it back together so that it would fit.

Then Major Marcel brought it to Roswell and that was the last he heard of it until the story broke that he had found a flying disk.

Brazel said that he did not see it fall from the sky and did not see it before it was torn up, so he did not know the size or shape it might have been, but he thought it might have been about as large as a table top. The balloon which held it up, if that was how it worked, must have been about 12 feet long, he felt, measuring the distance by the size of the room in which he sat. The rubber was smoky gray in color and scattered over an area about 200 yards in diameter.

When the debris was gathered up the tinfoil, paper, tape, and sticks made a bundle about three feet long and 7 or 8 inches thick, while the rubber made a bundle about 18 or 20 inches long and about 8 inches thick. In all, he estimated, the entire lot would have weighed maybe five pounds.

There was no sign of any metal in the area which might have been used for an engine and no sign of any propellers of any kind, although at least one paper fin had been glued onto some of the tinfoil.

There were no words to be found anywhere on the instrument, although there were letters on some of the parts. Considerable scotch tape and some tape with flowers printed upon it had been used in the construction.

No strings or wire were to be found but there were some eyelets in the paper to indicate that some sort of attachment may have been used.

Brazel said that he had previously found two weather observation balloons on the ranch, but that what he found this time did not in any way resemble either of these.

"I am sure what I found was not any weather observation balloon," he said. "But if I find anything else, besides a bomb they are going to have a hard time getting me to say anything about it."

18th June – Atlantic Ocean: Green light circles the ship

William Anderson:

> *"We were on our way to America. At 3.20pm I was on the bridge, when the lookout reported that we were being circled by a very large green light. I looked and saw this light under the surface of the water, about 80-100 feet across, keeping the same distance away from the ship.*

It kept circling us for about 45 minutes, before finally sinking out of sight. Other members of the crew watched it and I know that photographs were taken. Nothing showed on the radar screen aboard ship. The incident was reported by radio to the Air Ministry."

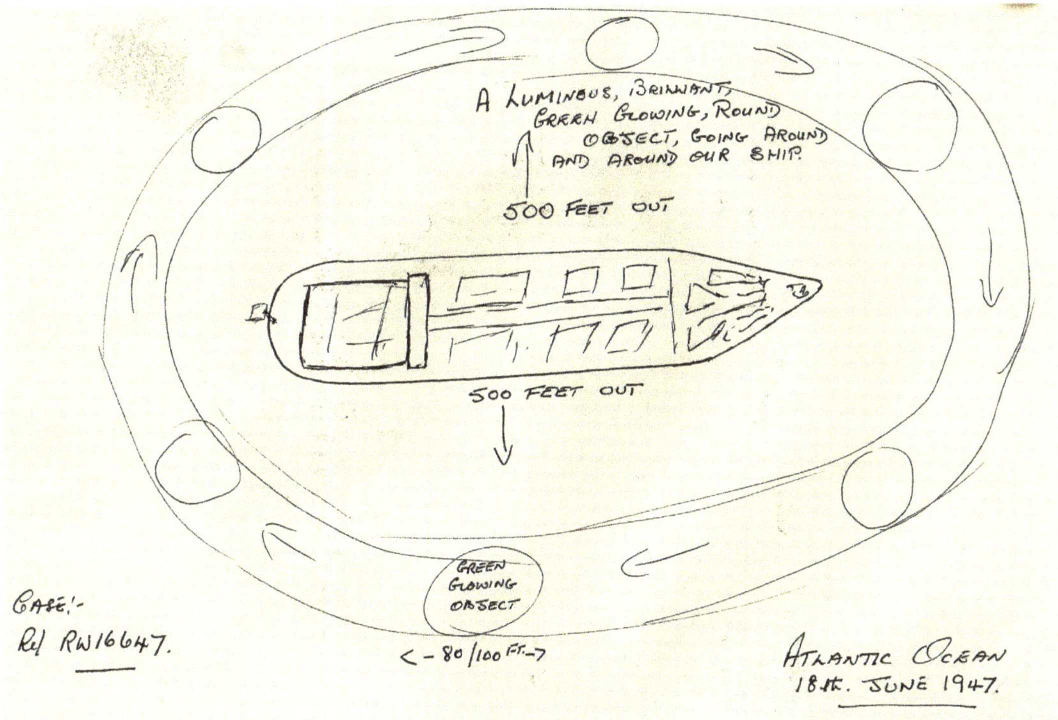

21st June – USA: Five UFOs

Five unidentified objects were seen in the sky over Maury Island, Washington State. One discharged what looked like metallic fragments, before heading out to sea.

24th June USA: UFO sighting by Kenneth Arnold

UNCLASSIFIED

Page 9

I have received lots of requests from people who told me to make a lot of wild guesses. I have based what I have written here in this article on positive facts and as far as guessing what it was I observed, it is just as much a mystery to me as it is to the rest of the world.

My pilot's license is 333487. I fly a Callair airplane; it is a three-place single engine land ship that is designed and manufactured at Afton, Wyoming as an extremely high performance, high altitude airplane that was made for mountain work. The national certificate of my plane is 33355.

Kenneth Arnold
Box 587
Boise, Idaho.

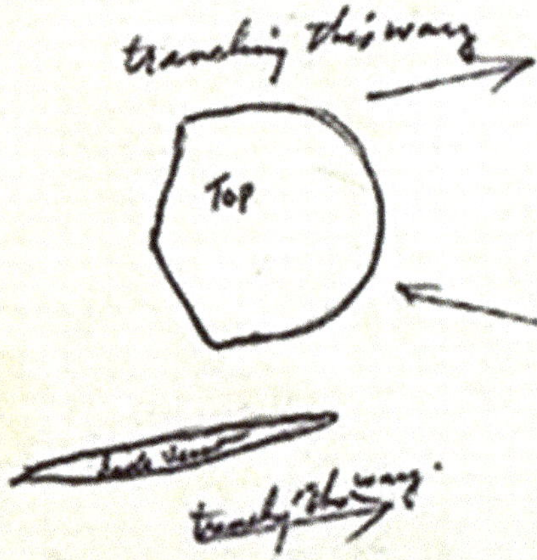

They seemed longer than wide their thickness was about 1/20th of their width

Mirror Bright

They did not appear to me to whirl or spin but seemed in fixed position traveling as I have made drawing.

Kenneth Arnold.

17

[redacted] UNCLAS[illegible]D

Pilot Sees 'Saucer-like Objects' Flying at 1,200 m.p.h. in Oregon

Pendleton, Ore., June 25.—(AP)—Nine bright, saucer-like objects flying at "incredible" speed at 10,000 feet altitude were reported here today by Kenneth Arnold, Boise, Idaho, pilot, who said he could not hazard a guess as to what they were.

Arnold, a United States Forest Service employee, engaged in searching for a missing plane, said he sighted the mystery objects Tuesday at 3 p.m. They were flying between Mount Rainier and Mount Adams, in Washington State, he said, and appeared to weave in and out of formation. Arnold said he clocked them and estimated their speed at 1,200 miles an hour.

He added he talked today with an unidentified man from Ukiah, south of here, who said he had seen similar objects over the mountains near Ukiah Tuesday.

"It seems impossible," Arnold said, "but there it is."

Arnold said he clocked the objects from Mount Rainier to Mount Adams, and estimated their speed at 1,200 miles an hour. He said they appeared to fly almost as if fastened together—if one dipped, the others did, too.

After the incident, he said, he talked to other pilots when he landed at Yakima, Wash., but none of them had seen anything similar.

Oregon is perhaps more concerned than many areas over reports of mysterious objects because of the wind-borne balloons launched from Japan during the war. One of the bomb-laden balloons fell near Lakeview, Ore., in May, 1945, killing six persons.

At Portland, Ore., Edward Leach, senior C.A.A. Aeronautical Inspector, said he could offer no explanation of the fast-flying objects reported by Arnold.

"If they were actually as described," Leach said, "I don't know what they could be. I rather doubt that anything would be travelling that fast."

Leach said he was not sure whether objects travelling at 1,200 miles an hour could be seen clearly enough to tell that they were weaving in formation, as reported.

In Washington, the War Department said it had no information on the Oregon sky mystery.

An Army spokesman expressed interest in any object which would fly at the estimated speed of 1,200 m.p.h., declaring:

"As far as we know, nothing flies that fast except a V-2 rocket, which travels at about 3,500 miles and hour — and that's too fast to be seen."

Moreover, the V-2s, unlike the saucer-shaped objects seen in Oregon, are cigar-shaped.

The spokesman said it was safe to say that the Army is not conducting any high-speed experimental tests in the area mentioned and is certainly "not shooting" in populated regions.

THURSDAY, JUNE 26, 1947

Lone Flier Only One to Sight Big Objects in Western Sky

Pendleton, Ore. - (AP) - Army and CAA spokesmen expressed skepticism Thursday over a report of nine mysterious objects—big as airplanes—whizzing over western Washington at 1,200 miles an hour.

Kenneth Arnold, a flying Boise (Idaho) businessman who reported seeing them, clung, however, to his story of the shiny, flat objects, each as big as a DC-4 passenger plane, racing over Washington's Cascade mountains with a peculiar weaving motion "like the tail of a kite."

An army spokesman in Washington, D. C., commented: "As far as we know, nothing flies that fast except a V-2 rocket, which travels at about 3,500 miles an hour—and that's too fast to be seen."

The spokesman added that the V-2 rockets would not resemble the objects reported by Arnold, and that no high speed experimental tests were being made in the area where Arnold said the objects were.

A civil aeronautics administration inspector in Portland, Ore., added, "I rather doubt that anything would be traveling that fast."

Arnold described the objects as "flat like a pie pan," and so shiny that they reflected the sun like a mirror. He said he was flying his own plane at 2:59 p.m. two days ago toward Mount Rainier, when they appeared directly in front of him 25 to 30 miles away, at 10,000 feet altitude.

28th June – England: UFO sighted over Birmingham

On 28th June 1947, George Thomas from Chase Road, Heath Hayes, Birmingham, was out playing with two friends, close to Five Ways traffic island. At 6pm, they noticed a strange light approaching their position.

> *"It suddenly swooped down, as if going to attack us. We screamed out in front and dropped to the floor. It sailed over our heads and moved away. I was so frightened I could hardly run. When I told my parents they laughed at me, as if I was making it up."*

(Source: Personal letter)

July – England: 'Flying saucer' landing at Hereford – entities seen

We are all familiar with the most publicized alleged UFO incident that occurred at Roswell, New Mexico, in July 1947, involving the alleged recovery of a downed alien spacecraft (later denied by the military authorities, who explained it away as a top secret high altitude research balloon). This is still the subject of fierce debate and controversy right up to the present day.

We spoke to Mollie Tilley from Tamworth, Staffordshire – a sensible, down-to-earth, friendly woman in her late 70s, who remains curious about her Uncle Frank Handford's close encounter, in July 1947, of a 'flying saucer' landing at the family farm in Fishpool Hill, just outside Hereford.

Mollie:

> *"My uncle and mother was not the sort of persons to make up wild stories. They were the exact opposite, not given to flights of imagination. My mother told me this story, many times over the years, and was adamant that Frank was telling the truth."*

■ UFO probe: *New look at 50-year-old mystery*

Did aliens land on a Herefordshire farm?

■ By *Bill Tanner*

DID extra-terrestrials find themselves in the sights of a Herefordshire farmer's gun as they took turf from his land?

This scenario, as unlikely as it may seem, is the subject of an investigation by two UFO-ologists who claim the contact could be among the most significant of the 'flying saucer' phenomena.

True to form, 'the authorities' are accused of covering up the county's very own alien X-file, but this does not deter Rob and Marilyn Aldworth, of Birmingham UFO Society, from taking on a task that would test Mulder and Scully.

The tale Rob and Marilyn relate took place in late 1947 when, in the early hours of the morning, a 'dome shaped disc-like object' is said to have landed in an orchard next to a farmhouse at a village nine miles from Hereford.

The farmer watched with his housekeeper as three 'small silver-suited beings' alighted from the craft and took up samples of turf, but, before he could draw a bead on them with his gun, they re-boarded and were heading for the heavens as swiftly and silently as their arrival. Only a circle burnt into the ground at the landing site was evidence that the 'aliens' were ever there.

According to a 'close relative' of the farmer, from whom Rob and Marilyn take their details, the police were called to the scene the following morning. They, in turn, alerted the Ministry of Defence who took soil samples and declared the landing circle radioactive. The two witnesses were then warned to 'forget' what they had seen and never to discuss it with anyone.

Subsequent inquiries into what occurred met with silence and no known records exist, but Marilyn hopes fresh questions some 50 years later may meet with answers.

"Our informant is elderly and, at this stage, unspecific on some details such as an exact location. However, if what has been described took place, it could be among the most important contacts in the history of UFO investigation," she said.

The year of the landing is significant in UFO lore. It was in 1947 that a 'spaceship' supposedly crashed at Roswell in New Mexico. Marilyn says the 'aliens' allegedly found after this event are 'remarkably similar' to those who may have come to earth in Herefordshire.

Anyone able to assist Rob and Marilyn in proving 'the truth is out there' can contact the couple on 0121 6816344.

According to Betty, Frank and Mrs Newman (his housekeeper) were disturbed by dogs' barking in the middle of the night. Fearing intruders, Frank loaded a pair of shotguns ready to defend them. When the pair went over to the window, overlooking the apple orchards,

> *"We saw the incredible sight of a dome-shaped craft, glowing with light, descending onto the ground, and watched as a pair of steps slowly came out of the craft, followed by the entrance of three silver suited 'beings', who stood next to the spaceship, picked up some apples and a piece of turf, before re-entering the 'ship' and leaving."*

The next morning they ventured outside and discovered a large circular impression burnt into the ground and scorching to a nearby wicker gate. Frank telephoned the police, who later arrived with men from the Air Ministry, as well as military personnel, These conducted a search of the area with a Geiger counter, *"which revealed high levels of radiation."* The men then left, after threatening Frank with dire consequences if he told anybody what had happened.

Police telephoned

Despite publicity in the *Hereford Times* about this incident and searches through local newspaper archives, we were unable to find any other witnesses. However, we were able to confirm a Mr Frank Handford living on Fishpool Hill, in July 1947. Local resident Andrew Bailey contacted us about the incident and conducted research into the matter. He discovered that the farmhouse located in Lower Fishpool Hill had been demolished in 1948, and according to the 1946-1948 Herefordshire Electoral Roll the

residents were Margaret E. Handford and Frank Handford, ordnance survey grid reference for the site being 603339.

Mr Bailey also took some photos of the present building, which was still under construction in summer 2008. He was accompanied by his partner and two young daughters, one of whom became very agitated and asked to leave.

(Source: Marilyn & Robert Aldworth, Birmingham UFO Society)

4th July – USA: Pilots sight UFOs

While over Emmet, Idaho, at 8.17pm, United Airlines Captain E.J. Smith, First officer Ralph Stevens, and stewardess Mary Morrow, sighted four objects with flat bases and round tops, moving at varying speeds; one was high to the right of the others.

(Source: Project Blue Book unknowns)

6th July – USA: UFO rolling across the sky

During the daytime at Fairfield-Suisan Air Base, California, Army Air Force Captain James Burniston and his wife watched, for one minute, an object – without any wings or tail – roll from side-to-side, three times, flying at speed across the sky heading towards the south-east direction.

(Source Project Blue Book unknowns)

7th July – USA: UFO crash landing at Roswell

Roswell Daily Record

RECORD PHONES
Business Office 2288
News Department
2287

RAAF Captures Flying Saucer On Ranch in Roswell Region

Claims Army Is Stacking Courts Martial

House Passes Tax Slash by Large Margin

Security Council Paves Way to Talks On Arms Reductions

No Details of Flying Disk Are Revealed

Ex-King Carol Weds Mme. Lupescu

Miners and Operators Sign Highest Wage Pact in History

'FLYING SAUCER' FOUND

EXTRA

Army Reveals Disc Picked Up In New Mexico

L. A. Woman Slain by Mystery Strangler

House Votes Tax Cut, 302 to 112

Passes by 2-Thirds Majority

Ezekiel the Prophet Foretold Flying Discs

Russ Defy U.N., Ask Troops Quit Greece

NUDE BODY FOUND IN CITY HALL AREA

Roswell Daily Record

Gen. Ramey Empties Roswell Saucer

Arrest 2,000 In Athens in Commie Plot

Ramey Says Excitement Is Not Justified

Brazel ranch near Roswell, New Mexico

8th July – USA: Two silver 'discs' seen over Air Force Base

At 9.30am, over Muroc Air Force Base, California, 1st Lt. Joseph McHenry, T/Sgt. Ruvolo, S/Sgt. Nauman and a Miss Janette Scotte, watched, for an unstated length of time, two silver 'disc'-shaped or spherical objects – apparently metallic – flying through the sky in a wide circular pattern. **(Source: Project Blue Book unknowns)**

9th July – USA: Black 'disc'

At 12.17pm, over Meridian, Idaho, Idaho statesman aviation editor and former (AAF) B-29 pilot – Dave Johnson – watched for over 10 seconds, from an Idaho Air National Guard AT-6, a black 'disc', which stood out against the clouds, made a half-roll and then a stair-step climb.

29th July – USA: Two UFOs sighted

At 2.50pm, Hamilton Air Base, California, assistant Base Operations Officer – Captain William Rhyerd, accompanied by Ex-AAF B-29 pilot – Ward Stewart, watched two round shiny white objects, estimated to be 15-25 feet in diameter, fly across the sky, 3-4 times the apparent speed of a P-80 aircraft, which was also in sight. One object flew straight; the other weaved from side-to-side, like an escort fighter. **(Source: Project Blue Book unknowns)**

July – England: Pilots sight 'spinning top' UFO over Carlisle

In the same month, an ex-Squadron Leader was instructing a pupil on a night exercise over Carlisle, Cumberland (now Cumbria). As they aligned the aircraft with the flare path on its final run, they were surprised to see a UFO hovering about 150 feet below them.

> *"It resembled a child's metal spinning top, with an astrodome on its top and a span of approximately 40 feet. We increased our speed, attempting to overtake the UFO, but when about 1,000 yards away (now 150 feet off the ground) it shot across the sky at such speed, ruling out any chance of*

pursuit. As we returned to straight and level flight, we flew into the space previously occupied by the UFO itself. It was as if we were flying into the slipstream of another aircraft."

When the two men landed they discussed the incident with the flight path controller, who told them they must have seen a reflection of light!

(Source: Peter Paget, *The Welsh Triangle*, Granada Publishing, 1977)

July – Scotland: Close encounter, Edinburgh – occupants sighted

Andrew Bryce Cherry (86), from Edinburgh, spoke to us about a frightening experience that took place at 5.30am, in July 1947, when aged 22 and employed as a factory worker at Woods Bottle Works, Portobello, in Edinburgh.

He was waiting for a bus on Baileyfield Road, near St. John's School, when:

"I caught sight of a very strange object high up in the sky, descending towards me. It had a bevelled observation window; behind was another identical craft. When it was about 300 feet above me, I was shocked to see what I took to be a man, just like you and I, wearing dark clothes, sat next to a control panel of some sort. There was another man in the craft but I didn't see much of him. The outside of the craft had a rough diamond finish to it – marled, that's the best way to describe it. I estimated the width being 12-15 feet across. I could hear a low hum, presumably connected with a flame being ejected from the craft – fan-shaped, brownish red in colour. It then tilted and shot off across the sky, accompanied by the other one, and headed towards the Fife area."

Andrew remains fascinated by the incident despite the passing of time which is still fresh in his memory, as if it happened yesterday. **(Source: Ron Halliday/Malcolm Robinson, SPI/Personal interview)**

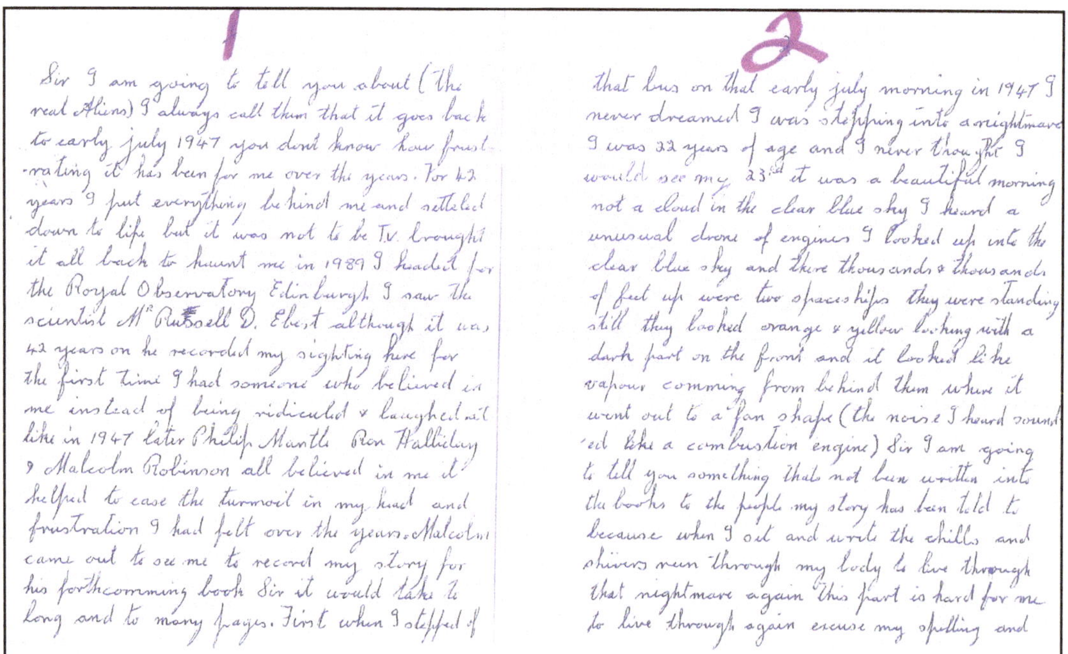

1

Sir I am going to tell you about (the real Aliens) I always call them that it goes back to early july 1947 you dont know how frust-rating it has been for me over the years. For 42 years I put everything behind me and setteled down to life but it was not to be T.V. brought it all back to haunt me in 1989 I headed for the Royal Observatory Edinburgh I saw the scientist Mr Russell D. Ebert although it was 42 years on he recorded my sighting here for the first time I had someone who believed in me instead of being ridiculed & laughed at like in 1947 later Philip Mantle Ron Halliday & Malcolm Robinson all believed in me it helped to ease the turmoil in my head and frustration I had felt over the years. Malcolm came out to see me to record my story for his forthcomming book Sir it would take to long and to many pages. First when I stepped of

2

that bus on that early july morning in 1947 I never dreamed I was stepping into a nightmare I was 22 years of age and I never thought I would see my 23rd it was a beautiful morning not a cloud in the clear blue sky I heard a unusual drone of engines I looked up into the clear blue sky and there thousands & thousands of feet up were two spaceships they were standing still they looked orange & yellow looking with a dark part on the front and it looked like vapour comming from behind them where it went out to a fan shape (the noise I heard sounded like a combustion engine) Sir I am going to tell you something thats not been written into the books to the people my story has been told to because when I sit and write the chills and shivers run through my body to live through that nightmare again this part is hard for me to live through again excuse my spelling and

3

writing its awesome unbelievable this is hard for me well hear goes they were about 4 miles up they must have been observing the bus then they dropped down to observe me they dropped down that fast my eyes could not focus they seemed to stop at about 3,000 ft for about 2 sec. then they dropped till they were about 300 ft above me in all it took about 6 sec. (phew that was hard) I am 74 now and its so vivid as if it just happened yesterday Sir I am the only one in the world who can explain (the real Aliens) and it scares me so you can imagine how frustrating it is for me to be believed I thought you only see them once in a lifetime but on June 1993 when I was out walking my dog I saw them flash through the sky the same silver white discs I saw in 1941 to disappear in sec. There must be hundreds of Aliens trying to reach us

4

but I doubt it. I will tell you things about (the real Aliens) it will kill a lot of myths for all time its been said Aliens are greenmen or little greymen eight foot giants dome headed freaks they rape make circles in fields eat cattle time stands still their space-ships are all shapes and sizes (bunkum) not even the one that was to have crashed in Mexico came from the same planet I have been wanting to get that of my chest for years well Sir I must protect (the real Aliens) can you imagine someone protecting Aliens when millions & millions of people dont think they exist I would shock U.F.O. scient-ists because my sensational story is true Aliens Definitley Definitley Exsist.

When they were about 300 ft I stood in awe and fear rooted to the pavement was I going to see my 21st birthday in those split sec. all thoughts were running through my mind as I stood there

5

looking up to there spaceships I could see right into the one nearest me but I could not see into the other one because it was right behind, it had a large observation window & instrument panel inside they were 10 to 12 ft com-pletley round what I thought was vapour miles up was a hut huge 10 to 12 ft behind where the fan shape was a brownish red flame about 6 ft the metal was marbled just like rough diamonds the combustion noise I heard miles up was the noise the flame was making it looked empty then he darted forward to the centre of the panel he seemed to pull some kind of lever he wore a darkish suit he must have been the leader because the flame cut of from both of them automatically then he darted forward to the front of the spaceship then he mocked me it sounded like whmmm but they were on the move there engine was a smooth hum very very

6

silent they shoot right up about 85° to dis-appear over the fife coast in sec. They were slightly saucer shaped to the slight bulg on there observation window they are silvery white when they spin away Aliens are just like us only more intelligent & hundreds & hundreds of years ahead of us and I think they only visit us in daylight I think what people are seeing are satellites some with a magnetic field to take back information to there planet where ours burn up or stay in space for all time where they can return theirs and there spaceships could not land on earth they would cause fires so they must have a docking area on there planet to descend the way they dropped down towards me they could never land otherwise there speed when they are on the move is awesome incredible they could never land on there planet (without docking.) Well Sir I hope I have given you the

7

insight to (the real Aliens) they dont mean us any harm just to observe us I was curious so I asked the scientist Mr Ebest how when I first saw them miles up they were orange & yellow looking he said it was the reflection of the sun (HA) how stupid I felt I knew he was correct. Its over 51 years comming up to 52 on july 1999 its been a long frustrating time for me someone who has the answers and could kill all myths for all time although I had put it behind me for 42 years but since 1989 its been a mile-stone round my neck not a night goes by since 89 I dont think about them Malcolm Robinson said I would never forget my nightmare in 1947 I have sent you a photo copy of my recorded sighting I dont want publicity but to give you the true facts about (the real Aliens) thanks

yours Truly
Mr Andrew B Cherry
10/2 WHITSON GROVE
EDINBURGH EH11 3BS
0131 443-1107

P.S Please keep my address secret

johndawn

From: "DAVID SANKEY" yonder.co.uk>
To: "johndawn" <johndawn@hansonholloway.fsnet.co.uk>
Sent: 03 August 2006 12:18
Attach: Test-Render-A-B-Cherry.jpg
Subject: Re: Render Test, A.B. Cherry Craft

Hi John,

Please find attached a test render for the A. B. Cherry case. If you could forward this on to Mr. Cherry and ask for his approval, and if any amendments are needed.

Dear Andrew
Can you have a look at this 'Test' Render and alter anything and send back so Dave can do the Background please.
John

Test Render Mr. Cherry

THEY SPIN AWAY ALMOST STRAIT UP 98 OR 85° TO DISAPPEAR IN SEC:
THEY MUST HAVE A DOCKING AREA ON THEIR PLANET THEY COULD NEVER LAND OTHERWISE THATS HOW THEY COULD NEVER LAND ON EARTH I THINK THEY JUST VISIT US IN DAYLIGHT IN TWO'S I HAVE SEEN THEM TWICE JULY 1947 & THE 23RD JUNE 1993
A.B. CHERRY

Regards
Dave

03/08/2006

8

1

Dear Sir

When you read my following story it will shock you and every U.F.O. scientist in the the world for someone who for over 51 years knows how (the real Aliens) spaceships operate for 42 years after being laughted at and ridiculed I had put it out of my head and got on with my life I have explained it all in my letter, Over the years since 1989 you have know idea how frustrating it has been for me to listen to dreams & fairy tales of some people on what they have seen but I am talking about the real thing that is (genuine and true then you have skeptics like Patrick Moore & Mark McAuley at the Royal Observatory Edin: and professor James at Oxford and many more. I was scared to go public in case of more ridicule till a story appeared in the people newspaper I was

9

raped by Aliens I was angry here for the first time I wanted to tell the world I wanted to protect them can you imagine some one protecting Aliens when millions & millions dont think they excist I wrote to the people and told them it was impossible with (the real Aliens) I sent my recorded sighting and told them to take a photo copy and send the original back to me after several more letters and a phone call it took them exactly two months to return it now I never let it out of sight I take photo copys myself it means so much to me. Sir I dont think anyone wants to know the truth even newspapers they would have no more crap to write about do you think for one minute I would give you my name & address if my story was not genuine Sir I am to well known. I wrote to channel 4 when I wanted to go public I got a reply on the 23rd Sept 1995 (thanks)

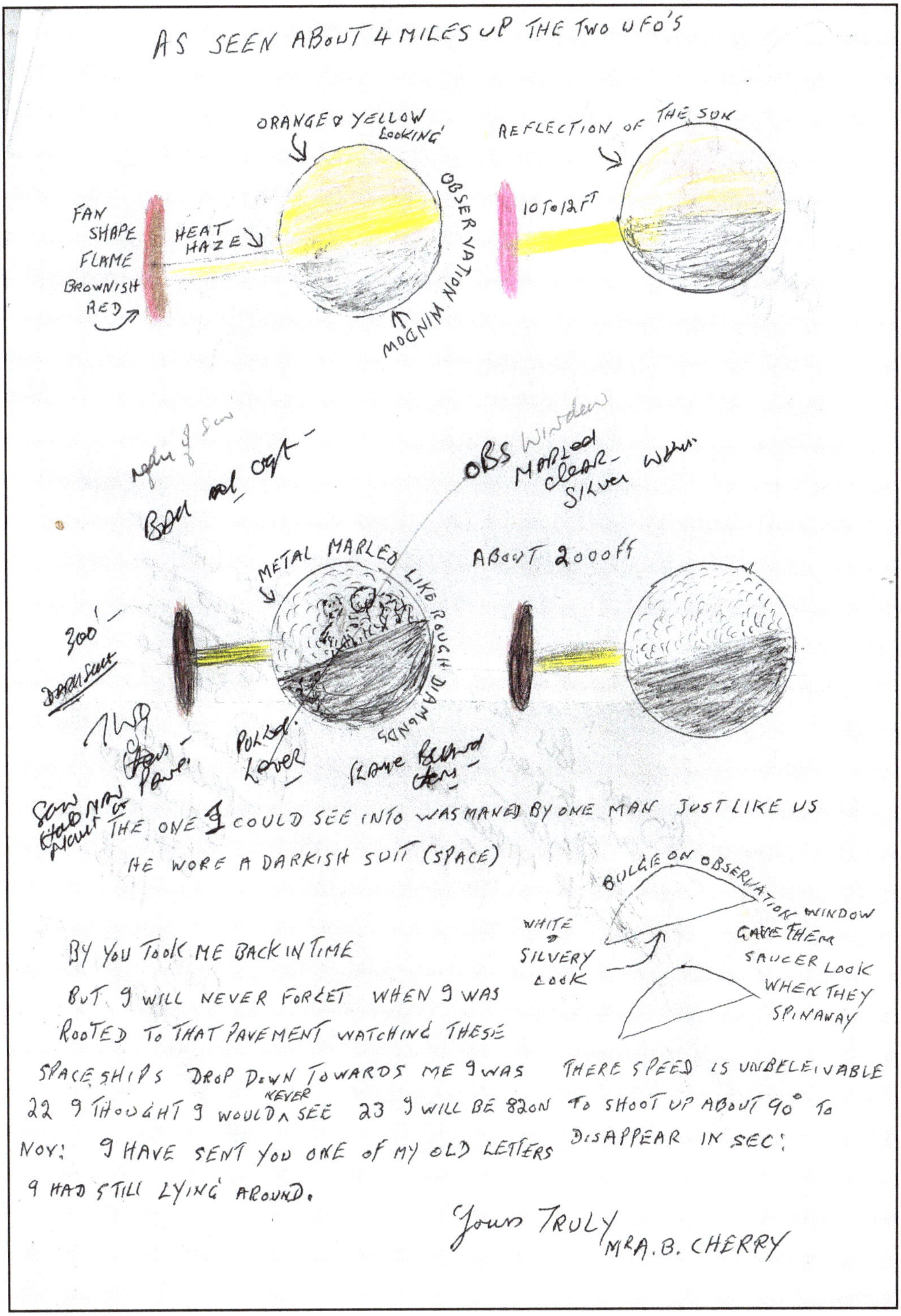
AS SEEN ABOUT 4 MILES UP THE TWO UFO'S
ORANGE & YELLOW LOOKING
REFLECTION OF THE SUN
FAN SHAPE FLAME
BROWNISH RED
HEAT HAZE
OBSERVATION WINDOW
10 TO 12 FT
OBS Window MARLED clear - Silver white
METAL MARLED
LIKE ROUGH DIAMONDS
ABOUT 2000 FT
300'
THE ONE I COULD SEE INTO WAS MANED BY ONE MAN JUST LIKE US
HE WORE A DARKISH SUIT (SPACE)
BULGE ON OBSERVATION WINDOW GAVE THEM SAUCER LOOK WHEN THEY SPIN AWAY
WHITE & SILVERY LOOK
BY YOU TOOK ME BACK IN TIME
BUT I WILL NEVER FORGET WHEN I WAS ROOTED TO THAT PAVEMENT WATCHING THESE SPACESHIPS DROP DOWN TOWARDS ME I WAS 22 I THOUGHT I WOULD NEVER SEE 23 I WILL BE 82 ON NOV: I HAVE SENT YOU ONE OF MY OLD LETTERS I HAD STILL LYING AROUND.
THERE SPEED IS UNBELEIVABLE TO SHOOT UP ABOUT 90° TO DISAPPEAR IN SEC:
Yours TRULY
MR A.B. CHERRY

Busty Taylor

England: UFO display over Andover

We spoke to Frederick 'Busty' Taylor – considered one of the world's leading researchers into the crop circle phenomenon – about what he saw whilst a primary school pupil in Andover, Hampshire, in 1947.

> *"I can clearly remember seeing, even as a child, hundreds of tiny 'silver balls' moving across the sky at high altitude. The oddest thing was they appeared to be playing 'tag' with each other and were accompanied by one or two larger objects heading towards the south-east. Not long after this my father, who worked for the MOD as a crane driver, was with some other men when they noticed an object, absolutely still in the sky, which vanished about ten minutes later."*

(Source: Personal letter/interview)

August – Wales: Frightening experience for young girl at farm

Margaret Lloyd recalled a disturbing, unforgettable experience, which befell her when aged six and living at the family farm in North Wales.

> *"I had been out walking and was crossing the courtyard to the farm, when I heard this weird whooshing noise, like helicopter blades coming from above the nearby granary roof. I looked*

up and saw this dark 'doodlebug-like' object, dark grey in colour, hovering over the building. I started screaming. My mother rushed outside, wondering what was going on. I pointed upwards and she stood with me in amazement as it slowly moved across the sky, towards the direction of Rhyl, leaving a glowing red vapour trail in the sky."

(Source: Personal interview)

3rd September – USA: Numerous silver objects sighted

Oswego, Oregon housewife – Mrs Raymond Dupui, sighted 12-15 round, silver objects, moving through the sky at 12.15pm.

14th October – USA: 'Flying wing'-shaped UFO

At 12 midday, 11 miles NNE of Cave Creek, Arizona, ex-AAF fighter pilot J.L. Clark – now a civilian pilot - accompanied by two other men, watched for about a minute a 3 feet 'flying wing'-shaped object, which looked black against the white clouds and red against the blue sky, moving at an estimated speed of 380 mph, at 8-10,000 feet, heading in a north-west to south-east direction.

(Source: Project Blue Book unknowns)

1948

7th January 1948

Death of Captain Thomas Mantell, pilot of F51 Mustang, killed in pursuit of red glowing 'saucer', at 20,000 feet above Godman Airbase.

1st April – USA: Turtle-back flying object sighted by pilot

This is a reproduced transcript of a report made by a pilot and subsequently brought to the attention of the Blue Book investigators. Air Material Command – INCOMING MESSAGE to Dept. of Army, Washington DC, to Wright Patterson AFB, Dayton, Ohio

> 'Report control is A-1917 Pilot 15 Air Force at 0955, 1st April 1948, heading 180 degrees, altitude 1,500 feet indicated at 124 degrees 3 minutes east, 12 degrees 52 minutes north. Weather scattered cumulus with a base, three thousand top 600 visibility unlimited, sighted flying object approximately 3 miles east, heading 360, altitude estimated one thousand feet below him. Unidentified object estimated speed at time 200 miles per hour. Pilot turned left, attempting to intercept unidentified flying object for more positive identification.
>
> At this time flying object made a turn of 90 degrees left, levelled out and accelerated, disappearing in approximately 5 seconds, heading off 270 degrees. Pilot had phenomenon under observations for about 60 seconds, described as having a turtle back and an indistinct dorsal fin. The shape of the object was that of a half-moon, closely resembling a 'flying wing' type aircraft, estimated wingspan 30 feet length 20 feet, colour silver. No exhaust trail was observed. Five seconds elapsed time for disappearing would indicate exceedingly high speed.'

Pilot Ensign Roland D. Powell attempts to intercept UFO

Interestingly, we discovered that this was not the first time UFOs had been reported over this location – During the summer of 1945:

US Pilot Ensign Roland D. Powell, based at the US Naval Station Pascoe, Washington, was one of five F6F Hellcat pilots scrambled to intercept a UFO, described as *"being the size of three aircraft carriers, side by side, seen hovering at high altitude above this top secret plutonium production facility"* for the world's first nuclear bombs at Hanford.

(Source: Tim Good, *Alien Base*, published by Century, 1998)

Although we found details of a UFO sighted near Hanford, in July 1952, we were unable to find any details of the above sighting contained within the files of Blue Book.

(Source: J.A. Hynek, *UFO Report*, Sphere Books, 1978)

5th April – USA: Two objects seen over airbase

During the afternoon, at Holloman Air Force Base, New Mexico, Geophysics Laboratory balloon observers – Mr Alsen, Mr Johnson and Mr Chance, sighted:

> *"...two irregular, round, white or golden objects, one of which was seen to make three loops and then rise upwards, disappearing rapidly; the other flew away in a fast arc, westward, thirty seconds later."*

24th July – USA: Torpedo-shaped UFO sighted by pilots

In the early morning hours of 24th July 1948, pilot Clarence Chiles and co-pilot John B. Whitted were flying an Eastern Airlines Douglas DC-3 from Mobile, Alabama to Montgomery, at about 5,000 feet in altitude. At about 2.45am, Chiles spotted a hazy red cloud, somewhat similar to aircraft exhaust. It was slightly above them and to the front-right of the DC-3 by about half-a-mile. Chiles saw an aircraft and, thinking it the source of the exhaust, pointed it out to Whitted and said, *"Look, here comes a new Army jet job"*. However, they quickly realised that the object was unlike a jet plane and was moving towards them at very high speed.

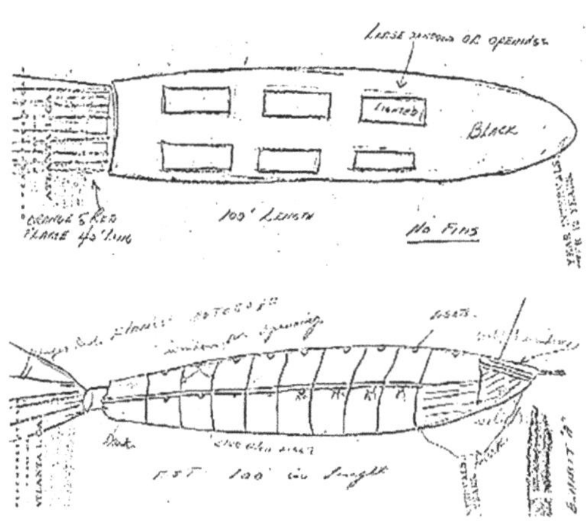

Within a matter of seconds, the UFO was now almost on top of them.

Chiles racked the DC-3 into a tight left turn. Just as the UFO flashed by at about 700 feet to the right, the DC-3 hit turbulent air. Whitted looked back just as the UFO pulled up in a steep climb. Both pilots obtained a clear view of the UFO and were able to later give a good description to Air Force intelligence.

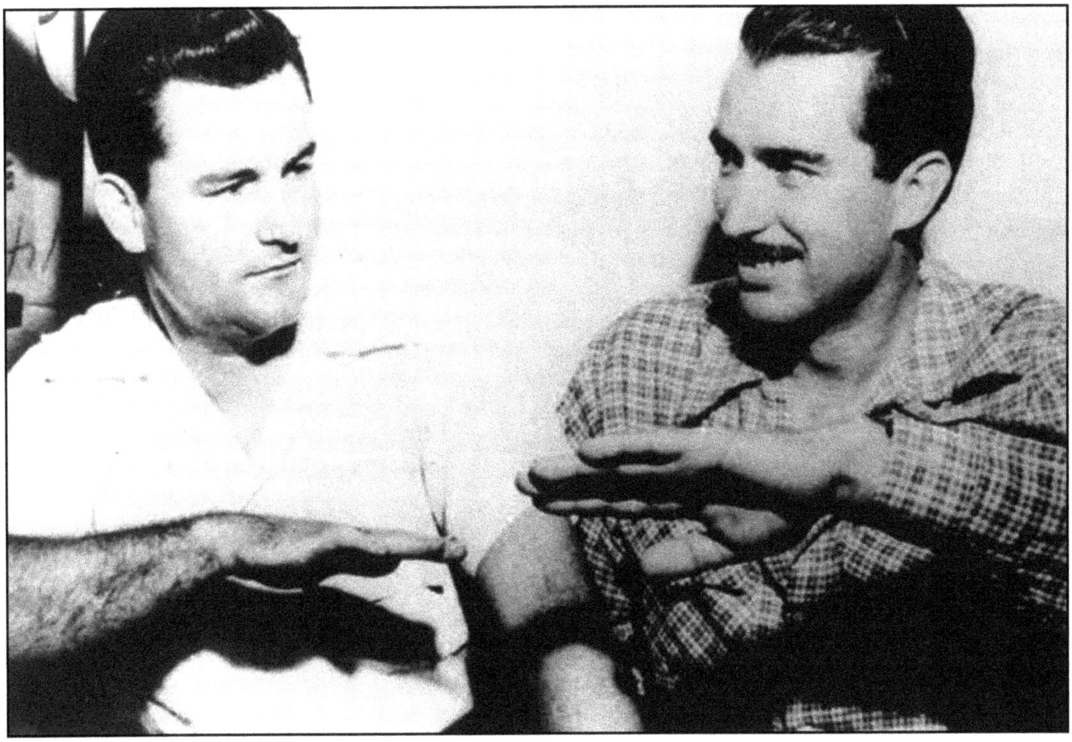

'Cigar' or torpedo-shaped object seen

Following the sighting that had lasted for about 10 to 15 seconds, both men described the object as:

> *"...'cigar' or torpedo-shaped, about 100 feet in length, and about three times the diameter of a B-29 Bomber. The 'fuselage' was entirely smooth, with no wings, projections or fins. A bright red-orange exhaust was emanating from the object's rear, and was more orange at the outer edges of the exhaust, but grew redder when it rose in altitude. The exhaust extended approximately 30 to 50 feet behind the object."*

They heard no sound from the object as it sped past the DC-3.

Intriguingly, the witnesses asserted the object had what appeared to be two rows of rectangular 'windows'.

A few weeks after the sighting, Chiles: *"There were two rows of windows, which indicated an upper and lower deck. From inside these windows a very bright light was glowing"*.

Blue glowing light underneath

Underneath the 'ship' there was a blue glow of light. The light from the object was so bright that both men were blinded by its intensity for a few seconds. There were only a few differences in the observations of the two men: Chiles thought he observed a conical shape at the object's nose that was somewhat similar to a radar pole, and he described a glassy window at the object's front that was somewhat similar to a cockpit window. Whitted thought the object was slightly further away than Chiles described, and he did not see the cockpit-like 'windshield' or the 'radar pole' at the object's nose. Chiles recalled the 'exhaust' as being less intense, and not flaring out as much as Whitted observed.

Most of the passengers were asleep

Given the early hour of the flight, most of the passengers were asleep. One of them – Clarence L. McKelvie – would later offer corroborative eyewitness testimony. He asserted that he saw an *"extraordinarily bright light from his window seat in the aircraft"*, describing it as unlike lightning.

He later told Project Sign investigators that the 'light' seemed to have moved parallel to the plane, but at a higher altitude. Within seconds of the close encounter, Chiles asked Eastern Airlines flight controllers, via two-way radio, if any known experimental aircraft were being flown in the region. There was none.

After landing

The flight landed at Birmingham a little before 4am. The pilots went to a hotel, only to learn that their sighting had already generated some interest. Within a few hours, they were interviewed at radio station WCON, and also by newspaper reporter William Key.

The UFO report earned national press attention. People had quickly suggested that the object had been a meteor, but the pilots both flatly rejected this: they had both seen many meteors in their careers, and this object was certainly not a meteor.

It was man made!

On the contrary, they insisted that the flying fuselage they had observed was *"a man-made thing"*. Within days, Sign investigators interviewed eyewitnesses Chiles, Whitted and McKelvie. In addition to the report from The Hague, Sign investigators discovered several eyewitnesses who seemed to have seen the same object Chiles and Whitted observed.

Eyewitness on the ground

One of them was Walter Massey, a ground-crew chief at Robins Air Force Base in Georgia, about 150 miles from Montgomery.

He claimed to have seen a very similar object about an hour before Chiles and Whitted's encounter. Like the pilots, he said it was:

> *"...a cylindrical object that seemed to be two or three times larger than a B-29, with a long stream of fire coming out of the tail end. I noticed a faint glow on the belly of the wingless object".*

Not a meteor

Massey was certain the object was not a meteor. Ruppelt also writes of another Air Force witness. A pilot, flying near the Virginia/North Carolina state line, reported that he had seen *"a bright shooting star"* in the direction of Montgomery, Alabama, at about the exact time that the Eastern Airlines DC-3 was 'buzzed'.

(Sources: Clark, Jerome, *The UFO Encyclopedia:* 2nd Edition; Volume 1, A-K; Omnigraphics, Inc., 1998, ISBN 0-7808-0097-4, *The Encyclopedia of UFOs*, Ronald Story, editor; Garden City: Doubleday & Company, Inc., 1980, ISBN 0-385-13677-3, *The Report on Unidentified Flying Objects* by Edward J. Ruppelt, 1956)

Inside the radar tower at Washington National Airport, Air Force Project Blue Book Captain Edward Ruppelt (center) is shown how UFOs positioned themselves over the Capitol. This flap in August, 1952, led to the CIA setting up the Robertson Report, which later debunked the subject.

31st July – USA: Domed 'disc'

At 8.25am over Indianapolis, Indiana, Mr and Mrs Vernon Swigert – an electrician by occupation – sighted a plain white object, described as resembling a cymbal or domed disc, about 20 feet across and six to eight feet wide, flying across the sky from horizon to horizon in about 10 seconds, shimmering in the sun as if spinning.

August – England: Fluorescent green object seen

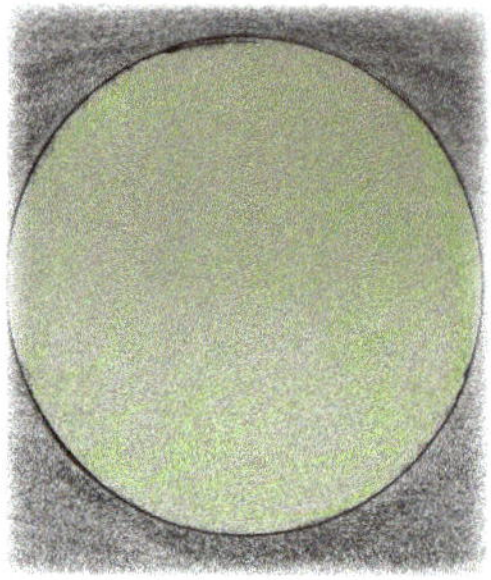

Clacton-on-Sea woman – Mrs Hollis (68 in 1995) contacted Ron West to tell him about what she witnessed, while walking home with her 18-month-old son and husband, when near Priory Park, when they saw a fluorescent green object dropping down behind trees.

> *"I was scared stiff; it was the size of a dustbin lid in the sky and hovered there for about five minutes."*

23rd September – USA: 'Amoeba' object seen

At 12 noon, Sylvester Bentham and retired US Army Colonel Horace Eakins were in San Pablo, California, when they sighted:

> *". . . two objects - one, a buff or grey rectangle with vertical lines; the other, a translucent 'amoeba' with a dark spot near its centre, heading at a fast speed across the sky".*

1st October – USA: Pilot chases 'light'

On the evening of 1st October 1948, Air National Guard Lieutenant Gorman was flying his F-51 Jet aircraft and returning from a cross-country flight with his squadron of North Dakota Air National Guard, when he saw an unidentified light source. He closed to within 1000 yards to take a closer look, later saying:

> *"It was about six to eight inches in diameter, clear white, and completely round without fuzz at the edges."*

For 27 hair-raising minutes, Gorman pursued the 'light' through a series of intricate manoeuvres.

The experienced Gorman was so shook up after the incident that he had to circle the airport twice before landing!

Project Sign investigates

USAF investigators from Project Sign were soon on the scene to interview Gorman and the other three witnesses. Their initial report found the pilot and witnesses highly credible and concluded *"that something remarkable had occurred"* in the skies over Fargo.

The investigators also discovered that Gorman's F-51 recorded an *"unusually high Geiger counter reading"*. They speculated that Gorman *"may actually have been pursuing an atomic-powered craft ".*

Project Sign later revised their findings, announcing that Gorman had first been chasing a lighted weather balloon and then the planet Jupiter!

The sighting attracted the attention of the media and also a vintage comic at the time.

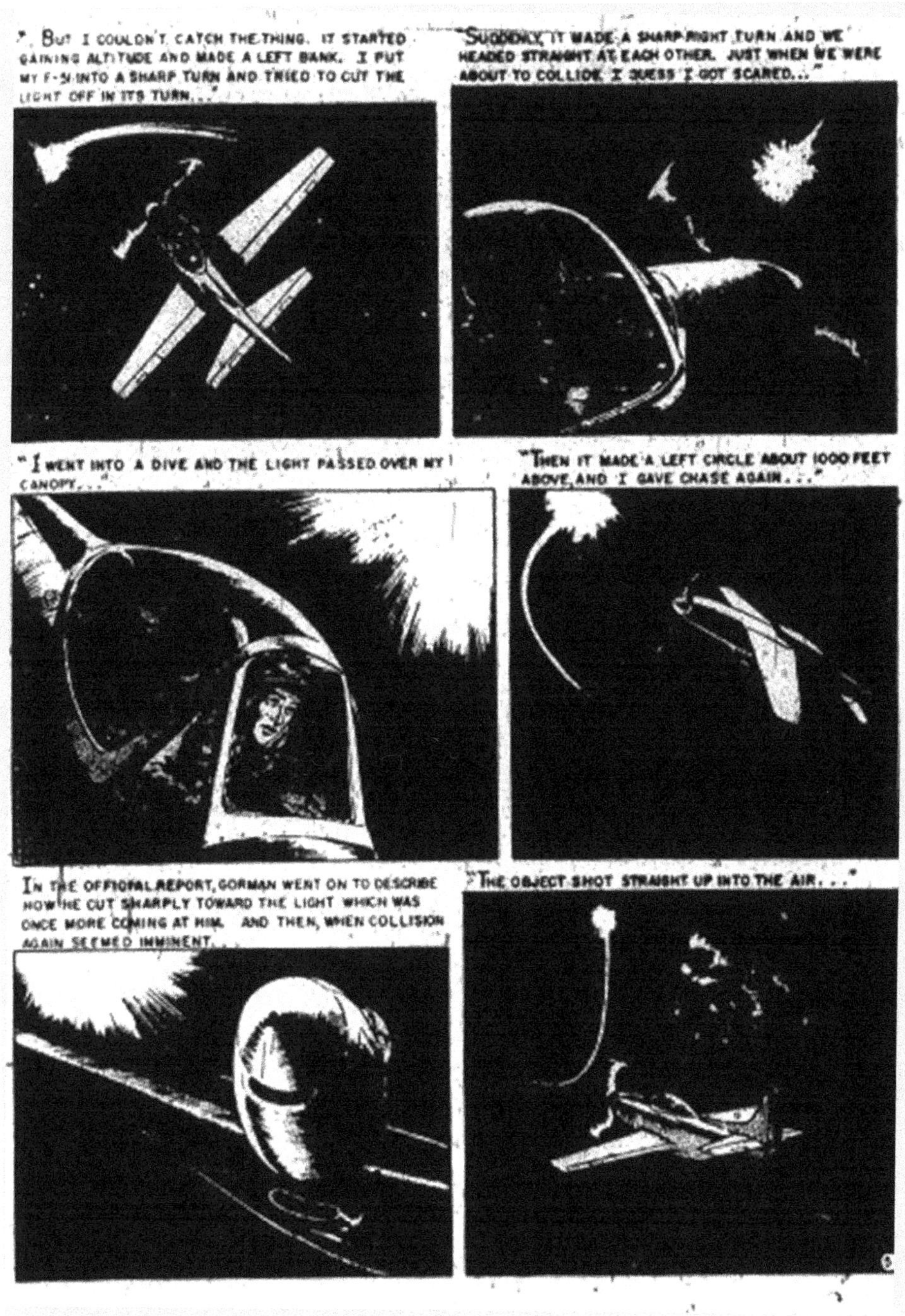

"Flying Saucers"

23 December 1948

3. CONTROL SYMBOL OR FILE NO.

4. REPORT OF FINDINGS

AGENT'S NOTE:

Records of the FBI and the Fargo Police Department disclosed no record of above informant and the police consider him an entirely reliable informant.

On 18 December 1948, Dr. A. E. Cannon, Eye, Ear and Nose Specialist, residing in Fargo, North Dakota, was contacted concerning the sighting of a "Flying Disk" over Fargo, North Dakota on 1 October 1948. Dr. Cannon stated that while he was flying in an airplane over a football field in Fargo, North Dakota on 1 October 1948 he sighted an Army plane flying in rather unusual tactics. The plane was obviously trying to contact a flying object that was, it appeared to him, nothing but a flying light. Informant landed as soon as possible, and since that time he has been contacted by officers of the United States' Army and representatives of various newspapers concerning the object sighted. Informant has been unable to give any more detailed information than that stated above.

(B-

AGENT'S NOTE:

It seemed that this informant had been interviewed by quite a number of people concerning the incident mentioned above, and he was unwilling to give any more information. The reliability of this informant was guaranteed by the local police. Informant has no record with the police nor the FBI.

'Flying Saucer' Chased by National Guard Flier While Three Men Watch

FARGO, N. D.—(AP)—A National Guard fighter pilot yesterday told a story of a 30-minute encounter with a mysterious flying object over this city in the darkness—and his account was supported by two control tower operators and another flier.

In a signed statement for Air Force intelligence, the pilot, Lt. George Gorman of the 178th fighter squadron, North Dakota Air National Guard, claimed he chased and did aerial maneuvers Friday night with a lighted, disk-like object which outran and and outmaneuvered him.

Watching him and the object with binoculars were Lloyd Jenson and H. E. Johnson, both of Fargo, control tower operators at Hector Airport here. Both said in statements yesterday that no other aircraft had reported to the tower besides Gorman's F-51 fighter and a Cub, whose pilot, Dr. A. E. Cannon of Fargo, also reportrd watching Gorman and the object dogfight around Fargo.

Gorman said he first caught sight of the lighted object between his ship and the city's lights at about 4,500 feet. The F-51 pilot said he attempted to intercept the object, making head-on passes, but that it outturned and outran him for nearly a half hour until he lost it at 17,000 feet. Gorman said his speed at various times throughout the engagement ranged from 270 to 400 miles an hour.

All four men identified the object as a round light, perfectly formed, with no rays leaving its body and traveling at a speed considerably faster than the F-51.

"I've never seen anything like it," Gorman said. "If anyone else had reported such a thing I would have thought they were crazy."

Major D. C. Jones, commanding officer of the North Dakota 178th Fighter Squadron said he would send Lt. Gorman's statements to Air Force intelligence but refused to comment further.

[redacted]

Interrogation Report No. 2, dated 4 Oct 48 (Cont'd) UNCLASSIFIED

As he flew into the pattern preparatory to landing, what seemed to be the tail light of another airplane passed him from the right. He called the tower immediately and complained that they had misinformed him, that there was a third ship in the air. The tower came back with the information that no other aircraft was reported out, that they had just checked with all other air fields in the area. Lt. Gorman, seeing the tail light run just outside the Piper Cub, pulled up and cut towards the moving light in order to identify what he thought to be another aircraft. He saw the Piper Cub plainly outlined beneath him against the city lights, but saw no outline of anything around the moving light. Lt. Gorman then proceeded to move toward the object (he thinks that he was about 1000 yards from the object at this moment), which appeared then to be about 6 to 8 inches in diameter. The light was clear white, completely round without fuzz at the edges, and was, until then, blinking on and off. He then proceeded to follow the light which suddenly became steady and pulled into a sharp left bank, making what he thought to be a pass at the tower. Lt. Gorman dived after the light, bringing his manifold pressure to 50 inches and realizing 2000 RPM, which increased at the finish of the dive to 3000. He was unable to catch up with the object which began to gain altitude.

Lt. Gorman continued to follow the object, in the meantime calling the tower and advising them as to what was going on. The object continued gaining altitude and again made a left bank. Lt. Gorman then cut his F-51 into a sharp turn and tried to cut the object off in the turn. By that time he was to an altitude of 7000 feet. The object then made a sharp right turn and Lt. Gorman turned about and headed straight at the object which had completed its turn and was coming toward him. At the point where acollision seemed imminent, Lt. Gorman got scared and went into a dive, the object passing over his canopy at approximately 500 feet. At this time he had 60 inches of manifold pressure and 3000 RPM. The object again made a left circle approximately 1000 feet above him and he again gave chase. He cut again sharply toward the object which was once more coming at him and, at the time when collision seemed imminent again, the object went straight into the air and he started climbing after it until he gained approximately 14000 feet, at which time his plane went into a power stall. The object then turned in a north-west northern heading and disappeared. It was then 2127 hours.

Lt. Gorman proceeded to return to the field, being so excited that he had to make two passes at the field before he could properly land. During these entire maneuvers, Lt. Gorman noticed no deviation on his instruments. His magnetic compass reacted normally, there was no interference with his radio. He heard no sounds, noticed no odors, and saw no exhaust trails.

13th October – USA: UFO sighted

In compliance with request contained in "Elements of Essential Information, Project, Sign", Miss FLORENCE BROOKE, on 1 December 1948 executed and signed the following statement.

THE STUDEBAKER CORPORATION
South Bend 27, Indiana

December 1, 1948

At approximately 11:45 AM on October 13, 1948, while looking out through our office window facing North, I noticed a very dark colored plane flying directly North, but it was so far away I could not determine what type plane it was other than the fact that I felt it was not a transport plane inasmuch as we see transports very frequently, they are sliver in color and travel East and West, or Southeast and Northwest while within our scope of vision from this location.

While I watched the above described plane fade from view, another object caught my attention. At first I thought this object was a piece of paper being blown along by the wind, however on closer observation, I noted that it was much higher than would be possible to see a piece of paper floating. Also the object was traveling at what seemed to be a very high rate of speed, although it was impossible for me to determine the altitude at which it was moving. The object was sliver in color and seemed to be turning or spinning so that the sun reflected on it. As it was traveling very rapidly and at what seemed a very high altitude, it was not possible to determine its shape, although I am certain it was not an airplane. It did not appear to be a smooth surfaced object because of the flashing of the sunrays against it. The object was traveling a direct course from Northwest to Southeast and was within my scope of vision for perhaps 15 to 20 seconds.

s/ Florence Brooke
t/ Florence Brooke,
Secy. to S. W. Sparrow,
V.P. in Chg. of Engrg.

3rd December – USA: Bouncing light

A USAF Sgt. Control tower operator, based at Fairfield-Suisan Air Force Base, California, was on duty at 8.15pm, when he sighted a round white 'light' that flew for 25 seconds, with varying speed, in a peculiar bouncing motion, before finally climbing upwards, erratically, and out of sight.

(Source: Project Blue Book unknowns)

1949

4th January – USA: USAF Captain sights UFO

At 2pm, over Hickam Air Field, Hawaii, USAF pilot – Captain Paul Storey, was on the ground. He saw:

> *"...a flat white, elliptical object, with a matt top, circling in the sky, oscillating to the right and left as it did so, before it sped away". 27th January – USA: USAF Captain sights a cigar-shaped object*

At 10.20pm, over Cortez-Bradenton, Florida, Captain Sames – acting chief of the Aircraft Branch, at *Eglin Air Force Base, and his wife, watched:

> *"...a cigar-shaped object – as long as two Pullman cars, showing seven lighted square windows and throwing sparks – descend and then climb back upwards, 25 minutes later, in a bouncing motion, at an estimated speed of 400 mph".*

March – England: Strange phenomenon over Staffordshire

Ronald Ratcliffe from Newcastle-under-Lyme – a man who was to see far more than his fair share of extraordinary things in the sky over the years – spoke to us of what he saw in March 1949.

> *"It was a cold and sunny morning, with a few trees still bare. I was looking out of the kitchen window at the time, while washing up, when I noticed what looked like a piece of white square material, like a tablecloth, flapping in the sky, about 200ft off the ground above the Stoke-on-Trent to Tern Hill railway line, which ran past our estate at the time. I watched and realised, with heart-pounding excitement, it wasn't just flapping about randomly.*
>
> *It appeared to be moving forward in a swimming movement – not unlike the breaststroke. I went outside into the backyard, so I could get a clearer view of what was going on, and noticed it was near to a small cloud, which seemed to be 'boiling' rather than inanimate in appearance. When the swimming object reached the clouds, it seemed to have quite a struggle to get into the cloud. When this finally happened the cloud disintegrated into pieces, blowing outwards across the sky, before disappearing from view."*

(Source: Personal interview)

March – England: Paratrooper sights yellow 'disc' in the sky

Ex-Paratrooper Mr Charles Holding from Blisworth, Northampton, was out poaching with two old army friends, just outside the village on a cloudless, hazy, Sunday morning in March 1949. One of his friends on the other side of the hedge shouted,

> *"Look Charles! We are being spied on", and pointed upwards in the sky.*

*Eglin Air Force Base is a United States Air Force base located approximately 3 miles southwest of Valparaiso, Florida in Okaloosa County. The host unit at Eglin is the 96th Test Wing. **(Source: Project Blue Book unknowns)**

Charles:

> *"I looked and saw a brightly coloured disc-shaped object, resembling a yellow moon, stationary in the sky, 5-10,000 feet in height, about the size of a Dakota aircraft. It appeared to descend, but abruptly took off at a tangent into the atmosphere and was gone from view. As it went through the haze it left a trail in the sky, which lasted for at least five minutes, before disappearing."*

(Source: Personal interview)

17th March – USA: Eight UFOs sighted

At 7.52pm, Guards of the 2nd Armored Division at Camp Hood, Texas – while awaiting the start of a flare firing – watched, for an hour, eight large, green, red and white flare-like objects, flying across the sky in generally straight lines.

3rd April – USA: Object, shaped like two plates

At 11.55am, Dillon, Montana construction company owner Gosta Miller, and three other unnamed persons, reported having sighted an object, shaped like two plates attached face-to-face; matt base with bright aluminum top, 20 feet in diameter and 4-5 feet in thickness.

> *"It rocked or rotated in six cycles, before finally moving away."*

4th April – USA: Curved UFO

At 10.20pm, William Parrott – former Air Force pilot and Major – was out walking with his dog at Merced, California, when he saw:

> *"...a round objects with a curved base and dull colouring, which made a clicking sound until overhead."*

5th April – USA: Triangular UFO sighted

Logan City Police officer Lt. Ronald J. Hadfield was standing on Main Street, at.9.50am, when he was approached by Lamar Bullock of the Cache Valley Electric Company, who directed his attention to something strange in the sky.

He looked upwards and saw:

> *"...something that had the appearance of a puff of smoke or vapour, about 15,000 feet above sea level, slightly west of Logan".*

This phenomenon was witnessed by a number of people who then contacted the FBI, at Salt Lake City, and the Logan Sheriff's Office.

They included Fred Sears, of Fred's Flower Shop, Logan, who was out playing golf at 9.45am, when he saw what looked like:

> *"...a tracer bullet, moving through the sky – faster than any plane I have ever seen – followed by the sound of an explosion."*

Frank Petersen of the Logan City Corporation Light Department also contacted the police, after he and his men saw something strange while working on clearing power lines of tree limbs, which he described as:

> *"...a triangular object descending through the sky, with the base downwards. It changed colours rapidly from blue to purple to orange, yellow, and finally very bright green, when it then disappeared from view."*

(Source: Declassified file)

8th April – USA: UFO with conning tower and three ports

At 2am, Mr Earl Baker of Kokomo, Indiana, was aroused from sleep by his dog. He went to the window and looked out, when he saw:

6th April – USA: 'Flying Discs' seen over Stapleton Airfield

6/4/49

DECLASSIFIED
Authority 923007
By BP NARA Date 7-26

Lt. Col Martin
Security CSI
Col. Carpenter
Capt. Koch

DEPARTMENT OF THE AIR FORCE
STAFF MESSAGE DIVISION
INCOMING CLASSIFIED MESSAGE

C[redacted]

THIS MESSAGE REQUIRES PARAPHRASE
SEE PARAGRAPHS 51D, 51i and 60A,
AR 380-5

OPERATIONAL PRIORITY

FROM: LOWRY AIR FORCE BASE, DENVER, COLORADO

TO : COMGEN AMC WPAFB, DAY TON, OHIO, (ATTN: MCIAXO-3CAD)

INFO: CHIEF OF STAFF USAF WASHINGTON, DC (ATTN: DIR OF INTELL.)
COMGEN ATC BARKSDALE AIR FORCE BASE, LA. (ATTN: INTELL OFFICER)
COMGEN TDATC SCOTT AIR FORCE BASE, ILL. (ATTN: INTELL OFFICER)

8 APRIL 1949

NR : LUGB 2102

Local FBI agent reported Flying Discs over Stapleton Air Field, Denver about 2000 hours MT 6 April 1949. Observations made from ground near highway and witnesses collected. 1 round shaped object, altitude 15000 to 25000 ft, traveling fast and gaining altitude, fadeing from view. This headquarters ground radar set SCR-584 operated continuously 12 hour period commencing 1800 MT on combination search and tracking basis. Set operated on "S" band approximately 3000 megacycles. No unusual objects noted in scope, no form of interference encountered. Weather analysis at 2000 MT, sky conditions clear visibility 40 miles or more, winds alogt 15000 feet NW 25 knots becoming NW 40 knots at 25000 feet. U.S. Weather Bureau Stapleton Air Field report upper Air observation consisting of tracking of weather ballon through optical means conducted from 2000 hours MT.

CLASSIFICATION CANCELLED TO UNCLASSIFIED
BY AUTHORITY OF THE DIRECTOR OF S...
KURT K. KUNZE, Capt, USAF
Historian
8 DEC 1975
DATE

OUT SECURITY DIV. OSI

IN 14 APR 1949 SECURITY DIV. OSI

APR 11 3 34 AM '49

OFFICE OF SPECIAL INVESTIGATIONS
24 1/85 64

INFO: OIN, CSI

CAF IN 1663 (9 April 1949) DTG

[redacted]

COPY No.

MAY 26 1949

THE MAKING OF AN EXACT COPY OF THIS MESSAGE IS FORBIDDEN

UNCLASSIFIED

U. S. GOVERNMENT PRINTING OFFICE 16—58692-1

"...a grey metallic 'disc', hovering in the sky. It was 50 feet in diameter and 15 feet thick; it had a top, shaped like a conning tower and three ports on the rim, giving off a blue light. It hovered for two minutes, and then flew away."

(Source: Project Blue Book unknowns)

14th April – USA: Four rectangular UFOs sighted

At 2.30pm, over Fort Monmouth, New Jersey, Army Master Sergeant James sighted four rectangular, amber objects, about 3 feet by 4 feet in size, moving rapidly through the sky. They were seen to change speed and direction as they did so, also moving in a curious rising and falling action during the 3-4 minute sighting. (Source: Project Blue Book unknowns)

24th April – USA: UFO sighted over Skyhook balloon

Mr J. Gordon Vaeth, aeronautical engineer – employed by US Naval Research Office – and Charles B. Moore were tracking a launched Skyhook balloon with a theodolite, when they saw a whitish ellipsoid higher up, with diameter of about 100 feet, altitude of 56 miles and speed of 25,000 miles per hour. Other accounts tell us that this took place at 10.30am over Arrey, New Mexico, and that witnesses were General Mills, meteorologist and balloon expert C.B. Moore, and others on a balloon launch crew.

24th April – USA: Sausage-shaped UFO

At 5.45pm, Howard Hann, Mr Hubert and Tex Keahey from Tuscon, Arizona, sighted a bright, sausage-shaped object in the sky for 40 minutes. 2nd May – USA: Three 'flying discs' seen by air traffic controller.

At 11.40am on 2nd May, CAA radio operator – Mr Small – using field glasses, saw 3 'flying discs', 30 feet in diameter, at 14,000 feet, heading south-west at 300-400mph, before making a left turn and depart ahead of a United airliner, taking off from Elko Airport.

At 10.15pm the same day, Mr Marvin Leroy Small – an airplane communicator with the CAA – sighted:

"... three objects, circular and flat (appearance of a pancake) looking like oxidized aluminum, moving at an estimated speed of 250-300mph. After being in straight flight for a couple of minutes, veered left, appeared to accelerate, and tilted."

(Source: FOIA; FUFOR Index)

5th May – USA: Two 'flying discs' seen by Army Majors

Army officers – Major Day, Major Olhausen and Captain Vaughn – sighted two oblong white 'discs' in the sky, at 11.40am, flying at an estimated 200-250 mph. During a 30-50 second observation, they were seen to make a shallow turn while in flight. 6th May – USA: Two 'flying discs' sighted. Mr C.G. Green of Livermore, California, was outside at 9.35am, when he sighted two shiny, disc-like objects, rotating around each other, before they banked away.

"One then shot upwards, leaving a grey trail, before rejoining the other. The sighting lasted five minutes."

9th May – USA: Two flat objects sighted over Tucson, Arizona

At 2.30pm, Master Sergeant Troy Putnam observed two, round, flat, silvery objects, estimated to be 25 feet in diameter, flying across the sky, at a speed estimated to be between 750-1,000mph.

18th May – USA: Silver 'disc' seen by housewife

On 18th May 1949, a New Orleans housewife was outside, watering her lawn, when she noticed a silver 'disc'-shaped object, resembling a dinner plate in appearance, approximately the size of a small aircraft, apparently travelling east to north-north-west direction, on the outskirts of the City, in the vicinity of Lake Pontchartrain, two miles away, at an angle of 45 degrees off the horizon.

21st May – USA: UFO over Hanford Nuclear Plant – Jets scrambled

On 21st May 1949, an F-82 Fighter aircraft was dispatched from Moses Lake Air Force Base, near Hanford, Washington, to intercept a 'flying disc' that was observed by personnel (and confirmed on radar) hovering in restricted airspace over Hanford Atomic Power Plant, at an altitude of 17-20,000 feet. Before the aircraft could take-off, the object shot away in a southerly direction at a speed greater than the Jet fighter.

Could the object have looked anything like this image caught over a chimney in Lincolnshire some years ago?

UFO over Hanford Atomic Power Plant

A short time later, another aircraft was observed on radar in the restricted area of the Hanford Atomic Power Plant. This one was positively identified as a commercial aircraft, dropping leaflets announcing a rodeo! Dr. Allen Hynek pointed out the Blue Book files carried this UFO sighting under the classification of aircrafts, based on the assumption that the UFO and aircraft were one and the same, despite the comment made by the investigating officer that two separate and distinct alert conditions existed on the afternoon of 24th May 1949.

(See *Denver Post* Newspaper report, 5.7.1952)

Hanford Atomic Power Plant

24th May – USA: UFO sighted over Rogue River

On 24th May 1949, at 5pm, three men and two women were out fishing in a boat near the mouth of Oregon's Rogue River, scanning the water with Navy binoculars for signs of jumping fish, on what was a clear day with the sun behind their backs, when they noticed a strange circular object approaching from the north-east.

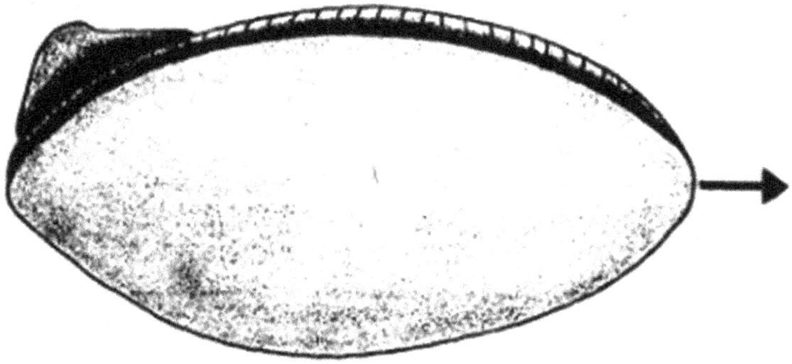

Illustration/diagram of the object from U.S. Air Force Project Blue Book Special Report 14 (Battelle Study) (Credit: UFOs at Close Sight)

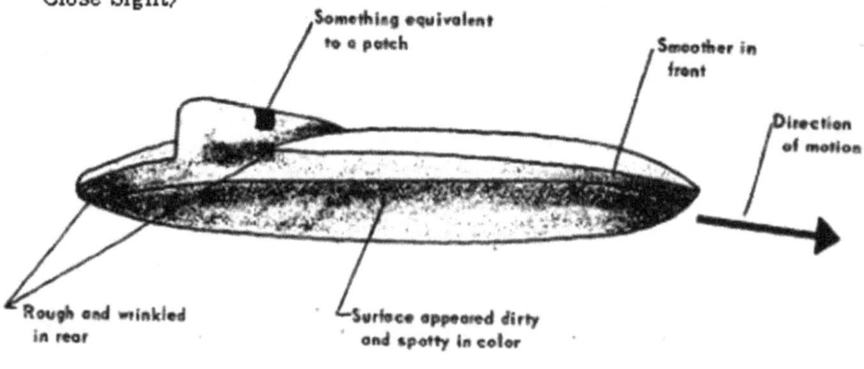

Rogue River

After watching it hovering in the sky to the east of them for about two and-a-half minutes, it shot away silently, at high speed, in a southerly direction. The fishermen (and women) – then employees of the Ames Research Laboratory at Moffett Field, near San Francisco – were able to look at the object through binoculars for about a minute each, when they saw an object they described as being:

> *"...circular and thin, relative to its diameter, with a shape similar to that of a pancake, with some sort of vertical fin on the upper surface at the trailing edge. No wings, antenna lights, propellers, engines, or exhaust ports, could be seen or heard; its trailing edge looked wrinkled and dirty."*

About three weeks later, the Ames employees reported their sighting to the security office at Moffett Field. The security office then requested AFOSI agents to investigate the sighting. Examination of Blue Book archive material reveals the Rogue River UFO report had been inexplicably split into two separate accounts; the one taken from Olive Elizabeth Macbeth, giving the address: PO Box 207 Gold Beach, Oregon, was not matched up with the other statements obtained from her companions – Dr. Gilbert Rivera, of California; and James Heaphy of 152, Sherman Avenue, North Bend, Oregon.

This no doubt contributed to the suggestion later made that the witnesses 'might have seen either an aircraft or a radar testing device, carried aloft by a gas filled balloon', neither of which can be treated seriously. Although we were unable to find any other sightings of similar 'craft' reported to Blue Book, we were to come across other reports of UFOs seen over American airspace during this period.

Dr. Bruce Maccabee

We contacted Navy physicist, optical analyst, and long-time MUFON member Dr. Bruce Maccabee, who is well-respected for his research into the UFO subject. 'Bill' Dillon had forwarded details of his 1957 UFO sighting to him and Jenny Randles, twenty years ago. Bruce then sent us three pages of Air Intelligence Information Reports, the source of the drawings contained in the special report #14 originally seen by 'Bill' Dillon, as submitted by Mr Heaphy to his employer at the Ames Jet Propulsion Laboratory, Moffett Field, California.

Rogue River UFO sighting – one of the best cases

Bruce:

> *"These are the original Air Intelligence Reports, which started off the whole thing. The AIR shows that copies of Heaphy's sighting report were submitted to some high level Officials, at NACA. In my humble opinion the RR case is one of the best, if not the best, of the simple*

> *(simple means no photos, no landing traces, no radar etc. – observation only) multiple witness cases of the early years because of the clarity of the report, the credibility of the witness, and the dynamics and shape of the object. I have discussed the arguments for credibility etc. in my web page paper, which was written long before the AIR report became available. The AIR only adds to the credibility of this case and, of course, the proposed explanation by the AFOS (Air Force Office of Specified Intelligence) and officially accepted by Project Grudge/Blue Book; namely a weather balloon, with radar reflector, makes no sense when compared to the details of the observations."*

The report into the Rogue River, Oregon sighting was submitted about twenty days after the incident took place to the security officer at the National Advisory Committee for Aeronautics at Moffett Field, who later concluded 'the observers who were familiar with high speed flight were undoubtedly competent'.

We wrote letters to the local newspapers in Oregon, hoping to track any of the witnesses, but never received any replies.

Bruce Maccabee

Bruce Maccabee received a B.S. in physics at Worcester Polytechnic Institute in Worcester, Mass., and then at American University, Washington, DC, (M.S. and Ph. D. in physics). In 1972 he began his career at the Naval Ordnance Laboratory, White Oak, Silver Spring, in Maryland, which later became the Naval Surface Warfare Center Dahlgren Division. Dr. Maccabee retired from government service in 2008. He has worked on optical data processing, generation of underwater sound with lasers and various aspects of the Strategic Defense Initiative (SDI) and Ballistic Missile Defense (BMD) using high power lasers.

Joined NICAP – State Director for Maryland

Maccabee has been an active ufologist since the late 1960s when he joined the National Investigations Committee on Aerial Phenomena (NICAP) and was active in research and investigation for NICAP until its demise in 1980. He became a member of the Mutual UFO Network (MUFON) in 1975 and was subsequently appointed to the position of state Director for Maryland, a position he still holds. In 1979 he was instrumental in establishing the Fund for UFO Research (FUFOR) and was the chairman for about 13 years. He presently serves on the National Board of the Fund.

Some of his investigations

His UFO research and investigations (which, he often stresses, are completely unrelated to his Navy work) have included the Kenneth Arnold sighting (June 24, 1947), the McMinnville, Oregon (Trent) photos of 1950, the Gemini 11 astronaut photos of September, 1966, the Tehran UFO incident of September 1976, the New Zealand sightings of December 1978, the Japan Airlines (JAL1628) sighting of November 1986, the numerous sightings of Gulf Breeze UFO incident, 1987–1988, the 'red bubba' sightings, 1990-1992 (including his own sighting in September, 1991), the Mexico City video of August, 1997 (which he deemed a hoax), the Phoenix lights sightings of March 13, 1997, 2004 Mexican UFO incident and many others. **(Source: Wikipedia)**

24th May – USA: Five to eight objects sighted by pilot

Joseph Shell was ferrying a SNJ trainer for North American Aviation, from Red Bluff, California, to Burns, Oregon. While over South Oregon, at 2.25pm, he saw:

> *"...five to eight oval objects, twice as long as wide, and one fifth as thick. They flew in trail formation with an interval equal to three to four times their length, except that the second and third were closer together".*

'Bill' Dillon and his English sighting of May 1957

There appears to be remarkable similarities with a UFO sighted eight years later (in 1957) over Luton, Bedfordshire, England, by then schoolboy William Dillon (now a personal friend), who remains intrigued by what he saw, well over half a century ago and is still trying to obtain sight of original copy sketches mislaid some years ago. (See Ramridge UFO sighting, 1957)

Summer – England: Silver UFO seen by cyclists over Lincolnshire

In the summer of 1949, Mr and Mrs I. Booth from Brookhill Street, Stapleford Nottinghamshire were out cycling along a country lane in Lincolnshire, when they were astonished to see a long gleaming, silvery, dirigible-shaped object, gliding westwards, about three miles away, at a height of about 20,000 feet.

> *"We cycled on, watching it all the time, and shortly overtook a neighbour. The three of us then walked half-a-mile and continued to keep our eyes on it, until it disappeared into the sunset. Imagine our amazement when we read about a similar object seen by the pilot and crew of a plane crossing America – all of whom, with their passengers, signed affidavits confirming the sighting. What we and they saw was a Mother spaceship for 'flying saucers' and not all the pundits and scoffers will ever persuade us otherwise."*

(Source: Letter to Richard Thompson)

24th July – USA: Seven UFOs sighted by pilot

Henry Clark – manager of a flying service – was flying a Piper Clipper over Mountain Home Idaho, at midday, when he saw seven delta-shaped objects, 35-55 feet in span, 20-30 feet long, and two to five feet thick.

> *"They were light coloured, except for a 12 feet diameter dark circle at the rear of each, and flew in a tight formation of twos, with one behind, and then made a perfect but unbanked turn. During the 10 minute sighting, they displayed decreasing smooth oscillations."*

The plane engine ran rough during the sighting, and after landing was found to have all its spark plugs burnt-out.

30th July – USA: Pilot and Air Traffic Controllers sight UFO

Northwest Airlines – Captain Thrush, two Portland Air Traffic control tower operators, and a flying instructor, sighted an object showing a white light and two red lights, at 9pm, over Mount Hood, Oregon. It was seen to manoeuvre and hover in flight.

August – England: 'Operation Bulldog' launched

In August 1949 'Operation Bulldog' was launched to test the resources of Britain's Defence chain of radar installations, stretching from Land's End in the south-west, to the north of Scotland. During this month, a UFO was tracked on radar by personnel at RAF Sandwich, in Kent, travelling roughly parallel to the coast, heading west to east. When at a position over the English Channel off the Kent coast it turned abruptly northwards, before being picked up by Martlesham radar station, Ipswich, at an estimated speed of 30,000mph, with a returning echo the size of a large passenger or freight ship, in the region of 15-20,000 tons.

Warned of breaking Official Secrets Act

It was last tracked by *RAF Bempton, before suddenly increasing speed and heading straight up into the sky – then vanishing off the radar screen at about 100,000 feet! The dozen or so employees were reminded of the requirements of the Official Secrets Act and told to forget what they had seen.

November – Strait of Hormuz: Three objects sighted under the sea

USN Commander J.F. Bodler was bound for India and traversing the Strait of Hormuz, when they observed the approach of a luminous green pinwheel – apparently pulsating as it revolved slowly under the water – estimated to be 1,000 to 1,500 feet in diameter. The ship passed over it without incident. As the submerged object diminished astern, a second and third appeared near the surface off the stern quarter heading in the same direction as the others.

(USA Sources: Project Blue Book unknowns)

*RAF Bempton was an RAF airfield during the First World War, situated at Bempton in the East Riding of Yorkshire, England, six miles north of Bridlington. During the Second World War, it was a radar station.

1950

5th February – USA: Illuminated cylindrical objects

FORMER US Navy serviceman – Marvin Odom, and Lt. Philip Foushee – pilot from Otis Air Force Base, and two others, were at Teaticket, Massachusetts, at 5.10pm, when they saw:

> *"...two thin, illuminated cylinders, one of which dropped a fireball. They then manoeuvred together and disappeared at speed, upwards, after 5 minutes observation".*

(Source: Project Blue Book unknowns)

24th February – USA: Elongated object

Over Albuquerque, New Mexico, Municipal Airport weather observers – Luther McDonald and Harrison Manson – sighted a white, slightly elongated object, heading in a straight trajectory across the sky, for one-and-a-half minutes, through a theodolite, at 1.55pm. 25th February – USA: Cylindrical UFO seen over New Mexico

At 3.55pm, twelve Atomic Energy Commission security inspectors from Los Alamos, New Mexico, sighted a silver, flashing cylindrical object, with tapered ends, flying in a peculiar manner – slowly, then fast through the sky – before changing course, seconds later – then lost from sight. Some of the witnesses only saw it for seconds; others, for up to two minutes.

(Source: Project Blue Book unknowns)

March – England: Three UFOs sighted in cloudless sky

Mr Peter Brooks (then aged 18) was stood near the promenade at Minnis Bay, Kent, looking out to sea across the end of the Thames Estuary, towards the North, at 4pm.

> *"I was wondering whether to walk home to where I lived, or to wait for a bus, as there was a north-easterly breeze blowing. I decided to wait 20 minutes for the bus and scanned the horizon for any vessels, when my attention was caught by the sound of a Jet aircraft overhead. I looked and saw a Meteor Jet flying over – a familiar sight, as RAF Manston was only a few miles away. It was climbing in a huge arc across the clear sky in an east to*

> *west direction. It then flew towards the sun, which was about 45 degrees off the western horizon and I could no longer follow its flight. Almost immediately it appeared as a dot in the sky – now heading back towards the eastern direction – which puzzled me, as it seemed an impossible manoeuvre. I was stunned to see a grey-black 'disc', at a height of about 4,000 feet, and kept my gaze locked onto the object. Its speed was the same as the Jet and was not a weather balloon, as it kept on a steady course heading southwesterly.*

By this time it was at an angle of 90 degrees to the coastline, when I became aware that there were, in fact, two of them – the second slightly behind the first. I continued my observations and was shocked to see three of them flying in a perfect 'V' formation, until they faded from sight into the blue haze of that cloudless day."

13th March – USA: Cylindrical UFO seen

At McClellan Air Force Base, California, USAF First Lt. B.J. Hastie, and a Mrs Rafferty, were outside the base when they saw:

> *"...a cylindrical object with twin tails, estimated to be 200 feet long and 90 feet wide, heading North at incredible speed, at 3.20pm. Two minutes later it was gone."*

(Source: Project Blue Book unknowns)

17th March – USA: Large number of strange objects seen

The Las Vegas Daily Optic newspaper (17.3.1950) – 'Saucers in Clusters', told of a large group of 'flying saucers' reported over Farmington that morning. Some people estimated them in their hundreds; others, twenty or so objects heading across the sky, high overhead. Former Army Captain, Mr Clayton J. Boddy – business manager of the *Farmington Daily Times* was one of those that witnessed the events.

> *"A large number of 100, or more, appeared in the sky over Farmington shortly before noon. At least twenty of them were close enough to be seen as flying saucer-shaped objects. They disappeared towards the north-east in a sudden burst of speed that could not be estimated."*

20th March – USA: 'Flying disc', with portholes, seen by pilots

At 9.26pm, Chicago & Southern Airlines Captain Jack Adams, and First Officer G.W. Anderson, was over Stuttgart, Arkansas, when they sighted a 100 feet circular 'disc', with 9-12 portholes along the lower side emitting a soft purple light, and a light at the top, which flashed three times in nine seconds, flying through the sky at a speed judged to be not less than 1,000 mph. It was seen for 25-35 seconds.

29th March – USA: Six objects seen over lake

At 7am, Real estate salesmen Whiteside and Williams were at Marrowbore Lake, Tennessee, when they saw 6-12 dark objects, shaped like 300lb. bombs, estimated to be five feet long, flying across the sky at a speed estimated to be 500 mph, before descending – making a noise like wind blowing through the trees.

27th April –USA: TWA pilots sight UFO

A Trans World Air Lines DC-3 flight 117 was ninety miles east of Chicago, cruising at 2,000 feet over Goshen, Indiana. In the left-hand seat, handling the controls was Captain Robert Adickes, with ten years' service in TWA (also a four-stripe captain), but on this flight he was in the right-hand seat, serving as First Officer or co-pilot to Captain Robert F. Manning.

Manning glanced out from the shadowy cockpit – South Bend was a spreading glow in the darkness. Clouds massed at 4,000 feet made a black sky overhead.

Strange red light seen

Suddenly at 8.25pm a strange red light moving swiftly near the horizon caught Captain Manning's attention moving toward the air liner, climbing up on the right, from a point some miles behind.

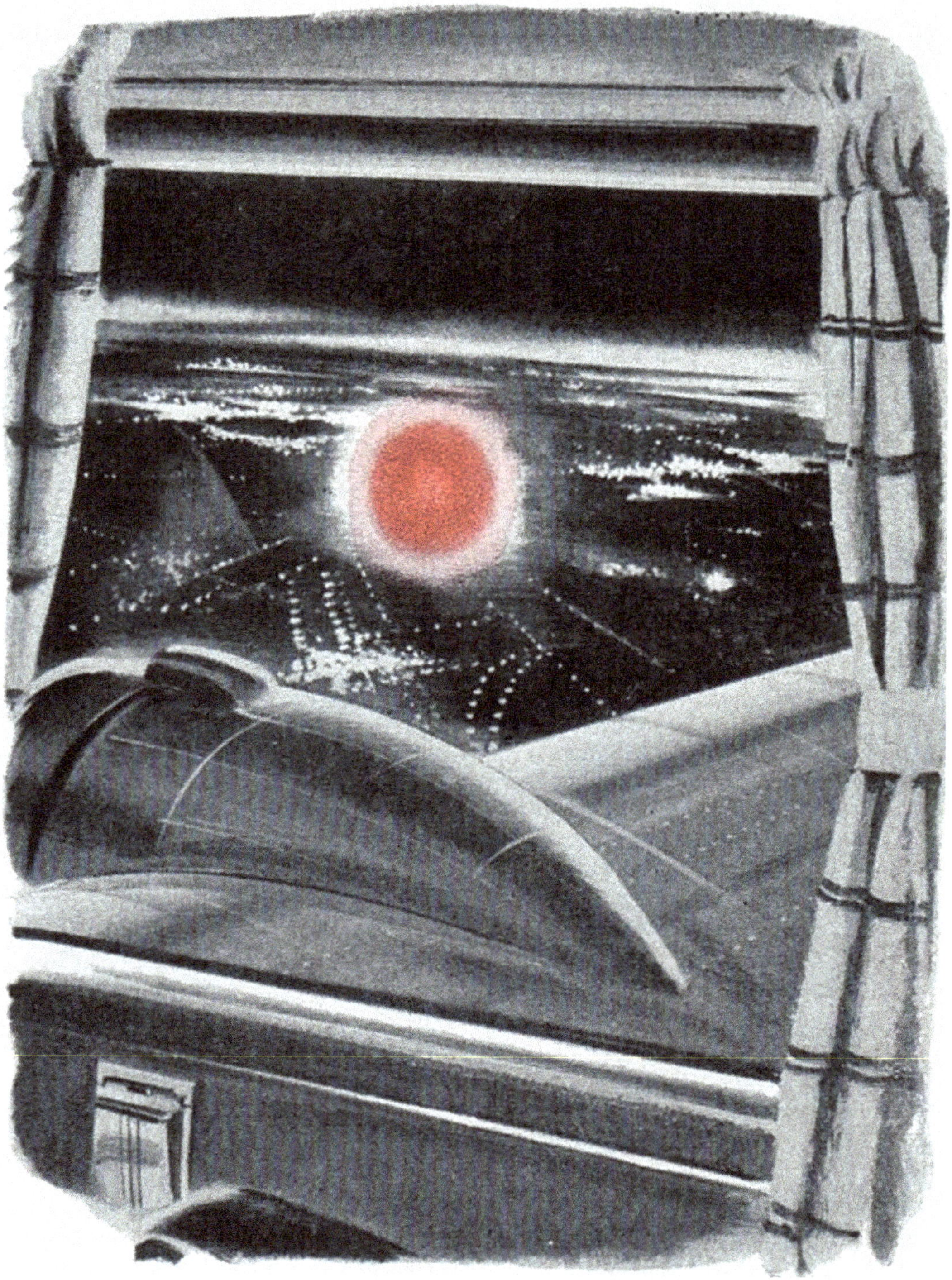

"This was no wing tip light — the strange red light was too bright. With growing astonishment, I saw that the light was increasing in size. Whatever it was, this was no conventional aircraft. The DC-3 was cruising at 175 miles an hour, but the mysterious glowing object was overtaking it rapidly. It was now an orange-red colour, like a round blob of hot metal sweeping through the night sky."

Captain Manning looked down onto a spherical-shaped object glowing brightly on top, its lower part in shadow. He asked Adickes to have a look and tell him what he made of it.

Captain Adickes turned, startled, and rose up and gazed through the starboard window. The thing was still climbing, not quite at the airliner's level. Over the top, he could see scattered ground lights, and below it, car lights on a highway. He could only guess at its size, but it looked to be at least twenty feet in diameter, probably closer to fifty. The two pilots stared at each other – then Adickes reached for his mike and called TWA, at Chicago.

Radioed TWA at Chicago

"We've sighted a strange object off the starboard wing," he swiftly told the dispatcher. *"Ask ATC if there's any traffic near us."*

In a moment, the answer came back. Air Traffic Control had no record of anything near their ship. Adickes and Manning looked out again at the 'saucer'. It appeared to be half-a-mile distant, now keeping pace with the plane. Adickes shook his head incredulously.

Banks the aircraft

"It looked exactly like a huge round wheel, rolling down a road, but how could a thing like that stay in the air? I'm going to try to sneak up on it," he told Manning.

He banked the ship gently, but the glowing 'disc' at once slid away, keeping its distance. He tried again, with the same result.

"Call the hostess", he said abruptly. *"I want someone else to see this thing."*

Back in the cabin, hostess Gloria Hinshaw caught the hastily flashing signal. She hurried up the aisle and entered the cockpit.

"Take a look out there", said Adickes. He pointed across the right wing. The amazed hostess stared out at the glowing 'saucer'. It was once more flying parallel with the plane.

"What on earth is it?" Gloria Hinshaw exclaimed.

"We don't know", said Manning.

"Go back and tell the passengers", Adickes said quickly. *"Get them all to look at it."*

Hostess alerts passengers

The hostess returned to the cabin. The first passenger, in a single seat on the right, was sound asleep. She turned to the two across the aisle – Clifford H. Jenkins and Dean C. Bourland, both Boeing Aircraft men.

"There's a 'flying saucer' out there. Look out the starboard side."

Jenkins laughed, and then he saw the look on her face. He jumped up and peered out of the opposite window, Bourland crouching beside him. From the lighted cabin, the shape of the 'saucer' was less distinct. To Jenkins, it looked like a blur of windows lit with a queer red light. It was unlike anything he'd ever seen – and he knew every type of plane.

While Jenkins and Bourland were gazing at the 'saucer', Captain Adickes came hurrying out of the cockpit. The sleeping passengers woke up, as Adickes leaned down to look out through his window.

> *"What's the matter - what's going on?"* he demanded.

> *"Look out there"*, said Adickes. *"See that thing?"*

He turned to the two Boeing men.

> *"Did you see it? I want plenty of witnesses to this"*.

The starboard-side passengers were watching the 'saucer' but on the port side aft, the hostess was having trouble.

When Adickes returned to the cockpit, Manning was putting down his mike.

> *"I called the South Bend radio range"*, said Manning. *"I told them to go out and see if they could spot the thing."*

Adickes took the controls, and made one more cautious attempt to sneak up on the 'saucer'. When the thing again slid away, he swung around quickly to give direct chase. Instantly, the glowing 'disc' dived. In barely more than a second, it went down to 1,500 feet, racing off to the north past South Bend. Its speed, Adickes estimated, was close to 400 miles per hour. For a few minutes longer, the weird light remained visible - a diminishing bright red spot against the ground. It then faded and disappeared. Adickes' radio flash to Chicago had been picked up by newspapermen.

Reporters were waiting at the airport, and the story was soon on the wires. It drew unusual attention. This was not just another 'flying saucer' story to be laughed off. Besides the crew, there were passenger witnesses. Adickes, recalling the ridicule other pilots had met, had carefully seen to that.

Donald E. Keyhoe launched a thorough and very professional investigation into this incident for True Magazine which involved tracking down many of the civilian witnesses and obtaining their eye witness accounts.

(Source: Project 1947 WWW Internet 2016)

April 1950 – England: 'Flying saucer' sighted over Lancashire

Donald S. Sharpe – a night waiter at Cordes Restaurant, Broadway, New York – contacted Blue Book in 1956 with regard to what he saw, while working in a circus in Blackpool, England, during April 1950.

> *"I and several of my co-workers were on one of the piers, when we noticed a luminous object in the western sky over the Irish Sea. This object hovered motionless for the first minute or two after it was seen. It appeared elliptical, the major axis horizontal and about equal in apparent size to the diameter of a full moon."*

Evidentially, it was actually a discoid object seen approximately edge on, since a row of four or five equally spaced 'portholes' could be seen .These 'portholes' emitted spreading beams of brilliant white light, illuminating the thin cloud layers underneath. The 'body' of the object glowed with a soft silvery luminescence around its far edge, which could be seen as a glow or halo. No other structural details were apparent.

> *"The object was not rotating presently; it began to move in a series of back and forth movements, rushing at great speed towards the observers and then back again, also performing vertical*

oscillations. After it had been under observations for a total of three to four minutes, it dashed out of sight at great speed."

According to Mr Sharpe, he was later told that something similar had been seen in the same locality on at least two other occasions during the previous twelve months. The investigator ruled out a number of theories and concluded the observation was rigorously authentic. Coincidently, on 26th May 2008, nearly 60 years later, a saucer-shaped object was photographed over the pier, confirming the authors' suspicions that UFOs appear to be indigenous to certain localities.

(Source: Project Blue Book)

Although we were unable to trace any other witnesses to this incident, or obtain any information from the BBC, we discovered that a mysterious object, displaying green and red lights, was seen travelling across the sky over Yorkshire, at a speed estimated to be in excess of more than 1,000mph, during the early part of 1950. Among the numerous witnesses were coastguards.

A subsequent investigation, launched by the RAF and scientists from Durham University (who discounted the theory that it was a meteorite), failed to come up with any satisfactory explanation.

29th May – USA: Pilot sights UFO

The Sperry UFO case was a sighting of an Unidentified Flying Object by the captain, Willis Sperry, and other crew of an American Airlines DC-6 airborne near Mount Vernon, Maryland on 29 May 1950.

Media exposure of the case helped to establish a popular perception of UFOs being reported by "credible" witnesses such as airline pilots; Sperry was interviewed for several newspapers and was later featured in Clarence Greene's 1956 semi-documentary film Unidentified Flying Objects: The true story of flying saucers.

Sperry's aircraft had left Washington Airport at 9:10 pm EST on a flight to Nashville and was climbing to 20,000 ft. Weather conditions were clear, with the ground obscured by haze, and a full moon around 25° above the horizon.

(Source: Wikipedia, 2016)

Captain Willis Sperry

Bright blue light seen

At approximately 9.30pm, seven miles west of Mount Vernon, co-pilot W. Gates alerted Sperry to a bright blue or bluish light ahead of them and increasing in size. In a letter to the Flying magazine, several months later, Sperry described the light as:

"...a brilliant, diffused, bluish light of fluorescent type [...] 25 times the magnitude of the brightest star".

To avert a possible collision, Sperry banked the aircraft and changed course 45 degrees to the right; the light appeared to stop before changing course to parallel the aircraft on the left.

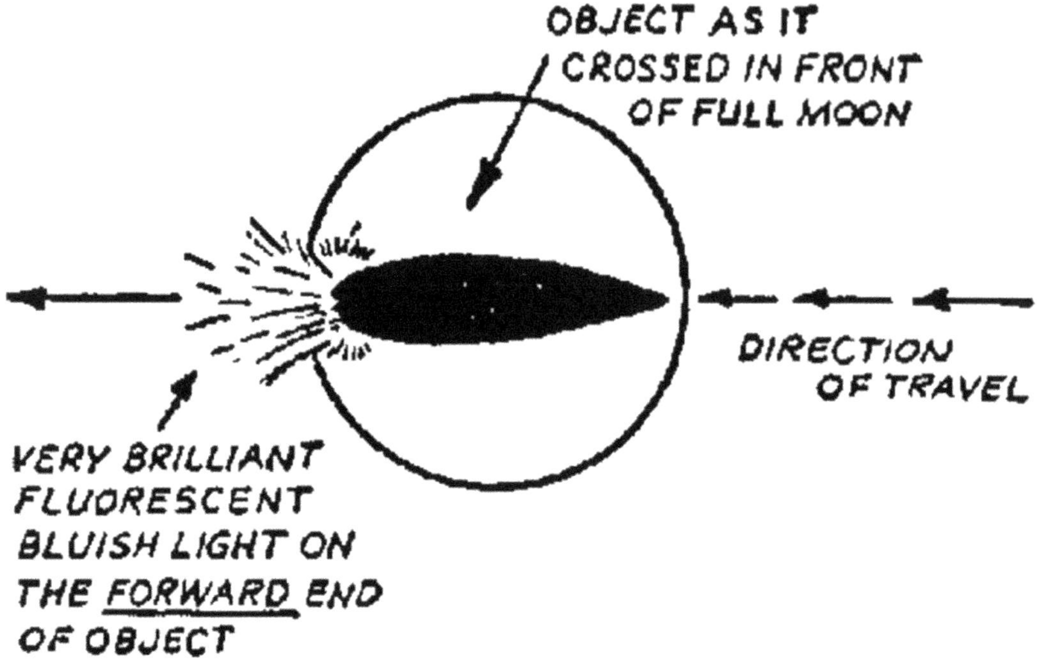

Object showing silhouette somewhat reminiscent of a submarine

During this period the light very briefly passed between the aircraft and the upper part of the moon, revealing an object with a long silhouette (somewhat reminiscent of a submarine) without visible wings or empennage. In his 1950 letter, Sperry stated the blue light was on the front of the object, which was also seen by the co-pilot and by flight engineer R. Arnholt.

The object having appeared to pass behind the left wing, the pilots banked to the left and resumed their previous course, but Gates spotted the light again through the right window *"as though it had circled behind them"*. The light then appeared to head eastwards behind the aircraft, and was observed again by Sperry towards the rear left, travelling in the direction of the Atlantic; he estimated the total time of observation as around one minute, during which time the light had appeared to be completely stationary at least twice.

Sperry reported his observations to Washington control tower, but they had observed nothing on radar. He also spoke to his passengers, stating that one man had seen an *"extremely bright light, passing the left side of the ship"*.

Later Interviewed by the Media

Apart from newspaper interviews immediately following the sighting, the press having been notified by control tower staff, and his appearance in the 1956 film (where the case was featured alongside the Mantell Incident, Gorman Dogfight and others, considered unexplained at the time), Sperry was also interviewed by KABC-TV in 1964. He and Arnholt were further interviewed in 1968 by the prominent ufologist - Dr James E. McDonald.

Sperry later learned that Hank Myers, subsequently pilot of President Harry S. Truman's plane, had been piloting another Washington-bound AAA aircraft between Nashville and Knoxville on the same night, and had witnessed a bright meteor which fell eastward from the zenith, but which then appeared to move horizontally for several seconds. Comparing the times and the relative position of his aircraft with that of Myers, Sperry felt that this was possibly the same phenomenon, or object, as he saw. Both he and Gates – the co-pilot – had, however, 'emphatically discounted' the possibility of the phenomenon being a meteor, due to its movements.

Spring – England: Man chased by orange 'globe of light' at Hereford

Something many will feel borders more on the paranormal, rather than UFO, took place in the spring of 1950 and involved Mr Owen .J. Gittings – a veteran of the Second World War, holder of the Burma Star and Atlantic Medal. He was then living in Lloyd Street, Tupley, in Herefordshire.

> *"It was my common practice to retire to bed early, as I worked the early morning shift. I can remember being awoken at 10.30pm by the sound of a terrific commotion coming from below. I raced downstairs and found my brother, Colin, in a shaken state. When I asked him what had happened, he told me he had just been chased by a 'great ball of orange light' along the street. Together with other family members, we sat down and tried to rationalise what Colin had seen. Various suggestions were made, including a possibility of a policeman's torch waving in the air. Colin would have none of this and insisted there was no natural explanation for what had taken place. I could see from his demeanour that this was no skylark, but decided to go back to bed. I remember waking up at about 1am. Looking through the window, I was shocked to see a perfectly formed, flat, almost two dimensional, glistening circle of yellow bronze light covering the whole of the house opposite me. Within a short time it had faded away."*

Still remains mystified

Owen still remains mystified by what he and his brother saw. What he finds strange is that after he sighted the 'circle of light', why didn't he alert the rest of the household, instead of getting ready for work? When he arrived, the timekeeper expressed considerable surprise as to his early arrival. When Owen told him what had happened he was stunned. Instead of the expected laughter or ridicule, the man told him about his own experience when, while fishing at Bishop's Meadow, he had sighted *"a great 'ball' of orange light appear in the sky, just as dusk was falling."*

(Source: Personal interview)

25/8/200

C.W Gittings
c/o St Martin Motor Services
81 St Martins St
Hereford

Dear Mr Hanson

In reply to your request, I will attempt to give you the information you require. It was many years ago I would estimate approx forty years. Home, was council owned on a good quality estate situated in a cul-de-sac which finished in a circle approx twenty yards in diameter ,the apparition which startled me was on the opposite pavement to my path a and when first noticed I was approx thirty yards away.
It was quite eerie, a pillar of fluorescent green which I would liken to a fog, Size is difficult now but I would think perhaps seven feet high and three feet width, whether round or square I cant say. Without a doubt it frightened me and I do know this was not a figment of imagination .I bolted on home locking the door behind me which in those days was never locked until the last one in, ran up the stairs to have a better look through my bedroom window which overlooked this area but whether the angles made a difference I do not know, it just disappeared . My late night arriving home was always a little apprehensive for some time after.
Hope this is of interest to you, but for Owen reviving it I doubt whether I would of ever mentioned it again.

Your Sincerely

Waveney Girvan on *Lord Louis Mountbatten

In chapter four of his book, *Flying Saucers and Common Sense*, published in 1955, Waveney Girvan reveals that Earl Mountbatten had written a personal letter to the editor of the *Sunday Dispatch* early in 1950. This letter followed an earlier article concerning a 'wave' of UFO sightings in America, in the town of Orangeburg. The letter read as follows:

> *"These extraordinary things have now been seen in almost every part of the world - Scandinavia, North America, South America, Central Europe, etc. Reports are always appearing and the newspapers generally try to ridicule them. As a result it is difficult for any seriously interested person to find out very much about them. I should therefore like to congratulate you on having had both the intelligence (and, incidentally, the courage) to print the first serious helpful article which I have read on the 'Flying Saucers'. I have read most other accounts up to date, and can candidly say yours interested me the most".*

Summer 1950 – England: 'Flying Saucer' over Yorkshire

During spring/summer 1950, Dennis Maycroft from Nottinghamshire was carrying out electrical installation work to the BBC transmitter at †Holme Moss, Yorkshire, a few miles from Holmfirth. He was working on a mast platform, approximately 600 feet off the ground, with Mr Frederick Binchell (a senior engineer from the BBC) and four steel erectors from the Birmingham area.

At 2.30pm they noticed something in the sky, roughly two miles away, over the Huddersfield area.

> *"It was shaped like an upturned saucer, silver in colour and approximately a hundred feet in length. We watched it move slowly up and down in the sky, noting that when it was in the 'up' position, the underside appeared dark. When it was 'down', you could see a bluish 'energy' around the top of it. Details of the sighting were passed by telephone to Mr Binchell, who was now on the ground."*

After some two hours had elapsed the saucer-shaped object climbed upwards at tremendous speed before being lost from view.

---

*John Hanson: *"I had the pleasure of meeting his Lordship, Lord Louis Mountbatten, and Prince Charles in the 1970s, during a dinner held to celebrate the annual gathering of the survivors of HMS Kelly, in London – thanks to my late father-in-law, Chief Petty Officer Ted West, who served under 'Captain' Mountbatten. 'Ted' lived in Selly Oak, Birmingham. Rest in Peace. I felt privileged when Lord Louis officiated at Ted's funeral."*

†Holme Moss transmitting station was built by John Laing & Son and became the BBC's third public television transmitter, launched on 12th October 1951. Of historic and technical interest, this operated on the 405 line VHF system, with black and white transmissions originally on British System A, Channel 2, with vision 51.75 MHz, 45 kW and sound 48.25 MHz, 12 kW. The mast survived until the end of the Band I TV broadcasts in 1985, with a replacement mast being constructed, adjacent, in 1984.The site is now owned and operated by Arqiva.

When Dennis returned to the ground he discovered that over twenty people had seen the unidentified flying object, including the senior engineer who had already left on his way to London to report the incident.

> *"A few weeks later, when somebody enquired about the sighting, he was told it had been a weather balloon. If this had been the case, how could it have hovered in the same position for two hours and moved at such fantastic speed?"*

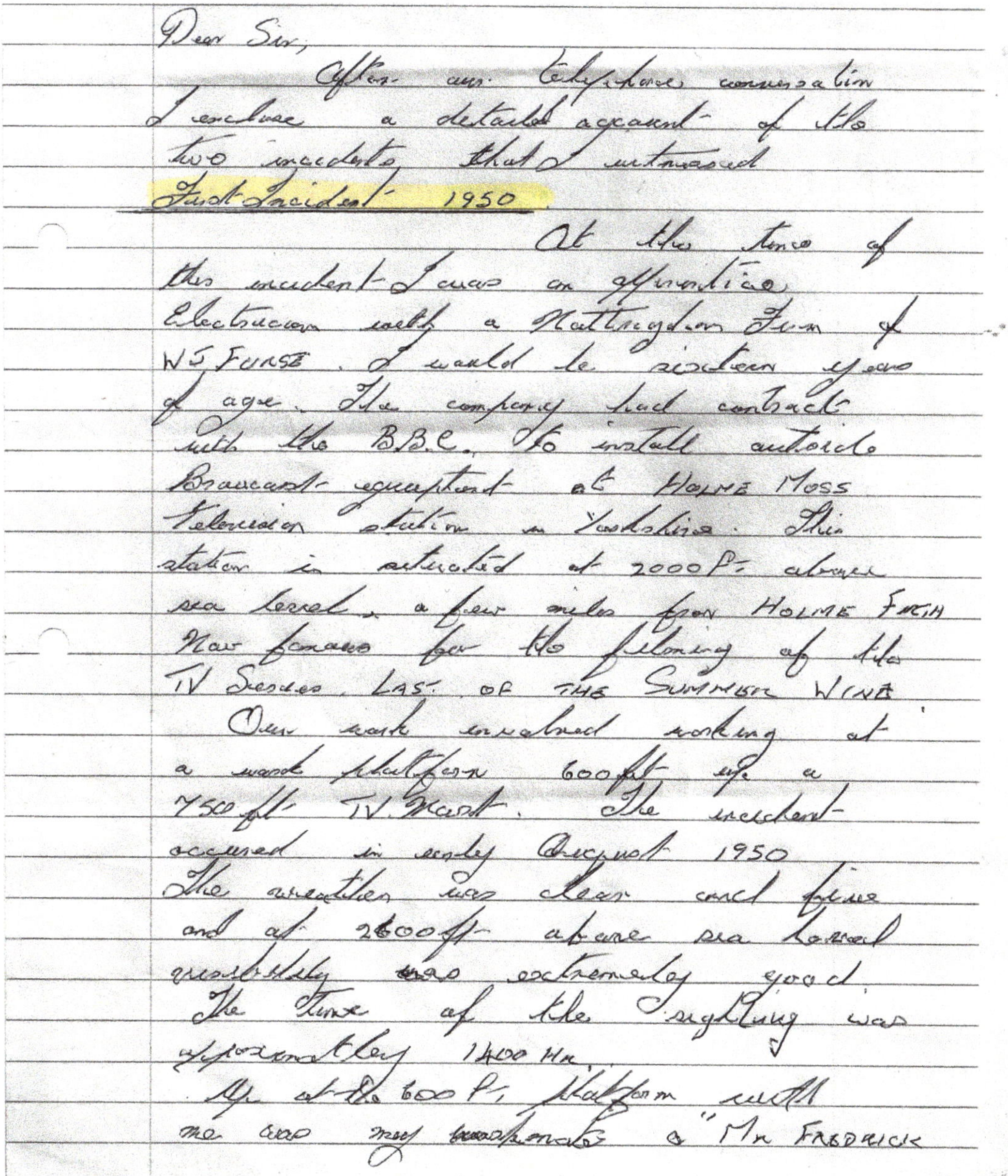

Dear Sir,

After our telephone conversation I enclose a detailed account of the two incidents that I witnessed

First Incident 1950

At the time of the incident I was an Apprentice Electrician with a Nottingham Firm of WJ FURSE. I would be sixteen years of age. The company had contract with the B.B.C. to install outside Broadcast equipment at HOLME MOSS Television station in Yorkshire. This station is situated at 2000 Ft. above sea level, a few miles from HOLME FIRTH Now famous for the filming of the TV Series LAST OF THE SUMMER WINE

Our work involved working at a work platform 600 ft up a 750 ft TV Mast. The incident occurred in early August 1950

The weather was clear and fine and at 2600 ft above sea level visibility was extremely good.

The time of the sighting was approximately 1400 Hr.

Up at the 600 Ft. platform with me was my workmate a "Mr FREDRICK

2

Birchall". There was also men
from a firm of Steel erectors from
Birmingham Area. If I remember
correctly there was four of them.
Also up the mast was a Senior
Engineer of the B.B.C. from London.
Looking out towards Huddersfield
we observed something in the sky.
we thought was about ten miles
away from us And to see it at
this distance with the naked eye
we estimated that It had to
be at least 100 ft across.
It was shaped like a upturned
Saucer and was silver in colour.
It appeared to oscillate up and
down. When it was in the up
position, the underside appeared to
be of a dark colour. When it was
downwards there appeared to be a
blueish ring around the top of the
upturned saucer.
When all of the people on
the work platform confirmed that
they could see the object we
all agreed on description. But
non of us knew what it was.
When you are working in the
Mast you can keep in contact
with the control room on the
ground by a telephone system.
The Senior Engineer phoned
through to the Control Room
and reported the incident

3

A number of staff came out and reported that the U.F.O. Could be see from ground level. The Station Manager was then contacted and told about the sighting. He then came out and confirmed that he to could see the U.F.O.

He was advised by the Senior Engineer, to report the incident to the Police. After this was done the Senior Engineer left us and returned to ground level.

We stayed up the Mast carrying out our work. But kept an eye on the U.F.O. between us. It was in full view for about two hours (2). It then started to climb at a tremendous rate of acceleration and vanished.

On our return to ground level it was the general subject of conversation. It seemed that about 20 people had seen the U.F.O.

We were told that after the Station Manager had reported to the Police. The Senior Engineer from London also reported the incident to someone. But we do not know who it was. All we could find out, that after his telephone call. He returned immediately to London.

A few weeks later we were told that what we had

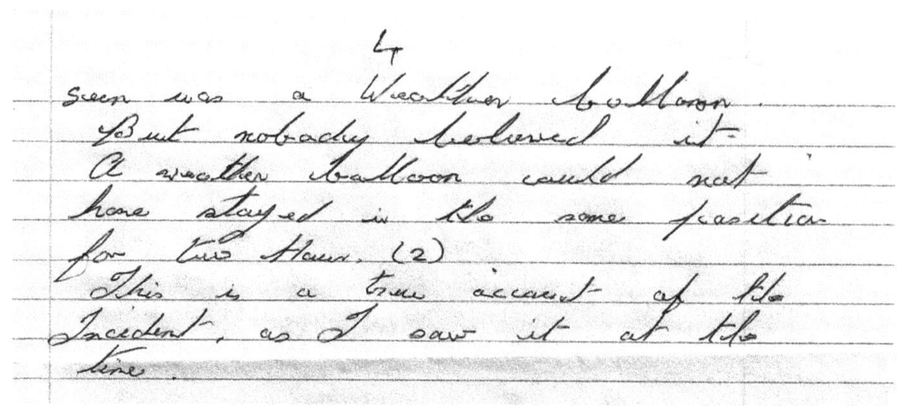
4

Seen was a Weather balloon.
But nobody believed it.
A weather balloon could not
have stayed in the same position
for two Hours. (2)
This is a true account of the
Incident, as I saw it at the
time.

England: RAF Wartling tracks UFOs on radar

Jack Baxter

We spoke to Jack Baxter – an ex RAF Radar operator, living in Herefordshire – who was quick to point out that while he had never personally seen a UFO, he was convinced they existed after having monitored many radar broadcasts involving pilots who had been scrambled to intercept, between 1949 and 1951, at RAF Wartling, near Pevensey Bay, Eastbourne, Sussex.

> *"We were divided into crews of four or five airmen, with a pilot officer in charge. Our task was to track and identify all aircraft movement in an area of the south coast. On many occasions, when these flying objects could not be identified, they scrambled Jet fighters, mostly Meteors, which had a top speed of some 640 knots, from places such as Tangmere and West Malling, to name just a few. Invariably, the pilots would report seeing strange circular objects, which veered away from them as they approached at speeds of 1,100 knots.*
>
> *On June 1st 1950, the pilot of a Meteor Jet from RAF Tangmere was flying at 20,000 feet on an easterly course over the Portsmouth area, at 2.30pm, when he sighted an object travelling at very high speed on a reciprocal course, 1,000-2,000 feet above him and roughly 1,200 yards to starboard. He described it as 'circular and of bright metallic appearance, moving at an estimated speed of 800 knots for a few seconds'."*

RAF Wartling

> *"Tangmere contacted the radar station at RAF Wartling about the matter and were informed that at about the same time as the pilot's 'report' the duty controller and three radar operators had observed an unusual response to the PPI, which appeared to be due to a 'target' moving at 1,300-1,650 knots, first approaching and then receding from the station. The controller stated that the 'response' looked to be very thick, leaving more afterglow than usual 'response' behind. The operator, observing on a separate display, said it was 'slim,*

short and weaker than aircraft, with a series of "shadows" appearing in the space between successive points'. As the receding course of the radar target could have tallied with the course of the object reported by the Meteor pilot, the people concerned were interviewed by a member of the Research Branch Fighter Command, from whose report the above data was taken. It was established that there was, in fact, a discrepancy of ten minutes between the times of the two reports, which were estimated as individually accurate to plus or minus one minute. It must therefore be concluded that there was no connection between the unusual PPI response and the pilot's visual observation.

We believe that the radar response can be very simply explained as due to interference from another transmitter – a phenomenon which has been frequently observed and which is described in detail in Appendix A. It is impossible to be entirely definite about the pilot's report. Assuming that he was not merely the victim of an optical illusion, the most probable explanation which is borne out by his description of the object as 'circular', implying a spherical body, is that he saw a meteorological balloon and greatly overestimated its speed. We find no reason whatever for adopting any less simple hypothesis."

1st June – England: RAF pilot sights revolving object in sky

We discovered the incident formed the foundation of a press release by the Air Ministry, in June 1950, when it was disclosed, quote: 'the First Officer's report of a 'flying saucer' seen over Britain' was being investigated by the Air Ministry, who reported a Meteor jet pilot, flying at 40,000 feet, told the Station Intelligence Officer at RAF Tangmere, near Chichester, Sussex, quote: 'a shining disc-like object, revolving and travelling at very high speed', and that his story could not be shaken under cross-examination.

A report of the incident, later sent to Fighter Command HQ, was checked by Senior Officers and weather experts.

12th June 1950 – USA: Eddie Rickenbacker

World War I flying ace [*]Eddie Rickenbacker – President of Eastern Air Lines – told the press that:

"Flying saucers are real; too many good men have seen them. If they exist, you can bet they belong to the Unites States Air Force."

Eddie Rickenbacker

The Air Force insists they have no such equipment.

[*]Edward Vernon Rickenbacker (October 8, 1890 – July 23, 1973) was an American fighter ace in World War I and Medal of Honor recipient. With 26 aerial victories, he was America's most successful fighter ace in the war. He was also a race car driver and automotive designer, a government consultant in military matters and a pioneer in air transportation.

14th August – England: RAF pilot sights UFO over RAF Farnborough

Two months later, on 14th August 1950, a spectacular sighting took place over RAF Farnborough, involving Stanley Hubbard – then a Flt. Lt. Test Pilot with the RAF.

> *"It was a warm day and unusually quiet for a base that normally resonated with the sound of general noise and aircraft engines.*
>
> *As I trudged across the runway, heading towards the Mess where I was billeted, I became aware of a strange sound coming from somewhere behind me. I stopped and turned around, curious as to the source of this noise, and was very much taken aback to see an object, looking like a 'flying sports discus', rocking from side-to-side in a regular rhythm of movement (approximately 20-25 degrees either side), heading across the sky at about a thousand feet off the ground. I watched as it moved over, noting that the exterior of the craft appeared to be light grey in colour – a bit like mother-of-pearl – blurred, rather than sharply defined. As it passed overhead, it allowed me to determine it was obviously reflecting light because, as it rocked, it reminded me of a pan lid, rotating segments of light. Around the edges were what looked like tiny crackling, sparkling lights, accompanied by a powerful smell of ozone. The next thing I was aware of was the arrival of the female dispatcher from the radio shack nearby. She was hysterical. She screamed out my name and said, 'Did you see that horrible thing go over?' I walked over to the Wing Commander's, office and explained what I had seen.*
>
> *He made a telephone call to the Air Ministry, who interviewed me a few hours later, following which I was advised not to make any enquiries about the incident, or discuss it with anybody else."*

3rd September USA: Three 'flying discs' seen

At 2pm over Spokane, Washington, Major R.J. Gardiner and his wife, along with a neighbour, saw what they described as metallic bronze 'discs', 20-30 feet long, by 2-6 feet thick, moving erratically in the sky for 5 minutes, although it appears the neighbour only saw one object.

(Source: Blue Book unknowns)

20th September – USA: Strange sighting over Colorado

At 10.49am two large, round, glowing UFOs with three smaller, internally lit objects, was seen hovering in the sky over Kit Carson, Colorado, for a minute, before moving away. As it did so, three smaller ones came from either behind or within the two larger objects, and the group shot off upwards and out of sight.

5th September – England: Lightning strikes twice!

Incredibly, Stanley Hubbard was to find himself, once again, sighting something unusual over the same airfield – this time on the afternoon of 5th September 1950. While with a group of men watching the sky, near the Flying Control building, waiting for the return of a Hawker P108 out on test flight, he noticed an object in the sky to the south, and grabbed hold of the nearest person – his civilian boss, Jack Spencer – and asked him what he thought the object was. When he saw it he shouted *"Oh, my God"*, and called for someone to fetch a camera. Nobody moved. He told someone to fetch a pair of binoculars and 'Taffy' Evans came up with a pair.

By this time a number of people were gathered watching the performance of this unidentified object, as it took off from what appeared to be an unstable hovering position to incredible speeds across the sky, in great angular steps of movement, ranging between 180-330 degrees. Once again, after bringing the incident to the attention of the Wing Commander, Stanley was interviewed by a group of men from the Scientific Intelligence Department.

Stanley said:

> *"What I saw was highly classified! They were very, very specific that I was not to discuss the matter with anybody, because it was highly classified."*

RAF test pilot, Stanley Hubbard

Over fifty years later, Dr. David Clarke searched declassified documents at the Public Records Office and found the report into the incidents, submitted by Scientific Intelligence. A copy was obtained and shown to Mr Hubbard, who was shocked to discover that both incidents had been explained away as either hallucinations or misidentifications!

During our communication with Mr Hubbard in 2006, about what he had witnessed, he told us he had been inundated by requests from TV and film-makers in the United Kingdom, including the BBC, to take part in further documentaries.

Stan:

> *"Such matters are now of no interest for me, especially after what I saw as a most embarrassing performance, broadcast by a group of total incompetents!"*

(Source: Personal interviews)

14. October, 2003

Dear John,

I am terribly sorry that my response to you has been delayed so long, but let me try to catch up.

I returned from a lengthy trip overseas with a return of the viral pneumonia that I thought I had got rid of the previous month, which laid me low for a couple of weeks. A quick recovery from that was further delayed by an accident I had while preparing our property here to withstand Hurricane Isabel, that left me with damaged hands and broken ribs which are taking a long time to heal, and this has been overtaken by another relapse of the pneumonia

Anyway, back to your letter of 26. June. You ask if I can approve a number of statements which quite clearly refer to a verbal report I gave to Scientific Intelligence representatives at Farnborough in 1950, but they certainly are not my words nor do they really describe what I reported at the time. So how can I in all good conscience approve those words. Those Scientific Intel. clowns that interviewed us couldn't, or were not allowed to, accurately report what I told them, and that miscarriage has caused much embarrassment. Dr. David Clark, whom apparently you know, has a copy of a paper I did for him on the subject some time back, and I'm sure he would talk to you about it..

Alas, the son-in-law you ask after, is no longer with us. He died back in 1980 along with my daughter, as a result of a head-on motor accident. I'm afraid I cannot help either with the name of the young lady who was the dispatcher at the Test Pilots School in 1950, you know that was a long time ago. Presumably the Frank you enquired about must be my old navigator who was with me at the time of the second sighting. He was a Flt.Lt. at the time, and a very fine Flight Test observer , and as far as I know he is now somewhere in South Africa. He also took part in the interviews we had at Farnborough a couple of years ago, which were put on the air by a group of total incompetents; a most embarrassing performance that I do not wish to repeat.

Now I am being inundated by requests from TV film-makers in the UK including the BBC to take part in a further series of documentaries. You may imagine my response to that nonsense. I will have no part in it.

I must thank you very much indeed for forwarding the material for my perusal. As you say there is an incredible amount of coverage of these phenomena, and it seems that public interest is being focused more onto it. I'm afraid I haven't the time to follow it closely, but I do wish you well in your endeavours.

Most Sincerely,

Stan

Stanley Hubbard

21st September – USA: UFO tracked on radar

MIT research associate and Air National Guard, Major M.H. Ligda, confirmed the radar tracking of an object during MIT tracking of USAF flight of F-84 or F-86 jet fighters, at 9.52am, over Provincetown, Massachusetts. *"The UFO's speed was 22 miles per minute (1200mph.) It was observed to make a turn of 11-12 Gs acceleration during the one minute observation."*

(Source: Project Blue Book unknowns)

September – England: Landed UFO seen in field at Surrey

Bernard Green (now in his late 60s) from Farnham, Surrey, was prompted to write to the Herald newspaper, Farnham (25.1.2002), after reading about Stanley Hubbard's sighting, wondering if what he had seen in September 1950, at Runfold, was connected.

> *"I was aged 16 and out walking when I spotted this mysterious object, which I took to be a balloon lying in a field at Whiteways Corner, Runfold. I then realised it was far too big. Apart from that, there were no cables or distinguishing fins that a barrage balloon would have had. All of a sudden it just accelerated at an incredible speed across the sky – out of sight in a few seconds.*
>
> *There appeared no sound or vapour trail seen. I thought, at the time, it may have been a seaplane being tested.*
>
> *Over the years I became experienced in flying, gliding, parachuting, and have flown aircraft, but never did I see anything like that again."*

(Source: Personal interview)

From: "Bernard Green" <bernard@bernardgreen.wanadoo.co.uk>
To: <johndawn@hansonholloway.fsnet.co.uk>
Sent: 15 May 2006 23:11
Subject: UFO

Dear John , I did not get your letter, I was not aware that the Herald printed a story of me sighting a UFO I wrote about a doodle –bug v1 which hit the farm adjacent to where I live. That was about 1945. However, I watched a UFO about 1949-195 . I wrote about it once a few years ago at the request of a friend. I did not tell any one before because I did not want to be considered mad. When I was young you could be locked away for less. I have no time to tell all at this moment. I am new to typing. I was about 15 yrs old and hiding from my father who wanted me to work.
It was a beautiful sunny day with a few high cumulus clouds. I was laying on my back in a field at Runfold, Farnham Surrey now GU10 1LZ. Above me was a barrage balloon - grey and shiny.
It was stationary, but the clouds were moving. Hang on. I thought. There were no vanes at the back or anywhere and no trailing wires, no basket. Then it accelerated NNE and out of sight ie 15 miles in seconds approx 4-5 secs . I thought that's from Farnborough RAE. But NEXT DAY the Daily Mirror paper front page showed that the day before was the first Test of the FLYING BEDSTEAD which was the start of the Jump Jet , IT WAS CHAINED TO THE GROUND WITH 20 FOOT CHAINS.
SOME TIME LATER I READ THAT MANY OFFICIALS , AIRMEN AND POLICE SAW WHAT I SAW.
What I saw had no sound, no lights, no windows, no smoke or contrail. I would estimate now that it was at about 3000 to 5000 ft elevation. The variant due to unknown size.
I knew what a balloon looked like , the Parachute Regiment trained in Aldershot.

Yours sincerely, Bernard Green. 01252 783100 evenings, my son Alfred Bernard Green was a Policeman , traffic at Guildford.

Plotting 'Bogeys' on Radar

Were the same 'hallucinations' tracked on radar at RAF Neatishead, Norfolk, in the same year, by Mrs Ena 'Stevey' Stevens, employed as an WRAF radar operator at the base? She had this to say:

> *"UFOs were frequently plotted on the radar scopes as unidentified, rather than 'Bogeys' – a term used to identify unidentified aircraft entering the wrong airspace. Contrary to the public's perception now, there was little excitement generated when UFOs were tracked on radar at the base on one of the four radar scopes, installed in the reposing cabin where l worked at the time.*
>
> *On one occasion I was plotting a Squadron of 24 Meteor Jets from RAF Marham, when, during a sweep, I noticed I was picking up twenty-five returning echoes, the last one being at a height of between five and one-hundred-thousand feet. I double-checked the information and then contacted the officer-in-charge, Squadron Leader 'Tiger' Shaw, ex 'Battle of Britain' pilot. After discussing the matter with him, I contacted the group leader of the formation by radio and asked him to confirm how many aircraft were operational. He replied, 'twenty-four'."*

Squadron Leader 'Tiger' Shaw consulted

> *"I then asked one of the pilots at the rear of the formation to obtain a visual image. He radioed back and said he could see what looked like a heat mist rising up and down behind the formation. As the aircraft began their landing descent, this 'heat mist' shot off upwards at a terrific speed, disappearing off both the height radar installations."*

Radar 'echo' picked up following cargo aircraft

Another commonplace occurrence relating to UFOs being tracked on radar, according to 'Stevey', involved the nightly flight of the Prestwick shuttle – a cargo aircraft that travelled between Prestwick, Scotland and London, Heathrow.

> *"Quite often the base radar would identify an echo trailing behind this aircraft, sometimes moving about rather than constant. This regular 'companion' became the subject of much conversation with other girls I worked with. Why it picked the shuttle and not other aircraft escapes me." (Source: Personal interview)*

The 'Sunday Dispatch' Newspaper

We should never underestimate the power of the media, or its capability to set the political agenda, even to the extent that it can drive government policy. This is as true today as it was in the post-war years.

This was the year that the newspaper headlines in the UK began to reflect growing concern about the number of UFO sightings brought to their attention. Prior to that there had, of course, been coverage, but this largely concerned US sightings and the reporting was often dismissive.

8th October – Major articles on UFOs by national newspapers

On the 8th October 1950 two major newspapers started a series of articles on the subject. *The Sunday Express* began to serialise Gerald Heard's book – *The Riddle of the Flying Saucers.* (The book was subsequently published in the US under the title – *Is Another World Watching?*) The rival *Sunday Dispatch*, a London paper, ran extracts from Frank Scully's – *Behind the Flying Saucers*, and Donald Keyhoe's – *The Flying Saucers are Real.*

However, it was not just the media who were clamouring for answers and pressing the Government for action. Some very senior Establishment figures felt that something should be done and lobbied on the subject, sometimes openly and sometimes behind the scenes. Some of these figures were quite prepared to express openly the view that some UFO sightings might well be extraterrestrial in origin.

12th October – England: Three 'flying saucers' seen over Lincolnshire

On 12th October 1950, four blazing 'orbs of light' were seen sweeping backwards and forwards in the sky over the UK – like the groundswell of some heavenly tide. A week later, on 19th October 1950, workmen at Tallington, near Stamford, Lincolnshire, reported having sighted three 'flying saucers', one of which was seen to break slowly away and head north-westwards.

(Source: Unidentified newspaper cutting)

15th October – USA: UFO, shaped like a bullet

At 3.20pm over Oak Ridge, Tennessee, Atomic Energy Commission Trooper Rymer, J. Money-maker, and Captain Zarzecki, sighted two shiny silver objects, shaped like a 'bullet' or 'bladder', leaving what looked like a smoky trail. One of them then vanished from view, leaving the other stationary in the sky, which was seen to leave and reappear several times further away.

(Source: Project Blue Book Unknowns)

20th October – England: Workman sights UFO over Isle of Wight

The catalogue of unexplained sightings continued with a report from a group of six workmen, who were taking their mid-morning break at Ramsey, Isle of Wight, on 20th October 1950, when one of them – Bob Marshall – noticed something unusual through a break in the clouds…

> *"…a long, narrow 'oblong', with rounded corners, clearly defined. The end of the 'oblong' was dark and solid looking, although the centre seemed almost transparent."*

(Source: Isle of Wight UFO Society/ *Daily Mail,* 21.10.1950 – 'Now Flying Saucers over Britain')

23rd October – USA: Three portholes on UFO

Ex-USAF pilot Frank Risher from Bonlee, North Carolina, was outside at 12.42pm when he sighted:

> *"…an aluminum object, shaped like a dirigible or Convair C-99 cargo plane, with three portholes, which arrived in the sky from the south-east and hovered 3-5 seconds, before flying away south-east 40 seconds later."*

Source: Project Blue Book unknowns)

25th October – Wales: Formation of UFOs seen

At 8pm on 25th October 1950, David Morgan from Lampeter was standing in the village of Bwichllan overlooking The Vale of Aeron, when he saw: "…what looked like five or six stars in formation, flying towards Cardigan Bay – bright and distinct."

30th October – Wales: Glittering 'stars' seen

Five days later, on 30th October 1950, two big glittering 'stars', showing long pointed 'tails', were seen moving slowly through the sky over Hirwaun, near Aberdare, Merthyr Tydfil, Wales, by a number of people in the town and surrounding areas, who contacted the authorities. Many of the reports told of seeing what looked like 'stars' either travelling together or 'attached to each other', approaching from the west and heading eastwards. Some people even described seeing them divide in flight.

(Sources: *South Wales News*, 31.10.1950 – 'Flying Saucers in Wales?'/*Western Mail*, 2.11.1950 – 'More say they saw Flying Saucer'/*Western Mail*, 4.11.1950 -'More about Flying Saucers'/ *Western Mail & South Wales News*, 4.11.1950)

30th October – England: UFO display over Devon

We learnt of a spate of UFO sightings that occurred on 30th October 1950 – this time over the Devon area – contained in a booklet entitled, *Flying Saucers Over The West*, written by Arthur Bearne, quote: 'Evidential reports of sightings of unidentified flying objects, over a period of 18 years, including that observed by the Authorities (October, 1950), Air Force personnel, and many other persons throughout the West Country and other parts of Britain.'

Mr Bearne described what he saw, at 7pm on 30th October 1950, while walking towards the kitchen door.

> *"I became aware of a light high over my head, westward of the direction of the house. Looking upwards, I was mystified to see a funnel-shaped stream of flames, chiefly white, descending pointed end first, in an absolute silent and peculiar manner. I stared most intently at this unusual and unaccountable sight, trying to think what it could possibly be. Was it a burning plane, which had caught fire and burst asunder (?), because it was not falling straight down but going at an unvarying angle and at a steady and apparently not fast speed, and there appeared something peculiar about the forward point of the flames, which at first I could not understand.*
>
> *After having been in my view for possibly a minute, the flames or flaming object, or objects, disappeared from my sight below the top of the roof of the house. In a very short while I saw it again but now, stranger*

Arthur Bearne

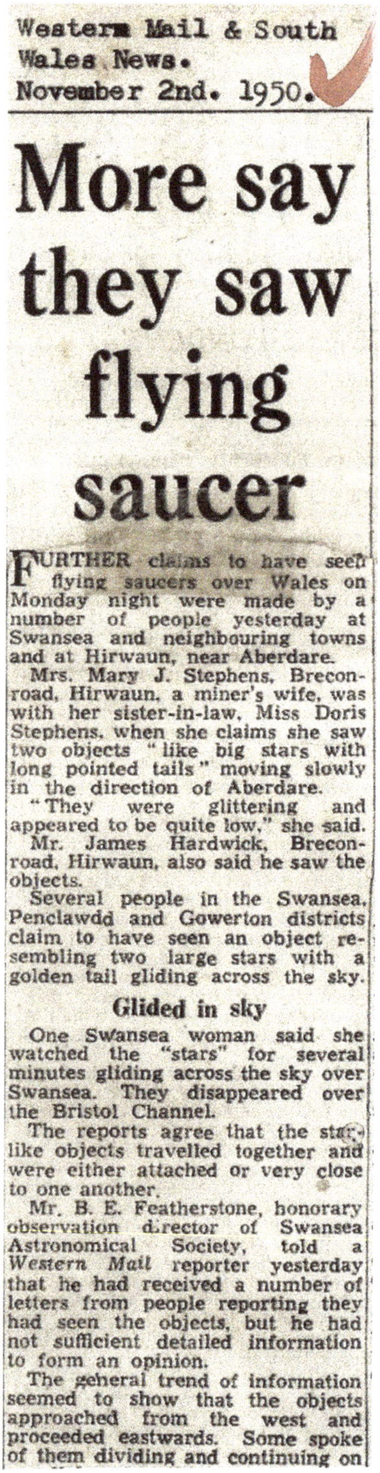

Western Mail & South Wales News. November 2nd. 1950.

More say they saw flying saucer

FURTHER claims to have seen flying saucers over Wales on Monday night were made by a number of people yesterday at Swansea and neighbouring towns and at Hirwaun, near Aberdare.

Mrs. Mary J. Stephens, Brecon-road, Hirwaun, a miner's wife, was with her sister-in-law, Miss Doris Stephens, when she claims she saw two objects "like big stars with long pointed tails" moving slowly in the direction of Aberdare.

"They were glittering and appeared to be quite low," she said.

Mr. James Hardwick, Brecon-road, Hirwaun, also said he saw the objects.

Several people in the Swansea, Penclawdd and Gowerton districts claim to have seen an object resembling two large stars with a golden tail gliding across the sky.

Glided in sky

One Swansea woman said she watched the "stars" for several minutes gliding across the sky over Swansea. They disappeared over the Bristol Channel.

The reports agree that the star-like objects travelled together and were either attached or very close to one another.

Mr. B. E. Featherstone, honorary observation director of Swansea Astronomical Society, told a *Western Mail* reporter yesterday that he had received a number of letters from people reporting they had seen the objects, but he had not sufficient detailed information to form an opinion.

The general trend of information seemed to show that the objects approached from the west and proceeded eastwards. Some spoke of them dividing and continuing on

still, I observed it not as a long stream of fire but a roughly spherical 'ball of fire', which was now travelling horizontally away from me in a southerly direction, towards Churston Ferrers and High Brixham – possibly not more than 500 feet high.

I observed this bunch aflame (by now some miles away) suddenly take an upward course and, to my amazement, I then saw ahead of the flames the forward portion of a huge 'disc', from which the flames appeared to recede as it climbed upwards (actually it could have been two 'discs', because in front of the 'disc' appeared to be a faint outline of a second 'disc')."

Telephoned the police

The next day Mr Bearne telephoned Paignton Police and reported the incident. He was then invited to visit the police station where he spoke to Chief Inspector G.H. Jewell, who told him they had received 'no other sighting reports'.

Sarcasm directed at him

As a result of some publicity given to the incident by the *Torquay Herald Express*, on 31st October 1950 ('Flying Saucer' seen at Paignton), Mr Bearne was to receive many sarcastic comments from his friends, although their attitudes changed when a number of people contacted him to corroborate his sighting, one of whom described seeing the object pass over Torquay, at 10.30pm.

Another witness was Murray Symons – the principal of an Okehampton firm. He was out walking with friends in Chagford, between 11pm and 11.30pm, when their attention was caught by what looked like a 'falling star' in the sky, some ten miles away from them, or thereabouts, at a height of some 2,000 feet.

> *"It suddenly pulled out of its rapid descent and flew horizontally across the July sky, followed by the sighting of a series of circular 'hoops of light' tapering slightly at each end, giving a cigar-like outline – the front of the object being brilliantly lit with a phosphorescent white light, followed by a mauve coloured light terminating in a red glow, like the exhaust at the end of a mechanically propelled machine."* **(Source: Richard Bearne)**

31st October – England: Cigar-shaped object over London

On 31st October 1950, a long cigar-shaped object, trailing sparks like hot ashes through the sky, was seen over Chiswick, heading towards Kent, and was later explained away as a shooting star.

2nd November – England: Police officer sights mysterious 'bars of light'

Two days later (2nd November), Detective Sergeant Ambrose, stationed at Gowerton, in Wales, sighted a single white 'ball of flame' crossing the sky during the evening – *"brighter than any star, which broke up into two 'stars', shedding sparks – resembling a bar of light, joined by two parts."*

5th November – England: Cigarette-shaped UFO seen over London

At 7am on 5th November 1950, Fred Wilkinson – staff manager for Pan American Airways, with previous experience in the RAF as an engineer, for some years – was supervising operations for a transatlantic flight, when he noticed:

> *"...a 'lighted body' approaching in the sky, heading east to west, at terrific speed. I thought, at first, that it was a jet, and then I saw from its shape and the presence of blue flame from the tail made this impossible. It flew in a straight line, rather than a curve as a shooting star or rocket would have done. I put its speed at 1,000 mph."*

Other personnel present confirmed the sighting. They included ex-anti aircraft gunner – Fred Perrier – who said:

Now—'Flying Saucers' over Britain

October 21, 1950.

By Daily Mail Reporter

SIX men saw what they claim was a Flying Saucer over Ramsey, Isle of Man, at 10.5 a.m. yesterday.

As far as is known no R.A.F. or civil planes were over Ramsey at the time.

The six, engineering workers, were having their mid-morning break by an open factory door when they saw the object.

Mr. Bob Marshall, 25, of Sulby, Isle of Man, said: "It first appeared in a break in the clouds. It was a long, narrow oblong, with rounded corners.

"It had a clear-cut outline. Each end of the oblong was dark and solid-looking, but the centre seemed to be almost transparent."

His workmates—Messrs. Brian Cottier, William Kelly, Michael Ball, Rex Bishop, and Clifford Skillithorne—confirmed his story.

> *"It was cigarette-shaped when I first saw it. It was not a jet aircraft, shooting star, comet, or firework."*

What appeared to be the same object was also seen by Mr P. Bell – a civil engineer from Didsbury, in Manchester, on 5th November 1950. He described it as *"circular, with a light shining from its underside."*

(Source:* Sunday Dispatch, 5.11.1950/*British Flying Saucer News Bulletin)

5th November – USA: Bean-shaped UFO

At 11.55am over Oak Ridge, Tennessee, Fairchild Aircraft illustrator – Don Patrick – sighted:

> *"...a translucent light-grey object with a dark core, shaped like a pear or bean, moving across the sky for 5-10 minutes in rapid, darting movements".*

6th November – England: 'Comet-like object' sighted over Southampton

On 6th November 1950, a 'flying saucer' or bluish comet-like object was seen travelling in an east to west direction, towards Southampton, at 7.35pm, followed by a similar object at 8pm.

7th November – England: UFO over Southampton

Was there a connection with another report of a 'flying saucer' sighted over London, at a speed estimated to be between 5-600 mph, by Mr Edward Leslie Docker (director of a firm), who was sitting in his office in Hindpool Road, Barrow-in-Furness, just before noon on 7th November 1950?

> *"Out of the clouds to the west came a huge 'thing', shaped like a cigar. The ends looked darker than the centre, which was aluminum in colour. It was flying at about 400ft, with a length estimated to be hundredfold."*

Another witness was ex-RAF serviceman – John Clarke, who pointed out that "it was too big to be an aircraft and had tapered ends". **(Source: *Daily Mail*, 8.1.1950 – 'Flying sausage is the latest')**

22nd November – England: Former RAF Officer sights UFO over Yeovil

Captain L. Nicholson of Yeovil – former RAF Officer, fully qualified in aircraft recognition – was standing in his garden, at 8.14pm on 22nd November 1950.

> *"It was a dark night, without a moon. Sounds could be heard a mile away, when I saw a dull red glow in the west, rather like a large 'ball of flame' rushing across the sky from just over the horizon. I called my wife and watched as it drew nearer and nearer. When I saw what it was I yelled, 'flying saucer', to my neighbour – Maurice Ring. We had a good view of it for between 15-20 seconds. It was a large circular disc, travelling at terrific speed, something in the region of 5-700mph, at a height of up to 1,500 feet, lit around the sides by a bluish flame. I have lectured many times on all types of British, American, and foreign aircraft, but have never seen any with the slightest resemblance of this object." (Source: Sunday Dispatch, 26.11.1950)*

1950 – England: Motorist overtaken by 'ball of light'

The intense publicity surrounding many UFO reports in that era were one of the reasons Joan Bygraves, from Oxfordshire, decided not to say anything about what she and her husband saw, while travelling home one evening, in 1950.

> *"It was pouring with rain, at the time, when all of a sudden, the road was lit up behind us – as if a car was going to overtake. I turned around to have a look, but could see nothing except darkness. In the split second it took to do this, a 'ball of light', about two feet in width, dropped from the roof, rolled down the windscreen, and then vanished. My husband and I*

talked it over and decided not to say anything, because of all the 'flying saucer' publicity. I'm glad that we didn't report it, because we now realise what we saw was more likely to be ball lightning than a UFO." **(Source: Personal letter)**

6th December – USA: 'Flying saucer'

At Fort Myers, Florida, former aircraft purchasing agent – Harry Lamp, and four boys, were outside using 10 x 8 binoculars, at 5pm, when they sighted a silver object in the sky with a red rim, 75 feet in length and 3-4 feet thick, showing a 'bubble' on top and two white and two orange jets along the side, During the time it was stationary, the centre of the object revolved. Suddenly, it took off very fast and disappeared from view. (Source: Project Blue Book unknowns)

10th December – England: Group Captain sights UFO over Kent

On 10th December 1950, Group Captain Cartmel was north-east of Sevenoaks, in Kent, when he saw a bright object heading across the sky, at approximately 150 mph and at a height of 3,000 feet.

1951

January – England: UFOs seen over Ipswich

WELL-KNOWN (at the time) Suffolk botanist and ornithologist *Irene Stubbings from Upland Road, Ipswich – happened to be looking out of her window at lunchtime, in January 1951.

> *"I saw what looked like two 'silver shillings', one behind the other, travelling high in the sky in a straight line, heading towards the south-west. They didn't appear to be going exceptionally fast, as I had them in view for over a minute."*

8th January – USA: Triangular lights

At 10.45pm, south of Fort Worth, Texas, Mr and Mrs W.J. Boggus, with other unnamed drivers and passengers in other cars, stopped to watch two groups of stationary red and green lights in the sky, forming a triangle, which were then seen to move away shortly afterwards.

12th January – USA: Fan-shaped UFO

At 10pm, over Fort Benning, Georgia, an illuminated object, showing a fan-shaped trail, was seen stationary in the sky by US Army 2nd Lt. A.C. Hale. After about 20 minutes it then sped away.

16th January – USA: Objects seen over research balloon

Two members of a balloon project from the General Mills Aeronautical Research Laboratory, Artesia, New Mexico, with the manager of Artesia Airport, and three pilots, were observing their 110 feet balloon, at an altitude of 112,000 feet, when a dull white, round object was spotted. It appeared larger than the balloon, but made no movement. Later, the balloon crew and the others saw two

*Irene Gertrude Nash was born at Lowestoft, Suffolk, in 1881, daughter of Arthur Nash, a fish merchant, and his wife Elizabeth Curtis nee Ling, who married at St. Saviour's, Southwark, in 1875. By 1891 the family had moved to The Lodge, The Elms, Ramsgate, Kent, where she studied at Ramsgate School of Art. Irene married at Margate in 1909, Arthur Edmund Stubbings, a manager in a confectionery business, and they moved to 13 Holly Road, Ipswich where Irene continued her studies at Ipswich School of Art, under George Rushton. She was also member of Ipswich Art Club 1935-1956 and a regular exhibitor. She died at Ipswich in 1956, aged 75.

objects from the airport, flying side-by-side; they circled the balloon and flew away to the north-east. The second observation lasted about 40 seconds. **(Source: Project Blue Book unknowns)**

26th February – USA: UFO seen hovering over airbase

At 7.10am, USAF Sergeant J.B. Sells, of Ladd Air Force Base, Alaska, sighted a dull-grey metallic object, estimated to be 120 feet long and 10-12 feet thick in the sky. "*It hovered, puffed smoke, and then shot away after 1-1½ minutes.*"

5th April – England: Triangular UFO seen over village

Retired Royal Navy Officer Richard Manders was living in Boarshunt – a small village near Portsmouth – and was driving home with his wife and friends, after having been to see friends at Bishop's Waltham, at 11.10pm. They were surprised to see three round lights, hovering above the village, and stopped the car to get out for a closer look.

> *"They formed a triangular pattern in the sky, one top, two bottom, roughly 200 feet apart; suddenly they all merged into one and shot straight upwards, disappearing from sight." (Source: Ron West)*

May – England: Formation of UFOs seen over Isle of Wight

Shanklin resident Cecily Tait was pushing Jack (aged two-and-a-half) in his pushchair, sometime between 3-5pm in May 1951, along the cliff path at Keats Green, Shanklin, towards the Chine end, on a clear, cloudless day.

> *"My attention was drawn to five white blobs, like little white round clouds, forming a rough 'V' pattern – apparently over the sea.*
>
> *I glanced away. When I looked back, they had gone – completely vanished in within 10-12 seconds of observation."*

(Source: Letter to Kath Smith, Isle of Wight UFO Society)

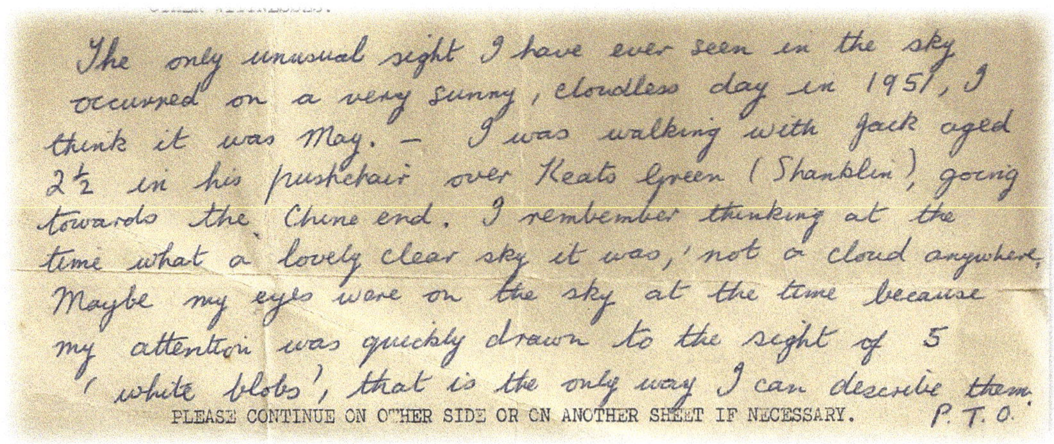

The only unusual sight I have ever seen in the sky occurred on a very sunny, cloudless day in 1951, I think it was May. – I was walking with Jack aged 2½ in his pushchair over Keats Green (Shanklin), going towards the Chine end. I remember thinking at the time what a lovely clear sky it was, not a cloud anywhere. Maybe my eyes were on the sky at the time because my attention was quickly drawn to the sight of 5 'white blobs', that is the only way I can describe them.

PLEASE CONTINUE ON OTHER SIDE OR ON ANOTHER SHEET IF NECESSARY. P.T.O.

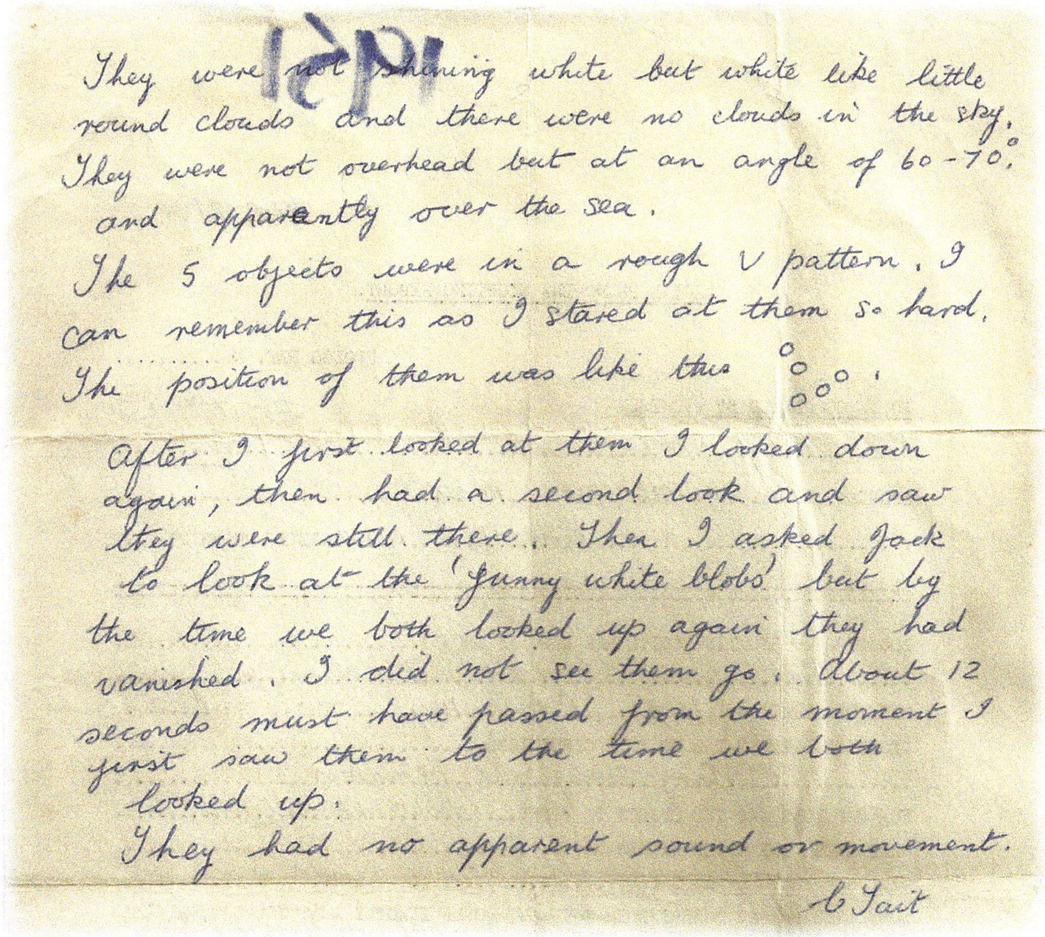

1951

They were not shining white but white like little round clouds and there were no clouds in the sky. They were not overhead but at an angle of 60-70°. and apparently over the sea.

The 5 objects were in a rough V pattern. I can remember this as I stared at them so hard. The position of them was like this °°° .

After I first looked at them I looked down again, then had a second look and saw they were still there. Then I asked Jack to look at the 'funny white blobs' but by the time we both looked up again they had vanished. I did not see them go. About 12 seconds must have passed from the moment I first saw them to the time we both looked up.

They had no apparent sound or movement.

C Tait

June – England: UFO over River Thames

From the archives of Project Blue Book, we discovered a letter sent to Captain (later Major) Hector Quintanilla by John G. Young – then living at Klamath Falls, Oregon:

> *"Dear Captain Quintanilla,*
>
> *I saw in the paper recently how you take UFOs seriously. I have had a little secret for about 13 years, but always feared of being labeled as a crackpot, but at this stage I couldn't care less. Our home in England was about 500 yards from the River Thames, half-way between the towns Kingston and Richmond, Surrey. I was home on a 3-day pass from the Army, in June 1951, when I happened to glance up and was startled to see a very big, bright, circular object. It stayed over our position above the river for what seemed a long time, although it may have been only a minute. I longed for a camera, or other witness, but there was none to be seen or heard. I had heard of 'flying saucers' with portholes around the side, but this was just a silvery bright object, size of an average parachute. It was as a plate, or saucer.*

After an eternity, I moved a couple of steps. (I was going to run for aid.) In a twinkling, it was gone. It was not a weather balloon – its brightness was from within.

Yours truly,

John G. Young"

It is clear then, as it is now, that reports of strange unidentified objects seen moving through our airspace were classified by the Air Ministry of Defence as being secret. This particular file was not released until 2001 – 50 years later!

Captain Hector Quintanilla

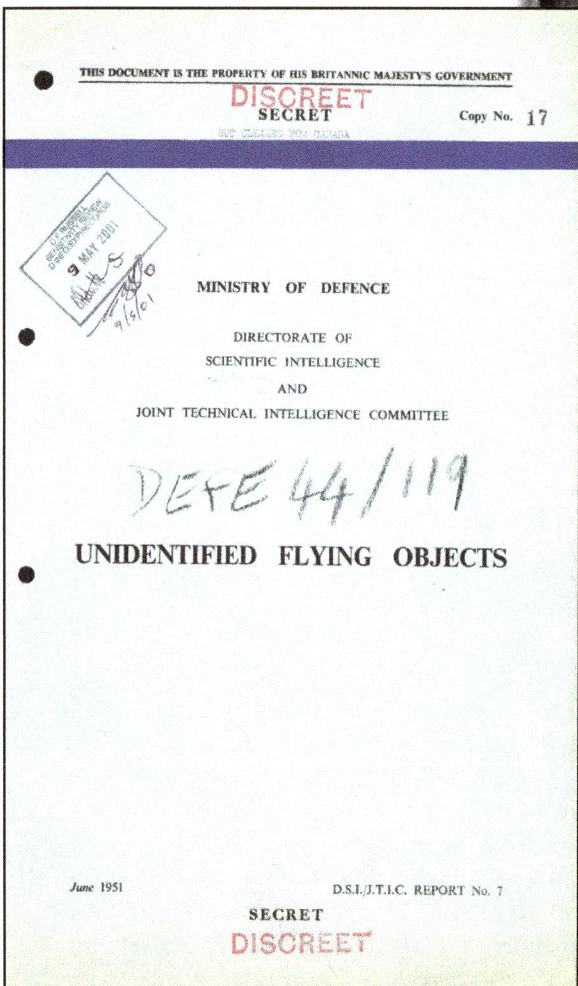

THIS DOCUMENT IS THE PROPERTY OF HIS BRITANNIC MAJESTY'S GOVERNMENT

DISCREET

SECRET

Copy No. 17

9 MAY 2001

MINISTRY OF DEFENCE

DIRECTORATE OF SCIENTIFIC INTELLIGENCE AND JOINT TECHNICAL INTELLIGENCE COMMITTEE

DEFE 44/119

UNIDENTIFIED FLYING OBJECTS

June 1951

D.S.I./J.T.I.C. REPORT No. 7

SECRET

DISCREET

1st June – USA: UFO over Niagara Falls

At 4.20am, over Niagara Falls, New York, M/Sgt H.E. Sweeney, and two enlisted men, sighted a glowing yellow-orange, saucer-shaped object, with arc-shaped wings. It then flew straight upwards and was lost from view, 30-40 seconds later.

24th July – USA: Tubular fin-shaped object sighted

Over Portsmouth, New Hampshire, Hanscom Air Force Base Operations Officer – Captain Cobb, and Corporal Fein, were on duty at 7.10am, when they sighted a grey 100-200 feet tubular object, five times long as wide, with fins at one end, showing 'many black spots on the body', flying through the sky at a speed estimated to be between 800-1,000 mph, at 1-2,000 feet altitude, leaving a faint swath as it did so – gone in seconds.

Summer – England: 'Flying disc' over Grimsby

In the summer of 1951, Mr J.P. Roddam of Roundway, Grimsby, who had seen service with the Royal Observer Corps, was with his mother and sister when they sighted:

> *"...a plain, flat, dull-grey coloured 'disc', with clean cut edges, moving irregularly through the sky over Durham, towards the north-east, in a sort of tumbling action, catching the sun – visible for over an hour, at an angle of 30 degrees off the horizon."*

(Source: UFOLOG)

31st August – USA: Pear-shaped object sighted

At 12.45pm, Mrs Tom Tilson of Matador, Texas, was with a another woman, when they sighted a pear-shaped object with a length of a B-29 fuselage (100 feet), aluminum or silver, with a port or some type of aperture on the side. It moved with smaller end forward, drifting slowly at about 150 feet altitude – then headed up in an arc across the sky and out of sight after a few seconds.

(Source: Blue Book unknowns)

Summer – Scotland: Orange UFO follows tractor

In early summer 1951, a farmer from Ballintuim, Scotland, was towing a trailer, with his two daughters. Suddenly, an orange object appeared at the rear of the vehicle and followed them, before disappearing over a nearby hill. The farmer described the object as looking like:

> *"...two soup bowls, joined together, with a rim around them. It was about 14 feet in diameter, 12 feet high, 100 feet away from us, and about 70 feet off the ground."*

(Source: Gemini Magazine)

England: RAF jets followed by white 'discs' over Norwich

Maurice Jackson from Attleborough, near Norwich, spoke of what he saw at Primary School in 1951:

> *"I was in the playground, at lunchtime, when I was amazed to see a group of RAF jets heading towards the north, being followed by two or three tiny white 'discs'. It never entered my mind they could have been 'flying saucers'. This was an unfamiliar term to me at the time. All I can tell you is what I saw. It has stuck in my mind ever since. I have no idea what these things were."*

July – England: RAF employee sights 'diamond' UFO

Mr Leonard Burrell from Kessingland, Suffolk, was completing his National Service at RAF Church Lawford, just outside Rugby, Northamptonshire.

> *"The camp was split into two sections by a country road. On one side was the main camp, consisting of a runway with perimeter tracks at both ends. On the other side what was loosely termed, 'The School', consisting of about ten Nissan huts in various stages of*

deterioration, and a single storey brick building containing Administration offices, linked by a cinder track to a large field, with trees all around. During the time I was there, the landing strip was only used by a couple of 'Chipmunks' (training aircraft doing 'circuits and bumps'). The School (run independently from the main camp) was used to give new entrants a preliminary grounding in the art of building emergency airstrips. Both 'sides' even had their own security guards.

'Bright light' seen in the sky

One Sunday, in mid-July 1951, I found myself in the unfortunate position of being posted to camp security as Guard Commander, supervising two rather green National servicemen, who had been in the RAF for ten weeks, in contrast to myself – an 'old hand' of eighteen months' service, at the age of 21. I spent Sunday morning finishing an oil painting, taking into consideration that our duties as Guards was not to walk around the camp like a guard, but to keep an eye on things. At about 12.25pm, I instructed the lads to fetch their lunch and off they went with mugs and 'eating irons' clutched in their hands in the regulation manner. I lay on my back, gazing at the sky, rather absent-mindedly thinking about my forthcoming marriage, when something caught my eye – a bright light, brighter than the sun behind it. It seemed to flash on and off at one second intervals, clearly visible against a blue sky with a few high feathery clouds far away on the horizon. I looked at my wristwatch (12.35pm), and continued to observe the object.

Diamond like object seen descending

Approximately ten minutes later, the object had descended low enough for me to make out precisely what it looked like. I estimated it to be between five and ten feet long and three to six feet wide in the middle. It was silver metallic in appearance, with a very high gloss to its outer surface, and seemed to have been constructed from glass-like material, with a mirror finish.

It reminded me of a very large diamond, with finely cut edges. The object was now at its lowest point, about 500 feet off the ground and 2-300 yards away, appearing to rest for a while, for several seconds, over a group of trees near the school buildings.

Suddenly, a number of birds that had been roosting in the trees flew up into the air and headed towards the UFO, as though attracted by it. None of them actually went near it but, within a split second, they all turned and headed away from the object, screeching as they went. The whole area around the school went completely quiet. You could not hear one bird until the object disappeared, when they started to sing again. As the birds flew off, the UFO began to move slowly upwards, still turning at the same speed and flashing regularly, with bright sunlight reflecting off each facet of its surface. Within 20 minutes it had gone."

Len contacted the nearest RAF weather station and explained what he had seen. They confirmed that no weather balloons were in the area that day, and could not offer any logical explanation for the sighting.

2/ Enclosed is the picture of yours truly as promised which was taken in September 1952, almost exactly two months after I spotted the UFO.
It was interesting to see the SUN headline's last week ---- "ARMY SPOT UFO's OVER SHROPSHIRE", perhaps you know more about it than recorded in the paper, unfortunately I never had an opportunity to read the actual article.

Incidentally, I am going to try and find an article I wrote about my sighting for a small amateur, local magazine call "The Lantern" that recorded strange happenings that had been experienced by local folk.

That was about 20 years ago, so you can compare the item with what I told you, and they should be identical, assuming the passage of time hasn't elaborated what was seen.

Anyway, I hope you get some good news soon from a prospective agent or publisher, and do please let me know when you do!

Sincerely,

Len

"I received the impression they thought I had 'a touch of the sun' and should have consulted a psychiatrist!"

Len pondered on why such a device should descend over a small British Aerodrome with no particular 'claim to fame', until he remembered something of great possible significance:

The perimeter tracks at Church Lawford were being used to store a great deal of plant and equipment, recovered from the disastrous 'Groundnut Scheme' (a Government blunder which cost the taxpayer millions of pounds and ended in utter chaos). Was it possible the UFO was attracted to something which, from the air, looked like two figure eights joined by a central lane, or was there another reason?

4th/5th September – England: UFO landing at Brighton – occupants seen

On the 4th or 5th September 1951, Mrs Sheila Burton – then in her late teens – was visiting her parents at Withdean, on the outskirts of Brighton, Sussex. After waking up at 6.30am, she went over to the bedroom window overlooking the long garden and was looking out over the early morning ground mist, as the sun began to rise, when she saw something large and flashing, followed by the landing of a silvery-green, light green, or lime-coloured dome-shaped craft.

Three entities came out of the object

Panel-like doors opened and out came three 'men', who moved in a straight line across the lawn.

"They were five to six feet in height, with bald heads, wearing a dark green khaki one-piece garment and holding what looked like a 'machine-gun device'. The 'men' continued walking for about 30 feet and then simultaneously began to walk backwards to the craft and re-

entered their respective panels, which closed. Red flashing lights restarted and the object shot upwards, vertically, and became lost from sight."

During further conversation with UFO researcher Andy Collins, Mrs Burton told him that she estimated the diameter of the craft to be 40 feet and 25 feet in height, and the red flashing lights to be six to seven feet below the apex, equally spaced around the perimeter of the dome. Nothing could be seen of the interior of the craft.

The occupants of the 'craft'

In respect of the occupants of the 'craft', the witness was able to supply a wealth of information:

"Their bodies were rather thin in proportion to their size; their legs seemed thick but short; they had long arms with hands similar to our own; faces were expressionless; the nose, small and pointed; mouth, small with no lips; eyes were small and deep-set; ears were also pointed; skin was similar complexion to ours; from the right shoulders down to the left-hand side were thick black bands, which joined onto a stomach belt, also black, of the same thickness."

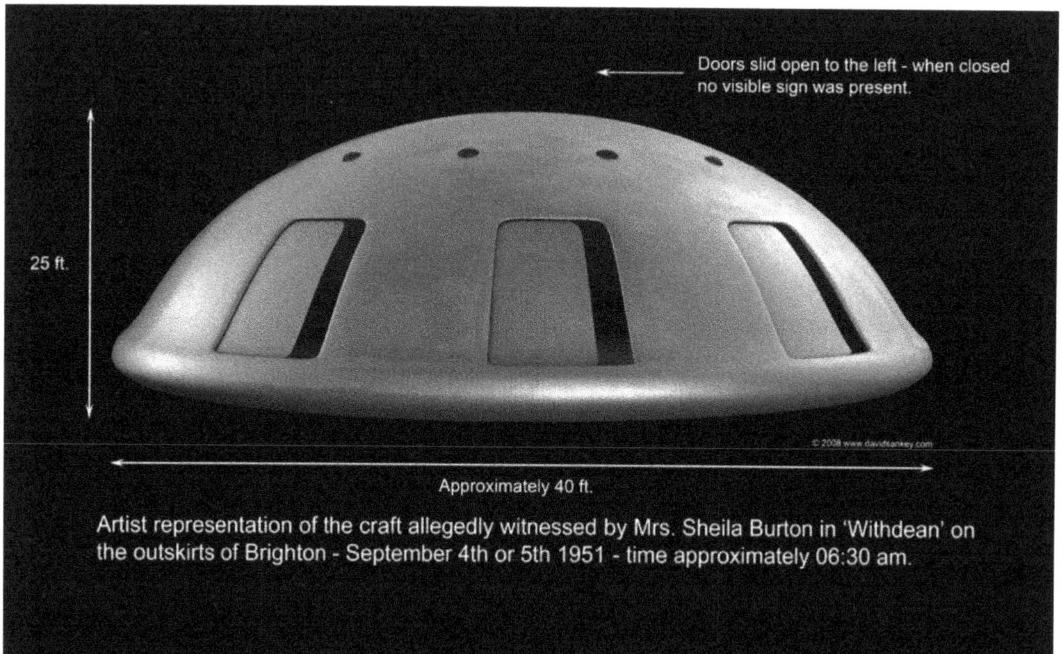

Artist representation of the craft allegedly witnessed by Mrs. Sheila Burton in 'Withdean' on the outskirts of Brighton - September 4th or 5th 1951 - time approximately 06:30 am.

Wearing devices resembling a black cylinder

"Each held a device like a machine-gun in shape – like a black cylinder, some twenty inches long by three inches in diameter, rounded off at the rear, with a point at the end. About a third of the way along the cylinder from the rear end was a black rectangular shape fitted onto its underside – like a magazine. Another shorter, wider, rectangle protruded from the top above the magazine; both rectangles seemed to have vertical engraved lines running down them. These devices were carried with both hands but they appeared to do nothing with them. Their movements were like mindless robots, carrying out pointless duty – an impression strengthened when they stopped and retracted their footsteps."

Without doubt this was one of the most impressively thorough descriptions we had ever come across of an apparent alien 'craft' and its occupants.

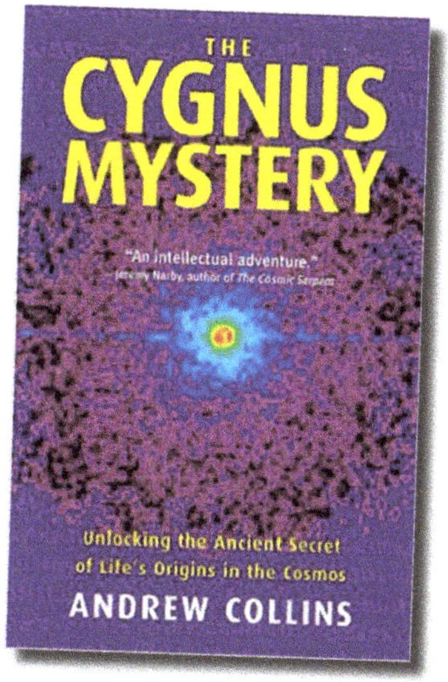

Whilst there are many who believe the sighting represents an example of interaction by an alien species, whose actions defy human conception and logic, we should be very careful in evaluating an intelligence that may well be as far removed from us as we are from them. We should also be mindful about dismissing, contrary to popular speculation, the myth that the UFO entities and their 'flying saucers' are not likely to be representative of an extraterrestrial intelligence, purely because of the distance involved.

We think it logical that during the history of the planet, 'alien' artifacts may have already landed and that it would be arrogant not to believe this. The problem lies with attempting to apply human traits of believed behaviour to an intelligence whose existence apparently flourishes side by side with man, rather than through visitations achieved by colossal journeys from far-off destinations light years away. But what if 'they' are able to manipulate time and space, taking into consideration their 'craft' has been plotted on radar moving at incredible speeds? How do we know what 'they' are really capable of? One thing is assured, if 'they' wanted to adopt a hostile attitude towards us, we would undoubtedly come off the worse.

Andy Collins

Andrew Collins was raised in the Essex town of Wickford. As a teenager, he became a UFO investigator, and in 1977 he investigated the first-ever missing time abduction case reported in the UK, and that investigation changed his life. He became a journalist with the magazine Strange Phenomena and openly sought the help of psychics in an attempt to better understand the relationship between UFOs, prehistoric sites, earth energies, and the human mind. As a science and history writer, he has authored a variety of books that challenge the way we perceive the past, including his best-selling The Cygnus Mystery, that delves into how ancient monuments and temples, that are still standing today, were built with an orientation towards Cygnus.

Purpose of sash or belt worn diagonally – unknown

In respect of the entities seen by the witness Sheila, the reader will come across countless other occasions involving the sighting of similar 'beings.' What part the 'sash' or belt worn diagonally across the chest plays, we do not know; perhaps the commonality owes more to the human belief system about UFOs than any standard 'uniform.'

6th September – USA: Six orange 'lights' sighted

At 7.20pm, over Claremont, California, S/Sgt W.T. Smith and M/Sgt L.L. Duel sighted six orange 'lights' in an irregular formation, flying on a straight course across the sky, before being lost in a bank of coastal fog a few minutes later.

(Source: Project Blue Book unknowns)

September – England: Twenty UFOs seen by family, over London

In the same month Monica Manders (30) of Shooters Hill Road, Blackheath, London, was out in the garden one bright sunny morning, with her parents, when their attention was caught by a strange object in the sky:

> *"It appeared to be a solid object, flying very high, moving slowly. It was roughly the shape of a rugby ball and to us – even at that height – it appeared to be two thirds the size of a rugby ball. It shone silvery white and was clear and distinct. It disappeared from our view a few minutes later, heading southwards. Then another one appeared, heading along the same route from the north-west direction. In all, we watched twenty of these objects moving across the sky before swinging sharply southwards. They looked like small oblong airships but with nothing suspended beneath them."*

2nd October – USA: UFO with clipped tail seen

At 6pm, Battelle Memorial Institute graduate physicist Howard Cross, from Columbus, Ohio, sighted a bright, oval-shaped object, with a clipped tail, flying across the sky – before fading into the distance, a minute later.

9th October – USA: Civil Aviation Authority Chief sights UFO

At 1.42pm, over Terre Haute, Indiana, CAA Chief Aircraft Communicator – Roy Messmore – was on duty at Hulman Municipal Airport, when he saw a round, silver object, flying directly overhead, reaching the horizon in 15 seconds. (Note: A very similar incident happened three minutes later, near Paris, Illinois, 15 miles north-west, and was also listed as 'unidentified' for several years, but was eventually reclassified.) **(Source: Project Blue Book Unknowns)**

11th October – USA: Balloonists sight UFOs

At 6.30am, balloon researchers from Minneapolis, Minnesota, including aeronautical engineer Mr J.J. Kaliszewski, aerologist Mr C.B. Moore, and pilot Dick Reilly, were aloft in the air, with Doug

Smith on the ground, when the flight crew saw the first object – a brightly glowing one, with a dark underside and a halo around it, moving high above them through the sky. It then decreased its speed and was seen to make a number of slow climbing circles, for about two minutes, before finally heading away, eastwards, five minutes later. A short time afterwards another object was seen, as confirmed by ground observers, using a theodolite. This, too, headed away at speed but was only seen for a few seconds. [Authors: Was it the same one?] **(Source: Project Blue Book unknowns)**

24th November – USA: Pilots sight UFO

At 3.53pm, USAF pilots W.H. Fairbrother and D.E. Stewart, in P-51 Mustangs, were flying over Mankato, Minnesota, when they sighted a milky-white object, shaped like a Northrop flying wing (broad, slightly swept-back wing with no fuselage or tail) with an estimated 8 feet span, heading in a straight trajectory across the sky – out of sight, five seconds later.

7th December – USA: UFO activity reported

At 8.15am, Oak Ridge, Tennessee, Atomic Energy Commission guard Mr J.H. Collins sighted a 20 feet square object – white-grey but not shiny – flying above the ridge towards the clouds and back again, twice, taking 30-40 seconds each time, during 30 minutes of observation. Later that afternoon, at 4.30pm, Sunbury, Ohio, amateur astronomer Carl Loar was looking through his telescope, when he saw a silvery sphere, with two specks at the sides. The object then appeared to explode and was replaced by a dark cloud with many specks.

Saucers Bob Up— Again In Reports

Ridge Informants Insist Object Seen There Was 'Big As A House'

By BILL ANDERSON

OAK RIDGE, Oct. 25—Reports that an object like a flying saucer was seen near the top-secret Nuclear Energy for the Propulsion of Aircraft project here grew stronger today.

But they are all second hand reports like so many of the other stories about flying saucers.

The NEPA project is a joint effort by the Air Force, the Atomic Energy Commission, and several aircraft companies to make a study of the application of atomic energy to the propulsion of aircraft.

The reports, all unofficial and from private sources, described the object as "silver—like an airliner, and apparently of aluminum construction."

"When in the air it was accompanied by the sound of jets," they said.

FIRST RIDGE REPORT

It was the first detailed report of such an object to appear in the atomic city.

AEC officials told The Journal that they have "no comment on such reports." The commission *recently passed out forms for guards* at the Los Alamos plant to fill out in case they saw flying saucers. The forms were not *distributed here.*

The reports started to filter into The Journal Oak Ridge Bureau two weeks ago. They were at first discounted, due to the fact that on the same day the reports started the story of the AEC queries in Los Alamos appeared in The Journal.

Yesterday two reports were re-

Continued on Page 9, Col. 1

Saucer Reports Bob Up Again In Ridge Reports

Informants Say Aluminum Object Rose Near Secret Project, Was 'Big As A House'

CONTINUED FROM PAGE ONE

ceived, both from usually reliable sources.

The saucer-looking object was seen late Thursday, Oct. 12—a few hours before the form story appeared.

The following description was given *of the object: "It was round* and big as a four-room house. The *color was silver*—like an airliner, and it was of aluminum construction, or an element looking like aluminum. There was a "blister" at the top of the saucer, and it had windows.

ROSE—AND SWOOSH!

"The object rose, very *slowly*, for about 100 feet, and then moved slightly forward. The *Journal* informant said. "Again it rose, about the same *distance up and forward* and then—swoosh! It was gone *at a fast rate* of speed."

The person added that the object, *during* its fast flight away from the vicinity, seemed to "flatten out."

None of the sources questioned by The Journal had seen the object; they had just talked to someone who said they had seen it. And it was *obvious that the persons* who said they saw it did *not realize what* they were telling might fall under the head of classified or secret information. Strict security rules cover *all* classified material.

While the official AEC statement *was "no comment," checks* with several other sources indicate a rumor of the *same object* has made its rounds of the government *buildings here.*

In a routine check with various officials connected with the project here, the following information was *given to them, and then* a series of *questions asked:*

"Several persons working near and *around the* NEPA project and the K-25 plant have stated an object, termed by them as a 'flying saucer,' was seen early Oct. 13 or late Oct. 12 in the K-25 area.

"Have you heard similar reports *of the same type objects* near that area or the NEPA project either at those times or at an earlier or later date?"

NO AEC COMMENT

Gordon Molesworth, assistant to the manager for Public Information here, said, "no comment" to the questions.

Will Cole, public relations at NEPA said "no."

Both offices said flatly that there had been no "official" information *passed on to them.*

The latest quarterly report issued by the Office of Public Information for the AEC has a lot to say about the atomic propulsion project, *but no recent information* as to progress at the *plant.*

Last week, one woman *reported* to The Journal that her neighbor had spotted what she had described as a flying saucer. Her description placed *the object flying* in circles over the area for some *length of time*. Earlier in the same day, a fighter plane, stationed in Knoxville for protectional purposes here, had been flying over the area.

Previous reports during the past year came from the usual run of reporting *flying saucers*. One scare turned out to be a weather balloon that had broken its ties with the local weather station. Several persons saw the balloon, which accompanied by air pockets and directional winds, plus a light for the weather *observers*, actually appeared to be a saucer.

Another case was two jet plane,

1952

January – England: UFO over Canterbury

VERA Mathews from Bramble Farm, Sturry, near Canterbury, was watching a beautiful sunset, one evening in January 1952, when she noticed something moving across the sky at a great height, from North to South.

> *"It appeared to be oblong in shape, two feet long and six inches deep. Its colour was golden and the nose of the object appeared to have flames shooting from it, as it ploughed through the sky. When it was over Canterbury, I lost sight of it but a couple of minutes later it reappeared – this time travelling from South to North, but I lost sight of it again as it went behind the woods, towards the direction of Whitstable. As an ex-WRAF Officer, I am familiar with many types of aircraft and can definitely state that what I saw did not fit into this category."* **(Source: Isle of Wight UFO Society)**

5th January – USA: UFO over lake

George Griffin was out fishing, near Lake Helen, when he saw:

> *"...a dark object about the size of a water bucket, travelling slowly high across the sky in a North to South direction. I watched it for 15 minutes and noted that it left a white trail – similar to smoke, though no flames were seen. This was still visible for 15 minutes after it had gone out of sight."*

(Source: *DeLand Sun News*, 6.1.1952 – 'Reports strange object in sky')

29th January – England: Pear-shaped UFO sighted over Hampshire

On the 29th January 1952, Gladys Keevil from Christchurch, Hampshire, was awoken by a bright light flooding the bedroom, between 2am and 3am. Knowing it could not be moonlight, because the moon does not shine on that side of the house, she got out of bed to see what it was.

> *"Hanging in the sky was an object, shaped like a pear, with the big end downwards, glowing with a red firelight glow; I went into my next room and awoke my son, and we watched it*

> *for a quarter-of-an-hour, until it faded away. It was a clear night and the object seemed a fairly good distance away."* **(Source: Isle of Wight UFO Society)**

11th February – USA: Pilots sight UFO

At 3am, while over Pittsburgh, Pennsylvania, Captain G.P. Arns and Major R.J. Gedson, flying a Beech aircraft trainer, sighted a yellow-orange comet-shaped object, pulsing flame for a few seconds, before it was lost from sight.

(Source: Project Blue Book unknowns)

20th February – USA: Red fiery object seen zigzagging in the sky

Mrs Mae Lee of Long Beach, and two other people, saw:

> *"...a 'fiery ball' in the heavens, while driving between Riverside and Corona, on the late afternoon. We parked and watched it for about 15 minutes. It seemed to drop straight from far in the heavens. Finally it began to zigzag, before going up into the sky."*

(Source: Project Blue Book unknowns)

21st February – USA: Three green 'balls of fire' observed

Richmond newspaper employee Robert Carruthers, along with a group of carrier boys, sighted three green 'balls of fire' in the sky, at dusk. **(Source: *Springfield Union*, Massachusetts, 21.2.1952 – 'Balls of fire are reported in sky by West Coast viewers')**

28th February – England: Student sights UFO over Cambridge

Keith B. Wedmore (19), at Cambridge University studying Law and History, was walking through the college at 10.40pm on 28th February 1952, when he noticed a bright round object in the sky travelling north-east.

> *"It was evenly bright all over a perfectly round surface, which presented me broadside on, except that at the bottom there was a particularly bright spot of light that made the rest of it look like a halo around a candle flame. I watched it for perhaps 15 seconds, until it went out of sight, and during this time it made no noise whatever. I could not tell what size, or what height it was."*

(Source: Letter to *Sunday Dispatch*, 20th April 1952)

Heavy UFO activity recorded over the United States for this period

20th March – USA: Saucer-shaped 'light' seen

At 10.42pm, a dull orange-yellow, saucer-shaped 'light' was seen moving across the sky on a straight trajectory over Centreville, Maryland, by WWl/WW2 veteran A.D. Hutchinson, and his son. Thirty seconds later, it was gone from view.

(Source: Blue Book unknowns)

23rd March – USA: Mysterious red fireballs sighted

At 6.56pm, the pilot and radar operator of an F-94 jet interceptor were over Yakima, Washington, when they sighted a stationary 'red fireball' in the sky, during a 45 second observation. At 7pm, another similar object was seen. Both were seen to increase in brightness and then fade, before being lost from view. [Project Blue Book Status Report #7 (31st May 1952) says target was also tracked by ground radar at 78 knots (90 mph) at 22,500 feet and 25,000 feet altitude.]

(Source: Blue Book unknowns)

24th March – USA: Tracked on radar

At 8.45am, 60 miles west of Point Conception, California, a B-29 navigator and radar operator tracked an unidentified target for 20-30 seconds, at an estimated speed of 3,000 mph.

(Source: Blue Book unknowns)

4th April – USA: Tracked on radar

At 7.30pm, two radar operators of the 147th AC & W Squadron, based at Duncanville, Texas, tracked an object for one minute by radar, moving at an estimated speed of 2,160 mph.

(Source: Blue Book unknowns)

5th April – USA: Three objects sighted over Phoenix

At l0.40am, over Phoenix, Arizona, Mr and Mrs L.G. Ryan, Mr R.L. Stokes, and Mr D. Schook sighted a large, dull-grey circular object, followed by two more, moving straight across the sky at high speed. On the same day – this time over Miami, Florida, at 9.15pm, Mr L.E. VanDercar and his nine-year-old son, sighted:

> *"...four dark circular objects, with fuzzy edges, crossing the face of the moon; each was half the apparent diameter of the moon".*
>
> **(Source: Project Blue Book unknowns)**

6th April – USA: Huge formation of 'flying discs' witnessed

At 2.59pm, it was reported that over Temple, Texas, a total of 50-75 grey-white 'discs' were seen moving through the sky, some changing position within the formation continually, tilting in unison every 12-15 seconds during the four minutes of observation. **(Source: Blue Book unknowns)**

14th April – USA: Pilots sight 'inverted bowl' UFO

At 6.34pm, over Memphis, Tennessee, US Navy pilots – Lt. Junior grade Blacky and Lt. Junior grade O'Neil – sighted what they described as an 'inverted bowl', 3 feet long and 1 feet high, with vertical slots, flying through the sky on a straight heading at speed, 100 yards from their aircraft, for between 45-60 seconds of observation. At 12.35pm, over LaCrosse, Wisconsin, several light coloured objects were seen by an unnamed pilot.

17th April – USA: Deep-orange coloured UFO seen

At 3pm, a group of army weather observation students at Yuma, Arizona, saw a flat, white, circular object, flying irregularly across the sky, leaving a brief trail – gone from view, seven seconds later. At 8.30pm, Mr S.B. Brooks, and engineer – Mr J.A. Eaton, sighted a round, deep-orange coloured object, flying through the sky over Longmeadow, Massachusetts, in an erratic manner, occasionally emitting a 'shaft of light' from the rear, during the 40 minute sighting.

18th April – USA: 'V'-shaped formation

At 11.30am, seven to nine circular orange-yellow 'lights', moving in a 'V'-formation, were seen flying overhead, silently, over Bethesda, Maryland, heading in a South to North direction – gone in a few seconds.

24th April – USA: Three UFOs sighted and other activity reported

At 5am, the crew of a USAF C-124 transport plane over Bellevue Hill, Vermont, sighted three circular, bluish objects, forming a loose 'fingertip' formation, twice flying parallel to airplane, during a 3-4 minute period.

At 2.30pm, three Cambridge Research Center electronics engineers, at Milton, Massachusetts, sighted two wobbling flat, red 'squares' moving across the sky. During just over a minute of observation, they were seen to climb and then level out.

At 8.10pm, later that evening, a USAF Surgeon – Major E.L. Ellis, at Clovis, New Mexico, sighted a number of orange-amber 'lights' – sometimes separate, sometimes fused – behaving erratically in the sky. Their speed varied from motionless to very fast during the five minutes sighting.

27th April – USA: Cigar-shaped objects observed

Mr H.A. Freytag and three male relatives, of Roseville, Michigan, were outside at 4.15pm, when they saw a silver, oval object in the sky; this descended and stopped. Two silver cigar-shaped objects were then seen to appear, followed by one departing to the east – the other west. A third silver cigar-shaped object flew by at high speed. The sightings lasted 45 minutes.

At 8.30pm – this time over Yuma, Arizona – Master Sgt. G.S. Porter, an off-duty control tower operator, and his wife, sighted bright red or flame-colored 'discs', appearing as large as fighter aircraft in the sky. It was learnt that they were not the only ones; apparently, seven other people witnessed this phenomena over a two-hour period.

29th April – USA: Pulsating UFO encountered

At 3:30pm over Marshall, Texas, Civilian pilot – Mr R.R. Weidman – reported sighting:

> *"...a round white object, which flew across the sky moving from side to side in flight, for about one and-a-half minutes."*

At 10pm, B-29 Bomber bombardier Lt. R.H. Bauer from Goodland, Kansas, saw:

> *"...a white fan-shaped object moving through the sky, pulsating 3-4 times per second. Seconds later it was out of sight."*

7th May – USA: UFO sighted over Nevada

At 6.45pm, Mr and Mrs George Smith, along with their grandson, sighted a silvery-white object hovering in the sky, at about 100 feet, 9 miles south of Ely, Nevada. The couple described it moving backwards and forwards as it did so.

Ten minutes later, it flew upwards and out of sight. **(Source: Project Blue Book unknowns)**

9th May – England: 'Blue bubble' sighted over Malvern Hills

What lay behind the appearance of a UFO seen flying through the sky over the Malvern Hills, Worcestershire, at 1.30am on 9th May 1952, by two unnamed members of the scientific community, based at the local Radar Research Establishment (a locality that was itself to be the venue for a number of UFO sightings over the years)?

> *"Suddenly, about 30 degrees to our left, appeared a circular object consisting of an inner circle, about seven feet in diameter, with a halo ten yards in diameter, both emitting a weird green phosphorescent glow, at a height of some 2,500 feet. It was travelling in a south-east direction, at a speed we estimated to be 600 mph, just above cloud cover, one mile east of the Malvern Hills, parallel to the Earth's surface. When it reached a point of 30 degrees to our right, it vanished. We felt its movements suggested some sort of controlling force. It was not a flare, distress signal, or aircraft."*

Another witness to the phenomenon was Mr Austin Stone – a retired RAF officer, then a writer – who was on his way home to Malvern, after attending a performance of his play Mystery in Pimlico at the Birmingham BBC Studio.

He said: *"It looked like a gigantic 'blue bubble' and only took five seconds to clear my line of vision".*

(Source: believed to be the *Sunday Dispatch*)

May – England: 'Flying disc' sighted over Kensington, London

In May 1952, a slightly blurred, milky-white, disc-shaped object was sighted by a Kensington, London man, a mere 30 feet away from his window. Shropshire UFO historian – Gavin Gibbons – interviewed the witness, who told him:

> *"It moved into an open space between the house and the one opposite, zigzagging backwards and forwards, several times, before heading north-west."*

Unfortunately, we do not know the actual date or time of the sighting.

Gavin Gibbons

Sunday Dispatch newspaper – Cigar-shaped UFO sighted

In its 1st June edition of 1952, the *Sunday Dispatch* newspaper – the front runner of publicizing UFO reports – told its readers about a strange cigar-shaped object, seen speeding across the sky to the north of Canterbury at 7.30pm, followed by what was described as something resembling a flattened ellipsoid, with a shiny surface, sighted over Aldershot three minutes later. One minute later, a glistening metallic object was seen over Poole, Dorset, accompanied by a sighting of what looked like 'a huge, shiny, 'egg' in the sky over Portland Bill'.

(Source: *Sunday Dispatch*, 11.5.1952 – 'Blue Bubble with halo that baffled them' (1.6.1952) – 'Flying Saucer is seen over the South again')

1st May – USA: UFO display over Washington

At 5.32am, over Moses Lake, Washington, two Atomic Energy Commission employees – Mr Eggan and Mr Shipley – sighted a silver object, without wings, heading through the sky – visible for one and-a-half minutes. On the same day – this time over *George Air Force Base, California – three men were out on the firing range, at 10.50am, accompanied by a Lt. Colonel, when five, flat, white 'discs' about the diameter of a C-47s wingspan (95 feet) were sighted, moving at speed across the sky.

They then made a 90 degree turn in formation, leaving three in front and two behind, which darted around for 15-30 seconds.

5th May – USA: UFOs sighted

At 10.45pm, Tenafly, a New Jersey resident – Mrs M.M. Judson – sighted six or seven translucent, cream-yellow, objects that moved in an ellipse through the sky; one was apparently stationary, while the others moved in and out.

7th May – USA: Silver cylindrical UFO

At Kessler Air Force Base, Mississippi, a group of servicemen that included Captain Morris, a Master Sergeant, a Staff Sergeant and an Airman First Class, were on duty at 12.15pm, when they saw an aluminum or silver cylindrical object, darting in and out of the clouds, during a five to ten minute observation.

9th May – USA: Arrow-shaped UFO seen

At 5.20pm (once again over George Air Force Base, California) a dull-white, arrowhead-shaped, object was seen moving across the sky – straight and level – for ten seconds.

10th May – USA: UFOs over Nuclear Plant

Over Ellenton, South Carolina, four yellow, 'disc'-shaped, objects were seen on five occasions, between 10.45pm and 11.15pm, by four DuPont employees at the Savannah River Nuclear Plant.

19th May – USA: Seven objects sighted by pilots

At 1.48am on the 19th May, while flying on a training mission in the vicinity of San Angelo, Texas, an RB-36 crew of the 31st Strategic Reconnaissance Squadron, 5th Strategic Wing, sighted seven UFOs ahead of their aircraft. The RB-36 was at a height of 18,000 feet, moving

*George Air Force Base is a former United States Air Force Base, located within city limits, eight miles north-west of central Victorville, California, about 75 miles north-east of Los Angeles, California.

at 189 mph when the sighting took place. The seven objects appeared at the 11 o'clock position to the aircraft and were stacked in a vertical column, the base of which was estimated to be 25,000 feet, the top being 60,000 feet.

20th May – USA: UFO sighted by pilots

At 10.10pm, over Houston, Texas, USAF pilots – Captain J. Spurgin and Captain B.B. Stephan – sighted a bright white oval object, moving from side-to-side in the sky, before completing a gradual turn over the next 90 seconds.

25th May – USA: White UFO with dark sections

Seven people, including John Hoffman, his family, and friends – residents of Walnut Lake, Michigan – were outside at 9.15pm when they saw a large white circular object, with dark sections on its rim, flying across the sky for 30 minutes.

28th May – USA: UFO display over city

Between 1.45pm and 2.40pm, two Albuquerque City fire department employees sighted two circular objects in the sky; one bright silver – the other, orange or light brown – performing manoeuvres in the sky.

29th May – USA: Tubular UFO sighted by Major

At 7pm, Major D.W. Feuerstein was on the ground at San Antonio, Texas, when he saw a bright tubular object, tilted from horizontal to vertical, moving across the sky. After eight minutes of observation the object slowly returned to horizontal, then once more tilted vertically and accelerated away. As it did so it appeared to lengthen and changed to red in colour – lost from view in a total observation of 14 minutes. **(Source: Project Blue Book unknowns)**

June – England: Climber sights small 'being' in Devon

In June 1952, a woman climbing Haytor, near Newton Abbot, was three-quarters of the way up, when she saw:

> *"...a small man, dressed in a brown smock, tied at the waist; he had brown material on his legs and a flat brown cap. He was about four feet tall and elderly looking. He stood there, his hand shielding his eyes from the sunlight. Suddenly, he dived out of sight".*

Haytor

An intriguing sighting! Was he one of the 'little folk', or just a small man, or dwarf? We do not know the answer, but the witness thought it was important enough to tell someone about what she had seen. **(Source: *Middle Kingdom*, MUFOB, Volume 6, No. 2)**

1st June – USA: Pilot sights UFO

At 1pm, ex-military pilot reserve – Major W.C. Vollendorf – reported having seen an oval object with a 'definite airfoil', climbing at speed through the sky for seven seconds.

Just after 3pm, three glimmering UFOs were seen by Soap Lake, Washington resident – Mr Raymond Lottman – over a ten minute period. At 6pm, aircraftsman Beatty and two civilians, from Rapid City, South Dakota, sighted:

> *"...at least five, long, silver objects, flying in a neat box formation across the sky, with a 'leader object', for 15-20 seconds."*

5th June – USA: Yellow objects seen

At 6.45pm, over Albuquerque, New Mexico, Staff Sgt. T.H. Shorey reported having seen a shiny, round object, which flew 5-6 times as fast as an F-86 jet fighter, for 6 seconds, across the sky.

At 11pm, over Lubbock, Texas, Dan Benson and Mr Bacon sighted:

> *"...eight yellow circular objects – like large stars – during 45 minutes of observation. The first two were in a trail formation; the others were seen singly".*

Other witnesses to unidentified aerial phenomena that day, at the same time, were 2nd Lt. W.R. Soper – a Strategic Air Command top secret control officer, former OSI agent; and two other persons from Offutt Air Force Base, Omaha, Nebraska. They told of seeing:

> *"...one bright red object, which remained stationary in the sky for four and-a-half minutes before speeding away, leaving a short trail."*

The length and breadth of the enormous 'wave' of UFO sightings that took place in the 1950s defies conception. It would be so easy to become complacent about the sheer volume which, in the main, now remains a forgotten part of the 20th Century.

However, each and every individual sighting created great excitement to those people involved. Sadly, many are gone without at least being able to answer what lies behind the continual movement of these objects still being reported, now over 60 years later. Without doubt it is the greatest unsolved mystery of our time.

7th June – USA: Rectangular object sighted by pilots

At 11.18am, the crew of a B-25 bomber over Albuquerque, New Mexico, flying at a height of 11,500 feet, sighted:

> *"...a rectangular, aluminum object, flying through the air, 300 feet below us."*

The crew estimated the size of the UFO as being six feet by four feet.

8th June – USA: Four shiny UFOs sighted

At 10.50am, Mr and Mrs J.D. Markland from Albuquerque, New Mexico, sighted four shiny objects fly across the sky on a straight and level course in a 'diamond' formation.

13th June – USA: Orange UFO seen

At 8.45pm, Mr R.S. Thomas – an Olmstead Air Force Base employee and former control tower operator, from Middletown, Pennsylvania – reported seeing a round, orange object in the sky, travelling south, which stopped for a second before heading eastwards. It then halted again and dropped downwards.

15th June – USA: Large cigar-shaped UFO

At 11.50pm, Mr Edward Duke – an ex US Navy radar technician from Louisville, Kentucky – reported to the authorities of having seen:

> *"...a large, cigar- shaped object with a blunt front, illuminated sides and a red stern, which manoeuvred in a leisurely fashion for 15 minutes across the sky."*

16th June – USA: Over Walker Air Force Base, New Mexico

At Walker Air Force Base, New Mexico, USAF maintenance specialist – Staff Sgt. Sparks – told of sighting five or six grey 'discs' travelling across the sky, at 8.30pm, in a half-moon formation, moving at an estimated speed of 5-600 mph. – out of sight, one minute later.

17th June – USA: Silver/yellow objects seen

At 1.28am, the pilot of a USAF F-94 jet interceptor, over Cape Cod, Massachusetts, reported that a 'light', resembling a bright star, crossed the nose of his airplane. Between 7.30pm and 10.20pm, a number of people around the McChord Air Force Base, Washington, reported seeing between one to five silver/yellow objects, flying erratically through the sky, in peculiar stopping and starting movements, which lasted for about 15 minutes.

18th June – USA: Crescent-shaped UFO seen

At 9am, a crescent-shaped UFO was sighted hovering in the sky over Columbus, Wisconsin, for several seconds, before heading away at speed.

At 10pm, over Walnut Lake, Michigan, Mr M. Hoffman and four relatives, using binoculars, sighted an orange light zigzagging across the sky and then hovering for an unspecified length of time.

21st June – USA: UFO rushes past B52 Bomber

At 12.30pm, while over Kelly Air Force Base, Texas, flight engineer training Sergeant Howard Davis, aboard a B-29 bomber, at 8,000 feet, sighted "a white, flat object, with a sharply pointed front and rounded rear, showing a dark blue centre and red rim, trailing sparks", as it shot past the B-29 at a distance of 500 feet in one second.

23rd June – USA: Giant 'soap bubbles' and 'flying discs'

Oak Ridge, Tennessee secretary – Martha Milligan – was out at 3.30am, when she saw a bullet-shaped object with burnt-orange exhaust, flying straight across the sky for a period of between 30-60 seconds.

At 10am, over Owensboro, Kentucky, National Guard Lt. Colonel O.L. Depp sighted:

> *"...two objects, looking like giant 'soap bubbles', reflecting yellow and lavender colours as it flew across the sky, leaving a trail in its wake that lasted for 5 seconds."*

Airport weather observer – Rex Thompson based at Spokane Airport, Washington – told of having seen:

> *"...a round 'disc'-shaped object with a metallic shine, flashing and fluttering like a flipped coin, for 5-7 minutes."*

Is it possible there was a connection with what was seen at 9pm, the same evening, over Mc-Chord Air Force Base, Washington?

Lt. K. Thompson reported seeing an unusual 'light', heading across the sky for a period of ten minutes.

25th June 1952 – USA: Egg-shaped UFO seen

At 8.30pm, over Chicago, Illinois, Mrs Norbury and a Mr Mathews sighted a bright yellow-white, egg-shaped object, which sometimes had a red tail, moving around the sky in a total of seven circles, over one and-a-half hour's observation.

26th June 1952 – USA: Three lights again!

At 11.50pm, over Pottstown, Pennsylvania, the assistant manager of the local airport reported three sightings of flashing lights over an half-an-hour period in the sky, involving two 'lights' separated by two miles, with a leader flashing steadily and the other irregularly. Their speed was estimated at 150-250 mph.

27th June 1952 – USA: Off duty pilot sights pulsating red UFO

At 6.50pm, over Topeka, Kansas, a USAF pilot was accompanied by 2nd Lt. K.P. Kelly, and his wife, when he sighted a pulsating red object, which changed shape from circular to a vertical oval as it headed across the sky. At one point it was stationary for about five minutes, before vanishing from view.

27th June – USA: UFO sighted

At 7.50am, Mr Terrell and Mr Yates – employees at Red River Arsenal, Texarkana, Texas – sighted a bright object, shaped like

> *"two dish pans, face-to-face, moving through the sky, then out of view in 4-5 seconds".*

27th June – England: Flashing UFO sighted in sky over Liverpool

On 27th June 1952, an object looking like a 'large flashing silver dinner plate' was seen moving over Liverpool, at high altitude, in broad daylight, by a number of people – including Mrs Ann Cox of Beswick, Manchester.

> *"I saw a small patch of blue in the sky, spasmodically flashing with white light. It appeared to wobble."*

29th June – USA:

At 5.45pm, three USAF air policemen at O'Hare Airport, Chicago, Illinois, sighted a bright silver, flat oval object, surrounded by a blue haze, which was seen to hover, and then move very fast to the right and to the left, and up and down, for 45 minutes.

5th July – USA: UFO over Hanford Atomic Power Station

Four Florida pilots – three of them Second World War veterans – spoke of seeing a 'flying saucer' hovering over Hanford Atomic Plant at Richland, Washington.

Captain John Baldwin of Coral Gables, who had 7,000 hours of flying time in the Pacific, said:

> *"My companions, and I, saw a perfectly round white 'disc' – almost transparent, with small vapor trails hanging off it – like the tentacles of an octopus. We were flying at 9,000 feet when we saw the object, about 10-15,000 feet above us. The object seemed to back away from us and change shape; it became flat, gained speed, and disappeared quickly. All of us have been flying a number of years and we have seen all kinds of clouds and formations, but never anything like this before."*

His account was corroborated by Captain George Robertson of Miami, Pilot D. Shenkel, and Steven Summers (co-pilots for Conner Airlines). The incident was reported to the Civil Aeronautics Administration Regional Office in Seattle, and Larson Air Force Base, Moses Lake, Washington. Both of them refused to comment.

3rd July – USA: Two UFOs sighted

At 4.15am two big 'lights', estimated at 20 feet in diameter, were seen to fly across the sky over Selfridge Air Force Base, Michigan, at tremendous speed.

At 11.50pm, two bright pastel-green 'discs' were sighted rushing through the sky at speed ,over Chicago, Illinois, by Mrs J.D. Arbuckle. Six seconds later, they were out of view.

5th July – USA: State policeman sights three dark 'discs'

At 7.58pm, State Patrolman Hamilton was over Norman, Oklahoma, in the State Patrol airplane, when he saw "three dark 'discs', hovering in the sky", before they flew away, silhouetted against a dark cloud 15 seconds later.

7th July-USA: Flying Saucers over Cincinnati

THE CINCINNATI ENQUIRER
FINAL EDITION
FIVE CENTS
20 PAGES
MONDAY MORNING, JULY 7, 1947
FLYING SAUCERS OVER CINCINNATI
Army Aircraft Search For Mystery Discs
CAMERAMEN Keep Vigil In Sky
Cops Would Be Wonderful Baby-Sitters, But Tiny Terrors Keep Them On The Run
SHUN ROLE Of Spoiled Child
DEADLOCK On Coal Unbroken
Tyke Found Asleep On Log In Woods; Hunted Three Days
TWO OF 'EM Seen Going North

9th July – USA: Aluminium UFO seen in the sky

At 6.30pm a farmer from Kutztown, Pennsylvania, sighted an aluminium, oval-shaped, object in the sky. It was then seen to change direction and altitude, before finally tipping on its end and departing 20 seconds later.

At 12.05pm, USAF pilot Major C. K. Griffin was over Colorado Springs, Colorado, when he saw a luminous white object, shaped like an airfoil less its trailing edge, in the sky moving slowly and erratically for 12 minutes.

At 3.35pm over Rapid City Air Force Base, South Dakota, Staff Sgt. D.P. Foster (and others) sighted – on three occasions – a single white, disc-shaped object, moving at speed across the sky – out of sight in five seconds.

12th July – USA: UFOs tracked on radar

At 3.30pm, Insurance Company president – William Washburn from Annapolis, Maryland – reported having seen:

> *"...four, large, elliptical-shaped objects, flying very fast through the sky. They stopped and turned 90 degrees in mid-air, before heading away seven to eight seconds later."*

At 9pm, Kirksville Air Force Base, Missouri, a number of radar controllers plotted several big blips on radar, at 1,700mph.

13th July – USA: 'Bow tie'-shaped object seen

At 5pm, two Alabama Redstone Arsenal employees, one of whom was Mr Washburn, sighted:

> *"...an object, like a bow tie, polished aluminum in appearance, flying through the sky. One of the 'triangles' rotated a quarter turn in the opposite direction, before returning to its original position. It then made a right-angle turn and accelerated away, 30 seconds later."*

14th July – USA: Eight UFOs seen over Virginia, later tracked on radar

At 8.12pm on the 14th July 1952, two Pan American pilots – William Nash, First Officer, and William Fortenberry – were flying on a heading of 60 degrees, near Norfolk, Virginia, when they saw eight objects in the sky, manoeuvring below their airliner, in formation, over Chesapeake Bay, near Old Point Comfort, Virginia.

Junior Freshie

The Miami Herald

Wednesday, July 16, 1952 No. 226 Florida's Most Complete Newspaper 42nd Year 48 Pages 5 Cents

Secret Papers Bare Reds' War Fears

See story on Page 7-D

'Glowing Like Hot Coals,' They Moved At 1,000 Miles An Hour

Miami Pilots Spot 8 Saucers Flying In Formation

By JOHN F. BONNER
Herald Staff Writer

Two Miami airlines pilots said Tuesday they saw 1,000-mile-an hour flying saucers in formation over Chesapeake Bay.

They said eight of the "things" 100 feet in diameter and "glowing like hot coals," passed directly beneath their Pan American Airways DC-4, wheeled sharply and zoomed out of sight.

First Officer William B. Nash 35-year-old veteran of 10 years with Pan American, said he and Fortenberry, 30, "watched the whole maneuver" for 10 or 12 seconds.

"We definitely saw them," Nash swore. "There is no doubt in our minds that we saw missiles of some kind operating under intelligent control.

"We feel, because of the way the missiles acted and because of all the other reports that have been heard, that they must be from some extra-terrestrial source," he added.

Nash's report drew implied support from a high Pan American official.

Santes Cayanes, manager of Pan American's Miami overhaul base and acting operations manager here, said the flying saucers Nash and Fortenberry saw "obviously were not a figment of their imagination."

It was the second report this month of Miami airline pilots having spotted the mysterious saucers.

On July 6, four non-scheduled airline pilots reported they saw a saucer hovering near the atomic energy plant at Richlands, Wash.

The four were Capt. John Baldwin of Coral Gables, Capt. George Robertson and D. D. Shenkel of Miami and Steven Summers of Hialeah—all of them veteran airmen.

Nash said when his plane landed about midnight Monday, he and Fortenberry immediately reported the phenomenon to Pan American officials and to "military authorities."

Fortenberry added: "We're not at liberty to divulge whom we made our report to, but I can assure you it is being taken care of by competent authorities. Flying saucer reports aren't falling on deaf ears."

Here is the story Nash told Tuesday:

He and Fortenberry, a Pan American pilot for 11 months, were co-pilots on a DC-4 en route from New York to Miami for overhaul. Aboard were 10 Pan American employees.

Capt. F. V. Koepke was in the passenger compartment as the ship neared Norfolk, Va., shortly after 8 p.m.

"The visibility was excellent, about as good as you could find," Nash said. "I was pointing out the city of Newport News to Fortenberry, since he had never flown the route before.

"We were both looking to the southwest when we saw them simultaneously—six of them flying toward us in echelon formation.

"As they neared us, they appeared to be solid bodies of light, a little more amber than automobile tail lights are. They were brilliant, far more intense than the ground lights.

"They had definite outlines, nothing [illegible] about them. And they [illegible] like hot coals.

"They approached us from the southeast of Newport on a northeast heading, going at an extremely rapid pace. We estimated their speed at far over 1,000 miles per hour.

"We were flying about 8,000 feet and the six things flew under us at about 2,000 feet. Fortenberry was looking directly down on them.

"When they got below us, they made a sharp, 150-degree turn. We were amazed. Their turn was almost instan-

Turn to Page 8-A, Col. 4

WILLIAM FORTENBERRY

WILLIAM NASH
. . . then the things made a sharp, 150-degree turn

—Herald Staff Photos

McKinney To 'Discourage' Any Draft-Truman Moves

Peace Near? Hopeful Air Pervades UN

High Officials See Truce This Summer

By The Associated Press

UNITED NATIONS, N. Y. — There was an air of hopeful expectancy at United Nations headquarters Tuesday. For good or bad something seems about to break in the cold war. The break may be in

President Gave Order, He Asserts

Doubts Stevenson Will Be Nominee

By International News Service

CHICAGO—Democratic Chairman Frank McKinney declared Tuesday he will discourage any draft-Truman move at the Democratic convention on the basis of presidential instructions given him just two days ago.

15th July – USA: Discus-shaped UFO

Mr J. Antoneff and two other persons from West Palm Beach, Florida, were outside at 10.10pm, when they sighted:

> *"...a greyish object, shaped like a discus, hovering in the sky over Palm Beach International Airport. It then began to follow an SA-l6 twin-engine amphibian and flew away after 40-60 seconds".*

19th July – USA: Seven UFOs plotted

At 11.40pm, on Saturday, 19th July 1952, Edward Nugent – an air traffic controller at Washington National Airport (today Ronald Reagan Washington National Airport) – spotted seven objects on his radar. The objects were located 15 miles (24 km) south-southwest of the city; no known aircraft were in the area and the objects were not following any established flight paths. Nugent's superior, Harry Barnes – a senior air traffic controller at the airport – watched the objects on Nugent's radarscope. He later wrote:

> *"We knew immediately that a very strange situation existed . . . their movements were completely radical compared to those of ordinary aircraft."*

Barnes had two controllers check Nugent's radar; they found that it was working normally. Barnes then called National Airport's other radar centre; the controller there – Howard Cocklin – told Barnes that he also had the objects on his radarscope. Furthermore, Cocklin said that by looking out of the control tower window, he could see one of the objects – *"a bright orange light. I can't tell what's behind it."*

Plotted over the White House

At this point, other objects appeared in all sectors of the radarscope; when they moved over the White House and the United States Capitol, Barnes called Andrews Air Force Base, located 10 miles from National Airport. Although Andrews reported that they had no unusual objects on their radar, an airman soon called the base's control tower to report the sighting of a strange object.

Airman William Brady, who was in the tower, then saw *"...an object, which appeared to be like an orange 'ball of fire', trailing a tail. It was unlike anything I had ever seen before."*

As Brady tried to alert the other personnel in the tower, the strange object *"took off at an unbelievable speed".*

Meanwhile, another person in the National Airport control tower reported seeing *"an orange 'disc', about 3,000 feet altitude".*

On one of the airport's runways, S.C. Pierman – a Capital Airlines pilot – was waiting in the cockpit of his DC-4, for permission to take-off. After spotting what he believed to be a meteor, he was told that the control tower's radar had picked up unknown objects closing in on his position. Pierman observed six objects – *"white, tailless, fast-moving lights"* over a 14-minute period. Pierman was in radio contact with Barnes during his sighting, and Barnes later related that *"each sighting coincided with a pip we could see near his plane. When he reported that the light streaked off at a high speed, it disappeared on our scope".*

Andrews Air Force Base

At Andrews Air Force Base, the control tower personnel were tracking on radar what some thought to be unknown objects, but others suspected, and in one instance were able to prove, these were simply stars and meteors.

However, Staff Sgt. Charles Davenport observed an orange-red light to the south; the light *"would appear to stop and then make an abrupt change in direction and altitude... this happened several times"*. At one point both radar centres at National Airport and the radar at Andrews Air Force Base were tracking an object hovering over a radio beacon. The object vanished in all three radar centres at the same time. At 3am, shortly before two jet fighters from Newcastle Air Force Base in Delaware arrived over Washington, all of the objects vanished from the radar at National Airport. However, when the jets ran low on fuel and left, the objects returned, which convinced Barnes that *"the UFOs were monitoring radio traffic and behaving accordingly"*. The objects were last detected by radar at 5.30am, around sunrise.

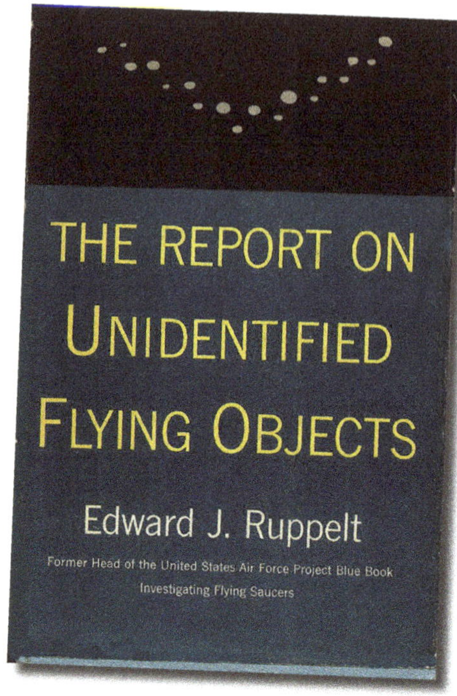

Five huge 'flying discs' seen

Mr E.W. Chambers – a civilian radio engineer – was in the Washington suburbs, when he observed *"five huge 'discs', circling in a loose formation. They tilted upward and left on a steep ascent"*.

(Sources: Clark, Jerome, *The UFO Book: Encyclopedia of the Extraterrestrial.* Visible Ink, 1998, ISBN 1-57859-029-9, Michaels, Susan, *Sightings: UFOs*, Simon and Schuster, 1997, ISBN 0-684-83630-0/Peebles, Curtis, *Watch the Skies: A Chronicle of the Flying Saucer Myth*, Berkley Books, 1994, ISBN 0-425-15117-4/Randle, Kevin, D., *Invasion Washington: UFOs over the Capitol*, 2001, ISBN 0-380-81470-6/Ruppelt, Edward, J. *The Report on Unidentified Flying Objects*)

USAF pilots sight three UFOs

During the same period of time, on a clear, cloudless day, two US Air Force Colonels, Lieutenant Colonel John L. McGinn and Lieutenant Colonel John R. Barton, both veteran fliers with distinguished military careers – [At the time, both men were assigned to the Pentagon with highly classified assignments and were familiar with even the most secret foreign and domestic aircraft designs] – had requisitioned a twin engine B-25 bomber at Hamilton Field, north of San Francisco, for a cross-country flight to Colorado. Between Sacramento, California, and Reno, Nevada, they entered the 'Green 3' aerial highway to Salt Lake City, Utah.

At 3.40pm, while at 11,000 feet (3,300m) over the Carson Sink area, east of Reno, the two pilots then sighted three objects make a left bank and fly quickly to within 400 to 800 yards (meters) of their B-25. The two men estimated the speed of the unknown aircraft to be, at the very least, three times that of the F-86. After four seconds, the aircraft sped away out of the vision of the pilots.

When they landed in Colorado Springs, they contacted Air Defense Command Headquarters and learned that no civilian or military aircraft had been anywhere near the Carson Sink at the time of the incident. The two men dismissed the suggestion that they had seen F-86 jets, since they were intimately familiar with the design of that craft.

Air Defense Command relayed the report to Ruppelt at Project Blue Book.

(Source: *The Report on Unidentified Flying Objects*, Edward Ruppelt)

18th July – USA: Silver 'bubble' and UFO display

At 11am over Miami, Florida, Mr E.R. Raymer and his daughter sighted an opaque, silvery 'bubble', flying very fast through the sky at right-angles to the wind direction; object out of sight 10 seconds later.

At 9.45pm, over Patrick Air Force Base, Florida, three USAF officers and four enlisted men sighted, over an hour period, a series of hovering and manoeuvring red-orange 'lights' in the sky.

19th July – USA: Elliptical-shaped object and UFO display

At 2.55am, an experienced Pilot Williston, over North Dakota, sighted an elliptical-shaped object with a light fringe, travelling fast through the sky, which was seen to make a 360 degrees turn and then a 180 degrees turn in five minutes.

At 11.35pm the same day, this time over Elkins Park, Pennsylvania, USAF pilot – Capt. C.J. Powley – and his wife, saw two star-like 'lights', which manoeuvred and hovered across the sky, for five to seven minutes.

20th July – USA: Strange lights seen

At 12.20am Lavallette, New Jersey, Seton Hall University chemistry professor – Dr. A.B. Spooner – sighted two large orange-yellow 'lights', with some dull red colouring, flying across the sky – which then turned and circled, for five to six minutes.

21st July – USA: Delta-shaped object

At 4.30pm over Converse, in Texas, the wife of USAF Capt. J.B. Neal sighted:

> *"...an elongated, fuselage-shaped object, which flew straight and level – then made a right-angle turn and went out of sight, at a speed I estimated to be in excess of 300mph, in three to five seconds".*

At 8.10pm, a military officer and two enlisted men from Rockville, Indiana, sighted an aluminum delta-shaped object with a vertical fin, which flew straight across the sky and then hovered, during three minutes of observation.

At 10.40pm, over San Marcos Air Force Base, in Texas, a USAF Lieutenant, two Staff Sergeants, and three airmen, witnessed the passage across the sky of a mysterious 'blue circle', leaving a blue trail, which was seen to hover and then accelerate to near-sonic speed, a minute later.

22nd July – USA: UFO activity increases

Just after midnight, Holyoke, Massachusetts woman – Mrs A. Burgess – sighted a yellow flashing light in the sky, which then dropped downwards.

At 10.50am over Los Alamos, New Mexico, control tower operator Don Weins, and two pilots, reported seeing eight large, round, bright aluminum objects flying across the sky, before beginning to dart around erratically over the next 25 minutes. At 2.46pm, Don Epperly – a Trans Texas Airlines station manager and weather observer from Uvalde, Texas, sighted a large, round, silver object flying through the sky, at more than 1,000mph, for 45 seconds, gyrating in flight as it did so.

At 10.47pm, the pilot and radar operator of a USAF F-94 jet interceptor, flying between Boston and Provincetown, Massachusetts, sighted a spinning 'blue light', which passed the aircraft.

23rd July – USA: Jet fighters sight increase in UFO traffic

On this day, crews of several USAF F-94 jet interceptors, heading from Dover Air Force Base over Pottstown, Pennsylvania, logged thirteen visual sightings and one radar tracking of blue-white 'lights' seen moving over the sky, during a two hour duration, beginning at 8.40am. The objects included reports of a large silver object – shaped like a long pear, with two or three squares beneath it – flying between 170-210 mph, while a smaller object – delta-shaped or swept back – flew around it, at 1,150-1,700 mph.

USAF Pilot – Capt. H.W. Kloth – was over South Bend, Indiana, at 11.35pm, when he saw:

> *"...two bright blue-white objects, flying together, then the rear one veered off after about nine minutes".*

At 12.50pm, the two-man crews of two USAF F-94 jet interceptors, at 35-46,000 feet altitude, over Altoona, Pennsylvania, sighted three cylindrical objects in a vertical stack formation, flying at an altitude of 50-80,000 feet for 20 minutes. [This may have been 12.50am]

24th July – USA: Three delta-shaped UFOs seen

USAF Lt. Colonels McGinn and Barton were aboard a B-25 Bomber, at 3.40pm, over Carson Sink, Nevada. Three silver, delta-shaped objects, each with a ridge along the top, crossed in front of and above the B-25, at high speed, in 3-4 seconds. Letter to the President by a President!

These sightings, which were reported in the Press, appear to have galvanized all manner of speculation and interest. One man even wrote to the President of the United States.

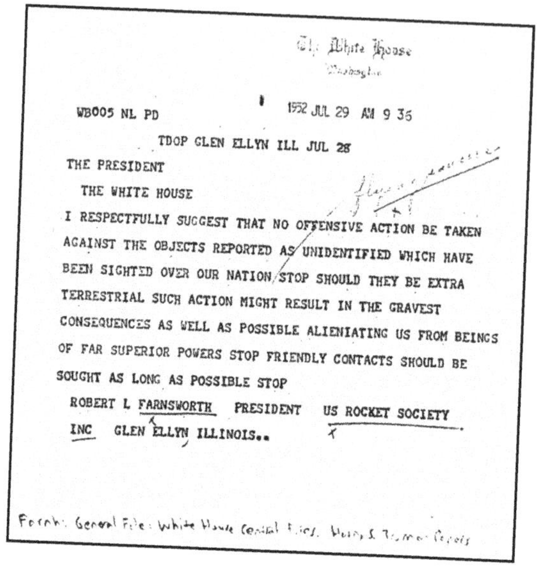

The White House

WB005 NL PD 1952 JUL 29 AM 9 35

TDOP GLEN ELLYN ILL JUL 28

THE PRESIDENT

THE WHITE HOUSE

I RESPECTFULLY SUGGEST THAT NO OFFENSIVE ACTION BE TAKEN AGAINST THE OBJECTS REPORTED AS UNIDENTIFIED WHICH HAVE BEEN SIGHTED OVER OUR NATION STOP SHOULD THEY BE EXTRA TERRESTRIAL SUCH ACTION MIGHT RESULT IN THE GRAVEST CONSEQUENCES AS WELL AS POSSIBLE ALIENIATING US FROM BEINGS OF FAR SUPERIOR POWERS STOP FRIENDLY CONTACTS SHOULD BE SOUGHT AS LONG AS POSSIBLE STOP

ROBERT L FARNSWORTH PRESIDENT US ROCKET SOCIETY INC GLEN ELLYN ILLINOIS..

25th July – England: Shopkeeper sights UFO over Southampton

Local shopkeeper – Mr Frank Paskins from Lockerley, near Southampton – was delivering from the back of his van on 25th July 1952, when he saw:

> *"...two objects, flying much higher than jets across the sky. At times they reversed, or flew sideways. I watched them for about three minutes, together with Mr and Mrs Menhennet, of Blackfield".*

(Source: *Southern Evening News*, 25.7.1952)

26th July – USA: Heavy UFO activity continues

At 12.05am, Airman First Class, J.M. Donaldson – stationed at Kirtland Air Force Base, New Mexico – sighted eight to ten orange 'balls', forming a triangular or 'V' formation, flying through the sky at a fast speed, for three to four seconds.

At 12.15am, USAF Captain H.A. Stone – and men in the control towers at Fairfax Field and Municipal Airport, Kansas City, Missouri – watched a greenish light for an hour, showing red and orange flashes, in the north-west sky. This was a continuation of extensive UFO sightings and radar tracking of UFOs reported throughout the Washington, D.C. area, all night long.

26th July – USA: UFO display over Washington

On Saturday, 26th July 1952, at 8.15pm, a pilot and stewardess on a National Airlines flight into Washington observed some strange objects above their plane. Within minutes both radar centres at National Airport, and the radar at Andrews AFB, were tracking more unknown objects. A Master sergeant at Andrews Air Base observed the objects; he later said:

> *"These lights did not have the characteristics of shooting stars. There was [sic] no trails . . . they travelled faster than any shooting star I have ever seen".*

27th July – England: UFO sighted over Liverpool

A flashing object – like a silver dinner plate – was seen over Liverpool, during the 27th July 1952.

Mrs Ann Cox, from Beswick, was the first to see:

> *"...a blue patch of blue in the sky that appeared to wobble, making white flashes of light. I told my daughter, Wenda, and nephew, Robin Williams, my neighbour, Mrs Murray, and her daughter. It disappeared behind clouds, six minutes later, in an eastern direction."*

(Source: Unknown newspaper – 'A Flying Dinner-Plate Flashes By')

On the same date but in the United States, at Selfridge AFB, Michigan, three B-29 Bomber crewmen who were on the ground sighted a number of round, white objects, heading across the sky at intervals, beginning with two seen at 10.05am, one at 10.10am one at 10.15am, and one at 10.20am. Each was seen for about 30 seconds. During the same evening, at 8.30pm, Mr and Mrs Adrian Ellis from Wichita Falls, Texas, sighted two 'disc'-shaped UFOs; fifteen seconds later, they were out of sight.

(Source: Project Blue Book Unknowns)

28th July – USA: Radar picks up UFOs in airspace

At 2.15am over McChord Air Force Base, Washington, Training Sergeant Walstead and Staff Sergeant Calkins, of the 635th AC & W Squadron, reported seeing a dull, glowing, blue-green 'ball' – the size of 'a dime at arm's length' – flying very fast across the sky, on a straight and level trajectory.

At 6am, over McGuire Air Force Base, New Jersey, Ground Control Approach radar operator Master Sergeant W.F. Dees, and other persons, were in the base control tower when the radar tracked a large cluster of very distinct blips. Visual observation was then made of *"oblong objects having neither wings nor tails, which made a very fast turn and, at one time, were seen in echelon formation"*. Unusually, the sighting lasted 55 minutes.

29th July – USA: Clusters and a larger UFO sighted

At 1.30am, Osceola, Wisconsin, radar operators on the ground and a pilot of an F-51 Mustang in flight, sighted several clusters of up to 10 small radar targets, heading south-west to east, at 60-70 mph, following each other through the sky. They were accompanied by a larger object,

The Alexandria Gazette

AMERICA'S OLDEST DAILY NEWSPAPER—ESTABLISHED 1784

CANCER IS YOUR FIGHT: ... Let's Do It Today.

VOL. CLXIX—NO. 151 ALEXANDRIA, VIRGINIA, TUESDAY, JULY 29, 1952 FIVE CENTS

EYE-WITNESS STORY OF "FLYING SAUCERS" SEEN ALONG ALEXANDRIA-CLARENDON AXIS

Planes To Take Off Over River

Proposal Made As Remedy For Low Flying Craft

Only Temporary Relief Seen For Area's Blistering Heat

Fairfax Men See Objects On Radar On Night Watch

By WILLIAM HAFFRON

Saucers Seen Again Early This Morning

Flying Saucers Seen Over Washington For 2nd Time In 4 Days

Washington, D. C., saw flying saucers again for six hours early today.

Eight to 12 objects showed on radar screens, flying a 10-mile arc around the capital. Radarmen estimated the objects, or flying saucers, were clipping along at about 120 miles per hour.

The last time the saucers were spotted over Washington, on Saturday, the air force sent jet fighters up to chase them, and when the word of the new appearance was flashed around, it was expected that the jets would be ordered up again, to try to shoot down the objects.

But the jets stayed on the ground. An air defense official explained, "We were too busy with other things, and besides objects aren't hurting anybody."

However, civil aeronautics officials did direct an Eastern air lines pilot to check the objects as he flew over the city. But the pilot didn't see a thing. The officials said the saucers disappeared from the radar screen when the plane reached the area where thy had been tracked.

So it remains a mystery.

The second appearance of the saucers in four days leaves th experts just as stumped as ever. Some think the saucers are space ships from another planet. Some think they're just natural phenomenon we haven't figured out yet.

The air force doesn't know what to think. But it's determined to find out. Top scientists have been called in to launch a major investigation.

moving at 700 mph. Duration of sightings one hour.

At 2.30pm at Langley Air Force Base, Virginia, USAF Capt. D.G. Moore, of military air traffic control systems, sighted an 'unknown object', which flew at an estimated 2,600 mph, below 5,000 feet altitude, toward the airbase, for about two minutes. Twenty minutes later radar picked up an object moving away, which stopped for two minutes, before heading away at high speed and off the scope in four minutes.

(Source: Project Blue Book unknowns)

18th July – USA: Two UFOs sighted

At 3.10pm over White Plains, New York, Mrs Florence Daley reported having sighted:

"...two round objects, bluish-white with brighter rims, flying in formation across the sky, making a sound like bombers – only softer."

Following an interview, made later, Florence stated she had what sounded like many feminine voices coming from the objects. [Authors: This is something one might have once dismissed away rationally, but not now!]

27th July – England: Wobbling UFO sighted over Liverpool

29th July –USA:

Discus-shaped UFO At 4.35pm Mr Herbert Mitchell, accompanied by another person, from Merced, California, sighted:

"...a dark, discus-shaped object, being trailed by a silvery light, two lengths behind. It then tipped on its side, dove, hesitated and then circled very fast during the two minutes observation."

At 12.30pm, USAF officials at Ennis, Montana, received information that UFOs were coming from the direction of Seattle, Washington. Two to five flat, 'disc'-shaped objects were then seen in the sky - one of which hovered for three to four minutes, while the others circled it over a 30 minutes observation time.

At 12.35pm the same day, Wichita, Kansas USAF shop employees – Douglas and Hess, at Municipal Airport – sighted a bright white circular object, with a flat base, that was seen to fly very fast through the sky before stopping in mid-air for 10-15 seconds, over the Cessna Aircraft Company plant, during a five minutes sighting.

(Source: Project Blue Book unknowns)

30th July – Germany: RAF pilot paced by silver UFO

On the 30th July 1952, RAF Flight Sergeant Roland Hughes was on a training flight over West Germany in a de Havilland Vampire FB9. As he was returning to base, he reported being intercepted by *"a gleaming silver, metallic disc"*, which flew alongside his aircraft before speeding off. The mystery object was also detected by RAF radars on the ground, which recorded it travelling at speeds far in excess of any known aircraft.

Here is another illustration shown from another pilot who saw this while flying over Mount Kilimanjaro.

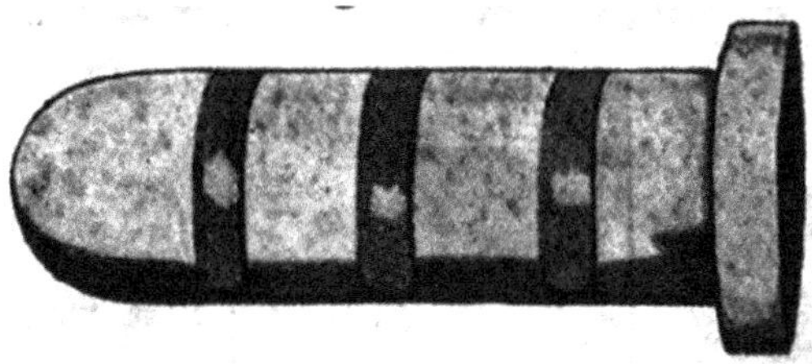

Sighting reported personally to Aviation Minister

Hughes reported the sighting to his senior officers, who sent him to see Duncan Sandys – the then Aviation Minister – to brief him personally. In one document – written a few days after the interview with the 23 year-old Hughes – The Minister tells the government's chief scientist – Lord Cherwell – about the meeting and states that he found the airman's account and the supporting evidence from radar "convincing". The sighting came shortly after a number of similar 'flying saucer' reports from US airmen, and added:

"I have no doubt at all that (Hughes) saw a phenomenon similar to that described by numerous observers in the United States."

Duncan Sandys, Aviation Minister

Lord Cherwell

Lord Cherwell had dismissed the US sightings as *"mass psychology"*, but in his memo Sandys takes him to task for this attitude and makes clear his position on the existence of UFOs. The minister, who was later promoted to Defence Secretary, went on:

> *"Until some satisfactory scientific explanation can be provided, it would be most unwise to accept, without further question, the view that 'flying saucers' can be dismissed as 'a mild form of hysteria."*

"Saucer Sam"

A 'FLYING DINNER-PLATE' FLASHES BY

28 JUL 1952

A FLASHING object " like a large silver dinner-plate " was seen flying high over Liverpool yesterday.

Four women and a man, an ex-R A F observer, told police they had seen it travelling east. After six minutes it disappeared behind clouds.

Said Mrs. Ann Cox Beswick: " I saw a small patch of blue in the sky . . . it increased . . . there were spasmodic white flashes. It appeared to wobble."

Mrs. Cox then told her 21-year-old daughter Wenda, her nephew Robin Williams, her neighbour, Mrs. Murray and daughter.

They, too, said they had seen the flashing object.

[*The Meteorological Office at Speke and coastguards reported that nothing had been seen.*]

In Washington jet fighters tried to intercept unknown objects spotted by radar. They failed.

Wales: UFO sighted over Berwyn Mountains

In July/August 1952, Gilbert Wilkinson was six and living on the western side of a mountain called Long Mountain, which was shaped roughly like a pig's back: long and rounded. It ran north to south, right on the modern-day border between England and Wales. It was just 30 yards from ancient Offa's Dyke, overlooking the river and Severn valley, with Powys Castle on the opposite hills.

On this particular evening he was watching the sunset over the Berwyn Mountains, with Cader Idris in the distance, when he suddenly saw what looked like a star appear in his line of vision, followed by another five 'points of light' forming a straight line across the sky. He knew this was unusual, because at that time of the evening the brightest stars were only barely visible.

> *"I dashed into the house and said to my mother, 'Come and look; God is turning on the stars'. She reluctantly came out, by which time, of course, there was nothing to see and I was duly scolded for telling fibs! It was only later in life that I came to consider the significance of what I had seen, all those years ago, which became indelibly burnt into my memory and totally unlike anything else I was to ever see again."* **(Source: Personal interview)**

1st August – USA: UFO display

At 1.14am, over Lancaster, California, Sheriff's deputies and others sighted two brilliant red lights, hovering in the sky and manoeuvring for 5 minutes. 4th August – USA: Doughnut-shaped UFO At 11.37am, a woman and her two children from Mt. Vernon, New York, sighted an object shaped like a doughnut, emitting black smoke from its top as it made a 15 feet arc in 1.5 minutes through the sky over a two hour period.

4th August – USA: Cylindrical UFO sighted by vessel

Ship's Master Nils Lewring and Chief Mate Jacob Koelwyn, Third Mate, of the motor vessel Marcala, were 100miles south of New York. 39' 35' N., 72' 24.5' W, at 10am, when they sighted:

> *"...a cylindrical object, estimated to be 10 feet in diameter, some 50-100 feet in height, moving through the sky in a churning or rotary motion. Fifteen seconds later it accelerated away and was lost from sight."*

(Source: Project Blue Book Unknowns)

7th August – USA: Four 'discs'

At 9.08am, over San Antonio, Texas, four glowing white 'discs' were seen in the sky; one was observed to make a 180 degrees turn, the other flew on a straight and level course, one veered off, the other circled the locality during the 70 minute sighting.

9th August – USA: 'Disc'-shaped UFO seen

At 10.50am, a 'disc'-shaped object was seen heading across the sky, at speed, over Lake Charles, Louisiana, by USAF Airman J.P. Raley. At one stage it halted for a few seconds, before continuing on its way during a five to six minute sighting.

18th August – USA: Police sight UFO

At 12.50am, three Police Officers from Fairfield, California, observed an object in the sky changing colour, like a diamond, and changing direction over a period of 30 minutes.

19th August – USA: Two UFOs seen

Red Bluff, California, Ground Observer Corps observer – Albert Lathrop – was on duty at 2.38pm, when he saw:

> *"...two objects, shaped like fat bullets, flying at speed in a straight line across the sky – gone in 25 seconds".*

21st August – USA: Three 'lights' over Texas

At 11.54pm Ex-artillery observer Jack Rosen, from Dallas, Texas, sighted:

> *"...three blue-white 'lights' in the sky, which hovered before descending; one and-a-half minutes later one of them descended more".*

23rd August – USA: Pulsing amber light

At 4.10am, USAF 2nd Lt. H.K. Funseth, a ground radar observer, and two US Navy men, reported having sighted a pulsing amber 'light', moving through the sky over a period of seven minutes.

24th August – USA: Pilot sights two silver balls

A Georgia Air National Guard F-84G jet fighter pilot – Colonel G.W. Johnson – was on patrol over Hermanas, Mexico, at 10.15am, when he saw:

> *"...two, six feet 'silver balls' in abreast formation; one of which turned grey rapidly, the other more slowly. One then changed to a long grey shape during a turn. They were lost from view about 10 minutes later."*

At 5.40pm, on the same day – this time over Tucson, Arizona – Mr and Mrs George White saw:

> *"...a large round, metallic, white 'light', moving in a dancing, wavering motion, for about one minute, with a vague lower surface, flying slowly through the air – then increasing speed."*

At 9.30pm Levelland, Texas, residents – Mr and Mrs Elmer Sharp – reported seeing an object, shaped like a spinning top, changing colour from red to yellow to blue, and with a fiery tail, hovered for 20 minutes, whistling – then flew away. It, or another like it, returned an hour later, at 10.30pm.

25th August – USA: Object seen

Pittsburg, Kansas, radio station musician – William Squires – was up at 5.35am, when he sighted:

> *"...a dull aluminum object, shaped like two meat platters, face-to-face, estimated at 75 feet long, 45 feet wide, and 15 feet thick, hovering about 10 feet above the ground, 100 yards off the road, with a slight rocking motion.*
>
> *Through a window in the front section of the object shone a blue light; the head and shoulders of a man could be seen.*
>
> *The mid-section had numerous windows, through which could be seen some kind of regular movement. A series of small propellers were spaced close together along the outer edge of the object, revolving at high speed. It then ascended vertically, with a sound like a large covey of quail starting to fly at the same time."*

At Holloman Air Force Base, New Mexico, civilian supervisor – Mr Fred Lee, and his foreman – Mr L.A. Aquilar, observed a round silver object, flying southwards in the sky, at 3.40pm. It then turned and flew north, before making a 360 degree turn and heading upwards, three to five minutes later.

26th August – USA: UFO over Nevada

At 12.10am over Lathrop Wells, Nevada, USAF Captain D.A. Woods sighted a large, round, very bright object with a 'V'-shaped contrail, showing a dark cone in the centre, flying at speed across the sky. On one occasion it stopped in flight and made an instantaneous 90 degree turn, followed by a gentle climb and finally sudden acceleration.

28th August – USA: Six UFOs seen over Air Force Base

At Chickasaw and Brookley Air Force Base, Alabama, USAF control tower operators, an officer from USAF Office of Special Investigations, and others, were on duty at 9.30pm when they saw six objects, varying from fiery red to sparkling diamond in appearance, motionless in the sky.

These were seen to move erratically in up and down movements for one hour and 15 minutes.

29th August – USA: Three UFOs sighted by pilot

At 8.35pm, Colorado Springs, Colorado Pilot C.A. Magruder reported having sighted:

> *"...three objects – 50 feet in diameter, 10 feet high, aluminium in colour with a red-yellow exhaust – flying in formation at an estimated speed of 1,500 mph, for four to five seconds".*

These may well have been the same objects sighted over Thule, Greenland, by two US Navy pilots, at 10.50am the same day.

1st September – USA: UFOs tracked on radar

At 4.45am over Yaak, Montana, a visual sighting by two USAF enlisted men, corroborated by radar tracking using AN/FPS-3 radar set, plotted two small, varicoloured lights, flying erratically for over an hour, which became black silhouettes as dawn approached. At 10.30pm two large objects, shaped like spinning tops and displaying red, blue and green colours, were seen flying side by side through the sky over Marietta, Georgia, leaving a sparkling trail in the air which lasted 30 minutes.

2nd September – USA: 40 targets

At 3am, a radar operative at Midway Airport, Chicago, Illinois, plotted forty targets flying in miscellaneous directions, up to 175 mph.

Two appeared to fly in formation with a DC-6 airliner. The sighting went on for a total of eight hours.

3rd September – USA: Dark ellipse

Over Tucson, Arizona, civilian pilots – Mr McCraven and Mr Thomas – sighted a shiny, dark, ellipse in the sky, which made three broad, curving sweeps in 1.5 minutes.

6th September – USA: Object seen

At 4.55pm, ex-congresswoman – Mrs Isabella King, and Bill McClain, were in Tucson, Arizona, when they saw an orange teardrop-shaped object, whirling on its vertical axis and descending fast through the sky. It then stopped and retraced its path upwards, while whirling in the opposite direction, before being lost from view one and-a-half minutes later.

12th September – USA: report of a monster seen in West Virginia

Wikipedia reports (2106) The Flatwoods Monster, also known as the Braxton County Monster or the Phantom of Flatwoods, is an alleged unidentified extraterrestrial or creature reported to have been sighted in the town of Flatwoods in Braxton County, West Virginia, United States. Stories of the creature are an example of a purported close encounter of the third kind.

Braxton Co. Residents Faint, Become Ill After Run-In With Weird 10-Foot Monster

Seven Braxton County residents Saturday reporting seeing a 10-foot Frankenstein-like monster in the hills above Flatwood.

They said they saw the monster Friday night when they climbed a wooded hill to investigate reports that a flying saucer had landed.

Mrs. Kathlyn May, Flatwood, said she and six boys, including a 17-year-old member of the National Guard, started to search for a bright object which her two small sons said they had seen come down.

However, State Police laughed the reports off as hysteria. They said the so-called monster had grown from seven to 17 feet in 24 hours.

The National Guard member, Gene Lemon, was leading the group when he said he saw what appeared to be a pair of bright eyes in a tree. At first he thought it was an oppossum or a raccoon but when he shone his flashlight on it, he said, he saw a 10-foot monster with a blood-red face and a green body that seemed to glow.

Mrs. May said Lemon let out a terrified scream and fell over backwards. She said the monster started toward them with a bounding motion.

All of the party agreed that there was an overpowering smell that burned the nostrils and made them sick. Several of the party fainted and vomited for several hours after returning to town.

A. Lee Stewart, co-publisher of the Braxton County Democrat, said he and several men armed with shotguns returned with Lemon about a half-hour to an hour later, and reported a sickening odor still present. He said there were also slight heat waves in the air.

"Those people were the most scared people I've ever seen," Stewart said. "People don't make up that kind of story that quickly."

Both Mrs. May and Lemon described the thing as having the shape of a man, blood-red face, bright green body, protruding eyes, and hand extended forward and appeared to give off an eerie light. They said it had a black shield affair in the shape of an ace of spades behind it and wore what looked like a pleated metallic shirt.

"It looked worse than Frankenstein," Mrs. May said.

At 7.15pm brothers, Edward and Fred May, and their friend Tommy Hyer (ages 13, 12, and 10, respectively) witnessed a bright object crossing the sky. The object appeared to come to rest on land belonging to local farmer G. Bailey Fisher. Upon witnessing the object, the boys went to the home of the May brothers' mother – Kathleen May – where they reported seeing a UFO crash-land in the hills. From there, Mrs May, accompanied by the three boys, local children – Neil Nunley (14) and Ronnie Shaver (10), and 17-year-old West Virginia National Guardsman Eugene 'Gene' Lemon – travelled to the Fisher farm in an effort to locate whatever it was that the boys had seen.

Pulsating 'ball of fire' seen – creature reported

Lemon's dog ran ahead out of sight and suddenly began barking, and moments later ran back to the group with its tail between its legs. After travelling about 0.25 miles the group reached the top of a hill, where they reportedly saw a large pulsating 'ball of fire', about 50 feet (15m) to their right. They also detected a pungent 'mist' that made their eyes and noses burn.

Lemon then noticed two small lights to the left of the object, underneath a nearby oak tree, and directed his flashlight towards them, revealing the creature – which was reported to have emitted a shrill hissing noise before gliding towards them, changing direction, and then heading off towards the red light. At this point the group fled in panic.

Sheriff's department contacted

Upon returning home, Mrs May contacted local Sheriff Robert Carr and Mr A. Lee Stewert, co-owner of the Braxton Democrat – a local newspaper. Stewert conducted a number of interviews and returned to the site with Lemon later that night, where he reported that *"there was a sickening, burnt, metallic odor still prevailing"*. Sheriff Carr and his deputy Burnell Long searched the area separately, but reported finding no trace of the encounter other than the smell.

Early the next morning, Stewert visited the site of the encounter for a second time and discovered two elongated tracks in the mud, as well as traces of a thick black liquid. He immediately reported them as being possible signs of a 'saucer' landing, based on the premise that the area had not been subjected to vehicle traffic for at least a year. It was later revealed that the tracks were likely to have been those of a 1942 Chevrolet pickup truck driven by local Max Lockard, who had gone to the site to look for the creature some hours prior to Stewert's discovery.

Civilian Saucer Investigation, Los Angeles investigates incident

After the event, Mr William and Donna Smith – investigators associated with Civilian Saucer Investigation, Los Angeles – obtained a number of accounts from witnesses who claimed to have experienced a similar, or related phenomena. These accounts included the story of a mother and her 21 year-old daughter, who claimed to have encountered a creature with the same appearance and odour a week prior to the 12th September incident.

The encounter reportedly affected the daughter so badly that she was confined to Clarksburg Hospital for three weeks. They also gathered a statement from the mother of Eugene Lemon, in which she said that, at the approximate time of the crash, her house had been violently shaken and her radio had cut out for 45 minutes, and a report from the director of the local Board of Education, in which he claimed to have seen a 'flying saucer' taking off at 6.30am on the 13th September (the morning after the creature was sighted).

September – 'Flying triangle' UFO reported by Allied Naval Fleet

In September 1952, NATO's first Exercise, 'Operation Mainbrace', was conceived by General Eisenhower to show NATO members Norway and Denmark that their land could be defended in the event of war with Russia. It involved the use of 200 ships from eight nations and over 80,000 men, and it was held in the North Atlantic, between Ireland and Iceland.

13th September – Triangular UFO sighted – three rays of light

During the night of 13th September 1952, Lieutenant Commander Schmidt Jensen and several members of his crew aboard the Danish Destroyer class Willemoes, were north of Bornholm Island when they saw an unidentified object, triangular in shape, emitting a bluish glow, moving at high speed towards the south-east, at an estimated speed of over 900mph.

> *"I was in charge of the bridge and the Captain had just turned in. The sky was clear when, suddenly, we heard a whistling sound and saw a 'flying triangle' passing at speed. It was luminous, with a greenish light, and flew with one corner pointing forward. From its rear*

Sunday Dispatc

151st Year. No. 7,872. 2½d. SEPTEMBER 21, 1952.

What Intruded Into 'Exercise Mainbr

'SAUCER' CHASED R JET PLANE

Say 6 Airmen

NOT Smoke-Ring Or Weather Balloon, Says Pilot

By Sunday Dispatch Reporter

SERIOUS investigation was being made last night by the R.A.F. into the mystery of a silvery-white object that chased a Meteor jet-plane over Yorkshire during "Exercise Mainbrace."

It was seen by two R.A.F. officers and three aircrew as they stood near Coastal Command Shackleton Squadron H.Q. at Topcliffe.

Here are five of the R.A.F. men who saw the Flying Saucer. Left to right standing: L.A.C. Grime, Sgt. T. B. Dewys, Master Sigs. A. E. Thompson, Flight-Lieut M. Cybulski, Flight-Lieut. J. W. Kilburn.

They had just landed after a flight and were watching a Meteor coming in to land at the neighbouring Dishforth R.A.F. station.

One of them, Flight Lieut. John W. Kilburn, 31, of Egremont, Cumberland, then spotted "something different from anything I have ever seen in 3,700 hours flying in a variety of conditions."

He told me last night:

"It was 10.53 a.m. on Friday. The Meteor was coming down from about 5,000ft. The sky was clear. There was sunshine and unlimited visibility.

"The Meteor was crossing from East to West when I noticed the white object in the sky.

"This object was silver and circular in shape, about 10,000ft. up some five miles astern of the aircraft. It appeared to be travelling at a lower speed than the Meteor but was on the same course.

GOLF MATCH OF THE CENTURY!

BEN JOHNSON & CO. LTD.

YORKSHIRE **Evening Press** LATE CITY

WORK OF QUALITY AND RELIABLE SERVICE

IDEAL LAUNDRY

SATURDAY, SEPTEMBER 20, 1952. A KEMSLEY NEWSPAPER.

TOPCLIFFE AIRMEN SIGHT A "FLYING SAUCER"

"Incredible Speed"

THE captain of a Coastal Command Shackleton aircraft at R.A.F. Station, Topcliffe, to-day told an "Evening Press" reporter about the "flying saucer" which he saw while he was standing near a hangar on the station.

He is Flight Lieutenant John William Kilburn (31), of Thornhill, Cumberland, who has been in the R.A.F. for 16 years, 11 of them as aircrew. He said: "I noticed a white object and assumed that its height was between 10,000 and 20,000 feet. It was five miles astern of a Meteor jet aircraft. It was silver in colour, circular in shape and looked to be solid. The sun was glistening on it.

"It appeared to be travelling at a much slower speed than the Meteor but on a similar course. It maintained its slow forward speed for several seconds before it started to descend, then began swinging with a pendulum action, something similar to a falling sycamore leaf.

"I thought it might be a parachute or an engine cowling at first sight.

"The Meteor turned towards Dishforth and this object followed suit. After a few seconds it stopped its pendulum motion and started to rotate about its own axis. It then made off at an incredible speed towards the west turning south-east before disappearing."

MATTER OF SECONDS

Flu? Grin And Bear It

A COMMITTEE of the World Health Organisation has spent five days discussing influenza, and its verdict—the world cannot control influenza.

The chairman, M. Pierre Lepine, reported that there are so many different types of influenza virus that experts never know which type of vaccine to prepare in advance.

The development of an epidemic is too swift for a vaccine to be prepared in time to deal with a particular outbreak.—B.U.P.

£500 Bail For Estate Agent

ARRESTED last night by Chief Inspector Bliss and other Scotland Yard fraud squad officers, Patrick Murphy (40), building contractor and estate agent, Fawley Road, West

12 Months For Crystal-Gazer

A CLAIRVOYANT, John D'Arcy (36), was sentenced to 12 months' imprisonment to-day, at Hastings Borough Quarter Sessions, and Ray Metcalf (31), a writer, to six months' imprisonment, on charges of conspiring to defraud a widow, who, it was stated, was told during a crystal-gazing incident at Bexhill that she would "marry a dark young man."

They were jointly charged with conspiring together between June 12 and July 18 to defraud Mrs. Agnes Frances Drake, of St. Matthew's Gardens, St. Leonards, "of such moneys as she might be induced to part with by false representations."

Metcalf was also charged with stealing a diamond ring value £165, the property of Mrs. Drake, and alternatively with fraudulently converting the ring given to him to have the gold taken out and made into a clip.

He was found not guilty on charges relating to the diamond ring. Both had pleaded not guilty.

When the case was resumed to-day, D'Arcy was questioned by Mr. Sidney Noakes, prosecuting, who asked, "Were you telling her she was likely to have a second husband?" D'Arcy replied, "Yes, I was. I described

CAR OUTPUT, EXPORTS ARE DOWN

THE Society of Motor Manufacturers and Traders announce that the average weekly output during July—7,500 cars and 4,530 commercial vehicles—showed a fall of more than 1,200 and 570 units respectively compared with the weekly average figures during the first half of this year.

The month's figures were, however, affected to some extent by strikes in the industry.

JULY FIGURES

July exports of cars, 25,942, valued at £9,500,000, although higher in volume and value than in June, were below the monthly average figures for the first half of the year.

Commercial vehicle shipments for July, 11,364, valued at almost £7,100,000, were higher than comparable figures a year ago.

jetted three rays of fire, backwards. I have no idea how high it was, so I could not judge either its size or speed but I believe it went at more than 1,500 km per hour. It disappeared in a north-westerly direction. I have studied some astronomy and have also learned to identify most of the modern planes and I am sure it was neither."

[Comment: Although this may appear to be a one-off case, the reader should be aware of a particularly heavy period of UFO activity taking place in the USA at that time, involving over 580 reports of unidentified flying objects seen beginning in July 1947. This information is taken from the files of 'Blue Book unknowns' kept at Maxwell Air Force Base. We should not overlook the importance of the description either, bearing in mind the countless times that witnesses to UFO activity have reported seeing three objects, three rays of light, three entities, and three craft.

(Source: Don Berliner Fund for UFO Research)

13th September – USA: Object like 'fat football'

UFO 'fat football' sighted in sky Mr W.A. Hobler was flying a Beech Bonanza over Allentown, Pennsylvania at 7.40pm, when he saw:

"...an object, shaped like a 'fat football', flaming orange-red in colour, descending through the sky, which then pulled up in front of the airplane; two seconds later it disappeared from view".

Fall River (MA) *Herald-News*, July 29, 1952

Jets Told to Shoot Down Flying Discs

Air Force Puzzled But No Longer Skeptical

By DARRELL GARWOOD

WASHINGTON, (INS)—The Air Force, stumped by the inability of 600-mile-an-hour jet planes to catch "flying saucers," turned today to a new type camera to solve the 5-year-old sky mystery.

Jet pilots are operating under a 24-hour nation-wide "alert" to chase the mysterious objects and to "shoot them down" if they ignore orders to land.

However, the Air Force confessed that none of its jets have come within shooting range of the blinking, enigmatic flying discs.

Several pilots, according to the Air Force, have tried to shoot down the mysterious discs but the "steady bright lights" in the sky have outflown the pilots by as much as a thousand miles an hour.

An AF spokesman said a new-type camera may be able to bring the mystery to an end. He said the camera photographs "luminous phenomenon." It uses the principle employed by astronomers in determining the composition of stars. Air Force scientists hope to determine the physical makeup of the phenomenon and identify its source.

Maj. Gen. John A. Samford, chief of Air Force Intelligence, said the new type cameras have been ordered and will be distributed to jet plane pilots as soon as they become available.

Meanwhile, as new reports continued to pour into the Pentagon of more sightings of mysterious objects the Air Force summoned several "saucer" specialists from Dayton, Ohio, for a conference today.

Called to Washington were Capt. E. J. Ruppelt and several fellow officers from the Air Technical Intelligence Center at Wright-Patterson Field.

The Air Force said it is receiving new reports of "flying saucers" at the rate of 100 a month.

The Air Force contended that its intensive investigation of more than 1,000 "saucer" reports has convinced it that they are not being sent over the United States by an enemy.

The AF added that its investigation indicated also that they are not being controlled by "a reasoning body."

Forty-eight hours of intensive investigation has failed to explain radar and visual observation of unidentified objects accompanied by brilliant white and colored lights on two successive weekends over Washington. The so-called "saucers" were seen on both Air Force and Civil Aeronautic Authority radarscopes. How the CAA sightings were made was described by a radar specialist, James M. Ritchey of the Washington Air Route Traffic Control Center.

"Dozen Objects"

"Until unidentified objects began moving onto our radarscopes, I thought people who reported flying saucers were just seeing things," he said.

"Now I don't know what to think. I have talked to representatives of the Air Force, and they say they can't explain the appearance of the flying objects.

"All we can do is tell you what we saw on our instruments, and

(Continued on Page Six)

(From Barry Greenwood newsclipping collection)

14th September – USA: Red cigar-shaped UFO seen

At 7pm, a member of the Ground Observer Corps – Mr L.W. Barnes, from White Lake, South Dakota – sighted a red, cigar-shaped object, with three 'puffs' of what is believed to have been smoke behind it, flying westwards. It then altered course to the south-west, changed direction to southwards, and was gone 30-40 minutes later.

At 8.40pm, while over Santa Barbara, California, a USAF C-54 transport pilot reported seeing a blue-white 'light' travelling in the sky adjacent to his plane, before if then headed upwards thirty seconds later.

16th September – USA: Five 'lights' seen and tracked on radar

At 6.22pm over Portland, Maine, the crew of a US Navy P2V Neptune patrol plane sighted a group of five 'lights', while a long, thin blip was being tracked on radar. Although some consideration was given to this being USAF KC-97 airplanes, involved in a refuelling operation, it appears unlikely to be the case. The sighting lasted 20 minutes. At 7.30pm the same day, three USAF officers and two civilians from Warner Robbins Air Force Base, Georgia, sighted two white 'lights' heading across the sky, side by side, at an estimated speed of 100 miles per hour, over a period of 15 minutes observation.

17th September – USA: Flat shining objects

At 11.40am on 17th September 1952 over Tucson, Arizona, Mr and Mrs Ted Hollingsworth sighted:

> *"...two groups of three large, flat, shining objects, flying in tight formations. The first group was slow, the second faster – both out of sight, two minutes later".*

19th September – England: RAF pilots sight UFO over RAF Topcliffe

On 19th September 1952, two RAF officers and three members of the ground crew were stood near Coastal Command, Shackleton Squadron, at RAF Topcliffe, watching a Meteor Jet descending to land at the nearby Dishforth airbase, at 10.30am.

In an interview later held with a reporter from the *Sunday Dispatch* (21.9.1952), Flight Lieutenant John W. Kilburn from Egremont, Cumberland, had this to say:

> *"It was something different from anything I have ever seen in 3,700 hours of flying in a variety of conditions. As the Meteor crossed from east to west, I noticed a white object in the sky. It was silver and circular in shape, about 10,000ft up, some five miles astern of the aircraft. It appeared to be travelling at a lower speed than the Meteor, but was on the same course. I said 'What the hell is that?', and the chaps looked to where I was pointing. Somebody shouted that it might be the engine cowling of a Meteor falling out of the sky – then we thought it might have been a parachute – but, as we watched the 'disc', it maintained a slow forward speed for a few seconds, before starting to descend. While descending, it was swinging in a pendulum fashion from left to right. As the Meteor turned to start its landing run, the object appeared to be following but, after a few seconds, it stopped its descent and hung in the air, rotating as if on its own axis. It then accelerated at an incredible speed to the west, turned south-east and disappeared. It was difficult to estimate the speed of the object, as it was all over within 15-20 seconds. During that time, we could see it was flashing in the sunshine. It appeared to be about the size of a Vampire Jet aircraft, at similar height. We were all convinced it was some solid object.*
>
> *We realised it could not be a broken cowling, or parachute. There was not the slightest possibility it was a smoke ring, or vapour trail from the Meteor or from a jet aircraft, nor a weather observation balloon. The speed of which it moved discounts this altogether."*

The other air crew – Flight Lieutenant Marian Cybulski, Master Signaller Albert W. Thompson, Sergeant Flight Engineer Thomas B. Dewey and Flight Lieutenant R.M. Paris – confirmed the account given by F/Lt. Kilburn. In addition, LAC George Grime told of seeing:

> *"...a sort of halo shining on the centre of the object; it appeared to be going round and shine as it turned. It was a solid object, with no marks on it."*

(Source: *North Evening Gazette*, 29.9.1952 – 'Flying saucer seen /*Sunday Dispatch*, 7.12.1952 – 'RAF's saucer – still a mystery')

September – 'Flying saucer' seen over Dishforth, by woman picnicking

Although we cannot say positively that this was the same UFO seen by Mrs Kathleen V. Wilson-Sharp of High Lawns, Colchester, who was enjoying a picnic with her husband near Crayke, in September 1952, it appears to have been very likely, bearing in mind the course of a conversation held shortly after, with the commanding officer of RAF Dishforth Aerodrome.

> *"I was watching some Fighters coming in to land at Dishforth Aerodrome, about 20 miles away to the North, when I noticed a circular object emerge out of two very dark clouds and hover above the Aerodrome. At first I thought it must be a weather balloon, as it appeared stationary, when suddenly it turned and streaked off in a very un-balloon-like horizontal and speedy manner. When I first saw the object, it caught the light of the sun. When it turned, it had a brilliant light of its own. Actually, it seemed to me to be more like an inverted cup and saucer, not unlike a lemon squeezer."*

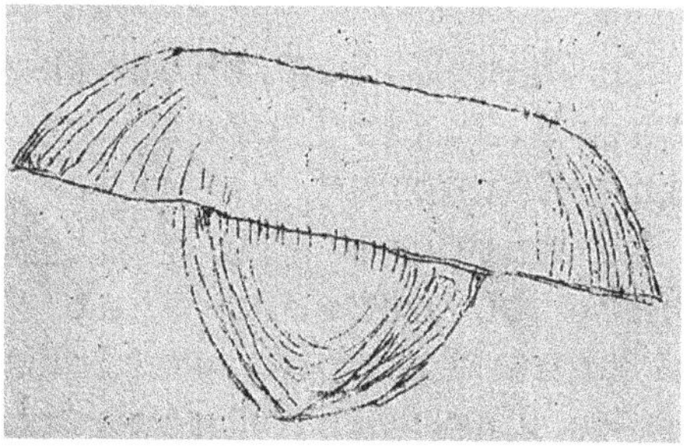

Mrs Wilson-Sharp was so puzzled about what she had seen that she wrote to the commanding officer at Dishforth Aerodrome, asking if anyone there had seen it. He wrote back by return, thanking her for the clear description of it and stating that six of his officers had seen it and that their description tallied with hers.

RAF Officer was writing a book on the subject!

He also told her that he was 'collecting all the evidence he could and had written and published a book on the subject' – What a pity we do not have a copy of this letter, or the book, never mind his identity! Mrs Wilson-Sharp wrote a letter containing the above information to Dr. Geoffrey G. Doel – a member of the Royal College of Surgeons – then involved with the London Unidentified Flying Object Research Organization (LUFORO).

'Saucer' hiding in the cloud

Following publication of her sighting in the London UFO Research Bulletin of 4th April 1962, Mrs Wilson-Sharp wrote back to Dr. Geoffrey Dole, explaining the object she had seen in the April edition was in reverse position to that printed, adding:

"A lumbering old bomber made its way between the two dark clouds, the wings being hidden in the dark cloud on each side and the fuselage quite clear between the clouds. As it came through the clouds, it must have disturbed the 'saucer', which was hiding in the cloud on the left from my view of it, and it seemed to roll over and present its brilliant side direct towards me and probably turn over on its dark side – then it seemed to roll over again, until it was in position a lemon squeezer would be when in use."

(Source: As above/*LUFORO Bulletin*, Volume 11, No. 4, April 1961)

Questions raised in the House about this matter, seven years later!

According to Hansard, on February 2nd 1959 (seven years after the Topcliffe sighting had taken place), Mr Mason asked the Secretary of State for Air – Mr George Ward – for the results of the enquiry into the unidentified flying objects sighted by airmen, during NATO's 'Operation Mainbrace', on 19th September 1952.

Mr Ward replied, *"No object was ever identified"*.

20th September – England: UFO seen over Sutton, Surrey

On 20th September 1952, a white object was seen in the sky over Sutton, Surrey, by Mr John S. Cracker, shortly after three RAF Jets had passed overhead.

21st September – England: UFO sighted by RAF jets

On the 21st September, a squadron of six RAF Jets – on manoeuvres over the North Sea, taking part in the ongoing Exercise 'Operation Mainbrace' – sighted a 'sphere' heading towards their position. When one of the jets attempted to intercept the object, apparently tracked on radar, it shot off across the sky at tremendous speed. Later that evening, at 10pm, Mr Thomas Higgins from Margate, Kent, was strolling along the jetty when he saw four 'flying saucers' cross the sky.

22nd September – England: UFO sighted by motorist

On 22nd September 1952, Mr C.E. Hading of Potters Bar was driving through Stony Stratford, Milton Keynes, about a mile away from Dunstable Road, when he saw an illuminated 'disc' travelling at considerable height.

"It looked like an illuminated dinner plate, or full moon, crossing the sky. Suddenly, it accelerated and darted away at tremendous speed."

24th September – USA: Flashing particles stream past B-29

At 3.30pm, the crew of a USAF B-29 bomber over Charleston, West Virginia, reported having seen:

"...a lot of bright, metallic particles, or flashes, up to three feet in length, streaming past the aircraft, for 15 minutes".

29th September – USA: Five or six objects seen in sky.

At 3.15pm, USAF serviceman T/Sgt. Mr B.R. Hughes was in Aurora, Colorado, when he saw:

> *"...five or six circular objects in the sky – bright white, not shiny, circling in trail formation – for five to six minutes".*

September – England: UFO tracked on radar

Frank Redfern described his duty in the RAF, serving under ex-Battle of Britain's 'Tiger' Shaw, at RAF Neatishead in the 1950s.

> *"In September 1952, during 'Operation Mainbrace', I was manning the radar screen when, just after 4am, the scope picked up an object, which at first I thought may have been an aircraft, travelling at 50,000 feet over the North Sea, and parallel to the English Coast. I then realised, due to its enormous speed, this could not be so. Aircraft from RAF Coltishall were scrambled to intercept.*

One of the jets attempted to intercept the object, but it shot off across the sky at tremendous speed, heading towards Norway.

The next day, a group of people from Coltishall arrived. They included a photographic team and additional radar equipment.

Frank Redfern (left) with UFO author son, Nick Redfern

To our surprise, the UFO showed up again on the scope and they scrambled the aircraft. As far as I know, they did capture it on film. The following day, the radar tapes and records kept of the incident were seized by a group from Coltishall, and that was the last I heard of it." **(Source: Personal interview)**

Ultimately Frank provided the trigger of curiosity for his son Nick Redfern now living in the States who is well known as an authority on the UFO subject and other strange phenomena. Nick has been a prolific writer of many books over the years and we wish him continuing success.

September – England: UFO over Bexleyheath, Kent

One September afternoon in 1952, Kenneth Fairman was on his way home from Bexleyheath School, with his friend – Roy Beadle – and his collie dog. As they approached the Warren (now Warren Road), they noticed a 'circle of lights' descending overhead about 20 feet away. They threw themselves onto the ground, with the dog lying between them, and watched, in stark disbelief, as a dark saucer-shaped object hovered silently above their heads. Suddenly the 'craft', estimated to be 20-30 feet wide, shot up into the sky and headed off towards London.

Kenneth:

> *"A few months after the incident, I was struck down with a mystery illness that baffled the doctors, causing paralysis of the lower limbs. Fortunately, it eventually cleared up."*

(Source: Personal interview)

England: Builder sights UFO over River Deben, Suffolk

Alec White – now living in Felixstowe, Suffolk – wrote to us about what he saw, in 1952, whilst plastering the inside of a house at Waldringfield that overlooked the River Deben, approximately five miles away from RAF Woodbridge.

> *"My mates left me to finish off the bathroom, while they went next door to erect some scaffolding. I was plastering around the window but began to feel hot, so I opened the window, glancing across the river, when I noticed this giant black object hovering just above the water. At first, I wondered if it was something dangling on the end of a crane. If this was the case, where were the cables? It then dawned on me that I was looking at something very unusual. Panicking, I ran next door, climbed up one of the ladders and shouted to my mates, 'Quick! Look out of the window'. All we could see was a giant ring of black smoke. They laughed at me – then a Lancaster Bomber appeared on its landing approach, attracting the comments that what I had seen must have been a flare, which I refused to accept."*

Alec, whose impressive knowledge of aircraft and their applications was triggered by early sightings of Spitfires painted in their pre-war white paint, confirmed he had made enquiries at Martlesham Airbase, shortly afterwards, with regard to the rare appearance of the Lancaster Bomber (then on test with two jet engines, rather than propeller), and remains convinced the crew of the aircraft must have seen the UFO as they flew overhead.

(Source: Personal interview)

Artist impression of the object seen over the River Deben by Alec White

England: Close encounter with mysterious 'bubbles'

Coventry resident – Mr I.P. Painter – was out for a stroll along a country lane where he lived, at 9pm, one pleasant evening in 1952. He was sitting down, smoking a cigarette, when he saw what he first took to be a 'soap bubble' moving across the sky in front of him, against the prevailing wind. He glanced around, expecting to see children – but saw nobody. Thinking a speck of material had settled in his eye, he stood up but was amazed to see a number of other 'bubbles' circling and moving up and down in front of him. To his astonishment, they drew together and seemed to:

> *"...merge into each other, until there was just one 'bubble' left, which reminded me of a goldfish bowl, dirty inside the glass – then it left so quick, it was gone. Was it my imagination? Certainly not! I cannot accept this as fact. I retraced my steps to see if I could find a possible explanation. Some people suggested I had dropped off to sleep and dreamed the incident. Not so, I was wide awake."*

(Source: Isle of Wight UFO Investigation Society)

1st October – USA: Pilots attempts to intercept UFO

At 6.57pm, USAF First Lt. T.J. Pointek of Shaw Air Force Base, South Carolina, was piloting a RF-8O reconnaissance jet, when he saw:

> *"...a white 'light', which flew straight along the sky. It then shot upwards vertically and hovered, before making an abrupt turn during the 23 minutes I attempted to intercept".*

Pascagoula, Mississippi residents Mr and Mrs C.C. McLean, and one other person, were outside at 7.40pm, when they saw:

> *"...a milky-white object, shaped like a powder puff, which hovered for 5-10 minutes – then flew away very fast, in an arc.*

A loud blast was heard at the start of the 22 minute sighting."

10th October – USA: Blinking white 'light'

At 6.30pm, a blinking white 'light' was seen crossing the sky in a pendulum movement, by a USAF S/Sgt. and two other enlisted men from Otis Air Force Base, Massachusetts, before shooting upwards into the sky.

17th October – USA: Ten 'lights' seen

At 10.15pm, Church Ministers Greenwalt and Kluck of Killeen, Texas, sighted ten 'lights' or a rectangle of lights, moving across the sky, for a period of 5 seconds.

19th October – USA: 'V'-shaped formation of three UFOs

Over San Antonio, Texas, ex-USAF aircrew man Mr Woolsey sighted:

> *"...three circular, aluminium objects, one of which was olive-drab coloured on the side, flying in a rough 'V' formation.*

One object flipped slowly; another object stopped, during the 3-4 minute sighting, at 1.30 pm".

21st October – England: RAF pilots sight three UFOs

Air Commodore Michael Swiney, OBE, from Norfolk, spoke of what he witnessed nearly 50 years ago, on the 21st October 1952, whilst a RAF Flight Lieutenant stationed at the Central Flying School, Little Rissington, in Gloucestershire.

At the time of the incident he was instructing Flight Lt. David Crofts – a naval officer – on a high-level exercise.

> *"As we broke cloud cover, I saw what at first I took to be three parachutes in front of the path of the aircraft. Instinctively, I grabbed hold of the control stick and pushed it to one side in an evasive movement, at the same time looking over my left shoulder and directing David Crofts' attention to what I had just seen. At this point, I realised the three objects were not parachute flares but two perfect circular objects, with a third object being on edge showing a fuzzy white. I contacted Little Rissington Control Tower by radio and told the Controller, after some deliberation, he had three UFOs in front of the aircraft, asking him what action should be taken. He replied they would contact the Senior Officer at the airbase for guidance. A check made with Box Radar Station, Wiltshire, confirmed the objects had been plotted on Radar as three 'blips', which then merged into one echo."*

The pilots made their way back to Rissington, flying back through their own contrail in an effort to establish whether they were being followed by the UFOs, bearing in mind the 'blip' on the radar scale had disappeared when the contrails did.

After landing at Little Rissington, they were interviewed separately about the incident but gave identical accounts of what had been seen.

Michael Swiney:

> *"I can't give any explanation for what we saw. I can't say it was any 'Alien' craft, or indeed, representative of any 'Alien' technology. All I can tell you is what we saw."*

Air Commodore Michael Swiney (seen here on the right)

Air Marshal Sir Peter Horsley

Air Marshal Sir Peter Horsley – a former Deputy Chief of Strike Command, later Equerry to HM the Queen and HRH Prince Philip – was to take an interest in this matter on behalf of the Prince, whom it is claimed has always been interested in UFO reports.

We wrote to the Prince's secretary, in 2008 enclosing a copy of the synopsis for this book, asking him whether he would be prepared to obtain the views of Prince Philip on the UFO subject.

Brancaster
KING'S LYNN
Norfolk.

2 March 08.

Dear Mr. Hanson.

Thank you for your recent letter; you caught me a bit 'short' over a photo, but I managed to find something which may do for your purpose. It has the merit of being taken over the time of my episode in Oct. 52 when on the staff at CFS; the glass was for purely medicinal reasons, of course!

The Felpham incident was certainly interesting, and it just goes to show that we're not all mad!

With best wishes,
Yours sincerely,
Michael Swiney.

Air Marshal Sir Peter Horsley (above and below, left) later Equerry to His Royal Highness Prince Philip

From: Mr Sebastian Cox

Head of Air Historical Branch (RAF)
Royal Air Force
Bentley Priory
Stanmore
Middlessex
HA7 3HH

Telephone (Direct dial) 020 8838 7828
(Switchboard) 020 8838 7000
(Fax) 020 8838 7375

Air Cdre M J E Swiney; OBE RAF Ret'd
Skipper's Piece
Brancaster
King's Lynn
Norfolk
PE31 8AA

Your Reference

Our Reference
D/AHB(RAF)8/10

Date
6 August 2001

Dear Air Commodore Swiney MJS. Ack. 17/8

I must first of all apologise for the very long delay in replying to your letter of 23 March 2001. As I believe you are aware your letter's arrival coincided with our having to move the Air Historical Branch from central London to our current home at Bentley Priory. The move was forced on us by the serious structural problems which had been discovered in our previous building, and with three kilometres of classified records to be safely transferred I am afraid it has absorbed the bulk of our efforts over the intervening period. However, we are now safely ensconced here and are steadily working our way through the backlog of mail that has built up in the meantime.

With reference to your quest for the report you submitted whilst at CFS we have been unable to locate any reference to it here in AHB. If, as most such reports were, it was submitted to Air Ministry intelligence, then it will have suffered one of two possible fates. Firstly, if it was considered of sufficient historical interest by the MoD record reviewers, it would have been transferred to the Public Record Office under the terms of the Public Record Act (i.e. the Thirty Year Rule). Assuming it was placed on a file I would expect it to be amongst the Air Intelligence files which are in the PRO as AIR CLASS 40. We have run a brief check on the PRO catalogue by searching under CFS and the date, but without success. If it was transferred it may, however, have been placed on another file perhaps with similar such reports, and I am afraid the only way to be sure of that is to go to the PRO and look at all the files with likely looking titles. There is no other certain method of establishing that it is not in the PRO. If the MoD record reviewers did not consider it worthy of permanent preservation then I am afraid it would have been destroyed, which I think is its most likely fate.

Again, I am sorry my reply has been so long delayed and that we could not be more helpful on this occasion.

Yours sincerely,
Sebastian Cox

Although the Prince's secretary found our letter 'interesting', he refused our request. Details of the incident were also outlined in a book written by Sir Peter Horsley – *Sounds from another Room* (Leo Cooper, 1997, page 177-179):

"Very seldom did visual and Radar match exactly but very occasionally this did occur, as happened in a report from RAF Little Rissington – the Central Flying School, responsible for training Flying Instructors.

An Instructor and his pupil Instructor were carrying out a high-level sortie in a tandem seat Meteor Mk VI – the pupil in the front seat, the Instructor in the rear. The front pilot observed a circular flying object, some distance away dead ahead, filling about three inches of his windscreen, which was approximately two feet across.

He had no previous knowledge or interest in UFOs. The object was so strange he immediately assumed that he had oxygen failure and informed his Instructor, who took over control and turned the aircraft through forty-five degrees. He then saw the object and the two pilots confirmed its description to each other. The Instructor immediately reported the incident to Little Rissington Air Traffic Control. The crew turned again towards the object, opening up to full power at Mach 8. They gained quite rapidly but when the circular object filled half their windscreen, it suddenly turned on its side 'like a plate' [their words] and climbed away out-of-sight at great speed. It was not possible to estimate its size because they did not know its distance. Their description was similar to other reports – circular and emitting an iridescent light around the edges.

Meanwhile, in Fighter Command, Southern Sector radar reported to sector operations an unidentified aircraft travelling through the sector. All unidentified blips were treated as hostile and positively identified and on this occasion a pair of stand-by fighters was scrambled from Tangmere.

At the sector radar head the Little Rissington Meteor appeared on the tube closing in on the unidentified blip, which then moved rapidly across the screen at an estimated speed of over 1,000 miles per hour. Unfortunately, as the Meteor closed, it disappeared into a patch of ground clutters, so it was never possible to measure the final distance between the two and estimate the size of the UFO.

The Tangmere aircraft never made contact with it. The incident was reported to me but, unfortunately, as I was just leaving the country on an overseas tour, I was unable to interview the crew."

Obtaining sight of the original report

In conversation with Mr Swiney about the version of events as given by Sir Peter Horsley, obtained from their original report, Mr Swiney still felt that while his memory of the event was reasonably accurate, he would have liked to have seen a copy of his original report, last seen by him in 1974.

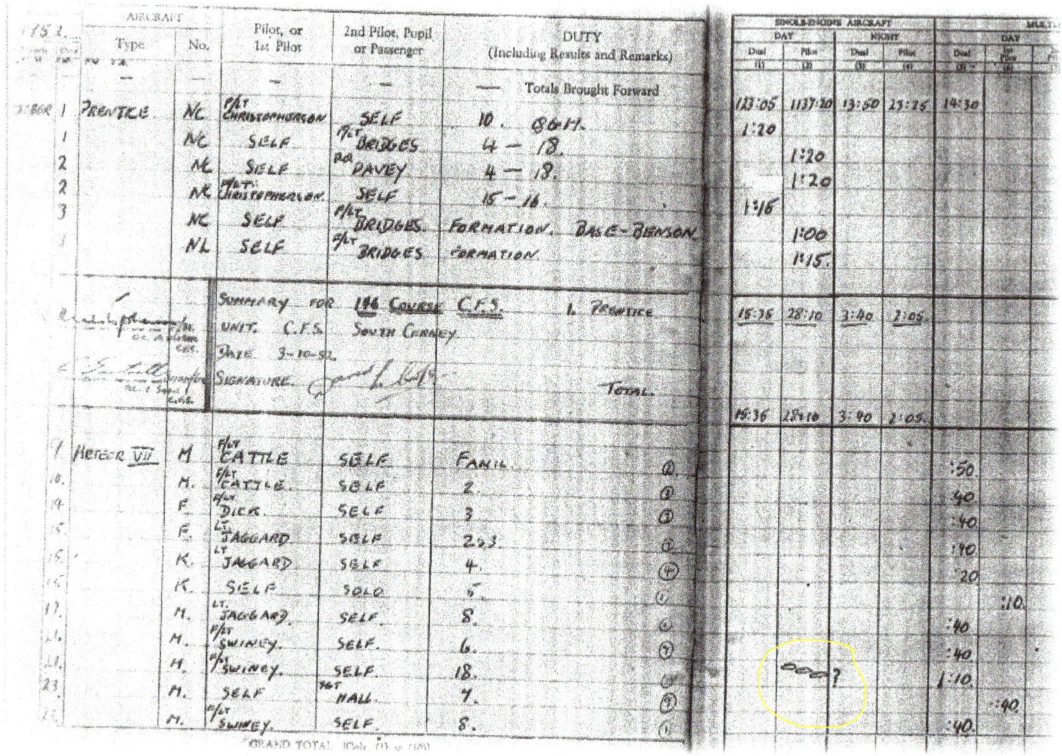

Date	Aircraft Type	No.	Pilot, or 1st Pilot	2nd Pilot, Pupil or Passenger	DUTY (Including Results and Remarks)	Day Dual	Day Pilot	Night Dual	Night Pilot	Day Dual	Day 1st Pilot
					Totals Brought Forward	123:05	1137:20	13:50	23:25	14:30	
1	PRENTICE	NC	F/LT CHRISTOPHERSON	SELF	10. 8&11.	1:20					
1		NC	SELF	F/LT BRIDGES	4 – 18.		1:20				
2		NL	SELF	P.O. DAVEY	4 – 18.		1:20				
2		NK	F/LT CHRISTOPHERSON	SELF	15 – 16.	1:15					
3		NC	SELF	F/LT BRIDGES	FORMATION. BASE–BENSON		1:00				
		NL	SELF	F/LT BRIDGES	FORMATION		1:15				
					SUMMARY FOR 186 COURSE C.F.S. 1. PRENTICE UNIT. C.F.S. SOUTH CERNEY DATE 3-10-52. SIGNATURE TOTAL.	15:36 15:36	28:10 28:10	3:40 3:40	2:05 2:05		
7	METEOR VII	M	F/LT CATTLE	SELF	FAMIL. ①					:50	
10		M.	F/LT CATTLE	SELF	2. ②					:40	
14		F.	F/LT DICK	SELF	3 ③					:40	
15		F.	LT. JAGGARD	SELF	2&3. ③					:40	
15		K.	LT JAGGARD	SELF	4. ④					:20	
15		K.	SELF	SOLO	5.						:10
17		M.	LT. JAGGARD	SELF	8.					:40	
21		M.	F/LT SWINEY	SELF.	6.					:40	
21		M.	F/LT SWINEY	SELF.	18.		⬭⬭⬭?			1:10	
23		M.	SELF	SGT HALL	7.						:40
		M.	F/LT SWINEY	SELF	8.					:40	

GRAND TOTAL

Operational Record Book

In the ORB (Operational Record Book) kept at the Central Flying School, Little Rissington, it contains the following entry, dated 2lst October 1952:

> *"Flight Lieutenant M.I.E. Swiney, Instructor and Lieutenant D. Crofts, Royal Navy, Student, sighted three mysterious 'saucer-shaped objects' travelling at high speed, at about 35,000 feet, whilst on a high-level navigation exercise in a Meteor 7. Later A.T.C.C Gloucester reported radar plots to confirm this but the Air Ministry discounted any possibility of 'extraterrestrial objects."*

Still trying to obtain sight of original report

As the years went by, Mr Swiney attempted to obtain sight of his original report but was informed that, in accordance with MOD procedure, all files had been routinely destroyed at five-year intervals (this practice was halted in 1967, the earliest records being from 1962), which meant his was no longer available for scrutiny – or at least this was the impression the MOD wanted to give!

Seconded to the MOD – original report obtained!

In 1974, during a posting to the MOD itself, Mr Swiney – now an Air Commodore – asked for sight of his original UFO report from 1952 and was handed the document, which contained his

From: David L. Crofts,

Alverstoke,
GOSPORT,
Hants   PO12

31 July 2001

John Hanson Esq.,
PO Box 6371,
BIRMINGHAM
B48 7RW.

Dear Mr. Hanson,

Thank you for your letter and enclosures dated 23.07.01 . Please excuse the delay. We spoke last evening. Your original telephone call was certainly completely unexpected, and since then I have reflected many times on the experience which my flying instructor (now Air Commodore M.J.E. Swiney O.B.E., R.A.F. (Rtd.)) and I shared.

I have spoken to him on the telephone and he forwarded to me his letter which failed to reach me because we had moved house two years ago. He had attempted to warn me that I might be contacted concerning this incident.

It is my opinion that given the passing of nearly fifty years, any report that I could now give you would perhaps be inaccurate to a degree. I believe the most sensible course of action would be for me to suggest that you visit the Public Records Office and consult the papers for 21st October 1952, since following the Thirty Year Rule any government documents are available for public scrutiny. This you could do with my blessing and you would then have the eye witness details to work from.

I shall be most interested to hear what success you have. Meanwhile I enclose a copy of two pages from the book I mentioned which refers to the incident.

Yours sincerely

David L. Crofts.

Encl.

and David Crofts' account, without any fuss, after being told it had been previously filed in the Air Intelligence Branch's Blue Book! After examining them, he placed the files into the out-tray and thought no more of it – until retirement in 2002, when he expressed an interest in having sight of the reports again, and wrote to the RAF's Air Historical Branch, now based at Bentley Priory. He was advised that UFO reports submitted to Air Ministry Intelligence could have been preserved for transfer to the PRO or, alternatively, marked for destruction – which was suggested to have been the likely fate in this instance.

Enquiries made with GCHQ

Dissatisfied, Mr Swiney wrote to the Director General of GCHQ to enquire if their department had retained a copy of the incident, and was later told that while a search of the archives had failed to find the document, his request had been passed to the MOD. They wrote to him explaining, quote:

> *"It was generally the case that before 1967, all UFO files were destroyed after five years but, since 1967, following an increase in public interest, UFO files are now routinely preserved. Any files from the 1950s and early 1960s are available for examination at the PRO."*

Michael Swiney:

> *"If it was generally the case that before 1967 all UFO reports were destroyed after five years, how was it that I actually saw and read it in 1974, some seventeen years later, while serving at the MOD?"* **(Source: Personal interviews)**

We spoke to David Crofts, now living in Hampshire, who corroborated the account given to Mr Swiney, adding:

> *"After a debriefing with two officers from the Air Ministry, I was told by them that the objects were moving at a speed of some 6,000 miles per hour."*

In 2015, we learnt that David had passed away. - Our condolences to his family.

On the same date but this time over Knoxville, Tennessee, employees at an airport weather station logged the sighting of six white 'lights', which were seen to fly in a loose formation for one to two minutes, and make a shallow dive at a weather balloon. Unfortunately, the time of this event is not known.

24th October – USA: UFO shaped like a plate, sighted by pilot

At 8.26pm, a USAF Pilot was flying a Beech trainer over Elberton, Alabama, when he saw an object,

> *"...shaped like a plate, with a brilliant front and vague trail, flying with its concave surface forward, for 5 seconds".*

31st October – USA: Orange UFO sighted

At 7.40pm, an orange blimp-shaped UFO was seen flying at rooftop level over Fayetteville, Georgia, by off duty USAF Officer – Lt. James Allen. The object – described as being 80 feet long and 20 feet high – crossed over Allen's car (at which time his radio had stopped playing), then headed way at a 45 degrees, making tremendous speed, a minute later.

3rd November – USA: Control tower sights UFO

A long, elliptical, white-grey 'light' was seen to fly at a very fast speed over Laredo Air Force Base, Texas, by control tower operators, who noted that it paused and then increased speed, during the three to four seconds observation.

4th November – USA: Whirling 'discs' sighted over New Jersey

At 5.45pm, Vineland, New Jersey housewife – Mrs Sprague – sighted two groups of 2-3 whirling 'discs of light', heading south-east, over a period of 30 seconds.

11th November – England: Oval object seen over Kent

At 4.15pm on 11th November 1952, around forty people living near Hither Green cemetery in Bromley, Kent, sighted 'an oval object in the sky, which constantly changed from oval to conical, before disappearing in a bright flash of light. Five minutes later, a police sergeant and twenty recruits, based at Dover, Kent (some miles away to the south), sighted an object on the western horizon, heading northwards. They described it as brilliant red with a long silvery tail, ten times the diameter of the main 'body'. After about ten minutes, all visibility was lost as the object entered a heavy stratus cloud layer.

(Source: From the files of Project Blue Book & the *Sunday Dispatch*, 23.11.1952 and 25.11.1952)

12th November – USA: Seen over prohibited area

At 10.23pm over Los Alamos, New Mexico, a security inspector sighted four red, white, and green 'lights', flying slowly over a prohibited area, for 15 minutes.

13th November – USA: Oval objects in 'V' formation sighted

At 2.20am, radar tracking by USAF 779th AC & W station, Opheim, Montana, picked up an unexplained track – which was plotted for 1 hour, 28 minutes, at an altitude of 158,000 feet (30 miles) and at a speed of 240 miles per hour.

At 2.43am over Glasgow, Montana, US Weather Bureau observer – Earl Oksendahl, sighted:

> *"...five oval objects, with lights all around them, flying in a 'V' formation, for about 20 seconds. Each object seemed to be changing position vertically, by climbing or diving – as if to hold formation. The formation, which had come from the north-west, made a 90° overhead turn, and then flew south-westwards."*

18th November – USA: UFO follows aircraft

At 3.20am, the crew of Capital Airlines DC-4 Flight 610 notified Andrews Air Force Base Senior air traffic controller – Tom Selby, that while over Washington DC they had seen an object, showing several 'lights' following the aircraft, for about 20 minutes.

20th November – USA: Close encounter with alien beings

George Adamski was out on a picnic lunch with six friends – Mr and Mrs Alice Wells, Mrs Lucy McGinnis, Dr. and Mrs Williamson, and Mr and Mrs Bailey – overlooking a mountain ridge, when a gigantic cigar-shaped 'silvery ship' was seen riding high and soundlessly over the ridge. After lunch had been consumed, they drove towards a hillock with the 'ship' apparently following them (and stopping when they stopped) where George set up his telescope and camera.

Beautiful 'craft' appears in sky

Adamski then asked his companions to leave him on his own. A short time later,

> *"My attention was attracted by a flash in the sky and, almost instantly, a beautiful 'craft' appeared to be drifting between the saddle of two of the mountain peaks and settling silently into one of the coves, about half-a-mile from me."*

Conversation with man from Venus

A short time later, he saw a man standing at the entrance between the low hills, about a quarter-of-a-mile away. On drawing closer, he saw that:

> *"...the person had long hair, and was wearing something like ski trousers. I realised he was a human being from another world. Following a long conversation, conducted through telepathy and hand gestures, I discovered the man was from Venus and was far advanced in knowledge and wisdom to us."*

Eventually, Adamski and the man from Venus made their way back to the small spacecraft, which was hovering about a foot off the ground beyond a small hill. He learned that this had come from the 'Mother ship' they had seen earlier.

Exclusive photo of George Adamski from 'Flying Saucer Review'

Impressions of the footmarks

During the walk, the 'visitor' pointed to some curious markings left by the soles of his shoes on the desert surface. (Adamski later took some plaster impressions of these marks, which are hieroglyphic in visual image.) Adamski then claims he received a shock, which jerked up his right arm and left a bruised numbness that was to last three months, after approaching close to the 'craft'.

The 'man' then climbed in and left, after asking if he could borrow one of the film canisters in George's possession, promising to return it at a later date.

(Source: Charles Davy, *The Observer*, 4.10.1953 – 'A Visitor from Venus')

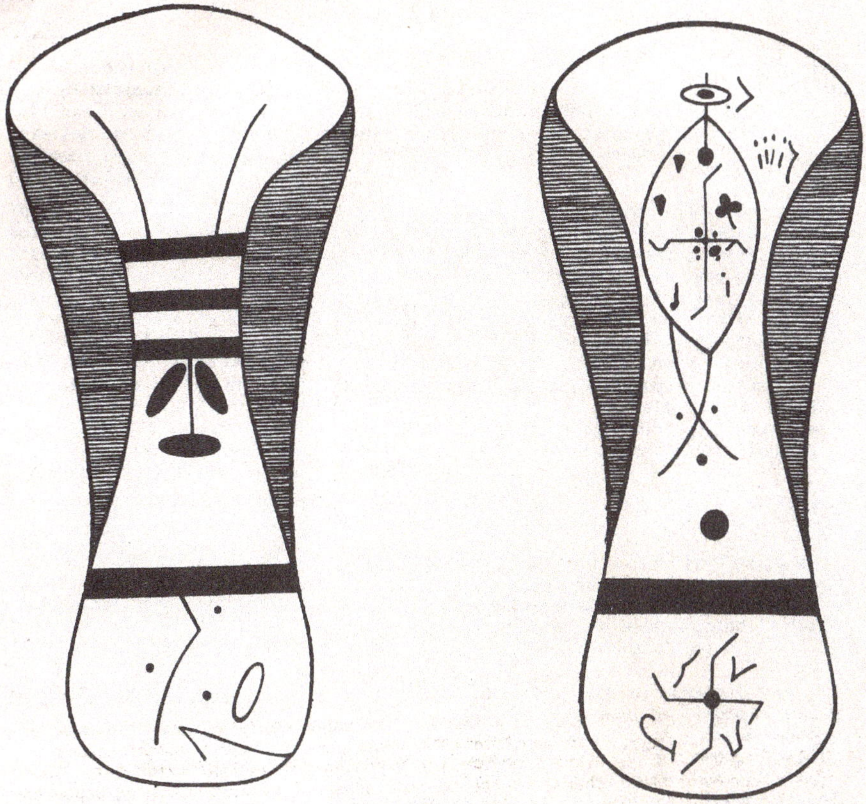

Left footprint   Right footprint

Drawings of the Footprints left in the Arizona Desert by a Venusian Space Visitor on November 20, 1952.

References: *Flying Saucers Have Landed* by Leslie and Adamski.
Other Tongues, Other Flesh by Hunt Williamson.

Published in June 1972, and again seven years later in May 1979
by VIEWPOINT AQUARIUS, c/o Fish Tanks Ltd,
49, Blandford Street, London W.1. England
Tel: (01) 935 3719

All of us earthlings are urged to interpret them: by the mathematics of The Concentric Key, by the Symbology of the Ancients by the Ideographs, the Emblems/Pictographs, the hidden colours/perfumes/harmonies, the seven-fold Keys of the Seven Planes of Consciousness. Mankind's enlightenment may hinge there-on: Space Mind/Full Mind/Manas calls.

Stichting
CENTRAAL PROJECTIE- EN LICHTBEELDEN INSTITUUT
AMSTERDAM-OOST
WEESPERZIJDE 112 - TELEFOON 747266

VLIEGENDE SCHOTELS
FLYING SAUCERS

396

19th December – return visit

At 9am, Mr George Adamski received a visit from his mysterious visitor, who landed to within 100 feet of his house and dropped the film out through a porthole. When the film was developed, the print was found to be covered in hieroglyphics. It was on this occasion that George took a number of photographs of the spaceship, which were reproduced in the book *Flying Saucers Have Landed*, by Desmond Leslie and George Adamski – (Publisher Werner Laurie, price 12 shillings and six pence).

We also learned that a friend – Sergeant Jerrold Baker – who was nearby photographed the 'craft' as it took off.

In his 'write-up' of the account given to him, Charles Davy – the reporter for *The Observer* newspaper – considers whether this was as the result of hallucinations or a hoax, perpetrated as a highly lucrative means of earning considerable monies, following subsequent publicity surrounding the highly unusual events that occurred. However this seems unlikely, bearing in mind the other witnesses who corroborated many parts of the encounter with the man from Venus; apart from that, the description of the 'craft' and its occupants are not unique to that time period and have similarities, too, with many other sightings contained within our books. Even after 60 years it has 'the ring of truth' about it.

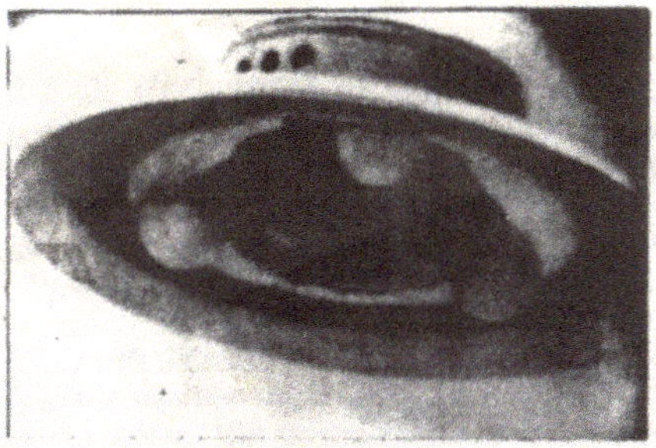

G. ADAMSKI - California - 1952

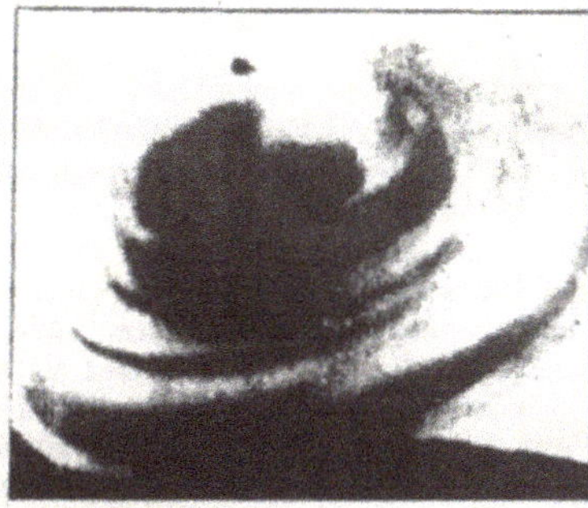

C. ALLINGHAM - Scotland - 1954

M. RODEFFER
Maryland - 1965

GEORGE ADAMSKI

G. ADAMSKI
California - 1952

G. ADAMSKI - California - 1951

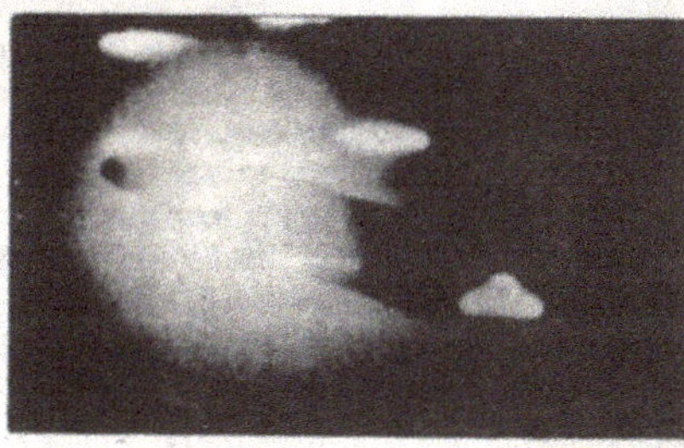

G. ADAMSKI - California - 1951

24th November – 'Flying tadpole' sighted over English Counties

On 24th November 1952, a brilliant 'light', described as resembling a 'flying tadpole or 'green beetle', was sighted moving through the skies over Yorkshire, Suffolk, Kent and Sussex. One witness was Mr Charles Henderson, who saw it from his sister's house in Chichester Road, Bognor Regis; others included Arthur Quick from Aldwick, Bognor Regis.

UFO with three blinding lights seen

Support for the theory that it might be a new top secret plane was given by Mr James Johnson of Westerton, near Chichester, who described seeing:

> *"...a sleek, powerful, jet plane with swept back wings, coming in over Tangmere Aerodrome, Sussex, with three blinding lights on its nose and wingtip."*

The RAF at Tangmere and the Air Ministry denied any experimental plane was based there. The same object also appears to have been seen by railway man – Mr Hardman of Drayton, near Chichester, who said:

> *"I have never seen anything like this before. The plane was equipped with three powerful headlights. They were amazingly brilliant."*

'Flying tadpole' seen over Bognor

Other witnesses included Bognor policeman PC William Keates, who spoke of seeing what he took to be the headlights of a car behind him.

> *"I turned around and saw what looked like a 'flying tadpole' crossing the sky horizontally, lighting up the whole town."*
>
> *Two police officers going off duty, at 6am, told of seeing the sky light up. One of them – PC Tony Cox – thought that sparks from an electric train must be the cause, until he turned around and saw, "...this queer thing speed across the sky, towards the north-east", whilst Frank Croft – a local newsagent – spoke of seeing "what looked like a rocket, which seemed to break up over Tangmere Aerodrome, or somewhere in that direction".*

24th November – USA: UFO characteristics of behaviour

At 6.30pm, over Annandale, Virginia, Mr L Brettner told of seeing a round, glowing object, flying across the sky – which was seen to make very fast, right angle turns and reverse its course, during the one hour sighting. England: Silver 'ball' sighted near Stratford-upon-Avon

In the same year, West Bromwich resident Alfred Mills – founder member of the South Staffordshire Metaphysical Society, employed as an estate clerk for the Birmingham Co-op Society and part-time journalist – was walking along the road close to Moreton Paddock Estates, Moreton Murrell (seven and-a-half miles from Stratford-upon-Avon), one morning at 6.30am.

> *"I saw this large grey silver 'ball' with shimmering edges cross the sky, heading SSE, about 300 feet up in the air. I closed my eyes and opened them. It was still there. It covered 180 degrees of arc in 5-6 seconds. I contacted the editor of the Stratford-Upon-Avon 'Herald' – Mr Grail – who told me a woman living 8 miles away from where I had seen it, had already contacted him about the sighting." (Source: Isle of Wight UFO Society/John 'Dennis' Llewellyn)*

27th November – USA: Mystery black smoke reported

At 12.10pm, the pilot and crew chief of a UAAF B-26 bomber were over Albuquerque, New Mexico, when they saw a series of black smoke bursts (4-3-3-4-3), similar to anti-aircraft fire, over a 20 minute period, up to 12.30am.

30th November – USA: Targets tracked

On this date, over Washington DC, radar operators at Washington National Airport tracked similar targets to those plotted on 26th July 1952.

1953

Stop Press! Chicago man chased in Canada by UFO

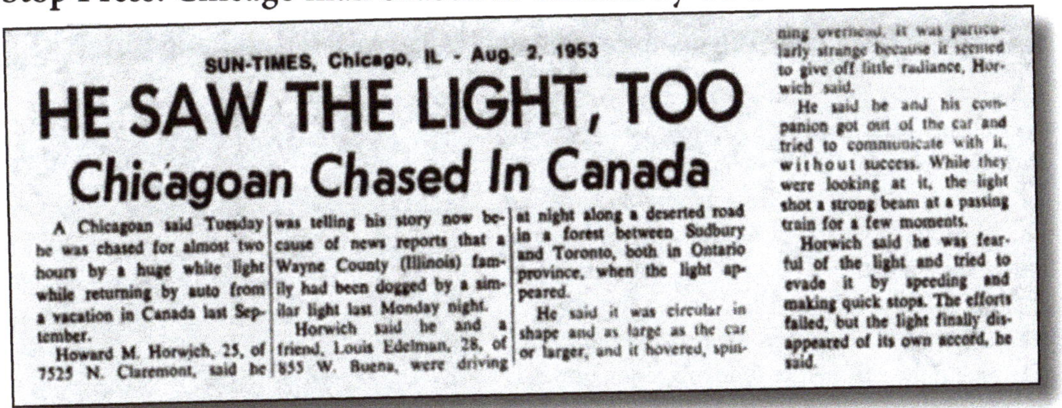

SUN-TIMES, Chicago, IL - Aug. 2, 1953

HE SAW THE LIGHT, TOO

Chicagoan Chased In Canada

A Chicagoan said Tuesday he was chased for almost two hours by a huge white light while returning by auto from a vacation in Canada last September.

Howard M. Horwich, 25, of 7525 N. Claremont, said he was telling his story now because of news reports that a Wayne County (Illinois) family had been dogged by a similar light last Monday night.

Horwich said he and a friend, Louis Edelman, 28, of 855 W. Buena, were driving at night along a deserted road in a forest between Sudbury and Toronto, both in Ontario province, when the light appeared.

He said it was circular in shape and as large as the car or larger, and it hovered, spinning overhead. It was particularly strange because it seemed to give off little radiance, Horwich said.

He said he and his companion got out of the car and tried to communicate with it, without success. While they were looking at it, the light shot a strong beam at a passing train for a few moments.

Horwich said he was fearful of the light and tried to evade it by speeding and making quick stops. The efforts failed, but the light finally disappeared of its own accord, he said.

1st January – USA: Saucer-shaped object seen

AT 8.45pm, Mr Warner Anderson – a Craig, Montana resident – and two women reported having sighted a silver, saucer-shaped object with a red glowing base, flying low over a river and then climb horizontally into the sky, at speed, ten seconds later.

8th January – USA: Green UFO seen by Air Force Officers

At 7.15am, over Larson Air Force Base, a number of men from the 82nd Fighter-Interceptor Squadron, including the squadron commander, were on the ground when they sighted a green, 'disc'-shaped or round object, flying south-west for 15 minutes, in a vertically bobbing motion and sideways movements, below the clouds.

10th January – USA: UFO display

Retired Colonel Robert McNab and Mr Hunter of the Federal Security Agency were in Sonoma, California, at about 3.45pm, when they saw:

"...a flat object, the size of a pinhead, which made three 360 degree right turns in nine seconds through the sky – then made abrupt 90 degree turns to the right and left, stopped before accelerating to its original speed, and finally flew out of sight vertically in 60-75 seconds".

England: Metallic 'flying saucer' sighted over West Yorkshire

Mr Lloyd Mason from Upper House, Hade Edge, West Yorkshire, was walking up a steep hill in the Don Valley, Brightside, Sheffield, in the early 1950s, at 6.30pm, on a clear but cold night.

"Suddenly I was surprised to see, about 500-1,000 feet in the sky above me, a bright orange coloured, large metallic-looking 'flying saucer', showing lights around its sides, with a dome, hovering in the air. It then suddenly shot off across the sky at incredible speed and vanished."

(Source: David Mason)

January – England: Pilot's wife sights UFO – warned to keep quiet!

In January 1953, Mrs M.L. Martin – wife of a RAF serviceman, stationed at RAF Marham, Norfolk – was looking out of the window at 3pm, when she saw what she took to be a jet aircraft, crossing the clear blue sky at high altitude. To her horror, both 'wings' left the fuselage. However, instead of crashing to Earth, they rushed across the sky, one behind the other, before coming to a halt, glinting as they caught the sun, before suddenly rising upwards and disappearing out of sight.

"When I later discussed what I had seen with my husband, he told me all personnel at the airbase had been warned not to breathe a word about a UFO which had, apparently, been seen by other airmen."

Was there a connection with what Mr J.B.W. Angus Brooks – a former RAF Intelligence Officer – sighted on 26th October 1967?

(Source: *Warnings from Flying Friends*, Arthur Shuttlewood)

28th January 1953 – USA: Flat white disc seen

Mr R.W. Love – owner of Love Diving Company, Point Mugu, California, – was engaged in retrieving radio controlled drones at 1pm, when he saw a 18-20 feet white, flat 'disc', heading through the sky overhead on a straight trajectory – gone six minutes later.

Twenty five green spheres seen later the same day

At 6.05pm the same day, still over California, USAF T/Sgt. George Beyer sighted:

> *"...five 25 feet green spheres, flying in 'V' formation through the sky. They then changed formation to one behind the other, the end objects turning red. They were kept under observation for 12 minutes".*

Over Albany, Georgia, at an undetermined time, radar maintenance personnel tracked a stationary target for 20 minutes.

January/February – Hong Kong: UFO tracked on radar – log destroyed

Mr Robert Eldred from Grimsby, South Humberside, was a RAF radar operative seconded to (Army) Bombardier 21, Fire Command Troop 27, Heavy Anti-Aircraft Regiment Royal artillery, near the Chinese border.

> *"The Duty watch operator drew my attention to an unusual fast track on the scope. We checked the set for any malfunctions – there weren't any. By this time, as part of normal procedure, the 'unidentified' target had been passed on to RAF Sector Operation Control. We were asked to clarify by making further checks. Once again, the track was confirmed.*
>
> *We continued to carry on tracking the target, when Sector Operations Control instructed us to delete all records from radar Log, and physically destroy them. The next day we received a visit by a RAF Officer, who I hadn't seen before; he asked to check the logs. He was unable to offer any explanation as to what it was that we had plotted."*

4th February – USA: White oblong-shaped UFO seen

Arizona Weather Bureau observer – Stanley Brown – was using a theodolite, at 1.50pm, when he tracked:

> *"...a white oblong object, flying straight upwards, which then levelled off in flight and was joined by a second, similar, object.*
>
> *The second object was seen to move away but return to the first object on two separate occasions. After five minutes, both were lost to sight behind clouds."*

13th February – Scotland: UFO over Inverness

During the afternoon of 13th February 1953, a grey, oval, object was seen in the sky over Inverness, by local resident George Macpherson.

> *"It turned sideways – now cigar in shape – and then darted backwards and forwards across the sky."*

(Source: *Glasgow Herald/Greenock Telegraph*, February 1953)

17th February – USA: UFO tracked on radar

Two officers and three airmen of USAF AC & W Squadron, Port Austin, Michigan, were on duty at 10.04pm, when they sighted both visually and by radar an object which appeared to be larger and brighter than any star, changing colour as it moved slowly across the sky for five minutes, until 10.09pm.

At 10.08pm, the radar picked up a target moving in a similar direction for 17 minutes, at a similar speed.

20th February – USA: USAF pilots sight UFOs

At 10.30pm, the crew of USAF *B-25* Bomber, flying over Pittsburg, Stockton, California, sighted an unusual bright yellow 'light' for 8 minutes, which flew on a collision course before dimming and accelerating away.

Apparently there was also a second 'light' seen during the same period, but the time when the incident took place is not known.

24th February – USA: Two bright red UFOs seen

At 7.43pm over Sherman, Texas, Warrant Officer and Mrs Alden saw two bright red round objects, with large halos, flying around in small circles; they were then seen to climb and fade away during the three to seven second sighting.

27th February – USA: Five UFOs performing grid pattern in sky

A USAF airman/private pilot sighted:

> *"...five, fluttering yellow 'discs', making circular turns in the sky over *Shreveport, Louisiana, at11.58am. Three of them then vanished, leaving the other two – which performed a number of erratic square turns for a total of four minutes."*

11th March – USA: 'Flashing light' over mountains

At 4am, Mrs Nina Cook – an experienced private pilot and wife of a Pan Am flight engineer – reported having seen a large 'light', flashing 10-15 times per minute, moving up and down along a mountain range at Hackettstown, New Jersey.

21st March – USA: Six 'flying discs' seen

At 3.05pm over Elmira, New York, a member of a Ground Observer Corps observation post sighted:

> *"...six 'discs' in a group, flying high across the sky – gone in a few seconds."*

25th March – USA: UFO display

At 3.05pm, a USAF Captain and a Mrs D.E. Cox from San Antonio, Texas, saw several 'lights' in the sky – some of which moved straight, others making 360 degree turns for one-and-a-half hours.

27th March – USA: Pilot chases UFO

At 7.25pm, a USAF *F-86* Jet fighter was flying at 700 miles per hour over Mt. Taylor, New Mexico, when the pilot saw a bright orange 'circle', moving through the sky at an estimated speed of 900 miles per hour. The plane gave chase but presumably lost it, four minutes later.

29th March – USA: Aluminium UFO sighted

At 3.45pm, Mr L.C. Gillette – a Spooner, Wisconsin resident – was outside when he saw an aluminium, circular, object flying high and fast through the sky, during which it was seen to reverse its course on two occasions over the 15 seconds sighting.

Mr Gillette said he had seen a similar object in 1938.

*Shreveport is the third largest city in the state of Louisiana and the 113th-largest city in the United States. It is the seat of Caddo Parish and extends along the Red River into neighboring Bossier Parish.

12th April – USA: Ten UFOs seen by co-pilot

Major Fred G. Padelford was co-pilot aboard a *C-47* at 10,500 feet, when ten objects were seen in a loose changing formation, flying at 140 miles per hour.

15th April – USA: Three orange 'lights' seen in the sky

At 5.45pm, three orange 'lights' were seen in the sky for three and-a-half minutes over Tucson, Arizona, by S/Sgt. V.A. Locey.

20th April – England: UFO display over Sheffield

On 20th April 1953, an object resembling 'two plates, face-to-face, trailing a red glow, performing a number of strange movements in the sky' was seen by three youths – Terry Platts, Brian Davies and Allan Green – over Rawmarsh, Sheffield. According to the boys,

> *"For most of the time it appeared edge on, but towards the end of the observation it banked and went away, and we saw its circular shape. On moving, it left a long trail of flame ending in black smoke; this stopped when the craft stopped."*

The boys were amazed how slow the object could fly, and the fact that it could dive and stop and start as it flew across the sky. Strangely, the sketch they submitted to the newspaper was not published; instead another one was showing what appeared to be rockert rather than saucer shaped was this Intentional or accidental?

(Source: *Star & Sheffield Telegraph*, 24.4.1953)

Witness' sketch. Newspaper's.

21st April – England: Mystery object sighted over football match

At 7.45pm on 21st April, a brightly lit object was seen hovering motionless in the sky over Norwich, by spectators at a football match, before being lost from view at 8.15pm. It is likely that this was the same UFO sighted by a member of the Royal Observer Corps, at 8.15pm, North of Lowestoft. Through the lens of a telescope, he saw *"what looked like a plastic lighter refuel capsule, with a sharp pointed end"*, move towards the south-west, before turning north-east and disappearing from view, 30 minutes later.

(Source: *Evening News*, Norwich, 25.4.1953)

26th April – USA: 'V' formation

At 7.35pm, Mr A.C. Carter Mr and Mrs H. Hopkins and their daughter, from Athens, Georgia, sighted fifteen to twenty yellow objects, flying across the sky in a 'V' formation, heading in a south to north direction – lost from view ten seconds later.

England: RAF Pilots sight cigar-shaped UFO

RAF/RNAZ Serviceman – Gordon Cammell – was stationed at RAF Coltishall, Norfolk, England, as a jet pilot, flying *Meteor* night fighters. During a routine night flying exercise one of our crews – Captain J. Allison and radar operator Flying Officer I. Heavers – reported sighting a cigar-shaped UFO, with internal green lights visible through windows.

> *"When this crew entered our flight room upon their return, they were both very excited and convinced that the object they had seen was extraterrestrial, because of its very high speed and unusual configuration. The next day we learned the crew of another night fighter jet of number 85 Squadron,*

> *flying near their base at RAF Maidstone, Kent (over one hundred miles from Coltishall), had reported an identical sighting only three minutes after our crew's encounter. Three minutes to cover a distance of 100 miles meant that the UFO was travelling at about 2,000 mph, which was well in excess of the capability of any aircraft in the UK at that time."*

(Source: Personal interviews)

In 1980, a security policeman at the airbase witnessed a diamond-shaped 'craft' fly over the base, preceded by a powerful banging noise.

May – England: Silver UFO sighted over Birmingham

In May 1953 a number of people living in the Birmingham area contacted the police, after sighting a silver coloured object crossing the sky in broad daylight. The sighting was later explained by Edgbaston Observatory as possibly being a leaking weather balloon. **(Source: UFOSIS)**

10th May – USA: Delta-shaped object

US Marine Corps Squadron Leader D.R. Higgin was flying an *F3D-2* Jet fighter over Elsinore, California, at 12.40pm, when he saw a dark gunmetal delta-shaped object, 22 feet long by 10 feet wide, showing a fin on the top. This was then seen to descend at a 25-30 feet angle under the lead airplane of the formation, and over the airplane of the Squadron Leader – gone in a few seconds.

25th May – England: 'Flying saucer' over Brighton

During Whitsun 1953 RAF serviceman – Mr R. Hayward – was on leave and was stood outside his house in Wiston Road, Whitehawk, Brighton, with a friend.

> *"It was a beautiful sunny day, with clear skies. From the direction of Race Hill, near Bear Road, appeared an object in the sky, heading towards the south-east. I have very little perception of height or speed, but at that distance and time I can say that the object, which made no noise, was flying fairly low and slowly. We went around to the back of the house and called my mother to have a look, which she did, before it disappeared from view in the direction of Woodingdean."*

Mr Hayward says that sometime after the sighting, an article on UFOs was published in the *Sunday Times,* accompanied by an artist's sketch, which was similar to what he saw. **(Source: *Sky-search*)**

27th May – USA: UFO display over Texas

At 8.30pm, a number of people living in the San Antonio area of Texas reported the presence of nine separate lights, seen 'meandering' in the sky over a period of 15 minutes.

Spring – England: RAF man sights wedge-shaped 'craft'

RAF Serviceman Sidney Yeakes – stationed at RAF Felixstowe, Suffolk – was cycling towards the town to meet his wife and son from an outing to the local cinema, in spring 1953. A short distance from the cinema, he noticed . . .

"...a dark, wedge-shaped 'craft', trailing six separate yellow and blue flames from its rear, at a height of about 7,000 feet – totally unlike any aircraft I had ever seen. Frightened, I dismounted and watched it move over, feeling the hair on the back of my neck stand on end, as the object disappeared in the sky towards the direction of Harwich."

(Source: Letter to Brenda Butler)

2nd June – England: Five objects seen on Coronation Day

In September 2006 we were contacted by Dawn Gould, (79) who had served in the Women's Land Army during the Second World War with the Civil Defence. She described what she saw at midday on 2nd June 1953:

"I was living at Melplash Court, Bridport, Dorset, and pegging the washing on the line, when I happened to look upwards and see five saucer-shaped objects, like white circles, high up in the blue sky, 'line abreast' – just hovering there. Before I could shout out or fetch someone, they changed to 'line astern' and moved forwards and upwards until out of sight. I've never forgotten what I saw."

Papers and photographs of Dawn Gould (née Yardy) of Weymouth, relating to her service with the Women's Land Army, her marriage to Egon Heinrich – a German POW, and field names at Melplash Court Farm can be found on the Dorset History Centre.

In January 2016 we emailed them, asking if we could obtain further information on Dawn and hopefully a photograph but have received no reply yet. **(Source: Personal interview)**

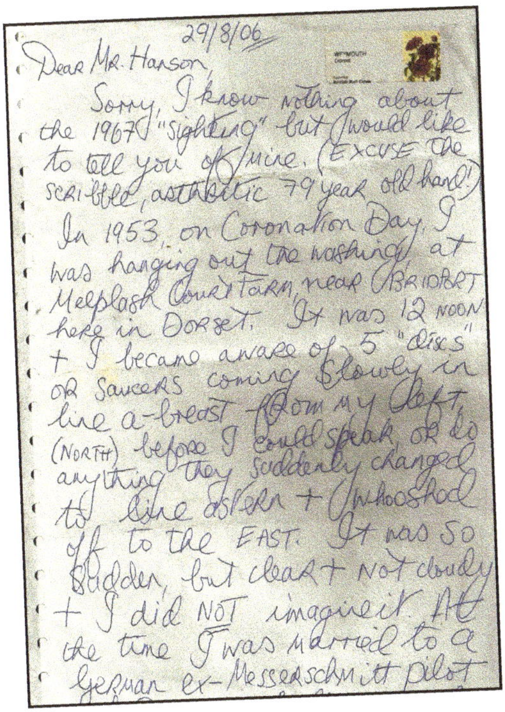

29/8/06

Dear Mr. Hanson,

Sorry, I know nothing about the 1967 "sighting" but I would like to tell you of mine. (Excuse the scribble, arthritic 79 year old hand!)

In 1953, on Coronation Day, I was hanging out the washing at Melplash Court Farm, near Bridport here in Dorset. It was 12 noon + I became aware of 5 "discs" or saucers coming slowly in line a-breast from my left (North) before I could speak or do anything they suddenly changed to line astern + whooshed off to the East. It was so sudden, but clear + not cloudy + I did NOT imagine it. At the time I was married to a German ex-Messerschmitt pilot

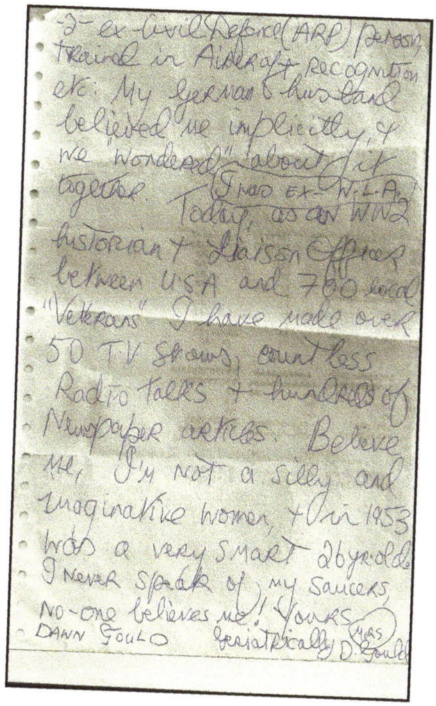

-2- ex-Civil Defence (ARP) person trained in Aircraft recognition etc. My German husband believed me implicitly, + we "wondered" about it together. (I was ex-W.L.A.) Today, as an WW2 historian + Liaison Officer between USA and 700 local "Veterans" I have made over 50 T.V. shows, countless Radio talks + hundreds of Newspaper articles. Believe me, I'm not a silly and imaginative woman, + in 1953 was a very smart 26 yr. old. I never speak of my saucers, no-one believes me! Yours geriatrically (Mrs) D. Gould

DAWN GOULD

21st June – England: Strange light seen over Gloucestershire

During the early hours of 21st June 1953, a column of vertical white light was seen forming above the horizon at Stroud, Gloucestershire, with a bright yellow and red object underneath, which slowly drifted downwards before disappearing from view.

(Source: Harold Wilkins)

25th June – England: 'Flying disc' over Cumbria

At 4pm on 25th June 1953, a metallic grey 'disc', leaving a vapour trail, was sighted over Windermere, Cumbria. This incident was followed by a highly unusual tropical storm, which struck the district the day after – caused, we believe, by violent turbulences in the atmosphere.

Was this a coincidence, or connected with the presence of the UFO? Although such a suggestion may appear preposterous, we were to come across other occasions when severe weather conditions occurred shortly after UFOs were seen in the locality.

On 31st July 1953, police and firemen made an unsuccessful search of the Llanberis area, after *"receiving reports of a UFO seen on the slopes of Snowdon"*.

June – Gibraltar: UFO lands in sea

John Tribbick, from Norwich, spoke to us about his amazing UFO sighting, while staying with friends in Gibraltar, during June 1953.

> *"It's something I shall never forget. I can still see it in my mind's eye. At the time I was talking outside my girlfriend's house, at 12.30am, when we saw this pale green circular object, motionless in the sky over Little Bay, Gibraltar. Suddenly, it slowly descended just over the water and then slowly sank into the sea, disappearing from sight. Immediately the water boiled up like a cauldron, with panic-stricken fish jumping up into the air. I even saw a pair of dolphins rise up out of the water. One of them charged straight at the sea wall and struck it. It was the strangest thing I had ever seen in my life."*

2nd August – England: Cigar-shaped UFO seen over Shropshire

On 2nd August 1953, Mr C.B. Philips from Weston Rhyn, Oswestry, and his friend, James Buckley, were walking through the village at 9.05pm, when they noticed a cigar-shaped object with a blue/white front, bright orange middle and dull red rear, crossing the sky, heading north-west, towards Chirk Castle.

(Source: Robin Gibbons)

The following day, the *Daily Herald* newspaper (4.3.1953) brought its readers' attention to a similarly described object, seen by a number of holiday-makers, at Rhyl, heading out to sea.

(Source: Gavin Gibbons)

3rd August – USA: Air Traffic Control Chief sights UFOs

Amarillo, Texas airport control tower Chief – Mr C.S. Brown – was on duty, at 12.04pm, when he saw:

> *"...a round, reflective, or translucent object flying across the sky, which stopped in flight for seven seconds, and then sped away before halting again. It was then joined by a similar object and both flew off in different directions, after a total of 56 minutes observation.*

August – England: UFO sighted over Essex

In August 1953, Valerie Frostick (15) from Orchard Road, Market Hill, Maldon, Essex, was on the way to bed, one evening, when she happened to look out of the bedroom landing window and noticed:

> *"...what I took to be a shooting star, moving across the sky. I stopped and continued looking, when I realised that this was no shooting star. It was a 'flying saucer', which was rotating, and had a smooth creamy metallic outer surface. As it passed opposite to me, I saw that it had a dome on top, with portholes all the way around. The 'saucer' then headed off, westwards. Instead of feeling frightened, I felt very peaceful and rather smug to think I had seen such a lovely object."*

(Source: Dan Goring)

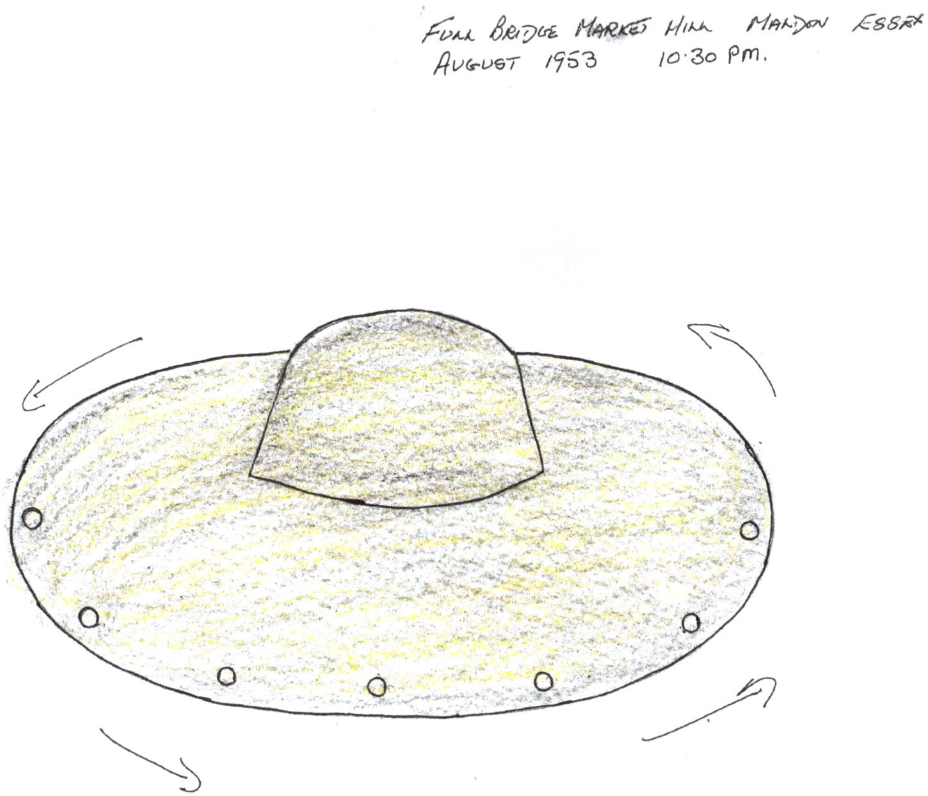

Summer 1953 – England: Orange 'globe' over Hertfordshire

At 4pm, Kenneth Jackson (in his early 30s) of Sheringham, Norfolk, with a degree in psychology, was motorcycling home from his job in Hoddesdon, in Hertfordshire, along Andrew's Lane, Goff's Oak, Waltham Cross.

> *"I acquired the thirteenth puncture that week, so once again dismounted and commenced*

to repair it. A man approached me and directed my attention to a 'globe of orange light', sat in the northern direction of the sky over Enfield Lock Way. I first thought it was a weather balloon, and stood watching it for about 45 minutes, when it suddenly shot away at terrific speed.

The next day, the newspapers were full of reports of UFOs seen by thousands of people living in the North London area." **(Source: Ron West)**

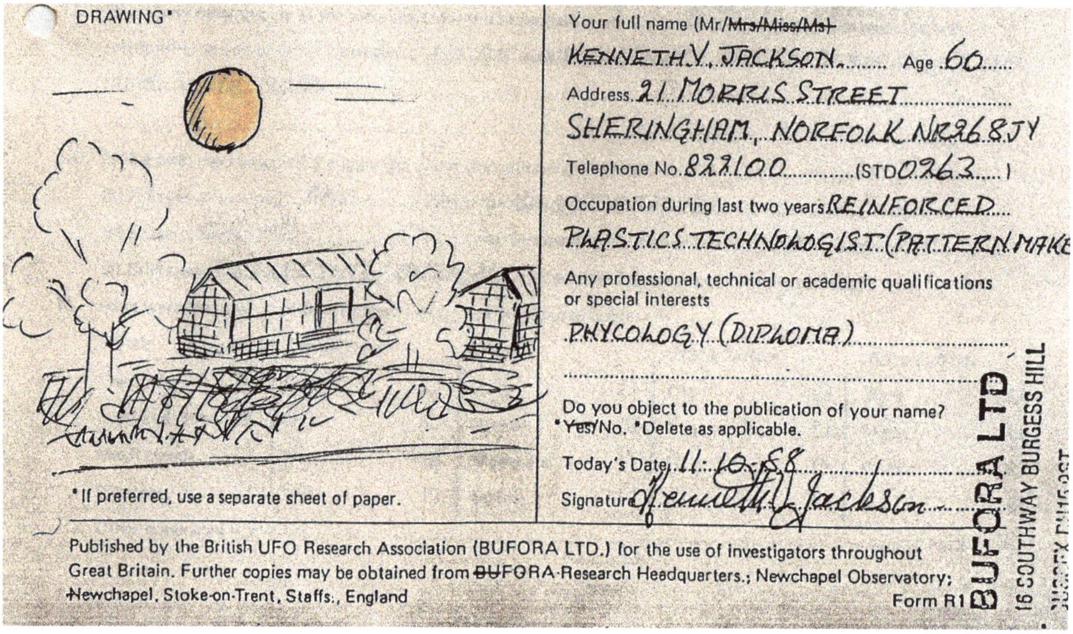
DRAWING*

*If preferred, use a separate sheet of paper.

Your full name (Mr/~~Mrs/Miss/Ms~~) KENNETH V. JACKSON. Age 60

Address 21 MORRIS STREET

SHERINGHAM, NORFOLK NR26 8JY

Telephone No. 822100 (STD 0263)

Occupation during last two years REINFORCED PLASTICS TECHNOLOGIST (PATTERN MAKE

Any professional, technical or academic qualifications or special interests

PHYCOLOGY (DIPLOMA)

Do you object to the publication of your name? *~~Yes~~/No. *Delete as applicable.

Today's Date 11.10.88

Signature Kenneth V. Jackson

Published by the British UFO Research Association (BUFORA LTD.) for the use of investigators throughout Great Britain. Further copies may be obtained from ~~BUFORA Research Headquarters.; Newchapel Observatory; Newchapel~~, Stoke-on-Trent, Staffs., England Form R1

BUFORA LTD
16 SOUTHWAY BURGESS HILL

20th August – USA: Aircraft 'buzzed' by UFO

The crew on board a *TB-29* Bomber/trainer aircraft were near Castle Air Force Base, California, at 9.05pm, when they saw a greyish, oval, object in the sky, which made four passes at the airplane (three times at 10-20 miles distance), before diving vertically as if two objects.

26th August – USAF Government warning

It may seem appropriate to bring the reader's attention to a USAF standing order, issued in the United States to military personnel, on 26th August 1953, quote: *'All genuine reports of UFOs must be kept from the public. Para nine informs ranking Air Force officers that they are warned not to probe beyond the first reporting stage. Under section 111 of a joint army, naval and air publication (JANAP.146B) and pilot who reveals an official UFO report, can be imprisoned from one to ten years and can be fined $10,000.'*

September – England: UFO sighted over Hertfordshire

At 3.30pm, in September 1953, Susan Brown (18) – a doctor's receptionist from Hertford – was about to cross over Dicker Mill Bridge, near Hartham Common, Hertfordshire, when she noticed a boy of about 12, and an elderly man, pointing upwards into the sky.

> *"I looked up and saw the wonderful sight, which still remains vivid to the present day, of a 'flying saucer' – a tremendous machine, moving at great height in the sky. It seemed so solid, like stainless steel. It was silvery-pink and predominantly lime-green in colour – then it just dematerialised, making me wonder if, in some way, it was supernatural or a ghost."*

Dan Goring interviewed Susan in 1977 about what she had seen, after she stood up at one of the meetings and told the audience what she had witnessed. Dan found her to be very level-headed and believable. This lady considers herself to be psychic and appears to have had other sightings of strange objects. She also alleged to have had a number of premonitions – traits of behaviour not uncommon to some UFO witnesses.

Son of RAF Officer sights UFO over West Midlands

Tony Day – the son of a RAF officer – contacted us about what he witnessed in September 1953, while living near Hilltop Farm, Handsworth Wood, Birmingham (now National Park adjoining Sandwell Valley Nature Park).

> *"I was aged 12, at the time, and very interested in aircraft, having spent a lot of time drawing the many aircraft my father had flown, while in the RAF. It was a beautiful day, with a cloudless sky, when I noticed what I took to be a jet aircraft moving towards me, about a mile and-a-half away. I was shocked to see that it resembled nothing like I had ever seen before. It had a number of swept back wings along a surface of highly polished material."*

Tony still ponders as to what it was that he saw all those years ago. We initially thought the aircraft might have been the *Miles M.52* – a top secret supersonic aircraft that was to be developed during summer 1942, by Whittle, to fly at a speed of 1,000mph, with an ability to climb to 36,000 feet in 90 seconds – but discovered Whittle was later taken over by Rolls Royce.

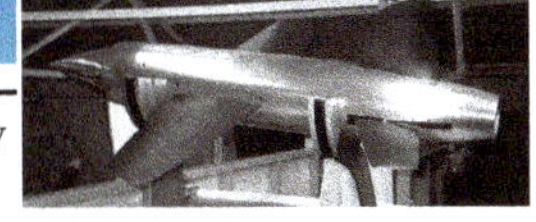

*Britain's supersonic project, the *M.52*, never flew over England; it was scrapped by the Air Ministry of Scientific Research in 1946. Clearly, this could not have been the aircraft seen by Tony Day.

October – England: 'Flying saucer' sighted over Surrey

In October 1953, Mr F.W. Underwood from Elstead, Surrey, was cycling home to Midhurst, late one evening, when he saw a bright light in the sky moving towards him – bright enough to light up the countryside.

> *"I saw an object 2-3,000 feet up in the air, spilling out this silvery blue light. It looked just like one of those 'flying saucers' you saw in the newspapers at the time, with what looked like portholes and a long trail of light passing behind it – then it stopped briefly, before carrying on. All of a sudden, it shot upwards into the sky and disappeared from view."*

(Source: Isle of Wight UFO Society)

6th October – England: 'Flying saucer' sighted over Norwich

Mr F.W. Potter from Norwich – then aged 34, owner of a local window cleaning business, with over twenty years experience as an amateur astronomer, member of the British Astronomical Association and the Norwich Astronomical Society – was in the process of leaving his house, with his wife, to attend a meeting on 6th October 1953. As the couple stepped out of the house, Mr Potter was the first to see a bright yellow 'star', moving slowly across the sky – unlike anything he had seen before.

The couple rushed back into the house and brought out a three-inch reflecting telescope, which they set up in the back garden. During an observation period, which lasted three and a half minutes, they were able to describe the following:

> *"It had a dark grey hull and a caged dome shape, with the cube of the dome hanging towards the ground, the flat side emitting a pulsating light that was much stronger when the object was stationary but decreased in luminosity when the object moved. In the centre of the caged dome was what looked like a conning tower, containing what looked like eight windows?"*

WHAT MR. POTTER SAW

WHAT was it that Mr. Frank Potter saw flying over his garden at night? Was it a flying saucer? -9 OCT 1953

The first time he saw it was three weeks ago. But The Object had gone before Mr. Potter, of South Park-avenue, Norwich, could get his telescope.

But, as a member of Norwich Astronomical Society, he was curious. "Every night since I have kept watch," he said yesterday. And on Tuesday night it came again.

The time: 7.15. Mr. Potter, who is a 36-year-old window cleaner, saw it through the telescope—for three-and-a-half minutes. Then he made a sketch of it.

"It was one large dome on which was mounted a smaller one," he said yesterday. "From eight hatches—four on each side—shone powerful rays.

"Round the edge of the larger dome, which was a dark grey colour, was a much lighter band. It glowed red underneath. It moved silently at a great height."

Mr. Potter's sketch is very similar to the picture published in a book by George Adamski, an American. Mr. Adamski claims to have seen a flying saucer land and to have spoken to the occupant, who came from Venus.

Mr. Potter is sending his sketch to the British Astronomical Society.

COMMENT by the Air Ministry: "It could have been an experimental jet aircraft. There are a lot around these days."

DAILY MAIL, THURSDAY, FEBRUARY 11, 1954

An amateur astronomer saw it through his telescope last October. It wasn't a meteor . . . or a weather balloon. Could it be . . .? This is the problem posed in this second of four articles on the Flying Saucer mystery.

Was it a 'Saucer' They Saw over Norwich?

by J. STUBBS WALKER

This artist's drawing is based on a verbal description and a sketch made by Mr. Potter of the mysterious object he saw in the sky.

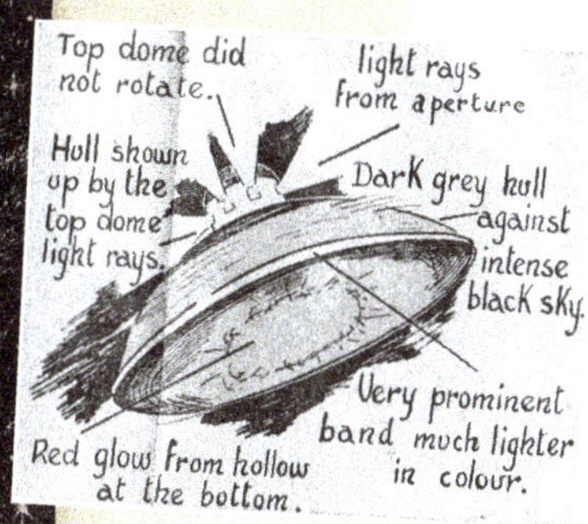

WHETHER you are a saucer enthusiast or what the "saucerers" call a heretic, you have to admit that the evidence of some of the sightings is sufficiently impressive to justify fully the detailed study the Air Ministry still give to the subject.

Take the case of Mr. F. W. Potter, a 34-year-old amateur astronomer, who runs his own window-cleaning business in Norwich.

For nearly 20 years Mr. Potter has been interested in astronomy. He is a member of the British Astronomical Association and of the Norwich Astronomical Society. His wife also is a member of the Norwich society, and their interest in astronomy is sufficiently alert for them to have bought, for their own personal use, a 3½in. refracting telescope—an expensive piece of equipment.

One night early in October last year Mr. and Mrs. Potter were leaving their home near Norwich to attend a meeting of the local society. It was a dark, clear night, and the time was about 15 minutes after seven o'clock.

A habit

AS they stepped from their porch, turning towards the garage, Mr. Potter looked up into the sky. "I always do," he says, "more or less out of habit."

He saw something which he first took to be a bright yellow star in a position where it should not have been. Then he noticed that it was moving, so he called to his wife to fetch from the house the big telescope, which they then set up in the front garden.

The object, however, was moving over their house, and they had to fold up the cumbersome telescope and its tripod and carry it through the house to set it up again in the back garden. There, for three and a half minutes, both Mr. and Mrs. Potter were able, they say, to make a close study of the "object."

"We were both pretty excited," Mr. Potter admits. At the same time, however, he was able to keep the telescope trained on the U.F.O., and his observation of detail was confirmed by his wife.

It was a dark grey hull against an intensely black sky, dome-shaped and with the curve of the dome hanging towards the ground. The flat side emitted a pulsating light which was much stronger when the object was stationary, dulling as the object moved. At the centre of the curved dome there was a kind of conning tower with eight windows through which light was beaming.

Excitement

"I HAVE seen hundreds of meteors," Mr. Potter told me, "and there was no question that this was one. Neither could it have been a weather balloon."

The Potters went on to their meeting at the Norwich Astronomical Society, arriving late and in a flutter of excitement.

Mr. W. E. Bennett, the honorary secretary of the society, confirms their state of excitement and confirms, too, that when members questioned the Potters their stories coincided in all detail. Mr. Potter immediately sketched for the members what he had seen. His wife agreed that the sketch was as accurate as she could remember.

Now, here is a strange thing about what the Potters saw and what Mr. Potter drew. The whole of his description is very much like the much-questioned photographs of a flying saucer supposedly taken at short range by Mr. George Adamski and published in his book "Flying Saucers Have Landed," except for the vital fact that Mr. Potter drew what he saw in his refracting telescope, *which reverses the image.*

Adamant

HIS flying saucer was not flying the same way up as those of Mr. Adamski, and no amount of arguing will make him change his mind. Mr. Potter had previously seen a representation of the Adamski saucer and was consequently aware that what he saw might be expected to be flying the other way up.

So far as I am aware, Mr. Potter's sighting has never officially been investigated. He himself refuses to call it a flying saucer, despite his detailed sketch of it. He and his wife have received scores of insulting letters, ridiculing and reviling them. As Mr. Potter points out, none of those letters of ridicule seems to have been written by anyone with any scientific training.

As a result of considerable publicity given to the sighting, with strong comparisons being drawn with what the Potters' had seen and a similar photograph of a 'flying saucer', taken by Mr George Adamski (as shown in his book, *Flying Saucers have landed*), the couple received scores of insulting letters, ridiculing them for having reported the incident – all of them having been written, according to Mr Potter, *"by people without any Scientific training"*.

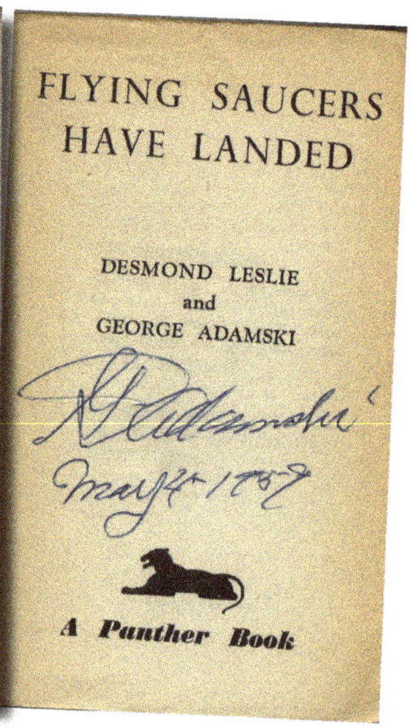

NOW REPRINTED

Now read what has happened to

GEORGE ADAMSKI

since he wrote the famous incidents in *Flying Saucers Have Landed*

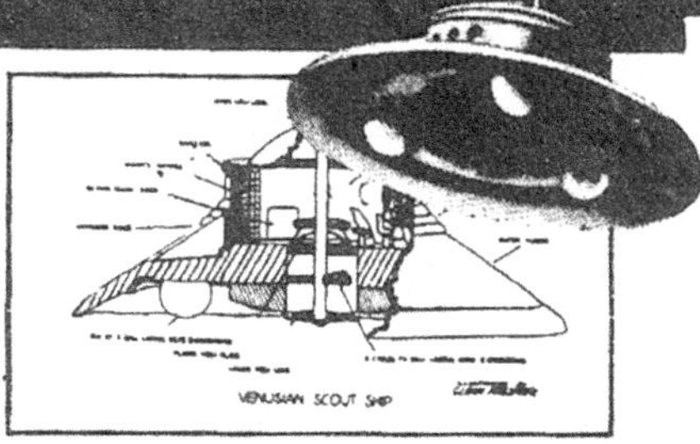

INSIDE THE SPACE SHIPS is Adamski's own story of what has happened to him since that memorable November 20, 1952, when he first made personal contact with a man from another world . . .

SINCE December 13, 1952, when he took the first, now-famous photographs of the saucer that brought his original visitor . . .

Now Adamski tells of his first meeting, a few months later, with a second man from another world — *his first meeting with one who speaks to him.* This second visitor takes him to a Venusian Scout (flying saucer) that in turn transports him to a mother ship. Later, he is conveyed in both a Saturnian Scout and a Saturnian mother ship. Adamski tells us what transpires in these space craft, and what the men and women from other worlds have told him.

Adamski's first book, FLYING SAUCERS HAVE LANDED, has now sold over 200.000 copies in the United States and U.K. and has been translated into Dutch, Spanish and French.

NOW, in INSIDE THE SPACE SHIPS, Adamski gives us 16 photographs and other illustrations, not only of the flying saucers, but of the great space ships from which they are launched. The main group of these photographs was taken in April, 1955—and neither the photographs nor a description of them has ever before been published!

TO GET YOUR COPY, FILL IN THE COUPON BELOW:

NEVILLE SPEARMAN LTD.
112 Whitfield Street, London W1

Please send me my copy of
INSIDE THE SPACE SHIPS

NAME ....

ADDRESS ....

....

I enclose 26/- postage

BY POPULAR DEMAND

ORBIT

JOURNAL OF THE TYNESIDE U.F.O. SOCIETY

Volume one. Number one.

APRIL 1959.

Editorial.

"----to Whirl through the Universe----".

Who Knows?

Can There be Life on Venus?

The London Airport Story.

Propulsion of Flying Saucers.

Food for Thought.

Cuttings and Quotations.

Acknowledgments.

EDITOR J. OTLEY
SECRETARY

41 DEANHAM GARDENS
FENHAM
NEWCASTLE UPON TYNE 5.
ENGLAND

POST FREE 1/6 PER ISSUE

"PHENOMENA"

FLYING SAUCERS

Do They Really Exist ?

You would like to know the answer to the above question ?

IS THERE ANY PROOF ?

A NEW MAGAZINE "PHENOMENA" - will try to find proof, or otherwise denounce the existence of such things . . .

Will you help us to find proof, etc.

HOW CAN I DO THAT ?

As you are well aware by now, UFO groups are going all out to obtain PROOF. They sometimes deny there is proof, in fact WE KNOW THERE IS NO REAL PROOF. In fact the biggest Ufo group today in the world is the I.S.S. and quite openly the organiser of this group confessed to the B.B.C. sound radio on June 1967 the following - that, " one can never say", What are the chances of seeing a UFO locally-) "It's fifty-fifty, but there have been a few sightings in the north London area, the last one was seen in Walthamstow, on a Sunday evening: UFO's explained Mr. Palmer, of the International Sky Scouts to the BBC- fly along invisible magnetic fields termed as LEY LINES. He thinks that certain areas of LONDON will be having more sightings soon. But said Mr. Palmer "Then they will be probably leaving there and going elsewhere."

Indeed, if this is the case, where will our space or dimentional objects appear next.

This is the searching question. Several other interested minds also set about answering these problems.

These people amalgamated to form yet another large investigating body and are now known as the BRITISH UNIDENTIFIED FLYING OBJECT RESEARCH ASSOCIATION for short-BUFORA.

But have all these people, some with qualifications found PROOF. _____ Someone remarked to Phenomena editor " PROVE THAT FLYING OBJECTS DON'T EXIST

So this leaflet was prepared by INTERPLANETARY NEWS- A magazine of down to earth FACT. We are advertising our new magazine, that is now going to print the TRUTH and PROVEN FACT about UFO's. We are going to read and study and interview all, and everything about this phenomena, what is more we would sincerely like you to help.

Our enquiries revealed that a number of other witnesses had also seen this unidentified object over the Norwich area, during the same evening.

7th October – England: UFO plotted on radar

One is bound to wonder if there was any connection with the saucer-shaped 'craft' seen by Mr Potter and other inhabitants of Norfolk and a UFO plotted on radar by RAF Neatishead, just before dawn, the following morning. According to an unnamed source, a UFO was tracked travelling northwards from Cornwall, at a speed of 36,000 mph.

(Sources: *Eastern Evening News*, 11.10.1953, Letter sent to Newspaper/*Daily Mail*, 11.2.1954 – 'Was it a Saucer they saw over Norwich?')

9th October – England: 'Flying saucer' seen over English Channel

Three days later on 9th October 1953, a saucer-shaped object was seen stationary in the sky over the English Channel, by the crew of a BEA Airliner en route from London to Paris. The incident later brought to the attention of the media involved Captain Peter Fletcher and his first officer – Mr R.L. Lemon. In an interview held with a reporter from the *Sunday Dispatch* newspaper, Captain Fletcher said:

> *"Our Elizabethan flight left London Airport at 9am. There was a certain amount of low cloud and fog, but when we climbed we found ourselves in an absolutely clear atmosphere with a clear blue sky. It was one of those rare days when you could see an aircraft 50-60 miles away. It was so clear that when we were over the English Channel, we could see aircraft over the Airport at Orly, 100 miles away. I reported our position to Control when we were over Seaford, Sussex, on a course of 150 degrees, who informed me of a Constellation aircraft overtaking on our left. I watched as it reached its cruising altitude of some 13,500 feet, immediately ahead of me and above.*
>
> *At this stage the relative position of my aircraft to the Constellation and the sun was such that the sun's light was reflected to me from the top surface of the aircraft's wing, making the lit surface very easy to see, while a darker shadow etched in the lower part. It was then that I noticed the 'flying saucer'. It was apparently another aircraft above the Constellation and a little away to the left and it seemed to have similar sun reflections.*
>
> *When the Constellation was getting on for 30 miles ahead of us, the irregularities of fuselage, engines and tail, could still be distinguished breaking up the reflecting surface of the top wing. But it's quite different with our 'flying saucers', which had the appearance of two shallow saucers, with their rims together.*
>
> *1. Its relative position remained unchanged for the whole of the 30 minutes we kept it under observation. It appeared to be still.*
>
> *2. The intensity of reflected light from the top surface remained absolutely steady until the last ten minutes of observation when it gradually dwindled away at a speed consistent with the changing position of the sun.*

Flying saucer over the Channel

TWO experienced British European Airways pilots have reported to London Airport that on a recent flight to Paris they watched FOR 30 MINUTES a mysterious object in the sky that might have been a "flying saucer."

"A solid object constructed of highly-polished metal"

Captain Peter Fletcher, of Putney, has been a pilot for 18 years, first with the R.A.F. and, since its beginning, with B.E.A.; First Officer R. L. Lemon, of Iver, Bucks, became a pilot in the R.A.F. 14 years ago. Both are therefore trained observers as well as skilled pilots.

Each described the incident technically and dispassionately. Neither has the least doubt that he saw an "unusual aircraft" of some description.

They agree, although they cannot prove it, that they were not deceived by a trick of light.

Here is their story, factual and unvarnished. It is told by Captain Fletcher:

Captain Fletcher and First Officer Lemon.

OUR Elizabethan flight left London on the morning of October 9. There was a certain amount of low cloud and fog, but when we climbed we found ourselves in an absolutely clear atmosphere.

The sky was intensely blue. There was not a cloud. The sun shone brilliantly. It was one of those rare days when you could see an aircraft 50 or 60 miles away.

It was so clear that when we were over the English Channel we could see aircraft over the airport at Orly, 100 miles away, and if we had been high enough we could have seen the Alps.

I had reported our position to Control when we were over Seaford, Sussex. We were en route for Paris on a course of about 150 degrees. London radar said that an aircraft was overtaking me on my left.

This aircraft, a Constellation flying some 50 knots faster than ourselves, passed on ahead and a few minutes later reached its cruising altitude of 13,500 feet and was in a position immediately ahead of me and above.

At this stage the relative position of my aircraft to the Constellation and the sun was such that the sun's light was reflected to me from the top surface of the aircraft's wing, making the lit surface very clear to see, while a darker shadow etched in the lower part.

First sighting

THIS is important in view of later observations.

It was then that I first noticed the "flying saucer." It was apparently another aircraft above the Constellation and a little away to the left, and it seemed to have similar sun reflections.

Bearing in mind that all airliners flying around Europe are basically of similar linear size—that is a wing span of 100 feet to 150 feet, I judged this other aircraft was flying at approximately 20,000 feet, and was about the same distance from me as the Constellation, or probably a further 20 miles away.

After watching the two aircraft—and I had no reason up to now to think that the other object was not an aircraft—it became apparent that there was a subtle difference between the two.

I must get a little technical here. Both my aircraft and the Constellation were on precisely the same course and therefore its bearing from me remained exactly the same, but as it was drawing away from me at a greater speed, its relative position to me slowly changed.

DURING Royal Air Force exercises last year two officers and three airmen reported seeing a silvery circular object following a Meteor jet which was landing at a Yorkshire aerodrome.

They said that the flying saucer" was at about 10,000 feet and after apparently revolving on its axis it sped to the westward at a terrific speed.

The R.A.F. made a serious investigation into the report and did not dismiss it as "meteorological phenomena."

Last month the Air Ministry said that the special department which was set up to investigate reports of "flying saucers" has received Captain Fletcher's report and experts are now evaluating it.

As slight irregularities occurred in the path of the Constellation's flight, the intensity of light reflected from the upper surface varied.

Even when the Constellation was getting on for 30 miles ahead of me the irregularities of fuselage, engines and tail could still be distinguished breaking up the reflecting surface of the top wing.

But it was quite different with our "flying saucer."

First Officer Lemon and I studied it intently. We had plenty of time.

"It seemed still"

IT had the appearance of two shallow saucers with their rims together. We noticed that:

- Its relative position to ourselves remained completely unchanged for the whole of the 30 minutes that we had it under observation. It appeared to be still.
- The intensity of reflected light from the top surface remained absolutely steady until the last ten minutes of observation when it gradually dwindled away at a speed consistent with the changing position of the sun.
- The top reflecting surface was smooth and unbroken. It was more highly polished than is normally the case with an aircraft's "skin."

At first I had automatically classified the "stranger" as the Elizabethan that had taken off two or three minutes before me bound for Nice and reporting his cruising altitude as 19,500ft. But on crossing the French coast at Dieppe this aircraft reported his position behind me.

No aircraft reported crossing the French coast at a time that would have put it in the position of the mystery craft.

I was at once interested in my unchanging neighbour and began to check up on the other aircraft in the vicinity.

I noted the following facts:

- Low fog had prevented aircraft not only leaving London Airport, but by and large most of the U.K. aerodromes up to approximately 8.40 a.m. and I was the fourth to take off from London.
- The three preceding me were a D.C.4 to Amsterdam, the Elizabethan to Nice, and D.C.3 to Brussels.
- No civilian aircraft leaving Northolt would comply with the height, direction, etc., of the mystery craft.

This eliminated all civilian aircraft flying from U.K. to France. I was left with the possibilities of a Service jet or an Air France Comet.

We ruled out the latter possibilities because neither a jet nor a Comet would maintain for 30 minutes a course exactly the same without showing some variation in apparent position relative to our own aircraft, for they would be flying twice as fast.

Remember also that we could see variation in the apparent position in the Constellation.

Not a balloon

THE most striking thing to both of us was the absence of fluctuation in the intensity of the reflected light.

I admit that at one time I toyed with the idea that it might be a balloon. But it would obviously have had to be an enormous balloon and later observation confirmed the elliptical shape. In this it had the properties of an aircraft wing, being roughly one-tenth as deep as it was long.

It was impossible to estimate the size of the object because we did not know how far away it was from us. The day was so clear that it could have been an extremely large craft up to 100 miles away.

Given the size of an object one can estimate its distance away. Given the distance one can estimate size. We knew neither.

It certainly looked as big as the Constellation and was farther away from us. How far we could not judge but we estimated that it was somewhere over Northern France.

Neither of us has any doubt about one thing: We were not deceived by a trick of light.

We have no doubt whatsoever that the object was solid, having a shape approximately that of an aircraft wing and that it was constructed of a metal similar to that used for aircraft construction only much more highly polished.

In 18 years of flying I have never seen anything like it. If it had been visible for a few seconds or even for a few minutes I would have dismissed it as an illusion or a trick of light.

But we had our "saucer" under observation for a full half-hour. We had time to consider it, to estimate its size. Our radio officer saw it and we brought along the steward to confirm what we saw.

Certainly we saw something material in the sky. Whether or not it was a "flying saucer" we cannot say.

But we will not dismiss it as a trick of imagination—not after 30 minutes of wondering what it could be.

If it wasn't another conventional aircraft, and I have given my reasons why we do not think it was, then what was it?

Maybe your guess is as good as mine, but we saw it.

Page 6 — WESTERN MAIL, November 5, 1953

> *3. The top reflecting surface was smooth and unbroken. It was more highly polished than is normally the case with an aircraft's skin. We had no doubt whatsoever that the object was solid, having a shape approximately that of an aircraft, and constructed of a metal similar to that used for aircraft construction – only more highly polished. In 18 years of flying, I have never seen anything like it before. If it had been visible for a few seconds, or even a few minutes, I would have dismissed it as a trick of the light."*

(Source: *Sunday Dispatch*, 18.10.1953)

2nd November – USA: Three UFOs sighted over Idlewild Airport

They included six flying objects, in two groups of three, seen hovering over Idlewild Airport, at 10.10pm on 2nd November 1953, by Police Patrolman Anton Stalder, who described the top portion of the cigar-shaped objects as having *"what appeared to be that of an inverted keel of a sailing boat, or the upper portion of a blimp's rudder"*.

(Source: Project Blue Book)

England: RAF serviceman ordered to photograph UFO

In autumn 1953, 'Jim Jones' – a senior RAF aircraftman (who asked that his real name be kept confidential) – was instructed by RAF Waterbeach control tower to photograph an object that had been picked up on radar approaching the airfield, at great speed.

It stopped short, about a mile from the end of the runway, at an estimated height of 1,000 feet, elevation 30-35 degrees.

Received burns to face

'Jim' obtained several feet of film, but during the procedure he received facial burns and singed hair as an *F86 Super Sabre* (USAF) took off to intercept the object, which immediately fled eastwards at great speed. On returning to control, the cameras and films were taken and sent away to the Air Ministry. The airman 'Jim Jones' was referred to the airfield hospital for treatment of burns sustained. He had this to say:

> *"The object was disc-shaped, silver in appearance, and was very prominent in the bright sunlight. The sighting took place roughly around 2.30pm. The UFO was in full view for about five minutes, before the object sped away as the F86 Super Sabre jet took off to intercept it. Air Traffic Control not only picked up this object on radar but saw it in the sky."*

'Jim' said the object's size could be compared to holding a five pence piece, at arm's length. He has no idea what happened to the film he took. Interestingly, he met the radar operator in the NAAFI, later, who told him *"We've had quite a few of these"*, and showed 'Jim' some UFO files in confidence.

(Source: Gloria Dixon, BUFORA/Malcolm Robinson, SPI)

3rd November – England: RAF pilots sight UFO over Kent

On 3rd November 1953, RAF Pilots – Geoffrey Smythe and Terry Johnson – were out on patrol over West Malling, Kent, in their *Vampire* jet fighter, at l0am.

Geoffrey Smythe

> *"We noticed a bright circular object, motionless in the sky, at a height of about 20-000 feet. Within thirty seconds, it took off – like a rocket – at a fantastic speed, in excess of anything we had seen.*
>
> *When we landed, we brought the sighting to the attention of our Commanding Officer. The result was electrifying. Rather than dismissing it out-of-hand, he ordered us to go to Fighter HQ, where we were interviewed by a Senior Staff Officer, who actually told us what we had seen could not be explained away as a balloon or aircraft movement. There was an enormous amount of interest in what we had seen. Prince Philip himself sent out a Squadron Leader (Sir Peter Horsley) to interview us."*

(Source: Personal interview/*Daily Express*, 10.11.1953 – 'Saucer's jet fliers see one from 20,000ft up/*Express* Air Reporter, Derek Dempster)

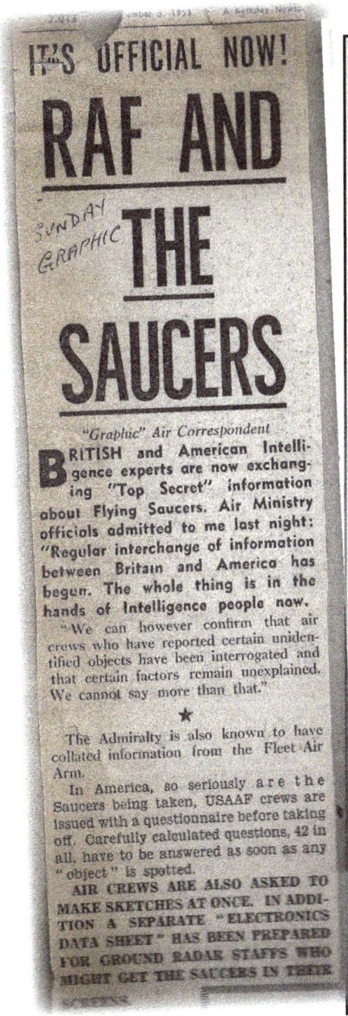

IT'S OFFICIAL NOW!

RAF AND THE SAUCERS

SUNDAY GRAPHIC

"Graphic" Air Correspondent

BRITISH and American Intelligence experts are now exchanging "Top Secret" information about Flying Saucers. Air Ministry officials admitted to me last night: "Regular interchange of information between Britain and America has begun. The whole thing is in the hands of Intelligence people now.

"We can however confirm that air crews who have reported certain unidentified objects have been interrogated and that certain factors remain unexplained. We cannot say more than that."

★

The Admiralty is also known to have collated information from the Fleet Air Arm.

In America, so seriously are the Saucers being taken, USAAF crews are issued with a questionnaire before taking off. Carefully calculated questions, 42 in all, have to be answered as soon as any "object" is spotted.

AIR CREWS ARE ALSO ASKED TO MAKE SKETCHES AT ONCE. IN ADDITION A SEPARATE "ELECTRONICS DATA SHEET" HAS BEEN PREPARED FOR GROUND RADAR STAFFS WHO MIGHT GET THE SAUCERS IN THEIR

Tel/Fax: (01242) 574535

11, Evelyn Close,
Greatfield Drive,
Charlton Kings,
Cheltenham,
Glos.
GL53 9BX

20th January, 2001

Mr. John Hanson,
The Flying Saucer Review,

Dear Mr. Hanson,

Many thanks for your letter and the 'bits' that came with it. My, wotta lot of people interested in the 'funnies'!

I'm sorry to have been so tardy in replying. 'Christmas' was the reason which caused me to be away from my WP.

There was a strange thing, an example of the Number 6 bus joke. No one had queried our 'exciting event' for years. Then, suddenly, I had two, the second of which was yours. I had just replied to the first which came from a northern university where they were doing a study into peoples' behaviour. The annoying thing is that I erased my reply just a moment before your letter arrived. Otherwise I could have instantly sent you a copy. Ah well!!

Be that as it may, herewith a chronicle of events. Firstly, I have to say our sighting was not especially exciting. It just got a lot of publicity.

It was the 3rd November, 1953. My colleague and I were flying a Vampire out of West Malling in Kent engaged upon practice interceptions. At the time we were at 20,000 feet somewhere south of Dover. Suddenly, my colleague, Johnson, shouted, "What the hell is that?". I looked up just in time to see 'something' – confirming that it was not a case of Johnson's imagination. But I could not give an accurate description. I just saw enough to say that it was circular or spherical. It vanished as quickly as it had appeared. Johnson's description was the same and he had seen it for a second or three longer.

Upon completion of our exercise, we returned to our base. It was then Johnson and I discussed the event. He thought we should report things unfamiliar. So we did.

At this point, I should explain that we were not 'new boy' aviators. I had been flying for over 10 years. Johnson a little less. Consequently, we did not imagine things that were not!

We reported to our CO. and were astonished at his reaction. He was 'electrified'!

A little explanation is necessary. 99% of similar reports to COs would have died a death at that point in time, and many probably did. But, our CO had had an experience during the war and had never fully recovered from the castigation and ridicule he suffered.

You may know that from 1944 we escorted Bomber Command aircraft at night on their forays over Germany – known as the 100 Group operation. Our CO was doing that in a Mosquito when, deep into Germany, he saw a strange light in the sky. It had to be German so he pursued it, and he pursued it, and pursued it, until he had to break off the 'engagement' to return home. In the meantime, he had actually achieved nothing. He had closed range on whatever it was because the light had became brighter, and his navigator had established a contact on his radar. But, whatever he did, the light and the radar contact seemed to be 'stuck' ahead and he could not get any nearer to it. Back at his base, he was routinely interrogated and he described what had happened. They thought he was 'going up the wall' and threatened with being taken off operations.

What he had seen became known afterwards as a 'Foo Fighter'. Quite a lot of our chaps saw them and had similar experiences. It was assumed they were something the Germans were playing with but, mysteriously, seemed harmless. What was most interesting, was that, after the war, we learned that the Germans were also seeing the same things and assumed it was something we were playing with. The Germans had a name for them, but I have forgotten.

Anyway, that was the reason our report did not die a death and was passed 'up the line'.

Consequently, Johnson and I were summoned to Fighter Command HQ where we were 'interrogated' by SASO (Senior Air Staff Officer). He informed us that the circumstances of our report had been investigated. Aicraft movements and the various balloon launches checked but there was nothing that tied up with the time of our 'sighting'.

In the meantime, 'word had got out' – probably through Malling's Auxiliary Air Foce connections.. There was a small paragraph in the Daily Express and a report in the Kent Messenger. That was followed by a TV interview onthe evening news.

But, then the 'proverbial hit the fan'! The War Office issued a statement that the object we had seen was also reported by an Army TA unit. They had found their radar was locked onto 'something' and through their telescope saw what we had seen. The Daily Express jumped onto it and the next day's issue bore the screaming headline on page one – 'Mystery at 60,000 Feet'!! All very exciting because iit was a second party confirmation of a UFO sighting.

But, it has to be said, we were famous over practically nothing. The matter came up in a debate in the Commons. With much hilarity, the sighting was described as 'All balloony'.

That was the end of our story except for some 'follow-ups'. Firstly, the Duke of Edinburgh was apparently interested in flying saucers and he sent his Equerry to interview us. He was a Squadron Leader who came to see us at West Malling. He listened to the story but did not seen terribly interested himself. However, very recently, the very same chap (by this time a retired Air Marshal) appeared on a TV programme about saucers and he expressed a lifetime interest (dating from?).

Immediately following our 'adventure' the Royal Air Force introduced a UFO reporting procedure.

One of the most interesting aspects was a letter either Johnson or I received shortly after all the publicity. It was from a Flight Lieutenant Mick Swiney. It said that he had had a similar experience to ours and he had suffered as a result. He hoped that we could all meet up sometime to compare experiences. We did not manage it at the time but 4 years later I was posted to a fighter squadron in Germany, and Mick Swiney was one of the Flight Commanders.

His sighting and experience was a very good one!

About the time of our sighting, he was a flying instructor at the Empire Flying School. On the day in question, he had taken off from his base in a Meteor 7 with a Navy Lieutenant doing an instrument exercise. On the climb up, the Navy man was flying with Swiney playing safety and monitoring. He then saw precisely what we had seen, a single sphere or disc, which seemed to be on a similar flight path to theirs.

Swiney then cancelled the training exercise and called the Navy man out from under the hood. He confirmed that Swiney was not imagining things. He decided to 'go after it'.

They were heading easterly at the time, with the object forward and above them. Swiney increased his rate of climb. He certainly got closer to it but could not say how close. But he could see that it was not a single object. There were 3. A large sphere or disc in the middle with a smaller disc or sphere on each 'side'.

There was no question of the objects being balloons. Even on the climb, Swiney's speed was in excess of 300 knots.

A strange thing was that when Swiney altered his heading, so too did the objects. Eventually, Swiney had to think about returning to his base and turned about to head westerly. So, too, did the objects, maintaining their same relative position.

In the meantime, Swiney had alerted the ground, the Air Defence organisation and its radars. They could see both Swiney and the objects.

Time came for Swiney to start his descent. The objects maintained their position but became smaller as he descended.

Suddenly, at around 25,000 feet, the objects vanished. He did not see them go. He arrived back at his base and landed. He was met by his Station Commander who ordered him to say nothing to anyone about his experience. He even used the words 'dismissal from the Service'.

However, Swiney did speak to the Defence people who described. how the objects, having left him, proceeded northerly at about the same speed as before, between 200 and 300 knots. Then, around the Manchester area, they turned about and headed to the south, increasing speed. Finally, they vanished from the Defence radars over France by which time their speed exceeded 20,000 knots.

That was a GOOD sighting!

Have not seen a single thing since – despite flying for a further 30-odd years!!

I hope it is of interest to you. Apologies for the typing!

Yours sincerely,

Geoff Smythe

G. SMYTHE

3rd November – England: Pilot sights UFO over Norfolk

On 3rd November 1953, Margaret Walker – a qualified pilot from Dereham, Norfolk – was standing outside her home address when she noticed a bright silver object, hovering in the night sky at a height of about 4-5,000 feet.

> *"This was no firework. It was far too large and stationary in the sky. I shouted to my neighbour to come and have a look. As my eyes became more focused, I was able to make out what looked like a platform around the centre – then it started to slowly move off towards the North, halted, before returning to its original position, then headed westwards, where it became lost from view."*

Was there a connection with a report from an unnamed Luton man, who spoke of seeing *"a long, cigar-shaped object, without any wings or tail, surrounded by rings of gas"*, over the town on the same day?

(Source: Luton Paranormal Group)

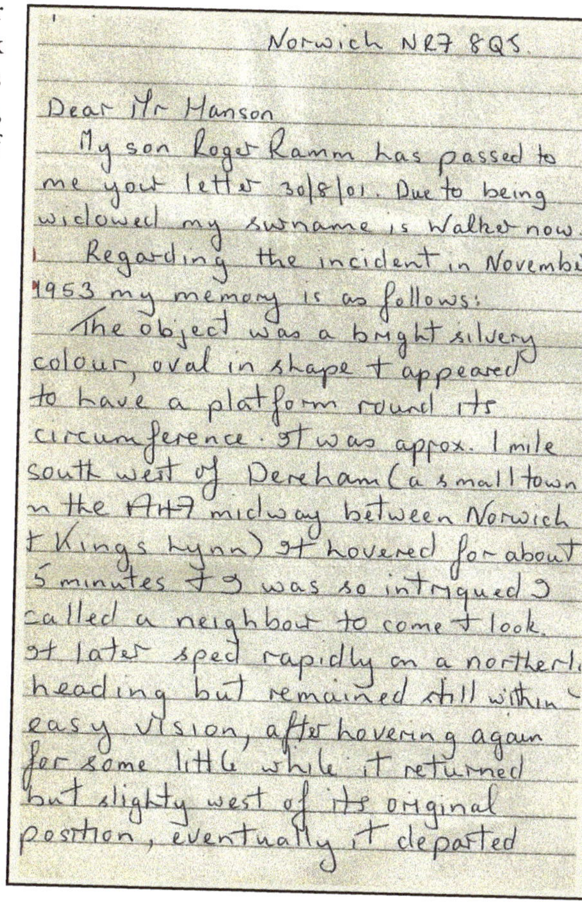

Norwich NR7 8QS.

Dear Mr Hanson
My son Roger Ramm has passed to me your letter 30/8/01. Due to being widowed my surname is Walker now.
Regarding the incident in November 1953 my memory is as follows:
The object was a bright silvery colour, oval in shape + appeared to have a platform round its circumference. It was approx. 1 mile south west of Dereham (a small town in the A47 midway between Norwich + Kings Lynn) It hovered for about 5 minutes + I was so intrigued I called a neighbour to come + look. It later sped rapidly on a northerly heading but remained still within easy vision, after hovering again for some little while it returned but slighty west of its original position, eventually it departed

3rd November – England: War Office claims UFO tracked on radar

On 9th November, the War Office disclosed to the public that an unidentified object, circular in appearance, had been tracked by Ground radar unit stationed at Lea Green, Kent, at 2.30pm on November, 3rd 1953. Calculations carried out, based on a radar bearing south-east, at 42 degrees, at a range of 30,000 yards, showed an object 200 feet across.

In addition to the signal received by the radar transmitter, a visual sighting made of the 'object' through a telescope, showed a brilliant white spherical 'object' stationary in the sky, at some considerable height.

Apparently, the mysterious 'object' was again plotted on radar by members of an anti-aircraft unit, stationed in Lewisham, who 'picked it up' at 2.45pm during that afternoon, on what was described as a particularly foggy afternoon, with poor visibility, over the London area. On this occasion, the 'object' estimated to be at a height of sixty thousand feet, moving slowly through the sky, was reported to the adjutant, who declined to say what the 'object' was because of the foggy conditions, although he admitted the strength of the signal indicated it to be of a colossal size. The War Office also admitted they had received details of three other objects tracked on radar, in daylight, between 14th and 22nd September 1953. In each case, the radar echo was equal to that given off by a large Bomber, and was between one to two hundred feet across, the heights of these 'objects' estimated to be between fifty and seventy thousand feet.

BBC broadcast story

On 13th November 1953, the BBC presented a newsreel describing the UFO encounter, involving RAF Pilots Smythe and Johnson, much to the surprise of the viewers, who watched the drama unfold on their flickering black and white television sets. Details of these incidents were also published by the *Daily Mirror*, in their edition of the 19th November 1953, by which time the Air Ministry had already declared that the 'object' sighted by the RAF and picked-up by the Radar Unit 'was a weather balloon' (an explanation not accepted by the RAF pilots, or members of the ground based Radar Unit).

They even made a film about UFOs this year!

Incident debated in House of Commons –UFOs load of 'ballooney'!

Subsequently, during a debate in the House of Commons about the incident, Mr Nigel Birch – Parliamentary Secretary to the Secretary of State for Defence – confirmed that the Government had accepted the weather balloon explanation for what had been seen, which attracted one comment, amidst much laughter, that it was all a load of 'ballooney'!

Over 60 years later the subject still dominated the newspapers!

Now over 60 years later, have we really learned any lessons? In the *Telegraph,* dated 5th August 2010, we learn of the following . . .

Winston Churchill 'feared panic' over Second World War RAF incident

Winston Churchill was accused of ordering a cover-up of a Second World War encounter between a UFO and a RAF bomber, because he feared public "panic" and loss of faith in religion, newly released secret files disclose.

The former Prime Minister allegedly banned reporting of the "bizarre" incident, off the east coast of England, for half a century amid fears disclosures about unidentified flying objects would create public hysteria.

4 NEWS

Winston Churchill demanded to know the truth behind flying saucers in 1952, when he was Prime Minister and sightings of Unidentified Flying Objects had plunged the world into a frenzy of conspiracy theories and rumours of alien visitors. Both the UFO images here were photographed over Salem, Massachusetts, one of them by a US Coast Guard named Shell Alpert.

AP

SECRETARY OF STATE FOR AIR
LORD CHURCHILL

What does all this stuff about flying saucers amount to? What can it mean? What is the truth? Let me have a report at your convenience

W.S.C

28 July 1952

How Churchill chased flying sau

by Paul Harris

SCIENTISTS and generals drew up a top secret report on Unidentified Flying Objects and then decided to cover up a wave of rumours and sightings that swept Britain in the 1950s, *The Observer* can reveal.

The existence of the UFO report, written in 1951 and later used to brief Prime Minister Winston Churchill, was denied by the Ministry of Defence for almost 50 years.

But the six-page document has recently been unearthed by UFO historians Andy Roberts and David Clarke as they researched a book on UFOs and the Cold War. The report has been a 'holy grail' of British 'ufology' and details the conclusions of a shadowy panel called the Working Party on Flying Saucers. This group was the idea of Sir Henry Tizard, one of Churchill's most trusted scientific advisers during World War II and a key figure behind the development of radar.

But anyone looking for an elusive 'X-file' that confirms the existence of aliens will be disappointed. The report concludes that all sightings were explainable by natural events, such as the weather or meteors, or were of normal aircraft.

But it does speak volumes about the scale of paranoia in Britain at the start of the Cold War. From 1950 onwards, hundreds of UFO sightings were reported across Britain and were regular front page news. Leading public figures, including Lord Louis Mountbatten, came out with their belief that Earth was being visited by aliens.

The phenomenon terrified the top brass on both sides of the Atlantic. Generals were worried that reports of flying saucers could be used by the Soviet Union to disguise an earthly attack or that the sightings were giving the Russians a clue that Britain's radar network was faulty and easy to penetrate – which was actually true but unknown within the Soviet bloc.

'This was a time of great paranoia and fear. The Government took a decision to throw a blanket over the UFO scare and say as little as possible about it,' said Clarke.

'There certainly was a cover-up, but what was being covered up was Cold War paranoia and our fears over our radar system. It was nothing to do with aliens.'

Despite the official silence, the UFO scares did not die down. In 1952 Churchill fired off a memo to his advisers in the wake of fresh UFO sightings in the United States. 'What does all this stuff about flying saucers amount to? What can it mean? What is the truth?' Churchill wrote.

Tizard's report was then used to brief the Prime Mi ter on the perceived lack real threat from UFOs August of that year. A months later an order w out expressly banning RAF personnel from cussing sightings with a one not from the military.

In trying to underplay sightings, Britain was foll ing the lead of the Un States, which had conduc several studies into its UFO sightings and adopted a policy of offi secrecy. When the Bri report was presented, a CIA scientist travelled ov the meeting to make sur conclusions of Ameri closest ally fitted in.

Secret meeting with President Eisenhower

He is said to have made the orders during a secret war meeting with US General Dwight Eisenhower, the then commander of the Allied Forces, at an undisclosed location in America during the latter part of the conflict.

The claims are contained in thousands of pages of declassified files on UFOs, released on Thursday online by the National Archives.

The 18 files, which cover from 1995 to 2003, are made up of more than 5,000 pages of reports, letters, and drawings drawn from correspondence with the public and questions raised in parliament.

Allegations made against Churchill in 1999

The allegations involving Churchill were made by the grandson of one his personal bodyguards, a RAF officer who overheard the discussion, who wrote to the Ministry of Defence in 1999 inquiring about the incident after his grandfather disclosed details to his family.

RAF crew photographed UFO

According to the series of letters, written by the guard's grandson, who is now a physicist from Leicester, a reconnaissance plane and its crew were returning from a mission over occupied Europe when they were involved in the war incident.

During their flight, on the English coast, possibly near Cumbria, their aircraft was approached by a metallic UFO which shadowed them. Photographs of the object, which the crew claimed hovered noiselessly near the plane, were taken by the crew.

Later, during discussions about the unexplained incident, the two men were claimed to have become so concerned by the incident that Churchill ordered it remain secret for 50 years or more.

During the meeting, a weapons expert dismissed suggestions that the object was a missile as the event was *"totally beyond any imagined capabilities of the time"*.

Sighting Classified

Another person at the meeting raised the possibility of a UFO, at which point Churchill ordered the report to be classified for at least half a century and reviewed by the Prime Minister to stop "panic" spreading.

> *"There was a general inability for either side to match a plausible account to these observations, and this caused a high degree of concern", wrote the scientist, whose details are redacted.*
>
> *Mr Churchill is reported to have made a declaration to the effect of the following: 'This event should be immediately classified, since it would create mass panic among the general population and destroy one's belief in the Church'."*

Apart from telling his daughter – the scientist's mother – about the incident when she was nine, the bodyguard, who was *"greatly affected by his experience"*, only disclosed the details to his wife on his deathbed, in 1973.

The scientist – also an expert in astronomy, who said he developed software for use in *"spacecraft thermal engineering"* – was told years later by his mother.

Stressing he was not a 'crackpot', he said he wanted to investigate the science behind the incident after his grandfather, who was bound by the Official Secrets Act, remained convinced that the object was secret technology being tested by a foreign power.

[Authors: ... and this was just one incident!]

MOD – UFO files before 1967 were destroyed after five years

After investigating the claims, a Ministry of Defence official said there was no evidence to support the claims, as *"all UFO files before 1967 were destroyed after five years"* due to insufficient public interest. This was supported by a Cabinet Office official.

Dr. David Clarke

Dr. David Clarke – author of *The UFO Files* and Senior Lecturer in Journalism at Sheffield Hallam University – said . . .

> *". . . the fascinating files showed the level of concern about such bizarre incidents during the war. It does tie in with what we already know, as you have to remember that this was also long before the phrase UFO was created. I suspect there is an element of truth to the statement".*

(Source: Andrew Hough and Peter Hutchison)

5th November – England: UFO seen over RAF Tangmere, Sussex

Other sightings of strange objects for this date included a report of a white object seen revolving above RAF Tangmere Airbase, Sussex, at high altitude, on 5th November 1953 – initially thought to be 'a white revolving meteorological balloon by the ground crew, until it flew off at high speed' on the same day as test pilot Neville Duke shattered the world speed record by flying at 723 mph at l00 feet, between Bognor and East Preston.

6th November – England: Was RAF jet on intercept with UFO?

On 6th November 1953, Mr Bridgend from Sevenoaks, Kent, was one of a group of men out working that afternoon.

> *"In an almost cloudless sky, at 3.15pm, I noticed what looked like two explosions in the sky directly overhead, followed by the appearance of a RAF Vampire jet pulling out of a steep dive. When the smoke gradually dispersed, it revealed a small white object, motionless in the sky, at high altitude. I pointed it out to others, who had trouble seeing it because of the height involved.*
>
> *At 4.30pm the object now began to flash, as if signalling – still in the same position. Suddenly, a smaller object appeared to break away from it and began to flash, as if signalling the other object."*

(Source: ***Kent Evening Standard*****)**

7th November – England: Close encounters with occupants of UFO!

Philip Molava was 13 years-old, and living in an orphanage at Shirley, near Croydon, Surrey, at the time when he was to encounter something so frightening it would be too easy to dismiss the whole matter as a dream or even a nightmare, with one essential difference – it was neither of those!

Philip was fond of rabbits and kept two larger ones and some young ones in a totally predator proof hutch. Unfortunately, over a period of four weeks, he had mysteriously lost about four baby rabbits, which had just disappeared from the hutch. There was no answer to this. None of the boys kept rabbits, and examination of the hutch revealed no sign of any interference or damage to the wooden surround. One accepts that there was, of course, a possibility that the rabbits had eaten their offspring – which seem unlikely, as rabbits are vegetarians – and if this had been the case, then one presumes there might have been some trace left in the hutch.

Decided to keep watch

Philip, by now extremely concerned that someone was managing to infiltrate the secured hutches and steal the rabbits, decided to keep observation. At around 1am or 2am on 7th November, after having spent an hour waiting, his efforts were rewarded – but not in the way that he ever expected!

> *"I noticed a silent white 'disc', flying or floating through the air, heading towards me at about five miles per hour. It was unlit and didn't have any markings or holes in it, and resembled two plates edge-on-edge, about the size of a large dinner plate."*

Jumped up and tried to touch it

It was so low that he jumped up to touch it but failed, and watched it sail through the air, over the hutch and away.

Unable to make any sense out of this, he did not tell anyone what had transpired. Sadly, he had no further trouble with the rabbits, as the person in charge at the Orphanage took it upon himself to drown the young ones and sell the others.

Unable to move, as if semi-paralysed

Over the course of the next 48 hours Philip suffered a strange malady, being unable to move a muscle and felt as if he was undergoing some form of paralysis. He tried to eat an orange, but was sick. He was then taken to the Infirmary and given an injection, but continued to suffer the illness.

Strange 'mist' forms over bed – Three 'beings' appear

At around 1am or 2am, he was lying in the dormitory bed *"waiting for something to happen"*, but didn't know what. He said:

> *"I saw a strange 'mist' forming at the foot of the bed, the size of the width of the bed, which moved up and froze parts of my body as it did so. It halted and three 'figures' materialised, dressed*

Philip Molava in 1978

> *in black wearing dark or black monk-like habits. They stood around me; two on one side, one on the other. They were over me and I thought they were benevolent and going to cure me. They froze my body but not my mind, and it was as if they were making me at ease with myself."*

He was unable to describe any of their anatomy, such as hands, and was unable to estimate how much time had passed. *"It was as if time stood still."* He tried to enter into communication with them, but they didn't answer. He then (as he puts it) *"flaked out"*.

The next day, Philip felt much better. Once again, he decided not to tell anybody – no doubt fearing ridicule – but did hear one of the boys claim he had heard voices during the night.

(Source: 'A case of rabbit snatching?', Janet and Colin Bord, *Flying Saucer Review*, Volume 24, No. 3, November 1978)

10th November – England: UFO over Knutsford, Cheshire

Miss Maureen Brockhurst – Head girl at Knutsford Secondary School – and her brother, were on Shaw Heath when they heard a whining noise – like an aeroplane – at 7.10pm on 10th November 1953. Looking upwards they saw a strange object in the sky ...

> *"showing a yellow glow behind it, with five or six lighted windows or ports, glowing with golden light, about the size of a full moon, fairly low in altitude, hovering in the sky before moving northwards at high speed, a short time later."*

They were not the only witnesses. A pilot reported having seen it over Ringway Airport. Other witnesses included villagers from nearby Toft and Barrington. The RAF later explained it away as having been a helicopter, or weather balloon!

(Source: *Flying Saucers Uncensored*, Harold T. Wilkins)

UFOs tracked on RAF Neatishead radar

We learnt that RAF personnel at Neatishead had also witnessed something on the radar scope during the same year, according to one airman plotter, who spoke of a particular night when, as the night fighters were due to be stood down, they began to receive new plots on the radar scope, originating in Cornwall and extending north-east to the North Sea, involving a track with six plots, with a time lapse between each plot of seven seconds. This indicated that whatever it was had travelled three hundred-and-fifty miles in thirty-five seconds – six thousand miles per hour!

20th November – England: UFO seen over Cheshire

At 2.15pm on 20th November 1953, a large metallic spherical object was seen motionless in a clear blue sky over Newton-le-Willows, near Barrington, Cheshire, hovering above passing jets from the nearby American airbase at Burtonwood, who denied it was either one of their jets or a weather balloon. (**Source: *Daily Mail*, 21.11.1953)**

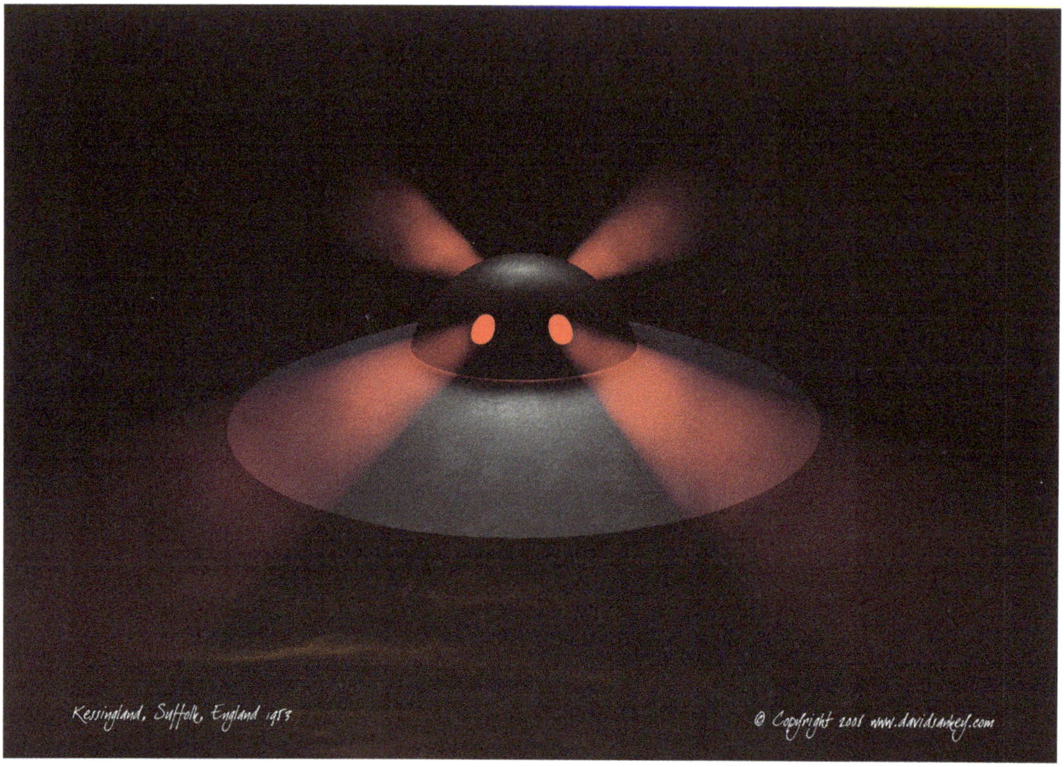

Winter – England: 'Flying saucer' seen over Norfolk

In 2005, we visited East Anglia UFO/Paranormal researcher Ivan W. Bunn, from Lowestoft – a friendly, helpful man, who had no objection to us referring to any of his material published previously by him in the *'Lantern'* series, kept in the reference section of the local library. From this we learnt of an interesting sighting that occurred in winter 1953. A member of the Royal Observer Corps was riding his motorcycle from Wrentham to Kessingland, along the old A12 road towards Latimer's Dam, at 6.45pm, when he became aware of a vibration like a low frequency hum in the air. Looking up into the sky he saw four rays of light approaching, the front two appearing to be shorter than the rear, perhaps due to the angle of the object, in contrast to the other thin silvery beams of light moving downwards. He decided to stop. As the object passed overhead, at a height of about two hundred feet, heading inland, he was able to obtain a clear view of it, before it disappeared behind nearby woods.

Ivan W. Bunn

THE KESSINGLAND U.F.O.

All maps and drawings are based on originals made by the witness and now in the files of B.S.I.G.

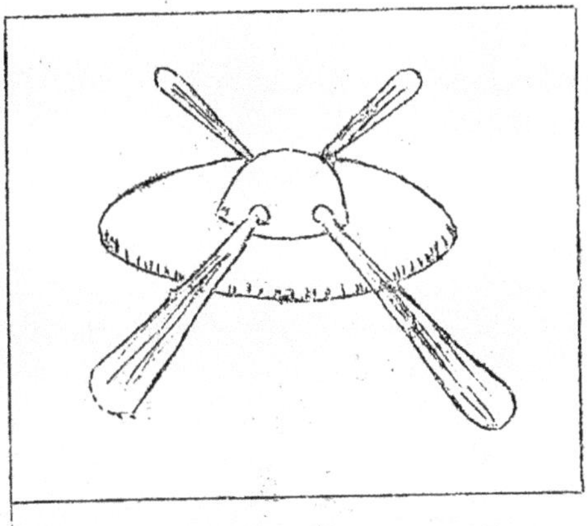

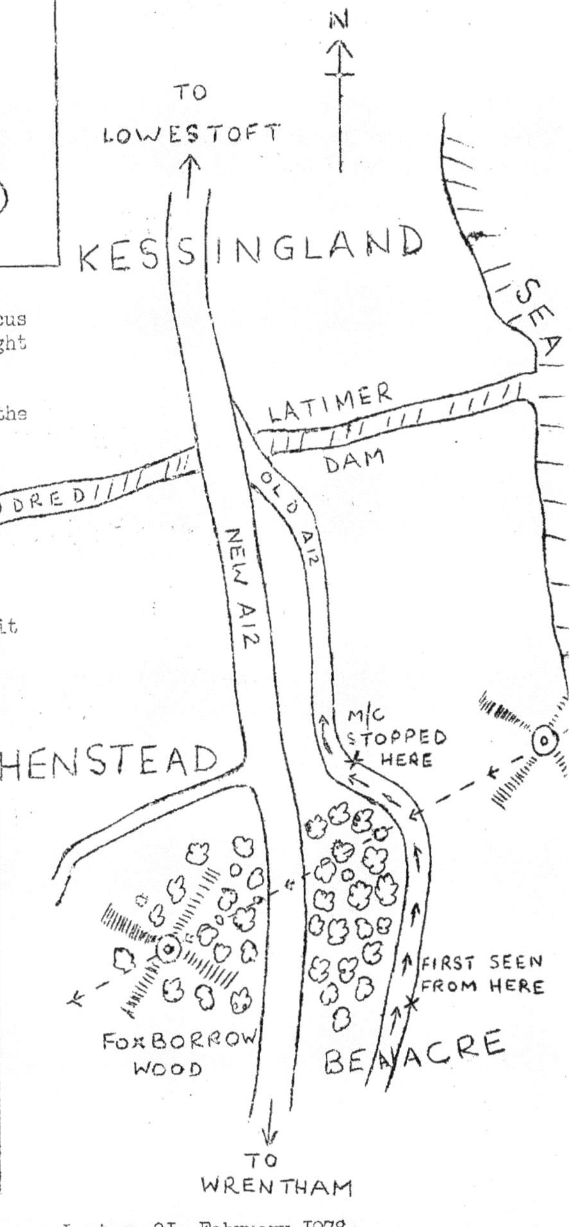

Above: Rough sketch of UFO; "Discus shaped object with 4 beams of light shining from dome."

Right: Rough plan or area where the UFO was seen.

Below: Witnesses view of UFO as it passed directly overhead.

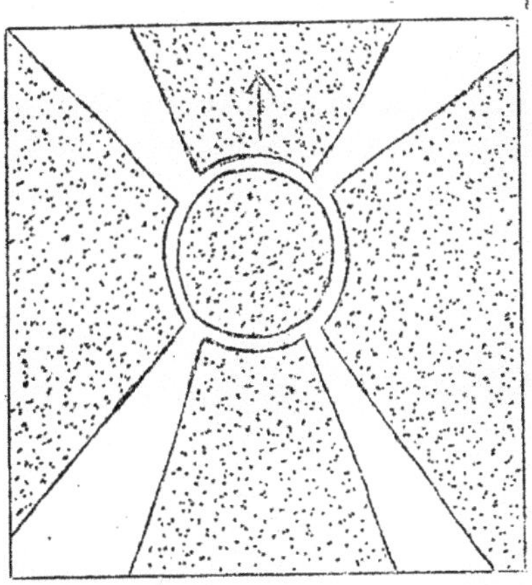

Borderline Science Investigation Group: Lantern 2I, February I978.

23rd November – England: 'Flying saucer' reports – 'humbuggery'

The *Evening Standard* (23.11.1953) published the view of the Astronomer Royal – Sir Harold Spencer Jones, FRS., about the 'wave' of sightings and also worldwide interest in reported 'Flying Saucer 'activity.

> *"The youth of today eagerly devour tales about space travel and interplanetary wars. There are reports from the United States of some of the 'saucers' having come to Earth, and of little men having come out of them. Though it is significant, no photographs of these reported visitations have been obtained. In these matters we have to be on guard against deliberate hoaxes to see how much a gullible public would swallow. I can say quite definitely and with absolute assurance that none of the 'flying saucers' can come from another planet."*
>
> **Venus** – *"Venus and Mars are the only two planets from which they might conceivably have come. Sufficient is known about Venus to be able to say that life of any sort on that planet is quite out of the question."*
>
> **Mars** – *"Mars, on the other hand, does show some traces of primitive type of vegetation akin to rock lichens on our Earth. Life on Mars appears to be in its last phase and to be on the verge of extinction."*
>
> **Moon** – *"This is a completely dead world; reports of little men having come from 'flying saucers' are therefore nothing but humbuggery."*
>
> **Secret Weapons** – *"On various occasions I have given it as my belief that most of the reports of 'flying saucers' can be attributed to observations of meteorological balloons. The USAF recently announced officially that most of the 'flying saucer' accounts are balloons, and that none are attributable to test of secret weapons."*
>
> **No Mystery** – *It is high time that the 'flying saucers' should be allowed to lapse into obscurity as the Loch Ness Monster has done.*
>
> *Let us be finished with them, for there is nothing mysterious about them. All the reported appearances are capable of a natural explanation. 'Flying saucers' are not secret weapons undergoing test: They are not spying craft from a potential hostile power: They are not spacecraft from a neighbouring planet. When these facts are generally realised, interest in 'flying saucers' will die a natural death."*

23rd November – USA: Pilot dies in suspicious circumstances

Wikipedia 2016 tells us of the fate of First Lieutenant Felix Eugene Moncla, Jr., (born 21.10.26), who was a United States Air Force pilot, who mysteriously disappeared while performing an air defense intercept over Lake Superior, in 1953.

This is sometimes known as The Kinross Incident, after Kinross Air Force Base, where Moncla was on temporary assignment when he disappeared.

The US Air Force reported that Moncla had crashed and that the object of the intercept was a Royal Canadian Air Force aircraft. According to the report, the pilot of the Canadian aircraft was later contacted and reported that he did not see the *F-89* and did not know that he was the subject of an interception.

On multiple occasions, the RCAF have denied that any of their aircraft were "involved in any incident" on that day, in correspondence with members of the public asking for further details on the intercept.

Unusual target tracked on radar

On the evening of 23rd November 1953, Air Defense Command Ground Intercept radar operators at Sault Ste. Marie, Ontario Michigan, identified an unusual target near the Soo Locks.

An *F-89C Scorpion* Jet from Kinross Air Force Base was scrambled to investigate the radar return; the *Scorpion* was piloted by First Lieutenant Moncla, with Second Lieutenant Robert L. Wilson acting as the Scorpion's radar operator.

Wilson had problems tracking the object on the Scorpion's radar, so ground radar operators gave Moncla directions towards the object as he flew. Moncla eventually closed-in on the object, at about 8000 feet in altitude.

Two blips appear to merge, then both vanish

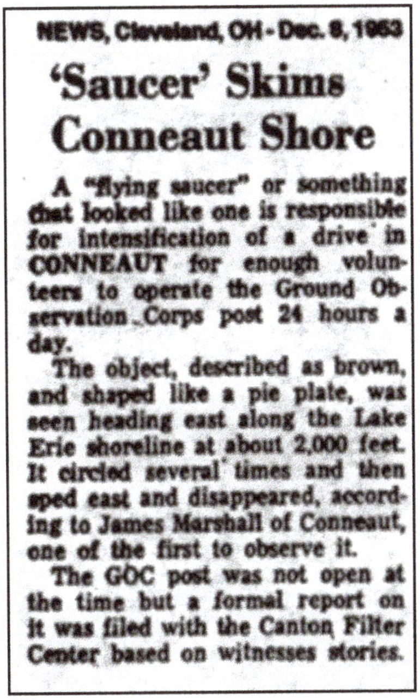

NEWS, Cleveland, OH - Dec. 8, 1953

'Saucer' Skims Conneaut Shore

A "flying saucer" or something that looked like one is responsible for intensification of a drive in CONNEAUT for enough volunteers to operate the Ground Observation Corps post 24 hours a day.

The object, described as brown, and shaped like a pie plate, was seen heading east along the Lake Erie shoreline at about 2,000 feet. It circled several times and then sped east and disappeared, according to James Marshall of Conneaut, one of the first to observe it.

The GOC post was not open at the time but a formal report on it was filed with the Canton Filter Center based on witnesses stories.

Ground Control tracked the *Scorpion* and the unidentified object as two 'blips' on the radar screen. The two 'blips' on the radar screen grew closer and closer, until they seemed to merge as one (return). Assuming that Moncla had flown either under or over the target, Ground Control thought that moments later, the *Scorpion* and the object would again

appear as two separate 'blips'. Donald Keyhoe reported that there was a fear that the two objects had struck one another 'as if in a smashing collision'.

Rather, the single 'blip' continued on its previous course.

Attempts were made to contact Moncla via radio, but this was unsuccessful. A search and rescue operation by both the USAF and the RCAF was quickly mounted, but failed to find a trace of the plane or the pilots. Weather conditions were a factor hampering the search.

1st December – England: Cyclist sights UFO over Norfolk

On 1st December 1953, at 5.30pm, Owen Moor from Beccles, Norfolk, was cycling home when he noticed an object moving across the night sky, at fantastic speed, heading towards the Midlands.

> *"It was like a shooting star but flying level in the sky. As it passed my position, I detected a peculiar humming noise. The first person I met was a railwayman. I asked him if he believed in 'flying saucers'. He answered, 'yes, you saw the thing go over?' I saw it discharging a blue/green light and turn towards Norwich, climbing at great height."*

(Source: Ivan W. Bunn)

They were not the only ones to sight something unusual in our sky. Strange silver 'balls of flame' were seen shooting across the sky at 6pm, over Nottingham and Leicestershire.

2nd December – England: Mysterious streaks of light seen

On 2nd December 1953, people living in the Birmingham area sighted fiery streaks of light crossing the sky. One witness described seeing what looked like *'a large sheet of flame flying towards the north-east, before breaking up into smaller pieces, at a height of 2-3,000 feet'*. Apparently, some charred fragments were seen to fall through the sky over Sutton Coldfield to the north of Birmingham, accompanied by a peculiar chugging sound likened to a World War Two aircraft. Even stranger was a report from Exmouth, Devon, of what *'looked like a dagger, seen travelling handle first across the sky, forming a letter Z'*.

8th December – USA: report of brown object skimming lake

13th December – USA: 'Spaceship'

George Adamski claims that he received a visit by a 'spaceship' near his home on Mount Palomar

14th December – England: 'Dagger'-like object seen

At 6.15pm, Anne Walsingham – editor of the *Exmouth Journal* woman's page – was talking to Miss Cristobel Battishall in St. Andrews Road, Exmouth, about the enormous halo around the moon, when they noticed a 'bright light' in the sky, heading at speed from the south-west. Within seconds it had gone from view. Miss E P. Buddulph of 6, Lion House, Exmouth – a nursing superintendent of Exmouth St. John Ambulances Brigade and Exmouth librarian – was also witness to the passage of the object. She said:

> *"I was walking down Saltereton Road from the hospital and looking at the huge halo around the moon, when suddenly across the sky, heading in a south-west to east direction, flashed an enormous object – shaped like a dagger – travelling 'handle' first, forming the letter* **Z,** *showing red orange and black. I wondered if it was a rocket than a meteor. Two ladies in front of me stopped short and made an exclamation."*

(Source: *Exmouth Journal*, 19.12.1953 – 'Four Exmouth women see 'dagger' in the night sky')

16th December – RAF issue '*restricted directive on flying saucers*'

Was the continuing public interest into reports of 'flying saucers', now seen all over the world, one of he reasons why RAF Fighter Command issued a restricted directive on 16th December 1953? The directive was ordering that 'sightings of aerial phenomena were to be immediately reported, in writing, to the Deputy Director of Intelligence, at the Air Ministry, together with a request for UFO reports to be made to them from the public'.

England: RAF pilot sights UFO over Salisbury

In the winter of 1953, Flt. Lt. Cyril George Townsend-Withers – principal scientific officer at Boscombe Down, Wiltshire, responsible for testing experimental aircraft radar equipment – was conducting tests with new radar installed into a *Canberra* aircraft, accompanied by his science officer. In an interview held with Peter Hough and Jenny Randles, of the Manchester UFO Research Association, he had this to say:

> *"We took off at 11am, and flew over the Salisbury area, gaining height to 55,000 feet, when a 'blip' appeared on the radar scopes, representing an object five miles behind us. After establishing the anomaly was not being caused by any malfunction in the equipment, I climbed up into the turret and, on looking back, saw a glistening object following us at the same speed. The pilot tried unsuccessfully to shake off the intruder, accelerating to speeds up to 225 knots, finally executing a 'U' turn to give us a better view of the UFO. Unfortunately, it also put us on a collision course. The object was very brilliant – almost fluorescent – with two stabilising fins at the rear and about the same size as a small jet fighter, with a thirty feet wingspan.*
>
> *As we approached within four miles of each other, it suddenly shot vertically upwards, at terrific speed, and vanished, 50, 60, and 70,000 feet – as quick as that! There wasn't even a vapour trail. Radar experts were very interested, but there was no reaction in the sense they thought it was an enemy aircraft, posing a threat. The attitude in those early days was 'we'll look into it, but if it isn't Russian then we are not really bothered".*

27th December – England: UFO sighted over Shropshire

Gavin Gibbons, Bachelor of Arts – a brilliant linguist, master of eleven languages and keen astronomer, renowned eccentric and author of numerous books devoted to the Welsh Border County – was cycling home from Llangollen along the A5, at 8.30pm on 27th December 1953, when he noticed a *"bright 'disc' in the sky, with a flattened right-hand edge".*

Spellbound, he stood watching the object as it hung motionless under the constellation of the Great Bear, before disappearing from view.

During conversation with his brother – Robin Gibbons – we

Robin Gibbons

Telephone :
Market Drayton

24th May 2007.

Mr J. Hanson,
31 Red Lion Street,
Alvechurch,
Worcestershire.
B48 7LG

Dear John Hanson,

Thank you very much for your letter and I am so very sorry not to have replied before. I do hope that it is not too late to give you the information that you need.

My Mother and I first became interested in Flying Saucers in the very beginning of the 1950s when we heard stories of Flying Saucer sightings and read the book "The Riddle of the Flying Saucers" by Gerald Heard. We told my brother, Gavin, about what we had discovered when he came home from his work in London and he became fascinated in the subject. Over the next few years, one of our main topics of conversation when talking to friends was about Flying Saucers. Over the subsequent years Gavin himself had well over a dozen sightings of Flying Saucers.

I have copies of both of George Adamski's books "Flying Saucers Have Landed" and "Inside The Space Ships". The second one he autographed when Gavin and I met him in Birmingham when we went to the talk he gave there.

As you will probably have noticed, there is a photograph of Wilfrid Daniels in Gavin's first book on Flying Saucers "The Coming of the Space Ships", which was taken in 1956. In Gavin's copy of the book Wilfrid Daniels has autographed the photo.

I enclose a couple of photos, as requested, one of Gavin and me, and the other of my Mother and me, both taken in the early 1950s.

Incidentally, we talk about Flying Saucer sightings going back some 60 or so years, but in point of fact they have been seen for a very much longer time than that. Did you ever read Julius Caeser's account of his invasion of Britain where he tells the story of a strange object flying over this country?

I hope all the above information is of some help to you.

Best wishes,

Robin Gibbons.

P.S. I have just re-read Michael Webb's correspondence and the article about Gavin which you left with me when you came here. I find there are factual mistakes in them. If you would like any further information, please feel free to contact me.

learnt that Gavin had originally dismissed newspaper accounts of UFOs as being unworthy of investigation, but was to develop an avid interest in the subject to such a degree that he later wrote a book entitled *The Coming of the Spaceships*. This contained a number of UFO sightings from the Staffordshire and Shropshire areas, including his investigation into the Jessie Roestenberg incident, when a 'craft' and its two occupants were seen over Ranton, Staffordshire, in October 1954.

28th December – USA: 'Saucer'

Marysville, California: Yuba County Airport Manager – Dick Brandt – was on duty, at 11.55am, when he saw:

> *"A 'saucer' in the sky – its brilliant blue light reflecting off a nearby building; it hovered briefly during the one and-a-half minutes observation."*

William Reich and UFOs

Wilhelm Reich (24th March 1897 – 3rd November 1957) was an Austrian psychoanalyst. Author of several influential books – most notably *Character Analysis* (1933), *The Mass Psychology of Fascism* (1933) and *The Sexual Revolution* (1936) – Reich became known as one of the most radical practitioners of psychiatry.

Reich's idea of "muscular armour" – the expression of the personality in the way the body moves – influenced innovations. He relocated to New York in 1939, partly to escape the Nazis, and soon after arriving invented the term "orgone" – from 'orgasm' and 'organism' – for a biological energy he said he had discovered, which he said others called God. In 1940 he started building orgone accumulators, devices that his patients sat inside to harness the reputed health benefits, resulting in newspaper stories about sex boxes that cured cancer.

After two critical articles about him in the magazines *The New Republic* and *Harper's* in 1947, the US Food and Drug Administration obtained an injunction against the interstate shipment of orgone accumulators and associated literature, believing they were dealing with a *"fraud of the first magnitude"*.

Charged with contempt in 1956 for having violated the injunction, Reich was sentenced to two years' imprisonment, and that summer more than six tons of his publications were burned by order of the court. He died in prison of heart failure just over a year later, days before he was due to apply for parole.

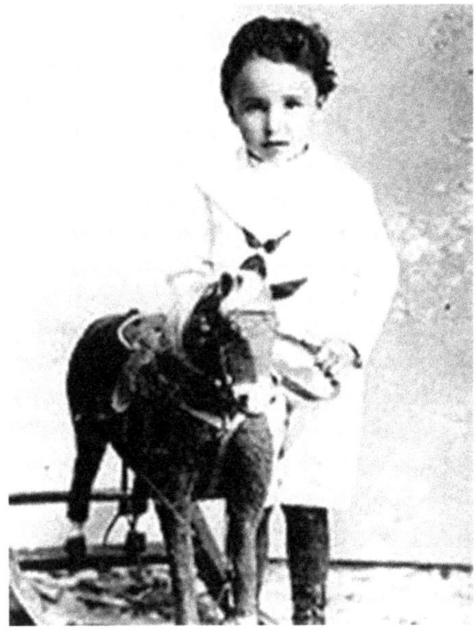

Wilhelm Reich c. 1900

Believed planet was being attacked by UFOs

From at least early 1954, Reich came to believe that the planet was being attacked by UFOs, or *"energy alphas"*, as he termed them. He said he often saw them flying over Orgonon – shaped like thin cigars with windows – leaving streams of black Deadly Orgone Radiation in their wake, which he believed the aliens were scattering to destroy the Earth.

He and his son, Peter, would spend their nights searching for UFOs through telescopes and binoculars, and when they believed they had found one would roll out the cloud buster to suck the energy out of it.

Claims of UFOs being shot down!

Reich claimed he had shot several of them down. Armed with two cloud busters, they fought what Reich termed a *"full-scale interplanetary battle"* in Arizona. In *Contact with Space* (1956), he wrote of the *"very remote possibility"* that his own father had been from outer space.(Source: Wikipedia 2016)

Sting operation

While Reich was in Arizona in May 1956, one of his associates sent an accumulator part through the mail to another state, in violation of the injunction, after an FDA inspector posing as a customer requested it. Reich and another associate, Dr. Michael Silvert, were charged with contempt of court; Silvert had been looking after the inventory in Reich's absence. Reich at first refused to attend court, and was arrested and detained for two days until an endorser posted bail of $30,000.

Hinted at conspiracies

Representing himself in the hearing, he admitted the violation but pleaded not guilty and hinted at conspiracies. During a recess the judge apparently suggested a psychiatric evaluation to Reich's ex-wife, Ilse Ollendorff, but this was not communicated to Reich.

The jury found him guilty on 7th May 1956, and he was sentenced to two years' imprisonment. Silvert was sentenced to a year and a day; the Wilhelm Reich Foundation was fined $10,000, and the accumulators and associated literature were to be destroyed.

Wilhelm Reich with his 'cloud buster'

Destruction of the accumulators

On 5th June 1956, two FDA officials arrived at Orgonon to supervise the destruction of the accumulators. Most of them had been sold by that time and another 50 were with Silvert in New York. Only three were at Orgonon. The FDA agents were not allowed to destroy them, only to supervise the destruction, so Reich's friends and his son, Peter, chopped them apart with axes as the agents watched. Once they were destroyed, Reich placed an American flag on top of them.

251 books then burned

On 26th June, the agents returned to supervise the destruction of the promotional material, including 251 copies of Reich's books. The American Civil Liberties Union issued a press release criticizing the book burning, although coverage of the release was poor, and Reich eventually asked them not to help because he was annoyed that they had failed to criticize the destruction of the accumulators.

In England, A.S. Neill and the poet Herbert Read signed a letter of protest, but it was never published. On 23rd July, the remaining accumulators in New York were destroyed by S.A. Collins and Sons, who had built them.

Six tons of books incinerated!

On 23rd August, six tons of Reich's books, journals and papers, were burned in New York, in the Gansevoort incinerator – the public incinerator on 25th Street. The material included copies of several of his books, including *The Sexual Revolution*, *Character Analysis* and *The Mass Psychology of Fascism*. Although these had been published in German before Reich ever discussed orgone, he had added mention of it to the English editions, so they were caught by the injunction. It has been cited as one of the worst examples of censorship in US history. As with the accumulators, the FDA was supposed only to observe the destruction. The psychiatrist Victor Sobey (d. 1995), an associate of Reich's, wrote:

> *"All the expenses and labor had to be provided by the [Orgone Institute] Press. A huge truck with three to help was hired. I felt like people who, when they are to be executed, are made to dig their own graves first and are then shot and thrown in. We carried box after box of the literature".*

1954

January – England: Damage to vehicles – unknown cause

WE came across an intriguing story reported in the *News Chronicle* (15.1.1954), which told of 83 separate incidents, involving damage caused to car windscreens and dented car bodies along a stretch of road at Cobham, Surrey, over a period of three years. A sample of white powder was recovered by Mr Bernard Sawkins, *"looking like minute pieces of tiny white paper, resembling ground up seashells"*, who confirmed a sample had been sent to New Scotland Yard for analysis (test results are unknown).

28th January – USA: Wilhelm Reich sights two UFOs

At 10am Mr Wilhelm Reich from Rangeley Main sighted two bright lights in the sky heading into a valley, seen against the mountain background, for 15 minutes.

14th February – England: UFO photographed over Cumbria

On 14th February 1954, Stephen Derbishire (13) and his cousin, Adrian Myers (8), set out to photograph bird life at The Old Man of Coniston, close to the Cumbrian village of Torva (the scene of a sighting involving strange 'figures', many years later).

At 12.30pm, an object was seen descending through the sky, glistening in the sunlight, its outline well defined, showing 'portholes', a hatch and a 'bump' on top. Stephen took two photographs of the object as it climbed rapidly upwards into the sky, accompanied by a swishing noise. He was later interviewed by the Duke of Edinburgh's secretary and invited to Buckingham Palace, where he spoke to the Prince about what had taken place.

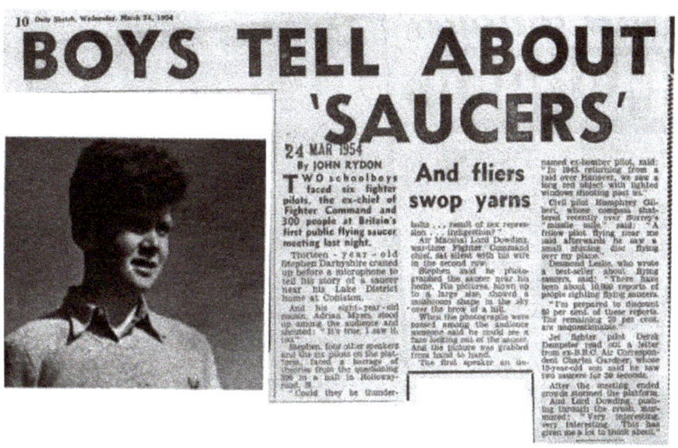

10 Daily Sketch, Wednesday, March 24, 1954

BOYS TELL ABOUT 'SAUCERS'

24 MAR 1954

By JOHN RYDON

TWO schoolboys faced six fighter pilots, the ex-chief of Fighter Command and 300 people at Britain's first public flying saucer meeting last night.

Thirteen - year - old Stephen Darbyshire craned up before a microphone to tell his story of a saucer near his Lake District home at Coniston.

And his eight-year-old cousin, Adrian Myers, stood up among the audience and shouted: "It's true. I saw it, too."

Stephen, four other speakers and the six pilots on the platform, faced a barrage of theories from the questioning 300 in a hall in Holloway-road, N.

"Could they be thunder-bolts ... result of sex repression ... indigestion?"

And fliers swop yarns

Air Marshal Lord Dowding, war-time Fighter Command chief, sat silent with his wife in the second row.

Stephen said he photographed the saucer near his home. His pictures, blown up to a large size, showed a mushroom shape in the sky over the brow of a hill.

When the photographs were passed among the audience someone said he could see a face looking out of the saucer. And the picture was grabbed from hand to hand.

The first speaker, an unnamed ex-bomber pilot, said: "In 1943, returning from a raid over Hanover, we saw a long red object with lighted windows shooting past us."

Civil pilot Humphrey Gilbert, whose compass shattered recently over Surrey's "missile mile," said: "A fellow pilot flying near me said afterwards he saw a small shining disc flying over my plane."

Desmond Leslie, who wrote a best-seller about flying saucers, said: "There have been about 10,000 reports of people sighting flying saucers.

"I'm prepared to discount 80 per cent. of these reports. The remaining 20 per cent. are unquestionable."

Jet fighter pilot Derek Dempster read out a letter from ex-B.B.C. Air Correspondent Charles Gardner, whose 15-year-old son said he saw two saucers for 30 seconds.

After the meeting ended crowds stormed the platform.

And Lord Dowding, pushing through the crush, murmured: "Very interesting, very interesting. This has given me a lot to think about."

Duke Wanted To Know More About Saucer

Dispatch Diary

S.D. 28 MAR 1954

THE boy who photographed a flying saucer with his box camera made a secret journey last week.

He went to Buckingham Palace to talk to one of the Duke of Edinburgh's secretaries. It was all very hush-hush.

At four o'clock that afternoon

This is Stephen's drawing of his "saucer."

young Stephen Darbishire was being interviewed by reporters. But, despite the barrage of questions, he kept his secret.

Half an hour later he was on his way to the Palace in a hired car.

Special Report

IT SEEMS THAT the Duke read about Stephen and wanted to know more.

So it was arranged that the 13-year-old schoolboy should talk it over with someone at the Palace and that a report of the conversation should be sent to the Duke in Australia. Hence Stephen's appointment at the Palace.

It was about four weeks ago that he photographed the flying saucer over Cumberland. Since then many people have examined the snapshot and agreed that it is one of the most convincing pieces of flying-saucer evidence yet produced.

Stephen's doctor father took him to London, ostensibly for a public meeting called to discuss these strange objects. Nobody mentioned the question of a visit to the Palace.

Stephen had a hunch– he took his camera

Flying Saucer snapshotter, schoolboy Stephen Darbishire, tells what he saw. His audience (left to right): Humphrey Gilbert, Colin Hodgkinson and Desmond Leslie. Below: The evidence from Stephen's camera of what he had seen

Stephen, thirteen, drew these sketches before the photograph (left) was developed. Right: Stephen and his cousin, Adrian Myer, snap the object

'Flying saucers' from Mars, according to Cedric Allingham

Omar Fowler

In stark contrast to what are believed to be genuine photos taken by Stephen Derbishire, Mr Cedric Allingham includes a rather bizarre presentation of a number of photographs in his book *Flying Saucers From Mars*, published in 1955. In addition to the sensationalism of Mr Allingham's photos of the alleged 'Adamski-type' craft and its 'Man from Mars', are we really expected to believe a lengthy discussion took place between a human being and his Martian counterpart, at Lossiemouth, in Scotland?

We believe this to be entirely fabricated.

We spoke to Omar Fowler; head of the Phenomena Research Association, whose dedication and knowledge of the UFO subject is second to none.

> *"The 'alien' [Martian] photographed near Lossiemouth (Scotland), was not an alien, but a Fleet Air Arm mechanic, wearing his working overalls (the belt with buckle on his back can be clearly seen on good copies of the photograph). I know, because I was in the Fleet Air Arm at the time, based at Arbroath down the road from Lossiemouth, and the buzz went around the base that some idiot had photographed his air mechanic mate on the airfield and then sent it to someone, claiming it was a Martian. It was the butt of considerable humour at the base."*

The true identity of Cedric Allingham – a man who shunned publicity and was never photographed in public – is still shrouded in mystery. What a strange attitude from a person one would have expected to be the focus of media attention, in order to promote the sales of his book. There was a suggestion that Mr Allingham had lectured to the Tunbridge Wells UFO Group in the spring of 1955, but our research revealed the guest speaker was, in fact, Mr Desmond Leslie.

George Adamski

Somebody else who took an interest in Cedric Allingham was Stratford-upon-Avon UFO researcher John Dennis Llewellyn, known to his friends as 'Dennis', wrote to George Adamski in 1965, and received the following reply:

> *"Concerning Allingham, a couple of years ago when I was in Europe, there was a complete search made for him by Lu Senstock of Switzerland, and as the report stated that he had died but no place in all of Europe could there be found any record of his passing on – which included such record houses in different nations, as well as convalescence resorts and sanatoriums – no one knows whether he passed on or is living quietly in some place, or was taken away by the Brothers."*

We met 'Dennis' and his charming wife, Ruby, at their family home and have kept in touch with

Ruby since 'Dennis' passed away, some years ago. Just before Christmas 2015, we spoke to Ruby (85) who told us 'Dennis' would have been pleased that his investigations into reported UFO activity around the West Midlands was finally published, instead of slipping away into obscurity.

Mrs Rhoda Mills

Interestingly we were to come across a letter from Mrs Rhoda Mills, who was then living in Somerset in 1982. At that time she was aged 70, which means she has passed away. She wrote about what she and her husband had experienced, while living in California, during the 'Adamski' era......

2 King George Road
Minehead
Somerset TA24 5JD

24 December, 1982

Dear

I just heard you talking on the radio about U.F.O's. I believe you said that you had written a book, although I gathered you have never seen one. Well, I have not written a book, but I certainly have seen many.

My husband and I recently came to live at above address after living in California for thirty years. In the fifties we were 'in the thick' of the flying saucer movement. I am now turned seventy. We knew George Adamski, George van Tassel, Angelucci, Geo. Hunt Williamson etc. I was secretary of a magazine on the subject. Each Spring we attended the huge Convention at Giant Rock in the desert. You may not have heard about these people, but they were very big names in those days. We actually have a snap of one of the spaceships over the desert.

As for sightings. Yes indeed! Many! Three in particular. One on the beach (which was deserted otherwise. We sat on the cliff and watched it for 45 minutes. A big glowing thing, pulsating. Then, as we gazed at it, it disappeared. It is all a matter of raising vibration. California was the centre of this sort of thing in the fifties, and that was long before rockets etc. were being sent into space.

The reason I am writing is because I could handle a local group if enough are interested. Before I left California I gave my son a batch of papers and sketches of alien beings. The sources have all been very very carefully checked. The American Government has a lot of information on this subject. They take it seriously.

Well, if you care to answer about running a group, my address is above. R.Mills Mrs.R.Mills

Mrs Rhoda Mills

26th February – USA: Silver 'disc' seen

Newburyport, Massachusetts architect – Mr R.M. Pierce, and marine engineer – George Avery, with one other person, sighted:

> *"...a silver disc, with a white trail, making a loud roaring noise as it crossed the sky, at 2.30pm, taking between 30-60 seconds to do so."*

1st March – England: Spinning UFO seen over Lowestoft

Mrs Edith Capes, from Lowestoft, contacted the local newspaper, The *Eastern Evening News* (2.3.1954), after sighting an object looking like a child's spinning top, with a light underneath it, travelling over the town, at 7.30pm on 1st March 1954. Later the same evening, Mr P. Goreham, from Norwich,

5 to 10 'Saucers' Reported Nightly By Airline Pilots

By JIM G. LUCAS
Scripps-Howard Staff Writer

WASHINGTON, Feb. 12—Commercial airline pilots report between five and 10 flying saucer sightings each night.

Representatives of major airlines will meet Wednesday in Los Angeles with Military Air Transport Service (MATS) intelligence officers to discuss speeding up saucer-reporting procedures.

The idea will be to "get the reports in the quickest possible way" so that the Air Force can send fast jet fighters to investigate.

TRAIL IS COLD

Heretofore, commercial pilots have landed and then reported to MATS through their companies. By that time, the trail usually is cold. Now, pilots are instructed to flash reports direct from the air to MATS intelligence in Washington or to the nearest Air Force base.

However several "bugs" have been found in this plan. Some pilots, for example, don't know how to contact MATS intelligence. Others don't think it important enough. That's one angle to be discussed at the Los Angeles meeting.

Airline pilots are asked not to discuss their sightings publicly or give them to newspapers.

Navy Capt. Bernard Baruch Jr., MATS intelligence officer, is in charge of the project. Capt. Baruch's headquarters are in New York, but MATS intelligence also maintains a large staff at Andrews Air Force Base, Md., near Washington.

NUMEROUS SIGHTINGS

One well-informed source said that until recently the largest number of sightings were from the Southwest Pacific. Saucer sightings have been particularly numerous around Australia, where the British maintain a guided missile range.

Recently, however, there has been an increase in saucer sightings in the North Atlantic, this source said. Simultaneously, the number of oil slicks and submarine lightings in this area has increased.

The same source said flying saucer sightings are "fairly common" throughout the non-Communist world.

2—ROCKY MOUNTAIN NEWS— Denver, Colo., Saturday, Feb. 13, 1954 reported having seen a spinning 'ball of light' in the sky, which changed into a 'triangle' as it headed across the sea.

2nd March – USA: Three UFOs sighted

In the vicinity of Harrisburg, Pennsylvania, research engineer – Mr R.C. Swengel, sighted three objects in the sky, at 10pm, each showing two lights, which flew in a straight trajectory for an unknown length of time.

24th March – England: What was it that blazed over Britain?

Terrence Scott – then a member of the Air Traffic Corps (Cadets), very adept at aircraft recognition, who had incidentally spent the previous weekend taking part in a glider training exercise, at RAF Hornchurch – was on his way to meet family members arriving by train, at Valkyrie Railway Station, London, at 5.50pm on 24th March 1955.

While walking along London Road, he felt a curious sensation come over him, as if something was going to happen. As he turned left into Hamlet Court Road, just before Annerley Road, he glanced upwards, towards the south, and saw, at an elevation of some 40 degrees to the left and slightly above a large medium cloud,

> *"...a huge object, displaying no wings or appendages, with a distinctive dark orange top and white underside moving approximately at the same speed as the cloud. I continued on my journey. I could see that it was moving eastwards.*
>
> *Suddenly, it gave a slight movement and totally disappeared from sight, travelling faster than the eye could follow. When I arrived at the Railway Station, I checked my watch, which showed 6.30pm. I looked around the sky, hoping to catch a glimpse of the 'craft', once again, and noticed a long flash of silver light in the north-west, some distance above the horizon. Looking back toward the south, I noticed a small cloud, low in the sky.*
>
> *Don't ask me why, but I just knew I would see it again near to the left of the cloud, which is what happened now. I could see that it was definitely the same 'craft', silhouetted against the sky, especially when it turned a little on its axis.*
>
> *I watched it change from orange to red – like the colour of dying embers of a fire – before gradually turning back to blood orange. Suddenly it slowed, stopped, went a little way again, before slowly fading out, glinting as it caught the rays of the sun on its underside – then finally gone."*

Mr Scott was not the only witness. The switchboards of the police emergency services were flooded with calls from the public, reporting what many took to be an aircraft on fire on that early evening.

The fiery object, with a red tail, was first seen zigzagging across the sky over Land's End, heading northward, sparking off numerous alerts to the Fire Brigade, who raced from one village to the next, fearing the inevitable was going to happen.

Chased by RAF jets

At 7.09pm, an object was seen heading over Manchester, at a height of some 20,000 feet, by a squadron of *Meteor* jets, from RAF Malling, in Kent, who attempted a pursuit in excess of 500 mph. All of a sudden, the object, described as looking like an 'orange ball of fire', vanished in a mid-air explosion. Another witness was Squadron Leader T. Storer – commanding officer of 610 Squadron, RAF Hooton.

He was flying at 20,000 feet, at the time, and thought it was an airliner coming down in flames. He said:

> *"If it was a meteorite, I have never seen anything like that before. It disintegrated so low, bright red and green lights were coming off it as it fell."*

Enquiries made, later, revealed that the object had covered a distance of 500 miles in forty-five minutes.

Other witnesses to the phenomena

Other witnesses to this phenomenon included a coastguard from Lancashire, who sighted a 'ball of fire' over the sea, a resident of Prestatyn, North Wales, who saw 'it' flying over the Vale of Clwyd, leaving a cascade of silver light in the sky; others described it pear-shaped, 'white hot mass', 'ball, with a stick at the end' (Blackpool), 'cascade of silver discs' (Merseyside), and 'large airliner', (Birmingham). A *Liverpool Post* reporter who was in Wallasey Drive, Liverpool, described it as being:

> *"...two 'discs', linked by a zigzagging trail. The left-hand 'disc' seemed to be over Great Orme's Head. As darkness fell the trail disappeared, followed by three of the 'discs'. A fourth 'disc' remained vivid until 7.31pm."*

Garage owner Mr Worthington from Dyserth, near Prestatyn, described the shape of it as rock-like.

It was a meteor!

An eminent professor from Jodrell Bank Observatory, Manchester, explained away the sightings as being a meteor – which seems odd, if you take into account the fireball was seen to travel in four different directions over the country, and estimated by another scientist to be a quarter-of-a-mile in diameter!

Mr Arthur Constance – Library of two million press cuttings

Somebody who always refused to accept this as an explanation was Mr Arthur Constance – a well-known journalist, author and broadcaster from Cheltenham, Gloucestershire, (died 15th March 1961), who possessed an impressive library of over two million press cuttings and sixteen thousand reference books devoted to strange phenomena, and whom it was said, at the age of 17, could recite 'almost the whole' works of Shakespeare and the Bible.

At the age of 69 (1960), Arthur had written nine million words, ten thousand articles, twenty-three books (including *The Inexplicable Sky*) and 260 Radio broadcasts. Arthur visited the Air Ministry, in May 1955, and handed over an 18,000 word report into his investigation of the events that took place on 24th March 1955, compiled from 180 different newspaper clippings.

Written nine million words and 260 broadcasts!

Mr Constance:

> *"The 'Thing' was seen by tens of thousands – probably hundreds of thousands of people. Dismiss mass hallucinations. Firstly, it could not have been a meteor, because it went in several directions. Secondly, it changed shape and colour. Thirdly, its speed was variable – in some places it hovered. Fourthly, the size of the 'Thing', apart from the trail, was far too great – it could not have been an earthly craft, or experimental device, its speed was far too great. When I went to the Air Ministry, I was received with courtesy and told it had been dismissed as meteorite, because the meteorological authorities said so!"*

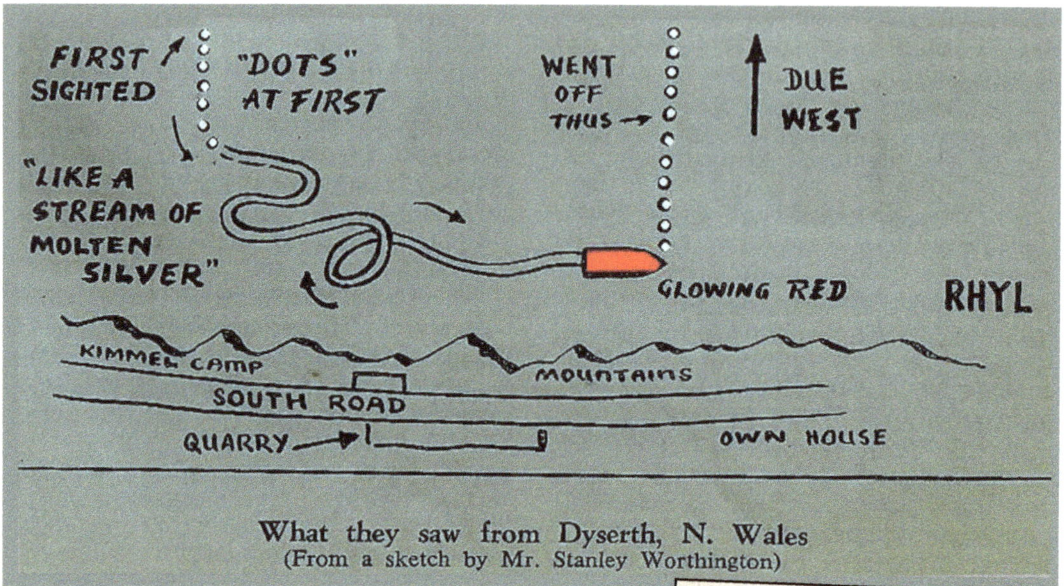

What they saw from Dyserth, N. Wales
(From a sketch by Mr. Stanley Worthington)

A lengthy report of the incident was published in the *Flying Saucer News,* in autumn 1953, by Arthur Constance.

Explanations: Meteorite or Northern Lights

Most people's first impression (including ours) would be that this was space debris or a meteorite. What we found odd was it took 45 minutes to travel up to Glasgow from a noted position, zigzagging as it did so. This means it was moving at 650 miles per hour rather than 2,000 mph, as reported in the newspapers. Some people claimed to have seen three 'explosion-like flares' accompanying it – green-orange, and then green again. An Air Ministry Official suggested, *"It was probably meteorite or a glimpse of the Northern Lights."*

Radicals of the ridiculous

An example of Arthurs's flair and brilliant mind can be seen in an article, entitled *Radicals of the Ridiculous,* published by him in the Tyneside UFO magazine *ORBIT,* in April-June 1960, of which we are delighted to present an extract, providing 'much food for thought':

> *"Conditioned as we are in this generation, by three dimensions not merely by three dominations, some preliminary (or more accurately preliminary) observations are necessary to this article. Our three dominations are closely identified with the three dimensions of our material world and (like them) are illusory. We are dominated by a spiritual up and*

down conception of reality quite as false as any height conception of space in a material sense. For we of this generation confuse arrogance with sublimity, humility with humiliation and the Supreme Being with the lowest demons in hell, so that we are as uncertain regarding which is right side up spiritually as we are regarding which humans are on their heads or heels on this supposedly spinning globe. I say supposedly, because all the evidence which seems to prove that our Earth speeds through space and spins is quite as relevant to a fixed earth as to a moving earth theory, both being mere theories of our spiderism which imply that we know what term such as 'speed' and 'spinning' mean, which we certainly do not.

Mr Arthur Constance

We are dominated by a spiritual forward and back conception of reality expressed in terms of 'evolution' and 'human progress' which is quite as false as any past-present future conception of what we call 'time' in an every day sense. For we of this generation cannot agree among ourselves whether we are progressing or retrogressing. Some of us press forward towards the past, other dream of the future. We are as ignorant regarding the meaning of the word 'length' as applied to human life or to the word humanity, as we are of the meanings of 'height' in our religious and political ideals.

We are dominated by a conception of spiritual 'breadth' which is quite as confused and illusory as any material conception of breadth as a dimension. We have our 'right' and 'left' opinions and are prepared to let others suffer or die for them, but there are so many degrees of 'leftness' and 'rightness' that no definitions of the terms can be other than relative - and when relatives quarrel among themselves they are notoriously irreconcilable. Narrow-minded people are often 'wider' that they may superficially seem. People who believe themselves to be 'broad-minded' are, often, as narrow as a razor's edge and as dangerous."

April - USA: Damage to cars, cause unknown

One cannot help but compare these inexplicable events with a similar spate of 'windshield activity' that occurred in the USA, during April 1954, when an 'epidemic' of 'attacks' were made on vehicle windscreens, covering an area of ten cities around the north-west of Washington, stretching from Bellingham in the South to Tacoma. Investigations made by the police revealed that, on occasion, they were being reported at around ten complaints per minute. Examination of the windscreens revealed no trace of any solid residue, such as one would expect from the discharge of pellets, although they did discover tiny globules of an oily, tar-like substance, which led to the theory that a rain of chemicals was eating into the windshields. This hypothesis appears to have been corroborated by two King County sheriff deputies, who claimed that they watched 'pit marks' appear on the windshield of the parked police vehicle while they stood next to it.

EVENING NEWS 30-6-54

JETS HUNT 'FLYING SAUCERS'

Squadron of Sabre jet fighters scrambled from Goose Bay, Labrador, to intercept "flying saucers" after they had been reported by Capt. Howard, pilot of London-bound B.O.A.C. luxury Monarch Straotcruiser. Capt. Howard, crew and five pasengers saw "the saucers." Monarch landed at London Airport to-day.

EMPIRE NEWS → 7-4-57

Mystery 'object' over Atlantic

RADAR operators throughout Britain were last night ordered to keep a special watch for a mysterious high-speed object picked up on long-range radar screens in Scotland.

Was it another "Flying Saucer"—a secret plane missing from its closely guarded base in Nevada, U.S.?—or a new long-distance Russian bomber on a reconnaissance flight by way of the North Pole?

The Air Ministry are taking the affair "extremely seriously," it was revealed last night.

Strict orders have been given to all R.A.F. personnel not to discuss with anyone the discoveries made at the West Freugh bombing range near Stranraer.

There the radio operators, scanning out into the Atlantic, found an unidentified aircraft.

Officers were called and, after studying the flight of the strange object, they asked for other radar stations, miles away at Luce bay, to help.

A report

All three stations plotted the course of the mysterious visitor, which was never seen by eyes.

A message was sent to the Air Ministry, who cabled for a detailed report.

Wing Commander W. P. Whitworth, in charge of the West Freugh station, said last night: "Other stations throughout the country have been asked to report."

In Nevada, U.S., a secret high-speed plane had earlier taken off and vanished.

The Air Force has asked for a maximum security guard on the plane if found.

It is believed to be the U-2, a single-jet plane with a huge swept-back wing which has been doing high-altitude research work and can possibly be used to detect particles in the air resulting from nuclear tests.

Report of 12 Cities

17 APR 1954

Many Pitted Windshields Baffle State of Washington

By the United Press

SEATTLE, April 16.—An epidemic of pitted automobile windshields has hit at least 12 northwest Washington cities and police today said they were at a loss to explain the attacks.

Seattle officers said they believed the mysterious pits were caused by chemical reaction rather than vandals. Police Chief H. J. Lawrence said it would take a small army of vandals to inflict the amount of damage reported.

Meanwhile, with the windshield phenomenon spreading from Bellingham south to Tacoma, law-enforcement officers decided to meet later today to compare notes.

Seattle officials said they could find no solid residue of any type of pellets which might have struck the windshields. However, they reported finding tiny globules of an oily tar-like substance which led to the theory that a rain of some chemical was eating into the windshields, which police said were made of a different kind of glass from other windows.

In some cases, officers said, windshield damage reports were believed to be the psychological result of publicity, which caused motorists to notice old pits not previously observed.

The Seattle Police Department was forced to put four extra officers on the complaint desk to handle windshield damage reports, sometimes coming in at the rate of 10 a minute.

Two King County sheriff's deputies reported they actually watched two pitmarks appear in the windshield of a truck.

At Tacoma, two reporters got out of their car for about five minutes to talk to a policeman and said that when they returned to the car it had four fair-sized pits that were not there before.

Gilbert Albrecht, a warehouse worker at Tacoma, said 34 pitmarks appeared on his windshield this afternoon.

8th April – USA: Landed UFO with occupant reported

At 4.30pm, a Chicago, Illinois resident – Lelah Stoker – claimed he had seen:

> *"...a white, round-topped 'disc', with a 'humanoid' suspended beneath it, skimming over the water. It then landed, and an occupant in a green suit walked around. Thirty minutes later, it took of at a very fast speed."*

23rd April – USA: Silver domed UFO

At 9.30am, Mr and Mrs F.E. Robinson from Pittsfield, Maine, sighted:

> *"...a silver dollar-shaped object, with a dome and a flashing light, accompanied by a sound – like a swarm of bees. It hovered and tilted, flew horizontally, then rose vertically without tilting. Stones underneath it moved. Four minutes later, it was out of sight."*

24th April – USA: Silver domed UFO

Hartland, Maine: Was this the same UFO seen the following day, by Mr D. Robinson, at 6.10pm? He described seeing:

> *"...a large, silver, oblong object, with a dome and a flashing light, that flew straight across the sky before heading straight upwards, 15 minutes later."*

27th April – England: UFO seen descending into sea off Bexhill, Sussex

On the morning of 27th April 1954, a blue/green-coloured object, with a moon-shaped top, was sighted sinking into the sea off Bexhill, Sussex, followed by a loud noise – like an aircraft – and a brilliant light seen moving from the direction of the object.

(Source: *Evening Standard*, 27.4.1954 – 'Moon in the sea')

Astronomer sights formation of UFOs over Surrey

In the same year, amateur astronomer Michael Wilson from Farnham, Surrey – who was to be technical director of Flight International during the 1970s – had just completed a six-inch reflecting telescope and was carrying out some final adjustments, in the evening, when he became aware of a series of 'lights' moving across the sky, from west to east.

> *"They had the appearance of first or second magnitude stars and were heading across the sky in groups of three. Speaking from memory [in 1971] there was probably fifteen or twenty of them taking 15-20 minutes to silently cross the sky. Coincidently there was considerable night flying activity going on with the RAF from RAF Odiham, some six miles away. I rang RAF Farnborough and they immediately sent a despatch rider and radio operator to Farnham, where I was living, since they were unable to pick up the objects themselves. It transpired, in conversation that they had alerted Odiham to the presence of unidentified aircraft and had sent up a flight of Hunter jets."*
>
> **(Source: Bob Tibbitts, Coventry UFO Research Group)**

April – England: Black sphere seen over RAF Church Lawford

Another serviceman who sighted a UFO over the airbase was Dennis Plunkett, whom we met and spoke to on a number of occasions over the years. His sighting took place in April 1954, when he was Head of the International Flying Saucer Bureau (UK), which had been formed by Albert K. Bender (USA) in 1952, from which the Bristol-based British Flying Saucer Bureau was formed in

1953 (an amalgamation of the British Flying Saucer Bureau and Flying Saucer Club).

When Dennis left for National Service with the RAF, in October 1952, his father – Captain Plunkett – took over the running of the organisation until his return. His father was actively involved, until his death in 1992. Sadly, we have to report that Dennis – who was still very much involved with the running of the British Flying Saucer Bureau – is now, in (2015), the subject of ill health and unable to carry on the work. Our thoughts go to his wife, Maureen. What a credit this man was to UFO research. He was always willing to help and very much the quintessential gentleman.

The Official Secrets Act

Dennis spoke about having seen:

> *"...a mysterious black sphere, moving in and out of cloud over the airbase, one day, and of a security notice posted on the wall at RAF Church Lawford, reminding the service personnel of the Official Secrets Act and the dire consequences of failing to keep quiet about any unusual airborne activity seen by the service personnel".*

12th May – England: Naval officer claims alien abduction in Derbyshire

During a number of visits made to Geoffrey and Margaret Westwood – both former police officers, living in the Harborne area of Birmingham, who were instrumental in running the Birmingham-based UFO Group, 'UFOSIS', during the 1970s – we discussed before her untimely death some years ago investigations into claims made of what appears to be an early report of 'Alien Abduction', brought to their attention, in 1976, by retired Chief Petty Officer Horatio Penrose – a married man with son, living in Lonsdale Road, Harborne – (although he actually addressed himself in rank of Commander).

Margaret Westwood

Margaret:

> *"He approached us after having heard of our organisation. (It wasn't until our third meeting, some weeks later, did he tell us about his 1954 experience, but only gave us the bare details.) We assumed his reason for contacting us was because he felt the UFO climate, both in public interest and the Press, had improved. By July 1976 he was no longer employed by the same firm and decided to tell us what had taken place, no longer fearing ridicule."*

From original interview notes, written by Margaret, we learnt that on 12th May 1954, he had driven his one year-old black Vauxhall Wyvern to an unnamed public house in Derbyshire, in order to meet an unnamed man who had expressed an interest in purchasing the vehicle (some 30-40 miles away).

Although an offer was made, Mr Penrose decided to think the matter over before committing himself and agreed to meet up with the same prospective purchaser, the following evening, to discuss the matter further – behaviour that may, to some, in this day and age, appear a little odd, accepting the distance involved (before Motorways), and one would have thought the interested party would have travelled to see the car, not the other way around. This was no short trip up the road, but a journey of some distance.

The following evening (14th May) Mr Penrose drove back to the public house in Derbyshire, where he met up with the prospective purchaser, who invited Penrose to his house for tea in order to discuss the matter further, taking into consideration that despite two visits and much time spent discussing the sale of the car, no agreement on price had been finalised. One almost gets the impression that the prospective purchaser was perhaps known to Mr Penrose. Would any normal person have gone to such lengths to sell their car to a complete stranger?

When they arrived at the house they found a meal laid by the man's wife. The couple were described as an ordinary English couple, but 'smaller than average' – the implications of which are lost, unless one is supposed to associate this couple with the mysterious events that were to take place, a short time later.

At 10.30pm, after still having failed to come to an agreement over the sale of the car, Mr Penrose told the couple he had changed his mind and left.

Bright 'light' seen – encounters grotesque creatures!

While driving along the Derby to Burton road, heading towards Birmingham, Mr Penrose noticed a very bright 'light', travelling towards him,

> *"...which at first I took be an oncoming vehicle, so I decided to slow down. The next thing I became aware of was it being over the car and on coming to an abrupt halt, throwing me forward in the driving seat, where I struck my head on the windscreen. Although dazed, I realised that something, or someone, had gripped the car on either side and lifted me into mid-air, before being lowered onto the side of the road. I felt myself being taken out of the car by a man in a one-piece suit, effortlessly, into an entrance on the underside of a large round vehicle which was hovering above us, and giving out a bright light. I was taken into a room, which contained other male and female occupants, distinguishable by their shapes, who had similar short hairstyles, whose facial expressions did not appear unusual. I was asked questions, telepathically, about my naval experience and work with radar. When I attempted some hypnotic regression, they seemed to become very confused. A woman injected some green fluid into my arm, after which I remembered no more, until I recovered consciousness in the Derbyshire Royal Infirmary and discovered I had been given stitches to a cut on the head."*

Mr Penrose also told of *"horrible tests of a medical nature being performed on me, by grotesque creatures, before being returned to my car."*

Reported to the 'Derby Telegraph'

Details of the accident were reported in the *Derby Telegraph* newspaper on 14th May 1954:

'Horatio Penrose was taken to the Derbyshire Royal Infirmary by ambulance, after suffering concussion and minor cuts and bruises, following an accident outside the Hilton Gravel works, Burnaston'.

The newspaper also told its readers that: *'Mr Penrose had been found by a passing motorist, and that his wife (Lillian) had travelled from Birmingham to see him, the following morning.'*

Whether this incident had anything to do with any subsequent divorce can only be speculation, especially as we don't know the grounds or the date when they split up. Mr Penrose told Margaret he

was kept in hospital for some months following the incident, after having sustained cuts to the head and face and loss of memory (which seems a rather long period of hospitalisation for what appears to be not any serious injuries), and that he had taken one of the nurses out socially as a gesture for looking after him.

RAC patrolman comes across the accident

After learning that a passing RAC patrolman had come across the incident and contacted the police, after finding Mr Penrose still sitting in the driver's seat of the car, we launched an appeal through the local newspaper (2004) to try and identify any of the people involved, such as the RAC man, police officers, ambulance men, and the breakdown service that had taken the vehicle away.

Senior police officer takes interest

Oddly, he also claimed after discovering a senior police officer had attempted to interview him at the hospital that the doctors had refused to allow this course of action to take place. What truths are there, if any, behind another suggestion made by Penrose that the police wanted to interview him because they had *'found an abnormally large amount of blood in the vehicle, following their arrival at the scene'*, indicating the likelihood of another person having been in the vehicle? – A matter that Mr Penrose denied emphatically.

We traced a witness who had seen the vehicle resting on top of the railings, but were unable to trace any of the personnel from the police or ambulance men who might have been able to throw some light on how the damage had been caused to both sides of the vehicle, causing the roof to buckle upwards – as can be seen from the photograph – strong enough to rip the driver's door away completely. Does this corroborate the version of events as given by Mr Penrose, or was the damage caused by heavy machinery used in removing the vehicle from the railings? Unlikely, we would have thought, as the rear of the car can be seen resting on a fence pole, a few feet in the air. Why was the car still in situ when photographed, the next morning? Were they waiting for lifting gear?

The Philadelphia Experiment

Margaret told us that Mr Penrose expressed a great interest in the Philadelphia Experiment (allegedly involving rendering the *USS Eldridge Destroyer DE-173* completely invisible in 1943) and carried a book with him, entitled *The Allende Letters*, by Brad Steiger and Joan Whritenour, published in 1961 (which referred to a mysterious Carlos Allende and his involvement with Dr Morris Ketchum Jessup – an astrophysicist author of a book, entitled *The case for UFOs* (1955), who was found deceased in his car from carbon monoxide poisoning in what appears to be suspicious circumstances, on the 28th April 1959).

Malcolm Robinson (left) with Peter Paget (right) at the Warminster Conference 2015

After being discharged from hospital, Mr Penrose went back to the scene of the incident and interviewed a railway signalman on duty that night (name not given), who described seeing a car, with an extremely bright light above it, go past the signal box.

Whilst there is every reason to question whether the 'close encounter' actually took place (after all, we only have Mr Penrose's word), there is no question about the validity of the accident and of the peculiar damage caused to the vehicle. Mr Penrose claimed he had made a return visit to the home of the interested purchaser, seeking some answers after he had recovered, when he was shocked to discover from enquiries made with the neighbours that the house was empty and the occupier was in prison.

Peter Paget and Mike Oram at the Warminster Conference 2015

Peter Paget

Somebody else who met Mr Penrose was Peter Paget – journalist and author of a number of books, which included *The Welsh Triangle* and *UFO UK*. He described meeting the 'Commander' in Birmingham, during the 1970s (probably August 1976/77), and of obtaining his account, which was later published in *The Welsh Triangle* (page 183-187).

We contacted Peter Paget hoping to obtain a photograph of Mr Penrose but were unsuccessful, although Peter remembered the incident well. Further enquiries were to reveal that Mr Horatio Rex Penrose (born 1918, Navy serial number PMX.12431758) had served on *HMS Royalist* during the Second World War as a Petty Officer, and was discharged from the Royal Navy on the 3rd February 1948. He had a wife, Lillian, and a son, Eric.

Traced niece, Mrs R Dunn

He also had a niece – Mrs R.M. Dunn – who later emigrated to Rochedale, Queensland, Australia, and was living there in 1977.

In 2010, we spoke to her. She told us:

> *"Their parents separated when my father was about six and Horatio two years of age. Dad and a middle brother came to Australia with their father, about four years later. In all that time they only had contact via a few letters during the war. They did not see each other again until my Dad visited Harborne, Birmingham, in 1977, nearly 60 years after their separation.*
>
> *Unfortunately, Horatio died a couple of years after the reunion, so they did not have much time to get to know each other. I have a photo of Horatio in his navy uniform."*

When we explained the reason behind our search to obtain a photo of him, she told us it was the biggest load of rubbish she had ever heard and refused to let us have the photograph.

Enquiries made with Mr R.Q. Jaggar, in 2001 – then a junior upper deck officer, now responsible for organising reunions with retired crewmates from *HMS Royalist* – revealed that Mr Penrose was remembered by at least two of the crew from the communications department, who described him as being a rather brash but keen and enthusiastic Petty Officer.

Hans Holzer

Margaret also brought to our attention that she understood Professor Hans Holzer – an American parapsychologist – had expressed an interest in producing a film of the incident, after having apparently interviewed Mr Penrose.

We spoke to Hans, in 2008, when he was living in New York and had penned a number of books on the UFO/Paranormal subject.

He denied any knowledge of Mr Penrose, or of producing any film in 2006.

Margaret Westwood showed us a file of mislaid documents, in September 2009, which contained a number of letters sent to her by Professor Hans Holzer, of the New York Committee of Paranormal Occurrence, dated October/November 1976, signed 'Aspera Ad Astra Productions Inc.', in which he thanked her for her offer of help, quote:

> *'We hope to start production by February 1st 1977, and in time I will let you know more exactly when I will be in England....'*

He was most anxious to undertake the hypnotic regression of the 'Commander' and was in the process of preparing a major documentary film along these lines.

In another letter, Professor Holzer stated that he had nominated Peter Paget as his production manager and that he was going to film the 'Commander', 'some time this fall'. Sadly, the film appears never to have come to fruition – perhaps one of the reasons why Hans had completely forgotten about his interest in Mr Penrose.

Regretfully, we had to bring our investigation to a close, feeling we had exhausted all avenues of enquiry. However, we still wondered who the other party in the vehicle was, and more importantly, what happened to them.

In 1953, Horatio E. Penrose, Royal Navy, and R.S.H Boulding, wrote a book, entitled *Principles and Practice of Radar.*

Hans Holzer (26 January 1920 – 26 April 2009) was an American paranormal researcher and author. He wrote well over 100 books on supernatural and occult subjects for the popular market as well as several plays, musicals, films, and documentaries, and hosted a television show, "Ghost Hunter" (not to be confused with Ghost Hunters, a separate show)

11th May – USA: Two 'bright lights' reported

Three USAF policemen, based at Washington National Airport, were on duty, at 10.45pm, when they saw two 'bright lights' on three occasions, heading across the sky on a straight trajectory, making 90 degree turns before fading away. Each sighting lasted about 45 seconds.

13th May – England: UFO over Cambridge

At 11pm on 13th May 1954, Mr G.V. Sales was standing outside Papworth Hospital, Cambridge, when he noticed a brilliant silver coloured object, oval in appearance, clearly visible in the sky. Ten seconds later, it disappeared from view.

(Source: Isle of Wight UFO Society)

14th May – England: USAF pilots scrambled to intercept UFO

At 3.45pm on 14th May 1954, three USAF fighters (from 91st. Fighter Squadron, RAF Bentwaters, in Suffolk, piloted by Captain Kenneth Scott, Jnr., Lt. Harry Joseph Eckes, and Lt. David Clarby) were scrambled by GCI Radar type seven at Bawdy, to intercept a UFO eight miles from their position. It was travelling at 240 knots, and had been sighted visually as 30 feet in diameter, silver/grey round object, showing a thin silhouette as it turned, at a height estimated between 50-60,000 feet. Unfortunately, the pilots were unable to get anywhere near the UFO. What the pilots would not have known is that, on the same day, Marine Corps pilots chased a formation of sixteen UFOs near Dallas, Texas. \

(Source: NICAP, *The UFO Evidence*, 1964/ Personal interview with Jill Clarby)

20th May – England: 'Flying saucer' seen hovering over field

Nigel Frapple was walking home from a dance at Wincanton, Somerset (a regular journey), at 2am on 20th May 1954, when he noticed an orange glow, low in the sky, which he took to be a farm or house on fire. Curious, he stopped near a farm gate, a short distance down the road, just past Redlynch crossroads, and crouched down to have a closer look.

"I was astonished to see this dome-shaped object, hovering approximately 40 feet off the ground in one of the nearby fields, a couple of hundred yards away. It had a cockpit in the centre, with three portholes, and was glowing with violet light. The outside of the 'craft' consisted of what looked like glass panelling, gun-metal grey in colour.

At one end I could see an orange 'ball', cascading with light – like the disco lights you now see. The curious thing was that it didn't appear to be attached to anything – just suspended in the air. Inside the cockpit were shadowy movements, indicating the presence of something or someone, moving behind the light, spilling out of the portholes. After five minutes, or so, it moved – as if it sensed me watching it. I stood up and took a couple of steps forward. To my surprise, it tilted and shot off across the sky.

When I arrived home in an extremely agitated state and told my brother what had happened, and later reported the incident to the police, at Bruton, 'all hell then let loose'. I was besieged by reporters from local and national newspapers, including the BBC, who asked me to show them the field. When we arrived there, we saw a blackened circle in the grass – still there 12 months later. I was bombarded with questions; somebody even asked me if I was drunk at the time! I told them that I had been drinking but had only consumed a couple of pints over the evening."

Nigel made some enquiries in the area and spoke to Mr Henry Toogood, who lived in a cottage lower down the hill. He confirmed having also seen the 'craft' that evening, but from underneath. He said:

> *"It looked like a huge dinner plate, with something resembling metal balls set into the underneath."*

Receives a visit from two men – threats made

About a week later, Nigel received a visit from two smartly dressed men.

> *"They didn't show any ID, but said they were from London. One of them was in his late fifties and wore a grey suit – he did all the talking. His companion was dressed in a dark pinstripe suit, wearing a bowler hat. He never said a word to me but kept his horrible 'black eyes' focussed upon me in a most disconcerting way, after I told them what had happened. Presuming they were from the Air Ministry, or branch of Government, the eldest of the two said, 'If you persist in telling these silly stories, we'll have to take you somewhere where you can't tell them anymore'. They say that time is a great healer and that, as you get older, you forget many things in life. My recollection of what those two said to me will forever remain crystal clear in my memory."*

Nigel Frapple

Mystery of The Air

Somerset Youth's Strange Story

(BY A *WESTERN GAZETTE* REPORTER)

What did 18 years old Nigel Frapple, of High-street, Bruton, Somerset, see "hovering in mid-air" over the Redlynch area of Bruton, about 2 a.m. on Thursday?

He makes no claim to be numbered among those who assert that they have seen a "flying saucer," but his description, in an interview with me as to what he is quite confident he did see, cannot be explained away very easily except that he saw something which answers to no known description. This is his story, which he accompanied with a rough sketch in my notebook.

He was cycling home from a visit to Wincanton and on reaching the area of Redlynch cross-roads says the air became illuminated with an orange light. Travelling along slowly at a height he estimates at about 75 feet was what he first thought must be a balloon on fire. He then saw that it was an object, he thinks about 30 to 40 feet across moving along more or less in front of him. This object hovered over a field. Dismounting from his bicycle he got to within about 50 yards of it and crouching behind a hedge had a good view.

The object, which made no sound, says Mr. Frapple, had a cockpit in its centre, with "sort of glass panels" and this was surmounted by a small revolving light. At one end was another orange light, which for want of a better description, he describes as a tall light, although he could see nothing connecting it with the main body, so that it seemed "suspended on nothing."

He endeavoured to get a closer look and the object commenced to move away slowly in a northerly direction and then vanished upwards at a terrific speed still making no sound except for a "whooshing noise." There seemed to him to be a kind of blue vapour coming from the craft.

Young Frapple is quite resigned to having no believers in his story, and was quite frank as to the difficulty of giving credence to what he is quietly quite confident that he saw.

Desmond Leslie and Captain Edward Plunkett

We discovered that Desmond Leslie had visited Nigel and interviewed him about his sighting, followed by the arrival of Captain Edward Plunkett of the British Flying Saucer Bureau and Flying Saucer Club, who was accompanied by a Mr Watts. He took some photographs and cine film of the location where it had taken place. Curiously, the British Flying Saucer Bureau did not publicise this incident – not that they had any doubt about the genuineness of the witness, but because of his involvement in a police court case. According to Edward, this policy was also adopted by the *BBC*.

At this stage we do not know if the *BBC* did run the story but it appears they may have done so, irrespective of other personal circumstances that had nothing to do with the UFO sighting.

Another witness contacts the newspaper

As a result of newspaper publicity, a Mrs Doreen Heffer from Five Oaks, Shobley, Ringwood, Hampshire, wrote to the *Western Gazette* newspaper on 4th June 1954:

'Sir,

With reference to your account of the 'Mystery of the Air', I should like to confirm that I saw exactly the same thing here, although not at such close range, about 11 o'clock at night. At first, a huge glow appeared which I thought might be a forest fire. When it topped the crest of a hill, I could see it was

"Mystery of The Air"

Readers' Experiences

To the Editor of the *Western Gazette*.

Sir,—Young Mr. Frapple, of Bruton, has one believer in his "mystery of the air." I saw the same type of thing in the sky about 15 months ago. We were living in a cottage at Pylle, Shepton Mallet — just fields opposite, no electricity. After dark I ran upstairs to fetch a book and went to the window to shut it. To my amazement there in the sky was a large orange light hovering over the fields. I gazed spellbound, but could see or hear nothing which could account for its presence over the fields. I shouted to the family to go and look in the sky. Then I rushed back to the window, but the object turned on its side and disappeared. My family were not in time to see it, they said they were rather scared by the tone of my voice. I am a middle-aged woman.—A. HODDER, 29, Chapel-lane, Blackford, Yeovil, Somerset.

(Our correspondent includes two drawings almost exactly like those drawn by Frapple in the reporters' notebook.—EDITOR.

Sir,—Perhaps Nigel Frapple may like to know of at least one person who can quite believe his story. I saw something so similar it must have been another such "object," during the early autumn of 1951 in Dorset. Military exercises were in operation a few miles north. It was a warm, still night, and after midnight. I noticed such an orange glow from my window that I went to discover what it could be. It was not quite such as a "fire" causes and for a minute I could not think what was making the lawn look so lurid, and then "floating" into view over the house was this glowing orange globe. It was so low I feared it was coming down on the roof and looked most alarmingly likely to explode, but it continued very slowly, lighting up the countryside very vividly and then disappearing in a northerly direction. I heard the "whooshing" noise, or almost "hissing," but this was only noticeable while it was quite near me. I was most relieved that it had "missed" the house: the "object" certainly seemed to be guided by some means.—READER.

Sir,—With reference to your account of the "Mystery of the air" I should like to confirm that I saw exactly the same thing here, although at not such close range. Here it was about 11 o'clock at night. At first a huge glow appeared, which I thought might be a forest fire. When it topped the crest of a hill I could see it was something moving forward. I thought a huge plane was on fire and expected something to drop off, but as it moved along, perfectly evenly on a straight course and did not loose height in any way it left me baffled. It was exactly as your Somerset reader described a yellow orange glow, with a deeper shade, which I imagine was the thing itself, and behind which looked as though it was following and too far to seem attached, was a sort of tall thing of orange fire colour. It was moving perfectly evenly, not very fast and travelling towards Ringwood. It must have been quite a few minutes before it got out of sight behind some trees.—(Miss) DOREEN HEFFER, Five Oaks, Shobley, Ringwood.

Summer/Autumn 1954 FLYING SAUCER NEWS 9

Saucer LOW - OVER HAMPSHIRE AND SOMERSET.

ON the night of May 19-20, two independent witnesses claim to have seen a huge circular flying machine, surrounded by a brilliant flame-coloured light. Both witnesses - Miss Doreen Heffer, of Shobley, near Ringwood, Hants.- and Nigel Frapple, of Bruton, Somerset- agreed on the salient features.

At least 50 ft. in diameter, it hovered gently at first, and then made off at speed. The only sound was a slight swishing.

Frapple claimed to have seen it whilst cycling home at 2 am. on May 20th - at a distance of only about 30 yards - when it appeared to have been about 20 ft. from the ground.

Miss Heffer has described the object she saw as flame-coloured with a deep red mark in the centre, and following - and seemingly attached - was another light, surrounded by a flame-coloured glow. She drew a diagram for FSC Representative, Mr. J. Ibson, which we reproduce here.

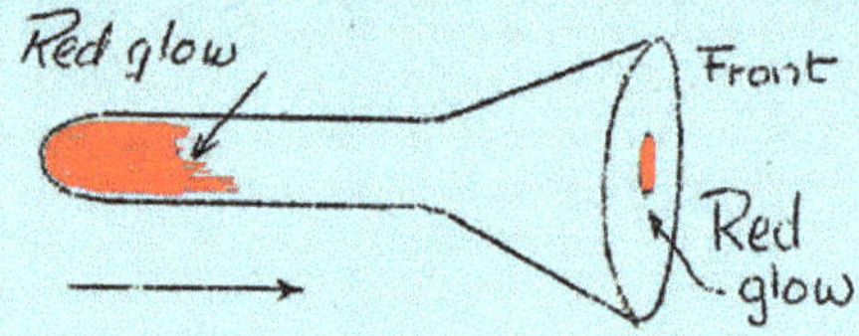

Seeing the glow from her window - which overlooks a large forest, she at first thought it must be from a forest fire, but this was ruled out when the glow was seen to move steadily forward on an even course, at about the speed of a transport 'plane. It followed the main Southampton to Bournemouth road in the direction of Ringwood.

Miss Heffer had seen the object some three hours earlier than Nigel Frapple, but had not reported it until she saw his claim in the local paper.

A full report of the object, it is understood, has been sent to R.A.F. headquarters at Uxbridge.

*****

something moving forward. I thought a huge plane was on fire and expected something to drop off, but as it moved along, perfectly evenly on a straight course and did not lose height in any way, it left me baffled. It was exactly as your Somerset reader described – a yellow/ orange glow, with a deeper shade, which I imagine was the thing itself."

Summer – England: UFO over Lincolnshire

In summer of the same year, Mr A. Alcock of Stamford, Lincolnshire, was driving towards Ketton, along the North Road, when he saw what looked like,

> *"...half a shining pea – flat at the bottom, curved on top – hovering in the air close to the Ketco Chimneys, then it rose slowly upwards and went out of view in two seconds".*

(Source: South Lincolnshire UFO Study Group)

30th May – England: 'Light' seen in the sky

A small globe-like light was seen to cross the sky over Canvey Island, Essex, and disappear towards the direction of London.

(Source: *Daily Herald*, 31.5.1954)

1st June – USA: Pilots sight 'unusual object in sky'

At 9pm, the crew of a USAF *B-47* Jet bomber, at an altitude of 34,000 feet, 400 miles south to Minneapolis, Minnesota, reported sighting an unusual object, 'showing lights', flying at a height of between 24-44,000 feet for 1 hour.

8th June – USA: Golden yellow light appears

At 1am (time not confirmed) Mr L.T. Prewitt – an employee of Red River Arsenal, Texarkana, Texas, reported seeing a golden-yellow 'light' flying over his house, making a "shhh" or buzzing sound for two minutes.

10th June – USA: Pilot sights white light

USAF pilot Capt. Bill McDonald, was over Estacado, Texas, at 9:09pm, when he saw:

> *"...a white 'light' descend at 45 degrees from great altitude, and then pass under my aircraft, before completing two 360 turns and then disappear from sight after 30 seconds".*

11th June – USA: Three UFOs sighted

Doctor H. Percy Wilkins – a noted lunar expert – was on a flight from Charlestown to Atlanta, Georgia, when he sighted two bright, oval-shaped, objects – *"like polished metal plates reflecting the sunlight"* – motionless above a bank of cumulus cloud.

Suddenly, a third object appeared and then headed away at speed, in an arc of movement, and disappeared behind clouds, leaving the first two still swaying gently.

15th June – England: Three lights seen

Over Four Elms, Kent, was a report of a bright yellow light, accompanied by two smaller blue lights on either side – apparently seen to rise up from the ground and head off slowly towards the London area. It moved in a curve and was accompanied by a curious 'rushing noise'. No firm shape could be detected behind the lights.

(Source: *Kent and Sussex Courier*, 18.6.1954)

23rd June – England: Cigar-shaped UFO sighted

At 9.15pm over Hengistbury Head, Hampshire, five people reported seeing:

> *"...a large, brilliant white, cigar-shaped object – larger than any aircraft – stationary in the sky for a few minutes, before it shot away at terrific speed".*

Other witnesses included people living in the St Catherine's Hill and Pokesdown areas. (Source: *Christchurch Times*)

24th June – England: 'Ball of fire' seen over Lyme Regis

At 3.30am on 24th June 1954, Lyme Regis resident, Mr M. Thomas – a radio dealer from Uplyme – and his wife, were awakened by an unusual noise. On going to the window to look out, he saw:

> *"...a 'ball of fire' in the sky – as large as the Moon, with a dark band across its face –*

before moving away in a series of jerking and hovering motions for about 25 minutes, before heading off in a westward direction".

(Source: *Devon & Dorset Reporter*, 25.6.1954)

25th June – England: Clergyman sights 'flying saucer' over Stafford

On 25th June 1954, the Reverend Cedric Wright – (vicar of Seighford, near Stafford) – and his wife and son, saw what they described as:

"...a great illuminated 'crab-like thing', with feelers, hovering like a helicopter, 80 feet off the ground; dome-like or half an orange in shape, with a halo of light sweeping the ground below with a backwards and forwards motion, about half a mile away."

(Source: Robin Gibbons/Gavin Gibbons, *Flying Saucer News*, page 8, Summer/Autumn 1954)

25th June – USA: Round object

Experienced private pilot – Mr John Mark – was flying a *Navion* light aircraft over Indian Lake, Ohio, at 5.05pm, when ATC radar at Dayton, Ohio Airport, tracked a very fast target at the same location. Mr Mark looked out and saw a . . .

"silver or aluminium round object with a flat base, raised front edge, and inverted cone on top. It had a diameter of about 60 feet and was flying horizontally to begin with, before halting in mid air. The object then climbed up steeply and was lost from view minutes later."

26th June – England: Flame coloured UFO seen

A flame coloured object was observed on the horizon over Leeds, at 10pm. Through binoculars, a cone-shaped object was seen, showing red and orange flames flickering from its base. It was also viewed by people living on the local moors for about 15 minutes as it manoeuvred, before heading away. **(Source: *Yorkshire Evening Post*, 28/29th June 1954)**

27th June – England: Group of people sight UFO over London

At 1.40am over Hindhead, Hampshire was a report of a 'bright light' seen moving rapidly across the sky. According to the eight witnesses, it appeared to speed up and slow down while in flight. It was accompanied by a noise like a jet aircraft, emanating from a point some distance away behind the object.

(Source: *Flying Saucer News* signed statements)

At 9pm on 27th June 1954, six people – including Eva Becke and her brother, Colin – sighted a strange object from their top floor flat near Regents Park, as the sun was setting. They described it as resembling a 'bowler hat' in the sky.

"It was a long way off, high up, and appeared to hover; other times, it moved slowly. Suddenly, two lines shot out from each side, with what looked like shimmering plates, at each end."

(Source: *The London Evening Newspaper*, 3.7.1954 – 'Golly! Was it a flying saucer?')

29th June – England: BOAC pilots sight UFOs

Two days later on 29th June 1954 (some accounts give the 30th), Captain James Howard was at the controls of his BOAC *Stratocruiser Centaurus* airliner on a flight from Idlewild Airport New York to London, at 9.05pm, accompanied by co-pilot First Officer Lee Boyd.

Other members of the crew included George Allen, navigating officer, Douglas Cox radio officer, Dan Godfrey engineering officer, and Bill Stewart another engineering officer also a veteran flyer, and Stewardess Daphne Webster. Captain Howard,

They were flying north over Seven Island, Quebec, heading north-east at about 230 knots, when he and five other passengers saw:

> *"...a large object, the size of an ocean liner, and six smaller ones definitely flying as a group to the north-west of us. Three of the smaller UFOs led the 'mother ship', the other three brought up the rear. They flew parallel to the BOAC for about 80 miles of our journey. Although the six 'escort ships' stayed the same, the 'mother ship' appeared to change shape occasionally."*

Pilot draws 'flying jellyfish'

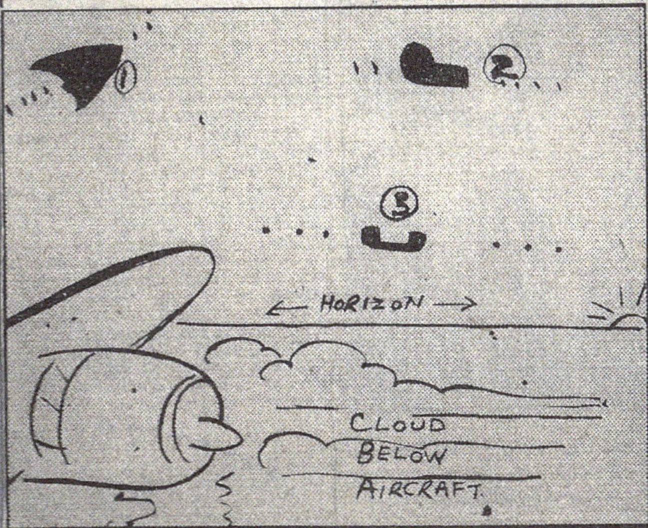

2/7/54 **By Daily Mail Reporter**

THIS sketch of seven mysterious flying objects was drawn exclusively for the *Daily Mail* yesterday by Captain James Howard, 33-year-old pilot of the BOAC stratocruiser, who saw them at 19,000ft. over Goose Bay, Labrador, on Wednesday.

The centre machine he described as a "flying jellyfish" because it appeared to be constantly changing shape. His sketch shows the three main shapes. The six smaller blobs —"they were dots in comparison"—altered their positions, sometimes three ahead and three astern, at other times one or two ahead and the rest astern.

At his Bristol home, Captain Howard said: "I'm still sceptical of the flying saucer theory, of piloted aircraft from other planets, and all the other tales. All I am willing to believe is what I saw and what my crew saw. Whether these objects were piloted craft or what they were I refuse to speculate. They were not like any plane I have seen before except for one short time when the larger object took on the shape of a delta-wing aircraft.

"In my 7,500 hours in the air, nothing like this has ever happened before. I am certain these objects were not the result of reflected light or mirages or any other usual phenomena one meets at high altitude. This really was something different."

Flying Saucer Camera will be used by Air Force to clear up saucer questions. One lens takes regular picture; the other separates light into colors so scientists can judge the source and make-up of saucers.

The crew of the BOAC radioed Goose Bay in Labrador, Canada, to find out if they had any explanation for what they were seeing, and were told nothing was showing on radar to explain the seven UFOs.

The tower then instructed a Royal Canadian Air Force *F94* Fighter jet to investigate the sighting, but shortly before its arrival the UFOs (according to eye-witness, George Allen):

> *"looked, to me, as though they went inside the big one, before vanishing from sight".*

By now the entire sighting had lasted eighteen minutes and covered 80 miles.

Stewardess Daphne Webster said:

> *"I have been flying for two years, but never seen anything like it before".*

During an interview with the *News Chronicle* reporter, a few days later, at his home in Coombe Dingle, Bristol,

Captain Howard said:

> *"There was a big central object which appeared to keep changing shape, sometimes wedge-shaped, sometimes like a dumb-bell, sometimes like a sphere with projections."*

1-7-54
1469

SAUCERS: 30 people in airliner watch 'seven of them'

NEWS CHRONICLE REPORTER

ECLIPSE day brought two mysteries of the air—one over the Atlantic; the other over the Channel.

NUMBER ONE—The crew of 10 and 20 passengers in a plane flying from New York to London report seeing a large flying saucer and six little saucers following them.

NUMBER TWO—The captain of an airliner saw a "giant white plane" floating on the water off Bournemouth. His radio call sent warships, lifeboats and helicopters scouring the sea in vain—and no plane is missing.

The transatlantic plane, a Stratocruiser, was flying at 19,000 feet, when B.O.A.C. pilot Captain James Howard suddenly sighted the objects—"obviously not aircraft as we know them."

Matter-of-fact Captain Howard, who has flown the Atlantic 265 times, said: "All appeared black. I'll swear they were solid.

"I've never seen anything like them before."

Tailed for 80 miles

For 18 minutes (80 miles) the seven objects flew parallel with the eastbound Stratocruiser.

They disappeared only when [illegible] intercepting [illegible], from Goose [illegible] called up by [illegible] radio-telephoned [illegible] miles away and [illegible]

Captain [illegible] at his home in [illegible] Drive, Coombe Dingle, Bristol, last night: "The formation of objects was between five and 50 miles distant.

"There was a big central object which appeared to keep changing shape—sometimes it was wedge-shaped, sometimes like a dumb-bell, sometimes like a sphere with a projection.

"The six smaller objects dodged about either in front or behind the 'parent.'

"But they all faded away rapidly when the Sabre jet fighter contacted us."

Optical illusion is thought to be "difficult to understand." All members of the plane's crew saw the same things—and so did 20 of the passengers. Thirty others were asleep at the time.

Captain Howard wrote a special report for B.O.A.C. while his aircraft was homeward bound from Goose Bay, flown by his co-pilot, First Officer Lee [illegible]

Daphne Webster, stewardess aboard the Stratocruiser, said: "I have been flying for two years—but I have certainly never seen anything like it before." Aged 28, she comes from Hounslow, Middx.

White plane SOS

The white plane mystery—an optical illusion caused by the eclipse of the sun—set in motion a full-scale air-sea rescue operation in the English Channel.

The "wreckage" of a giant white-painted aircraft, apparently floating in the sea about 25 miles south of Bournemouth, was spotted at 12.37 by a Portuguese pilot, 39-year-old Captain Marciano Veiga.

He took his London-bound D.C.4 down several thousand feet for a closer look, spotted the "wreck" again, and then lost sight of it in the haze. He radioed a report to the Ministry of Civil Aviation control station at Uxbridge.

Then although no civilian or R.A.F. planes had been reported missing or overdue, the rescue machinery was set in motion:

Two Naval helicopters from Gosport, and one from Lee-on-Solent, made sea sweeps;

The pleasure steamer Isle of Sark, bound for the mainland from Jersey, was diverted to join the search;

A B.E.A. pilot flying to Jersey was asked to keep a look-out;

Lifeboats from Swanage and Weymouth set out;

Radar ship helps

And five Naval craft—the frigates Veryan Bay, Porchester Castle and Tyrian, the destroyer Finisterre, and the radar ship Boxer—converged on the area.

But they found nothing and the search was called off at 4.45 p.m.

The official explanation? What Captain Veiga had seen was a B.E.A. plane, piloted by Captain G. J. Rice, flying through the haze several thousand feet below him, also bound for London.

The unusual eclipse conditions made the white-painted top of the B.E.A. plane appear to be stationary in the water.

NEWS CHRONICLE

In the December 11th issue of 'Everybody's Weekly', Captain Howard:

"It was a solid thing, I'm sure of that, manoeuvrable and controlled intelligently – a sort of base ship, linked somehow with the smaller attendant satellites. There is no rational explanation, except on the basis of spaceships and 'flying saucers'. On that basis, it must have been some weird form of spaceship from another world. If so, then another world was watching the Centaurus as it flew over Labrador that night, in June, watching, waiting maybe … For what? One day we shall know and that day, I'm sure, will be pretty important for the human race. I hope I'm here to see it."

Interviews set up by the British Flying Saucer Bureau

A member of the British Flying Saucer Bureau contacted Captain Howard, in order to set up an interview. Unfortunately, he was in the process of moving house to Wokingham, in Berkshire, and was unable to be the principle guest speaker at their July meeting.

Some time shortly afterwards, an interview was arranged with him by Graham Knewstub – the Vice President and research Chief of the Bureau.

On 7th July, Mr Lee Boyd and navigator – Mr Allen – were guest speakers at the monthly general meeting at Carwardine's Café, Baldwin Street, Bristol. A record crowd was present, despite attempts by local aircraft designer – Mr Wintle, to explain away the sighting as a form of mirage, due to the eclipse in the local press. Mr Wintle declined to attend the meetings and face the witnesses with his claim. Mr Lee Boyd and Mr Allen accepted the offer of honorary members of the Bureau, Captain Howard having already been granted this accolade.

(Source: *Evening News,* 30.6.1954 – 'Jets hunt Flying Saucers'/*News Chronicle,* July 1954 -'Flying Saucer – 30 people in Airliner watch seven of them')

30th June – USA: Woman photographs UFOs

MARTIANS OVER LAKE VIEW? Mildred Maier, 3812 N. Ashland, thinks so. Miss Maier took the above photo from her window on June 30 when the sun eclipsed. She, and scientists are puzzled over the "flying objects" which showed up on either side of the sun in her photograph.

2 Seen in Photo of Eclipse

Millie Maier's Shot Mystifies Experts

The Martians may be watching you, neighbor!

At least, that's the assumption presented by photos taken the morning of June 30, when the sun eclipsed over Lake View.

Early that day, neighbor Mildred Maier, 3812 N. Ashland, an amateur photographer, looked out the east window of her home. She aimed her camera at the sun, and took a picture.

Because she shielded her eyes, the photographer didn't see too much of the eclipse. But when she developed the photographs, Miss Maier discovered two "unidentifiable objects" flying on either side of the sun.

She quickly examined all of the photos she had taken to see whether or not the pictures had reflections in them. Since the objects showed up in even the darkest prints, she decided that the objects were real! If they had been reflections, they would have disappeared in the darker prints.

Unable to believe her eyes, and afraid of jumping to conclusions, Miss Maier sent the photos, with a letter of explanation, to National Geographic and Life magazines, and to Frank Edwards, news commentator for WGN.

All three photos were returned with letters that told Miss Maier to see a scientist or astronomer. Edwards asked to see the negative, with which Miss Maier refused to part.

In order to clear up the question of "Flying Saucers in Lake View," Miss Maier took the pictures to the Adler Planetarium.

A spokesman at the planetarium told Miss Maier that there was no evidence that the objects were "flying saucers." She reported the spokesman as saying, "We are told to debunk such theories."

Next, Miss Maier tried Northwestern university, where she was told that Dr. Kaj Strand, astronomer, was in Arizona taking photographs of Mars.

The Lake View woman has lived in this neighborhood for 17 years, is known throughout the city for her work in radio, television, and on the stage. For many years she and her sister, Marie, were known theatrically as the Gale Sisters. The two women live with their mother, Marie Maier, at the Ashland address.

Miss Maier, who has been taking pictures for 15 years, said that photographing a flying saucer is an entirely new experience for her.

When taking the "questionable" pictures, Miss Maier used a yellow filter and sun shade on a Speed Graphic camera.

Miss Maier and the scientists don't understand how her pictures showed two "flying saucers" when hundreds of newspaper pictures taken of the eclipse failed to show the objects. Miss Maier doesn't know what the "objects are" and neither do the scientists. Do you?

2nd July – USA: Did a jet crash after attempting to intercept a UFO?

The *Flying Saucer News,* in their edition of summer/autumn 1954, gave information on what they regarded as a parallel with the Mantell case, when they disclosed that a USAF jet had crashed after attempting to intercept a UFO over New York. According to official sources, the USAF had confirmed there had been a successful intercept, but declined to identify what had been intercepted because of the active nature of its mission. Ironically there had been an intercept all right, when the plane crashed into a car and buildings, killing four people, after the crew baled out when the cockpit had become unbearably hot.

A ridiculous explanation for the surge of 'flying saucers' reported in the press was offered by *The Lancet,* who wondered if some 'flying saucers' might have been *"froth blown from sewage works on washdays, when suds go down the drain"* – no doubt an explanation based on an article in the *Ludlow Advertiser* (15.7.1954), relating to a report from a garage man working near a sewage farm, who claimed he had seen six 'flying saucers' take-off over the area.

2nd July – England: Crescent-shaped object seen

A crescent-shaped UFO was seen turning in circles in the sky over Wallsend-on-Tyne, at a great height. It was seen to spin several times almost on its 'nose', before shooting away silently at high speed. **(Source: *Daily Mail,* 3.7.1954)**

7th July – England: 'Question mark' UFO seen over London

On 7th July 1954 a huge object, resembling a 'question mark', was seen drifting in the sky at an estimated height of fifteen miles above London, sparking off thousands of calls from the public. In one hour, the *Evening Standard* received over 2,000 calls from concerned citizens, who caused traffic jams after getting out of their cars and gazing upwards into the sky. The incident was later explained away as being a cosmic ray balloon, with a width of 600 feet and depth of 200 feet, released by Bristol University, at Cardington, Bedfordshire. **(Source: *Evening Standard,* 7.7.1954)**

8th July – England: Amateur astronomer sights UFO display, Wigan

We spoke to Mr Harold Hill from Orrell, near Wigan, Lancashire, whose interest in astronomy goes back to 1935, and who is responsible for cataloguing some interesting UFO reports from around the Lancashire area.

On 8th July 1954, at 9.20pm, he was watching the night sky, as the sun began to set, when he noticed a bright object, five degrees off the southern horizon. Looking through binoculars, he saw what looked like a ball-bearing, moving slowly northwards across the sky, gaining height. After some difficulty in attempting to locate the object with a low power eyepiece, he was staggered to see, instead of a single object, two – apparently oscillating around each other, like dancing partners,

> *"...one being larger than its companion and flashing intermittently, catching the rays of the setting sun. At this stage, I noticed the appearance of between 13-15 smaller objects, the shape of which I was unable to make out."*

Harold submitted a detailed account to the British Astronomical Association, who completely ignored his letter, irrespective of the fact that he had been an active member of their organisation – an attitude we were to experience for ourselves, 51 years later. Nothing appears to have changed!

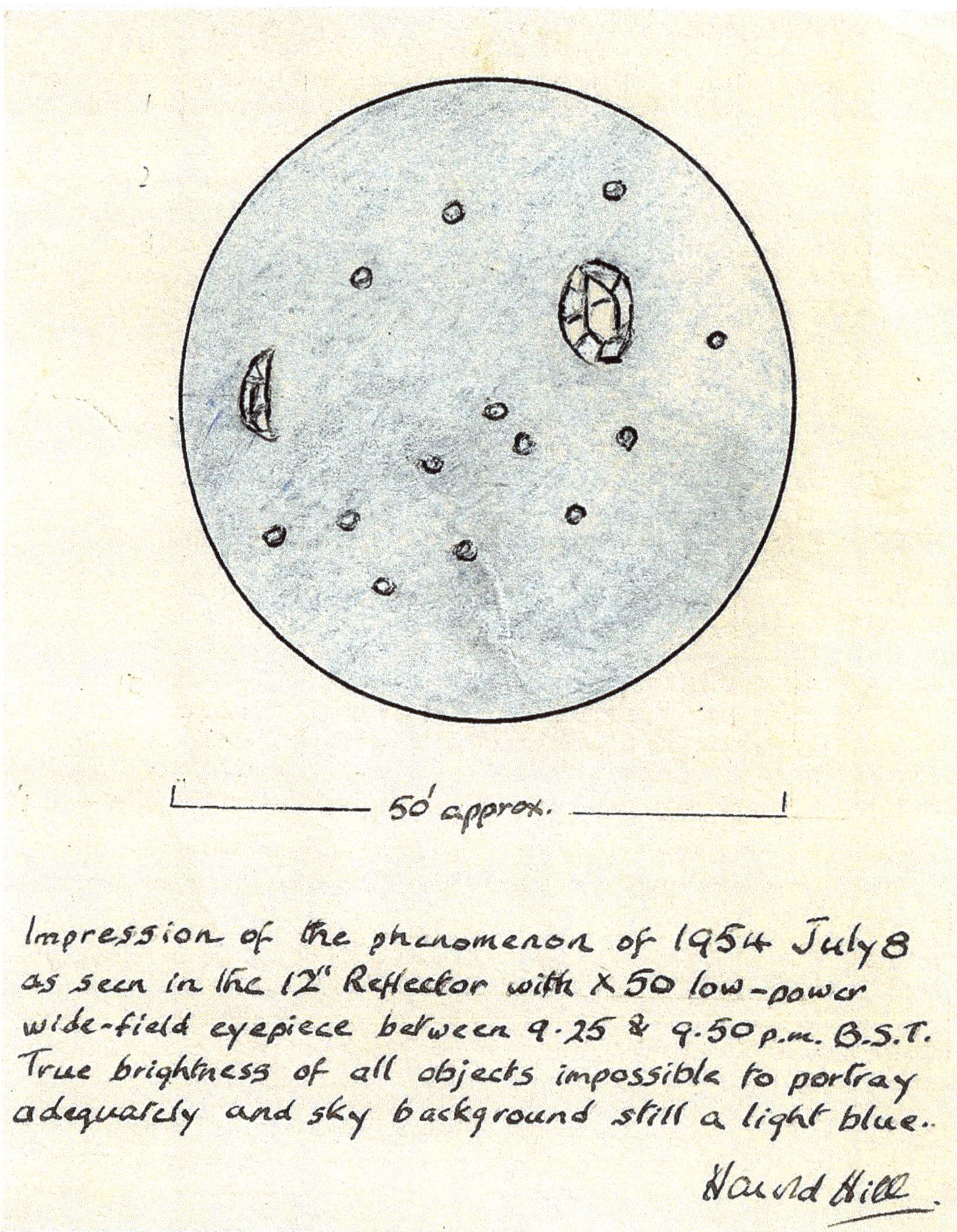

Summer/Autumn 1954 FLYING SAUCER NEWS 7

STRANGE SIGHT
seen over..... WIGAN

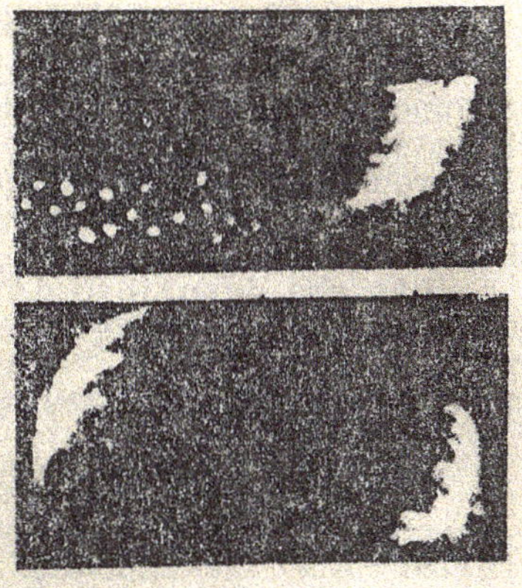

WIGAN amateur astronomer, Mr.Harold Hill, has sent a full report of the strange sky phenomenon he observed on July 8th., to the British Astronomical Association.

He first noticed it as a bright, star-like object, but under high powered binoculars, it was seen to be a small, bright metallic-looking globe.

Mr.Hill dashed to his observatory and trained his 12" reflecting telescope upon the strange object, which was by this time seen to have shifted its position, being higher in the sky. What he then saw was as amazing as it was unexpected:

"There was a principal bright silvery object, of indeterminate shape, accompanied to the left by a cluster of what appeared to be minute stars. The components numbered from 15 to 20 although it was very difficult to estimate the precise number because the members of the cluster constantly changed their positions independently of one another. The whole scene gave the impression of being one of great activity...."

Clouds intervened for a short time, and on clearing, another surprise was in store, for now there were TWO bright objects close together, the cluster of small objects having either disappeared or gone out of the field of the 'scope.

"They were gradually seperating and not only appeared to be gyrating and flashing, but exhibited a slow, pendulum movement about ea ch other in a manner rather like dancing partners - a truly amazing sight! One of the members was decreasing in brightness, and probably both - because they were now lost to view to my wife, who still had the binoculars trained...."

"The impression given was that the phenomenon was at a tremendous height, probably in the upper reaches of the stratosphere - or even beyond - because the small star-like objects of the cluster had shown no sensible size, even with the power of x 50. The two principal members defied description; they flashed as they gyrated as though metallic surfaces were reflecting the rays of the sun. Probably the closest analogy to what was seen is to be found in the flashing of the facets of a diamond as it is turned in a strong light".

The total time of the observations was from 9.30pm to 9.55pm, when clouds finally obscured the objects from view. It is stressed that the sketch is only a <u>rough idea</u> of what was seen; as already s tated, the objects defied description. Mr. Hill has been an amateur astronomer for nearly 20 years, and a member of the B.A.A. for 11 years and is convinced that the phenomenon was NOT of astronomical origin. His report and sketches were supplied to the Wigan Flying Saucer Club, of which he is also a member - and have now been passed on to B.F.S.B's Director of Research.

Dear Mr.Hanson,

It was pleasant to have a chat over the phone with you the other day on a subject of some mutual interest and from which I realised that in all probability you are much better informed than myself in these matters and especially as regards the more recent developments. I was quite impressed that you knew that Patrick Moore was behind the Cedric Allingham hoax because it was not generally known for quite some time after the book appeared. I gained the glimmering of a hint when he dealt with F.S. briefly in one of his Sky at Night TV episodes showing the picture of the 'Martian' and adding "... if you look closely you can even see his braces!' He spoke scornfully of F.S. generally and the impossibility of life existing elsewhere in the solar system. In this respect I found him as arrogant as Sir Bernard Lovell F.R.S. in a debate about UFOs with Gordon Creighton of F.S.Review refuting all arguments put to him by Creighton, sweeping them aside with disdain. I recorded the debate from the BBC programme on my old Grundig so it would be sometime in the 50s or 60s and Lovell seemed to become more and more insufferable everytime I played it over! Likewise, Moore also took part in a TV debate presided over by David Jacobs, a well known interviewer/commentator at that time. The protagonist was Desmond Leslie who had previously approached me to give an account of my 1954 sighting but unfortunately I was unable to go to the London studio on account of a severe attack of lumbago. Stephen Darbishire and his father, a medical doctor, took part and the boy gave an unvarnished, perfectly straightforward account, but in detail, of his experience in photographing what was evidently an Adamski-type scoutcraft*. Viewers could not have failed to be ~~impr~~ impressed by the obvious sincerity and conviction of Stephen's experience but even in this instance Moore was utterly dismissive and it struck me how incredibly hide-bound the man must be. My sighting was mentioned as evidence of the phenomena from an astronomical colleague but I cannot recall Moore's reaction to this - certainly he knew me as a contemporary with whose work in his own particular field he was well acquainted, and whose account was beyond reproach.

Leslie was much the more measured and cool in the debate and pointed out towards the end that an admitted 90% could be explained away as meteorological phenomena, balloons etc., but Moore's riposte to this was "You are only 10% out" in a most unnecessary sneering manner.

I was highly dubious about the Adamski part of the book "F.S. Have Landed" but after submitting the Darbishire photo with those of Adamski to an orthographic projection analysis on the drawing board -(I used to be a draughtsman)- I was convinced it was a similar, if not identical craft.

July – England: Bus conductor sights UFO over Hertfordshire

In July 1954, Raymond Logan was a bus conductor and on his way to the café at Harpenden, Hertfordshire, at 5.22pm, when he saw something strange in the clear blue sky and decided to forgo his cup of tea, and observe.

> *"I saw one small cloud in the sky, high over the town. Underneath it was a small object, completely stationary. Suddenly about a minute and-a-half later, it shot silently to a new position away from the cloud. It then stopped dead in the sky for about the same length of time, and rushed off once more. It repeated this process three times, completing a triangle. A short time later it moved away in a straight line, towards the horizon, very fast, and out of sight in seconds."*

Raymond reported the matter to the Air Ministry. **(Source: Margaret Fry)**

10th July – England: Strange white object seen in Channel

The *News Chronicle*, dated 10th July 1954, brought its readers' attention to a report made by a *DC-4* Portuguese Airline captain, Marcianao Veiga, who sighted what he took to be the wreckage of a giant white painted aircraft, apparently floating on the sea below him, twenty-five miles off the coast of Bournemouth. The incident was later explained away as being a BEA Aircraft, bound for London, piloted by Captain G.J. Rice, flying at several thousand feet below the Portuguese airliner.

12th July – England: 'Flying dustbin lid' UFO seen over Cheltenham

A silver object, resembling a 'flying dustbin lid', was seen moving at fantastic speed over Cheltenham on 12th July 1954.Seconds later, according to the witness, a RAF Jet was sighted passing overhead, at speed.

(Source: *Daily Mail*, 13.7.1954)

13th July – England: Farmer sights 'flying discs' following aircraft

On 13th July 1954, a startled Leicestershire farmer from Great Easton contacted the newspapers after seeing a 'flying disc' following an aircraft over Market Harborough, described as looking like a full moon in appearance, but almost flat in width.

(Sources: *Leicester Evening Mail*, 14.7.1954/ *Daily Mail*, 15.7.1954)

24th July – England: Couple sight 'hissing' UFO over Holcombe

On 24th July 1954, at 4.10pm, James Clayton and his wife, Mildred, were enjoying a picnic beside the road between Holcombe to Helmshore, in Lancashire, when they noticed a silver/grey circular object in the sky, giving off smoke and fire.

> *"It looked like two soup plates, one on top of each other, making a hissing sound – like escaping steam. It travelled backwards and forwards across the sky, several times, at various heights, at an estimated speed of 500 mph, before disappearing upwards into the sky".*

We spoke to Mildred in 2006, (now in her early 80s). She had no difficulty in remembering such a vivid incident. Sadly, we were unable to speak to her husband, James, who passed away some years ago. **(Source: Personal letter)**

25th July – USA: Black cylindrical object seen

Attorney Mr L.B. Tussing was out at Middle Sister Island, near the US-Canadian border in western Lake Erie, at 7.12pm, when he saw:"

> *...a black cylinder, 12 times long as wide, moving fast along the surface of the lake".*

26th July – England: Two lights

Two lights were seen in the sky over Maidstone, at about 10.30pm, which then merged into one and headed away towards Tonbridge, before disappearing from view. They reappeared again over the Tunbridge Wells area and kept moving *"to and fro, like a gnat"*, according go the witness.

30th July – USA: Pencil-shaped UFO sighted by pilots

Hughes Aircraft test pilots Englert and Peterson were flying a *B-25* Bomber over Los Angeles, California, at 10.15am, when they saw:

> *...a metallic, pencil-shaped object heading across the sky, slowly, which hovered for a length of time."*

July – England: 'Flying saucer' with aerials seen, Lancashire

Mr E.G. Emery from, Bristol, was driving his van, in July 1954, when he noticed a saucer-shaped object in a patch of blue sky, at a height of between 1,000 and 2,000 feet.

> *"The bottom of the object appeared to be red hot and radiating a heat haze. It had a turret on top and projections similar to wireless aerials. I stopped the van to get a closer look – then it just disappeared."*

(Source: *Bristol Evening Post,* date not known – 'Strange machine seen over Bristol Channel')

July – England: Strange close encounter with landed UFO, Kent

Sometime in July 1954, after hearing a strange, loud, deep, humming noise for two or three minutes, between 4am and 5am, lasting a period of several weeks, Dover resident – Harold Carpenter – decided to investigate further and set off walking to a wooded area – known locally as 'Sunny Calvert' – determined to finally track down the source.

With the humming noise still audible, apparently emanating from the south-west, Harold clambered down a deep slope to where the sound seemed to be coming from, and peered down. He was shocked to see a strange grey device, resembling a mushroom without a stem, hovering about eight to ten feet above the ground.

After making his way to a vantage point amongst the trees, he was able see the underside of the 'craft', definitely hovering above the ground, estimated to be about fifteen to twenty feet in diameter across the base, which housed what looked like a lip on the inside base.

Reported seeing five entities near 'craft'

Even more startling was the sight of up to five 'peculiar-looking beings' gathered underneath the 'craft' on the surface below.

These 'beings' were about four to five feet tall and carrying what looked like 'pound jam jars', with a handle in one hand and an implement resembling a pair of tweezers in the other.

The 'beings' used these to pick up bits of twigs and leaves, before placing them in the clear jars. They wandered around picking up various samples, while keeping close to the 'craft' which hovered silently above – the humming sound having now ceased.

Snout-like nose, resembling a pig

All wore the same one-piece grey, flexible-looking suits, which stretched over their feet and covered their heads – much like a balaclava – leaving their faces exposed, allowing Harold to:

> *"...see they were human in appearance, totally devoid of expression with normal human-like eyes, but the facial resemblance to humans ended with a snout-like nose, resembling that of a 'pig'. Their mouths were similar to humans and so were their hands, until [Harold] noticed they didn't appear to have thumbs. No ears could be seen owing to the nature of the one-piece suit, which hid them from view".*

'Craft' takes off

While observing all this detail, in fascination, Harold suddenly realised he was only within ten feet of the 'craft'. At this moment one of the 'beings' suddenly looked up with the same expressionless face and stared directly at him.

Without so much as a sound or movement, it somehow, in some way, alerted the others to Harold's presence, for they all suddenly stopped what they were doing and slowly began to retreat to the 'craft', which had descended, hovering now barely two feet off the ground. One by one the 'beings' disappeared underneath the 'craft' by means of its 'lip'.

The 'craft' then began to rise, at which point Harold saw one of the 'beings' climb through a type of 'gate', housed on the inside of the 'lip', which then closed. The 'craft' slowly continued to climb, moving slightly to one side, towards a clearing among the trees. It gradually gained altitude and speed, before suddenly emitting a flash of light and departing at incredible speed.

(Source: Chris Rolfe, UFOMEK)

Summer – England: 'Alien being' discovered in house, Kent

Another incident involving the appearance of a 'strange person' seen inside the family home, took place in the summer of 1954, according to Mrs Maureen Garner – a housewife from Kent – as told to Norman Oliver, Vice Chairman of BUFORA, on Sunday, 3rd February 1969.

"The experience occurred in 1954, when I was living with my husband, who was serving in the RAF in a little village called Tenterden, in the heart of Kent.

I had just come out of the lounge and was walking towards the kitchen, when I found my way blocked by a man, standing on the landing in front of me, preventing me from walking any further. I wasn't at all frightened, or amazed even, to see him.

Ordinarily, if I saw a strange man in my house I would be very nervous – I've only got to stand at the sink, washing up, and my husband comes in very quietly and peeps round the corner at me, and I jump out of my skin, but I didn't on this occasion. I was surprised to see him, yes, but I wasn't nervous. What surprised me most of all was the height – I am nearly six feet tall and I had to tilt my head back quite a bit to look up at him. He was over seven feet tall and was wearing a one-piece 'siren suit', but it wasn't brown like George Adamski's men, described by him some months before in the papers, (which I had read about), but a metallic, blue, 'siren suit', though it didn't seem to be made of metal – more of a soft, nylon sort of material.

It glimmered, but not like Lurex material does these days – it just glimmered with a soft, metallic light. I didn't look at his feet – I didn't have the time. What I looked at nearly all the time were his eyes, his face, and his features – and features is the operative word in this experience – not because he was a man, but because he was a strange looking man. He had a very high, broad forehead – I don't remember noticing his nose. I suppose he had one since if he hadn't he would have looked ugly, and he wasn't ugly. He had a slit for a mouth. I say a slit, because the lips weren't protruding like ours do… they might have turned inwards – I don't know. He had high cheek bones but they weren't protruding; the bones were 'heavy' underneath the skin. His eyes were very large. His jaw was a different shape – there was no jaw bone to see at all but the shape of his face underneath the eyes was pointed. There was a chin, yes, but below his eyes and down to his chin the skin was absolutely immobile, as if he hadn't opened his mouth for ages.

Face, resembling a blunt edged triangle

The dominant shape of his face was a blunt-ended triangle with his chin the blunt end. His eyes were deep blue. He had pupils and the expression in his eyes was something that I shall never forget – I can remember the man now as distinctly as I saw him then. His ears weren't visible, nor any hair, because covering his cranium and his head and ears was a very tight-fitting helmet, and this helmet was made of what seemed like Perspex.

It was a translucent material you could not see through, not an astronaut's helmet, though. The suit fitted his neck, fitted the waist – there was no belt around the middle; he was definitely a man. There weren't any seams, fastenings or buttons, or anything else like that in his clothing. His skin was

> *pink. He was a white man. He didn't say anything – he just stood and looked at me and I looked at him. If he was trying to give me a message, I don't know what it was. I didn't have the impression of receiving anything from him. I felt compelled to look in his eyes, though there was no specific expression in them.*
>
> *He had no eyebrows, or wrinkles in his skin, and one got the impression of great intelligence – wisdom even. I had no idea how old he was but I had the impression he knew everything about me there was to know. Why did this man materialise in front of me? I say materialise, because I didn't hear or see him come into the house, and when he left he just left.*
>
> *One second I saw him, the next I didn't see him. He didn't disappear in a cloud of vapour or anything like that – just suddenly he wasn't there anymore. He could have 'put me to sleep' whilst I was standing there and quietly left – I don't know. I've asked myself the question over the years, why did this man come to my home? The only reason I can think of is that he wanted me to see him and remember him. The only people I've told about this before have been relatives and close friends."*

In answer to questions put to her by Norman, Mrs Garner told him the man would have been standing in front of her for about half a minute. At no time did she touch the man, nor did he touch her – to be exact, she said her right arm was about three inches away from his left elbow. He didn't move his hands at all – he stood there with them at his side, but she didn't really look at them. He made no bodily movement at all – just his eyeballs moved and she could see the reflection of the landing window in them.

Asked whether she felt he was actually 'present in the flesh', Mrs Garner replied:

> *"He appeared to be flesh and blood. I certainly couldn't see through him. He wasn't a 'projection' and was solid."*

The incident took place in the daytime, though Mrs Garner is not quite sure of the exact time.

Prior to her meeting she had been dusting the lounge in the flat. Asked whether there had been any emotional upset prior to the incident; Mrs Garner replied there had been none, she was feeling perfectly wide awake, and was not tired. So far as she was concerned, up to the point of her confrontation, it had been a perfectly normal day.

The whole of the above transcript was taken from a recording made by Mrs Garner, at her request, in the presence of her husband and Norman Oliver.

(Source: Norman Oliver, 2008/*COSMOS 7* Magazine, January 1970)

2nd August – USA: Metallic UFO

An ex-AAF *B-17* gunner, who had flown 19 missions, was north-east of Schroeder, Westlake, Ohio, at 5.17pm, when he saw:

> *"...a thin, bright ellipse – like polished metal – hovering in the sky for 5-8 seconds, before dropping down to a height of 3,000 feet in a few seconds; it then hovered again and faded away 20 seconds later".*

August – England: UFOs sighted over London

During August 1954 a number of UFOs were seen passing over London – matters brought to the attention of Number One Strike Command HQ at Bentley Priory, who were unable to offer an explanation.

David Strudwick from Kent – an engineer and

member of the Scientific Institute, with a lifetime's experience of sorting out the 'teething problems' associated with the early Nuclear Power Stations of the 1950s – was walking home one evening, through London. *"I noticed a curious glow, travelling east to west over the East End. It had no definite shape to it. I can't say what it was, or where it had come from, but I don't think it was an aircraft, or fireball."* **(Source: Personal interview)**

6th August – England: 'Flying dumb-bell' seen over Barry

George Hartropp contacted us in 2003, while recovering from a triple heart bypass, about what he and his companion saw, at 5.45pm, on 6th August 1954. They were sitting on the pebble at the 'Knap', enjoying the afternoon, when their attention was caught by a stationary object in the sky over the Bristol Channel, towards the south-west, well out towards Rhoose Point.

> *"It was brilliant silver in colour and conveyed the impression of a light reflecting on chromium, or silver plate. The thing that struck us was, although there was a slight westerly wind, the object continued to remain stationary. The weather was perfect that evening, with an exceptionally blue sky, apart from one or two small patches of fractocumulus cloud. During the time we were watching the object, it altered its shape to a silvery dumb-bell before eventually disappearing from view, two hours later."*

George discovered they were not the only ones to see this object. Two security guards, stationed outside the main entry gate to the BP Chemical Plant, also witnessed the incident.

A few days later he learnt, through the national press, that a number of experienced observers from RAF St. Athan and Rhoose, including a flying officer, reported having sighted an object resembling a large double convex lens, viewed in vertical profile, stationary in the sky.

LOTS of people believe in flying saucers—and lots of others don't. Maybe the saucers are just another form of spots before the eyes. Or perhaps they really are space ships carrying strange beings from other planets. It is one of the world's biggest controversies.

● That is why we are publishing this amazing prediction by Agnes Bernelle, one of the believers.

● We hope that you will enjoy the article, whether you believe in flying saucers or not.

THE EDITOR

FLYING SAUCERS WILL LAND HERE NEXT YEAR!

says **AGNES BERNELLE**, *West End stage star*

WEEK END MAIL AUG 26 1954

"IF all goes well there will be flying saucer landings in England next year. . . ."

Those are the words of my husband, Desmond Leslie, written from the Californian desert, where he and an American investigator, George Adamski, are watching the sky in search of flying saucers.

Last year, you may remember, Desmond wrote a book with George, entitled: "Flying Saucers Have Landed," which was widely publicised in the English Press.

At that time he had never seen a saucer. But now he has.

A few days ago he cabled me: SAUCER SCORE NOW 12. And in a letter to me from their lookout point he wrote:

"Coming into San Diego we saw a beautiful, golden ship in the sunset, but brighter than the sunset.

"I had ten-power binoculars with me, and was able to study it for a half a minute from the halted car.

"It slowly faded out, the way they do."

That letter reached me in my London flat as I was rehearsing for Salome, the rôle that Rita Hayworth made famous in Hollywood.

I felt a chill of fear inch its way up my spine. I knew Desmond would never exaggerate, and the space ship sounded horribly eerie.

But Desmond assured me that we have nothing to fear from the men in the saucers. He and Adamski have been in close contact with them, and have learned many of their secrets.

"We have been given their simple philosophy," he told me. "It runs parallel to the original teachings of Jesus."

And Desmond explained to me that the space visitors do not seek trouble.

"If attacked, they would prefer to let themselves be destroyed rather than kill," he wrote.

How will we make contact with these beings?

Desmond wrote, excitedly, on July 4:

"They have little discs which can pick up our thoughts, and others which translate our vibrations and tones into their own language!"

[In his book "Flying Saucers Have Landed," Adamski said he had been able to communicate with spacemen by telepathy.]

G228 ESCONDIDO CALIF 22 16 1130A 36 SOUTH LODGE
LT LESLIE GROVE END RD
CUNNINHAM 4615 LONDON
10 0 58 NWB.
SAUCERSCORE NOW TWELVE —— ALL LOVE
DESMOUND

DESMOND'S CABLE

'100 landings'

In his letters from California Desmond has told me of landings already made on the earth.

"Altogether over a hundred [illegible]

He described their ships too. "The first one I saw was oval, with a dome on top," he told me. And in the same letter he gave me the amazing news that he and George have actual knowledge of the interior of the saucers.

"We now have plans and blueprints," he wrote, "of the interior layouts of four or five different types of craft.

"And we have details of the landing arrangements and instruments which, believe me, are out of this world!"

Perhaps you are wondering if I myself believe in flying saucers? Yes, I do.

I have thought it all out, and, from what I have learned from my husband, I think there is no doubt that they do exist.

Desmond has told me: "Everything the spacemen say is so very true. Their description of events is beyond our wildest science fiction."

Until Desmond had had actual contact with the men from the other worlds I doubted their existence. But his letters are full of facts which have amazed and shaken me.

What is more, I share my husband's belief that the present "cold war" conditions in the world may flare up at any time, and that the saucer men will probably be our only means of salvation.

A MESSAGE FROM VENUS?

COLUMBUS, Ohio, Saturday.—Dr. John Kraus, a radio-astronomer, has reported hearing new radio signals which "presumably originated on Venus."

Dr. Kraus, Director of Ohio State University's radio observatory, said the new signals had "many of the characteristics of signals from a terrestrial radio telegraph transmitting station."

June 23 1956

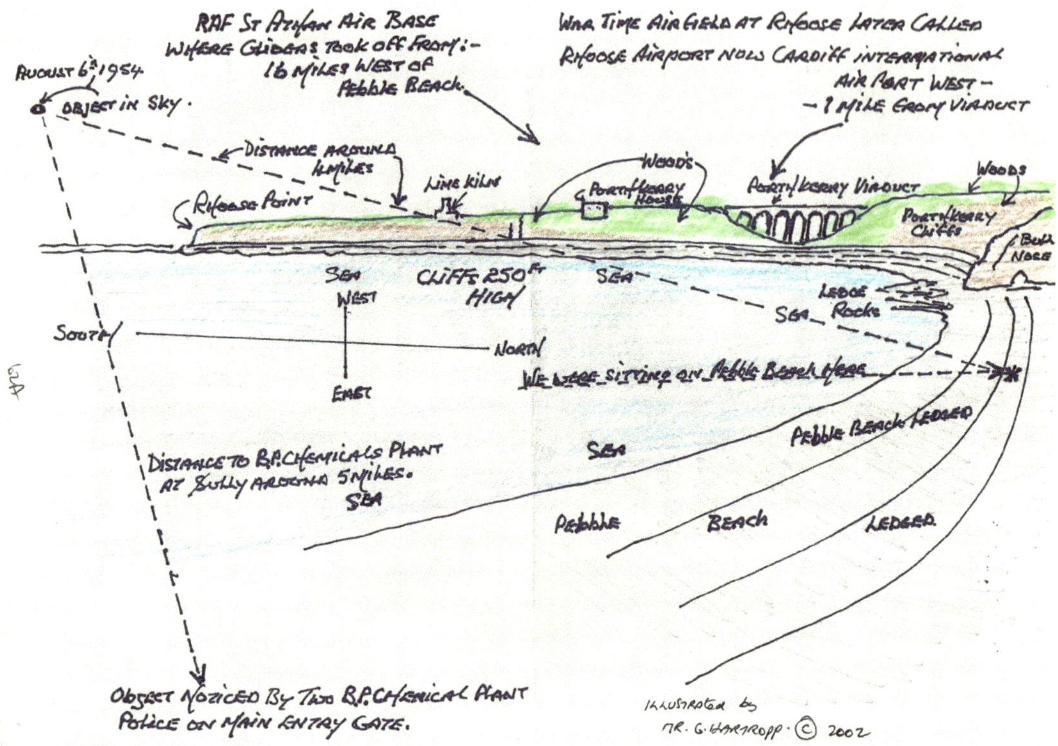

Confirmation

At 7.15pm, the same date, Eric Jones – a keen amateur astronomer – was at his home address, looking through the lens of the telescope at Barbridge Road, Hesters Way, Cheltenham, when he saw:

> *"...two circular objects – silver coloured, apparently solid – moving through the sky, heading south-west. The large one was inclined at an angle of 10 degrees and later flattened out, making the top of the object visible. The smaller object was rising and falling while on its journey, as if 'playing tag' with the larger object."*

(Source: Mr D.C. Jones)

Wrote to Lord Clancarty

George wrote an account of the incident and sent it to Lord Clancarty (formerly the Hon. William Francis Brinsley Le Poer Trench, born 18th September 1911, died 18th May 1995) – a major figure in British UFO research – who spoke on the subject in the House of Lords and wrote many books on the UFO subject. He was editor of *Flying Saucer Review* from 1956 to 1959, and founded the worldwide organisation 'Contact' while Vice President of BUFORA (The British UFO Research Association).

He wrote back to George, informing him that the UFO sighting would be referred to during a debate on the subject in the House of Lords.

George Hortop
22 Wyndham St
Barry.
Vale of Glam.
18.10.2001

Dear Mr Hanson.
Sorry at not writing sooner but as you may have thought I may have not been up to it. yes I have been exhausted the passed 4 to five weeks:- and have just feeling more with it after my Operation
I have enclosed a few items of which my be of interest to you including a photo copy letter from Lord Clancarty, also a drawing for you of the area known as Cold Knap:- Many thanks for your enclosed write ups: found them very interesting
Very best wishes yours sincerely
George Hortop

August 5. 1954. 1167

Letters to the Editor

Letter published 1956.

PEBBLE BEACH U.F.O. – A MYSTERY RECALLED

SIR, — Noting with interest the article in your newspaper by Neil Hyde, under the heading "Girls Saw U.F.O." published in your last edition, recalls to my memory an incident my fiancee and I witnessed.

The flying saucer incident we witnessed occurred on August 6th, 1954, in the early evening: time noted down as 1745 hours. Both of us were sitting on the Pebble Beach at the The Knap, Barry, when our attention was taken by a stationary object over the Bristol Channel in a S.W. direction, well out past Rhoose point.

This object was a brilliant silver colour and conveyed the impression of a strong light reflecting on a chromium or silver-plated body.

The thing that struck us was that although there was a slight westerly wind the object (disc shaped) was not moving, the weather was perfect for any August evening; the sky was exceptionally blue and clear of cloud apart from one or two small patches of fracto-cumulus cloud, so more or less broad daylight as you can imagine.

Also take note that this sighting was witnessed (as we both found out later on in the week through the national Press) by a considerable number of keen and experienced observers at R.A.F. St. Athan and Rhoose Airport.

Members of the R.A.F. Gliding School were completing a series of flying operations from St. Athan airfield at the time.

OTHER WITNESSES

The commanding officer at the time, several instructors and a number of air cadets were present, all of whom bore witness to the entity that appeared over the Bristol Channel that August evening in 1954.

A flying officer, it was stated, took off in a glider with a pupil to investigate the object from a closer angle and I quote his words: "The form I observed was that of a large double-convex lens viewed in vertical profile; it was not possible to estimate its true size or distance at which it was stationed, but on the southern and eastern legs of the first circuit of which I flew, the object was perfectly clear against a blue sky and very sharply defined and a bright silver colour."

Another thing that impressed the officer flying near the object as he stated was the immobility of the thing, it remained quite stationary and was seemingly unaffected by wind or air currents.

This, of course, was also the talking point between my fiancee and I watching it from the Pebble Beach.

The officer landed after one circuit and took off again with the same cadet for a second circuit similar to the first.

During this flight towards the object they found it was in the same position but had altered its shape to that of a silvery dumb-bell.

There was no apparent approach or recession or lateral movement of the form over the critical six to seven minutes of observation from the glider, this discounted the idea that it could be light from a conventional aircraft.

The immobility of the object equally discouraged the idea that it was a free meteorological balloon; from the beach we could not see it changing shape but could pick out the glider near it.

On this last circuit by the glider, the object suddenly vanished: on the beach we had been watching this object for an estimated two hours, when we noticed it disappeared.

This aerial phenomena really baffled us both; for a daylight sighting this was unique, as it is for an aircraft to get such a good close-up of such a phenomena.

Yours etc.,
GEORGE HORTOP.
22 Wyndham Street,
Barry.

6th August – USA: White 'light'

Over San Antonio, Texas, a mechanical engineer – L.H. Hormer – was outside, at 6pm, when he saw an intensely white elliptical 'light', which was seen to change to yellow, orange, and pink, four or five times, while heading across the sky over a period of five minutes.

15th August – USA: Dark oblong object seen

At 10.20pm, USAF Major W.J. Davis, and Captain R.D. Saunders, were flying a *C-47* transport plane over San Marcos, Texas, when they sighted a dark blue oblong object pacing their plane. It then veered away, and crossed in front of them before being lost from sight five minutes later.

16th August – England: UFO over Shropshire

On 16th August 1954, renowned Shropshire historian – Gavin Gibbons – was cycling from Cressage to Shrewsbury, when he saw a silver-white object moving across the sky, at what he estimated to be thousands of miles per hour. Over the course of the next few weeks a number of UFO sightings were brought to Gavin and his brother Robin's attention, involving objects resembling 'Mexican hats', 'flying grapefruits' and sightings of 'flying saucers', all over the county.

26th August – England: Upside-down 'saucer' over Bath

At least five people saw a bright, shining, object in the sky over Bath, between 6.30pm and 8.15pm. One man said:

> *"It seemed to be a shiny oblong, with a light shining through. When viewed binoculars, it looked like an upside-down saucer. Around the bottom rim there was a white light and it appeared to stay in the same place for some time. At intervals it flashed red and blue light. It then started to fade as it moved away towards Bath. After it had left, there was still a ring of white light where the edge had been."*

(Source: *Bath Chronicle*, 30.8.1954)

On the same evening an object, described as looking like *"a figure eight, upright and hexagonal, projecting a blue and green flame"* was seen at an altitude of 8-10,000 feet over Plymouth.

26th August – USA: Two glowing objects

At 615am, Reverend W.L. Shelton from Danville, Virginia, contacted the authorities after sighting:

> *"...two glowing silver or orange domed ellipses, estimated to be 20 feet long by about five feet, hovering in the sky; two minutes later they were out of view".*

27th August – USA: Seven UFOs sighted

At 1pm, seven large, white, teardrop-shaped objects were seen in the sky over Dorchester, Massachusetts, flying in align formation. They turned blue as they headed away, increasing speed during the two minutes sighting.

28th August – England: Oblong UFO sighted

Between 6.30pm and 8.15pm on 26th August 1954, at least five people saw a bright, shining, oblong object,

> *"...as if cut out, with light shining through it, in the sky over Bath. Through binoculars, it looked like an upside-down saucer. Around the bottom rim was a white light. Occasionally, you could see flashes of blue and red lights. It then faded away, leaving a ring of white lights where the edge had been."*

(Source: *Bath Chronicle*)

On the same evening, at 9.30pm, a number of people in Birmingham city centre sighted a bright bluish light in the sky, about the size (from the ground) of an orange, leaving a trail of sparks. Others reported seeing a 'vivid green object, with white rings around it, leaving a white trail with red sparks'.

Similar sightings took place over West Bromwich, Oldbury, Tyseley, Leamington Spa and Belbroughton – not forgetting a report of an object seen over Stourport, travelling towards Birmingham, described as resembling

> *"a ball of fire, shaped like a saucer, coloured blue with red edging".*

Object resembling 'figure of eight'

Again on the same evening, an object resembling a figure eight, or hexagonal in shape, was seen in the sky over Plymouth showing a comet-like tail, at a height estimated to be 8,000 to 10,000 feet. Other reports told of what looked like a rocket hovering 50 feet above the ground, hissing loudly, before fizzling out over the direction of Woodland Court.

RAF Mountbatten launches appeal

Unusually, Group Intelligence at RAF Mountbatten launched an appeal in the local newspaper (*Western Evening Herald*) asking for members of the public who had seen something strange to contact them. (Over 70 letters were received.)

(Source: *Flying Saucer News,* winter 1954/1955)

31st August – England: UFO seen over Bournemouth

A white balloon-shaped object was seen stationary in the sky over Bournemouth, for approximately 90 minutes, on the 31st August 1954. Later the same evening, *"a glowing object, showing a dark patch in the middle, making a high-pitched whistle, some 200 feet off the ground"*, was seen by others, including the driver of a car who drove off the road, according to the *Bournemouth Times* (3.9.54) and other newspapers that covered the story.

2nd September – England: Silver 'disc' seen over Kent

On 2nd September 1954, a huge silver 'disc' was seen at 7.20pm, hovering in the sky over Gillingham, in Kent.

(Source: *Whitstable Times,* 4.9.1954)

Other sightings for this day included reports of a bright light with a red 'tail' seen moving across the sky over Hereford, at speed, at 9.35pm.

4th September – USA: Twenty to thirty lights seen in the sky

At 3am, Mr J. Faltemeier – a C.A.A communications specialist from Butler, Missouri – reported having sighted:

> *"...twenty to thirty lights – as if on a string – flying across the sky, for about one and-a-half minutes".*

5th September – USA: UFO spotted again

Unbelievably, Mr Faltemeier, the C.A.A communications specialist was to sight something very odd, the following night.

This time it involved a silver or white object with a slightly swept-back leading edge seen in the sky, before veering off in a south-west to south direction, 30 seconds later.

7th September – England: Silver 'ball' seen over Derby

On 7th September 1954, a silver 'ball' was seen by four railway workers at Derby, rising upwards and hovering in the sky.

The matter was later reported to the *Daily Mail*, who attempted to connect the sighting with reports of the 'flying bedstead'!

(Source: *Daily Mail,* 8.9.1954)

12th September – England: 'Dumb-bell' UFO seen over Lancashire

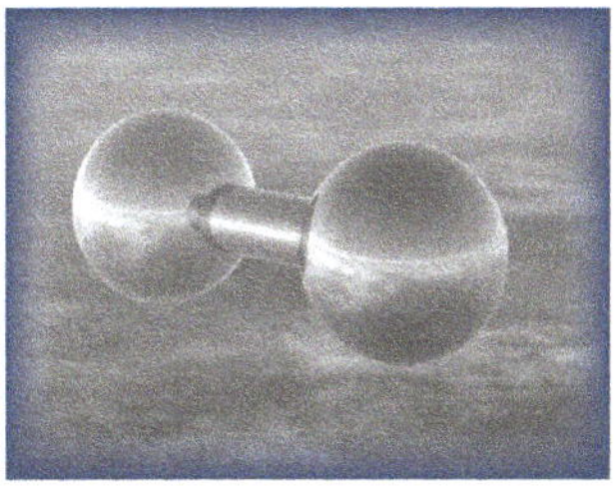

At 11am on 12th September 1954 a bright silver object, shaped like a dumb-bell, was seen flying slowly through the sky over St. Helens, Lancashire, by Mrs Rimmer,

> *"...catching the sun like a mirror, as it moved westwards".*

15th September – England: Spinning top UFO and RAF jet

At 11am, a man was working on a scenic railway on the beach at Great Yarmouth, Norfolk, when he heard a jet engine and saw:

> *"...a RAF Meteor jet heading towards the north-east, at about one thousand feet off the ground.*
>
> *This was followed almost immediately by the appearance of a bluish-grey cigar-shaped spinning object, which came out of the cloud and began to hover, changing shape as it did so. It stayed there for about five minutes and vanished from view."*

The man looked around him and was stunned to see the object hovering over the sea, before it finally vanished from view.

When he told people what he had seen they dismissed it as being a balloon, irrespective of the fact that balloons were launched from the jetty earlier and had been seen to fly away towards the south-east. This was no balloon!

(Source: Ivan W. Bunn)

18th September – England: UFO seen over Lancashire

Mr Roy Smallshaw and Miss Teresa Mulvaney, of Upholland, were watching the motor car reliability trials at Ashurst beacon, near Wigan, during the day, when they saw a bright object hovering in the sky in front of them, about the size of a pen at arm's length, some 10-20 miles away.

After some time it rose steadily, until it was lost from view.

(Source: UFOLOG)

21st September – USA: Red-orange 'ball of light' seen

At 12.23am over Barstow, California, two local policemen, four US Marine Corps police, and a highway patrolman, sighted a red-orange 'ball', giving off sparks, accompanied by a smaller 'light', making a zigzag descent through the sky, before halting in mid-air and disappearing 20 minutes later.

22nd September – USA: Revolving UFO lands

A private pilot – Mr J.N. Williams, and a colleague – Mr E.J. Ash, were out at 9am when they saw a thin, translucent revolving boomerang-shaped object, which then descended down behind some trees. Marks were later found in the dirt. This sighting lasted 15 minutes.

23rd September – USA: Two wheel-shaped UFOs sighted

At 9.45am, two bright silver, wheel-shaped, objects were seen heading in a north to south direction, by Gatlinburg, Tennessee resident, Mr David Owenby – out of sight two minutes later.

28th/29th September – England: UFO activity continues

Several people reported having sighted 'flying saucers' over Morecambe on 28th and 29th September 1954, following a report of a previous UFO sighting the week before. The sightings included 'a pure white glowing cigar-shaped object', seen by at least three people, at 6.45pm, over the bay at high altitude, *"like a saucer on end"* – gone in a few seconds.

At 3.30pm on 29th September 1954, a bright 'star', *"resembling a saucer in shape, with an aluminium surface"* was seen in the sky, heading south-westwards.

6th October – England: Air Traffic Controller sights UFO

A black circular object was seen hovering over Dartmoor on 6th October 1954, by an Air Traffic Control officer at Roborough Airport, at an estimated height of 5,000 feet, described as *"a typical 'flying saucer' shape"* – a matter reported to RAF Intelligence, who were quoted as saying they weren't interested!

(Source: *Cornish Evening Telegraph*, 6.10.1954)

11th October – RAF chase 'flying saucers' over Kent and Essex

On 11th October 1954, Mr Barry Boulton from Eynsford, in Kent, was one of a group of men working in Priory Lane when they sighted an object moving against the wind, heading north-east, at 4.20pm.

> *"It was spherical in shape, the top half highly polished aluminium, with a dark underside, and flying much higher than a jet plane, travelling across the wind at the time. About a dozen jet fighters then came into view, heading toward the direction of the UFO, at which point the object climbed rapidly and disappeared."*

Mr David Manners from Southend was watching balloons being released over the coast, one morning, when he saw a RAF *Meteor* jet fighter heading towards the north-east, at a height of about 1,000 feet.

> *"On looking around, I was shocked to see a blue/grey object come out of the cloud and stop dead in the sky, spinning on its axis, changing shape from cigar to 'disc'. It stayed there for about five minutes and then just vanished. I looked around, once more, and saw it hovering a short distance above the sea – then it disappeared, once again, in the blink of an eye.*
>
> *When I told people what I had seen, they suggested it must have been a balloon. If that was the case, it must have been a very fast and large balloon to travel against the wind and spin on its axis."*

14th October – England: RAF pilot encounters UFOs on patrol

RAF Auxiliary Officer, Flight Lt. James Salandin, MBE, (89 in 2015), who was stationed at RAF North Weald, Essex, near Epping (then attached to 604 County of Middlesex Squadron), described the mysterious encounter he had while on an air test, climbing towards Southend, Essex, on 14th October 1954 – *"still vivid in my memory, despite it having happened over 50 years ago"*.

Flight Lt. James Salandin

Mr Salandin, to whom we had the pleasure of speaking, many times over the years, spoke about his service with the Fleet Air Arm and the RAF, having logged 1,800 hours flying time on a variety of aircraft, including 300 hours in the famous *Spitfire*.

"I took off at about 4.15pm. Flying conditions were perfect. When at a height of some 16,000 feet, I noticed a number of contrails in the sky, approximately 30-40,000 feet over North Foreland. Through the middle of these trails I could see three objects, which at first I took to be aircraft, although there was no sign of any vapour trail that one would associate with the movement of an aircraft in high atmosphere.

When they got within a certain distance, two of them went off to my port side; one was gold in colour, the other silver. The third object headed towards me and closed to within a few hundred yards, almost filling the middle of the aircraft windscreen, before departing towards my port side. I tried to turn and follow but it had disappeared from view. The object I saw through the front cockpit of my Meteor 8 Jet aircraft was saucer-shaped, with a 'bun' on top and underneath. I didn't see any portholes, windows, or other exterior extrusions that one would associate with the passage of an aircraft through the air. There weren't even any flames coming from the objects."

Meeting James Salandin

In 2008, we met up with James Salandin at his home in rural North Yorkshire and had the opportunity to discuss personally with him what he had seen.

"It is now 54 years since my sighting of three UFOs in October 1954. At the time I was bound by the Official Secrets Act and, if it hadn't been for leaks, nothing more would have been heard of the incident. I have always said that I know what I saw and my story has never varied over the years – the picture is still clear in my mind. However, I have not at any time given an opinion as to my thoughts on the subject, but I feel that now is the moment

20.I.2014
To John & Dawn
Well done keep
the Volumes Coming!
Happy 2014
Best Wishes
James.

LET'S talk SPACE

WEEK-END PILOT IN NEAR COLLISION WITH FLYING SAUCER

IF Flight-Lieutenant J. R. Salandin, a week-end pilot of No. 604, County of Middlesex Squadron, Royal Auxiliary Air Force, had not been sceptical about Flying Saucers before his near collision with one last October, the Air Ministry might have had one of the first authentic cine records ever taken and been closer to solving the riddle of the unidentified flying objects than ever before.

Flight-Lt. J. R. Salandin climbs into his Meteor fighter.

Reporting for duty after lunch on October 14, Jimmy Salandin climbed into a Meteor Mk. 8 jet fighter and at 4.15 took off from North Weald, Essex.

The sky was blue and cloudless, and as he climbed in a southerly direction towards the Thames Estuary he spotted two Meteors in formation high above him leaving vapour trails behind them.

As his aircraft climbed, Salandin kept his eyes on the two fighters and every now and then checked his instruments and position.

The altimeter was reading just over 16,000 ft. and Southend was just looming up beneath him when he saw two circular objects streaking between the two Meteors, travelling in the opposite direction.

He watched them until they reached nine o'clock high—a position high on his port beam—when they disappeared beyond his range of vision. Reporting the incident later, Salandin said: "One was silvery and the other gold in colour."

But the shock was yet to come. When he turned to look through his windscreen he was horrified to see another object coming straight for him at his own level.

"The thing had a bun-shaped top, a flange like two saucers in the middle and a bun underneath," he said, describing it later. "It was silvery in colour and could not have been far off because it overlapped my windscreen."

A Meteor fighter's 37-ft. span wings just fill the windscreen at 150 yards.

As it closed in the object changed direction and passed Salandin on his port side.

"It was travelling at a tremendous speed," he reported and added: "I was so shaken I had to fly around quietly for about ten minutes to recover. I told control over the R/T (radio / telephone) what had happened."

What gripes Jimmy Salandin now is that he did not press his camera-gun button. "The thing was right in my sights," he says wistfully. "Next time I'll be on the ball."

At 150 yards the 37 foot span wings of a Meteor fill the windscreen.

2

to do so. Since my wife, Margaret, passed away nearly two years ago I've had plenty of time to reflect and would like to voice my true feelings, as most people appear to be sceptical or just not interested in UFOs. I was a volunteer in the Fleet Air Arm, from 1943 until demob in 1947, my flight training being with the United States Navy, after which I served with 604 County of Middlesex Fighter Squadron 'R' Auxiliary Air Force from 1947, until we were disbanded in 1957. The last five years of my service I was 'B' Flight Commander. During this decade, 604 were equipped with Spitfires, Vampires, and Gloster Meteors, the Squadron motto being, 'Si vis pacem para bellum', (If you want peace prepare for war!) I mention all of this because I was an experienced pilot and I have never seen, in all the years of my service, anything like I saw on that day."

James and late wife Margaret

The Coach House, Levisham, Pickering, YO18 7NL, North Yorkshire.

18th February 2004.

Dear John

Nice to hear you over the 'phone last evening and apologies for being so long with a reply to your most interesting letter and enclosures on the subject of UFO's.

As mentioned I have managed to find a couple of photographs which I had copied on Friday last. You will have to decide which one to use.

With regard to your text, I have made one or two alterations in pencil.—Hope you don't mind! Also the photos have captions on the reverse side.—I am not sure of the AVM's name on one; I think it was Reynolds, but am not sure, so it is better not to print, unless verified!

Incidentally, I have added AE after the MBE you showed. It means more to me than the former.-- Stands for Air Efficiency Award. – You don't have to print either, but, if you do, I would prefer the two.--- Awaiting the final draft. ---

With best wishes to Dawn and yourself

Sincerely,

James.

James R Salandin.

Derek Dempster – another man of courage

Another man to whom we spoke, also keen to set the record straight, was Derek Dempster, M.A, RAF test pilot with the North Weald Squadron from 1948 onwards, and personal friend to James – who inspired his interest in UFOs. Derek was educated, initially, at the French Lycee Regnault, in Tangier, and completed his schooling in England, in 1942, when he then volunteered for the RAF and was sent to Southern Rhodesia for pilot training.

On his commission, after receiving his 'wings', he qualified as a flying instructor. In the mid-1950s he left the RAF and took up a position as air correspondent for the *Daily Express* newspaper. He was then able to sift through reports of UFOs and decide whether further investigations should be carried out. He was asked to review a copy of *Flying Saucers have Landed,* by George Adamski and Desmond Leslie, which increased his curiosity into the UFO subject. Unfortunately, owing to a disagreement with the editor of the newspaper over the grounding of the world's first passenger jet, the *Comet*, he left the *Daily Express* and started his new job as first editor of Flying Saucer Review, at Werner Laurie Publishers, in Doughty Street, London. He was assisted by the following people: Waveney Girvan (publisher), Lewis Barton (editor of *This Week*, illustrated magazine), The Honourable Brindsley Le Poer Trench (an accountant at the South African Embassy), Dennis Montgomery (librarian) and Gordon Creighton (diplomat).

Derek Dempster:

> *"We held meetings at Westminster, Caxton Hall, near Scotland Yard. We believed these things were coming in from outer space, and we were trying to prove this with science. We had some allies, such as Peter Horsley, who had been Station Commander at North Weald, and was then equerry to Prince Philip. We received collaboration from Henry Chinnery, who was Horsley's successor.*

Derek Dempster M.A. (Cantab)
16 Archery Square
Walmer Deal Kent CT14 7HP
Tel : 01304 367791
e-mail : Derek..Dempster @ uwclub.net

Dear John,
Forgive me for the delay in answering your copious letter - a difficulty caused by rather serious illness. I hope, now, to be on the mend and able to give proper attention to your mammoth task.

First things first, though. I was horrified to see Denis Montgomery's bio about me. Or do I malign the poor bugger ?

I have rewritten the first two paragraphs, which you can integrate with the other introductory matter. I have written a lot more about myself than you need (*yellow copy)* so you have my OK to cut out whatever you want. It's not relevant to UFOs.

Air Marshal
Sir Peter Horsley's successor at the Palace was Squadron Leader Henry Chinnery, formerly the trainimg officer on my old Squadron (No 604 County of Middlesex) I mention this because he is referred to in Para 5 as **Chilsory.**

I am having trouble finding pictures of Desmond Lesley.I put them away in a safe place, and cannot now find them, Otherwise I enclose ~~some~~ one of self.

My PC printer has broken down, so I'm continuing this by hand. My P.C. guru spends Wednesday visiting sick computers. He was already booked up for today when I called him.

Let me link the 3 paras marked (A) on pink copy No 1 with the following:
Soon after joining the Express "copy-tasters" began passing any reports they received about things in the sky for

P.T.O.

my scrutiny and if worth investigating following up.

Among the things they passed to me was "Flying Saucers Have Landed" – the Adamski/Leslie book. (For Review

Coincidentally, one of my 604 Squadron colleagues – i.e. Jimmie Salandin – was involved in the encounter you already know about. I immediately contacted the publishers and met Desmond Leslie. My interest was immediately switched on to full.

At more or less the same time the Comet Jet airliner disaster was unfolding and I was in the middle of it.

Take in Montgomery copy (B)) Pink Page 2.

★

Ignore my biographical notes that have nothing to do with UFOs and take in (C) which relates to my literary output. ★ Not essential to include, but there if you want it.

★ Pink Page 4

Dan Lloyd – shorthand writer for Lord Louis Mountbatten

Both men had a keen interest in keeping the Palace posted on 'flying saucers' and we used to exchange files with them. There was also a shorthand writer for Lord Mountbatten, named Dan Lloyd, who was an ex-Royal Navy man. He was also very interested in 'flying saucer' matters and shared this interest and new research material with Mountbatten. It was said, at the time, that Mountbatten kept lever files of UFO photographs to show visitors on the bridge of the warships when he was at sea. I met George Adamski at this time.

I could see how terribly keen everybody was to embrace people like him, who claimed he had travelled to Venus. I was sceptical of him but wished to remained objective. What we were all living on, then, was hope and expectation. We kept being shot down due to the activities of the lunatic fringe, who began to attach themselves to Ufology. I had to leave FSR because of the effect it had on my business interests in the aviation industry; apart from that, I was being regarded as a 'nutcase', whose opinion in aviation matters was in question."

Derek's literary output includes *The Inhabited Universe* and *Worlds in Creation, The Tale of the Comet* with Kenneth Gatland, and the award-winning *The Narrow Margin* with Derek Wood, which served as a source book for the film *Battle of Britain*.

Derek passed away on the 25th January 2012.

Lord Louis Mountbatten took my father-in-law on his final journey

John Hanson:

"I met Lord Louis Mountbatten myself, during the 1970s, at an HMS Kelly reunion dinner, as my father- in-law was retired Chief Petty Officer 'Ted West', who shot down a German Stuka dive bomber at Crete, in 1943, as the ship foundered. I found Lord Louis a charismatic figure and was saddened of his assassination by the IRA in later years, but proud of the fact that he [Lord Louis] officiated at the funeral of Ted, when his ashes were cast into the sea at Portsmouth. What an honour that truly was!

Obviously, then, I had no inkling of the existence of UFOs. If I had, no doubt I would have been regarded as a 'nutcase' as well, by my fellow police officers."

(Source: Personal interviews held with Mr Salandin/Derek Dempster/*Flying Saucer Review*, Volume 1, No. 1, 1955/*Flying Saucer Review*, Volume 3, No. 2, 1984/ *Above Top Secret*, Timothy Good)

15/16/17th October – USA: Fifty objects seen

At Kingfisher, Oklahoma, a total of fifty objects with illuminated bases were seen flying very fast through the sky in a 'V' formation, at 8.45pm, on successive nights.

16th October – England: Girl encounters landed UFO, Essex

Patricia Hennessey from Chase Road, Southend, was walking home at 10.35pm on 16th October 1954, when she saw:

> *"...a silver-coloured cylindrical object, with a large corrugated tube or scaled pipe attached to one side, approximately six to twelve feet in height by ten feet in width, standing across Park Lane, its silver light blocking out the street light." (Other accounts mention the location as Caldwell Park.)*

We discovered that Mr Alex S. Jennings had carried out an investigation into the incident, which had attracted the attention of the press, whom it was said visited the location and found dark patches on the road – apparently neither oil, nor grease. Unfortunately, we were unable to obtain any details of the current whereabouts of Mr Jennings, or what appeared to be a fascinating close encounter, despite a number of appeals and lengthy searches made through old newspapers covering that period. Another source of information came from Cheltenham UFO researcher David Jones – a member of LUFORO and NICAP – who told of a number of villagers living in Hesters Way on the outskirts of Cheltenham, who sighted an object resembling a 'flat dish', surmounted by a dome, during 1954. One is bound to speculate on whether there was a connection with what James Salandin had seen. Could this have been his 'UFO', or was this a coincidence?

(Source: *Sunday Express*, 17.10.1955/Alex S. Jennings, *Flying Saucer News*, winter 1954/1955)

21st October – England: Staffordshire housewife's close encounter

In 1954, housewife – Mrs Jessie Roestenberg – was living at a farmhouse in rural Ranton, Staffordshire, with her husband, Tony (a Dutchman by birth), and their children, Karin (2), Ronald (6), and Tony. On 21st October, she witnessed something that was to totally change her conceptions of life on this planet – still very much evident when we met and interviewed her, over 50 years later! When we spoke to her, the events she described were still crystal clear in her mind.

Interviewed by Gavin Gibbons

She had first been interviewed in November/December 1954, by Shropshire UFO Researcher – Gavin Gibbons – and local UFO Researcher – Wilfred Daniels – (later published in an edition of *Flying Saucer News*, Winter 1954/55). Needless to say, what was told to Gavin was identical to what she was to tell us, half a century later. In the version of events given by Gavin, he outlines the arrival of what Jessie and her boys first took to be an aircraft. They watched it hovering over the chimney of the farmhouse, after hearing a noise like 'water being thrown on a fire'. They described the object as a dome, part divided vertically and horizontally, making four sections, the front two being transparent in material, the back two metallic, with an upper revolving part – like aluminium/silver.

> *"The 'saucer' tipped at an angle, creating an impression it was going to land, causing the children to throw themselves to the ground, enabling them to now see two 'men' – skin like ours, with very high foreheads, their features being in the lower part of their face, with shoulder-length hair, dressed in what looked like ski suits, with a stern and forbidding expression on their faces, wearing something resembling 'glass bowls' over their heads, with what looked like breathing apparatus.*

After about 15 seconds, the 'machine' ascended at an angle of 45 degrees, showing a flashing blue/purple light mounted on its front, and began to move away."

Jessie dashed into the house to draw what she had seen, thinking it had gone – but it then circled the house in an anticlockwise direction, leaving a trail – like jet plane, before heading upwards and northwards – soon out of sight.

We visited Jessie – a very down-to-earth, likeable woman – on a number of occasions throughout the years, who is now 90 (in 2016).

Mrs. Roestenburg, with her two sons keeping close beside her, points to the place where, she says, she saw the flying saucer hovering near her home.

This is a sketch, made today by Mrs. Roestenburg, of the strange object that she states she saw above her garden. It appeared to be built of "a dull silver metal," and the outer rim seemed to be revolving.

Wife says: "Terrified by flying saucer"

A RANTON, near Stafford, woman today told the "Express and Star" that she and her two children had been terrifield by a flying saucer, carrying "two long-haired, human-like creatures in tight-fitting jerseys."

The machine hovered over the garden, she stated.

When she heard a noise like a crashing aircraft, yesterday, Mrs. Jessie Roestenburg, of isolated Vicarage Farm, Ranton, ran out into the garden. She found her two children lying prostrate and terrified.

The next house to Vicarage Farm is about two miles away.

Above the children was a huge, saucer-like object with a dome, the front part of which was transparent, stated Mrs. Roestenburg.

Staring at the children from the machine were two "unsmiling, human-like creatures, with long faces and long hair."

Mrs. Roestenburg told our reporter that she ran to the back of the house in fright. The object then moved over the house, hovered there for about 15 seconds, and then shot off at high speed.

In June of this year, the vicar of nearby Seighford, the Rev. Cedric Wright, reported seeing a flying saucer over the vicarage at about midnight.

He said it was like a "giant illuminated spider," and estimated it to be about 25ft. in diameter.

Today, Mr. Wright said: "I was not lucky enough to get such a close-up view, as was Mrs. Roestenburg.

"It seems to me that these things are in the habit of frequenting our district. It cannot have been more than a couple of miles away from where I saw mine."

When Mr. Roestenburg, an architect's assistant, employed by Staffordshire County Council, returned home last night he found his wife and children in a state of terrified excitement.

So convinced was he of his wife's account that today he reported the matter to Stafford police and handed in a sketch of the object.

Telling her story today, Mrs. Roestenburg said: "The whole experience has left me sick with about five o'clock yesterday when there was a terrific noise like an aeroplane about to crash.

"I ran out and saw my children, Tony, aged eight, and Ronnie, who is six, lying on the ground.

"Above them, and looking as though it was going to drop and crush them, was this huge saucer-like affair, about 15 to 20 feet in diameter.

"I rushed to the other side of the house to get a better view of it, and it seemed to tilt.

"To my horror, I then saw two people looking out at us from the transparent dome.

"They were wearing tight blue jerseys.

"The machine at this time was making no noise at all.

"IT HOVERED"

Mrs. Roestenburg added: "The outer section of the object seemed to be revolving. It hovered over the house for what seemed like hours, but was probably only about 15 seconds.

"Then it increased its height circled twice and shot away, leaving a vapour trace and exuding a violet light.

"The boys were so terrified that they would not go out again last night. The dog was nowhere to be seen. I think it must have bolted."

Asked today what he felt about his experience, eight-year-old Tony Roestenburg said: "I did not like it a bit. At first I thought it was a jet that was going to crash."

He said he had not read any spaceship comics for months.

Mr. Roestenburg is anxious to get in touch with a scientific body interested in flying saucer sightings.

SPACE-MONKEYS

An explanation was given, a few days ago, of some of the stories about "flying saucer passengers" in America.

It was stated that monkeys were being used for experiments in the stratosphere. The unhappy animals were sent aloft in rockets, often with instruments attached for testing their physical reactions.

When they finally fell to earth,

An eventful life – *On a clear day*

She described an eventful life, including joining the British Army motor transport section in 1944, at the age of fifteen, then serving in the Women's Land Army.

Lately she was kept very busy, with a keen interest in poetry which developed after the UFO sighting and completion of her book – *On A Clear Day*, which described the mysterious events – a befitting title; it is also inscribed poignantly into the headstone of her now late husband Tony's grave.

Winter 1954/55 FLYING SAUCER NEWS 9

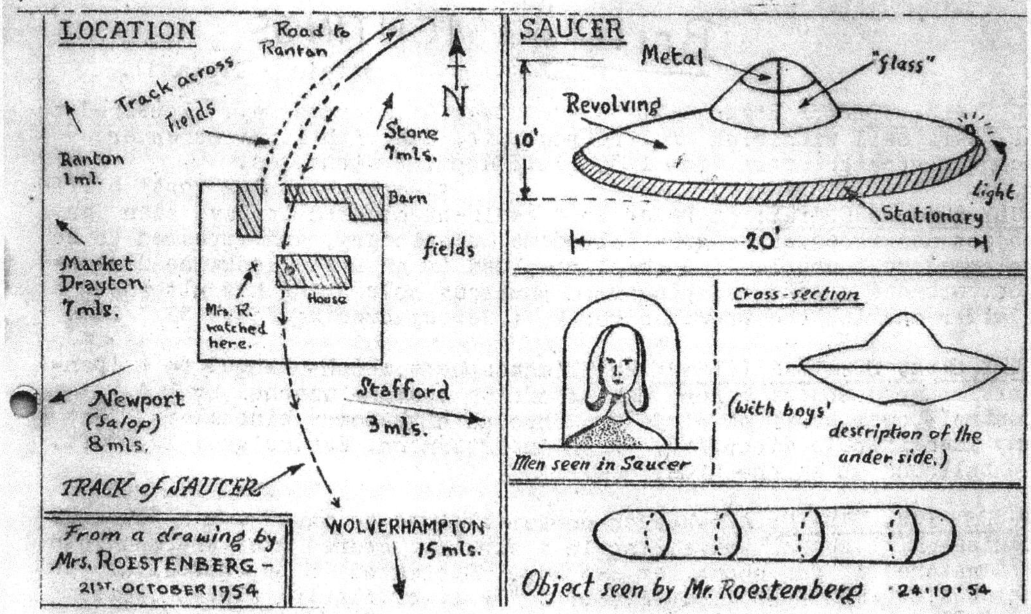

ONLY WHEN MOVING HORIZONTALLY DID IT LEAVE ANY TRAIL*. Mrs.Roestenberg thought it was a jet at first - and one was in the sky at the time. It was just beginning to get dark, and the saucer's trail appeared like a pencil line against the blue sky. It was a perfect day, with not a cloud in the sky.

Intrigued by his wife's experience, the following Sunday, October 24th, after lunch, Mr.Roestenberg climbed up to the chimney over which the saucer had hovered; partly to see if there were any trace of anything interesting - which there was not - but mainly to see if he could see anything in the 'space-ship' line. Believe it or not, his wish was almost immediately granted!

Suddenly, to the South East, he saw a cylindrical, sausage-shaped thing, about 25-30ft long, aluminium coloured and divided into four or five segments. His wife, called out to look, said it was the same colour as the saucer, but a friend staying with them insisted that there were dark patches where the wings ought to have been (the object being about the size of a fighter plane). However, Mr.Roestenberg examined it intently and could see neither wings nor tail; only the lines round it separating it into segments. It appeared South-east of where they were and was about 30° high. It flew round in an anti-clockwise direction, and then went into a bank of cloud.

* * * * *

*Editor's note: Contrails are normally only produced by aircraft flying at fairly high altitudes, apart from certain American jet types (such as the Sabre) which emit a smoky ('burnt paraffin') trail. This, however, is quite tenuous and disperses quickly.

8 FLYING SAUCER NEWS Winter 1954/55

EXCLUSIVE!
Full Report on the Ranton affair 1954

From GAVIN GIBBONS, our Roving Investigator.

RANTON, Staffordshire, England; October 21st. 1954.

Mrs.Roestenberg, of Vicarage Farm, her two sons aged eight and six, and her little girl aged 2½ were in the house when at about 5.45 they heard a terrific hissing noise, just as if water had been thrown on the fire, only much louder. They all rushed out and were astounded to see a strange object in the sky above them. "It's a jet!" cried one of the boys, and they rushed to the back, ready for it, but it didn't come. Turning round, they were amazed to see it hovering just above one of their chimneys. "It seemed to be moving very slowly for an aeroplane", said Mrs.Roestenberg, when I asked her what her first impression had been when she had run out of the front door at the first sound of the thing.

It consisted of a dome over a saucer. (See sketch). The dome - part was divided vertically and horizontally, thus making four sections. The front two sections were of some transparent material, and the back two were metallic. The upper side of the saucer itself was revolving (she couldn't remember which way) and the lower part remained stationary. Mrs.Roestenberg did not herself see the under side, but the boys said it stuck out a little. They were definite that there were no landing spheres as on the Adamski and Coniston Saucers. The colour was brilliant aluminium silver. She could not remember the colour behind the two men in the transparent panel....

The saucer tipped at an angle, presumably so that the crew could look at Mrs.Roestenberg and the children. All thought it was going to land and the children flattened themselves out as they would in an air raid. The two men in the saucer appeared to have skins much the same as ours, but had very high foreheads, the features being in the lower half of the face. Their hair came down to their shoulders, she said, and they were dressed in what seemed to be ski-ing suits. They never moved, and looked stern and forbidding. They had "glass bowls" over their heads, and the boys thought they could see breathing apparatus. After the terrified foursome had stared at the spectacle for about 15 seconds, the machine ascended at an angle of 45° - making no sound as it moved.

A flashing, purple-blue light (flashing at about the rate of the red aircraft beacon on the Wrekin) - mounted on the 'front' of the saucer came into action when the thing moved, and kept on all the time. Thinking the craft had gone, Mrs.Roestenberg dashed into the house to draw what she had seen. But after ascending in a Southerly direction it suddenly began to circle the house in an anti-clockwise direction and left a trail like that of a jet-plane. When it had circled the house one and a half times - by which time the boys had called her out again - it suddenly streaked up at 60° in a northward direction until lost to sight. "I've never seen anything move so fast!" said Mrs.Roestenberg, "much faster than the fastest jet".

Jessie:

"At about 4.30pm, I experienced a peculiar sensation – like a tingling in my nose and throat, as if I was going to catch a cold, but put it to the back of my mind, while waiting for the boys to arrive home from school. At 4.45pm I was beginning to worry where the two boys had got to, because they should have arrived home at 4.30pm. Suddenly, I heard what sounded like a giant cauldron of water being poured into a fire. I rushed outside, thinking an airplane was going to crash, and noticed the two boys lying flat on the ground. They shouted to me, 'Look, Mummy! Mummy, there's a 'flying saucer'!' I told them not to be silly and get up, but realised from their facial expressions that something had frightened them.

They grabbed hold of my skirt on either side of me and we walked up the side of the house, instead of going in by the side door I had just come out of. I seemed to be in some way drawn or compelled to the top of the garden – almost as if I was being manipulated by an outside influence, of which I had no control."

Occupants seen

"I glanced around and saw the amazing sight of this 'flying saucer' shaped object, hovering 40-50 feet above the roof of the house. Inside the 'saucer' I could clearly see what looked like two humans, wearing long golden hair down to their shoulders. I felt a mixture of emotions; amazement and fear run [sic] through my body, followed by the thought, 'God will wipe away all tears'. Immediately, all the tension left me (something I have never disclosed to anyone before, because of its religious significance). I turned to my sons and asked them if they had seen the 'flying saucer'. They replied, 'yes'. When I looked back, the 'saucer' was no longer there but a few minutes later we saw it circle the house, three times, before it shot upwards – like a rocket against the blue of the darkening sky."

Confused and unsure of how to deal with what had occurred, Jessie gathered the children together, hid under the kitchen table and waited for her husband to arrive home, when she explained what had taken place.

Tony telephones police

Tony wisely spoke to the boys individually, and then telephoned the police at Stafford. They sent a sergeant and five constables.

Jessie was very perturbed to see the following local newspaper headlines, boldly declaring, 'Staffordshire housewife sees hairy men from outer space'.

Strange rash appears

After the sighting she felt revitalised for a short time, until discovering a strange rash covering her face and front part of her body.

She also lost a considerable amount of weight over a relatively short period, which was cause for concern. Jessie sought the advice of her doctor, who was well aware of the UFO incident and intimated there was something wrong with her mental health. Offended by this suggestion, Jessie contacted psychiatrist – Dr. Wilson, who confirmed, after a medical examination, that there was nothing wrong with her mental state.

Jessie:

"He asked me if I had been given a chest x-ray and blood tests. When I told him this had not been done, he personally escorted me to hospital, where a chest x-ray was taken but found to be clear. Unfortunately, blood tests showed the blood count was very

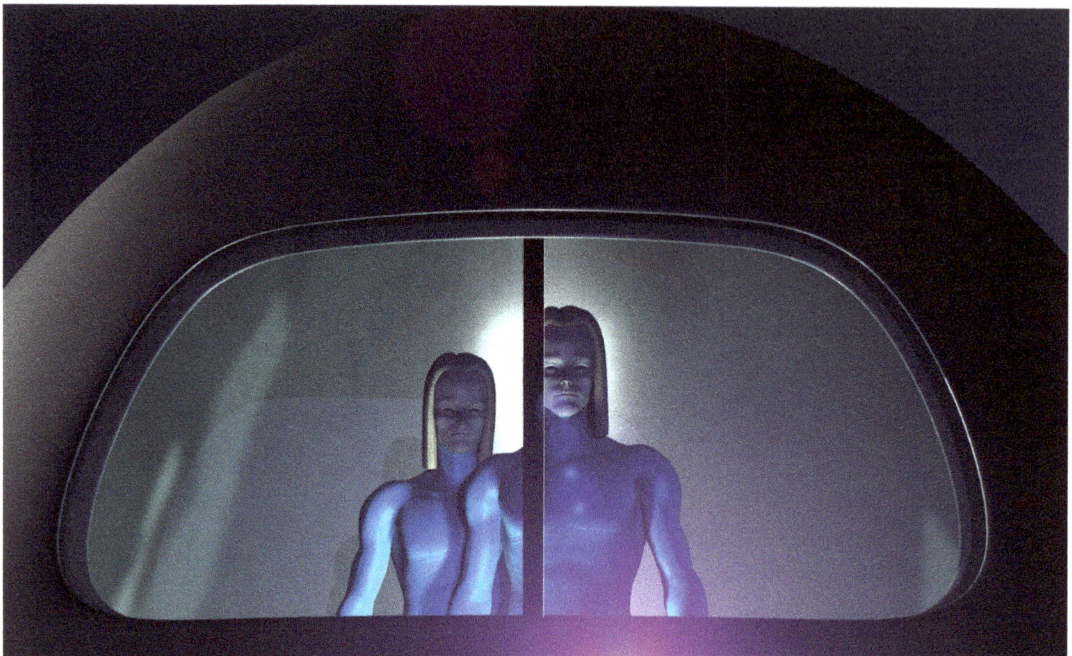

low. The haematologist said to me, 'If it didn't sound so ludicrous, I would say you have been exposed to a massive dose of radiation'. I was given injections of iron, twice a week, which caused all sorts of problems before the correct dosage was established."

History was to record that Jessie and her two children were not the only witnesses that afternoon.

Another witness traced

According to the Wolverhampton edition of the *Express & Star* (25.10.54), Mr Patrick Kennedy - then a teacher at St. Mary's Roman Catholic School, Fallings Park, Wolverhampton - described seeing an identical 'flying saucer' travelling over the town, just after 5pm on the same afternoon:

> *"We had watched a jet plane go over and then there was a noise - like another plane. It was like the drone of a petrol engine machine, not the whistle of a jet. I, and a ten year-old boy, named Guest, looked up and saw a circular object similar to the drawing made by Mrs Roestenberg, who saw it flying over Ranton. It shot across the sky at a speed - much faster than a jet plane - and seemed to be 5,000 feet up. It came from the Stafford direction and was travelling in the opposite direction taken by the jet plane, which had passed over at twice the height. It seemed to be a dark reddish/brown colour. Although the sun was shining, it did not gleam."*

Tony Roestenberg with Wilfred Daniels – 12-3-1955

The veracity of this statement, made by a witness who had nothing to gain, speaks volumes for itself. Not only does it corroborate with what Jessie saw, but raises the question of whether the jet aircraft had been scrambled to intercept the UFO. We shall probably never know, but wouldn't have been surprised.

She was also interviewed by Stafford UFO researcher Wilfred Daniels shown here on the right of the photo.

Over the years we have had the pleasure of meeting Jessie who has a crystal clear recollection of that eventful day, now 60 years ago

WOLVERHAMPTON EXPRESS AND STAR 25·10·54

W'ton teacher: "I saw flying saucer"

A WOLVERHAMPTON teacher and a ten-year-old boy claim that they saw the "flying saucer" reported to have been seen by a woman and her two children at Ranton, near Stafford, last Thursday, the "Express and Star" learned today.

Just after 5 p.m. on that day, Mr. Patrick Kennedy (34), c/o 58, Oldfallings-lane, was with about a dozen children and other teachers in the yard of St. Mary's Roman Catholic junior school, Fallings Park.

Normally school ends at 4 p.m., but they had stayed behind for netball and football practice.

Mr. Kennedy said today: "We had watched a jet plane go over, and then there was a noise like another plane.

"It was like the drone of a petrol-engined machine, not the whistle of a jet.

"I and a ten-year-old boy, named Guest, looked up and saw a circular object similar to that drawn by Mrs. Roestenburg, who said she saw the flying saucer at Ranton.

"It shot across the sky at a speed much faster than the jet plane. It seemed to be about 5,000ft. up.

"It came from the Stafford direction and was travelling in the opposite direction to that taken by the jet plane, which had passed over at twice the height.

"It seemed a dark reddish-brown colour. Although the sun was shining, it did not gleam.

"I SHOUTED"

Mr. Kennedy added: "I shouted: 'There's a flying saucer.' Other teachers and boys looked, but in that second it had travelled so quickly that it was already only a speck in the sky. Others, however, saw the speck.

Many people would not believe him, commented Mr. Kennedy, and he was inclined to dismiss the matter until he read of Mrs. Roestenburg's experience and saw her drawing of the "saucer" in the *Express and Star*.

The time at which he saw the object also tallied with Mrs. Roestenburg's account. She stated that she saw it hovering near home at about 5 p.m.

Space Ships a' Coming

TONY ROESTENBERG is a Dutchman, a solid, reliable type of man who settled in this country after World War II with his pretty Manx wife. They set up house at Vicarage Farm, which is close to Ranton village in Staffordshire. It is a small cottage, partly half-timbered, partly whitewashed brick, set in rather lonely surroundings at the end of a bumpy track across a field. Stafford itself lies three and a half miles to the east and there Mr. Roestenberg works as an assistant architect. The young couple have three children, two boys and a girl, and until the advent of that exciting day in October, 1954, they were indistinguishable from any other happy little family.

Little Karin, their two-year-old daughter, played happily in her own tiny, exciting world and waited until her two brothers arrived home from school to join in her games. At 4.15 in they came, six-year-old Ronald, and Anthony, a bright youngster of eight.

Half-an-hour went by. Suddenly there came from outside a tremendous hissing noise—a noise as if a huge kettle were pouring water upon a mighty fire. Rushing out of the house, they were astounded to see a large object moving very low overhead, going southwards.

"It's a jet!" cried one of the boys, and they all ran around to the other side of the house and looked in the direction that the object was going. There was nothing to be seen. Where had it gone? Bewildered, they looked up and their blood chilled when they realised why they could not see the object still moving across the sky. It was hovering over the house! Very low and completely silent, a queer round thing was standing in the air immediately over the little cottage. It was no jet—it was a vimana!*

Brilliantly it shone in the sky, so low that they could make out every detail of its body. They could see that the upper part of the disc was revolving and the lower part stationary. Stationary above that aluminium-coloured disc was a dome, the back aluminium coloured but the front consisting of two transparent panels. With a catch in her breath, Jessie Roestenberg saw that looking through those transparent panels at her were two men. They had tipped the Saucer slightly forward so that they could see downwards the better, and from this angle they silently regarded her.

She recalls that they looked very like earthly men, with white skins and long hair down to their shoulders. Their foreheads seemed immensely high, with the features almost entirely in the bottom half of their faces. Their heads were enclosed in what appeared to be some sort of transparent helmets and they were dressed in clothes of turquoise blue that resembled ski suits that Mrs. Roestenberg had seen. But what appeared strangest of all to the little group of watchers on the ground was the unsmiling expression on the faces of the men from the sky. Sternly they gazed down at the Roestenberg family, not in an unkindly fashion, but almost sadly, compassionately.

The terror of that little group can be imagined. They had only vaguely heard of Flying Saucers (their father had read a magazine article on the subject a year earlier) and the two boys had not read a space comic for months. Their heads were in a whirl. Who were these peculiar visitors and where had they come from? They assumed immediately that they were not of this planet, and their fear, though momentary, was very great. The children flattened themselves on the ground, pressing themselves down against the cool, comforting earth, away from the menace that stared down at them from the skies. The dog, which had accompanied them into the garden at the first alarm, shot off howling down the track that led into the village. Yelping, he scudded along, impelled by the one thought of escaping from this strange thing that he could not understand, away to the comforting sights and smells of the humans that he knew and loved.

As Jessie Roestenberg watched, appalled, the vimana began to move, flashing a purply blue light from the front of it as it did so. At an angle of 45° it started to ascend, making no sound as it moved, but continuing the flashing the whole time. With a gasp of relief Jessie ran into the house, intent on finding pencil and paper to sketch what she and the children had seen. As she looked for the stub of a pencil, the boys called out again from the garden. With fear returning once more to her heart she ran outside to see the Saucer coming back again, this time from north to south. It circled the house in an anti-clockwise direction one and a half times and then streaked skywards. It had gone at last. Mrs. Roestenberg had never seen anything go so fast. "It was going much faster than the fastest jet I have ever seen," she told me later.

At the time of the sighting it had begun to get dark and the vimana's trail—like that of a jet aircraft—showed like a shadowy pencil line against the blue of the sky. There was not a cloud in the heavens. Mrs. Roestenberg took one last look round and then ushered her children into the house to await the coming of her husband.

Mr. Roestenberg was absolutely astonished to hear his wife's story, but the way in which it was told, the obvious terror of his children, the absence of the dog, the pencil sketch that Jessie had made of the vimana, all convinced him that something very much out of the ordinary had happened in his absence and sent him hurrying to the police.

When they arrived they seem to have been very impressed by the story. One big constable rubbed hard at his head with his knuckles. "Well," he said, after a pause, "I never have believed in these here Flying Saucers, but I certainly do now."

* *Author's term for certain type of U.F.O.*

Condensed from the book "The Coming of the Space Ships" by Gavin Gibbons (13s. 6d.) by kind permission of the publishers Messrs. Neville Spearman & Co.

OTHER NEW BOOKS

We've said it before and we'll say it again, **The Observer's Book of Aircraft** (Frederick Warne & Co., price 5s.) is the best five bobs' worth of aircraft gen available. This new 1957 edition is similar in style to last year's annual, and is bang up to date with the

(*Continued on page* 105)

102

1954 (approximately) – England: UFO landing, with occupants

Gladys Spencer (82 in 1996), who was then living in *Thurnby Lodge, Leicestershire, with her dog named 'Scruff', was to tell of an amazing encounter with a 'craft' and its alien occupants, back in the early 1950s. It began one morning, when, while sitting on the wall on the corner of Dudley Avenue, taking in the morning air, she saw:

> *"...a 'thing' just appeared – as if from nowhere – and landed in the middle of the road, completely filling the sides of the road. It was like a glass globe or ball, with a flat green base, and contained people inside. There were two steps that led into the 'craft', and four people sat on green slatted seats.*
>
> *One of them came over to me; he was human looking and was wearing normal everyday clothes – a suit, I seem to remember. He said, 'Are you alright?' I wasn't scared and felt drawn to the object. It then took off and headed away towards Uppingham.*
>
> *Shortly afterwards I heard that scorched ring marks had been found on a nearby field and wondered if there was any connection."*

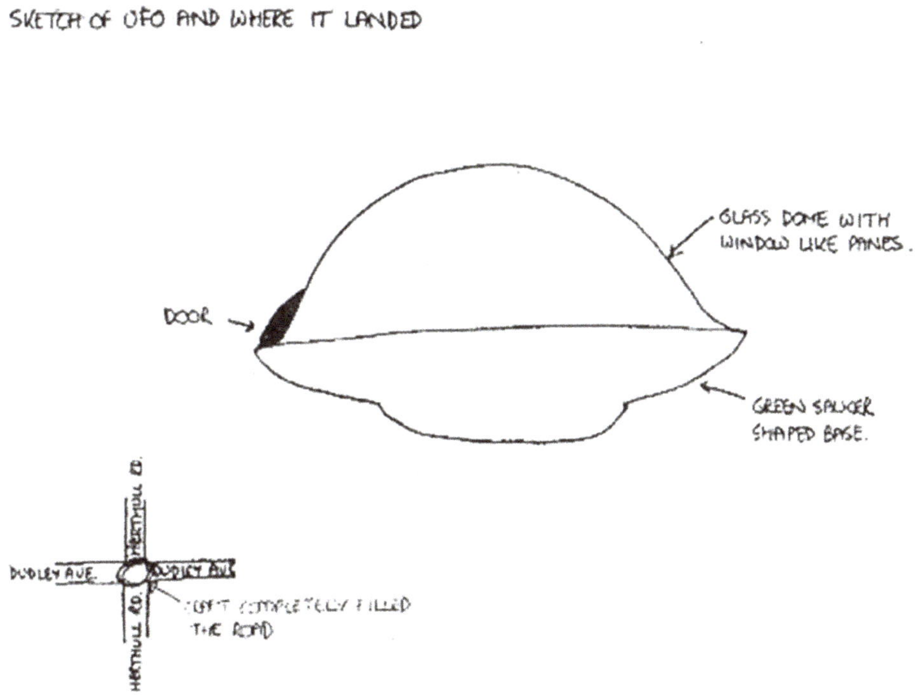

*Thurnby Lodge is an estate in eastern Leicester, England. Roughly, it consists of the area inside the city boundary which is north of the Uppingham Road, east of the A563 outer ring road, and south of Scraptoft Lane. Since the core area around Thurncourt Road is a council estate with an average reputation, many, particular those around the western and southern fringe, would disassociate their area from Thurnby Lodge. It is near but not part of Thurnby (to the south-east), after which it is named. Other nearby places are Humberstone (north and west), Scraptoft (east), Evington (south) and Goodwood, Leicestershire (south).

22nd October – USA: 'Angel hair' falls over Ohio

We contacted Susan Kienbaum at the Marysville Library, Ohio, in 2009, and obtained details of the incident, previously published in the *Marysland Evening Tribune* newspaper, on the 25th October 1954 – 'Saucer experts stumped'. Susan told us her former neighbour was one of the witnesses to the event that occurred at 3.13pm on 22nd October 1954, when . . .

> *"6th, 7th and 8th graders from Jerome Special School, Marysville, Ohio, sighted a brilliant silver cigar-shaped object, moving across the sky at terrific speed, shedding a blanket of what looked like vapour",*

which they brought to the attention of the school principal – Mr Warwick – and teacher – Mrs Dittmar. Mr Warwick watched the object for a brief period, before it shot off horizontally across the sky and disappeared.

Unfortunately, by the time Mrs Dittmar made her way to the fire escape to look out into the sky, the UFO had gone – though she and Mr Warwick did see, while driving home all the way to the Columbus Road, the trail of web-like material which the object had left, described as

> *"strung from one side to the other over telephone wires along the road, in long strands, covering bushes and trees, resembling Christmas tree decorations – long spun glass fluff".*

This is often referred to by UFO researchers as 'Angel hair', so named for its similarity to fine hair, or spiders' webs. Reports of this substance are mainly from the USA, Western Europe, Eastern Australia and New Zealand; it is quite rare in the UK.

Principal Warwick said:

> *"It looked like asbestos and felt like asbestos. You could catch the two ends and make a long thread but, within less than a minute, the substance would disappear. Oddly, when you touched one end of the strand, it would roll into a ball before disintegrating. Even more stranger is that, after touching it, your fingertips would turn green. As an experiment, I didn't wash my hands and noticed they broke out into a cold sweat but, after 30-45 minutes, the green faded away. I have never seen anything like it, or heard anything like it, before. It was the most unusual sight I have ever seen. No one was frightened."*

(Source: *The UFO Evidence*, NICAP, 1964)

24th October – England: Tony Roestenberg sights UFO over Shropshire

Two days later, on 24th October 1954, Tony Roestenberg – still pondering on what his wife had seen – wondered whether anything had been dropped or discharged from the 'saucer' onto the roof of his house. Making his way onto the roof from an upstairs window, he inspected the chimneys over which the UFO had hovered, and the slates, but found nothing of any significance.

Casually, he scanned the skies. It was just after 2.30pm on a pleasant October afternoon. Suddenly, something caught his eye towards the south-west. He was staggered to see, flying slowly along in a great semicircle, a cigar-shaped object. Frantically, he shouted for his wife to come out and see it, which she did, observing for herself the huge 'craft', estimated to be no more than a mile away, before it eventually disappeared into a bank of cloud to the north.

They agreed, when discussing the situation a short time afterwards, that the unidentified object had been 'aluminium in colour, and

Tony Roestenberg

appeared to be divided into four, or five, segments'. Tony asked Jessie whether it was the same 'craft' she had seen previously, to which she replied in the negative, although she admitted it was the same colour.

Other witnesses traced

Following our appeal in the local newspaper for any other witnesses, we were contacted by Mr Tony Goodwin – a civilian, employed by Staffordshire Police – who told us he and his father had been out in the back garden of their house, one afternoon, some 50 years ago, when they noticed an object 'just stuck' in the sky under cloud cover, which they estimated was at a height of about 5,000 feet.

Tony:

"Through a pair of binoculars, it resembled 'something like a plaice', roughly triangular with rounded edges, as opposed to sharp ones – more like an image seen through a mirror, rather than a structured 'craft', and larger than the Horsa gliders often seen flying over the area. Suddenly, the object hovering over the Ranton area shot off upwards into the sky, at a frightening speed – far too fast for the human eye to track – ruling out any possibility, in my opinion, that this was of earthly origin."

31st October – England: Two objects sighted over Shropshire

Between 8pn and 10pm, Gavin Gibbons – UFO researcher and author of books on the subject – sighted:

"...a large, round, object – about half the size of the moon, over 'The Queen's Head' – moving slowly towards the south-west.

It seemed to come up against an unseen obstacle as it changed to roughly eye-shaped, before ejecting faint sparks and what looked like smoke, and vanishing from sight. Seconds later, a similar object appeared on the same course. The skies were clear at the time."

11th November – England: Mysterious noise heard over Lincolnshire

On 11th November 1954, a housewife from Saxilby, Lincolnshire, was getting ready to attend a Women's Institute meeting in the early evening, when she heard an unusual 'chug-chug' noise in the sky.

"It didn't sound like an airplane, and appeared to be travelling west to east. I looked out over the sky but couldn't see anything."

On the same day, a small 'fireball' was seen moving up and down in the air, glowing with red light before entering cloud cover, at a height of between 5,000 and 7,000 feet, over Whitstable, in Kent, by many people – including one housewife, who was so excited she dropped a dish!

(Source: *Daily Sketch*, 12.11.1954 – 'Saucer breaks a dish')

11th November – England: Silver 'cigar' over Suffolk

On the same day, Harleston men – Harry Reeve and Ernest Hudson – were fishing at a flooded pit near to the former site of a watermill at Weybread, when they saw a strange object pass through the sky overhead.

Mr Reeve:

> *"It formed an almost perfect, vivid silver 'cigar', with a prominent middle 'bulge'. At times, it appeared to remain almost stationary and would then move off again, at speed, whilst retaining its original course. After being temporarily lost from view, it was seen again on an entirely different course. It then moved upwards, at an angle of 45 degrees in the opposite direction, before making a sharp left-hand bank, nose-diving towards its original position, before resuming its journey. During the course of its flight across the sky, the 'bulge' gradually diminished, leaving a shape like a smooth cigar. As we watched its extraordinary journey across the sky, we noticed the appearance of two or three RAF jet aircraft flying through the air, some considerable distance away, and wondered if there was any connection."*

Mr Albert Smith – Humming noise heard

Mr Albert Smith, from South Carlton, was outside with his wife, at 11pm on 11th November, when they heard a humming noise. Looking up, they saw a 'flying saucer' disappearing into the clouds. The couple also told the newspaper that the incident was witnessed by an 'American couple', who confirmed having seen 'something' fading away into the clouds.

12th November – England: RAF pilot sights UFO

Ex-RAF fighter pilot Neville Berryman, of Nettleham Road, contacted the local newspaper after what he saw.

> *"I am not going to tell anybody I saw a 'flying saucer', because I don't believe in them, but I saw through my bedroom window, in the morning, a most peculiar thing I can't explain away. At 7.45am on 12th November 1954, I was sitting up in bed, drinking my early morning cup of tea, when, to my surprise, I saw a spherical object – golden in colour, like the sun – about 5,000 feet up, pass across my bedroom window, at fantastic speed.*
>
> *I have always scoffed at people who claim to have seen 'saucers'. I had a good laugh at a Scampton RAF Officer this week, who told me he had seen one. I tried to reason out what I had seen. It couldn't have been a balloon. No balloon could have travelled at about 15,000 mph."*

(Source: *Lincolnshire Echo*, 12.11.1954 – 'Seeing things'/Evening Echo 13.11.1954 'Not a saucer but what was it?)

15th November – USA: Ten gold objects sighted

Mr N. Gallant – manager of radio station *WFAV* at Augusta, Maine, sighted ten gold, circular objects, flying in a vertical 'V' shaped formation across the sky, for three minutes.

17th November - England: RAF radar tracks multiple targets

The London *Sunday Dispatch* newspaper told of a strange pattern of 'blips' which normally appeared at midday on inland radar screens. These blips were flying in an east to west direction at about 12,000 feet. They would first appear in a 'U' or badly shaped hairpin formation, but after time would converge into parallel lines, then into a 'Z' formation, before disappearing. These objects were invisible to the naked eye, but on the radar screen the 'blips' represented between 40 and 50 echoes, and covered a wide range of the sky. A War Office spokesman said they always followed the same pattern. He said the sets had been checked and they were not faulty. The *Sunday Dispatch* reporter spoke to one of the men who had been involved. He was told that the matter was subject of utmost secrecy.

30th November - England: Huge orange object seen in the sky

Miss Lavinia Philips of Gathurst, near Wigan, Lancashire, was about to enter her house, at 11.55pm, when she noticed:

> *"...a huge, luminous, orange object in the sky. The moon at the time was in front of me and to the left.*
>
> *After being motionless in the sky for a short time, it rose suddenly and maintained its upward direction, until no longer distinguishable. Curiously, the cat - although part wild - was transfixed by the appearance of the object."*

Sunday Dispatch Newspaper and Lord Louis Mountbatten

Its editor - Charles Eade - had served as Press Liaison Officer for Lord Mountbatten, during World War Two; distribution was up from 800,000 to over 2 million copies per edition, in 1947.

In 1950 – in late summer, the *Dispatch* was partly responsible for launching the 'flying saucer' debate in the UK, when in a circulation battle with the *Sunday Express*. Both papers competed to serialise the seminal books by Major Donald Keyhoe - *Flying Saucers are Real,* Frank Scully's - *Behind the Flying Saucers,* and Gerald Heard's - *Riddle of the Flying Saucers.*

Eade had been encouraged to promote 'flying saucer' stories by his friend – Lord Mountbatten, whom he had served as Press officer during the Second World War. The *Dispatch* later reported on the 1951 Mount Kilimanjaro incident and the West Freugh incident, in April 1957.

3rd December - USA: Rotating UFO seen

At midnight, Mr and Mrs S.P. Mellen - residents of Gulfport, Mississippi - sighted a translucent grey, round, flat object, rotating on its vertical axis at high speed, for 30 seconds.

15th December - England: RAF scrambles jet fighter!

Other reports, involving the scramble of RAF jets, took place on 15th December 1954, this time over the Staffordshire area, when Tony Roestenberg - now extremely interested in the UFO subject since his previous sighting - was outside the family home at Ranton. He saw a 'ball of fire' moving slowly across the sky, at an angle of about forty-five degrees above the horizon, heading north. When he looked at the 'object', a very short time later, he noticed it had increased in size considerably and was now almost stationary to the north-east.

As he stood there, wondering what to make of this, he heard the sound of military aircraft approaching. A RAF jet was then seen to fly towards the curious 'fireball', at which point the 'object' shot northwards at an incredible speed, disappearing from sight over the horizon within seconds.

Late December – England: Boy photographs UFO

On 28th or 29th December 1954, Harold Cummins – then a 16 year-old schoolboy, from Wednesfield, near Wolverhampton – was looking out of his window, hoping to photograph wild birds at about 3.30-3.45pm, when he noticed a large object appear in the sky. He first took it to be a large bird. To his amazement it stopped and began to hover in the sky, showing a classic 'flying saucer' image.

Reacting quickly, he picked-up his camera and took a photograph through the glass. In the time that he looked away to put the camera back on the sill, it had gone.

The sighting and photo were originally published in a report written up by *Flying Saucer News,* in spring 1955 (Editor, Richard Hughes), which expressed the opinion that it was a genuine photo, although, quite rightly, the British Flying Saucer Bureau representative pointed out that further analysis would have to be carried out on the photo.

In 2009 we spoke to Dennis Plunkett about this matter, hoping to obtain further information regarding the whereabouts of the photo and any other developments, after finding another mention in *Flying Saucer News* (autumn 1955), when it was disclosed that 'the reports into the matter, by Denis Plunkett and George Watts, had not yet been finalised'.

People 4.5.58

Riddle of 'flying sun' at night

A RAF officer yesterday broke a five-month silence to tell of the astonishing event at Toppler's Hill, near Biggleswade, in Bedfordshire.

The district has been seething with stories of the "flying saucer" that shot across the sky on the night of December 2.

Flight-Lieut. Jack Hunter, a technical officer taking a guided-missiles course at Henlow, Beds., saw the object. He did not think anyone would believe him. So he kept silent.

Not a stunt

But yesterday he was challenged by "The People" to confirm or deny the local rumours.

He confirmed that he HAD seen an unexplained object in the sky. It COULD NOT have been an aircraft or missile and COULD NOT have been sent up as part of a stunt.

That remarkable testimony comes from a man who has spent 24 years in the Service and says: "I was a sceptic about flying saucers."

And Flight.-Lieut. Hunter was only one of a team of observers that witnessed the strange event on Toppler's Hill.

The man who brought the team together is 34-year-old Mr. John Whitworth, who keeps a shop in Shefford, Beds.

1955

British Government's attitude towards reports of 'flying saucers'

MANY people wrote to the Ministry of Air wanting to know their views on the question of whether 'flying saucers' existed, taking into consideration reports published in the Press. This was a matter brought to the attention of Parliament. The under-secretary of State for Air, Nigel Birch, stated that:

> *"Flying saucers do not exist. Reports of flying saucers, as well as other abnormal objects in the sky, are investigated as the come in, but there has been no formal enquiry. About 90% of the reports have been found to relate to meteors, balloons, flares, and many other objects. The fact that the other objects are unexplained need be attributed to nothing more sinister than lack of data."*

[Some sources give a figure of 15,000 sightings between 1947 and 1954 – only a few have survived.]

1st January – USA: UFO *"Like two pie pans"*

At 6.44am over Cochise, New Mexico, an instructor and student pilot in a USAF *B-25* bomber/trainer sighted:

> *"...a metallic 'disc', shaped like two pie pans, face-to-face, 120-130 feet in diameter, pacing the B-25, showing both its edge and its 'face', for five to seven minutes".*

23rd January – England: Flying Saucer Club, London

On the 23rd January, Air Marshall Lord Dowding told the Flying Saucer Club, in London:

> *"It's rude to fire AA guns and send fighters to shoot them down; you never know what they could do to you. I believe these objects come from planets hundreds of years ahead of us in scientific knowledge; there is no material we know that could travel 9,000 miles per hour, which was the recorded speed of one saucer, without becoming white hot."*

30th January – England: Ball of fire sighted

At 6.30am, a huge green fluorescent 'ball of fire' was seen heading through the sky, eastwards, over the Malvern Hills, by early morning workers, including milkmen and police officers.

Another witness was Gavin Gibbons, who was out cycling through west Felton, towards Oswestry, when he saw:

> *"...a brilliant light appear in the sky in front of me, at an angle of 20 degrees above the horizon, towards the north-west direction – its brightness somewhat exceeding that of Venus. It vanished in seconds, without making any sound."*

(Source: *Oswestry and Border Counties Advertiser,* 6.2.1955 – 'Strange Phenomenon')

1st February – USA: Foo fighter?

Instructor Capt. D.F. Ritzdorf, accompanied by aviation cadet F.W. Miller, was flying over Cochise, New Mexico, at 7.55pm, in a *TB-25* bomber/trainer. A red and white 'ball of light' was seen hovering off the left wing of the *TB-25* for 5 minutes, before making a very fast climb 8 minutes later.

2nd February – England: UFOs sighted

At 7.30am, Leonard Scott from Immingham, Lincolnshire, was in the process of getting his car out of the garage when he saw a bright object, at great height, in the sky. He first thought it was a star, until it dropped down from the sky and then stopped.

Leonard carried on his journey and picked up a colleague – Charles Lambert. As they drove along, both men saw:

> *"...the object moving at terrific speed across the sky, constantly stopping and starting, before finally swerving at speed, horizontally, and shooting upwards and out of sight."*

Swindon, Wiltshire

According to the *Swindon Evening Advertiser* (2.2.1955), several people reported sighting a strange white object in the sky over the town, at 9am. One person said:

> *"It had a curved end, like a boat, and something like a turret on top."*

Officials at the control tower of Vickers Armstrong Limited, and RAF bases nearby, commented that they had not seen anything untoward in the sky.

2nd February – USA: Highly polished sphere seen in the sky

USN Commander J.L. Ingersoll of Miramar Naval Air Station, California, was outside at 11.50am, when he saw:

> *"...a highly polished sphere, with red-brown colouring, which fell – then instantly accelerated to 1,000-1,500 mph".*

7th February – USA: Pilot sights three white lights

Pilot Captain Charles Elmore, reported seeing three bright white 'lights' due south of the DC-6B, at 8.35pm, as they crossed Biscayne Bay at 1,200ft.

> *"The lights were 15° higher than the plane and had fuzzy edges and were round. They appeared to hover with the front two connected by a line of light between them. Suddenly they blinked out. The tower also saw them, but couldn't identify them."*

(Source: Mr H.B. Williams/The *Daily Telegraph*, 7.2.1955)

10th February – USA: Half-moon shaped UFO sighted

Mr E.J. Stein – employed as a model maker at Bethesda, Maryland, at US Navy ship design facility – saw an object,

> *"...shaped like a small portion of the bottom of the moon, with a radiant yellow colour, hovering in the sky at 10.03pm, for 30 seconds. Its base then changed to a funnel shape. The total sighting lasted 1-2 minutes".*

24th February – USA: Green fireball seen over Texas

Streaking silently through the sky, the mysterious object was observed by thousands – including three control-tower operators at Pound's Field, one of whom was Mr J. N. Aber, who said:

> *"It was about midnight; this light seemed to pop out of the sky directly over us, like a huge electric arc. It was greenish, like the tip of a welder's torch. It was a blinding light, the brightest that I ever saw. The whole room lit up for a second."*

All three operators agreed that the fireball was moving so swiftly that it crossed the horizon in little more than a second. Its fiery glow was seen as far east as Jackson, Mississippi.

30th April – USA: Four black objects seen

Four black objects in a cluster, making a whooshing sound like a zephyr, were seen in the sky over Travis County, Texas, at 7.30am, by USAF Wing Intelligence Officer Major L.J. Pagozalski. A few seconds later they were out of view.

23rd May – USA: Two vertical rectangles above horizon

At Cheyenne, Wyoming, USAF Airmen I.J. Shapiro and E.C Ingber reported (over a five minute period, beginning at midnight) having watched two slender, vertical 'rectangles', low on the horizon, and two 'ovals' with tops (dark, with dark blue illumination), which then flew higher and out of sight.

25th May – England: UFO seen over Surrey by airline crew

On the 25th May 1955, the crew of a Portuguese Airlines 'Sky-master' aircraft landed at London Airport, and told of having sighted, *"...a long, silver, cigar-shaped object, without wings, pass under the nose of the plane"*, while flying between Epsom and Dunsfold.

Summer – England: UFO sighted over Warren Street, London

We visited John E. Ben – a bio-scientist by occupation, and member of MENSA – at his home address in Nottinghamshire, after learning of his interest in the UFO subject, during a 'wave' of sightings around the Warminster area. He talked about a childhood strewn with fond memories of growing up in the post-war period of London, when his grandparents kept the *'Rose'* Public House, in Warren Street, near Kennington Oval, London – the scene of extensive bombing during World War Two.

> *"I can't be absolutely sure of the exact year. It may have been the summer of 1956. I was walking home from the Henry Fawcett School, where I was a pupil, at the time, on a glorious hot summer's day. I remember crossing the main road – even then a busy one, and entering *Kennington Park along a footpath (known locally as Midnight Walk) and had only gone a couple of hundred yards, when I became aware of a deep throbbing noise. I looked upwards and saw something that terrified me, resembling a slightly flattened shuttlecock, glowing orange in colour, with the rounded part at the top, with a fine purple filament stretching downwards, completing the cone. I was so scared I jumped into some bushes and lay there, trembling, until whatever it was had gone. After a short time, I managed to regain my composure and continued on my journey past the bombed out houses, near Warren Street.*
>
> *Suddenly, to my horror, I heard that horrible sound once again – so loud I could see the corrugated sheets, used to board up the broken windows, shaking from their fixings. I ran home. My grandparents took one look at my soiled state and put me straight in the bath, blaming what had happened on the summer heat... but I knew different."*

(Source: Personal interviews)

5th June – England: UFO seen off the Dutch coast

The crew of the Lowestoft trawler *Grasby* – then 20 miles off the Dutch coast – sighted what looked like a 'shilling' in the sky, as it crossed overhead, at a height of about 10,000 feet. In five minutes if was gone from view – no vapour trail was seen. The time of the incident is not known.

27th June – England: Sighting over Merseyside

On this date, many people living in the Merseyside area sighted what appeared to be a stationary star in the sky – until it headed away at terrific speed – *"Circular in shape, transparent, lit up inside, showing red exhaust. An ordinary aircraft was seen to pass by."*

---

*Kennington Park is a public park in Kennington, London, and lies between Kennington Park Road and St. Agnes Place. It was opened in 1854 on the site of what had been Kennington Common, where the Chartists gathered for their biggest 'monster rally' on 10th April 1848. Soon after this demonstration, the common was enclosed and, sponsored by the royals, made into a public park.

Kennington Common was a site of public executions until 1800, as well as being an area for public speaking. Some of the most illustrious orators to speak here were Methodist founders George Whitefield and John Wesley, who is reputed to have attracted a crowd of 30,000.The common was one of the earliest London cricket venues and is known to have been used for major cricket matches in 1724. Kennington Park hosts the first inner London community cricket ground, sponsored by Surrey County Cricket Club, whose home – The Oval, is close to the park. In the 1970s, the old tradition of mass gatherings returned to the park, which was host to the start of many significant marches to Parliament. Today, this tendency is opposed by a few locals, who prefer the model of the Victorian Park. The Friends of Kennington Park, FoKP, provide a local forum for this struggle. **(Source: Wikipedia)**

3rd July – USA: Close encounter with strange creatures

Mrs Wesley Symmonds of Cincinnati, Ohio, was driving home through Stockton, Georgia, on the way to Florida, when she was astonished to see what she described as being:

> *"...four bug-eyed creatures near the road. They had thin arms, large eyes and pointed chins. Two in the background appeared to be turned away from me; one was bending over with what appeared to be a stick in its hand, the other had its right arm raised and was facing me. He had large bulging eyes, a cap-like affair on his head (or what appeared to be cap), no visible mouth, a long pointed nose, and a chin that came to a sharp point. He had long thin arms, which ended in a claw-like appendage."*

(Sources: Coral Lorenzen, *ORBIT* Civilian Research, Interplanetary Flying Objects Organisation (CRIFO)

7th July – England: 'Flying saucer' over Lowestoft

At mid-morning on 7th July 1955, Ruth Murray from Beccles, near Lowestoft, was cycling through the town with her young son, Roy, when he pointed upwards into the sky and said, *"Look at the lovely star in the sky"*.

Mrs Murray looked for herself and saw 'a flat, glistening silver coloured object', heading silently, at tremendous speed, towards the south-east. She said:

> *"I was so surprised I very nearly dropped the cycle, with my son in the back seat. It was the most beautiful thing I had ever seen. It couldn't have been an aircraft, nor was there any smoke. I watched it for a few seconds, and then it turned black and disappeared."*

(Source: *Lowestoft Journal,* 15.7.1955)

10th July – England: Silver 'disc' sighted over Hammersmith, London

At 4.30pm on 10th July 1955, Mr and Mrs Byway were watching a cricket match at Hammersmith, London, when they noticed a silver 'disc' travelling level with cirrus cloud, at an estimated height of 25,000 feet.

> *"The odd part about it was that there appeared to be two of these things close together, as though they were on top of each other."*

14th July – England: 'Flying saucers' sighted over Bexleyheath, Kent

Unreservedly judged as one of the most important post-war UFO incidents we were to ever come across was the near landing of a UFO in a public street in Bexleyheath, Kent, during a heatwave, in the summer of 1955.

It began with a sighting of something peculiar by local woman – Doris Jacques – who happened to look out of the open French windows at the rear of her house, in Hythe Avenue, at 4pm on 14th July 1955.

Doris:

"I happened to glance upwards and see this glowing orange, dome-shaped, object in the sky, just above the roof of a nearby house. Underneath it was a number of smaller grey, cigar-shaped, objects. After about ten minutes, the little 'cigars' went into the orange dome and, whatever it was, moved away out of sight. My daughter, Pamela – then a pupil at Bedonwell School, behind Brabourne Crescent – arrived home excited, at 3.30pm. Her first words to me were, 'Mummy, did you see the 'flying saucers'?

They were over the school playground, with a bright domed object moving about in the sky, with a lot of other smaller objects – then these moved into the bigger one, which flew away'."

Doris Jacques (left) with Daughter, Pamela Rossiter

In 2006, we spoke to Pamela Rossiter (nee Jacques), who was still living in the London area.

"It all seems so long ago. I suppose my memory of what I actually saw is fading, but the actual event is still clear. I remember being in the playground with other children, when something caught our eye in the sky."

REPORT FORM FOR U.F.O. SIGHTING (No. ....1955 SISM) 586

This organisation has been set up to investigate, collate and analyse reports of Unidentified Flying Objects. It will be of great value if you will kindly give precise details of your observation on the date of BETWEEN 12TH & 15TH JULY, 1955

SECTION A. FULL ACCOUNT OF OBSERVATION

I was sitting reading in my back room facing the garden by the french windows, at about 3pm. when I looked up and gasped. For there was this object glowing in the sky. At the time it was very hot and there were no clouds in a deep blue sky and there it was the only object visable just above & between the roof tops of houses at the bottom of the garden.

I was so astonished that it did not occur to me to go out into the garden, But I did not see it through glass as it was so hot all the windows & french door was open. After about 10 minutes the small grey cigars just went into the orange dome. As soon as they went in it took off in a flash!

My daughters (Pamela) school is just behind Brabourne Cresd The children including her were having an afternoon break in the play-ground when they also saw exactly what I did. When it was time for her to come home she came in excited and said "Mummy did you see the flying Saucers"

I would like to mention my mother-in law about a week earlier saw exactly the same objects over at the back of Marion Park. Charlton S.E 18,

---

At approximately 3.00 one afternoon in the summer of 1955, I was in the school playground when I saw in the sky a large bright dome-shaped object. This was surrounded by a number of smaller objects. After a short time as other children and I were watching, the smaller objects seemed to go into the larger object, and after a few minutes it began to move away until out of site.

MRS PAMELA ROSSITER
33 DULVERSTON ROAD
NEW ELTHAM
KENT

To the best of my knowledge and ability this is a true account of what I saw.

Signed: ..Mrs D. Jaques......... Date: ..11/2/78.........1978
6 HYTHE AVENUE

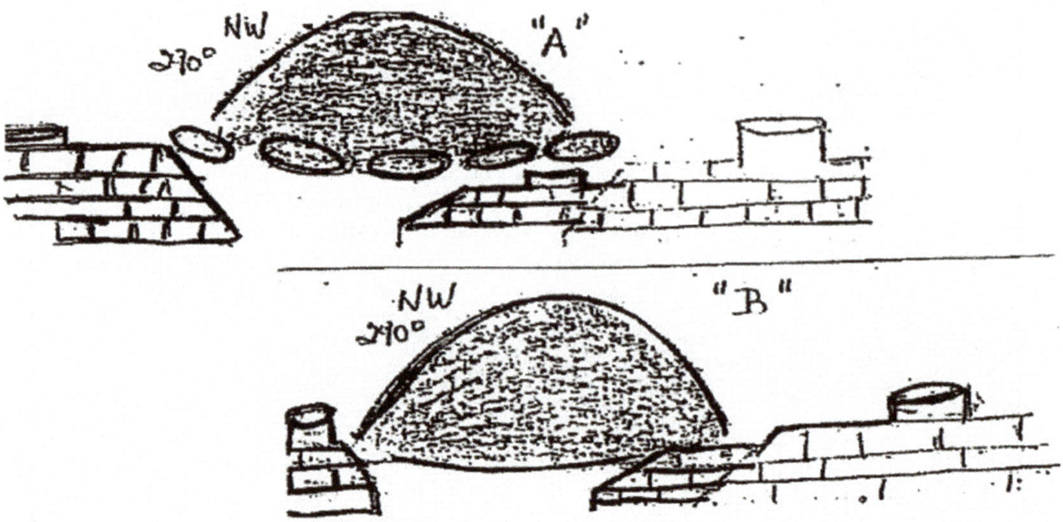

However, she did have a much sharper recollection of a conversation held with her grandmother, Eleanor Jacques, who told her about a cigar-shaped object she saw over Marion Park, Carlton – one of a number of UFOs apparently sighted by her mother, over the years.

17th July – England: UFO causes car to come to a stop

On Sunday 17th July 1955, Margaret Fry – then a young housewife, also living in Hythe Avenue, Bexleyheath, Kent, and on friendly terms with Doris – was on her way to the doctor's surgery, in King Harold's Way, accompanied by the emergency locum, Dr. Thukarta, who was on his way to the surgery to collect some medication for her son, Steven, taken ill with suspected sunstroke.

Black shadow falls over vehicle

Within minutes into the journey, the 'Austin 7' car was plunged into darkness as a black shadow fell across it, cutting off the bright sunlight.

> *"We turned right into Chessington Avenue. The engine of the car began to splutter. The car then came to a halt, near the junction with Ashbourne Avenue and Whitfield Road.*

Margaret Fry

Three objects resembling ball-bearings seen in base of UFO

Wondering what on earth was going on, we got out of the car, to be confronted by the amazing sight of a light-grey elliptical mass, with well-defined edges, about 25 feet in length, sprawled across the junction, roughly 20 feet above our heads.

Out of the base of this grey-silver pewter coloured object – which was divided into sections, apparently riveted together – descended three objects resembling huge ball-bearing wheels, which then retracted upwards, followed by a swishing noise as it began to spin.

Ron and Margaret Fry

Group of children arrive at scene

After a few minutes it rose slightly off the ground, by which time a group of children had arrived. They shouted, 'flying saucer!' Doctor Thukarta kept saying, 'I don't believe what I'm seeing. It's not happening'.

News Shopper (Bexleyheath + Welling) 4 September

www.newsshopper.co.uk **NEWS** BW September

BEXLEYHEATH: *Author appeals for information from 1950s youngsters who saw 'flying saucer'*

UFO kids urged 'phone home'

by LINDA PIPER
lpiper@london.newsquest.co.uk

A FORMER policeman who is researching UFO sightings in Britain is trying to trace a group of Bexleyheath children.

John Hanson, who lives in the West Midlands, is writing up a journal of UFO activity between 1941 and 1982.

He believes the children, now well into their 50s and 60s, could have been witnesses to an extraordinary sighting in Bexleyheath in 1955.

The incident took place on July 17 that year, in King Harold Way, when Margaret Fry, who lived in Hythe Avenue, was making her way to her doctor's surgery.

She and the doctor, Dr Thukarta, both saw what she described as an "enormous craft" hovering over the doctor's car.

She described the craft as saucer-shaped with a "blue/silver/grey/pewter texture, yet, none of those colours."

Mrs Fry said it also had what looked like three spheres inset into its base, one of which "flopped out", landing on the ground at the junction of nearby Ashbourne and Whitfield Road.

A group of twelve children who were playing nearby saw it and went over to have a closer look, before it rose up from the ground and into the sky, disappearing from sight after a few minutes.

Dr Thukarta died in 1965 but Mr Hanson has spoken at length to Mrs Fry, who now lives in North Wales, about her experience.

They would both like to know whether anyone else remembers this incident, particularly the children.

If you were one of those children or know anything about the incident, email Mr Hanson at hanson45@btopenworld.com or write to him at PO Box 10467 Kings Norton, Birmingham B30 1WF.

Alternatively, call News Shopper on 01689 885723.

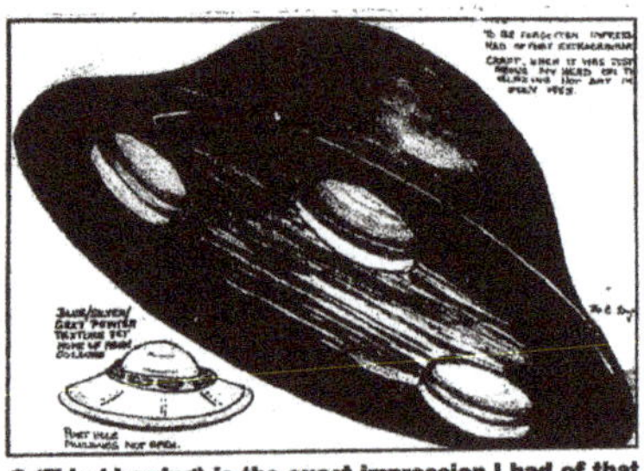

● **'This (drawing) is the exact impression I had of that extraordinary craft, just 18ft above my head on that blazing hot day in July 1955,' wrote Margaret Fry**

Gift troops a good Xmas

WITH the summer almost over, thoughts will soon turn to the next holiday — Christmas.

And once again Ennis Smith, from Crayford, will be collecting Christmas parcels to send

Hair-raising stunts help raise funds for centre

A MAN'S fundraising activities resulted in a close crop during the World Cup, which gave way to a red and white St George flag style, all to raise cash for the Carlton Resource Centre, in Sidcup.

So there were plenty of England flags around when

A few minutes later, it tilted at an angle and rose up to about a hundred feet, where it stopped still in the air. A porthole opened. It then immediately moved quickly upwards, making a 'swishing' noise, and rose about another hundred feet, where it began to slowly rock backwards and forwards, before heading away and out of sight."

Colin Howard

As a result of an appeal launched in the local *Kent News Shopper*, during 2004, asking for any witnesses to come forward, we were contacted by Colin Howard, a long-term resident in the area.

"I remember seeing an identical UFO pass over Bexleyheath in the 1950s. Unfortunately, I can't remember the exact year, or date. It was only when I saw the illustration of the object in the local paper that I decided to break the view of self imposed silence about what I saw, knowing that nobody would have ever believed me."

David Philips

Retired Postman – David Philips – also contacted us.

"I was living on a council estate in Bexleyheath, during July 1955, about a mile away from your publicized incident at King Harold's Way. It was a beautiful hot summer's day, with patchy cloud, when I noticed a 'disc' or saucer-shaped object, hovering a few hundred feet above the ground, about a mile away. Suddenly it tilted, revealing what looked like three ball-bearing-shaped lumps, set into its underside. I was so excited I ran to the house, shouting for my mother and father. As they came running out, whatever it was shot off across the sky – like a black streak of lightning, towards the London area – and was gone."

A visit made to the scene of the incident in 2004

On a visit to the locality, some years ago when we met up with Margaret Fry, Dan Goring and Alan Hilton, we called round to see retired serviceman Rodney Maynard – then aged 15, at the time, and employed as a labourer for a construction company at the Stream Way, Bexleyheath, working on a culvert to stop it flooding, as in those days it was mostly open farmland rather than the busy suburb of today.

"One hot summer's day, in July 1955, I was sat eating my lunch, when I heard the sound of excited voices and people running past. I asked what was happening. Someone mentioned an incident at King Harold's Way. I hadn't a clue what they were on about, but decided to take a look. I ran along Bedonwell Road into King Harold's Way, where I was literally 'stopped in my tracks' by the sight of the most peculiar thing I had ever seen, or was to see, in my life."

To our astonishment, a short time later Margaret proceeded to post leaflets into nearby houses, appealing for any further witnesses to come forward, 49 years after the event, in an act of unparalleled determination to discover further information. Talk about 'true grit' – she epitomised what UFO research was all about, despite suffering from osteoarthritis and life-threatening illnesses. We felt privileged to be there with her.

Did you see the UFO IN 1955?

A WOMAN who claims she stood over a large UFO on a sunny afternoon in Bexleyheath in 1955 returned to the scene last week to search for those who shared the experience with her.

SCOTT SINCLAIR reports...

FOR the first time in two decades Margaret Fry, who now lives in north Wales, stood on the exact spot where, almost 50 years ago, she says she had stared with other excitable residents in bewilderment at the 'pewter coloured object' before her.

Mrs Fry, who used to live in Hythe Avenue, Bexleyheath is desperate to speak with those children who had shouted: "It's a flying saucer", after it had flipped and landed at the T-junction of Ashbourne Avenue and Chessington Avenue, on Sunday, July 17, 1955.

Researcher

Mrs Fry, who has been a UFO researcher for 38 years as a result of her experience, said: "This is the first opportunity I have had in 22 years to come to Bexleyheath to try and jog the memory of those people who had lived in this area all those years ago.

"There are parts of the event I can not remember but some memories will never leave me.

"That week, there had been a heatwave. Temperatures touched 101 degrees. My eldest son had sunstroke and the doctor who came to tend to him suggested we go in his car to King Harold's Way surgery for medication.

"It was about midday. As soon as we left our house, there was a heavy shadow over our Austin car and the engine stalled. We got out and there was this thing spinning about 16ft above our heads. It just flipped and flopped on to the road.

"I remember there were children playing hopscotch on the pavement and they all came and stood around this craft.

"It was the traditional bell shape, which people may have probably seen on the TV.

"We were all aghast and they were yelling that it was a flying saucer. It stayed perfectly still for about sever minutes. Then it flew upwards and away. It took about another six or seven minutes for it to be out of sight.

"The doctor who was with me did report the incident to the British Medica Board. He was a locum for our GP, Dr Lobo, of Parsonage Manor Way.

"I am trying to trace one of those children who saw this thing with us.

I have tried off and on for the last 49 years to trace them. They must all be in their 50s now.

"Taough I understand that this is hardly believable, there are no doubts in my mind that we saw an extra-terrestrial craft that day."

'There were children playing hopscotch on the pavement and they all came and stood around this craft'

Margaret has now teamed up with UFO researchers John Hanson and Dawn Holloway, who are attempting to help Mrs Fry in her search.

Mr Hanson is writing a book on the subject, compiling the testimonies of dozens of individuals who have made sightings down the years.

He said: "If anybody had told me during my youth that I would be involved in the UFO subject, I would have dismissed this suggestion out-of-hand, believing that flying saucers and UFOs were representative of science-fiction, rather than reality.

"But after researching this subject during the course of the last nearly 10 years, along with my companion Dawn Holloway, it is apparent that the UFO phenomena is very much alive."

SEARCHING FOR CLUES: Margaret Fry. contributed picture

● If you would like to get in touch with Margaret Fry, contact Scott Sinclair at the *Kentish Times* on 020 8269 7000 or e-mail scott.sinclair@archant.co.uk

Dots seen over surface of 'craft' (see sighting 27th April 1956)

"I wasn't scared. My first thoughts were that somebody must have put it there. It never entered my mind that it could have been a 'flying saucer'. It just lay there on the gravel, making no noise, surrounded by at least sixty people, including many children, who stood there watching as it flashed with light, at second intervals - so bright it hurt to look for too long. On top of the object was this oval-shaped protrusion that reminded me of a nipple. I decided to get closer to the structure, which looked like beaten silver, with tiny dots all over it [and] with these massive suckers underneath. I shouted out to my brother.

We were so close, we could have touched it. The object began to wobble from side to side, the suckers drawing in slightly.

People started to shout, now alarmed.

In a blur of movement – too fast for the eye to catch – it left, leaving an image on the retina, which lasted for a few seconds.

I looked across the sky and saw it tilt, before coming to a halt in mid-air over Bedonwell School, where it stayed for about two hours."

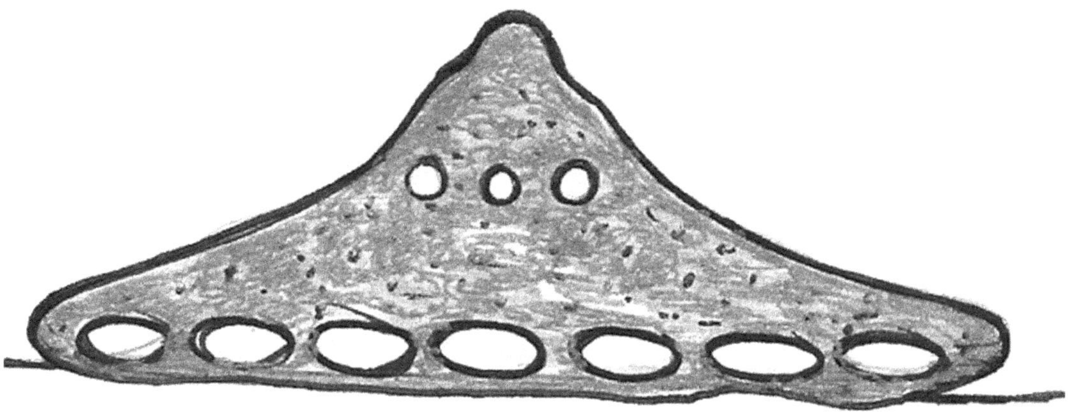

Police warned him to keep quiet

Rodney told us, some weeks after the incident, that he received a call from the local Police Constable, who warned him to keep quiet and not to talk about it to anybody – which is what he did, until he came forward to speak to us.

We asked Rodney if he had noticed any medical problems following the incident. He replied:

"Not really, but I did notice a number of unusual marks on my body, a few months later – something the doctors were unable to diagnose. The marks are still prominent on my body to this present date."

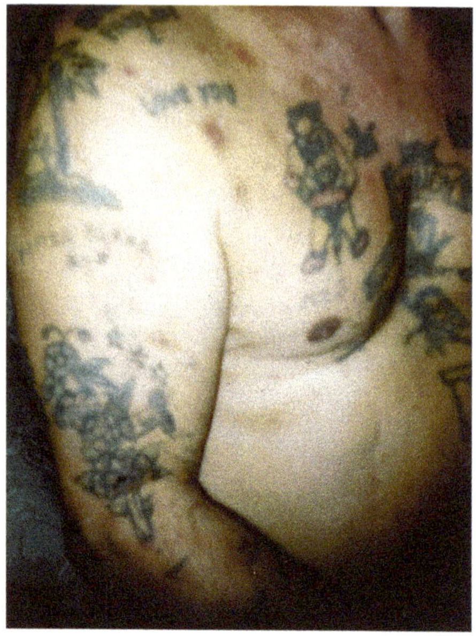

Rodney named a number of 'children' present at the scene in the local newspaper, including his brother (who had passed away). Unfortunately, despite publicity and our own research, through electoral rolls, we were unable to find those witnesses and felt he was apparently genuine, understanding the similarity in description between what he and Margaret had seen, but there was one flaw with his story. Rodney said he was working at the time, which meant it was unlikely to be a Sunday (as in those days Sunday was sacrosanct, unlike today). However, if the work was vital to prevent flooding, maybe he was working on the Sunday (?) – Surely unlikely, as this was a hot summer, rather than a wet winter, and with no danger of flooding. Is it possible that he saw the object on the same day as Mrs Jacques? If so, why did the landing take place at the same location, and why did both incidents involve children? Could there have been two separate near landings? We think there were.

Police Constable Jim Streek

Jim Streek – a retired police officer from the Kent Constabulary – contacted us about an incident he witnessed, while on duty at Sidcup Police Station, Kent, in mid-July 1955.

> *"I was on duty and assisting in the return of property to some women, when I overheard a conversation about a 'flying saucer' that had landed in King Harold's Way. I told the station sergeant what I had heard. He laughed at me and told me it must be a 'load of baloney'. My curiosity was aroused and, after completing my shift, I changed into 'civvies' and went to have a look, as the women had seemed serious.*
>
> *When I arrived in King Harold's Way, after cycling there, I noticed a small group of children talking to two smartly dressed men (one of whom had a clipboard with him) standing next to a large black car. As they looked like officials from a government department, I decided not to announce myself and left. It was only after all those years later, when I read about the article in the newspaper, did I realise the connection."*

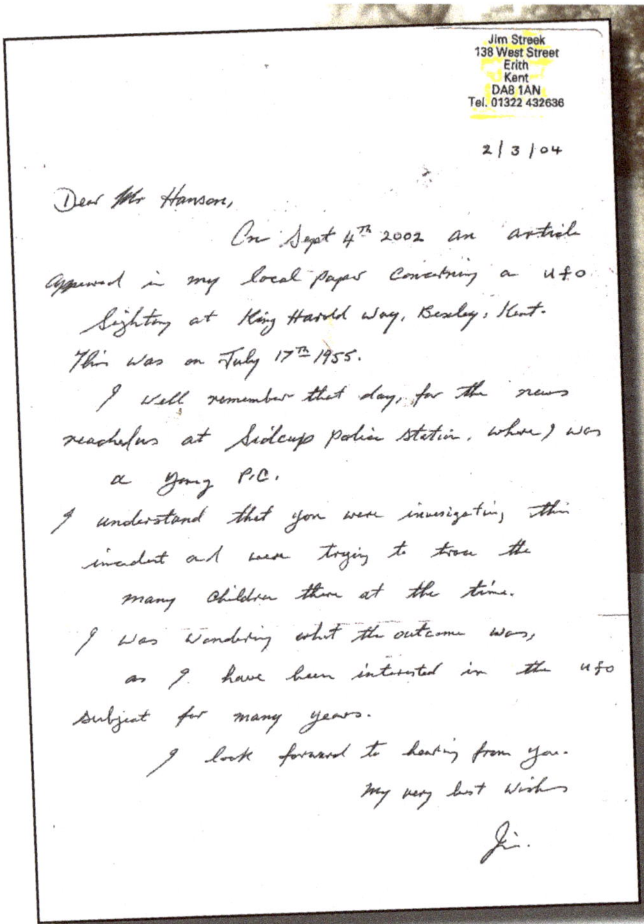

Jim Streek
138 West Street
Erith
Kent
DA8 1AN
Tel. 01322 432636

2/3/04

Dear Mr Hanson,

On Sept 4th 2002 an article appeared in my local paper concerning a UFO Sighting at King Harold Way, Bexley, Kent. This was on July 17th 1955.

I well remember that day, for the news reached us at Sidcup police station, where I was a young P.C.

I understand that you were investigating this incident and were trying to trace the many children there at the time.

I was wondering what the outcome was, as I have been interested in the UFO subject for many years.

I look forward to hearing from you.

My very best wishes

Jim.

Police Constable Jim Streek

Another witness

Another witness to the strange events that occurred on the 17th July, 1955, was a young man, whose details we have withheld – then living in Meopham, Kent. He told Margaret Fry:

> *"I was walking my dog on 'The Green', when I saw an object resembling a huge grey 'cigar', with a line of horizontal portholes of frosted glass along its length, motionless in the air, about a hundred feet above me, with what appeared to be 'figures' gazing down at me."*

Sadly, tragedy was to strike the man down, after he was seriously injured while holidaying in the Rocky Mountains, a few months later, and was brought back to England in a coma, where he died at Dartford Hospital, followed – bizarrely – by the death of his fiancée, who fell from a horse in Australia.

Unsigned letter from Erith woman

In 2005, Margaret received an unsigned letter with an Erith, Kent, postmark, from a woman, who had this to say:

> *"Dear Mrs Fry,*
>
> *I will tell you what I experienced and will leave it at that; hence why this letter has no address and name.*

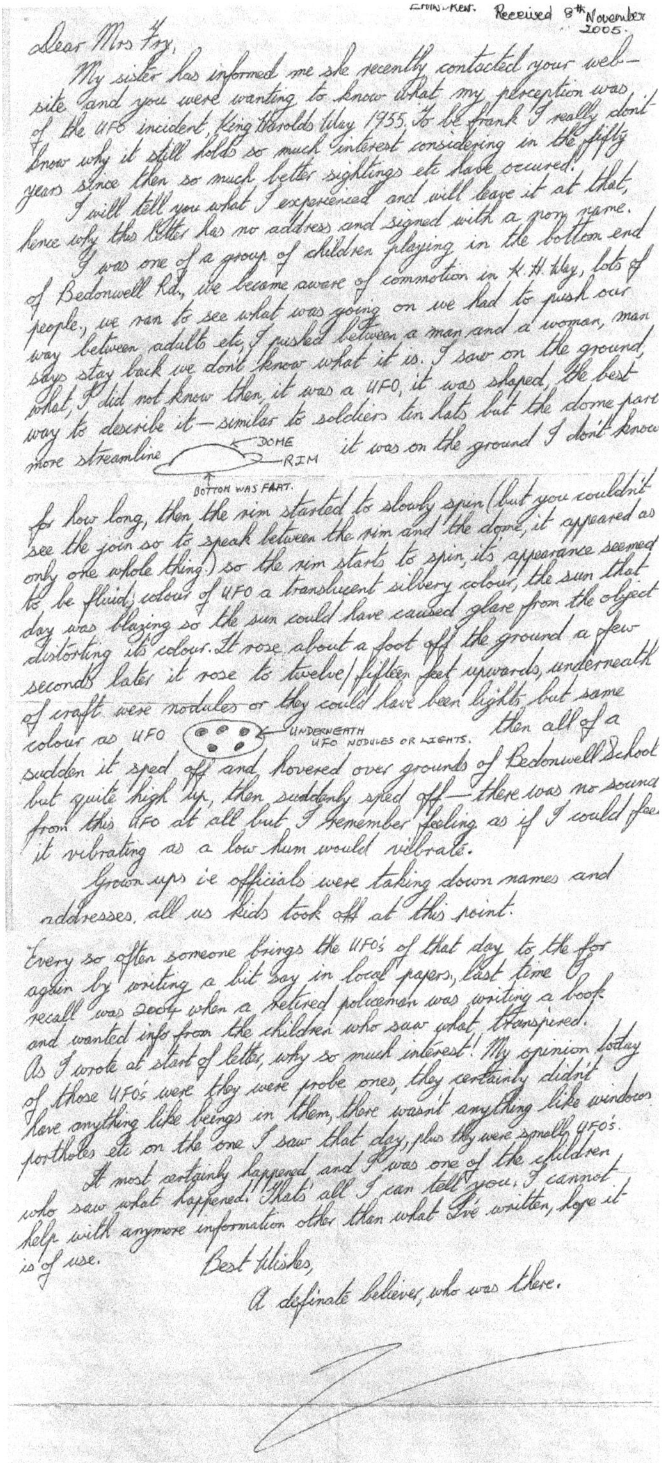

EMIN-KENT. Received 8th November 2005.

Dear Mrs Fry,
My sister has informed me she recently contacted your web-
site and you were wanting to know what my perception was
of the UFO incident, King Harolds Way 1955. To be frank I really don't
know why it still holds so much interest considering in the fifty
years since then so much better sightings etc have occured.
I will tell you what I experienced and will leave it at that,
hence why this letter has no address and signed with a nom name.
I was one of a group of children playing in the bottom end
of Bedonwell Rd., we became aware of commotion in K.H. Way, lots of
people, we ran to see what was going on we had to push our
way between adults etc, I pushed between a man and a woman, man
says stay back we don't know what it is. I saw on the ground,
what, I did not know then, it was a UFO, it was shaped, the best
way to describe it — similar to soldiers tin hats but the dome part
more streamline [sketch: DOME, RIM, BOTTOM WAS FLAT.] it was on the ground I don't know
for how long, then the rim started to slowly spin (but you couldn't
see the join so to speak between the rim and the dome, it appeared as
only one whole thing) so the rim starts to spin, its appearance seemed
to be fluid; colour of UFO a translucent silvery colour, the sun that
day was blazing so the sun could have caused glare from the object
distorting its colour. It rose about a foot off the ground a few
seconds later it rose to twelve/fifteen feet upwards, underneath
of craft were nodules or they could have been lights, but same
colour as UFO [sketch: UNDERNEATH UFO NODULES OR LIGHTS.] then all of a
sudden it sped off and hovered over grounds of Bedonwell School
but quite high up, then suddenly sped off — there was no sound
from this UFO at all but I remember feeling as if I could feel
it vibrating as a low hum would vibrate.
Grown ups ie officials were taking down names and
addresses, all us kids took off at this point.
Every so often someone brings the UFO's of that day to the for
again by writing a bit say in local papers, last time I
recall was 2004 when a retired policemen was writing a book
and wanted info from the children who saw what transpired.
As I wrote at start of letter, why so much interest! My opinion today
of those UFO's were they were probe ones, they certainly didn't
have anything like beings in them, there wasn't anything like windows
portholes etc on the one I saw that day, plus they were smally UFO's.
It most certainly happened and I was one of the children
who saw what happened! That's all I can tell you. I cannot
help with anymore information other than what I've written, hope it
is of use.
Best Wishes,
A definate believer, who was there.

I was one of a group of children, playing in the bottom end of Bedonwell Road, when we became aware of a commotion in King Harold's Way, involving lots of people. I ran to see what was going on and had to push my way between a man and woman.

Object like a tin soldier's hat seen on the ground

The man said, 'Stay back, we don't know what it is'. I looked and saw on the ground an object in shape similar to a soldier's tin hat, but the dome part more streamlined. It was on the ground I don't know how long, but then the rim started to slowly spin. You couldn't see the 'join', so as to speak, between the rim and the dome. It appeared as one whole thing; the rim started to spin.

Nodules on the body of the 'craft'

Its appearance seemed to be fluid – a translucent silvery colour. The sun that day was blazing, so the sun could have caused the glare from the object distorting its colour. It then rose about a foot off the floor. A few seconds later, it rose 12-15 feet. Underneath the 'craft' were nodules; they could have been lights, but same colour as the UFO.
All of a sudden, it sped off and hovered over Bedonwell School, but quite high up, then suddenly it sped silently away, but I remember feeling a low hum vibration. There were grown-ups taking children's details, so all us kids took off at this point.

My opinion, today, of those UFOs are that they were probes. There certainly didn't look anything like 'beings' in them. There wasn't anything like windows, portholes, etc., on the one I saw that day, plus they were small UFOs. It most certainly happened and I was one of the children who saw what happened. That's all I can tell you. I cannot help with any more information, other than what I've written. Hope it is of use. Best wishes,

Signed,
A definite believer"

Whilst we have no idea whether the author of this letter is genuine, we felt our quest to discover further information about what had, after all, been a spectacular landing of something inexplicable, and the whereabouts of some of the other 'children', were drawing to a close – although Margaret remained eternally optimistic that 'her children' would come forward.

Doctor Thukarta

We wrote to the British Medical Board, hoping to obtain a copy of the report submitted by Dr Thukarta. They had no such knowledge – not surprising under the circumstances.

Margaret Fry, 2016 – now published two books

"You might wonder how a person feels after an experience like this. For weeks afterwards, I felt in two worlds, as to speak. I also felt isolated, as there was nobody I could really discuss it with, but you have to put it out of your mind and get on with your life. What happened to me was to trigger off a lifetime's interest in the UFO subject. I began by joining BUFORA and met the Earl of Clancarty, who asked me to join Contact International – which I did. I still represent them today. In October, 1993, Gary Rowe of Rhyl, and I, formed the Welsh Federation of Independent Ufologists."

Since then Margaret has published two books one of which covers this sighting, and has been the subject of newspaper appeals with regard to tracing any further witnesses to that event – now 60 years on.

During her visit to Bexleyheath Margaret also met up with long life friends Alan Hilton (now sadly passed away) and Dan Goring ex editor of the UFO magazine *Earthlink*.

One cannot help but contrast the visual image of what was seen here by a number of witnesses and that described by Mr George Adamski –whatever you think of his encounters one shouldn't ignore the evidence presented by so many others over the years that can appears to corroborate his version of the events which took place.

Dan Goring with Margaret

Dawn Holloway with Alan Hilton

Another example of a similar craft is shown here which was seen to land by the witnesses at Gosport in Hampshire during 1965.

July – England: Two silver 'disc'-shaped objects over Coventry

In July 1955, Mrs Barbara Anderson from Binley, Coventry, was at her home address when her husband shouted out:

> *"Quick! Look outside. There are two 'flying saucers' going over!"*

Mrs Anderson:

> *"I carried on with my work, thinking he was messing about. Out of interest, I looked up in the sky. There was nothing to be seen. I thought no more about it until we were returning home, at 10pm, on a clear night, when I remembered the incident and jokingly said out aloud, 'We might see your UFOs', at which point an incredible thing happened – above our heads appeared two silver coloured 'discs', which turned and moved out of sight."*

(Source: Bob Tibbitts, Coventry UFO Research Group)

22nd July – England: Bright objects over Leicester

A formation of bright spherical 'balls of light' was seen flying over Leicester, at 11pm on 22nd July 1955, heading in a north- east direction. As they passed overhead, they changed formation.

24th July – England: Three objects seen over Leeds

Three mysterious objects – two of them silver, the third amber in colour – were seen heading across the sky, over Leeds, by a man walking along Leith Street.

> *"I first saw them as two pear-shaped silver objects, which turned to one side in flight and glinted in the sun. A similar object but amber in colour came into view and spiralled around the other two, and moved back at tremendous speed in a reverse direction. Four minutes later, they were out of view."*

(Source: *Flying Saucer News*, autumn 1955)

25th July – England: Silver metallic object seen over Essex

On 25th July 1955, a silver-grey metallic object, rounded on one side and covered with white haze, was seen flying slowly across the sky over Shoebury, in Essex, heading towards the north-east, before vanishing from view. During the same day, William Drury from Walsall, West Midlands, contacted the *Walsall Observer*, after he sighted:

> *"...a glittering, silver object, which passed in a leisurely manner over my back garden, and made off towards the direction of Walsall Aerodrome. It then disappeared, after a dark round cloud seemed to envelop it."*

26th July – England: Dark 'boomerang' UFO seen over Hampshire

On 26th July 1955, a dark 'boomerang'-shaped object – estimated to be 40 feet from tip to tip – was sighted by officials at Lasham Airfield, in Hampshire, to be hovering in the sky for about thirty seconds, at a height of some 3,000 feet above Britain's gliding champion *Philip Aubrey Wills, before heading off in a north-westerly direction, at speed. Details were forwarded to the Air Ministry and appeared in the local and national press. One of the witnesses in this matter was Mrs Yvonne Bonham – Secretary of the Gliding Association. She said:

> *"I estimated it to have a width of 40 feet and was hovering at 3,000 feet. I saw it for thirty seconds."*

Philip Aubrey Wills

*Philip Aubrey Wills, CBE (26th May 1907-16th January 1978) was a pioneering British glider pilot. He broke several gliding records and was the 1952 Open Class World Champion. He remained a regular member of the British team until 1958. He was second in command of the Air Transport Auxiliary, during World War Two. He was chairman of the British Gliding Association for 19 years and was awarded the CBE and the Lilienthal Gliding Medal for services to gliding.

26th July – USA: UFO hovers over Airport – knocks lights out

A brilliant, circular UFO – leaving a trail, four or five times its own length – flew over Washington National Airport, stopping and hovering as it did so. It was caught in the beam of searchlight, and then the searchlight went out. The UFO also caused the ceiling lights at the airport to go out, but these lit up again after it left.

27th July – England: Object seen in the sky

At 8pm, a cylindrical object was sighted over Liverpool, hovering over the Lever building, by Mr Jones and a number of his dock worker colleagues. On the same evening, a retired headmaster from Ellesmere Port, and his neighbour – an unnamed *Liverpool Evening Express* sports columnist – watched a mysterious object in the sky for some five minutes.

29th July – USA: Four orange flashing lights reported

At 10.45pm, Columbus, Nebraska resident – Maurice Raymond – sighted four orange flashing lights and one white flashing light,

> *"...moving up and down like yo-yos in the sky", for five to six minutes.*

15th/16th August – England: 'Flying saucer' over Yorkshire

During the evening of 15th August 1955, a number of strange objects were seen moving through the sky over the Yorkshire area.

A golden 'ball of light' was seen trailing smoke and sparks over Ilkley, by the witness – David Fletcher, of Raikes Hill, Silsden, near Bradford. This was followed by a report of a white 'streak of light' seen flashing along the water's edge at Heysham Harbour, and an illuminated multicoloured cigar-shaped object sighted over Bradford.

Alec Clarke – Chief Reporter for the 'Chronicle'

Mr Alec Clarke – the Chief Reporter for the *Chronicle* newspaper – was in his garden at Willaston, at about 8.15pm, when he saw a 'bright light' streaking across the sky.

> *"It was no more than a mile up. In fact, it seemed much less and went across the sky – like a rocket from a fireworks display and petered out in the same way."*

He contacted Jodrell Bank Radio Experimental Station, who told them they had not received any other reports, pointing out there had been many 'bright lights' in the sky, part of the Perseids meteor shower prevalent in the sky at that time.

> *"With regard to Mr Shaw's object, we are of the opinion it was a jet plane, as one was actually in the vicinity. It is surprising how people are easily deceived in that way. It was probably the rays of the sun reflected on the plane."* **(Source: Gavin Gibbons)**

August – Wales: Close encounter with panelled UFO

Mr Leonard Ferriday was out walking along a mountainside trail, near Maesteg, Mid Glamorgan, in August 1955, at 6.00am, on what was a clear, fine day – blue skies, with an early morning thick mist obscuring the valley below him – when he noticed a small 'spot of light' in the sky towards the west. Suddenly, without any further warning, to his utter amazement, and in a matter of seconds, he was confronted by the appearance of a saucer-shaped object, hovering in the air, 40 feet away from him, before descending to a height of some 20ft off the ground.

"It was about the size of a transit van and silver coloured, with patches of blue, pink, green and brown, covering the outside surface. There were about a dozen vertical panels moving around the middle row, left to right. On the top was a translucent dome. It hovered silently in front of me. I didn't know what to do and just stood there and watched it for about 30 minutes, before it launched itself into the sky, making a whooshing noise, and disappeared over the mountain." **(Source: Personal interview)**

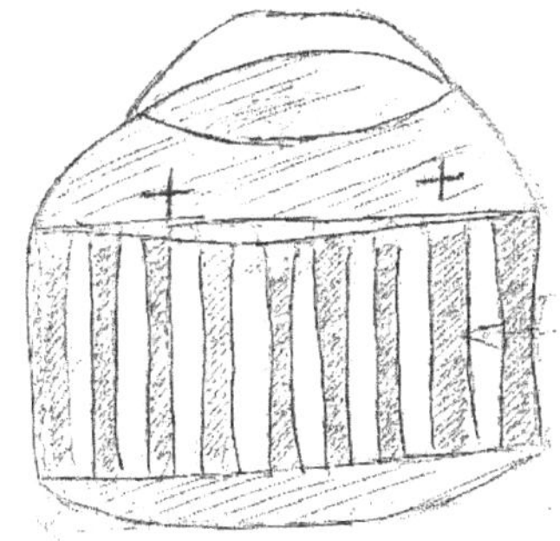

15th August – England: 'Flying saucer' over Cheshire, RAF scrambled

At 7.30pm on 15th August 1955, Geoffrey Shaw – a sub-postmaster, living in a small village on the A531, situated halfway between Crewe and Newcastle-under-Lyme, Cheshire – sighted, on a bright sunlit day, what appeared to be a 'flying saucer', two to three miles away, about a mile high, in the sky.

"My attention was attracted by an extreme brilliant point of light in the sky – like the reflection from a mirror. It seemed to come from a dome-shaped object, either highly polished glass, or metal. I watched it remain perfectly stationary for about three minutes. As my eyes became accustomed to the glare, I could make out the shadowy outline of a circular background. I then noticed a jet aircraft approaching from the east, its vapour trail showing. By now, the object, nearly circular in shape, was moving directly away from me – its brightness diminishing, the reflective surface turning almost a leaden colour, showing a bright rim and knob to one side – which may have been part of the dome – still visible to the eye. As it vanished into the far distance, the jet roared over the spot where the object had been and turned towards Ternhill Aerodrome."

Interviewed by Gavin Gibbons

In an interview held with local 'flying saucer' researcher, Gavin Gibbons, Mr Betley handed over a sketch of the 'craft', which appears similar to what was seen by Mrs Margaret Fry, on the 17th of July 1955. Interestingly, he also described seeing the three rings in its base, as it hovered overhead. Another witness to the event was Mrs Piggott, from a different part of the village, and Mr Kenneth Steventon.

"What I saw is a distant memory now, but I remember seeing a 'bright light' in the sky to the south-east, while walking down towards Wrinehill at about 7pm. I later passed on the information to Mr Shaw." **(Source: Personal interview)**

16th August – England: Encounter with humanoid at Bradford

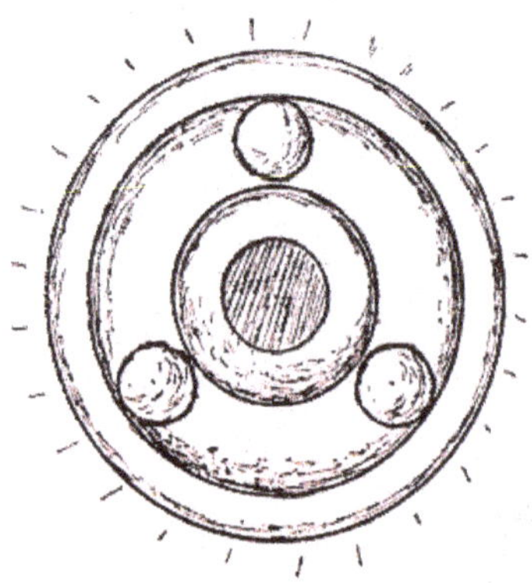

Shortly before 4am on 16th August 1955, Bradford lorry driver, Ernest Suddards (35), was on his way home, after collecting the firm's lorry from the garage where it was kept overnight, accompanied by his son Raymond (13).

As they drove down Roundhill Street, a short distance from the family home, they saw something or someone approaching in the glare of the headlights.

Mr Suddards:

> *"It looked about 4 feet tall, dressed in skin-tight black clothes, with arms close to its sides, with feet together, and hopped or jumped forwards, in a series of jerky movements. On its chest was a circular silver disc, with holes cut into it, below the throat. It then turned down a nearby passage. We were literally paralysed by the sight. After arriving home, we talked about it and then contacted the police, who had a look around but found nothing."*

WAS IT A FLYING SAUCER? 8/60

Brilliant object over Crewe

REPORTS of an oval-shaped object in the sky, about a mile high, on Monday night has revived local interest in flying saucers.

One report, given to "The Chronicle" on Tuesday morning, came from Mr. G. Shaw, sub-postmaster at Betley. He was exercising his dog at about 7.30 p.m. and walking in the Wrinehill direction.

He said, "My attention was suddenly attracted by a brilliant yellow light in the sky about five to six thousand feet high. It was oval-shaped and appeared to be perfectly stationary for about four minutes. It then turned on its side and went away in the direction of Chester, vanishing into the evening sky."

Immediately afterwards, said Mr. Shaw, a jet plane appeared from the Tern Hill direction, as if it was chasing the object

"From anywhere"

"The Chronicle" got into touch with Tern Hill but the Station adjutant said he had received no report of such an object and there was no jet plane from his station in that vicinity at that time. "If there was a plane it could have been from anywhere," he said.

About three-quarters of an hour after the incident reported by Mr. Shaw "The Crewe Chronicle" chief reporter, Mr. Alec Clarke, was in his garden at Willaston when he suddenly saw a bright light streaking across he sky. According to Mr. Clarke, "It was no more than a mile up—in fact, it seemed much less— and it went across the sky like a rocket from a fireworks display and petered out in the same way."

"The Chronicle" got into touch with Jodrell Bank Radio-Astronomical experimental station who had not seen or received any report of the object. It was stated that during this past week there had been many bright lights in the sky and that most of them were part of the Perseid meteor shower prevalent at this time.

"Unlikely"

Asked whether it would be possible for such showers to peter out like a rocket at 6,000 feet, the Jodrell Bank expert said it was most unlikely.

With regard to Mr. Shaw's object, they were of the opinion that it was a jet plane, as one was actually in the vicinity. "It is surprising," they said, "how people are easily deceived in that way. It was probabaly the rays of the sun reflected on the plane."

The Jodrell Bank people added that they had received a report of a brilliant light at 11 p.m. that night but that was probably a part of the Perseid meteor shower.

Did a SPACE-VISITOR Land in BRADFORD?

BY JACK IBSON

The night of August 15th saw considerable saucer activity over Yorkshire. A golden ball was reported from Silsden, in the direction Ilkley; a white streak was seen flashing along the water's edge at Morecambe, travelling towards Heysham harbour, and a cigar-shaped object was observed travelling slowly across the sky over Wakefield, which seemed to be flourescent and illuminated in various colours.

The strangest story, however, concerns the "Thing" that a Bradford lorry driver and his 13 year old son say they saw hopping up Roundhill Street at 4 o'clock the following morning. Our correspondent JACK IBSON interviewed the witnesses and here is his report:

ERNEST SUDDARDS, a matter of fact type, lorry driver, aged about 35, married, with two children, said he himself always laughed at unusual news reports such as Flying Saucers etc., but this incident had him completely shaken. He and his son had just been to collect the lorry from a garage about a mile away. They were coming down Roundhill Street, and as they were almost a few yards from their home, their blood chilled and their hair almost stood on end—for, approaching them in the glare of the headlights was—the **"Thing."**

Mr. Suddards described it as being **like a boy, or small human being, 4ft. tall, dressed in skin tight black clothes, arms down by sides and feet together.** It did not walk, but "hopped," or, more correctly **jumped** in jerky movements, both feet together—and seemed dazzled by the headlights.

Most revealing feature, which shone distinctly in the headlamps was a **circular silver disc**, perforated with holes, and situated on the chest, just below the throat. The "thing" moved forwards another few yards, then turned abruptly right into a passage, below Mr. Suddards' home. He and his son sat in the cab of the lorry, stunned and unable to move, for some time, and Mr. Suddards remarked to me that he would not have gone up that passage for a thousand pounds.

Eventually, they went home, and Mrs. Suddards confirmed to me that they had been shaky, pale and looked as though they had seen a ghost. They were fully half an hour in recovering and deciding what to do.

The "Thing"

The police arrived a few minutes after being telephoned, and questioned both Mr. Suddards and his boy separately, and since both gave the details with great clarity the Officer decided there " must be something in it " and organised a search of the neighbourhood. However, nothing at all was found. Mr. Suddards told me how he was derided and laughed at by his workmates the next day; " But they can say what they like—**I did see it !** " he affirmed. He didn't report it to the local newspaper, but they came to see him after seeing the Police report.

NOT OF EARTH

The only evaluation, to my mind, can be that Mr. Suddards was telling the truth, and that the details were correct. Animal ? I don't think so—not moving in jumps—there being no loose Kangaroos in the area !—and in any case what animal has a silver perforated disc on its chest ? Boy ? It could have been—but what child would be out at that time in the morning **with hands and feet tied ?**

Moving in jumps is very tiring—I tried it. No ; we have to recognise that it was some strange form of humanity—but not, apparently, of this world. The perforated disc could have been a breathing aid—and moving in jumps may be quite common on some other planet—with perhaps less gravity than ours.

SEQUEL

The matter may well have rested there, but a little while later, I had a phone call from Mr. Suddards, who told me he had met a Mr. Joseph Wood in the " local," and Mr. Wood, after being told of Mr. Suddards' experience, then recounted having seen a strange thing in a field about three or four days after the report of the " Thing." I called to see Mr. Wood, and found him to be an unimaginative type ; warehouseman, aged about 30 —not familiar with saucers or space theories.

He was walking along a short-cut, near Bowling Park, at about 11.30 p.m. on August 19th, when he saw, reflect-

ing a nearby street lamp, a bright (" like chromium plating ") silver bullet shape, stood upright behind a small hillock. The height was about 12ft—though the base was not visible—and the diameter about 4 or 5 feet.

From it was coming a high-pitched buzzing—like a radio set out out of order. Mr. Wood said he went cold, and shivers ran up his spine. He hurried away as fast as he could, but passed again on his return journey (he'd been visiting a friend) at about midnight, he saw the object was still there. A horse approached it but suddenly started back and raced away.

The area in question is within half a mile of Roundhill Street, where the Suddards' " Thing " was seen.

• • •

FOOTNOTE : The latest rumour about landings has been one put over by Dorothy Kilgallen, well known American columnist. She stated that, on a recent visit to Britain she learned that a saucer had crashed in this country, and from the wreckage British officials had deduced that it had been manned by beings about 4ft. tall.

Of course, no confirmation whatsoever can be obtained concerning this report, from any source, but it is interesting to note that the similarity in height ties up—and the description by the Suddards also bears a startling resemblance to the creatures described by Marius Dewilde, who claimed to have encountered two strange beings in France last year. (See " F. S. News " No. 7)

We spoke to Ray Suddards some years ago about this matter, who was himself a lorry driver by occupation.

> *"I remember it clearly – like it was yesterday. It had this silver plate, with holes on its chest, hopping up Roundhill Street. After my dad reported what we had seen, he was subjected to a lot of ridicule. A few days later, he picked up a newspaper and read about a similar 'figure' being seen in Horton Lane, close to where we had seen it."*

The sighting led to much speculation. Some people believed that what the Suddards' had witnessed was the lone occupant of a downed 'flying saucer'; others thought it might have been a ghost.

Following an appeal in the *Bradford Telegraph & Argus*, we were contacted by Detective Sergeant Paul Jackson (retired), who recalls the incident very well, because his partner, at the time, was P.C. Victor Briggs – the officer who interviewed them and made a search of the area.

> *"He (Police Constable Briggs) often brought up the subject in conversation, as he believed they had genuinely sighted something highly unusual."*

On the same day people living in the Gloucestershire area contacted the police, after sighting an ovoid or cigar-shaped object at 8.20pm. The object was described as being bright and leaving sparks behind in flight. It had a pale-green centre and silver at the edges. It also displayed an orange light – others claimed blue lights – and was last seen heading in a north-west direction.

19th August – England: Landed UFO at Bradford

On 19th August 1955, Mr Wood – a warehouseman, from Bradford – was walking past Bowling Park, about half-a-mile from Roundhill Street, at 11.30pm, when he noticed a bright silver bullet-shaped object, approximately 12 feet in height and four feet in width, standing upright near a hillock, making a high-pitched buzzing noise.

Upon his return, thirty minutes later, the object was still there, according to Mr Wood, who found its appearance very frightening and spoke of seeing a horse approach the object and then run away, clearly disturbed. Was there a connection between what the Suddards' saw and the mysterious UFO, or is there a rational explanation?

21st August – USA: Alien or ghostly spectres?

There have been numerous books, documentaries and debates, regarding this incident, which alleges a close encounter with extraterrestrial beings on the 21st August 1955. The incident became famous and well-publicized.

STAR, Indianapolis, IN - Aug. 23, 1955

Theye're Stealing Our Stuff

'Little Green Men From Spaceship' Give Family In Kentucky Night Of Terror

Hopkinsville, Ky. (UP) — A Kentucky farm family near here had local, county and state police in a quandary yesterday with reports of a visit from a "spaceship with little green men" aboard.

Cecil Sutton, his family and several relatives said they were up all night fending off the little men who glowed with an inner illumination while climbing trees and crawling about the roof of his home.

Hundreds of neighbors and curiosity seekers thronged the Suttons' yard and the neighboring fields yesterday and some returned last night to see if the spacemen come again.

Kentucky State police and local sheriff's officers who investigated the weird reports from the Sutton home six miles north of here were unable to find any trace of the "space visitors."

"That is because they used lights all over the place." Sutton said, "you can't see them except in the dark."

WHEN ASKED IF they expected the spacemen to return, Mrs. Sutton said, "That's what I'm skittedy about. They might be back."

The Suttons told this tale of the nightmarish visit:

About 7:30 Sunday evening, Bill Taylor, a visiting relative, went to a well near the home and came back to the house excitedly talking of a "spaceship" in a nearby field.

A few minutes later, "a little green man" approached the house. "He was about 3 feet tall, with eyes like saucers and set about 6 inches apart, with hands like claws and glowing all over," Sutton said.

About five feet from the door of the house he stopped and retreated when the Suttons fired a shotgun off into the air.

BUT SOON HE returned again, and the Suttons fired at him. He fell down from the blast, and then ran off into the fields.

Later more of the men returned and climbed about the trees and on the roof of the house which the beleaguered Suttons watched furtively.

After about three hours, the Suttons ran for their car and went into Hopkinsville to call the sheriff.

Deputy George Batts and two state troopers failed to find any clews to the visit during a thorough search of the grounds, but after they left the Suttons said the little men were still there and remained until dawn.

The police officers said there definitely was no one drinking at the Sutton home Sunday night.

Seven adults and three children were in the home during the reported visit from outer space.

From FRANK GARVAN in New York

'SAVE US FROM THE LITTLE GREEN MEN'

'Flying saucers' have been photographed — many times. But no-one has yet proved they come from anywhere but earth

Was it a flying saucer that landed in a Kentucky field and terrified a farming family . . . or were they just seeing things?

DO you believe in little green men with eyes like saucers, hands like claws, pointed ears and nickel-plated chests?

Would you reckon they came out of a flying saucer or an upturned bottle. Before my holiday in Kentucky I would have plumped for the bottle. Now . . .

Moonmen or moonshine? Listen to the story . . . and you be the judge.

Shortly before midnight on August 21, 1955, a couple of cars roared into the small Kentucky town of Hopkinsville.

They pulled up outside police headquarters. Their passengers rushed wildly into the station and babbled a story so fantastic that the folk of Hopkinsville still talk of it today.

Cecil "Lucky" Sutton, who lived with his family and his mother, Mrs. Glennie Lankford, in an isolated farmhouse at Kelly, nine miles from Hopkinsville, told police how a flying saucer had landed in a field behind his home and 12 or 15 little men had emerged from it

house kitchen, Chief Greenwell cross-examined the family to find out if their story was a hoax.

The farm was an old structure, set back about a mile off a highway. A long hall ran through the centre of the house, with screen doors at either end.

That night some relatives and a friend, Billy Ray Taylor, had been visiting the Suttons. There were 10 people in the house.

Around 7 p.m. one of the men was standing at the end of the hallway, looking out of the back screen door.

Suddenly, he said, he heard a hissing sound and saw a brilliant light. Some bright object seemed to have landed in a field a few hundred yards from the house.

Advancing

STARTLED, he called the others. When they came to look they saw three or four weird-looking creatures coming towards the house.

The creatures were about four feet tall. They had huge eyes, claw-like hands and long arms that hung almost to the ground. Their ears were pointed and their bodies green.

"What were they wear-

window. Sutton let go with his shotgun. The face disappeared.

Thinking they had wounded one of the creatures, the men decided to go cautiously outside to investigate. Taylor walked down the hall and out the door.

As he stepped under the low-hanging roof Sutton yelled, "Look out! He's trying to get you." A hand reached down and grabbed a fistful of Taylor's hair.

Taylor managed to pull

how he had knocked one of them off a barrel with his .22. He heard the bullet strike the creature, then whine as it ricochetted off.

The tiny figure tumbled to the ground, rolled like a ball, then floated off in the direction of the spaceship. The battle went on for nearly four hours before the terrified occupants of the house saw their chance to escape to their cars and go for help.

Taylor took Greenwell round to the back of the

or two at a Hopkinsville bar. But I didn't leave it at that. I did a bit of digging.

I popped in to see Police Chief Greenwell. A veteran police officer, he struck me as a level-headed man.

"Don't ask me to explain it," he said, "but *something* frightened those people. They weren't hopped up on Hopkinsville corn liquor or anything like that.

"They weren't a drinking family. No, sir. We could never prove or disprove their story, but there were a couple of odd things. One of my men reported seeing a light in the woods. But he found nothing.

"And a state trooper said he heard a loud swishing noise which sounded like a meteor as he drove up to the farmhouse, yet s[...] nothing."

Vanished

I'D have liked to hav[...] talked with the Sutto[...] but—and here's anot[...] mystery — they disappea[...] bag and baggage less th[...] 48 hours after the alle[...] invasion.

They just vanished i[...] thin air.

Why?

Was it a hoax that [...] out of hand? Chief Gre[...] well didn't think so.

Was it that they [...] couldn't stand to [...] around the place wh[...] they had had that terrify[...] experience in case the lit[...] men came back?

Or perhaps the little [...] *did* come back . . .

It occurred at Gaither McGette's rural farmhouse rented at the time by the Sutton family, located between the hamlet of Kelly and the small city of Hopkinsville, Christian County, Kentucky. Many people believe that it had nothing to do with any alien incursion and more in keeping with a paranormal report, involving some sort of demonic presence.

While there is no reason to suppose this was a hoax, it is worth considering whether you and I would have seen the same thing. I believe we probably would. Some claim it was investigated by the United States Air Force, which may well have been the case, bearing in mind the sketch of one of the 'creature's' released by the American Air Force in 1969 and later redrawn by Pauline Bowen.

The seven people present in the farmhouse claimed that they were terrorized by an unknown number of 'creatures' – often referred to as the *'Hopkinsville Goblins'*. The residents of the farmhouse described them as:

> *"...around three feet tall, with upright pointed ears, thin limbs, long arms, and claw-like hands or talons. The creatures were either silvery in colour, or wearing something metallic. Their movements on occasion seemed to defy gravity with them floating above the ground and appearing in high up places, and they 'walked' with a swaying motion as though wading through water".*

How it all started – Billy Ray Taylor sights disc-shaped object

Billy Ray Taylor of Pennsylvania and his family were visiting the Sutton family of Kentucky. There were a total of eleven people in the house that night, including the children of the two families. As the Sutton farmhouse had no running water. Billy Ray Taylor went outside to the water pump for a drink, at about 7.00pm, when he noticed unusual strange lights in the sky to the west, which he described as *"disc-shaped in appearance, and featured lights on its side that had all of the colours of the rainbow."*

He ran back to the house excitedly, telling the others about a flying 'saucer' but no one believed him, thinking he was mistaken.

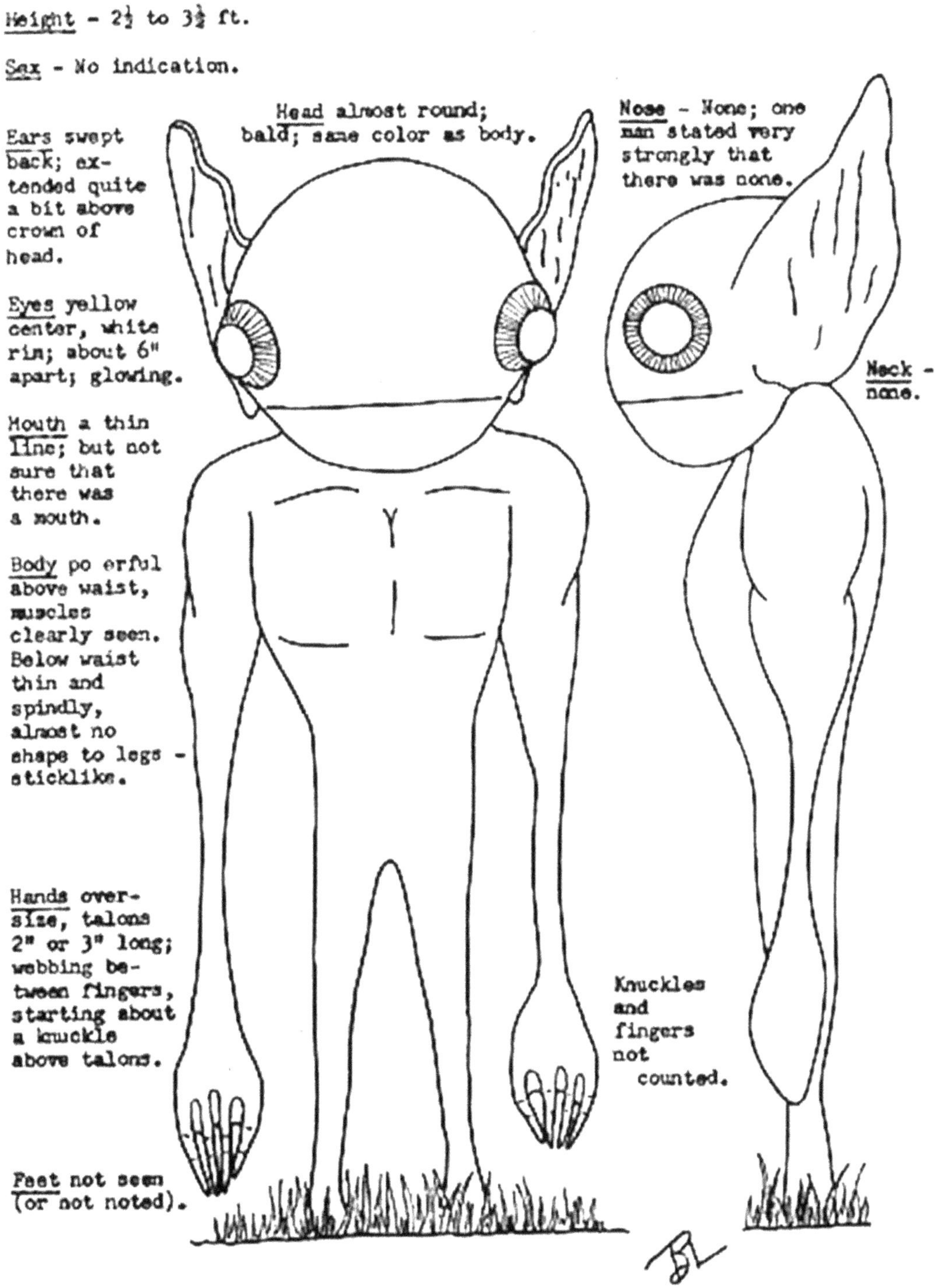
Height - 2½ to 3½ ft.
Sex - No indication.
Head almost round; bald; same color as body.
Nose - None; one man stated very strongly that there was none.
Ears swept back; extended quite a bit above crown of head.
Eyes yellow center, white rim; about 6" apart; glowing.
Neck - none.
Mouth a thin line; but not sure that there was a mouth.
Body po erful above waist, muscles clearly seen. Below waist thin and spindly, almost no shape to legs - sticklike.
Hands over-size, talons 2" or 3" long; webbing between fingers, starting about a knuckle above talons.
Knuckles and fingers not counted.
Feet not seen (or not noted).

Strange noises heard

At about 8.00pm, the families began hearing strange and unexplained noises outside, followed by the Sutton family dog (which was in the yard outside) barking loudly; it then hid under the house, where it remained until the next day. Going outside a few minutes later with their guns, Billy Ray Taylor and Elmer 'Lucky' Sutton then told of seeing a strange 'creature' emerge from the nearby trees.

Shoot first, ask questions later!

When the 'creature' approached to within about 20ft, the two men began shooting at it; one using a shotgun, the other man using a .22 rifle. There was a noise *"sounding like bullets being rattled about in a metal drum"*; it then flipped over and fled into the darkness and shadows. Believing they had wounded it, Lucky and Solomon went out to look for it. As the men were stepping from the porch, they saw one of the 'things' perched on an awning and fired at it, which they claimed knocked it off the roof. This was followed by the rattling noise, although the 'creature' was apparently unharmed by the weapons. [One speculates if it might have been the sound that caused them agitation, rather than the bullets themselves.]

Lucky and Solomon returned to the house in a disturbed state. Within minutes, Lucky's brother – J.C. Sutton – said that he saw the same 'creature' (or at least a similar one) peer into a window in the home; J.C. and Solomon shot at it, breaking the window, whereupon it, too, flipped over and fled.

The 'creatures' could be heard loudly scurrying about on the roof, and scratching, as though trying to break through. On occasion, when 'hit' by gunfire, they would float, rather than fall, to the ground.

The Siege begins

For the next few hours, the witnesses asserted that the 'creatures' repeatedly approached the home, either popping up at the doorway or at windows in an almost playful manner, only to be shot at each time they did. The witnesses were unsure as to how many of the 'creatures' there were; except for one sighting of two at the same time. All other sightings were of only one, although the first story claimed twelve to fifteen. At one point the witnesses shot one of the 'beings' at nearly point-blank range, and again would insist that the sound resembled bullets, striking a metal bucket.

Story Of Space-Ship, 12 Little Men Probed Today

Kelly Farmhouse Scene Of Alleged Raid By Strange Crew Last Night; Reports Say Bullets Failed To Affect Visitors

All kinds of investigations were going on today in connection with the bizarre story of how a space-ship carrying 12 to 15 little men landed in the Kelly community early last night and battled occupants of a farmhouse.

Most official of the probes was reportedly being staged by the air force.

More than a dozen state, county, and city officers from Christian and Hopkins counties went to the scene between 11 p.m. and midnight and remained until after 2 a.m. without seeing anything either to prove or disprove the story about the ship and its occupants.

went out of the house to get a bucket of water. He saw what looked like a flying saucer come over the trees and land in a field at a point about a city block behind the house. There was no explosion, only a semi-hissing sound, and the watcher returned to the house with the bucket of water.

A short time later somebody reported some little men with big heads and long arms were approaching the house. The men were described as having huge eyes and hands out of proportion to their small bodies. The visitors were wearing what looked to be metal plate.

The floating 'creatures' legs seemed to be nearly useless, and they appeared to propel themselves with a curious hip-swaying motion, steering with their arms. Although the 'creatures' never entered the house, they would pop up at windows and at the doorway, waking up the children in the house to a hysterical frenzy.

Alan Hendry, who was one of a number of people that investigated this matter, reported that *"Mrs Lankford counselled an end to the hostilities"*, feeling that the 'creatures' had never seemed to try harming anyone, nor had they actually entered the house. Between appearances from the 'creatures', the family tried to temper the children's growing hysteria.

At about 11pm, the Taylor-Sutton family decided to flee the farmhouse in their cars and arrived at the Hopkinsville Police Station, 30mins later. Police Chief Russell Greenwell judged the witnesses to have been frightened by something *"beyond reason, not ordinary; these were not the sort of people who normally ran to the police. Something frightened them, something beyond their comprehension."*

At about 11pm, a State highway trooper, near Kelly, independently reported some unusual *"meteor-like objects"* flying overhead, *"with a sound like artillery fire coming directly from them"*.

Police Officers visit the scene

The families returned to the farmhouse with Sheriff Greenwell, Deputy Sheriff George Batts (Patts?) and twenty officers, who saw for themselves evidence of the struggle and damage to the house, as well as seeing strange lights and hearing noises, although they did not see any sign of the mysterious 'creatures'. The Police left at about 2.15am, and not long afterwards it was claimed the 'creatures' made their return. Once again, Billy Ray fired at them, breaking another window in the house.

Newspaper/Radio Stations coverage

Kentucky New Era published an account of the incident on 22nd August 1955, and claimed 12 to 15 'little men' had been seen, when, in fact, the witnesses were unable to say how many were actually observed, but it appears there were at least two. On this date, Andrew 'Bud' Ledwith, of *WHOP* radio, interviewed the seven adult witnesses in two different groups. He judged their tale of the events as consistent, especially in their descriptions of the strange glowing 'beings'. Ledwith had worked as a professional artist, and sketched the 'creatures' based on the witnesses' descriptions. These were generally consistent, though the female witnesses insisted that the 'creatures' had a somewhat huskier build than the male witnesses remembered, and Billy Ray Taylor was alone in insisting that the 'beings' had antennae.

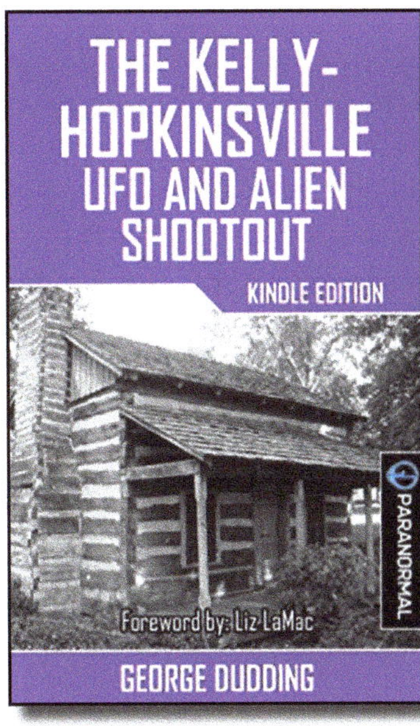

Ridicule directed at family

Not surprisingly, as time went by, the family became the target of considerable ridicule, especially as public opinion tended to view the story as a hoax and showed only a brief interest in

the event. Some residents of the local community, including members of the police department, were sceptical of the Sutton's story and believed that alcohol (possibly moonshine) may have played a part in the incident, although, to date, no evidence was ever found to support this allegation. Others claimed the whole thing was a hoax, after learning some of the witnesses had been employed by a carnival. The farm became a tourist attraction for a brief period, which upset the Suttons, who tried to keep people away by later attempting to charge people an entrance fee to discourage them. Soon they became fed up and refused to have any contact with UFO researchers – apart from, it is said, Isabel Davis of Civilian Saucer Investigation.

It was a monkey!

In 1957, US Air Force Major John E. Albert concluded that the Kelly-Hopkinsville case was the result of the witnesses seeing *"a monkey painted with silver that had escaped from a circus"*, and that Mrs Lankford's imagination had exaggerated the event. This Air force Officer was on his way from Gracey to Campbell Air Force Base when he heard a radio broadcast at 8am about the incident and decided to go to the scene and interview Lenny Langford. The explanation lacks substance as there were no bodies of any monkeys found at the scene. Isabel Davis rejected this explanation as not only entirely speculative but absurd, and published a details account of her investigation into the matter. Others suggested it was misidentification of a Great Horned Owl!

Police investigation

Police interviewed neighbouring farmhouses, whose residents were also distressed and reported to the police strange lights, strange sounds, and of hearing the gun battle at the Sutton farmstead. Police and photographers who visited the home saw many bullet holes and hundreds of spent shells, and further discovered what appeared to be an odd luminous patch along a fence where one of the beings had been shot, and, in the woods beyond, a green light whose source could not be determined.

Though the investigation was inconclusive, investigators did conclude, however, that these people were sincere and sane and that they had no interest in exploiting the case for publicity. The patch sample, although photographed, was never collected and had mysteriously disappeared by noon the next day. In 2002, Lucky Sutton's daughter – Geraldine Hawkins – who believed her father's account, said:

> *"It was a serious thing to him. It happened to him. He said it happened to him. He said it wasn't funny. It was an experience he said he would never forget. It was fresh in his mind until the day he died. It was fresh in his mind like it happened yesterday. He never cracked a smile when he told the story, because it happened to him and there wasn't anything funny about it. He got pale and you could see it in his eyes. He was scared to death."*

A claim is also made for another encounter with allegedly the same 'creatures' in another part of the United States, along the Ohio River, a week prior to the incidents in Kentucky, which itself had numerous witnesses.

There were dozens of eyewitnesses to the incidents, which included two families present at the farmhouse, and others in the area; other civilians, some of whom had no connection to the families at the farmhouse; and even one in another State.

With matters such as these, we believe it would be beneficial to examine not only the surrounding area for a clue as to why these 'entitles' manifested, but the backgrounds of the people involved. It is possible that one of them could have been the trigger for what took place and have experienced strange phenomena before? However, we are at a disadvantage as we only know some of what took place and were never there! Knowing that many photographs were taken of the scene by the police, we emailed the Kentucky State Police in 2014, hoping that they might have retained this file in their Police Museum, and also contacted the local Library, wondering if they had a file on this matter. Despite a number of emails and letters sent we never received any reply!

23rd August – USA: UFO display over Virginia

At 10.45am, Mr G.M. Park from Arlington, Virginia, watched through his 400x telescope, for 30 minutes, several orange 'lights' moving singly or in groups, circling and stopping through the sky.

(Source: *Project Blue Book*)

US fighter jets scramble to intercept UFO

At 12.10pm on the same date, according to Leonard H. Stringfield, editor of *ORBIT,* Fighter aircraft from Lockbourne Air Force Base, Ohio, were scrambled to intercept three UFOs, which had been hovering over the control tower. The aircraft climbed to 20,000ft, but the UFOs shot away at incredible speed.

Officials at Forestville and Loveland also told of having sighted the erratic behaviour of UFOs on the same day – described as round, brilliant white spheres and discs. [**Authors:** 'Three' objects reported again! This description dominates our extensive files – whatever the period.

The significance of this should be of major importance, bearing in mind that the UFO sightings reported in the 1980s – now referred to as triangular UFOs – have far more in common with earlier reports than we may think.]

25th August – England: Fifteen UFOs seen over Birmingham

At 7.30pm on 25th August 1955, former Royal Navy Volunteer Reserve Lieutenant Dennis Thursfield, of Frederick Road, Aston, was sat in his garden, when he saw the first of approximately fifteen UFOs crossing the sky, glowing with incandescent light.

In an interview, held later with a reporter from the *Evening Standard*, he had this to say:

> *"They moved across the sky in formation, in a stately sort of manner, from the north-west on a southern course. There were about 15 of them. I would describe them as unexplained phenomenon, rather than 'flying saucers'."*

(Source: Letter to Wilfred Daniels/*Evening Standard*, 26.8.1955 – 'Stately things in the sky')

26th August – England: 15 UFOs flying in formations of threes

Fifteen glowing, cigar-shaped, UFOs were seen flying in formations of threes, over Birmingham, by a number of witnesses, including a former Royal Navy Lieutenant. They were kept under observation for a total of thirty minutes.

28th August – England: RAF conduct mock battle against UFOs

Reflecting the public's interest in 'flying saucers' was a mock battle held at RAF Mountford, Wellesbourne, Warwickshire, as part of the station's open day, when the public were treated to a Bank Holiday display, with blue and white flares (representing 'flying saucers') and attacking Vampire jets, whose missiles proved ineffective against the alien craft – until the arrival of Valiant 'V' Bombers, which destroyed the enemy! The harsh reality was, and still is, so different.

31st August – England: 'Flying saucer' over Newcastle area

Andrew Thomas (12) and his three friends – Robert Esau, Ian Nicholson (12) and David Thompson (11) – were in Runnymede Road, Ponteland, Northumberland (near Newcastle-upon-Tyne) sat outside, playing, when they were astonished to see an object,

> *"...like a plate with another plate on top of it upside-down, low in the sky. Around the outside were little black dots, which looked like windows. We heard a high-pitched droning noise and it vanished; it was as big as a jet aircraft".*

The boys ran to the local Police Station, where they reported it to the Police Officer's wife. Later, an officer told the *Evening Chronicle "that they had been told about it, but there's not much that we can do"*.

(Source: *Evening Chronicle*, 31.8.1955 – 'Boys tell Police of flying saucer')

Other witnesses to this phenomenon were children in Villa Place, off Westgate Road, Newcastle, who contacted the local *Sunday Sun* newspaper to tell them about having seen what they described as what looked like:

> *"...two humbugs, stuck together, whistling low in the sky as it flew over the locality".*

Yet another witness was Kathleen Burrill of Barton Hill, Whitwell, in Yorkshire. She said she had seen what appears to have been the same 'flying saucer' that had flown over Ponteland, earlier.

It is possible there was a connection with what was seen by Isobel Armitage from 228, Hexham Road, Throckley – a teacher at Todd's Nook School, Newcastle, who sighted:

> *"...a strange object whirl across the sky, after being awakened by a whirring, roaring, clanging, ringing, noise".*

She looked out and saw, *"a black object, about five feet long, followed by other objects looking like a backbone of a kipper."*

9th September – USA: Brown almost square UFO seen

At 12 noon, near Alcoa, Tennessee, Mr M.N. Dawkins (using binoculars) observed a brown, almost square object, circling around the sky for 10-15 minutes.

Late September – England: RAF engineer sights UFO

In late September 1955, an ex RAF engineer, and his wife, were walking in Epping Forest, south of Eagle Lane, Woodford, at 10pm, when they noticed an orange-red, circular object, hovering just above the trees towards the north-west direction. The object then began to zigzag on a course of 8° each through a total angle of about 60°, moving from SW to NE, between 5-10mins. According to the witness:

> *"It was not very bright but had a clearly defined edge and looked solid. There was no sound, the weather was clear and warm, and no stars or moon were visible."*

The matter was brought to the attention of the Cambridge UFO Group, who suggested he might have seen ball lightning!

17th September – USA: UFOs seen over Titicus Reservoir

During a dark and breezy night, Frank and Eileen Bordes, of The Bronx, were out fishing on Titicus Reservoir, near Bush Pine, New York State.

Eileen was the first to see an iridescent pink mushroom-shaped object rise about 2ft above the water, before disappearing below the surface. She brought this matter to her husband's attention and then asked him to row ashore. When this was done, the couple looked out into the darkness, which was illuminated by twinkling stars. They then noticed a light, followed by two long lights below this, apparently emanating from an elongated object some 15ft long, which was partially submerged, around which appeared a good deal of turbulence. Frank and Eileen rowed along the shore, feeling they were being watched in some way. They also remarked on the curious fact that whenever they headed towards the object(s), it would speed towards them; when they moved back, so did it. **(Source: Dr. Paul Gray)**

Air Chief Marshal Hugh Caswall Tremenheere Dowding

The start of a global 'wave' of UFO activity, including what may well have been the first sighting of an 'alien vehicle' and its occupants, over the Staffordshire area the subject of startling disclosure by Lord Dowding (24th April 1882 – 15th February 1970), Commander-in-Chief of Fighter Command, during the 'Battle of Britain' 1940. He said a 'flying saucer' had landed in Scotland, during February 1954.

The monumental admission was made during an interview with the *Daily Sketch* (3.10.1955) by Lord Dowding (then aged 73), quote:

"I have talked to eye-witnesses personally. I am quite convinced they're sincere and reliable a 'flying saucer' landed at Lossiemouth, in Scotland, in February last year."

This was neither the first nor the last time Lord Dowding made his feelings known about UFOs. In a subsequent interview by the *Sunday Dispatch* (11.7.1954)

More than 10,000 UFO sightings reported up to 1954

"More than ten thousand sightings have been reported, the majority of which cannot be accounted for by any scientific explanation, e.g. that they are hallucinations, the effects of 'light refraction wheels' falling from aeroplanes, and the like. They have been tracked on radar screens and the observed speeds have been as great as nine thousand miles an hour. I am convinced these 'objects' do exist and that they are not manufactured by any nation on Earth. I can therefore see no alternative to accept the theory they come from some extraterrestrial source... I think that we must resist the tendency to assume they all come from the same planet, or that they are actuated by similar motives. It might be that the visitors from one planet wished to help us in our evolution from the basis of a higher level to which they had attained. Another planet might send an expedition to ascertain what have been those terrible explosions which they have observed, and to prevent us from discommoding other people beside ourselves by the new toys with which we are so light-heartedly playing. Other visitors might have come solely on scientific discovery and might regard us with the dispassionate aloofness with which we regard insects found beneath an upturned stone."

Alleged to know of six crashed UFOs

We also came across an article written by Hermann Hieminz, of Munich, who quoted Lord Dowding, in 1960, as having allegedly said:

"I am convinced these 'aircraft' come from outer space, the material from which the machines are made and the propulsion mechanisms are known but it has not been possible to manufacture the material or copy the drive.

Reports are available to us which show that several 'discs' crashed. I personally know of six crashes, one in Venezuela, two in the USA, one in England; the RAF immediately sealed off the area concerned hermetically, the fragments were taken into safe custody and subjected to thorough examination, one in Norway and one in Germany."

(Source: *Orbit*, Volume 2, No. 1, February 1960)

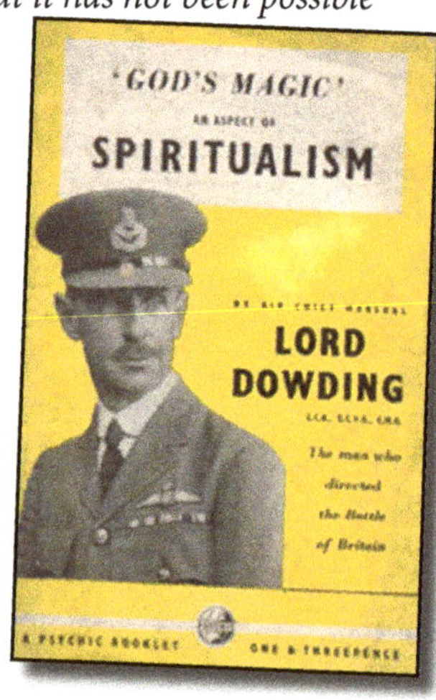

Man of courage

The opinions expressed by Lord Dowding, especially in the face of adversity, are to be applauded.

Crash-landed 'flying saucers'

Over the years, numerous rumours and myths have claimed knowledge of crash-landed 'flying saucers' and their 'alien' occupants being secretly retrieved by the military and shipped back to Government installations. This has led to the belief that glass fibre optics – and a number of other technologies, such as the microwave oven – was developed by humans from seized alien technology!

It seems ironic that while we see no reason to disbelieve the many genuine encounters contained within the pages of this book, involving the sighting of humanoid figures and saucer-shaped 'craft', we tend to view with suspicion stories of downed 'saucers' and their alien crews, when, for all we know, given the ancient history of this planet (and the vastness of space), it is logical to suppose artefacts from other planets may well have crash-landed onto Earth.

Stepson – David Whiting

We contacted David Whiting, who told us:

> *"I should make it clear I am not related by blood to Hugh, but a member of the family who has, for many decades, tried to preserve for posterity the Air Marshal's memorabilia (and keep his name alive). My connection with the RAF is through my father, P/O Max Whiting, who was killed when his Lancaster from 630 Squadron was shot down by a German night fighter over Denmark, on 22nd May 1944, on a mine laying mission.*
>
> *I did not meet Lord Dowding until 1946, when he used to visit my mother, Muriel, at our home near Tunbridge Wells.*
>
> *Hugh had a very good way with children; an engineer at heart. He used to enjoy helping me with my electrical experiments, model trains and aeroplanes. Later, I was furious with my mother and complained why had she gone and married my best friend.*
>
> *Hugh and I were very close, although he was old enough to be my grandfather. Although I had ambitions to join the RAF and fly, Hugh realised this would not be possible due to my defective colour vision, so he started me off on what became a fascinating engineering career with the Aeroplane Company at Filton."*

'Flying saucers' and fairies

Although the incident at Lossiemouth is now judged as fabricated (with the all too easy benefit of hindsight), how many people now know that in addition to Lord Hugh Dowding's belief in the existence of 'flying saucers' and fairies, (which he accepted would attract ridicule and question his sanity), he was an avowed spiritualist and member of the Theosophical Society?

> *"The evidence for the survival of physical death by animals is just as good in quality, if less massive in quantity, as that for the survival of human beings".*

Lord Dowding was also the author of four books: *Many Mansions* (1943), *Lychgate* (1945), *God's Magic* (1946) and *The Dark Star* (1951).

Champions of animal welfare

Incredibly, he claimed to have been the leader of a Mongol tribe in a previous life and, with Muriel, championed the cause of animal welfare, being staunch anti-vivisectionists. An evangelist, with a belief in life after death, he wrote in *Lychgate* of meeting dead 'RAF boys' in his sleep – spirits who flew fighters from mountain-top runways made of light, invariably attracting comments as to his state of mind by those who still continue to deny the evidence of a phenomenon that *may have nothing to do with the affairs of everyday man, but much to do with what happens afterwards.*

(Source: *Dowding of Fighter Command,* Vincent Orange, Grub St. Publishers, London)

October – Scotland: Three globed 'disc'-like objects seen at close range

In October 1955, Ex RAF serviceman Maurice Brazier was driving his van through the Galloway Hills late one evening on what was a bright moonlit night. As he neared Murrays Monument near Newton Stewart he saw an object which

> *"banked sharply right and then left before passing to the left of the van no more than 50feet up in the air. It was moving at about 40miles per hour and was 60-70feet in diameter. Its direction was south to north. Then it flew up the road heading east and west. When only 50 yards away I heard a high pitched buzzing noise and then a clicking as it banked. This grew louder the more the object banked. It had three things underneath which I can only describe as bilges with curved surfaces. It was a perfect circle in shape surrounded by a ring of light about 12inches from the edge. The top was smooth. This ring of flame appeared to vibrate and travel around in a clockwise direction. The disc did not revolve this was proved by the fact that the three blobs underneath were clearly visible as single objects. Oddly the engine on the van stated as it approached."*

This was a very interesting sighting bearing in mind the strong similarities with other UFOs brought to our attention including of course the now famous sighting in Bexleyheath Ken in July 1955.

Ship dive-bombed by UFO fireball at sea

What lay behind a letter, written by Mr W.I. Morris – member of crew aboard the motor vessel *Atlantic City* – outlining a bizarre event that occurred at sea, when the ship was dive-bombed by a 'ball of fire', just before dawn, approaching Newport, Wales, sometime in 1955?

> *"It was a warm morning, with calm seas. As I stood chatting to the officer on the watch, the man let out a yell as the ship began to deviate from its course – a highly unlikely manoeuvre, as it was on automatic steering. I stood there, pondering on what the problem was, when all of a sudden, we saw what looked like a fireball heading towards us on a collision course. I went to jump over the 'wind dodger' on the fore deck, but was pushed downwards by my companion as the fireball swept over the ship. When we got up, we saw the sea was now very turbulent. Dashing down to the wheelhouse, I discovered that the gyro and binnacle compass were out of action."*

(Source: Letter to Isle of Wight UFO Society)

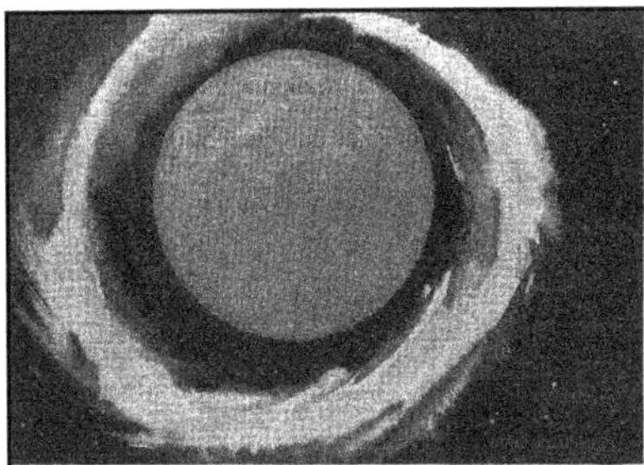

MAURICE BRAZIER DESCRIBES HIS SAUCER

"IT looked for all the world as if it would crash right on top of me." That's what Maurice Brazier said of the flying saucer he saw at Murray's Monument near Newton Stewart Galloway last October.

Now FLYING SAUCER REVIEW brings you an artist's impression of the u.f.o. drawn from sketches provided by Mr Brazier together with details omitted in the report published in the November December issue of the Review.

"It came right on until it was only about 20

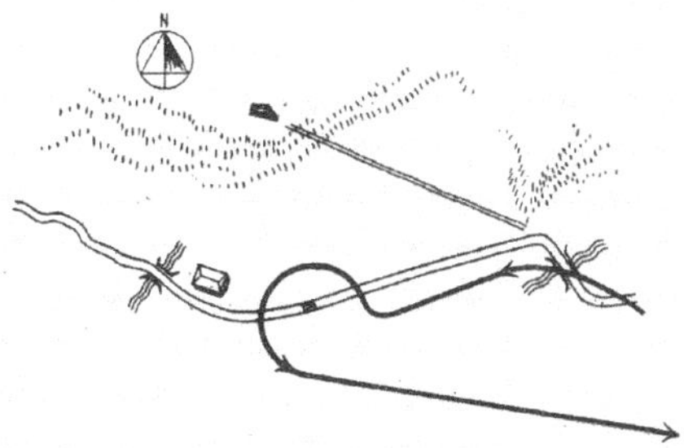

Fig. 1
Top side

Fig. 2
Side view

Fig. 3
Under side

yards away," said Mr Brazier, "banked sharply right then left and passed round to the left of the van no more than 50 feet up and at about 40 miles an hour. Sixty or seventy feet in diameter it went off in the direction whence it came.

"It was a bright moonlit night" he added "although it had been raining a few hours before, and when I first saw the u.f.o. it was travelling from south to north. Then it changed direction and flew up the road which runs east and west.

"When it was only 50 yards away I could make out a high pitch buzzing noise and as it banked I heard a clicking that became louder as the bank increased."

Altogether Maurice Brazier had the saucer in view for about five to six minutes. It had three "things underneath which I can only describe as bulges with curved surfaces" he said. When it turned to the left around the van it banked vertically between the van and the hill. It was a perfect circle in shape surrounded by a ring of light about 12 inches from the edge. The top was quite smooth.

The Galloway hills were noted for the way in

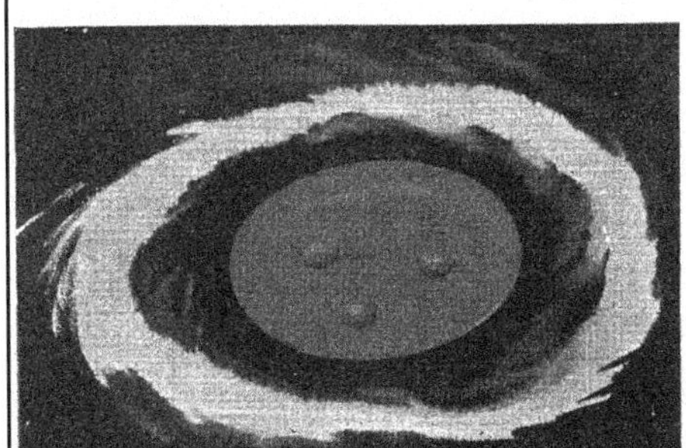

8

Richard B. Russell Jr

4th October – Russia: US Senator sights UFO, while on Soviet train

One of the most powerful US Senators in modern history – *Richard B. Russell Jr., chairman of the Armed Services Committee – witnessed two UFO sightings while on a fact-finding trip in Russia, during October 1955. Not unsurprisingly, the US government classified the sightings as top secret for more than three decades, until releasing them in 1985.

'Disc'-shaped UFO

Richard was on a Soviet train when he spotted a disc-shaped 'craft', taking off near the tracks. He hurriedly called his military aide and interpreter to the window and they saw the UFO, plus another one that appeared a minute later. The astonished trio reported the sightings to the US Air Force as soon as they were out of Russia.

Air Force Intelligence

The Air Force Intelligence report says Russell and his two companions spotted the UFOs on 4th October 1955, while travelling by rail across Russia's Transcaucasia region.

> *"One 'disc' ascended almost vertically, at a relatively slow speed, with its outer surface revolving slowly to the right, to an altitude of about 6,000 feet, where its speed then increased sharply as it headed North. The second 'flying disc' was seen performing the same actions, about one minute later. The take-off area was about 1-2 miles south of the rail line."*

No such things as UFOs!

In his report on the incident, Colonel Ryan called the sightings, *"an eyewitness account of the ascent and flight of an unconventional craft by three highly reliable United States observers.*

He added that Colonel Hathaway said,

> *"I doubt if you're going to believe this, but we all saw it. Senator Russell was the first to see this 'flying disc'. We've been told for years that there isn't such a thing, but all of us saw it."*

Fund for UFO research

Dr. Maccabee, of the Fund for UFO Research, believes that Senator Russell and his group never publicly revealed their incredible sightings because:

*Richard Brevard Russell, Jr. (November 2, 1897 – January 21, 1971) was an American politician from Georgia. A member of the Democratic Party, he briefly served as speaker of the Georgia house, and as Governor of Georgia (1931–33) before serving in the United States Senate for almost 40 years, from 1933 until his death from emphysema in Washington, D.C. in 1971. As a Senator, he was a candidate for President of the United States in the 1948 Democratic National Convention, and the 1952 Democratic National Convention. Russell was a founder and leader of the conservative coalition that dominated Congress from 1937 to 1963 and at his death was the most senior member of the Senate. He was for decades a leader of Southern opposition to the civil rights movement.

"...they were no doubt advised not to talk. These documents provide startling new evidence that UFOs exist.

These long secret documents are of major importance, because they show, for the first time, that one of the most powerful US Senators witnessed and reported a UFO. Russell saw the first 'flying disc' ascend and pass over the train, and went rushing in to get Mr Efron (Ruben Efron, his interpreter) and Colonel Hathaway (Colonel E.U. Hathaway, his aide) to see it, the report said.

Colonel Hathaway stated that he got to the window with the Senator in time to see the first (UFO), while Mr Efron said that he got only a short glimpse of the first. However, all three saw the second 'disc' and all agreed that they saw the same round, 'disc'-shaped craft as the first."

Incident denied

Mr Tom Towers, in his 20th January 1957 column, *Aviation News*, for the Los Angeles, California Examiner, printed the contents of a letter from Senator Russell, which was in response to a request for information about the sightings in Russia.

Mr Towers had originally contacted Senator Russell's office by letter, with the request that he be given permission to 'break' the story. The Senator wrote:

"Permit me to acknowledge your letters relative to reports that have come to you regarding aerial objects seen in Europe last year.

I received your letter, but I have discussed this matter with the affected agencies of the government, and they are of the opinion that it is not wise to publicize this matter at this time. I regret very much that I am unable to be of assistance to you."

The letter was dated 17th January 1956.

Can we trust official files?

In a *Just Cause* two-page report, dated March 1993, Lawrence Fawcett and Barry Greenwood outline this incident. They refer to a triangular object, showing three lights on each point. It was seen to make approximately seven fast spirals in the air, after which it climbed fast at a 45 degree angle, until it achieved high attitude and was then presumably lost from sight.

11th October - USA: Deep roaring noise heard from UFO

At 4pm over Point Lookout, Maryland, a round white object was seen in the sky, which then turned red with sparks. It was kept under observation by two men, for two and-a-half hours, accompanied by a deep roaring noise – unlike any aircraft.

18th October - England: Strange 'craft' over London

During the early morning, people living in the North Devon and Cornwall areas reported sighting a blue and white object – about the size of a dinner plate, with red flames emanating from it – moving through the sky.

At 4.10pm on the 18th October 1955, the Reverend Pitt-Kethley, from West London, was travelling on an Uxbridge train to East Harrow, London, when the train was halted by a signal at West Hampstead Viaduct.

As he casually looked through the window, he saw a strange 'craft' approaching in the sky, at a height of about 120 feet, described as being reddish-brown and grey in colour, reminding him of:

> *"...a German troop carrier, about the size of a small bus, containing about 30 immobile helmeted figures, with human faces, all apparently dressed in khaki uniforms – some of whom were seated and staring fixedly forward. I was puzzled how such an object, with its low trajectory, could possibly clear London."*

Sightings of strange aerial 'craft' like this are fairly unique, but not rare. Who can say what mission this strange vessel was on, or even guess, in our wildest dreams, where they were from? This is chilling in its implications, but fascinating none the less.

(Source: Jonathan M. Caplan/*FSR*, Volume 15, No. 3, May/June 1969, Gordon Creighton)

At 10.45pm, a mysterious flash – believed to be a meteorite – was sighted from the flying control tower at the Royal Naval Air Station, Culdrose, before disappearing in the direction of Redruth. It was suggested this could have been the same object which came down into the sea, about 20 miles off the Cornish coast.

19th October – England: Strange light plunges into ocean

At about 12.30am a strange light, accompanied by a sizzling sound, was seen by Mevagissey fisherman, which illuminated the coast over a wide area before plunging into the sea.

(Source: *Flying Saucer News*, autumn 1955)

17th November – USA: Twelve UFOs sighted

At 6.10am over St. Louis, Missouri resident – Mr J A Mapes, reported having seen:

> *"...twelve round, flat, objects – silver on top, with a dark base – flying across the sky in a 4-deep formation, tipping in pitch and rolling for 45 seconds".*

20th November – USA: Two UFOs seen

At 5.20pm, Lake City, Tennessee, Operations Officer – Captain B.G. Denkler, and five men of the USA F663rd AC & W Squadron, sighted two oblong, bright orange, semi-transparent objects, heading through the sky in a 'to and fro' movement.

The objects were seen over a period of between 4-15 minutes, by others. Like so many thousands of UFO sightings involving similar objects, their identities remain unknown although the behaviour characteristics are identical.

25th November – USA: US State Senator sighted UFO

At 10.30am over La Veta, Colorado, State Senator Mr S.T. Taylor sighted:

> *"...a luminous green-blue dirigible-shaped object in the sky – showing a fat front, tapered toward the tail, and 'jelly-like' in appearance – diving at a 45° angle, then changing to 30° and then gone in five seconds".*

15th December – England: 'Spinning top' UFO over Cambridge

Cambridge schoolgirl Jacqueline Jones (12) was walking home from school with friends, at 5pm, when they saw:

> *"...a huge, round, spinning object in the sky, making a humming sound. It seemed to be giving off white light."*

The object appeared to drop behind some houses and that was then the end of the sighting – no flash of light or further noises. Interestingly (and not altogether surprising) was the later revelation that another member of the family, Derek Jones (25) reported seeing a brilliant object in the sky, some miles away from where Jacqueline and her friends had sighted the spinning object.

16th December – England: 'Flying saucer' seen over Yorkshire

Mr H.S. Deburgh, from Scarborough, was exercising his dog, during the evening, when he saw what he took to be a 'flying saucer' rushing through the clear night sky.

> *"It was gold in colour and made a whirring sound. It had a dull red glow about it that seemed to flash intermittently.*
>
> *It then veered off, at tremendous speed. I watched it for about a minute longer, before it dwindled into a point of light over the horizon."*

18th December – England: Three shining UFOs sighted

At 12.30pm on 18th December 1955, three shining circular objects, *"resembling a smaller version of the full moon, one after the other"*, were sighted moving across the sky over Otley, in Yorkshire, by Mr and Mrs H.J. Cooper. **(Source: UFOLOG)**

21st December – USA: Golden 'disc'

At 11pm, Caribou, Maine resident – Mr Roberta Jacobs – sighted a round, very bright gold, domed 'disc'-shaped object, climbing in the sky. It then rotated, hovered, and accelerated away, six to eight minutes later.

29th December – England: Three UFOs seen over the moor

A circular object, giving off a brilliant white light, was sighted streaking across the sky over Birkdale, near Liverpool, at a height of about 2,000 feet (time not known). After passing over Formby it turned towards Ireland, leaving behind it a thin white trail.

In the adjoining County of Yorkshire, Mr H.J. Cooper from Chapel Allerton – who had served with the RAF as a navigator – was out hiking on the moors.

> *"The sky was blue and bright, when I saw what looked like two silvery balloons, at a height of about 3,000 feet and almost stationary. A third suddenly appeared and all three began to move. The speed increased to about 500 mph. The objects then assumed an oval shape; the whole incident was over in fifteens seconds."*

The Air Ministry was consulted. They confirmed the objects were not weather balloons, but suggested the explanation to be reflections!

(Source: *Flying Saucer Review*, Volume 2, No. 1, Jan/Feb 1956)

1956

2nd January – England: Cigar-shaped object seen over Yorkshire

MR James Donoghue of Broadcarr, Glaisdale, near Whitby, Yorkshire, was out walking with a friend, when they saw:

> *"...a bright cigar-shaped object, moving in a north to south direction."*

They watched it for 90 seconds, before it faded from sight.

(Source: *Flying Saucer Review*, Vol. 2, Jan/Feb 1956)

12th February – Pilots sight UFO, tracked on radar

Over Goose Bay, Labrador, Canada, *F-89* pilot Bowen, and radar observer Crawford, sighted a green and red object that rapidly circled their aircraft, at 11.25pm, which was also tracked on radar during. (We hadn't intended to catalogue Canadian sightings but felt it was necessary on this occasion taking into consideration the events that took place the next day in France.)

13th February – France: UFO tracked on radar

Emphasising that while lack of space prevents us from including all UFO sightings which occurred on both sides of the Channel, this one incident is of interest, bearing in mind it was not only tracked on radar but seen visually.

At 10.50pm an 'echo', twice as large as any aircraft, was picked up on the radar at Orly Airport, near Paris. Further scrutiny revealed it did not fit into any scheduled traffic pattern for Paris. In addition, it behaved in a manner unlike anything the operator had experienced before. He wasn't the only one to record this – the radar operator Mr Beaupertuis – on board a *Douglas Dakota* flight from London to Paris – was shocked to see an enormous, glowing, object through the portholes of the aircraft.

The Captain also witnessed the object and said:

> *"For a full 30 seconds we watched it, without being able to decide exactly on its shape or size. It was no civil airliner, for it didn't carry any navigation lights. I was then warned by Orly that it had moved to our left-hand side, so I turned towards it. I was then instructed that it had left and was heading towards Le Bourget."*

Oddly, neither Le Bourget nor Paris Observatory picked it up on their radar, despite its 'waltz' over a radius of some 50 kilometres (30miles) being tracked for about four hours.

4th April – USA: Fat oblong-shaped object seen

Retired US Army Captain Roy Hall, colleague Charles Anderson, and others, observed (through a 6-inch telescope and 55-200x telescopes) a fat, oblong object, with two lines around its middle, which remained stationary for six hours in the sky, over McKinney, Texas, at 3.15pm.

19th April – England: Triangular UFO over Derby

At 1pm on 19th April 1956 – a clear day, with sparse cloud – ex RAF serviceman Robin Gibbard was carrying out repairs to a house in Allestree, Derby, with another workman, when they heard the sound of an approaching aircraft.

> *"I looked up to see an Anson propeller twin-driven radial engine aircraft – the type used for reconnaissance – slowly approaching our position, flying at a height of about 2,000 feet. To our amazement a black delta/triangular winged aircraft appeared fairly close in the sky near the Anson, actually circling around the aircraft on at least two occasions, before breaking away in flight and heading off at fantastic speed in a long curve across the sky, and gone in seconds."*

Contacted by 'Paramount Studios', Hollywood!

During conversation in 2008, Robin told us that after having initially reported the sighting to Omar Fowler – Head of the Derbyshire Group (PRA – Phenomenon Research Association) – he was contacted by *Paramount Studios,* in the United States, who were producing a film on UFOs and wanted to interview him about his sighting. Unfortunately, he was never given the opportunity to see the film, which was apparently only shown to American audiences.

Robin:

> *"I have to say I now believe there is every chance that what I saw was more likely to have been an example of top secret technology, rather than any alien spaceship. I base my conclusion on an experience in the RAF, when stationed at 90 Maintenance Unit, Freckleton, between Preston and Lytham St. Annes, next to the English Electric Lightning works.*
>
> *One night I was on guard duty, checking the hangars in which the prototype English Electric Canberra Aircrafts were kept – an aircraft, by the way, I saw fly on its maiden flight on the 13th May 1950, and happened to wander into one of the officer's rooms and see a model of the later released 'Lightning' jet on his desk. Thinking no more of it, I constructed a small model of the aircraft. During a kit inspection, the officer saw the model and instructed me to destroy it – presumably as I shouldn't have seen the model, which was*

> *not supposedly in production at the time." (The 'Lightning', known as the English Electric P.1A, was developed as a supersonic research aircraft, by W.E. 'Teddy' Petter and first flew officially in August 1954)*

Coult it have been this film? Who knows?

19th April – USA: Pilots sight mysterious 'light'

At 6.07am, the crew of an Eastern Airlines *Super Constellation* sighted an intense 'white light', moving 4-5 times the speed of the airplane, over Houston, Texas.

27th April – England: UFO seen over Wolverhampton

On 27th April 1956, racing pigeon enthusiast – Mr Reynolds from Limehouse Lane, in Wolverhampto – was studying the sky, looking for a missing pigeon, at 8pm, when he noticed a brilliant silver coloured object, heading south-east across the sky, with one accord – *"the whole flock cocked their heads as the object passed over"*.

Mr Reynolds shouted for his wife, who came rushing outside. The couple stood watching as it passed overhead, low enough to see, "*...the outer surface was chequered,* ***covered with small dots,*** *like rivets, similar to those seen on a water tank*", before it was lost from view as it headed into a cloud, making a humming noise. **(Source: Wilfred Daniels, Stafford)**

10th May – England: UFO over London

At 7.55pm on the 10th May 1956, Mr R. Russell was leaving his house in Hornsey, London, when he saw an unusual bright white object in the sky to the west. Through 8 x 30 binoculars he was able to see its shape, which was at first oval and then ellipsoid, until it eventually drifted away out of sight. It was not Venus, which later rose up from the horizon.

26th May – England: UFO over Bristol

At 10.45pm on the 26th May, Mr Fred Jones was on the roof of his house, when he saw:

> *"...a long, silver, cigar-shaped object, lit up along its entire length. I watched it through binoculars for a couple of minutes, as it flew eastwards on a straight course, at a speed of what I estimated to be 1,600 mph."*

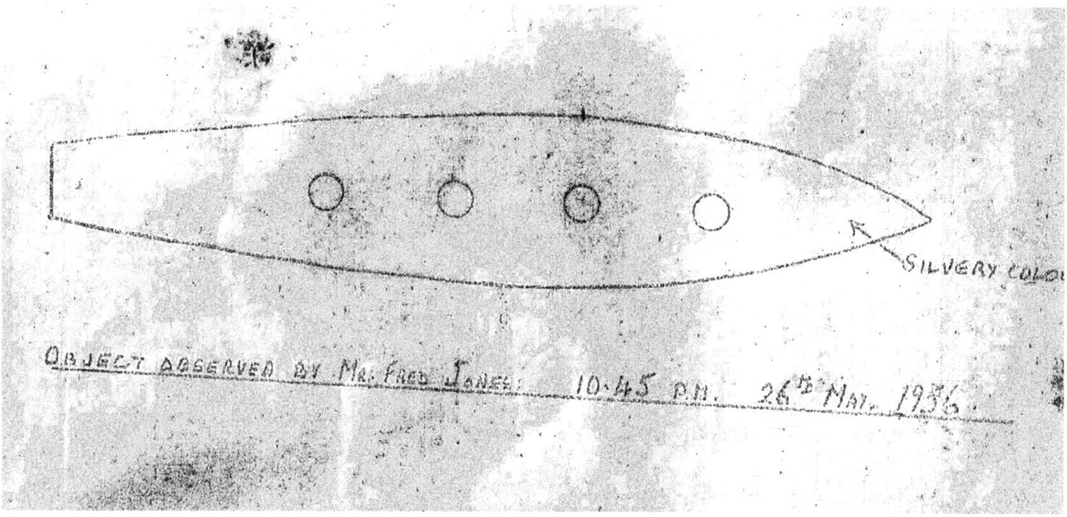

Mid 1950s – England: UFO display over London

James Millen (at the time of writing, in his late 60s), from London – who has been very much involved in counselling UFO witnesses, over the years (known to the authors personally) – described what he saw, while living near the Chelsea border with London in the mid-1950s.

> *"I was sat outside, talking to my uncle (who kept pigeons), when the whole flock turned their heads to look at something in the sky.*
>
> *We looked up, expecting to see a bird or airplane, and were stunned to see a huge metallic looking 'disc' in the sky, hovering in mid- air, towards London. We watched in amazement, as*

a number of smaller 'discs' tumbled out of the larger one and flew off in different directions, before returning. I think there were about eight of them. A few minutes later, the whole spectacle vanished in front of our eyes."

England: Cylindrical UFO seen over the *River Thames*, London

In the early part of 1956, former RAF serviceman Peter Weston – Radio Operator/Radio Navigator, who served with a number of Squadrons (including Lancaster Squadron 186, at RAF Stradishal) during World War Two, in Malaya and Korea – was number three in a line of four aircraft returning to base, east of London, near the *Thames Estuary*.

"A few miles before London, the lead aircraft reported seeing an unidentified flying object to port and told us to keep our eyes open. He described it as a long cylinder, with light shining through portholes, and a reddish glow at the rear. We acknowledged this, and then number two in line broke in to say they could see something. We thought we had seen something, but neither of us could be certain. While chatting back and forth on the radio, a voice came out of the blue, identifying itself by saying, 'This is Thames Radar. Maintain your height and speed and do not deviate from your route. This transmission is finished'. We didn't have a clue as to who was monitoring our transmissions, but were aware of a clandestine radar system covering the East Coast."

(Source: Jane Veinot, daughter)

June – England: UFO activity over Gloucestershire

David Jones

In June 1956, UFOs were sighted over the town of Cheltenham Spa and the surrounding area. On another occasion, an object *"showing blazing lights streaming out of its square windows"* was seen at 11.30pm, over Bishop's Cleeve – a high point overlooking the town (the scene of other UFO sightings over the years). **(Source: David Jones)**

6th June – USA: Silver 'disc' seen over California

At 5.30am over Banning, California, a Mr Bierman saw:

"...a thin 'disc' with a small dome, shimmering silver, hovering in the air about 100 yards away, for 8-10 seconds, before it shot upwards into the sky".

13th June – England: 'Closed ring' in the sky near Birmingham

At 8.25pm on 13th June 1956, Mr F. Scott and Mr T.C. Leighton were looking towards Barr Beacon, Birmingham, near Leacroft Colliery, when they saw what they took to be the shadow of a low aircraft, or smoke ring, travelling at great speed.

It was then seen to tilt upwards and vanish from sight.

(Source: Mr Wilfred Daniels/*Express & Star*, Wolverhampton)

14th June – England: Yellow 'star' seen in sky

A number of residents living in Wolverhampton left their homes, the next evening, at 10.45pm, to look up into the night sky, after being alerted to a strange object seen. A number of reports described a yellow 'star', heading slowly through the air from the North direction. By 11.30pm, it was over the southern horizon. One of the witnesses was Mr David Osborne, from the Birmingham and Midlands Institute Observatory. He told of seeing an aircraft and two RAF Jet fighters moving across the sky. The matter was brought to the attention of the USAF, who explained it away as a refuelling exercise. **(Source: Wilfred Daniels)**

Summer – England: Three 'flying discs' sighted over Southampton

Ron Lucas was taking his lunch break at Four Post Hill, Southampton, in the summer of 1956 when he noticed a silver object revolving in the sky.

> *"I managed to get a pair of binoculars and looked through them. It literally took my breath away when I saw three flying discs appear and take up a position next to the first object. After about three hours the spectacle vanished in front of our eyes."*

Many miles away on the Gower Peninsular, South Wales, Alan Titley was on the beach with his girlfriend, looking out to sea, enjoying the summer sunshine when:

> *"All of a sudden an enormous, clear, shaped object appeared in front of us, a few hundred yards away, hovering above the sea. We watched in disbelief as it slowly moved behind Worm's Head, where we lost sight of it, although we saw it once more, heading towards the mainland."*

The couple later discovered, from newspaper reports, that a number of people in the Swansea area had sighted a UFO over the city during the same week. **(Source: Personal interview)**

Summer – England: Over London

Brian O'Neil was visiting a friend on Warwick Avenue, situated adjacent to the canal at Paddington, London, in the summer of 1956. It was a beautiful clear early evening when he saw:

> *"...a cigar-shaped object, estimated to be 100 feet in diameter, move from behind a tree on the other side of the canal, before halting, moving upwards, and disappearing from view."*

(Source: Personal interview)

8th July – England: UFO sighted over Surrey

At 3.30pm on 8th July 1956, a white 'disc' with a small white dome on top, was seen passing across the sky over Surrey. Within a short time it changed to half white and brilliant red, before shooting straight up into the sky and ejecting two spheres or globes as it did so. **(Source: UFOSIS)**

10th July – England: Two spheres seen over Oxfordshire

On 10th July, an object resembling 'two spheres or globes, apparently joined by a bar-like structure', was seen over Stonewall, Oxfordshire, in broad daylight.

Another sighting of a saucer-shaped object took place in the same year, involving Mr P.J. Hurney from Somerford, Hampshire, who described seeing:

> *"...something moving across the sky, in an east to west direction, showing all the colours of the spectrum; it looked like two large plates, joined face to face".*
>
> **(Source: Fred Smith, Isle of Wight UFO Society)**

31st July – England: Silver cigar-shaped UFO over Buckinghamshire

Mr G. Robinson of Clifton, Bristol, was sat outside on Piggott's Hill, near Hughenden, Buckinghamshire, at 11.30am, when he saw a bright silver metallic in appearance, cigar-shaped object, passing between the clouds, for five seconds, before it disappeared behind another cloud. It was last seen in the western sky, heading North, on what a clear day with scattered clouds. The sun was shining and the moon was also visible. Calculations made revealed that the object was flying at 175 mph.

(Source: British Flying Saucer Bureau, *Bulletin* No. 4)

5th August – England: Strange 'light' in the sky over Bristol

Mr and Mrs E. Snaith from Filton, Bristol, were walking home, at 10.45pm, when they noticed a 'light', flashing alternatively red and green in the sky. At first they took it to be an aircraft – particularly as it was close to Filton Aerodrome – but changed their minds when the 'light' continued to hover for a period of ten minutes, without any change in apparent brightness. Secondly, the time interval of red and green, although fairly regular, was not exact and varied between half a second to one on each colour. It was a clear night, but no sound was heard. It was seen on a bearing of 350° at an elevation of 30°. It was eventually lost from view behind buildings.

(Source: British Flying Saucer Bureau, Investigator Mr R. Hetherington)

August – England: Three UFOs sighted over Bolton

Maurice Hart wrote to us about a strange incident that took place, while he was working the night shift at an engineering works in Bolton, overlooking the *River Tonge* in August.

> *"I was on my way back from break, at 2am, when I noticed a group of workers gazing intently upwards into the night sky. Curious, I stopped, looked upwards and was flabbergasted to see three huge brilliant blue 'spheres' absolutely motionless in the air. I could sense the awe as we all stood there, mesmerised by what we were seeing. I asked some of the men (whom I knew had served with the RAF) if they had any idea what the things were. They told me they had never seen anything like it before."*

Suddenly the interlude was broken by the arrival of the foreman, who came running over, demanding to know why they weren't at work. When Maurice told him, he glanced upwards and almost in the same breath, ordered the men to get back to work. From the look of his face, he was clearly frightened.

> *"When I finished my shift, I learnt from some of the other workers that the objects had been there all night but faded away at dawn.*

As I left the factory, I encountered the foreman. Instead of the usual 'good morning', he said, 'you been seeing 'little green men' as well?"

8th August – USA: Pulsating 'light' seen

Attorneys Mr W.B. Buttermore and Mr J.W. Smith were twenty miles south of Quartsite, Arizona, at 11pm, when they saw a blue and white pulsating 'light' flying across the sky, over a period of 5-7 minutes.

13th August – England: Light bulb object seen over Kent

A strange object was seen crossing the sky, during the late morning of 13th August 1956, by Eric Rush – then living near St. Mary Cray Railway Station, just off the A224, at Bexleyheath, in Kent.

"We lived close to Biggin Hill Aerodrome, so it was a common sight to see Spitfires and other aircraft flying across the sky, with the occasional sound of jet aircraft, which were pretty rare in those days. I was shocked to see what looked like a light bulb, crossing a gap in the blue sky – faster than anything I had ever seen before.

When my father arrived home, I told him what I had seen. He suggested I contact the Daily Mirror newspaper, which I did, but despite scouring the papers over the following days, I never saw my letter – although I was sent a ten shilling Postal Order and a thank you note for reporting the sighting of a 'flying saucer'.

Children's comic – 'Countdown'

Some years later, I came across a children's comic, called Countdown. It told of a UFO sighting, which took place in August 1956, written by Charles Bowen – editor of 'Flying Saucer Review'. I've often wondered if it was the same object I saw."

13th August – England: 'Flying saucer' over power Station, Manchester

At 5pm on 13th August 1956, Paul Porcher from Flixton, Manchester, was leaving work when he noticed a red object in the sky, framed between the two roofs of the nearby Barton Power Station.

"It was about 50 yards across, a few hundred feet up in the air, and seemed to have bevelled edges, resembling an upside-down cup and saucer. After about 15 seconds, it moved away towards Eccles. I don't claim to have seen a 'flying saucer'. I can't say what it was that I saw."

(Source: *Flying Saucer Review*, 1956, Volume 2, Number 5, Sept/Oct. 1956)

Three UFOs tracked on radar over East Anglia – RAF scrambled

At 9.30pm, radar operators at RAF Bentwaters and Lakenheath tracked a group of 'dots' moving in over the East Anglia coast, from the direction of Holland. The 'dots', which could also be seen visually, were then 50 miles distant and closing at nearly 5,000 mph – well over the speed of sound, but failed to produce any sonic boom. At this point the radar then picked up a number of other 'blips', showing as an irregular group of twelve to

fifteen in number, heading north-east at a much slower rate, *"being led by three UFOs, forming a triangular formation"*.

At 10pm, a United States Air Force jet was scrambled to intercept but returned to base, a short time later, after failing to make contact. Fifty minutes later, a UFO – described as 'an oval-shaped white light' was seen crossing the sky over RAF Bentwaters, at speed, apparently connected with the report of a similarly described object seen hovering over RAF Lakenheath, for a short time.

A RAF *Venom* night fighter aircraft, already on patrol over the Bedford area, was instructed to intercept the UFO.

After making airborne radar contact, the object began to zigzag behind the jet – both 'vehicles' being tracked by ground radar.

Despite a number of high-speed manoeuvres, the plane was unable to shake off the UFO until another fighter appeared.

According to the *Daily Express* (22.2.78), quote:

> *"The UFO was seen to shoot off at right angles and split into two separate objects, before locking onto the tail of the fighter in a deadly game of 'hide-and-seek', before eventually disappearing."*

Freddie Wimbledon

We contacted Freddie Wimbledon – the flight controller on duty that evening, at RAF Neatishead – who told us:

> *"The incident was released into the media by a retired USAF Officer NCO, who wrote his version of what happened, twelve years after the event, which became known as the Lakenheath incident. The article in the Daily Express was full of errors and inaccurate conversations. The Venom was not a single seater and did not possess the onboard capabilities to apply to any gun lock onto the target.*
>
> *I can tell you that details of the matter were brought to the attention of the Sunday Times, who contacted the MOD but denied any knowledge of the incident. Apparently the American ambassador was advised the same.*

Requirements of the Official Secrets Act

> *Because of the restrictions of the Official Secrets Act, I wasn't even allowed to discuss what had taken place – even with my wife. However, as the years passed and more servicemen came forward to tell what had happened, I became pestered by people who wanted to ask me questions about this incident. When I explained my position to them, some of them became quite nasty towards me. My memory of the event: I was chief controller on duty at RAF Neatishead, East Anglia, on the night of 13th/14th August, 1956.*
>
> *My duties were to monitor the radar picture and scramble the battle flight, which were on a 24-hour call-out to intercept any intruder over British airspace, not possibly identified in my sector of responsibility.*

Mr John Hanson
31 Red Lion Street,
Alvechurch
Worcestershire B48 7LG

3 Feb. 04

F. H. C. WIMBLEDON
CHILWORTH
GUILDFORD
SURREY

Dear Mr Hanson,

Thank you for your letter and all the "bumph". A bit late in my reply but I only left hospital after a heart attack very recently. I appreciate that you had the decency to write to me, whereas so many authors have quoted from printed extracts and bald statements said to come from me when I have never spoken to them in my life. When I have complained and even threatened litigation, they point out that legally they are entitled to use anything that appears in press. Hence I have variously been referred to as "Mr", FLT.LT, SQUADRON LEADER, FLT CONTROLLER, ATC officer etc etc!

You must remember (or possibly before your interest was developed) that the story was "blown" by a retired USAF N.C.O. who wrote his version of what happened 12 years after the event which became known as the "Lakenheath Incident" and who had "listened in" to the radio. This was pounced upon by the Sunday Times who queried it but were told by the M.O.D that they "had no knowledge of this incident". The American Ambassador was told the same and every step was taken to deny any knowledge.

As for people like me who ~~was~~ had been involved, we were under the Official Secrets Act forbidden to mention it. I never even told my wife!

Nevertheless, snippets began to emerge and I was pestered by various organisations, by callers, telephone calls, faxes, letters galore etc etc, even some people who became rather nasty because I would not tell them anything!

I'm afraid I reacted rather hastily and told the Sunday Times what I thought of them. This didn't help of course but because of my anger and the fact of my memory letting me down, I made the mistake of including one sentence which with later hindsight and contact with the RAF navigators* I have deleted this in the account you sent me and would ask you to print only the correct version if you use it at all. Preferably, don't use it!

* which should never have been included.

M.O.D continued to try to squash any reference to the "Incident" but inevitably more revelations occurred when people such as Pilots, Navigators, Sector Controllers and others concerned were found or started to make their own stories available. There was no stopping it, but somebody "high up" in authority issued a statement saying "all the papers in this case have been accidently destroyed". If you believe that, you will believe anything! Undoubtedly this was the most important scientific example of ~~alien~~ extra-terrestrial existence ever known. With witnesses from the ground, from RAF and USAF Radar and the experience of R.A.F personnel in highly equipped aircraft especially designed for that purpose. Is it likely all this would be destroyed?

I am convinced now as much as I was in 1956 that something occurred then was no imagination in the minds of those involved. It happened and that was it. Every logical explanation otherwise has been thoroughly checked and double checked.

Yours sincerely

Freddie Wimbledon

P.S. I did see the Jenny Randles film years ago and thought it complete twaddle! David Clarke I first met about 2½-3 years ago but have not heard from him for over a year now.

Many years ago I knew a very learned and sincere man who had lived most of his life in Nepal. He was quite convinced that the minds of the, for this letter, call them "orientals" are quite different from ours. and capable of travelling in (again we can call it this) a different world! Personally I do not query this a bit, the brain is a very curious piece of apparatus.

Lakenheath USAF contacted me

I remember Lakenheath United States Air Force Base contacting me, by telephone, to inform me there was something buzzing their airfield. I scrambled a Venom night fighter from the battle flight, through sector and my controller. The interception cabin then took over. The interception control team would consist of one fighter controller (an Officer, Corporal, tracker and height reader), consisting of four highly trained personnel, in addition to myself, who could clearly see the object on our radar scopes. After being vectored onto the trail of the object by my interception controller, the pilot called out 'contact', and continued to close on the target, but after a few seconds and in the space of one or two 'sweeps' of our scopes, the object appeared behind our fighter. Our pilot called out, 'lost contact – more help'.

He was advised the target was now behind him and given fresh instructions. I then scrambled second Venom, which was vectored towards the area, but before it arrived on the scene the target had disappeared from our scopes. Although we continued to keep a careful watch, nothing further was seen again. The fact remains that at least nine RAF ground personnel and two RAF crew were conscious of an object, sufficiently solid to give returns on radar. Following a report made of the incident, a senior officer from the Air Ministry came down and interviewed us about what had taken place."

Ivan Logan – Retired RAF Navigator 23 Squadron

Mr Ivan Logan – a retired RAF Navigator from 23 Squadron – one of the pilots involved in the incident – was also anxious to bring to our attention the subsequent exaggerations in the public domain, which included the ridiculous suggestion that one of the *Venom's* was chased by the UFO.

"At the time, we didn't consider the incident to be of any great significance. According to my log book, we took-off at 02.40 hours, on the 14th August 1956. My pilot was Ian Fraser-Kerr, and we were airborne for 45 minutes. On this particular night we were the second Venom aircraft used to attempt an intercept and were scrambled at low level, 2-3,000 feet, looking for a target near RAF Lakenheath (USAF). Normally we were controlled by RAF Neatishead or Trimingham , but on this occasion, we were with RAF Lakenheath Control Approach Radar, who advised us where the 'target' was, rather than controlling us. The difficulty with low altitude operations was the amount of ground clutter produced on the radar when we turned, or scanned low.

We had no radar 'lock-on' facility. It was all done manually, moving the scanner by means of a tiny joystick – pointing up, if turning towards the target, and down if we were turning away, the amount depending on how much bank the pilot was using. You can imagine the difficulty involved with trying to manually strobe the 'target' and, at the same time, advising the pilot, verbally, about visual height and target positions. I remember picking up a contact, several times, usually at about three to four miles. It may have been the same one, as it appeared to be virtually stationary. We were unable to turn behind it, as it was closing at high speed. Eventually, we were forced to return to base, as fuel was running low."

From: Ivan Logan

Kent
TN2

18th March 2004

John Hanson
31 Red Lion Street
Alvechurch
B48 7LG

Dear John,

In reply to your letter dated 11th March, I hope the following will be of some use.

1. I attach a copy of my version of events which I wrote in Oct 2000. I can't improve on this, however, I will be happy to answer by telephone any questions which may arise. For instance , why was I the first contact point on all this in 1996. With regard to the names mentioned in my report: Colin Smith died last year, I have no address for Ian Fraser-Ker (my pilot on the night) but I know Dr David Clarke had some success. John Brady: 6 Hinshalwood Way, Costessy, Norwich, Norfolk , NR8 5BN. Dave Chambers: 10 Sunnymede Avenue, Chesham, Bucks, HP5 3LE. If you need help in further contacts you can always speak to me first as I have quite a lot of information on ex- 23 Sqn members.

2. With reference to the reports you sent me, I can only comment on page 134 and the para ' An RAF Venon single seat fighter' etc. That says it all, Venom spelt wrongly and it was a two seater night/all weather fighter. All that bit is rubbish and I think it is the same piece I refer to in the final para of my attached report.

3. I enclose some photos which may be of use. I have nothing suitable from the late fifties.

4. Thanks for the address of the other Ivan Logan. I don't plan to follow it up.

Yours sincerely,

Ivan Logan

PS. I would like the large photos back in due course.

On the night in question I recall picking up a contact several times usually at about 3 or 4 miles. It may have been the same one. As it appeared to be virtually stationary we could not turn behind it as it was closing at high speed (our speed) probably 300 kts or so. Our targets were normally travelling at our speed and when in behind we synchronised speeds at visual range. In this case it was impossible. Eventually we returned to base as our fuel was low, at low altitude fuel consumption is much higher). We chatted with Dave Chambers & John Brady over coffee afterwards and compared notes although I don't remember filing a special report. I think at the time we thought that it was a met balloon or something similar and I don't recall considering UFOs neither do I remember either pilot talking about visual sightings on any lights although at low level there would have been plenty of lights to confuse.

I have no idea where Ian Fraser-Ker is today. He was a South African married and living in the UK. After about 1958 I do not know where he went as he was not my regular pilot and he is not on the Squadron Association books. Dave Chambers & John Brady are at the addresses I gave. Dave left the RAF to become an airline pilot and John stayed in the RAF retiring as a sqn ldr.

I can't find the Eastern Daily Press cutting I mentioned. It was sent to me about 6 or 8 years ago by Colin Campbell Smith who lives near Norwich. It was about the Lakenheath incident and Colin remembered I was one of the Navs and sent the cutting. The EDP may well be able to trace the article.

Finally, I have a couple more cuttings and letters which I will show you. One American article which you may have seen is gives an exaggerated account of the whole incident and quite frankly it is simply not true. It says that one of the Venoms was actually chased by the UFO!

I hope this is of use.

From: Ivan Logan

Tunbridge Wells
TN2
23 Oct 00

Thank you for your letter dated 20 Oct 00.
You will appreciate that my recallection of the events of 13 Aug 56 are very sketchy not only because it was so long ago but also, at the time, we did not consider the incident to be of any great significance. Certainly, we were not aware then of what was reported earlier at RAF Bentwaters (USAF).

My log book entry reads: 13 Aug 56. Take-off Time 0240 (Actually it would have been 14 Aug by then) Pilot: Fg Off Fraser-Ker, Details: 'Scramble', Airborne: 45 mins.

We were normally based at RAF Coltishall in Norfolk but once or twice a year a squadron was detached to RAF Waterbeach in Cambridgeshire for QRA (Quick Readiness) duties. Two aircraft were always on standby with crews in cockpits to get airborne in two minutes to intercept unidentified aircraft usually Eastern Block or occasionally friendly aircraft who may not have filed a flight plan.

On the night in question I believe that we were the second aircraft scrambled as the first had no success in intercepting.

Usually when scrambled we climbed to high level for 'trade' 100 miles or so over the North Sea. In this case, we were at low level 2-3000 feet I think, looking for a target near RAF Lakenheath (USAF). Normally we were controlled by RAF Neatishead or Trimmingham GCIs but on this occasion we were with RAF Lakenheath Approach Control Radar who were simply telling us where the targets were rather than controlling us. One difficulty at low altitude was that ground clutter on the radar tube (AI Mk 21 American Westinghouse kit) reduced the radar range of pick up. The tubes flooded with ground returns when we turned or scanned low. We had no radar 'lock on' facility, it was all done manually moving the scanner by means a a tiny joystick. Pointing up if turning towards the target and down if we were turning away, the amount depending on how much bank the pilot was using. Having to manually strobe the target and at the same time talk the pilot into a visual (say 50 yards) position by means of a standard commentary giving speed, height and turning orders as well as target position indications. It was a one armed paper hanger situation.

"After landing, we met up with the other crew – pilot David Chambers and his navigator, John Brady – in order to debrief. I don't remember UFOs being mentioned as the cause of the scramble. There was certainly some conversation about the possibility of it having been a Meteorological balloon, or something similar

We contacted Mr Chambers about the incident but there was little he could tell us, other than of a faint signal picked up on the corner of the radar screen and that no visual of the object was made.

Pilot John Brady

"At the time I was a navigator on 23 Squadron, equipped with the De-Havilland Venom NF3 night fighter, based at Coltishall, but attached to Waterbeach, near Cambridge, where it provided quick reaction alert to protect the integrity of UK airspace in that area. About an hour or so before we took off, my pilot – David Cambers, and I, were on two minutes' readiness.

At about 2am on 14th August, the controller at Neatishead asked for a Venom aircraft to investigate a contact for the Americans near their Base, at Lakenheath. After scrambling, we were instructed to climb to 7,000 feet, where we were handed over to Lakenheath, who gave us indications as to where the contact was positioned.

On the first search I saw nothing, but on the subsequent three or four runs I obtained a contact of around four miles. However, the contact was not as strong or bright as a contact from a large aircraft, but it was quite firm. The approach speed was high and gave the impression it was stationary, but at the same level as our aircraft.

From: John Brady.

1407

Costessey
Norwich
Norfolk

29th April 2004.

John Hanson,
31 Red Lion St,
Alvechurch
Worcestershire
B48 7LG.

Dear John Hanson,

Thank you for your letter of 10th April about the event at Lakenheath on the night 13/14 August 1956.

I was pleased to see Ivan Logan's report and I agree with his comments in his letter. I am sure he will have given you a good insight into the events that night – he and I have discussed these matters in the past. I will just outline for you what I can remember of our flight that night.

At the time, I was a navigator on 23 Squadron which was equipped with the de Havilland Venom NF3 night fighter. The squadron was based at Coltishall in Norfolk but was detached to Waterbeach near Cambridge where it provided quick reaction alert to protect the integrity of UK airspace in the area.

Just about an hour or so before we took off my pilot David Crowther, and I were put on 2 minutes readiness. A minute or two before 0200 on 14 Aug, the controller at Neatishead asked for a Venom to investigate a contact for the Americans near their base at Lakenheath. So, we were scrambled and were off at 0200. Neatishead vectored us towards Lakenheath and we were instructed to climb to 7000 feet. Shortly we were handed over to Lakenheath who gave us indications as to where the contact was positioned. On the first search run I saw nothing, but on the subsequent three or four runs I obtained a contact at around 4 miles. However, the contact was not as strong or bright as a contact from a large aircraft but it was quite firm. The approach speed was high and gave the impression that it was stationary but at the same level as our aircraft. The Americans confirmed at one stage the the contact was stationary. Unfortunately, you cannot intercept a target like that and my pilot could see nothing in the dark. The Americans did not offer close control but what they did was sufficient, and our radar – AI 21 – was good enough to obtain a contact. At the end of the fourth or fifth run we heard that another Venom had been scrambled so we returned to Waterbeach, landing at 0255.

At the debrief, Ivan and I agreed that we had obtained good contacts but could not come up with much idea as to what it was. My own belief is that it was probably a met baloon.

Little was made of this incident at the time and it was soon forgotten about although the usual debriefings took place. We certainly had no idea of any other events that night.

I have heard recently that this was the first time an RAF aircraft had been scrambled to intercept a UFO. I have to say that I do not believe in the 'Alien' classes of UFOs but on this night I did have a firm contact.

I doubt that my few words will help you much in your research but I wish you both the best of luck.

Yours sincerely

John Brady.

UFO was stationary

The Americans confirmed, at one stage, the contact was stationary. Unfortunately, you cannot intercept a target like that and my pilot could see nothing in the dark. The Americans didn't offer close control, but what they did was sufficient and our radar AIZI was good enough to obtain a contact.

At the end of the fourth or fifth run, we heard a Venom aircraft had been scrambled, so we returned to Waterbeach, landing at 02.55 hours.

At debrief, Ivan and I agreed that we had obtained good contact but could not come up with much idea as to what it was. My own belief is that it was probably a Meteorological balloon, but little was made of the incident at the time and it was soon forgotten.

Firm contact was made

I heard, recently, this was the first time a RAF aircraft was scrambled to intercept a UFO. Whilst I do not believe in the existence of alien craft, I did have a firm contact that night."

August – England: UFO sighted over Northumberland

Was there any connection with this ongoing 'alert' over Suffolk, and an incident that occurred at midnight on the same date (13th/14th August, 1956)?

It involved national serviceman Ken Young – then aged 18, on guard duty at Otterburn Army Camp, Northumberland, just outside the barracks, facing south-east. He saw what he described as:

> *"...a big, round, and very bright object, moving up and down in the air, lighting up the ground and trees around it – still there at 1am when I went off duty".*

Ken decided to keep quiet about what he had seen, because he wanted to leave the Army. Although it would be tempting to believe Ken had seen the same UFO as tracked on radar, many miles away, it appears he may have misidentified the planet Venus, seen through a temperature inversion, according to UFO researcher Jenny Randles, to whom the incident was later reported.

14th August – England: Three orange objects sighted over Leicester

At 7pm on 14th August 1956, David Hester and Brenda Wagstaff were waiting for a bus in London Road, Leicester.

Brenda:

> *"We noticed a curious orange glow in the sky, followed by the appearance of three orange coloured lights – one much bigger than the other – two of which appeared from different directions, before meeting up over Oadby.*
>
> *A green flare then appeared and faded from view."*

fsr FLYING SAUCER REVIEW

Vol. 16, No. 2 March/April 1970 Five Shillings

UFO OVER LAKENHEATH

See page 9

UFO intercepted by RAF Fighter

THERE have been many suggestions that "flying saucers", or UFO's, operate under intelligent control. The observed behaviour of some of these objects would seem to confirm such ideas, yet there are numbers of people, including some in authoritative positions, who scoff at such notions. How, they ask, can things which do not exist be intelligently controlled? Be that as it may, I wonder what *you* think of the following account of remarkable events over East Anglia on the night of August 13-14, 1956?

With our map to help you follow the events, here is a summary of the various reports:

● At 9.30 p.m. on August 13, 1956, a Ground Control Approach (GCA) radar of the U.S.A.F. at Bentwaters picked up a target moving at an estimated 4,000 mph. The target was lost at about 20 miles to the NW.

● A few minutes later, until 9.55 p.m., a sergeant operator picked up a group of "unknowns" 8 miles SW of Bentwaters. Checks on the radar set indicated normal operation. A scattered group of a dozen targets, proceeded by three in triangular formation, moved towards the NE at speeds ranging from 80 to 125 mph. At 40 miles to the NE the several echoes were seen to merge into one ("several times larger than the echo from a B-36 bomber"), and this remained stationary for 10-15 minutes before moving 6 miles NE, stopping again for 4 minutes, and then going "off-scope".

● At 10.00 p.m. an unidentified was located 30 miles East of Bentwaters. This moved at well above 4,000 mph to a point 25 miles W where it disappeared out of the radiation pattern.

● At 10.55 p.m. an object moving at more than 2,000 mph was tracked from 30 miles E of Bentwaters. It passed directly over the station and was *observed by alerted observers on the ground* looking up, *and by crew members of an over-flying C-47 aircraft at 4,000 ft* looking down. No sonic boom was reported. At this stage Bentwaters GCA alerted Lakenheath GCA, where ground observers saw a luminous object come out of the NE at low altitude, stop, then move off eastwards out of sight.

● Soon after that the Radar Air Traffic Control Centre (RATCC), a separate unit at Lakenheath, was tracking objects which performed *right-angle turns* when travelling at 600-800 mph, as well as stopping dead, and "starting with amazing rapidity." Ground visual observers also watched objects perform stops and course reversals at dizzying speeds, and also saw two objects merge into one.

● These unprecedented activities prompted a request to the Royal Air Force to scramble fighters to investigate the unknowns. At about midnight (and therefore into August 14) a *Venom* single-seat night fighter with nose radar, took off from Waterbeach RAF station. It arrived over Lakenheath and was vectored by the ground radar operators to a target six miles to the East. In the official report it is stated that the pilot *saw* the glowing object, but later lost contact both visually and by radar.

● The *Venom* was next directed by the RATCC to a new target some 10 miles E of Lakenheath, at between 10,000 and 20,000 ft. The pilot radioed: "Roger . . . I've got my guns locked on him." There followed a pause, then came the exclamation: "Where did he go? Do you still have him?" RATCC replied: "Roger . . . it appeared he *got behind you, and he's still there.*" Another pause, then the pilot acknowledged the reversal of positions, and for ten minutes he dived, climbed, circled and rolled, while the UFO stayed as if glued behind him. During the whole of this time the operators watched two distinct echoes (aircraft and UFO) on the ground radarscopes. Low on fuel, the RAF pilot decided to return to Waterbeach. The UFO followed him for a few miles, then stopped playing "tag", and stayed stationary. By this time a second *Venom* had scrambled. The U.S.A.F. operators heard the two pilots talking over their radio-phones:

"Did you see anything?"

"I saw something, but I'm damned if I know what it was."

"What happened?"

"It got behind me . . . I did everything I could to get behind him, but I couldn't. . . . It's the damnedest thing I've ever seen!"

The second *Venom* then developed a fault on its engine and returned to Waterbeach. The ground radars continued the watch until contact with UFO's was finally lost at 3.30 a.m.

The 1956 events at Bentwaters and Lakenheath, in which the Royal Air Force and the United States Air Force were involved, remained secret until 1969. They became known only when the findings (known as the Condon Report) of the U.S. Air Force-sponsored Colorado University Commission on UFO's, headed by Dr. E. U. Condon, were published.* Alerted to the incidents by a letter from a retired U.S.A.F. radar operator who had been stationed at Lakenheath RAF station in 1956, the Commission studied reports of the incidents in the files of the U.S.A.F. Project Blue Book, which were found to confirm the radar man's story.

In the Condon Report, the case history appears under the misleading name "Greenwich" (Case No. 2, pages 248-256), and the names of the RAF stations, and other details, are omitted. However, in pages 163-164 the events are discussed under the names Lakenheath/Bentwaters. So we are not breaking security!

A "GENUINE UFO"

In his opening remarks in his Report, Dr. Condon recommends that ". . . further extensive study of UFO's probably cannot be justified in the expectation that science will be advanced thereby", which doesn't seem to make sense when it is seen that his experts concede that the Lakenheath/Bentwaters events are inexplicable (as are several other cases in the Condon Report), and concluded ". . . the probability that at least one genuine UFO was involved appears to be fairly high."

Next week we will take a look at a photograph of a UFO which reveals strange effects unseen by the human eye.

1. Cromer 2. Great Yarmouth 3. Lowestoft 4. King's Lynn 5. Ely 6. Thetford 7. Bury St. Edmunds 8. Aldeburgh 9. Felixstowe 10 Colchester

The de Havilland Sea Ve..om Mk. 22, photographed in 1956.

* *Scientific Study of Unidentified Flying Objects*, Dr. Edward U. Condon, Scientific Director; Daniel S. Gilmore, Editor. Bantam Books, New York, Toronto, London.

by Charles Bowen
Editor of Flying Saucer Review

16th August – England: 'Flying saucers' sighted over Reading

At 1.30am on the 16th August 1956, a red 'star' was seen motionless in the sky over Sonning, Reading, Berkshire, by Mr H. Wheeler – extremely likely to have been the same object as witnessed by Susan Hoyle, who was with her boyfriend – David Summers, on the common, when they noticed:

> *"...a strange, oval, object surrounded by a silvery glow, heading north-west. The 'saucer' was about three times the size of the moon and was followed by another of a similar shape... then a third came into view, slightly larger than the other two, with small dark circles appearing to be continually merging with one another in the first two objects, while the third contained one large circle, slowly revolving."*

27th August – USA: Domed UFO sighted

Juniata, Pennsylvania resident – Mrs R.S. Pope, saw:

> *"...a bright 'disc' with a clear dome, flying vertically across the sky, which then headed away northwards".*

She reported having experienced a very cold breeze, which apparently originated from the object, during the few minutes' sighting, which commenced at 9.55pm.

29th August – England: 'Halo of light' over Bristol

As the sun sank towards the horizon, at 6.30am, a Brislington man sighted a round, orange-white object, *"like a vision or halo"*, passing through the clouds, heading westwards, towards Knowle. After five seconds it disappeared from view, but reappeared later for a few seconds.

(Source: British Flying Saucer Bureau, Mr R.W.G Anstee)

30th August – England: Strange 'light' over London, plotted on radar

At 10pm on 30th August 1956, an unidentified object was plotted on radar over London. Thirty minutes later, Flight Lieutenant Harry Goldstone – navigator on board a *Meteor Mk.X1* – was preparing to land at West Malling, in Kent, at 2,000 feet, after being asked to look out for an unidentified 'light' in the sky that could be seen visually by Ground Control.

> *"The light was a few thousand feet above us, but it didn't have a star's intensity of light. I don't subscribe to 'flying saucers', but I don't know what this 'light' was, nor does anyone else."*

(Source: *Flying Saucer Review*, World Roundup of UFO Sightings and Events)

31st August – USA: Dog bone-shaped objects seen over Montana

The *Minneapolis Star* told of a UFO sighting brought to their attention by Mr J. Gordon and his family, who were flying at 8,000 feet, between Sheridan, Wyoming, and Billings, Montana, at 8pm. At the time they were 40 miles away from Billings and flying at 180 miles per hour, when Scotty (10) directed his father's attention to something strange he could see in the sky. Mr Campbell looked, thinking they were overtaking another aircraft.

> *"I saw this 'thing' heading towards us, at a terrific rate of speed; it was huge. I called*

the Billings Control Tower, but they couldn't pick it up on radar. It looked like a black dog bone. When it was about a quarter of a mile away, it looked 150 feet long. During that time it seemed to hover close to us. The object then shot away, covering 55 miles in three seconds, meaning an equivalent speed of 1,000 miles per hour."

Incredibly four more similar UFOs appeared and hovered near the aircraft. Once again, Mr Campbell contacted Air Traffic Control but they were still not picking them up on radar. Mr Campbell landed his plane at Billings and, while telling people what had taken place, one of the objects flew over the airfield! Mr Campbell learned, from further enquiries, that this UFO had been sighted by others in the locality. Can any association be made between these objects and what was seen by the crew of the BOAC aircraft on 29th June 1954?

31st August – France: Three UFOs sighted

People living in Orly, France, sighted two luminous orange objects, moving side by side westwards, at high speed across the sky.

After disappearing in the east, a third object turned up several minutes later. Enquiries with Orly Radar revealed they had not picked up anything untoward on the radar.

(Source: *Space Bulletin*, Volume 1, no. 2, May/ June 1962, 'Radar and the UFO by Brinsley Le Poer Trench)

1st September – England: UFO tracked on radar, RAF scrambled

On 1st September 1956, radar stations in the UK were put on alert after an unidentified 'blip' appeared on the screen. Aircraft were scrambled but failed to sight anything, despite flying straight through the plotted location. This appears to have been explained away on 3rd September, by a statement from the Air Ministry, who blamed electrical storms.

(Source: *Evening Chronicle*, 3.9.1956 – 'Radar image was due to storms')

3rd September – USA: Cigar-shaped UFO sighted

On 3rd September, almost exactly 36 hours after a previous UFO sighting at the Dayton Country Club, a 30-year-old TV repairman also viewed UFO activity over the City of Dayton.

3rd September – USA: Shining 'discs' seen

A New Jersey newspaper informed its readers, on the 3rd September 1956, about 'shining discs' seen over Irvington, New Jersey, by Thomas Gann, private pilot, and Joseph Malenowski – both employees of RCA – who reported seeing two mysterious objects while driving.

Gann:

"We saw a Piper Cub, at about 3,000 feet altitude, coming in for a landing. Then we noticed two shimmering 'discs', hovering about 4,000 feet higher than the plane. After a moment, they both shot away with incredible speed into space."

An object was also seen in the sky over Silver Spring, Maryland, on the 3rd, described as

"a round white object, which shot upwards into the sky".

This was catalogued by *Project Blue Book* – explanation: Light reflection.

On the same date, at 9pm, over Jersey, four schoolboys – looking out for Mars through their telescope – sighted a huge, red 'disc' and smaller white one, which moved westwards and then changed colour to red, before disappearing. The larger one was seen to fly over a factory, before heading southwards in a blaze of light, ten minutes later.

4th September – USA: UFO display over Atlantic Ocean

Mary Mann and Amey Hoag were enjoying the night air on a terrace at Melbourne, Florida, observing the sparkling stars, when they noticed some glittering star-like lights moving around in the sky. One 'ball' of red and yellow light did something remarkable:

> *"It began a weird pixie dance toward the North. From a pinpoint of light, it suddenly seemed to accelerate and elongate, until it looked like a six-inch worm humping along through a starry garden, gaily doing somersaults and loop-the-loops. Its bright, segmented body twisted and turned and finally faded."*

At 9pm, over Dallas, Texas, US Marine Corps T/Sgt. R.D. Rogers, and his family, saw a large, star-shaped object, which changed to red in colour, which was stationary in the sky for 20 minutes, before heading away westwards, at an estimated speed of over 200 miles per hour, at 9.23pm.

5th September – Northern Ireland: UFO over Parliament

At Stormont, several people saw an irregular-shaped object moving 'fast and slow' through the misty sky. It was seen to hover over the Parliament buildings for two hours. Official explanation: Cloud.

6th September – Northern Ireland: UFO falls to ground

Undoubtedly, one of the oddest things brought to our attention involved an object which landed on a rural farm in Loup, County Derry, Northern Ireland – unusual enough to be included in this book as it was so strange.

It had been raining all day. For Irish farmer Thomas Hutchinson from Loup, it was of the dampest days he had ever experienced.

Mr Hutchinson owned a small place in the country 'Rallyniel', at Loup, close to the village of Moneymore.

At midday, on 7th September (some accounts give the 6th), Mr Hutchinson was doing indoor chores with his wife, when he happened to glance out of a window and see an object fall from the sky and land in a field, about quarter of a mile away.

Curious, Mr Hutchinson put on his rubber boots and wet weather gear and set out to investigate. Because a small stream and a hedge blocked his way, it took the Irish farmer almost 10 minutes to reach the 'landing site' – a muddy, sodden field in a small valley.

Discovered a red object on the ground

The first odd thing Mr Hutchinson noticed was a red coloured object, resting lightly on a tiny cushion of grass that kept it dry, or reasonably dry, since the rain fell unceasingly. The object remained motionless, so Mr Hutchinson walked up to it and looked it over. If the thing was a 'true UFO', it was one of the oddest ever described in UFO history.

> *"Immediately I picked it up, it started to revolve silently at very fast speed. I could feel the wind on my cheek coming from its whirling action. I carried it to the end of the field to bring it home. I put it down to open a hole in the hedge to get through. Immediately I let go, it rose straight up and disappeared in the clouds – leaving me very disappointed."*

Interviewed by the British Flying Saucer Bureau

Mr Hutchinson was contacted by the British Flying Saucer Bureau about the matter and was interviewed by Miss Isobel Potts, from Portadown, from which it was ascertained that the object was about three feet in height by 18 inches in diameter. The colour was light red, with three dark stripes across its upper half. From a distance, the object looked silver.

It was not warm to the touch and felt as if it were made of fine rubber, covered with very light canvas. At the top was a little knob, which was always turned to the sky. At the base was a peculiar structure which felt like rubber, from which projected a little spike by which Mr Hutchinson had carried it.

It was by apparently pinching this spike which may have restarted the internal mechanics. Weather experts at Aldergrove RAF Station suggested this was an off course meteorological balloon – an explanation offered by some of the Irish newspapers. Fortunately, enquiries made with RAF Aldergrove by the *Bristol Evening Post* revealed they had no idea what the object could have been!

The Royal Ulster Constabulary at Ballyronan were also notified, but never told the result of any findings following their investigation – no doubt because there weren't any.

8th September – England: Flickering object seen over London

At 8.44pm on 8th September, Charles Longcroft, from London, was waiting to catch the train at Box Hill, Surrey, with some friends, when they saw a round, scintillating object in the sky, flickering with light and constantly changing in colour from white to red, red to white, white to green and green to white. After seven minutes they lost it in cloud cover, but saw it again at 9.20pm. Apparently the object was also seen by other rail passengers as well as the porter.

(Source: *Flying Saucer Review*, Sept/Oct. 1956, Volume 2, No. 5)

14th September – USA: UFO display

At 1am, two police officers from Highland, North Carolina – one of whom was Officer O.S. Gryman – sighted:

> *". . . fourteen yellow-to-red round objects, with tremendous exhaust, flying in a vague formation south-west to east, before changing to north-east, then back again, while moving up and own in the sky over a period of one and half hours."*

17th September – Scotland: UFO sighted by schoolchildren

On 17th September 1956, pupils and staff were travelling to school at 8.30am, through Glendean (seven miles from Dunoon), when 'five flat half circular objects, with aluminium-like surfaces', were seen stationary in the sky.

We came across an original report from a number of files sent to us by Lincoln UFO Researcher – Dick Thompson, including a sighting by Janet Redman, in September 1956, to whom we spoke over 40 years later.

> *"I was aged fourteen and can never forget what happened. I saw this cigar-shaped object, motionless in the blue sky over the town, one afternoon, close to a very odd looking cloud. I was shocked to see a number of smaller objects come tumbling out of the 'cigar' and go back into it, before it shot off across the sky at a terrific speed."*

England: Silver object seen hovering over ground in Berkshire

Ex-World War Two, German sailor Fritz Ruffler – then living in Burghfield, Reading – a man who had 'diced with death' on many occasions during the Second World War – was cutting the hedge in a field close to a church at Trash Green, situated between Theale and Burghfield, in September 1956, when he felt the hairs on his neck bristle and a spine-tingling sensation.

> *"I turned around and was frightened to see what looked like a silver translucent raindrop, about four to five feet in height, a couple of feet in diameter, hovering just above the ground, about 50 to 60 feet away. All of a sudden it climbed upwards and disappeared into the sky, heading eastwards, out of sight in seconds, leaving me hardly able to walk home, shocked by what I had witnessed. I later found out that someone had published my sighting in a magazine – a matter I knew nothing about. Amazingly, they even depicted me with a full head of hair, which I have never had!"* **(Source: Personal interview)**

22nd September – England: 'Sphere' over Cleethorpes – RAF scrambled

What lay behind the mysterious appearance of a 'sphere', seen high in the sky at Cleethorpes? It looked like a glass globe, with something inside it, and was estimated to be 80 feet in diameter. It was seen by thousands of people all over the town, on the afternoon of 22nd September. The object, plotted at a height of 51,000 feet, remained still in the sky – despite a wind of 40 mph at that altitude. A spokesman from RAF Manby told reporters:

> *"We have no idea what it was, but it isn't a weather balloon. Two fighter jets were scrambled. By the time they had arrived, the object was nowhere to be seen."*

(Source: *Daily Herald*, 23.9.1956 – 'They're seeing saucers'/*Sunday Times*, 24.9.1956/ *Grimsby Evening Telegraph*, 23.9.1956)

23rd September – England: UFO sighted – RAF jets ordered to intercept

The *Sunday Times* (24th September) reported to its readers that:

> *"A 'flying saucer' was sighted both visually and by radar over Manby, in Lincolnshire, yesterday afternoon. The object was at 54,000 feet and remained apparently stationary for about an hour, though there was a wind of 40 mph at that height. Meteorologists calculated the diameter as being 80 feet.*
>
> *Two fighter aircraft were sent up to investigate. When they arrived at the location they found nothing, nor could it be seen anymore from the ground."*

Enquiries into this established that a cosmic ray balloon, 80 feet in diameter, released on the 21st September, failed to burst when the instruments were jettisoned and was last seen over Kent, at a height of about 90,000 feet. It appears that this was likely to be the answer.

(Source: Mr J.F. Wightman, *Flying Saucer News Bulletin*)

24th September – England: Object seen over Bolton Abbey

On 24th September 1956, a huge white bird was seen in the sky over Beamsley Beacon, near Bolton Abbey, Yorkshire, by a party of hikers – one of whom was Mr B. Henser:

"Simultaneously, Mr Elliot and I saw a bright, round, orange sphere. It hovered there for about five minutes, disappeared, but reappeared while we were some way from the top of the summit. When we eventually arrived at the top, there was nothing to be seen."

(Source: *FSR*, Volume 2, Number 6, November December, 1956)

26th September – England: Black UFO seen in the south-west sky

At 8.55am, Mr R. Brooks of Bedminster, Bristol, was working at the Bristol Infirmary when he noticed:

"...a round, black object, with a blurred fuzzy outline, apparently motionless in the sky to the south-west. It appeared to be the size of a pea, held at arm's length, and was silent. I watched it for four minutes and took my eyes away for about 30 seconds. When I looked back again, it had gone. The moon was just visible through the mist."

(Source: Mr Watts, British Flying Saucer Bureau)

9th October – England: UFOs over RAF Base

A glowing object was spotted in the night sky over RAF Little Easton, Essex. It was about half the size of the moon in size and at times pulsated, emitting five or six rays of light across the sky; a second smaller object appeared, which descended towards the first and then disappeared. The officer who witnessed this was Lt. Commander Pollack. **(Source: NICAP)**

23rd October – England: Retired Squadron Leader sights UFOs

Retired Squadron Leader Ernest Booker, from Lower Hill Road, Rugby, sighted two very bright 'lights' moving across the sky towards Coventry, at a height of some 1,500 feet, on 23rd October 1956.

"The lights could not have been attached to balloons, drifting with the wind, because the wind was blowing in another direction, and they would not have been on gliders, as they were travelling at a leisurely speed and were brighter than normal aircraft lights. When one changed course, so did the other."

25th October – England: Ex-RAF man sights UFOs over Warwickshire

On the evening of 25th October 1956, ex-RAF employee – Mr Christopher Orton of Stocks Lane, Thurlaston, in Rugby – sighted:

"...two exceptionally bright yellow/orange 'lights', which seemed to be attached, fore and aft, to something quite out of the ordinary. Not a sound was heard, as the lights swept to the south of my house and turned sharply, eastwards, disappearing behind the lights of the radio mast at Rugby."

26th October – England: RAF fighter scrambled to intercept UFO

The following evening, a RAF jet fighter pursued what he thought was a huge flying object, near Coventry, but had to give up the chase when it out-distanced him. The unnamed pilot told of:

"...climbing to 25,000 feet, when two bright amber 'lights' appeared above me, situated to the front and rear of some very large object, displaying no navigation lights."

(Source: Bob Tibbitts, Coventry UFO Research Group)

1st November – USA: Pilot sights orange 'light'

USAF Captain W.M. Lyons was flying a *T-33* jet trainer, 60 miles east of St. Louis, Missouri, Illinois, at 5.30pm, when he reported having sighted:

> *"...an orange 'light' with a blue tinge, flying across the sky for two minutes."*

7th November – Paris: Two UFOs sighted

At 6pm, many thousands of Parisians were in the City, taking part in a Pro-Hungarian and anti-communist demonstration, when two brilliant objects were sighted, for several minutes, over the City. The phenomenon was reported to the Observatory of Paris.

8th November – England: Two diamond-shaped objects seen

At 2.25pm on 8th November 1956, Adrian Mills was in North Row, London, when he sighted an object moving slowly through the sky, but lost sight of it as it passed behind buildings, opposite, blocking his view.

At 3.40pm, after having completed his business for the day, Mr Mills was in the process of leaving the building, when he was astonished to see two milky-white diamond-shaped objects in close formation, travelling eastwards.

(Source: *FSR*, Nov/Dec.1956, Volume 2, No. 6)

8th November – USA: Two UFOs seen behind jet fighter

At about 9am on 8th November, several witnesses in Coco Beach, Southern Florida, observed two UFOs, move in behind an *F-100* Jet Fighter. Through 7 x 50 binoculars, and also with the naked eye, they watched as the jet moved across the sky. The UFO came up fast and the jet pilot made a tight turn, but couldn't catch the object. It was learned, later, that the same object was seen earlier, pursuing a rocket launched from Cape Canaveral.

(Source: National UFO reports)

14th November – USA: UFO display over Alabama

Capt. W.J. Hull, veteran Capital Airlines pilot – who was a UFO sceptic and had written an article, entitled *The Obituary of the Flying Saucers,* for the *Airline Pilot* magazine – was flying over Alabama at 10.10pm on Capital Flight No. 77, approaching Mobile, Alabama, from New York City. Suddenly, he and his co-pilot – Peter Macintosh, noticed a bright 'light' through the upper part of the windshield. The plane was on a south-westerly course, and the object – looking like a meteor – was railing across their path, from left to right. However, instead of burning out, the 'meteor' halted abruptly, directly in front of the plane.

"What the hell is it, a jet?" Macintosh shouted.

As the UFO remained a constant distance in front of the plane, Captain Hull grabbed his microphone and called Air Traffic Control Mobile Tower.

> *"Bates Tower, this is Capital 77. Look out toward the north and east and see if you can see a strange white 'light' hovering in the sky."*

Bates responded, saying that a thick cloud layer was obscuring vision, and asked Captain Hull if he thought the object was in the vicinity of Mobile.

> *"Affirmative", Hull replied. "It is directly ahead of us and at about our altitude or slightly higher. We are right over Jackson and have descended to 10,000 feet."*

Immediately after the radio exchange, the UFO began to move. It darted back and forth, rising and falling, making extremely sharp turns – sometimes changing course 90 degrees in an instant. The colour and size remained constant.

> *"Macintosh and I sat there, completely flabbergasted at this unnerving exhibition", Captain Hull reported.*

After 30 seconds, or more, the object ceased its violent manoeuvres and again appeared to hover ahead of the plane.

Tried to raise Brookley Air Force Tower

About this time Mobile Tower called back:

> *"Capital 77, we are trying to raise the Brookley Air Force Base Tower".*

At this moment, the UFO began another series of 'crazy gyrations', 'lazy 8's', 'square chandelles'... and then shot out over the Gulf of Mexico, rising at a steep angle. It diminished rapidly to a pinpoint and disappeared in the night. Elapsed time: At least two minutes.

Captain Hull stated:

> *"The one thing, which I can't get over, is the fact that when it came, it came steeply downward; when it departed, after its amazing show, it went steeply upward!"*

17th November – England: 'Light' over Lancashire – RAF jet arrives

Jimmy Gee of Farnworth, near Bolton, was making early morning deliveries in his van at Walkden, Manchester, on 17th November 1956, when he saw a long, bright yellow strip – not unlike a bright fluorescent light – which turned, dropped horizontally, and headed towards Walkden. Shortly afterwards he came across a man and his two children, who told him they had just seen a 'flying saucer' going towards the Manchester area, with vapour jets trailing flame.

Ten minutes later, in what now already seems a familiar game of 'cat and mouse', a RAF Jet appeared in the sky and headed towards where the object had been.

(Source: *Bolton Evening News*, 19.1.1956)

25th November – USA: Police officers chase egg-shaped UFO

Police officers – Don Kelm and Jack Peters – of the South Dakota State Highway patrol, were driving along highway 34, at 12.15am, when they were astonished to see an egg-shaped object with a rounded base, illuminating the road with red light, hovering alongside the cruiser. The officers 'gave chase' over six miles but the object remained ahead of them, criss-crossing the highway.

They managed to take some photographs which, when processed later, showed a half-moon shaped object, with a bulbous protuberance at one end three times the diameter of the moon, which was also captured in the frame concerned.

A heavy period of UFO activity, covering the areas of North Dakota, South Dakota and Minnesota, began on 8th November.

The sightings – during nearly every hour of the day and night – continued until 2nd December. More than 85 separate visual sighting reports from some 60 different localities were received from the three State areas. Due to the unusually large number of reports, it was possible, in some instances, to determine that the same phenomenon was seen at widely separated areas. In other cases, the sighting reports

indicate that a great number of different objects were aloft at one time over different areas.

Busiest Day

The busiest day in the 25-day concentration was the 16th. From 9.30am, until late that night, reports streamed in from towns in Minnesota and South Dakota – many sightings obviously of the same individual object. During the day and evening of the 16th, 13 reliable witnesses described objects over the cities of St. Paul and Detroit Lakes, Minnesota; Peever, Oelrich, Wall, Hermosa, Minot, Mobridge, Glenharn and Milbank, South Dakota, and over Des Lacs, Bismark and Englevale, North Dakota.

UFO followed freight train – phones knocked out

A Lemmon, South Dakota, telegrapher saw an object – like a 'ball of flame' – that followed a freight train into the Lemmon's yards, at daybreak. It was estimated to be 25 feet from the ground. It swooped low over the stockyards, turned, and sped away. Seconds after turning, a noise – as if lightning had struck – was heard in the depot. The telegrapher, Calvin Goats, tried to call the next station – only to find the railroad phones, the Western Union service and the automatic block system, were mysteriously dead.

Shortly thereafter, they started functioning again – just as mysteriously. The object was about three feet in diameter.

30th November – England: 'Flying discus' seen over Northants.

Kettering residents – Mr Keith Manning, who was a member of the Royal Observer Corps, and Mr Maurice Holloway – were cycling home after completing work, and near the town centre, when Mr Manning spotted a mysterious object glowing in the night sky. They made their way up Market Street, to obtain an unobstructed view.

Mr Holloway:

> *"It was now clearly visible. It was circular in shape and had a hole in the centre. It appeared to be travelling sideways – like a discus – and at about the speed of a jet aircraft; we couldn't hear any sound. We stood watching, as it headed away towards Corby."*

(Source: International UFO Observer Corps)

Also on the same date (given the time differentials) was a report from Charleston Air Force Base, South Carolina aerial navigator – Major D.D. Grimes, who sighted 'an unspecified object' flying at an estimated 100 feet altitude, over water, for 10 minutes,at 12.48pm.

11th December – England: Bright green 'ball' over Yorkshire Moors

Peter Lawson (21) and Alan Owen (17), from the Haworth area of Yorkshire, were out motorcycling on the moors between Bolton Abbey and Addingham, at 8.15pm, when they were amazed to see:

> *"...a bright green object hovering in the air, about 2,000 feet, shaped like a ball, about 20 feet in width with yellow flames coming from it. It stayed there for a couple of minutes, before slowly descending – its light persisting, for some minutes."*

Another witness was Miss Gwen Verity of Station Road, Grassington:

> *"I had just left the house, when my attention was caught by a green object – which appeared to be circular – in the Blubberhouses direction. It appeared to travel straight down from the sky."*

(Source: International UFO Observer Corps)

30th December – England: UFO over Reading

Mrs Doris Dinnage of 4, West Hill, Reading, was in the garden, at 6.15pm. She happened to look up into the sky and saw what she described as:

> *"...an object – like a fish but without the tail, in the eastwards direction – zigzagging across the sky like a bird."*

She rushed into the house and told her husband, Charles, and the rest of the family. By the time they reached outside, it had gone.

(Source: *Flying Saucer Review,* March/April 1957, Volume 3, No. 2)

1957

1st January – England: Ring-shaped UFO and orange object seen

AT 3.30pm on 1st January 1957, Mrs G. Rhodes, Mr G. Thompson, Mr G.A. Langdale, Mr J. Hari, Mr A. Hunter, Mr A. Jadwatt, Mr M..P. Pattel and Miss A. and J. Rhodes were in the front room of Mrs Rhodes' house at Mill Lane, Sutton, St. Helens, Lancashire, posing for a family photograph, when a 'flying object' was seen by the group through the window. Everyone rushed out to have a look at it. They described it as being an enormous, grey, ring-shaped object, with defined inner and outer margins, seen moving northwards across the sky, before shooting upwards and vanishing from sight a minute later.

Glowing orange UFO seen over Staffordshire

At 4.30pm the same day, a glowing orange 'cigar' was seen in the sky over Ranton Staffordshire, by Mrs Jessie Roestenberg, who alerted her next door neighbour – Mrs D. Osborn. The two women watched as it crossed the sky, heading westwards, leaving a trail twice its length. *"An RAF jet appeared in the sky and approached the object, which then ascended vertically and vanished into the sky."*

Scotland – UFO drops silver object over landscape

In early January 1957, a resident of Lanarkshire, Scotland, was returning home when he noticed a bright star, moving northwards across the sky. A second 'star' then appeared alongside the other object, before heading towards his position.

Hurrying up the hill to a bridge, he noticed a slight mist was falling. Glancing upwards he saw the two 'stars' were now above him.

> *"Suddenly they halted in flight, enabling me to see a very large, black, oval-shaped object, and then there was a flash of orange red light, allowing me to see a silver, oval object, descending from the larger. The objects began to move away, accompanied by a faint whirring noise. After travelling for about a quarter of a mile, they stopped again – there was another flash of light. Once again, a small silver object dropped downwards. Finally, the larger object moved out of sight."* **(Source: Glasgow UFO Research Society)**

3rd January – England: UFO display over Hampshire

Unable to sleep during a stay at the Royal South Hampshire Hospital, Southampton, Mrs I. Hurcoop looked out of the window of the Cowan Ward, at 2.20am on 3rd January 1957, and noticed:

> *"...an unusual bright 'star', moving slowly across the night sky. I shouted for the night duty sister and attendant nurse, who stood watching with me, as the 'star' slowly disappeared below the roof line of the Grimston Ward, followed by the appearance of several more 'stars', which began an aerial display lasting until 5.30am."*

Eight hours later

Eight hours later, two boys from Halifax – David Weeks and David Tracey – reported sighting two 'solid' silver or grey oval objects, spinning on their axes, about the size of a moderate plane, heading eastwards over the town.

9th January – England: Two UFOs seen over Halifax, Yorkshire

Just under a week later, on 9th January, Mr I.D. Gale – a former lecturer on aircraft recognition with the Territorial Army, in Dorset, previously employed by the Air Ministry as a radar operator – was walking through Seville Park, Halifax, Yorkshire, at 11.39pm, when he noticed two objects hovering in the sky; one in a vertical plane, the other horizontal. By the time he shouted out to his friends, the objects had accelerated towards the south and were out of view.

(Source: *The Halifax Courier & Guardian*, 3.1.1957)

January – Scotland: UFO sighted over Lanarkshire

John Hanney of Lesmahagow, Lanarkshire, was walking home from Bible class, one Sunday morning in early January 1957, when he noticed a bright star-like object towards the North, moving slowly across the sky.

> *"To my amazement, a smaller object appeared alongside – then both of them headed towards my direction. As they did so, I noticed a strange mist falling onto the ground underneath them. I ran to the railway bridge to obtain a closer look and saw they were now about half a mile above the rooftops of houses, very close to where I was stood. As they hovered silently overhead, I was able to see a large oval shaped, black object, flashing a red light, illuminating the appearance of a silver, smaller, oval object, which descended from the larger one – now making a faint whirring noise. I watched them slowly move across the sky, but when about three quarters-of-a-mile away they stopped. There was another flash of light and another oval-shaped object descended out of the larger again."*

(Source: Glasgow Unidentified Flying Objects Research Society)

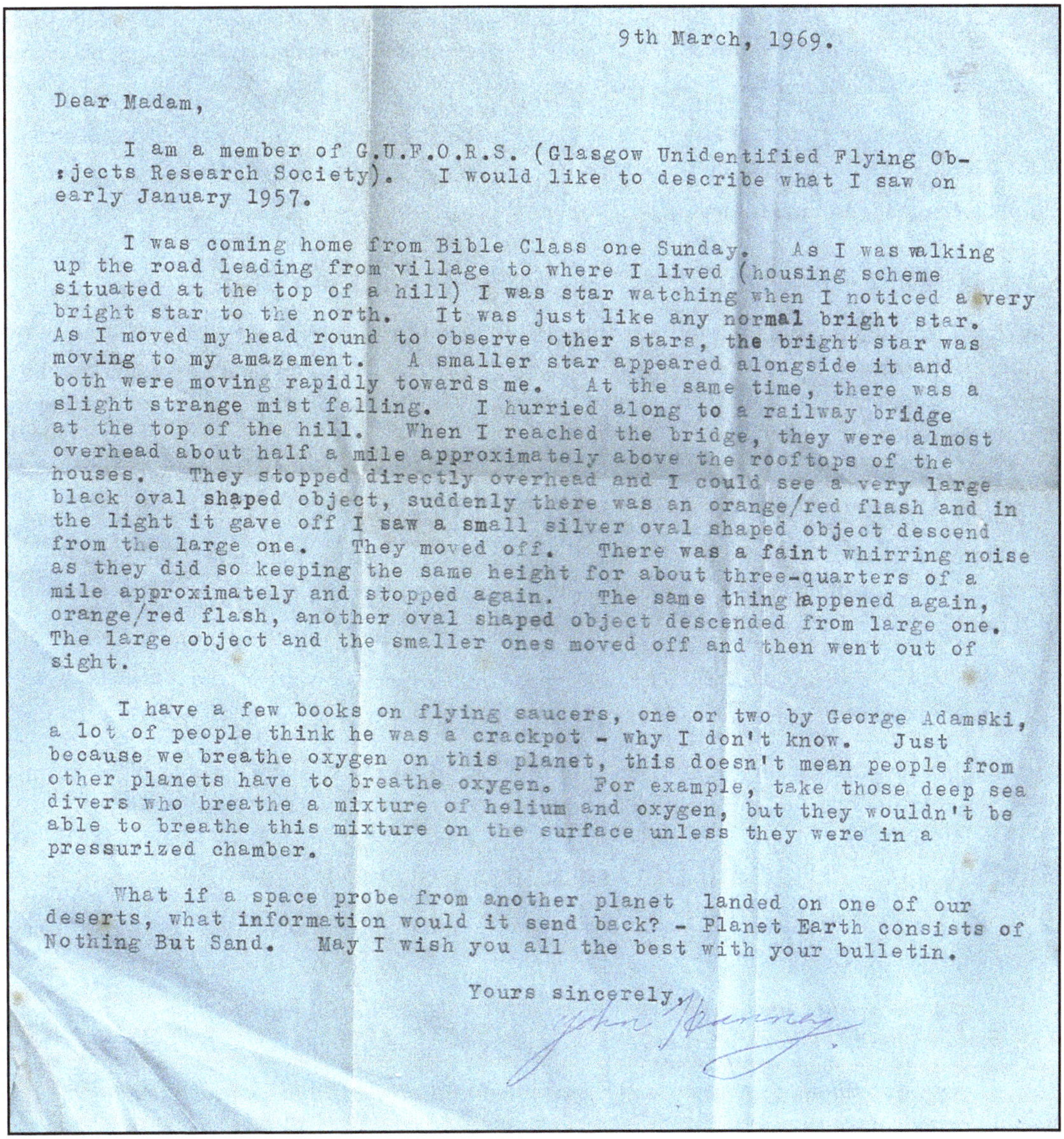

9th March, 1969.

Dear Madam,

I am a member of G.U.F.O.R.S. (Glasgow Unidentified Flying Ob-:jects Research Society). I would like to describe what I saw on early January 1957.

I was coming home from Bible Class one Sunday. As I was walking up the road leading from village to where I lived (housing scheme situated at the top of a hill) I was star watching when I noticed a very bright star to the north. It was just like any normal bright star. As I moved my head round to observe other stars, the bright star was moving to my amazement. A smaller star appeared alongside it and both were moving rapidly towards me. At the same time, there was a slight strange mist falling. I hurried along to a railway bridge at the top of the hill. When I reached the bridge, they were almost overhead about half a mile approximately above the rooftops of the houses. They stopped directly overhead and I could see a very large black oval shaped object, suddenly there was an orange/red flash and in the light it gave off I saw a small silver oval shaped object descend from the large one. They moved off. There was a faint whirring noise as they did so keeping the same height for about three-quarters of a mile approximately and stopped again. The same thing happened again, orange/red flash, another oval shaped object descended from large one. The large object and the smaller ones moved off and then went out of sight.

I have a few books on flying saucers, one or two by George Adamski, a lot of people think he was a crackpot - why I don't know. Just because we breathe oxygen on this planet, this doesn't mean people from other planets have to breathe oxygen. For example, take those deep sea divers who breathe a mixture of helium and oxygen, but they wouldn't be able to breathe this mixture on the surface unless they were in a pressurized chamber.

What if a space probe from another planet landed on one of our deserts, what information would it send back? - Planet Earth consists of Nothing But Sand. May I wish you all the best with your bulletin.

Yours sincerely,

21st January – England: 'Red glow' flashes across sky over Bristol

At 10.30pm on 21st January 1957, a fast-moving 'red glow', looking like *"a large fire, in the sky, with several rays running through it"*, was seen flying across the Bristol area, ruining television reception for many viewers – who contacted the BBC after the screens dissolved into wavy patterns and jagged edges, between 10pm and 10.30pm, followed by reports of an object seen over Downend, Portishead and Clevedon, a few minutes later – lighting up the sky with red light, before moving over Whitchurch.

The sighting was explained away by Filton Meteorological Office as likely to be the Aurora Borealis, although it seems unusual for it to be visible this far south. One witness – Mr Ronald Anstee from Fishponds, Bristol – told of a noise like *"a vast armada of heavy bombers, lasting for several hours, making* [his] *wife quite ill"*.

Was there any connection with a sighting of a large metal 'ball' or 'disc', which was reported over an army base in the United States on the same day?

(Source: NICAP/Personal interview)

23rd January – England: UFO display over Southampton

The Royal Hospital in Southampton was to be the focus of further UFO activity, during the early hours of 23rd January (just twenty days after the first one here, mentioned earlier in this chapter), when a number of bright 'stars' were seen performing a series of movements across the sky, before ending the display at 5.30am.

24th January – England: UFO seen next to aircraft over Wiltshire

At 11am, Mr F Todd of Corsham, and his friend were walking up Station Road, towards Chippenham, facing the direction of Lyneham Aerodrome, when they saw a *De Havilland Comet,* flying at a height of about 12-15,000 feet in a westerly direction, from Lyneham.

> *"When it was almost overhead, at its stern appeared a round grey object with a black line on it. Fifteen seconds later, it suddenly disappeared from view."*

Mr Todd had spent seven and-a-half years in the Fleet Air Arm and was sure the object was nothing to do with the airplane, or a metrological balloon. He reported the matter to the Air Ministry.

8th February – England: UFO seen in sky over Portsmouth

At 10.15pm on 8th February 1957, a UFO was seen moving quickly across the sky over Eastney, Portsmouth, by Mrs Freda King.

> *"The object seemed to enclose a dark form of some description, surmounted by a lighted spar – somewhat like a radio mast.*
>
> *The whole appearance vaguely resembled a humming top, in black and white. I'm convinced I saw a 'flying saucer'."*

(Source: Nicholas Maloret/*Southampton & Echo* Newspaper, 4.1.1957)

11th February – England: Black tailed UFOs seen over Nottinghamshire

On 11th February, as the light faded, *"five tadpole-shaped objects, dark in colour, with black tails"*, were seen flashing across the sky over Mansfield, Nottinghamshire. One of the witnesses spoke of seeing them:

> *"...stationary, and silhouetted against a clear sky, before two of them broke formation and shot upwards into the sky, leaving blue and white streamers."*

Was the sighting connected with reports of severe earth tremors (Force 8), which affected eleven counties in the UK on the 11th February 1957, stretching downwards from the Lake District to the outskirts of London? Its epicentre was later discovered to be Diseworth, halfway between Loughborough and Derby.

15th February – England: Egg-shaped object seen to descend into sea

On 15th February 1957 at 11.40am, a partly transparent, glittering, egg-shaped object was seen to descend into Sandstone Harbour, Portsmouth, by three boys – Geoffrey Bolt, Dudley Heywood, and John Whiting – who were on a school cross-county run, at the time.

(Source: Nicholas Maloret, WATSUP, Southampton)

15th February – England: UFO seen over Lancashire

At 10pm, Mrs Dorothy Fitton from Wardle, near Rochdale, Lancashire, was one of several witnesses that saw a large circular, glowing, object in the sky, underneath which was a second object that blinked white and red alternately.

> *"It was moving in a straight line, towards my house from the brow of the hill. After halting for a few minutes, it headed towards the direction of Littlborough."*

MP notified

Shortly after the sighting, snow fell. Oddly (or maybe not) on the 26th February, Mr J.A Leavey – MP for Heywood and Royton – tabled a question to the Secretary of State for Air, following incidents brought to his attention, which included a report of a commercial aircraft seen flying over Wardle, allegedly taking the same route as the UFO, and the discovery of a minute radio transmitter belonging to the Air Ministry, suspended for a meteorological balloon. Then two boys found another piece of meteorological equipment attached to a parachute, lying on Brown Wardle – also on the flight path of the UFO.

Not effected by the elements

None of the objects were affected by snow and were not believed to have been there earlier. One has to ask why these objects were recovered after the UFO incident. The answer is no doubt obvious, taking into consideration that when the tabled question was answered on the 20th March, in the House of Commons, the answer given by Mr Orr-Ewing was that the witnesses actually saw a pair of small hydrogen filled toy balloons, illuminated by a flashlight bulb, released by Mr N. Robinson – a laundry mechanic at Rochdale.

Dr. Clifford Thornton

According to Dr Clifford Thornton, who carried out an investigation into the matter, this explanation could be discounted, as Robinson was unable to confirm the release of the balloon. An investigation made by the local press revealed that the diameter of the balloon would have been 12 inches at

maximum. In addition, the light given off by the bulb would not have been anywhere near the source of illumination given by the UFO, understanding that some of the witnesses had been up to two miles away when they saw the object, which was accompanied by two smaller alternating lights underneath – certainly no toy balloon – but this was the explanation given in the House of Commons!

We learned that an Air Ministry spokesman visited the location and, after interviewing some of the witnesses, warned those to keep quiet.

Mr Robinson passed away in 1999.

Enquiries made, however, during more recent years, revealed that according to his cousin – Geoff Butterworth, Mr Robinson had been very skilled in electronics and had served in the RAF during the war. It is claimed that in the 1950s, he had pioneered an infra-red alarm system and was much occupied with inventions – in short an intelligent man, who it was also claimed had launched an Air Ministry weather balloon obtained for use in his experiments to develop a model airship. It appears that this may well have been the explanation, following investigations into the incident by Dr David Clarke.

Someone else who has now passed away was Paul Gregory from Newcastle-under-Lyme. In a letter to Bob Tibbitts he mentioned he had researched into the Cynthia Appleton incident. Sadly, the results of his findings are not known. *(See letter opposite).*

PAUL GREGORY
25 Wye Road
Clayton
Newcastle-under-Lyme
Staffordshire
ST5 4AZ
Newcastle-under-Lyme 69658

Mr R.W. Tibbetts,
43, Tanners Lane,
Tile Hill Village,
COVENTRY,
CV4 9HX.

19th April 1971.

Dear Sir,

In a recent letter from Norman Oliver, he mentioned the contact claim of Mrs Connelley from Coventry.

I do not think that I have heard of this case before, the reason being that I have for some considerable time been wrapped up in my own researches on the contactee theme.
I have made extensive researches into the Cynthia Appleton case, and anything as close to Birmingham is of interest to me.

We in the North Staffordshire area keep in close contact with regard to UFO incidents and I for my part liaise with groups and individuals in the Midlands.
I feel that since we in the Midlands are so scattered that co-operation between groups and individuals is a necessity.

With best wishes,

Paul Gregory

27th/28th February – England: UFOs over Surrey

Mrs Maureen Law of Godalming, Surrey, wrote to *Flying Saucer Review*, in 1957, telling them about a 'Flying Scout UFO' she had seen,

> *"...heading across the sky, at 8.30pm, in a south to north direction – high enough to see that it was round and emitting sparks in its trail. The next night, at 6.10pm, a friend of mine was at Milford, a little south of here, when a strong light in the sky was seen.*
>
> *Out of the haze appeared a large object, which was slowly descending, resembling a gigantic light bulb. When he arrived home, his son (who had been out in the north of the town) asked him if he had seen any peculiar light in the sky. When they 'swapped notes', they discovered that they had seen the same thing."*

28th February – England: 'Flying saucer' sighted over Weymouth

During the afternoon of 28th February 1957, Mr K. Maskery from Reddish, Greater Manchester, sighted a saucer-shaped object in the sky, showing many coloured lights, with flecks of red shooting out from its edge.

At 6.07pm, a 'flying saucer' was seen over Weymouth, by Mr C. Fooks and Mrs E. R. Newman, who said:

> *"I have never seen anything like it before. It seemed to come from out of a cloud, larger than any star. Its sheer brightness impressed me the most".*

Repeat performance

The following Sunday night (3rd March), Mr Maskery was returning home at l0pm, when he was surprised to see the strange blue 'light' in the sky once again. He called out to his neighbours – Mr and Mrs Longshaw – who stood watching with him, as it moved from right to left in the sky. At 11pm, a small blue 'light' was seen to move towards the object, which promptly vanished.

10th March – England: Mystery object seen in sky over Bristol

A similar (if not the same) object was seen by Paul McCormick from Fishponds, Bristol, who was observing Jupiter on 10th March, at 7pm, when he noticed an extremely bright object north of the planet.

> *"I focused my telescope on the object, and saw two separate lights; one red, the other white. Every so often, a reddish flash danced from the red light to the other, by which time the phenomenon was clearly visible with the naked eye, on a course that was taking it between the pole star and Ursa Major – now directly overhead. I listened carefully, but couldn't hear any noise. It seemed to drift over, like a ghostly shadow, and yet it conveyed the impression of power. As it passed the pole star, it faded and vanished from sight."*

(Source: *Flying Saucer Review*, May/June 1957, Vol. 3, No. 3)

13th March – England: Cigarette-shaped UFO over Scarborough

Three days later on 13th March, an object – resembling a shining silver cigarette – was seen hovering just over the sea at Scarborough, by a group of men out fishing, at 5.45pm.

21st March – England: UFO sighted over London

A large circular object, similar in size to a large star, was seen moving soundlessly through the sky over South Audley Street, London, by Miss Unity Dutta and a friend. It moved in an arc of approximately 20 degrees, paused, and then descended steeply, before stopping again and receding in size – getting smaller, until it disappeared from view.

(Source: *Flying Saucer Review*, Volume 3, No. 4, Page 6)

23rd March – USA: UFOs tracked on radar

The first of four UFOs appeared on the radar scope at a civilian airport in the Los Angeles area, at 1.50pm. According to the C.A.A operator:

> *"...it was moving faster than anything I had ever seen; about 40miles north-west it came to an abrupt halt, and then reversed its course in just a few seconds."*

Five minutes later two more UFOs appeared, also heading in the same direction. These were tracked at a distance of 30miles in 30secs, at 3,600mph, before they disappeared off the scope. A fourth 'target' appeared and also went off the scope at 3,600mph; by this time some of the objects were at 10,000ft, or lower.

Eight members of the NICAP Board of Governors, Rear Admiral Herbert K. Knowles, USN (retired), Colonel Robert Emerson, USAR, Dr. Earl Douglass, *Frank Edwards, Professor Charles A. Maney, the Reverend Albert Baller, and the Reverend Leon Le Van, confirmed having seen the signed radar report. Explanation: malfunction of equipment!

*Frank Edwards (August 4, 1908 – June 23, 1967) was an American writer and broadcaster, and one of the pioneers in radio. He hosted a radio show broadcast across the United States in the 40s and 50s. Late in his life, he became additionally well known for a series of popular books about UFOs and other paranormal phenomena.

In 1948, Edwards received an advance copy of *"Flying Saucers Are Real,"* a magazine article written by retired U.S. Marine Corps Major Donald E. Keyhoe. Though already interested in the UFO reports that had earned widespread publicity since 1947, Edwards was captivated by Keyhoe's claims that the U.S. military knew the saucers were actually extraterrestrial spaceships.

Photo taken inside 'Saucer Post' (courtesy of www.nicap.org) showing mail response following the Frank Edwards radio broadcast May 18, 1954.

Major Donald E. Keyhoe

Frank Edwards

26th March – England: UFO tracked on radar by RAF Church Lawford

RAF Church Lawford, Rugby, reported having tracked an object from a stationary position in the air to 1,400 mph.

A copy of the radar plot was requested by the Air Ministry. **(Source: Declassified MOD records)**

4th April – Scotland: UFOs tracked on radar

On the morning of 4th April 1957, radar operators at the Ministry of Supply Bombs Trial Unit, West Freugh, near Stranraer, in Scotland, picked up, on radar, five stationary 'objects' at 70,000 feet – the size of battleships – later explained away by an Air Ministry spokesman as an air balloon, sent up from Aldergrove Airport in Northern Ireland. This hardly seems in character with the attitude of the base commander – Wing Commander Whitworth – who was quoted as saying:

> *"I was not allowed to reveal 'its' position, course and speed"*, adding:
>
> *"From the moment of picking 'it' up, it was well within our area. It was an 'object' of some substance – quite definitely not a freak. No mistake could have been made by the Ministry of Supply civilians, who operated the sets – they are fully qualified and experienced Officers"*

– a different picture to that depicted, at the time, when investigators of the Deputy Directorate of Intelligence (Technical) confirmed a stationary 'object' had first been tracked on radar at Balmalloch, at heights varying from fifty thousand to seventy thousand feet, and another radar station, twenty miles away, had 'locked on' to the target.

Later, four more targets, moving 'line astern', were plotted by both radar stations. The size of the radar echo was considerably larger than would be expected from normal aircraft – more like the size of a ship's radar echo. Even if balloons had been in the area, these would not have accounted for the sudden change of direction and the high-speed movement against the prevailing wind.

The report concluded that the incident was due to the presence of *"five reflective 'objects' of unidentified type and origin"*.

(Source: AIR 20/9321.DDI.Tech., 30.4.57/*Sunday Dispatch*, 7.4.57)

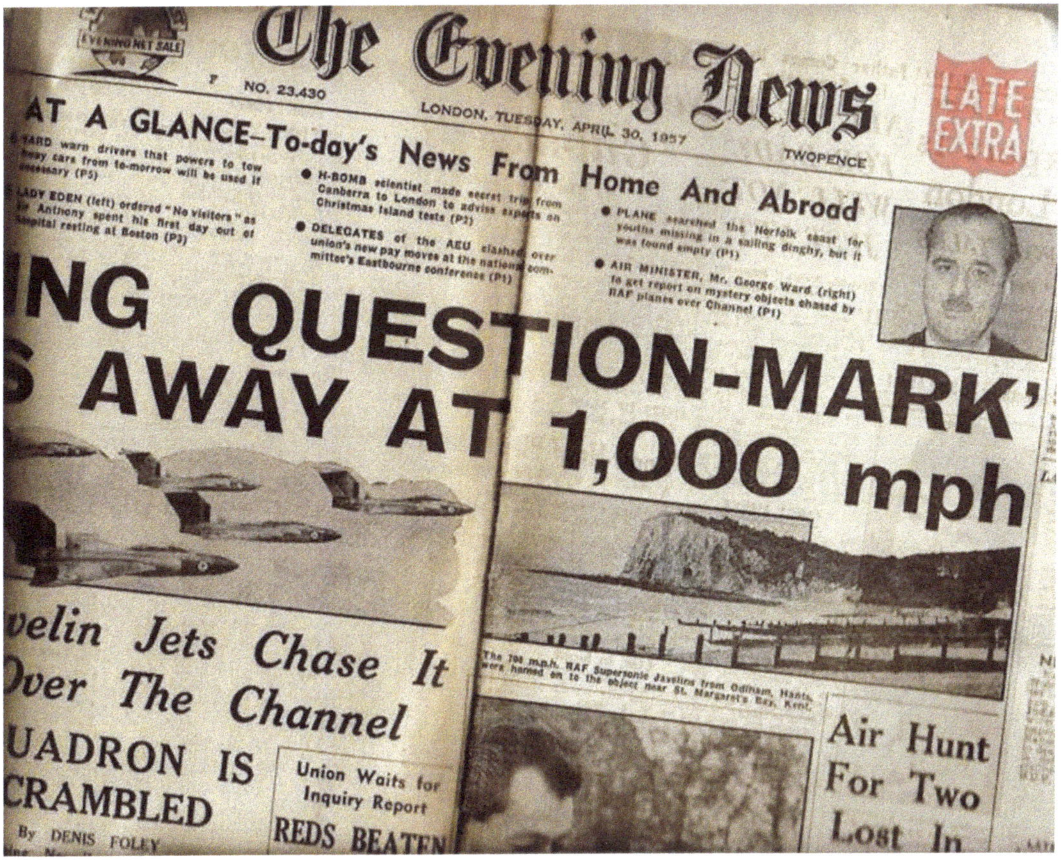

The Evening News

EVENING NET SALE

NO. 23,430 LONDON, TUESDAY, APRIL 30, 1957 TWOPENCE

LATE EXTRA

AT A GLANCE–To-day's News From Home And Abroad

Yard warn drivers that powers to tow away cars from to-morrow will be used if necessary (P5)

LADY EDEN (left) ordered "No visitors" as Sir Anthony spent his first day out of hospital resting at Boston (P3)

● H-BOMB scientist made secret trip from Canberra to London to advise experts on Christmas Island tests (P2)

● DELEGATES of the AEU clashed over union's new pay moves at the national committee's Eastbourne conference (P1)

● PLANE searched the Norfolk coast for youths missing in a sailing dinghy, but it was found empty (P1)

● AIR MINISTER, Mr. George Ward (right) to get report on mystery objects chased by RAF planes over Channel (P1)

ING QUESTION-MARK'

AWAY AT 1,000 mph

The m.p.h. RAF Supersonic Javelins from Odiham, Hants, were homed on to the object near St. Margaret's Bay, Kent.

velin Jets Chase It Over The Channel

UADRON IS CRAMBLED

By DENIS FOLEY

Union Waits for Inquiry Report

REDS BEATEN

Air Hunt For Two Lost In

UFO sighting later that evening

Later the same evening, Mr James Emmerson – a tanker driver by occupation – was driving thirty miles south of Penrith, at 11.30pm, when he noticed a reflection in the windscreen of his vehicle, which he took to be the headlights of an approaching vehicle. Seeing nothing arrive, he pulled in to the side of the road and switched off the tanker's lights. He was shocked to see:

> *"...a yellow, glowing object, in the shape of a perfect half-moon, with a distinctive gold rim and a straight edge on top".*

Was this one of the UFOs tracked earlier on radar at West Freugh?

It is worth bringing the readers' attention to a strange phenomenon which occurred at Ypsilanti Michigan United States), in early 1957, where, during some research work on a radar scope, 'points of light', resembling circular ripples, were seen to

Evening Standard Air Reporter 30-4-57

Two RAF Javelin all-weather fighters were sent up last night when radar screens covering the London area picked up an unidentified object over the Channel.

The object, which appeared to be streaking through the sky at great speed, is believed to have been a meteorite.

The Javelin crews found nothing.

The "object" was travelling westwards at considerable height. Its speed might have been as high as 1000 m.p.h.

This discounts any suggestion that it might have been a Russian bomber. The Russians have no bombers which fly faster than ours or the Americans'.

It's their job

Why were the two Javelins —the RAF's newest 700 m.p.h. delta-winged day and night fighters — sent up from Odiham, Hants, fighter base?

An Air Ministry spokesman said this afternoon: "It is the job of the RAF to take an interest in unidentified objects, even if we do know that about 99½ per cent of them are afterwards accounted for."

The RAF's defensive radar watch is maintained round-the-clock.

The Javelins carry far-reaching radar equipment. Their radarscopes located nothing last night.

An unidentified object which was recently picked up on an airfield radar set at West Freugh, Scotland, was found to be a weather balloon.

The RAF checks all such radar sightings.

15-5-57

MYSTERY OBJECTS OVER CHANNEL WERE HUNTERS

Evening Standard Reporter

The mysterious flying objects over the Channel on April 29 were two Hunter jet fighters of Fighter Command engaged on a training exercise. MPs were told this in the Commons this afternoon by the Secretary of State for Air, Mr. George Ward.

Their movements, as tracked on radar, seemed unusual and aroused the suspicions of the radar operators, he said.

Mr. Frank Beswick, Soc., Uxbridge, said there was a certain amount of apprehension about these false alarms.

'Not certain'

Had the Minister speculated about what would happen if such a missile was a nuclear weapon? he asked.

Mr. Ward said it was because the radar-controlling reporting system was not absolutely certain that the object was friendly that an investigation was started.

Replying to further points, he said that five flying objects reported this year were as yet unidentified.

They were still under investigation and might be identified later.

This total compared with six last year, none in 1955 and six in 1954.

NEWS CHRONICLE 8-4-57

News Chronicle Reporter

THE first report on the unidentified object picked up by a Scottish radar station last week will arrive today at the Air Ministry's hush-hush department.

Full details from the three radar stations which checked and cross-checked the object's speed and course follow within two days.

Top R.A.F. intelligence officers will examine both reports and then submit their conclusions to the Air Minister, Mr. Nigel Birch.

Until then the mystery will remain a mystery. "Don't talk" orders have been issued to the two radar operators, James McVey and John Kolosky, both of Stranraer, who picked up the object on their screens.

What might the object have been? A runaway meteorological balloon? Unlikely. A meteorite? Possible. A high-flying bomber? Also possible. A Russian reconnaissance aircraft? Not ruled out.

appear – some extending for 20 miles. Two years later, these 'ring formations' were observed on radar sets in Britain and the Unites States.

5th/7th April – Scotland: UFOs seen motionless in sky over Glasgow

On Friday, 5th April 1957, two UFOs – looking like silver three-penny bits – were seen motionless in the sky over Glasgow, followed by a report, on 7th April, of three silver 'globes' seen over Rothesay Bay by golfers on the course.

10th April – England: 'Flying saucer' over London

At 4.50pm, three people living in the Kensington area of London sighted what appeared to be a 'flying saucer' in the sky above them. They were James Collins of Dancer Road, Fulham, Mr B. Kell of York Street, and Mr J. Colly of Bridge Buildings, Hammersmith. All three of them described seeing:

> *"...an elliptical object – like two saucers, rim to rim – suspended in mid-air, swaying slightly in a pendulum motion."*

(Source: *Flying Saucer Review*, Volume 3, Number 4, July/August 1957, Page 6)

14th April – England:

EVENING CHRONICLE APRIL 15TH 1957.

I saw a flying saucer over City, claims girl

A FLYING saucer was reported seen over Newcastle at 9.50 last night.

Twenty-two-year-old Miss Maria Mallick, of 166 Rye Hill, Newcastle, claims to have seen it.

Miss Mallick told an "Evening Chronicle" reporter that she was sitting at home watching television. There were other people in the room with her, but she was the only one who sat facing the window.

She says she saw the saucer—"it looked just like the flying saucers they show you"—coming low from behind her house and swooping up high as it went along.

It was brightly lit, and it was the lights on the saucer which first caught her attention.

She said that no one else in the room saw it, as the others were facing the other way.

No other reports of the saucer have been received.

27th April – England: Black object over Taunton, Somerset

At 11.30am on 27th April 1957 – a bright sunny day, with a slight wind – Mr K. Solomons of Taunton, Somerset, was standing by his van, when he sighted:

> *"...an unusual, black silhouetted object – apparently stationary in the sky – glinting brightly, a quarter of a mile away. It then moved off, gathering speed and disappeared in the north-west direction, before dropping down behind some houses. I estimated its speed to be about one and-a-half times that of a jet plane."*

(Source: *British Flying Saucer Bureau/Flying Saucer News Bulletin*, number 9)

29th April – England: RAF scrambled over Hampshire

Two days later, at 8.50pm on the 29th April, a squadron of Javelin Jet aircraft were scrambled from RAF Odiham, Hampshire, in response to anomalous radar returns tracking an object over Orr, St. Margaret's Bay, Kent. No contact was made, owing to the extreme speed of the UFO.

Declassified MOD documents (AIR 20 9994) tell of two metallic objects sighted in the sky, at an estimated height of 30,000 feet, by Shanklin, Isle of Wight, resident – Mr L. Humphreys – and that no visual was made of the objects.

It is alleged the presence of the UFOs caused heavy interference to TV sets, during the screening of 'Come Dancing'.

Were UFOs signalling to each other?

At 9.30pm, Mrs Olive Webb of Leckhampton (just outside Cheltenham, Gloucestershire), noticed what she took to be the *Comet* airliner, moving low over the sky, and called her husband. The couple watched it for several minutes, noting:

> *"...superstructure on top, showing three lights, went faster in a reverse direction, without appearing to turn around.*
>
> *When near to the crest of Leckhampton Hill, it rose at a slight angle and was joined by a second object, both blinking at each other – as if signalling one another. Both objects then closed on each other and were gone."*

Mr Ian C. Walters investigates

Further investigation by Mr Ian C. Walters – a Cheltenham-based UFO investigator, who interviewed the witnesses – revealed the following additional information:

> *"The cigar-shaped object had a blue metallic grooving, like a gramophone record; the second object appeared from over the hill and approached the 'cigar' at high speed, slowed down as it neared the object, blinked, and disappeared up into the underneath of the 'cigar'."*

The couple was not the only ones to sight UFOs that evening. According to *Flying Saucer Review*, they were to receive numerous reports of UFOs sighted over the south of England, during the same evening.

(Source: Personal interview/*Gloucestershire Echo*, 7.5.1957/Ian C. Walters)

30th April – England: Spinning object over London

At 11.31pm, a round, red/orange object was sighted over Fulham Palace Road, London, by a party of six people. They included Mr T. Barton, his brother John, and his wife. The object was seen to perform two complete circles in the sky, apparently spinning as it did so, before heading away in a southerly direction.

At 11.48pm, Mr Brian Philips of Brookside South, East Barnet, sighted a strange object in the sky, heading northwards. At one stage the object turned through 360 degrees.

Brian telephoned the Police to report what he had witnessed, which lasted about a minute.

(Source: Gordon Creighton)

1st May 1957 – England: *Daily Sketch,* 1.5.57 'The 1,000 mile Wotsit'

In what one can only regard as light-hearted response to the events of the 29th May 1957, this was the banner grabbing headline!

Daily Sketch Reporter

JET fighters chased a mystery "raider" along the South Coast at 700 mph—but were left standing, the Air Ministry said last night.

The UFO (Unidentified Flying Object) was shown on radar as flying high at about 1,000 mph.

IT may have been a meteorite — or a guided missile — or a secret new Russian jet bomber.

One that got away puzzles the RAF

Favourite theory last night: A meteorite.

An Air Ministry official said yesterday: "We just don't know what it was.

"We are not trying to hide anything."

WHERE'S UFO?

The radar screen picked up the object flying in a westerly course south of London on Monday night.

Within second the UFO was being plotted on the screens of the secret underground Early Warning HQ.

Fighter Defence swung into operation.

Next air base in the track of the UFO was Odiham, Hants.

Twin-jet Javelins of 46 Squadron were scrambled.

Pilots rushed to their machines and were airborne in seconds.

Standing on their tails the Javelins climbed upward.

But the UFO raced West and no pilot was able to make contact.

And farther along the coast it shot off the radar screen and contact was not picked up again.

At the Air Ministry yesterday experts worked on the radar stations' reports.

The Russians are known to have a new type jet bomber which may be able to fly at more than 1,000 mph.

The only British aircraft capable of chasing this bomber is the record-breaking P1 fighter, which has not yet come into squadron service.

TO THE MINISTER

1st May – England: UFO over Cambridgeshire

During the early morning, Jack Martin (51) from Stow Road, Wisbech, Cambridgeshire, was outside when he happened to look upwards and see:

> *"...an object – the size of a dinner plate – flat in appearance and gold in colour. It disappeared over the village of Guyhirn, flying in a peculiar jerking movement."*

It was also seen by several other men in the same locality.

Domed-shaped object sighted over Cornwall

At 11.30am on 1st May 1957, ex-Royal Navy Petty Officer Eric Pengilly was delivering mail in the Coverack area of Cornwall, when he sighted *a dome-shaped object in the sky,* flying slowly from west to east, for ten minutes. When it reached the coast, just north of Manacle Point, it tipped at an angle of 45 degrees and shot upwards, climbing faster than any jet would have done. It then disappeared from sight. Eric later received a visit from RAF Intelligence Officers, who questioned him for a couple of hours on what he had seen. **(Source: *Flying Saucer News*, no. 9)**

May – England: Close encounter on airfield runway, Devon

We were to come across details of another incident that stirred our imagination: the discovery of a mysterious glowing 'craft', seen on the disused runway at RAF Winkleigh, twenty-three miles from Exeter, Devon, in early May 1957, by John Payne – a milk tanker driver, employed by Wincanton Transport of Yeovil.

John was driving from Weston-Super-Mare to Torrington, in Devon, as part of a regular journey, when he decided to pull in to the abandoned airfield to drink some coffee, half-an-hour before sunrise.

> *"On the morning in question it was fine, dry, with good light. I pulled onto the perimeter track, at 4.50am, at Winkleigh Aerodrome, North Devon, to have a drink. After some minutes, I noticed what appeared to be a 'submarine' at the end of the runway. My first thoughts were: how did that get up there? Also, it looked very new. I watched for some*

minutes, and then thought I would take a closer look, and got out of the cab and walked towards it.

After getting to within some 200 yards, I found it impossible to get any closer. It was like walking into sunshine. This was the very first intimation of anything out of the ordinary. It then went straight up, like an elevator, for about 1,200 feet, and headed towards the North Devon coast.

The speed was terrific. There was never any noise of any sort. There were no windows, exhaust, movement, that I could see. Possibly, the tail fins were just a little more fluorescent when in motion. No 'green men' – nothing. Please, I am not a crank – just a lorry driver. I make no claims as to its identity."

John Payne

UFO researcher Richard Farrow

Another account of the incident was obtained by Torbay UFO researcher Mr Richard Farrow – now living in Norway – who at that time only identified John as 'JP' but included an illustration of the craft.

Mr Ronald Toft of 'Pegasus Magazine'

Some one else who became interested in this matter was journalist Mr Ronald Toft – then editor of *Pegasus*, the magazine of the Surrey Investigation Group on aerial phenomena. We contacted Mr Toft, after learning details of the case, which had been passed to him by Omar Fowler (then National Investigations Coordinator for BUFORA). Mr Toft disclosed that he had written to John Payne (who had expressed a wish to remain anonymous, at the time) and that details of the incident were published in the May/June 1970 issue of *Pegasus* – of which we were unable to trace a copy. Frustratingly, all the other back copies were there; this was the only one missing!

Mr Toft:

> *"John described a force field, completely surrounding the object. When he approached to within 90 yards away, it was like walking into an invisible air cushion you could actually lean on. After the object took off, Payne (who was able to walk without any difficulties) discovered a faint black powdered circle on the ground, approximately 50 feet in diameter, like black carbon in appearance, which he didn't touch."*

In his communications with Mr Toft, John wrote:

> *"My personal feelings were one of intense relief at its departure. Mentally, it felt as if a weight had been lifted from me but, physically, I felt no pain, shock, tingling, loss of memory, or any other ill effects, but discovered, when I arrived at the Torrington factory, that my watch was 20 minutes slow. I believe that many other people also witnessed the passage of this object through the air and saw one other person on the runway, who didn't want to get involved, believing people would call him a crank and subject him to ridicule."*

John decided to forget what he had seen. However, nine years later, his wife Sylvia – suggested he report it to BUFORA.

Following an appeal in the local Yeovil newspaper, in July 2006, we were contacted by Janet Gough – an ex-neighbour of Mr & Mrs Payne, who told us her late father had also worked for Wincanton Transport, with John Payne. She knew of the 'UFO encounter' and had no reason to disbelieve John's version of the strange events.

Sadly, 'Jack' Payne, as he was known to Janet, died in January 2006, after suffering ill health for a number of years.

The *Evening News* (8.5.1957) told of receiving several reports of UFOs from the public. They included a bright orange object, seen over the London/Kent areas, a bright orange golf ball-shaped object over Hendon, and an orange object over Bexleyheath, Kent.

At 8.30pm on 10th May 1957, hundreds of people living between Stamford and Northampton watched an object looking like a huge star, or *'flaming inverted onion'*, pass overhead.

At 8.45pm, it was seen passing over the Northampton area, by Geoffrey P. Gaston – now visible as a circular object, bluish-green in colour, with yellow light coming from above and underneath.

9th May – England: Three objects reported

10th May – England: Strange object seen in the sky

During a cross-country run held in the Stamford, Northampton area, hundreds of people sighted what looked like a 'silver star' moving through the sky, at 7pm.

At 8.30pm, Nicholas Thrapston (13) of Rockingham Road, Kettering, saw it heading westwards and climbing as it did so.

Minutes later, Mr H. Clarke of Barons Way, Welford Road, Northampton, C.O. of the local sea cadets, was out gardening when he saw through his telescope what looked like "*...an inverted flaming onion in the sky*".

Two of his neighbours came over; one of them – Eric Cooper – looked through the telescope and declared it was a *'flying saucer'*. The party watched the object until out of sight, at 9.45pm.They were not the only ones; others in the Northampton area reported sighting the phenomena.

11th May – England: Black 'disc' sighted over Oxfordshire

We met up with Douglas Edgington – a veteran of the Second World War – who told us what he saw, while working on open farmland near Armscote, Oxfordshire, on 11th May 1957.

> *"I was with another worker, at the time, clearing back some trees, when I felt this peculiar sensation creep over me – as if I was being watched. I looked around, but nobody could be seen. I looked upwards and was shocked rigid to see a dense black 'disc', hovering in the sky above us. I shouted for my partner to look up. We watched in amazement as it floated there, a few hundred feet up in the air, towering above us. It then shot off across the sky, towards the direction of Stratford, leaving us shaking with excitement and a little frightened. We decided not to tell anyone what we had seen, knowing they wouldn't have believed us.*
>
> *A few days later, I came across a newspaper article about a party of golfers, who were playing on the*

EVENING NEWS 8-5-57

'Orange Light In The Sky'

"Evening News" Reporter

TWO young people who reported seeing a "Flying Golf Ball" in the sky have started a big night search among Londoners. Several people have written to "The Evening News" saying they have seen similar objects.

Mr. A. G. Bannister, of Jevington-way, Lee, says that he saw "a bright orange object" above his head which suddenly accelerated towards the west accompanied by a faint whine.

The "Flying Golf Ball" was also seen by **Mr. G. R. Overhead,** of Telford-road, Hendon.

"It was certainly larger than any star and indeed was orange coloured," he said.

Just before midnight **Mrs. L. Norris,** of Balcombe-street, Marylebone, saw a light pass over her house.

INTO CLOUD Then it Turned

Two 14-year-old schoolboys, **Colin Sharp,** of Dorcis-avenue, Bexleyheath, Kent, and **Robert Houston,** of Horsham-road, Bexleyheath, noticed an orange spherical object overhead three nights later.

They said: "It entered a small dense cloud then turned 90 degrees south and again turned to resume its original course. It was not a meteor or an aircraft."

From Gravesend **Mr. A. W. Beavis,** of The Grove, reported that he watched "an orange coloured light" approaching from the north-west through a pair of binoculars. It disappeared in 30 seconds.

Miss V. K. Smith, of Avery Hill Park, Eltham, and a friend saw "three bright balls in the sky." She heard no noise although it was a still and clear night.

course at Stratford-upon-Avon, the same day, when they saw two 'flying saucers' moving across the sky, at a height they estimated to be 2,000 feet.

13th May – England: Mysterious 'light' seen in sky

A mysterious 'light' was seen, by a number of people, crossing the sky over Nottingham, at 10.30pm on the 13th May 1957, followed by a second, thirty seconds later, during an eclipse of the moon. Others told of sighting a red and white 'light' moving over the County, at 11.30pm on the same date, and a yellowish-white object seen in the sky over Ashton-under-Lyne, between 11.30pm and midnight, which according to the witness, stopped still and then shot away towards the north-east, before disappearing

(Sources: Gavin Gibbons/British Flying Saucer Bureau, Shrewsbury/Isle of Wight UFO Society)

At Tollerton, Nottinghamshire a red and white lights were seen in the sky (initially believed to be an aircraft returning to Wymeswold, situated to the North of Leicester, with its engines cut out); other reports told of strange 'lights' seen the sky over the area of Bunny.

(Source: Isle of Wight UFO Society)

At 11.30pm, an unnamed *Nottingham Evening News* reporter saw a bright 'light' heading across the sky, from north to south – while looking through binoculars at the eclipse – which he thought was a shooting star, except that it was hardly moving across the sky.

(Source: *British Flying Saucer Bureau Bulletin,* No. 9/ Gavin Gibbons)

Major Patrick Wall, MP

On 15th May 1957, Major Patrick Wall, MP, asked the Secretary of State for AIR:

"How many unidentified objects had been detected over Great Britain this year, as compared with previous years, and whether the object picked-up on radar over the Dover Straits, on the 29th April, has been identified?"

A further question was put to the Minister, by Mr Frank Beswick, as to what the nature of the aircraft, or other aircraft, sighted on the Radar Defence screen, which occasioned the dispatch of Fighter Command, (Air 20/9321/1957).

Mr Ward replied, (*Hansard* 1957/393/4):

"that five flying objects reported this year are, as yet, unidentified, compared with last year – none in 1955 and six in 1954. The object sighted in the Channel, on the 29th April, turned out to be two of a large number of 'Hunters' of Fighter Command, engaged on a training exercise. Their movements, as observed on radar, were somewhat unusual and aroused the suspicion of the Radar." (Air 20/9322/57)

Further Answers: (At a later date)

In 1955-6, they had received 64 reports of unusual aerial phenomena. These had been classified as 26 balloons, 16 meteors, 8 aircraft, 2 planets, 3 flares, 1 mock sun, 1 fireball [sic] and one contrail.

The unexplained cases, which all occurred in 1956, were: The navigator of a Vulcan obtained a radar contact for 1 minute 15 seconds with an invisible object.

On 19th March, Lakenheath radar detected a target moving at 2,000-4,000 knots, which then stopped and hovered at a high altitude; a 'Venom' was scrambled to intercept, but saw nothing. It could have been inversion and reflection from the ionosphere ('angels' and 'a prop'). RAF Wethersfield vectored two interceptors onto a radar target, and one obtained a brief visual contact. No other radars could see it; a member of the Royal Observer Corps reported something with insufficient information to identify it as any particular thing. A B.Sc. reported an object at 12,000ft, which may have been a balloon. A man saw a round object, emitting rippling waves – like heat shimmer; it was not known what it might have been.

In 1957 up to April, there had been 16 reports, classified as 1 radar fault, 2 aircraft navigation lights, 1 meteor, 2 flares, 1 private experiment and 3 newspaper reports (one, the Jersey UFO in the *Daily Sketch* of 6th April, had been admitted to be a fake).

Unexplained cases

The 'West Freugh' case, Wigtownshire. On 4th April, a stationary target was observed by the Balmalloch radar to rise vertically from 50,000 to 70,000ft in 10mins. The object was automatically plotted by two radars alternately, as it moved off slowly to the north towards a second radar station, 20 miles away. After travelling 20 miles, it made a very sharp turn to the south-east and picked-up speed to 240mph, at 50,000ft. The second radar also picked-up a target in the correct position, which split into into four objects at 14,000ft, travelling in line astern, about 4,000yds apart. When the single object passed beyond Balscalloch's range, they also could see these four. The echoes were much larger than normal aircraft; in fact, nearer to those of ships. There were no known aircraft or balloons in the area (in any case they had made sharp turns against the wind) and a passing V-bomber had been correctly tracked at the same time.

16th May – England: Three lights sighted in sky over Tyneside

During the late evening of the 16th May 1957, three bright white illuminated objects were seen below cloud cover at Tees Bay, Tyneside, before heading east, at tremendous speed, according to the witness, who told of seeing one of the 'lights' split into two.

The same three lights were also seen over Ormsby and Hartlepool, by a number of people who contacted the police and MOD.

One of them was Mr A.T. Gyllespetz, who told:

> *"...of seeing them hovering in the sky. They looked solid and weren't aircraft. After zigzagging through the air, they sped off over the sea – as if looking for something".*

Other witnesses were Mr S. Proudlock and Miss V. Ward, who were taking their dog out for a walk along Oakland Avenue when they saw the lights.

Mr Proudlock:

> *"They were not aircraft. Two of them stood still in the sky for a full five minutes – then another came up from underneath them and turned around. After that they went out to sea."*

At 9pm Bradford man Mr Robert Holstead – a van driver from Dover Street – was called out by his neighbour – Hilda Bowers, who asked him to come outside. He went out and saw a strange object flying across the sky.

> *"It was fluorescent and much larger than an aircraft heading at high speed in a south to north direction."*

20th May – England: Workman sights 'flying disc' over refinery

At 2.15am on 20th May 1957, Mr L. Wetland from Blackfield Road, Fawley, near Henley-on-Thames, was working on top of a fuel tank at the Esso Refinery, Fawley, when:

"I happened to look up at the sky and see this object, shaped like a 'disc', flying in an arc, south-east to south-west, at 45 degrees elevation, high up. It went through the 'arc' in about four seconds and was elliptical – like a black ring, with a reddish/orange glow in the centre and around the edge. It appeared to be spinning, like a 'Catherine wheel'. In a few seconds, it had gone out of sight. I've served in the RAF and Merchant Navy, but never seen anything like that before".

(Source: *Echo* Newspaper, 20.5.1957)

20th May – England: UFO researcher Frank Marshall

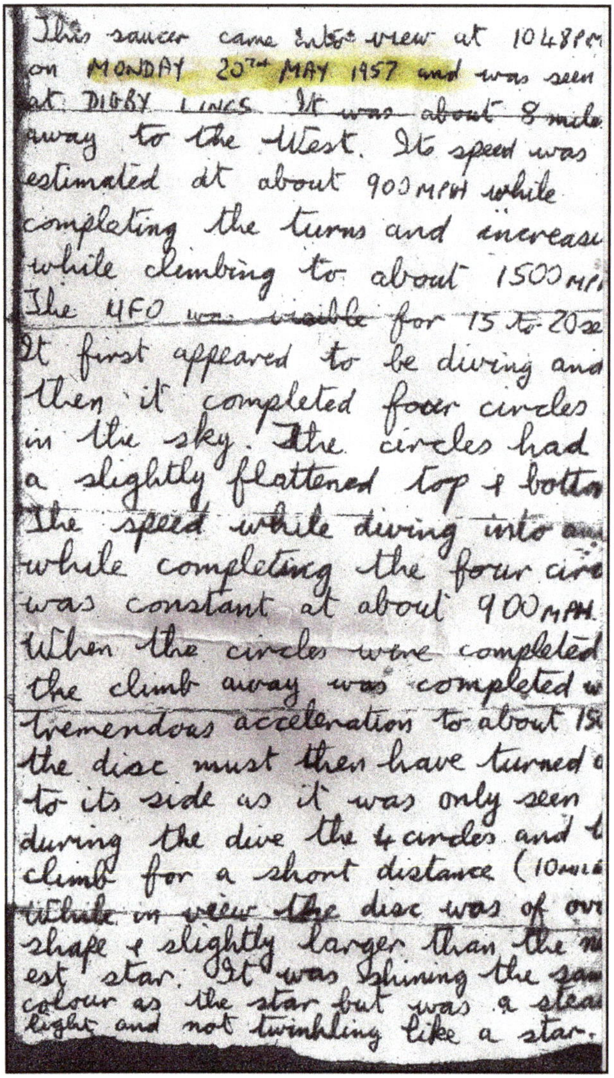

This saucer came into view at 10.48PM
on MONDAY 20TH MAY 1957 and was seen
at DIGBY LINCS. It was about 8 miles
away to the West. Its speed was
estimated at about 900 MPH while
completing the turns and increase
while climbing to about 1500 MPH
The UFO was visible for 15 to 20 se
It first appeared to be diving and
then it completed four circles
in the sky. The circles had
a slightly flattened top & botto
The speed while diving into an
while completing the four circ
was constant at about 900 MPH.
When the circles were completed
the climb away was completed w
tremendous acceleration to about 15
the disc must then have turned o
to its side as it was only seen
during the dive the 4 circles and t
climb for a short distance (10 mil
While in view the disc was of ov
shape & slightly larger than the n
est star. It was shining the sam
colour as the star but was a stea
light and not twinkling like a star.

During a visit to see veteran UFO Researcher Frank Marshall, living in the Dorset area – a friendly man, who allowed us access to his UFO files and memorabilia, collected over the last 30 years (despite a failing eyesight, which didn't dim his enthusiasm and knowledge of the UFO subject) – we came across a handwritten letter sent to Frank, many years ago, by an unidentified Airman, whose account is of great interest – as it took place on the same evening when two USAF *F-86D* jets from the Fighter Intercept Wings were scrambled to intercept a UFO.

Unidentified airman

"This 'saucer' came into view at 10.48pm on Monday, 20th May 1957, over Digby, Lincolnshire, about 8 miles away to the west. Its speed was estimated at about 900mph, while completing turns, but increased when climbing to

about 1,500 mph. The UFO was visible for15 to 20 minutes. It first appeared to be diving and then it completed four circles in the sky. The circles had a slightly flattened top and bottom. When the circles were completed, the 'disc' must have then turned onto its side, as it was only seen during the dive. It was of oval shape and slightly larger than the nearest star, shining bright rather than twinkling."

20th May – England: USAF pilot ordered to open fire on UFO!

What a pity we do not know the identity of the Airman concerned, as the letter was not signed. Can we say this was the same UFO tracked on radar in the late evening, over East Anglia, initiating an order sent to pilots from the 4069-111 Fighter Wing, based at RAF Manston, to intercept? Extremely likely, in our opinion, notwithstanding that over 50 years later, in interviews held between Milton and UK UFO Investigator – David Cayton (following information supplied to him by Harry – Manchester-based researcher, Harry Harris, 2008), it was established that the likely date given for the incident, from review of the personal flight log, may have been 27th April 1957, rather than 20th May 1957, although the contents of a letter written by the unidentified Airman to Frank Marshall, during the early 1960s, suggests the likelihood it was 20th May 1957, as opposed to the earlier date.

Milton Torres

We contacted Milton Torres – now a Professor of Engineering, with over 260 hours spent flying combat missions over Vietnam – to find out what had taken place on that night.

"The 406th FIW (Fighter Interceptor Wing) were committed to Metropolitan Sector (RAF) to have F-86Ds standing by as an operational requirement. I can clearly remember the call

to scramble, although I don't remember such specifics as the actual vector to turn after take-off. We were airborne, well within the five minutes allocated to us, and basically scrambled to about flight level 310, our vector taking us out over the North Sea. Normally, the other pilot would take the lead. However, for some reason, I was leading Pilot. I was advised by GCI (Ground Control Intercept site) that they had been observing, for some considerable time, a 'blip' on radar, orbiting over East Anglia.

From my conversation with GCI, I was told that all normal procedures of checking with the other controlling agencies had revealed the UFO, with a very unusual flight pattern, was motionless in the sky for long intervals. Their instructions came to select the afterburner, to expedite the intercept, and to proceed to a height of 32,000 feet. By this time, the aircraft radar was on and I was looking for any sign of the UFO. I was asked to report any visual observation, which would have been highly unlikely – as the weather had closed in, with very poor visibility. I complied with the instructions given to me by Ground Control, predicted to reach some theoretical point for a lead collision course type rocket release. At this time, the aircraft was travelling at Mach .92, which is as about as fast as the aircraft could travel.

Pilot given permission to fire on UFO

At that time, I was only a Lieutenant and very much aware of the gravity of the situation. 1 asked for authentication of the order to fire and received it! This further complicated my difficulty, as the matrix of letters and numbers to find the correct authentication was on a piece of printed paper, about 5 x8 inches, with the print not much bigger than normal type – not forgetting that it was totally dark, with the lights down for night flying. I used my flashlight while trying to watch the radar which, as you will appreciate, was no easy task. The authentication was valid and I selected 24 'Mighty Mouse' rockets on salvo. The final turn was given, with instructions to look 30 degrees to port, the UFO exactly where I had been told it would-be, at an angle of 30 degrees, 15 miles distance. The 'blip' was 'burning a hole' in the radar with its incredible intensity. It was similar to 'blips' received from B-52Bombers and seemed to be a magnet of light.

What followed next, I remember with much clarity. I ran the range gate over the 'blip' and the 'jizzle band' faded, as the marker superimposed over the 'blip'. I had a 'lock on' that had the proportions of a flying aircraft carrier – by that I mean the radar return was so strong, it could not be overlooked by the fire control system on the F-86D. The larger the aircraft, the easier the 'lock on' – this almost 'locked on' by itself. It was one of the best targets I could ever remember having locked onto. I called to the GCI, 'Judy', which signified that I would take

DR. MILTON J. TORRES

John Hanson and Dawn Holloway
31 Red Lion Street,
Alvechurch,
Worcestershire,
B48 7LG
UNITED KINGDOM

Dear John Hanson and Dawn Holloway,
Having read your literature I must bring you up to date quickly for you to understand the incident in question. Your request to tell Dave Roberson about your interest will meet with minimum interest from him as I am convinced I approached the wrong man. I am trying as hard as I can to find out who is the correct man that flew my wing that eventful evening is now my primary goal. I have talked to Dave on several occasions and I am absolutely sure he is not the man and the mission he described is another of those light in the sky that we ended up chasing. Since Dave Roberson and I flew so much together that when I was searching for the data that correlated to the things that occurred that I called him and both of us with our form 5's checked for night weather time and we came up with a flight of the same duration with the majority of the NW time as we were running on fumes by the time we reached Manston. This seemed like the correct flight so we both accepted it as fact.

As I stated David and I frequently flew together but in retrospect not this night! While I was talking to him he didn't recall the order to fire (we selected 24 rockets) nor him being with me on his own intercept. Too many discrepancies existed and much too important to mistake. I am certain he recollects another flight that we did have. He did not recall that in the in place turn the Met sector people swapped out positions in order to facilitate the intercept.. He normally flew lead, but on this occasion to facilitate the intercept I handled all the lead duties. This included the verification of the order to fire. This was the only time in my 20 year career that I ever used the matrix for verification and that by itself was unique. I was not too far from my date of return to the U.S. and we only stood alert a few times. We had some new pilots in the squadron and I am sure it was one of them. I have been talking to a UFOLOGIST (British) by the name of Harry Harris of Manchester (a solicitor) and he is aware that I have been looking for a hypnotist to see if we can come up with the unknown pilot. I think I have located one that I can use and I will try to schedule an appointment with him. Of the event, there are some clear recollections and some not so clear. BUT of this I am sure ---it happened pretty much as I described. I have instituted a search for a picture of me from the same period and have a few more places to look. I will not hold up this letter for it and I will send it off as well as e-mail it to you ASAP

My comments to you is that all those events you wrote about probably occurred just as you wrote them. I am convinced that other life exists in this universe and refuse to block out their existence due to lack of information.

DR. MILTON J. TORRES
Research Scientist

DAILY STAR, Wednesday, March 20, 1991

How fighter pilot took on a giant alien space ship

MY DOGFIGHT WITH A UFO!

By DICK DURHAM

TOP GUN fighter pilot Milton Torres has spoken for the first time about how he came within seconds of zapping a massive UFO over British airspace.

TOP GUN: Pilot Torres and his Sabre

all further steering information from my onboard radar computer, rather than depending on instructions from GCI. At this point I was travelling at about 800 knots, with 'dot' centred on my radar screen requiring only the slightest correction of course. At 20 seconds before launch of the missiles, the circle on the radar screen began to shrink, requiring increased precision to keep the 'dot' centred, while keeping the trigger depressed. At 10 seconds from the 'target', I noticed that the overtake position was changing its position. It moved rapidly to 6 o'clock – 3 o'clock, then 12 o'clock, before coming to rest on 11 o'clock position. This indicated a negative overtake of 200 knots. There was no way of knowing what the actual speed of the UFO was.

It could have been travelling at very high Mach numbers and I would only see the 200 knot negative overtake. The circle, now down to about one and-a-half inches in diameter, started to open up rapidly. Within seconds, it was back to three inches in diameter and the 'blip' was visible in the blackened 'jizzle band', moving up the scope. This meant it was going away from me. I reported this to GCI. They asked me, 'Do you have a tally-ho?' I told them I was still 'in the soup' and could see nothing.

Highly classified warned to keep silent

By this time, the UFO had broken lock and I saw it leaving my30 mile range, (soon off the radar screen at GCI). Following my return to RAF Manston, I was advised that the mission was considered classified and approached by a civilian in the Squadron operation area. He asked me a number of questions about the mission and told me it was highly classified and not to discuss it with anybody – not even my Commander – threatening me with a National Security breach if I ever breathed a word about it to anyone."

This is an incident which still captivates Milton's attention, who is now actively involved in organizing annual RAF Manston reunions. Like us, he wonders on whose authority that order was given and what precedence was in force for allowing the discharge of weapons over civilian airspace.

David Cayton

Tony Dodd with David Cayton (left)

According to UFO Researcher, David Cayton:

> *"In response to my FOI request to the MOD's Air Historical Branch (RAE) confirmed this to be the RAF's Sector Operational Command Centre cold war bunker, at Kelvedon Hatch, in Essex, responsible for controlling the Military London Metropolitan Sector area, at the time (now open as a privately run museum). This Unit had advised Milton the target 'blip' had entirely gone off the scope in just two sweeps of the GCI, and then instructed him that the mission was considered classified. The next day, he was debriefed by an Officer from the National Security Agency. The Commanding Officer, at Kelvedon Hatch, would report up to the ADOC (Air Defence Operations Centre), at Fighter Command HQ, Bentley Priory, Stanmore.*

Bentley Priory

> *I believe that almost certainly the order to fire would have been authorised by the ADOC, at Bentley Priory. The order would have been issued by the Met. Sector, Kelvedon Hatch, and then related to the pilots via the GCI Signal Unit, at Bawdsey. This would have been the chain of command. Milton knew for certain that his USAF 406th Fighter Wing was operating under the RAF's control and the USAF would most definitely have not been allowed to independently fire missiles over the UK airspace."*

Milton was never really sure who the other pilot was. He seemed to think that it might have been Major Dave Robertson, but then rejected that idea. Whether this was because the officer had chosen not to get involved would be pure speculation.

The Daily Star 20.3.1991- 'How fighter pilot took on a giant alien spaceship! 'MY DOGFIGHT WITH A UFO' this was the sensational headlines in the newspaper on their take on the incident by the journalist, Dick Durham, who said...

> *"Major Dave Robertson was also alerted that night in his own Sabre jet. He recalls leaving RAF Manston and then landing at RAF Bentwaters at Bawdsey, Suffolk, to have his jet armed with live rockets."*

Nick Pope seen here with Professor Milton Torres

I was advised that more than one ground control site and multiple UFOs were involved and that the area extended into Scotland, I gave chase to several of the UFOs but was unable to maintain radar contact long enough to go to lock on"

May 1957 - England: Cigar-shaped UFO sighted over Bedfordshire

Although many years had elapsed, and the dates unsure, Bill Dillon from Bedfordshire (now settled in Cornwall) had no difficulty in describing exactly what he saw, while a pupil at Ramridge Primary School, Turner Road North, Luton, Bedfordshire – a sighting which was to have a profound impact on his life – still very evident today (2016) – during many conversations held with him about the matter, bordering on a passionate, almost obsessive, desire to recover his original illustrations, compiled by him in 1981 – inadvertently mislaid by an English UFO researcher over the years, and to identify what this object was and its purpose over English soil on that day, in May 1957.

Ramridge Primary School

Consultation with Bruce Maccabee regarding this case

What makes this extraordinary case so important are the remarkable similarities with a UFO sighted at *Rogue River*, Oregon, in May 1949 – a sighting contained within the pages of Brad Steiger's book, *Project Blue Book* – matters that were brought to the attention of the eminent UFO USA Researcher, Bruce Maccabee, by Bill, who improved substantially on the visuals as shown in *Project Blue Book*. He endorsed the sighting made by Bill on that day as being very authentic and said:

> *"I think it was a real event, involving a craft similar or identical to the* Rogue River *craft. I am no longer the MD director for MUFON, as I now live in Ohio."*

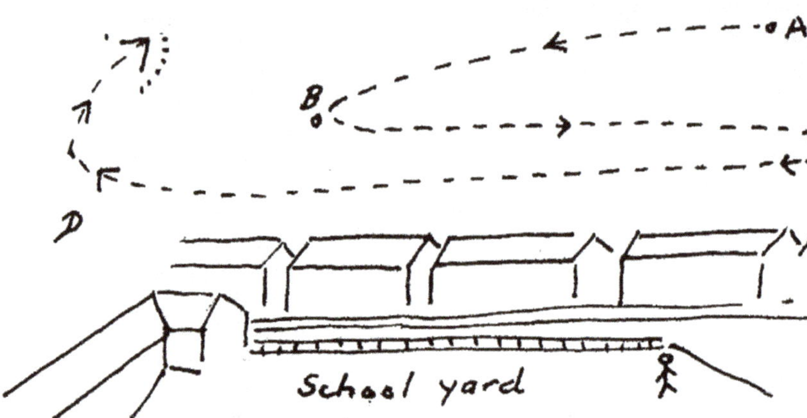

Bill Dillon's 1957 encounter

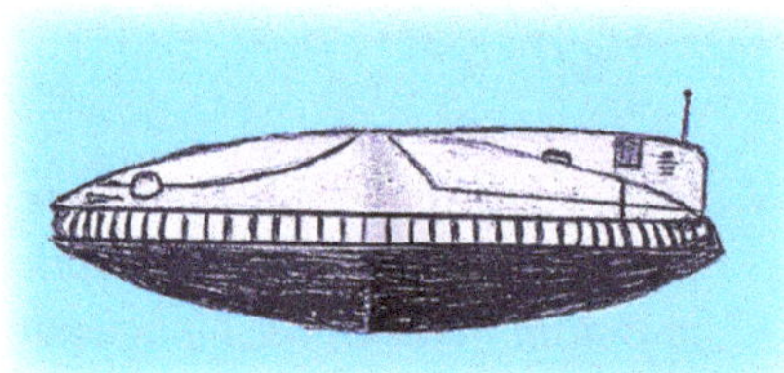

Bill Dillon

Bill Dillon:

> *"Along with other children, I had just finished my lunch and was assembling in the playground, when our attention was caught by a 'falling, glittering' effect in the sky, just ahead of an approaching weather front that I took to be associated with the movement of an aircraft, heading in a westward direction.*
>
> *The UFO was not perfectly circular but slightly ellipsoidal, or lozenge-shaped. It had a wrinkled, mottled, and generally dirty appearance. The struts leaned to the left in the region shown in the sketch. They resembled a common matchstick in appearance.*
>
> *It looked like a small dark line, seemingly too slow to be aircraft, as it moved across the sky, before retracting its previous path, (in a sort of a 'S', or' Z' shaped movement), and then began to head towards us over by Waulud's Bank – an important archaeological site. It vanished from view behind the main school building but was seen again as it gained altitude, allowing a fine view of its topside. Soon it was high in the sky, towards the south-east, standing on its edge and stationary. Suddenly, in a split second, it was gone."*

Teacher Eric Cousens shaken by the incident

> *"I looked around and noticed Eric Cousens - a teacher in the playground. From the shaken look on his face, I knew he must have seen it. I watched him make his way into the school, brushing past several of the children."*

Bill also sent us a photocopy of the teachers shown on a group photo, taken at Ramridge School in1956/57. This was useful, as it helped us to trace some of them, including Gordon Toy and Hugh Leader – now living in Braintree, Essex.

Ramridge Primary Shcool, teachers circa 1957

Teacher Hugh Leader confirms knowledge of sighting

Hugh Leader:

> *"Yes I was a teacher at the School. Bill was a pupil in another class of what was a big school, with approximately 700 children. To be honest, it's all a bit vague now, but I do remember being in the stateroom at the School one lunchtime, in the summer of 1957 (I'm certain of the year), when someone came in and told me about an extraordinary thing seen from the playground. The baffling part of all of this is that I can't remember why I didn't go out to have a look. It still puzzles me all these years later."*

Teacher Gordon Toy – No recollection

Gordon Toy:

> *"I'm sorry; I don't recall any such event. I have spoken to a colleague, who was at school then – Edna Mills. She, like me, has no memory of any UFO incident. My own feeling is if we had seen what Bill Dillon said he saw, why wasn't it known at the School? It would have spread like wildfire. You asked me about Eric Cousens – he was a friend of mine. We shared a flat together. If Eric had seen a UFO, way didn't he tell me? Unfortunately, Eric passed away some years ago."*

BARRY DEARMER

21ST MAY 2007.

AS A PUPIL OF RAMRIDGE JUNIOR SCHOOL SOME FIFTY YEARS AGO, OBVIOUSLY EXACT DETAILS AND RECOLECTIONS OF ANY SPECIFIC EVENT THAT LONG AGO ARE BOUND TO BE SKETCHY.

HOWEVER I DO RECOLLECT SEEING A STATIONARY OBJECT IN THE SKY, I REMEMBER WE WERE ALL ON THE SCHOOL PLAYING FIELDS IT WAS A VERY HOT AFTERNOON IT WAS CRICKET OR SOMETHING IN OUR SPORTS PERIOD. SOMEONE IN MY CLASS NOTICED THIS STATIONARY OBJECT QUITE HIGH IN THE SKY, IT WASNT MOVING THIS I REMEMBER, CAUSED QUITE A LOT OF INTEREST AMONGST THE CLASS SOMEONE POINTED THIS OUT TO OUR TEACHER (WHOS NAME ESCAPES ME) BUT HE DISMISSED IT AS BEING A WEATHER BALOON AND TO ALL GET ON WITH OUR GAMES. HOWEVER WEATHER BALOONS DONT APPEAR ONE MINUTE AND DISAPEAR THE NEXT. NO EXPLANATION WAS EITHER ASKED FOR OR GIVEN TO MY KNOWLEDGE AND THE INSIDENT WAS SOON FORGOTTEN.

BEST WISHES

B M Dearmer

Stephen Clarke sighted silver coloured sphere

Somebody who responded directly as a result of the newspaper appeal made by us, seeking any other witnesses, was Stephen Clarke – a former pupil at the School – still living in Luton.

> *"Bill's account was from the playground. I was actually on the playing field, with my class and a teacher, when I saw what I believe to have been the same object, except this one was stationary in the sky and only 80 feet, or so, above us – and some 60 feet from the fence where Bill Dillon would have been. It was a clear blue sky.*
>
> *We were playing cricket, if I remember rightly, when this silver coloured sphere was seen in the sky. It stopped everybody on the playing field in their tracks!"*

Barry Dearmer sighted a silver egg-shaped object

Thanks to Steven, we received a letter (opp. page) from Barry Dearmer – also a pupil at Ramridge School, in May 1957:

> *"As a pupil at Ramridge Junior School, some fifty years ago, obviously, exact details and recollections of any specific event that long ago are bound to be sketchy. However, I do recollect seeing a stationary object in the sky, one hot afternoon. I was playing cricket or something like that in the sports period, when someone noticed this stationary, silver egg-shaped object, high in the sky; it caused quite a stir amongst the class. Someone pointed it*

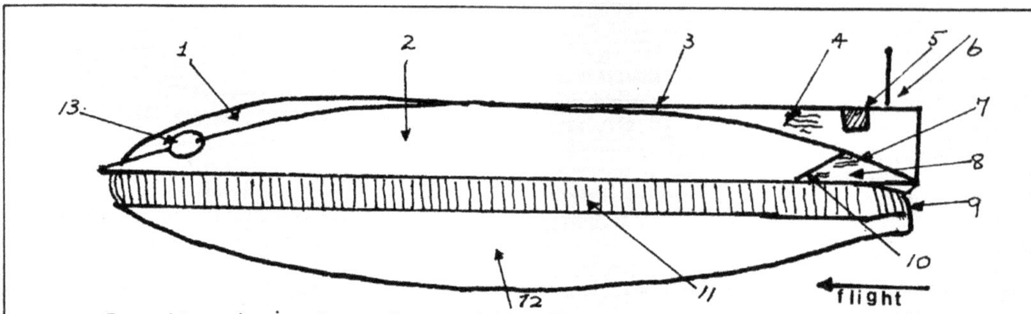

Ramridge Junior School UFO of 1957

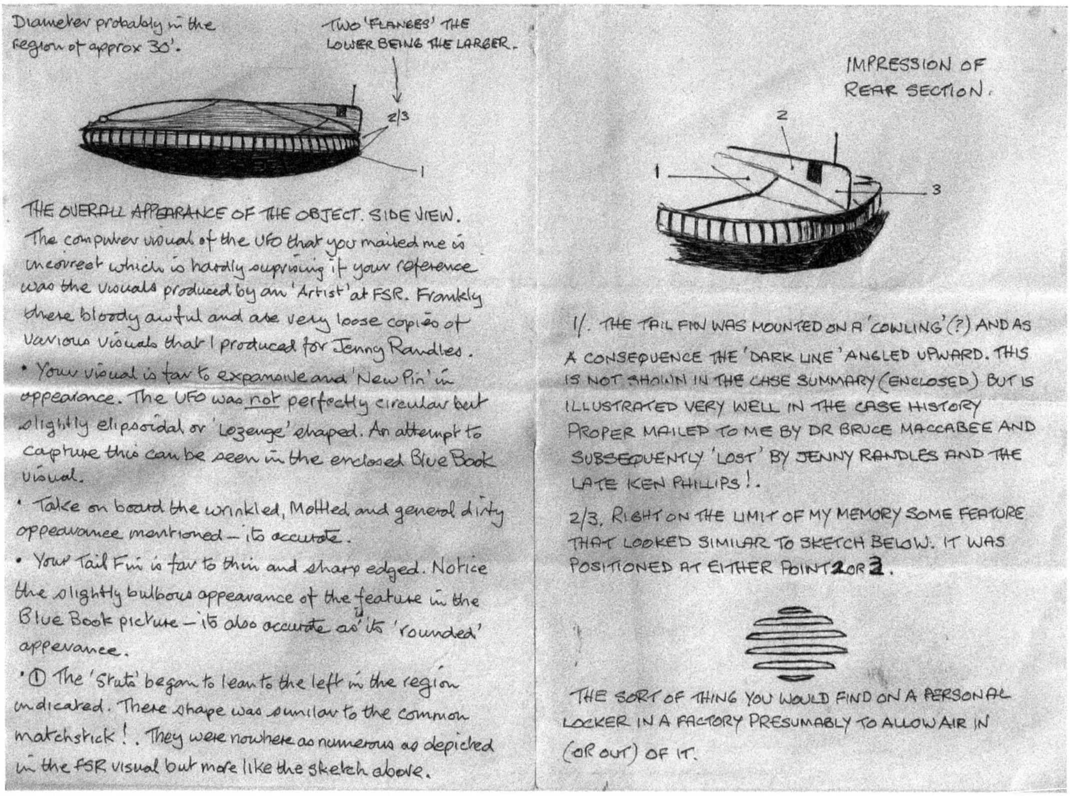

Diameter probably in the region of approx 30'.

TWO 'FLANGES' THE LOWER BEING THE LARGER.

2/3

1

THE OVERALL APPEARANCE OF THE OBJECT. SIDE VIEW.

The computer visual of the UFO that you mailed me is incorrect which is hardly surprising if your reference was the visuals produced by an 'Artist' at FSR. Frankly there bloody awful and are very loose copies of various visuals that I produced for Jenny Randles.

• Your visual is far to expansive and 'New Pin' in appearance. The UFO was not perfectly circular but slightly elipsoidal or 'Lozenge' shaped. An attempt to capture this can be seen in the enclosed Blue Book visual.

• Take on board the wrinkled, Mottled and general dirty appearance mentioned – its accurate.

• Your Tail Fin is far to thin and sharp edged. Notice the slightly bulbous appearance of the feature in the Blue Book picture – its also accurate as is its 'rounded' appearance.

• ① The 'Struts' began to lean to the left in the region indicated. There shape was similar to the common matchstick!. They were nowhere as numerous as depicted in the FSR visual but more like the sketch above.

IMPRESSION OF REAR SECTION.

2

1

3

1/. THE TAIL FIN WAS MOUNTED ON A 'COWLING' (?) AND AS A CONSEQUENCE THE 'DARK LINE' ANGLED UPWARD. THIS IS NOT SHOWN IN THE CASE SUMMARY (ENCLOSED) BUT IS ILLUSTRATED VERY WELL IN THE CASE HISTORY PROPER MAILED TO ME BY DR BRUCE MACCABEE AND SUBSEQUENTLY 'LOST' BY JENNY RANDLES AND THE LATE KEN PHILLIPS!.

2/3. RIGHT ON THE LIMIT OF MY MEMORY SOME FEATURE THAT LOOKED SIMILAR TO SKETCH BELOW. IT WAS POSITIONED AT EITHER POINT 2 OR 3.

THE SORT OF THING YOU WOULD FIND ON A PERSONAL LOCKER IN A FACTORY PRESUMABLY TO ALLOW AIR IN (OR OUT) OF IT.

out to the teacher (whose name escapes me), but he dismissed it as being a weather balloon and told us to get on with our games. All I can say is that, as far as I know, weather balloons don't just appear one minute and disappear. No explanation was either asked for or given, and the incident was soon forgotten."

Although Bill initially considered whether Stephen may have seen something different from what he saw, he now believes the distinct possibility of a connection, taking into consideration the angle of observation, height, and distance away.

It may be tempting to make a connection with Cardington Airbase, 30 miles away, as an explanation for what Bill had seen, except for the fact that its behaviour hardly matched the flight characteristics of any airship.

Similar UFO seen over 'Rogue River' by scientists in 1949

Secondly, if what Bill saw was the same 'craft' seen over *Rogue River,* many thousands of miles away, eight years previously, surely the witnesses – who were employed on Top Secret supersonic jet flight work, at Ames Research Centre, (founded in December, 1939), aircraft research laboratory for the National Advisory Committee for Aeronautics, (NACA), to become the National Aeronautics and Space Administration, in 1958, (NASA) – would have known the difference between an airship and what they saw?

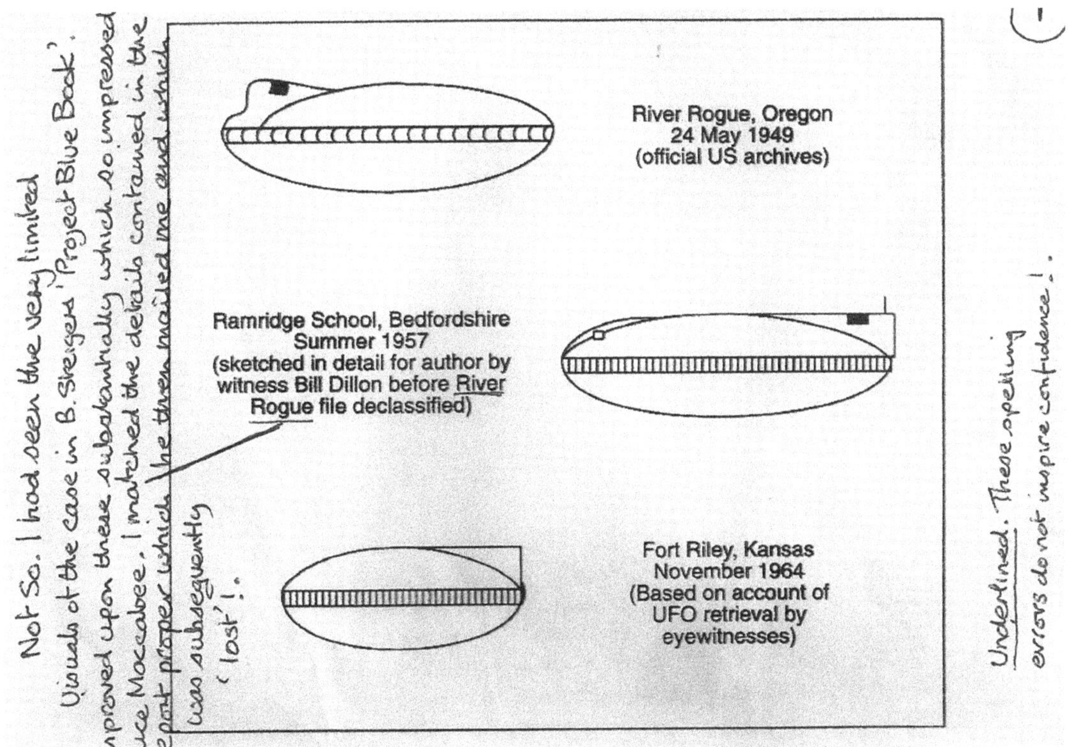

A comparison between the UFO seen at Rogue River, Rambridge, and Fort Riley.

Bill and the authors have been instrumental over the years in trying to raise the attention of the media with regard to what was seen despite suggestions it was a weather balloon!

The passing of the years

During the years that have elapsed this very intelligent likeable man has striven to let people know through the media and radio stations what happened on that fateful day. He has met with the Lord Mayor as shown in one of the photographs, and discussed the incident with Dr Allen Hynek.

The late Lord Mayor Frank Lester being presented with a portrait of himself, painted by Bill Dillon

Dr. Allen Hynek with Bill Dillon

Bill is also a very good artist and amateur astronomer and lives quietly in Newquay. He is a credit to the chosen subject and has always been there for myself and Dawn Holloway.

GOING BACK IN TIME

Man aims to unravel UFO saga

A PSYCHOLOGIST aims to unravel a sensational flying saucer mystery in Luton.

Malcolm Scott will use hypnosis to take amateur astronomer Bill Dillon back to his childhood.

Bill said he saw a flying saucer over Ramridge Junior School, Luton, in 1957, when he was 10 years old. He was with about 300 other children in the school playground.

●Going back in time. Psychologist Malcolm Scott, left, and Bill Dillon.

By JOHN RAFFERTY

Bill became passionately interested in astronomy and has become one of the country's leading ufologists.

He filed his report of the flying saucer sighting with UFO research bodies but has been unable to get his fellow

Together they hope to obtain concrete evidence for Bill's experience which he believes should be recognised as Britain's greatest UFO mass sighting.

There has been a huge interest in UFOs since the film Close Encounters of The Third Kind, now re-released and showing in Luton as a special edition.

WE SAW A UFO SAY 5 POLICEMEN

by IAN McKERRON

Because of the darkness he could not see an exact outline

4 Wednesday, June 21, 2006 LN

'I've never been more serious about anything'

UFO eyewitness: 'I regret nothing and retract nothing. I'm going to maintain this until the day I die'

by Andy Gayler

FEW of us can say we have seen something that is completely out of this world that has had a truly profound, life-changing experience on us. But when Bill Dillon was only 11 that is exactly what happened.

He was in the playground at Ramridge Junior School with fellow pupils, and the duty teacher Eric Cousins, waiting to go back into the building when he spotted something in the sky.

"I took in as many details as I could in a limited moment but in the passage of time your memories do fade," Bill said.

"We had just finished our lunch break and were assembling again in the playground. I happened to look up towards the west and caught sight of what I thought was an aircraft. At first the object looked like a small dark line and seemed too slow for an aircraft."

The object was travelling at a speed of

field of vision, as well as stopping still for a while, before finally disappearing.

"I felt that I was observing something extraordinary – a flying saucer," the 60-year-old added.

"I looked around quickly at the scene in the playground and noticed that the most visible effect was being registered on the face of the single teacher. Clearly shaken, and still glancing up at the stationary object, he brushed his way past several of the children and went into the school buildings.

"I would say it was over towards Wauluds Bank. The place is one of the most important archaeological sites in Britain – probably second in importance to Stonehenge – and many make connections to ancient archaeological sites and UFOs."

Bill said as an adult he was able to track down at least one teacher who was at the school when the event occurred.

She told him that she remembered the duty teacher coming back into the school

LIFE-CHANGING: Bill Dillon, pictured above in the '80s, witnessed a flying saucer as a child. Right, his UFO sketches

ing into the classroom and said: 'We've just seen something absolutely extraordinary'. She said he was in a mildly distressed state."

The former Vauxhall worker added that other children of the time had admitted to him they remembered the incident, but they were not willing to openly discuss it for fear of ridicule.

"I've just resigned myself to the fact that I'm the only vocal witness," said Bill, who is now living alone in semi-retirement in the West Country.

Around the same period there were other reports of UFOs in and around Luton, although many were explained away as weather balloons. The town was even known as playing host to the first widely reported car-stop encounter in the 1960s.

But, until now, the Ramridge sighting has only featured in specialist publications that came as a result of Bill's efforts to bring the story to people's attention.

He believes that what he saw almost half a century ago may be born of a force that has always been with us on the planet.

He also thinks humans themselves may play a part in when the objects appear and to whom.

"I'm going out on a limb," he said, "but the possibility exists my mental state was answered by an actual agency that was here.

"At the time I was living in Hollybush Road. It was extremely rural then, and dark. Even at that age I was into astrology and there was one thing I would have liked to see at that time – a flying saucer. So, I don't dismiss it as coincidence that in the fullness of time that's exactly what I saw.

"I doubt that we've ever seen the face of the agency behind these events. It's deeper and more complex than people think. It could be an entirely natural phenomenon that we have no knowledge of."

Bill's story came to the attention of The Luton News after a writer in Worcestershire wrote to the paper in the hope of finding the Ramridge event's one and only public witness.

With our help, the two men are now in contact and Bill's account of that sighting in June 1957 will probably feature in John Hanson's six-volume tome on UFOs in the UK soon to be completed.

Anyone who begins to hear the stories of people like Bill cannot help being somehow affected, and the project has been a 10-year labour of love for John.

But for the witness himself, it is not just a hobby. "It's had a complete life interest pursuit impact on me," Bill said. All I can do is encourage your readers to take the subject seriously – there is a case to be answered.

"I'm never more serious about anything in my life and I regret nothing and retract nothing I've said. I'm going to be maintaining this until the day I die."

■ Have you ever seen a UFO? Please drop us a line with the details. Our contact information is on pages 2 and 12.

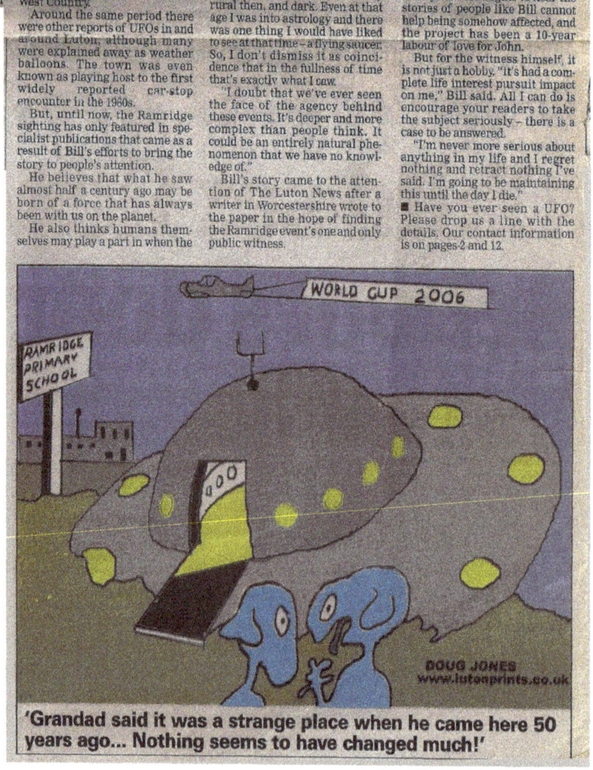

'Grandad said it was a strange place when he came here 50 years ago... Nothing seems to have changed much!'

Some of Bill's artwork

Search for witnesses to UFO

BOOK REKINDLES BIZARRE MEMORIES

BIZARRE events in the skies over Luton when a flying saucer "buzzed" children in a school playground have appeared in a new book on UFOs.

And a witness of the strange phenomenon is hoping that now someone else will come forward to confirm his story of what happened 30 years ago as he played with friends.

By MARCUS PENNELL

Bill Dillon, 41, was a 10-year-old pupil at Ramridge Junior School in Ashcroft Road, Luton, in the early summer of 1957 when something happened which changed his whole life.

"It is 30 years ago, but the event is indelibly stamped on my memory," said unemployed graphic artist Bill, of Hollybush Road, Luton.

Skywatcher

Bill's tale features in a new book called the UFO Conspiracy by professional skywatcher Jenny Randles. She draws comparisons between the object Bill saw and a similar sighting in Oregon in the USA in 1940.

"I am hoping that this book will make people remember. There were dozens of us in that playground and somebody else must remember what happened," said Bill.

"We had been running around and it was getting on for the end of the lunch break, when I looked to the west and saw something glittering in the sky. Several other people saw it and we thought it was a glider catching the sunlight or an aircraft crashing in flames," he said.

"Then I saw the object. It was a dark line in the sky that was descending at an angle and travelling slowly, west of us and travelling south.

"It changed course and started coming towards us, passing about 200 yards away and about 100 feet up. It was moving very slowly.

"We just stood there in open-mouthed amazement and then the whole playground erupted into noise with the kids jumping about and yelling. I just assumed this was something I would get one chance in a lifetime to see and stayed still, consuming every detail."

Shaken

The object then accelerated away over the school buildings — Bill can't recall it making any noise at all — in the direction of the airport which was then little more than a private aerodrome.

"The teacher on playground duty looked shaken to his foundations. He ran into the school, maybe to telephone someone, call another member of staff, or watch the object from the other side of the building.

Disbelief

"My parents treated me with complete disbelief when I got home, but that event sparked a lifelong interest in UFOs," he said.

Bill has been trying to find that teacher on playground duty for years, as any schoolfriends from those days he has met have only hazy recollections of the events.

"I believe the teacher's name was Eric Cousins and that he went to America then came back again, but I have been unable to find him," he said.

● How it looked – a drawing by Bill of what he saw in 1957.

● Searching for other memories – Bill Dillon who can remember the UFO passing over his school.

● *The UFO Conspiracy by Jenny Randles is published by The Blandford Press, price £10.95.*

No.5375 LUTON NEWS THURSDAY, August 20, 1987

Watch out for aliens

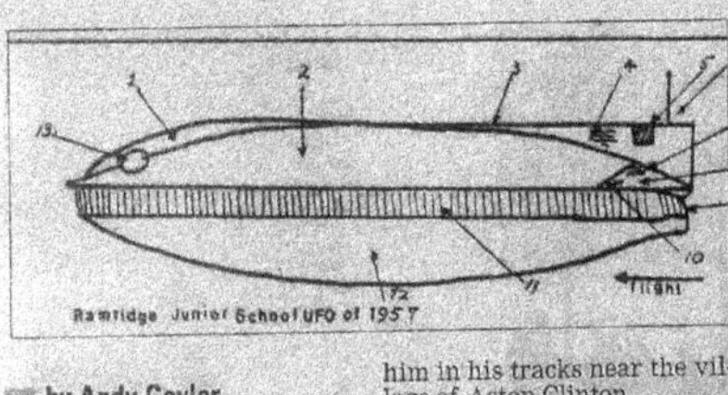

Ramridge Junior School UFO of 1957

SKY WATCH: Bill Dillon, a witness to the

by Andy Gayler

FORGET conspiracy theories – a good old dose of public humiliation will work wonders for forcing people to keep their "wacky" experiences very much to themselves.

And it's the reason that a number of Lutonians reading our summer stories about UFO sightings were happy to tell The Luton News they had seen something extraordinary, but

him in his tracks near the village of Aston Clinton.

"It was about 20 or 30 feet above the ground and at least 40 feet across," he said.

"There was a haze round it, like a halo round the the moon. As soon as I came within 20 yards of it, the speed of my car dropped right down to about 20mph. I changed into second and put my foot flat on the accelerator. Nothing happened.

"I'm a motor mechanic and I

John,

A photo of me as requested. On the steps of Luton Town Hall presenting a portrait to the then Mayor the late Frank Lester. Everyone was very pleased with my work. I made the front page of 'The Evening Post' paper with the enclosed.

1/. It was myself and NOT Peter Davies who attained the Peter Drew case. Peter Drew and I were both members of Luton Astronomical Society of which I am a founder member.

2/. Please make a point of including Bruce Maccabee's supportive endorsement, its adds to the accounts credibility. Thanks.

3/. In the same year the Canberra Bomber crews sighting of a very similar object while setting a new World altitude record. The aircraft was stationed at Luton Airport, very close to Ramridge School, and was owned by the John Napier company.

4/. To be confirmed. As the Ramridge incident terminated three Supermarine Swift aircraft arrived from the north and screamed at low altitude over the playground heading towards the general direction of where the UFO 'vanished on the spot'!.

5/. The comparitively recent Alderney (?) to Bristol aircraft who's pilot and passengers witnessed a UFO so similar in appearance to the Ramridge object.

Please consider these as candidates for inclusion. Thanks.
Phone me if you require any further assistance.

Regards, Bill

Dear Bruce.

I'm very pleased to be back in touch with you after such a long time via John Hanson. Your recollections concearning the state of proceedings when we last corresponded seem to be very good indeed. The only information on the Rogue River sighting that I had at the time of meeting you in London (1981?) was that which appeared in Brad Steigers 'Project Blue Book'. The visuals were pretty limited but showed enough for me to realize at once that this was the (same) UFO we observed at Ramridge. Naturally I'm delighted that I managed to supply other details not shown in the book but known to yourself to your satisfaction.

Perhaps I'm being unfair on myself but I have always been rather disappointed that I couldn't recall the fact that the tail fin was placed on top of a 'Cowling'(?) standing slightly clear of the rear upper hull. Please try and appreciate that the UFO is a 'detail rich' object and I (we) only had one opportunity to consume all available details and somehow try and retain them. Over the years I have tried manfully to do just that. Are any details available concearning the forward upper section?. I'm as confident as I can be in the circumstances that I'm going to be shown to be correct about this region also.

At Rogue River there does not seem to have been any interaction between the UFO and the local environment. This was not the case at Ramridge. Having passed us and beginning its climb the UFO passed through some cloud which was now increasing (beginning of a rain front) and as it did so the cloud displayed a magenta colour (excitation of atmospheric hydrogen?) and when the UFO was last seen in an area of open clear sky positioned to the left of the sun the sky for some distance around just didn't look natural.

MR. J. Hanson,
PO Box 6371
Radnal
Birmingham,
B48 7RW

11 Lincoln Road,
Skellingthorpe,
Lincoln
LN6 5UT
Tel. 01522 682717
26.4.02

Dear MR. Hanson,

UFO Appeal

I read with interest your letter in the Lincolnshire Echo recently. Whilst I have not had a sighting of a UFO in Lincolnshire, you may be interested in what I saw in Nottinghamshire way back in the '50's, somewhere between 1954 and 1959. I don't have a record of the exact year, unfortunately.

I was working in Nottingham at the time and had just got off a bus at the old Huntingdon Street Bus Station with a travelling companion when I heard a jet aircraft passing almost overhead. It was probably a Meteor. We both instinctively looked up into a clear blue morning sky at about 08.50 hours. I guess the jet would have been flying at about 7-10,000 ft. It was flying approx. West to East. As we watched there was a type of explosion from the rear of the jet (we heard no noise) and as the jet sped off to the East there was an object left hanging in the air where it had left the rear of the jet. It was cylindrical in shape and shone golden in the morning sunlight. To our surprise, seconds later it turned round on it horizontal axis and it started to move off in a Westerly direction, roughly towards Derby. It quickly gained speed and it soon disappeared from sight.

Had we not seen the object leave the rear of the jet aircraft it would certainly have been a UFO. I never saw a report of the sighting in the local Nottingham paper so it perhaps passed un-noticed to all but the two of us.

I should add that it retained its cylindrical shape throughout – there was no sign of any wings nor of any vapour trail.

I never reported the sighting other than to family and friends at the time.

I hope you may find this information of use in your journal. If you can throw any light on what it may have been, obviously I will be interested to hear from you.

Yours sincerely.

Ivor McNish.

22nd May – England: Cigar-shaped object sighted over *Bletchley

A 'short fat cigar' shaped object was seen hanging vertically in the sky over Bletchley, at 3.30pm on 22nd May 1957, attracting the attention of shoppers and local children, who stood watching the object – which remained completely motionless, despite a strong breeze blowing. At 5.10pm, it altered its position to that of horizontal and, within seconds, was heading towards Leighton Buzzard and soon out of sight.

25th May – England: RAF hold Exercise *'Operation Vigilante'*

On 25th May 1957, the RAF held an Exercise, named *'Operation Vigilante'*, over the Nottingham area – hardly likely to be connected, one would have thought, with the appearance of a rectangular object seen over Woodthorpe, at 11am, occasionally catching the rays of the sun, before disintegrating into what looked like white cloud.

This was followed by the spectacular sight of two silver 'discs', seen to fly out of this 'cloud' and then head off across the sky, leaving now what looked like purple vapour to drift downwards onto nearby rooftops.

During the same month, a British Airliner, flying at 5,000 feet over Rochester, Kent, suffered a total radio blackout, after encountering an oval-shaped object moving through the air, at 7.17am.

(Source: *Flying Saucer Review*, Volume 3, No. 6)

We can't be sure if there was a connection with what was reported by Mr Ivor McNish over Nottingham but one presumes it might be possible (see letter on previous pages).

England: RAF jet seen over Nottingham. Was the other object a UFO?

Incidents involving RAF Jets attempting to intercept UFOs will be, and already have been, documented, on many occasions, in the now eleven Volumes of *Haunted Skies*. An inexplicable incident, involving an RAF jet, occurred during the later 1950s – according to Mr Ivor McNish.

> *"My companion and I had just alighted from the bus, at Old Huntingdon Street Station, when we heard a jet aircraft – probably a 'Meteor' from the sound of it. Instinctively, we looked upwards into the sky and saw the jet passing overhead, at approximately 7-10,000 feet, heading west to east. We watched it go over. Suddenly, there was some sort of silent explosion from the rear of the jet. The next thing that happened was the jet sped away, leaving a cylindrical object in the sky, shining gold in the morning sunlight.*
>
> *We thought, at first, it might have been part of the aircraft when, to our surprise, it turned around on its axis and began to move west, towards Derby, leaving no vapour trail."*

Mr McNish strongly rejected our suggestion that he might have been mistaken about the object leaving the airplane when, in fact, it had been pacing the aircraft on its blind side, thus creating this

*Bletchley is important to those who study the history of espionage in Britain. Bletchley Park, also known as Station X, is an estate located in the town of Bletchley, in Buckinghamshire, England. During World War II, Bletchley Park was the site of the United Kingdom's main decryption establishment and the Government Code/Cypher School. Ciphers and codes of several Axis countries were decrypted there; most importantly ciphers generated by the German Enigma and Lorenz machines.

impression. Mr McNish was adamant this was not the case. He had seen an explosion and something appear, which was clearly visible as cylindrical in form, prompting the unanswered question: Did the object collide with the jet? If so, what happened to the jet aircraft?

26th May – Scotland: Cigar-shaped UFO seen over Ben Lomond

A yellow cigar shaped object was seen in the sky, east of Ben Lomond, diving and climbing in the air, between 4.00am and 5.00am on 26th May 1957, by two Police Officers on patrol near the Torpedo factory, at Alexandria.

(Source: *Flying Saucer Review*, July/August 1957, Volume 3, No. 4)

8th June – England: International 'Flying Saucer' Sighting Day

June the 8th was designated as a worldwide International 'Flying Saucer' Sighting Day. It attracted the attention of the *London Daily Herald, The Yorkshire Evening Post*, and numerous others.

At 5.35pm, Margaret Millington of Alexandra Road, London NW8, accompanied by her father, sighted:

> *"...a circular, apparent solid object, showing a flat base with the upper part mushroom-shaped, clearly visible against white cloud in the sky".*

(Source: *Flying Saucer Review, Volume* 3, No. 4)

11th June – Cape Canaveral: Test rocket explodes on test flight

A 1,600 mph. inter-continental ballistic missile was launched from Cape Canaveral, Florida. The missile, designed to carry a nuclear warhead, was making its first 2,200 mile journey test flight, when at 3.5000feet the booster rocket fell away.

At 5,000 feet it levelled off and then exploded in a 'ball of fire'. Speculation was rife as to the cause of the disaster; it is alleged one press photographer shouted out *"Good heavens, it's being plucked out of the sky".*

Another reporter said he had seen a violent-orange 'mushroom' diving towards the rocket, just before it exploded.

Later than night, twelve red objects were seen travelling through the sky over Glasgow, heading westwards, scattering sparks of light, by many people from Bridgeton, Govan, Govanhill, Blairdardie, Whitecraigs, Uddington, Bishopbriggs, and Coatbridge.

13th June – England: 'Flying saucer' sighted over the Humber

Edward George Watson of Rosmead Street, Hull, was out shooting on the night when he saw:

> *"...a 'flying saucer' over the Humber, travelling very fast, at about 4,000 feet. It was in view for about a minute, before disappearing up river. I told five other people what I saw."*

(Source: Isle of Wight UFO Society)

14th June – England: 'Flying saucer' seen over Nottingham

At 9.15am on 14th June 1957, plumber Mr Albert Brown was returning home to Long Eaton, Nottingham, when he sighted an unidentified flying object . . .

> *"resembling an artist's impression of a 'flying saucer' – aluminum, or silver, in colour – about a thousand feet up in the air, over the road bridge at Chilwell".*

Later that day, at 10.30pm, an object was seen zigzagging across the sky over Ilkley, Yorkshire, followed by a green flare-like object – roughly square in shape, with a piece missing at the rear – by Mr E. Gregg, while visiting Middleton Hospital.

At 11pm, Mr R.F. Andrews from Malabar Road, Truro, was sat in his garden when it lit up – as if a powerful searchlight was shining on it.

> *"I heard a swishing sound and looked upwards to see a cigar-shaped object pass overhead, throwing out sparks, with a very bright glow from the one end. It left a thin wisp of smoke in the air after it had gone."*

Other witnesses to this event were local brothers – D. and E. Drew – who were walking from Tregolls Farm, at 11pm.

> *"We were walking down the lane; there was no moon. Suddenly, the place was lit up by a brilliant light and I stepped into the side of the hedge, thinking a car was coming. My brother turned around and pointed at the sky. I looked up and saw a cigar-shaped object, glowing red at the head and throwing out a very brilliant light from its 'tail'. The object was travelling at terrific speed, approximately 300 feet in the air."*

(Source: Mr I. Ibson)

15th June – England: Cyclists sight unusual light in sky over Lancashire

At 6.15pm on 15th June 1957, Mr G. Marsden from Chorley, Wigan, was standing at the side of the road, taking a break from cycling with his son, near Mawdesley, when he noticed a silver point of light, with a bluish tinge to it, moving north-west, at a height of 6-7,000 feet.

> *"It appeared to be 25 feet in diameter and moving at 600 mph. We watched it for about twelve seconds in horizontal flight, until it whisked vertically upwards. In seconds, it had gone."*

(Source: *Uranus*, Volume 14, Number l, August 1957)

On the same evening, Mr and Mrs L.H. West were driving along the road, between Norbury and Hungerford, when they saw what looked like a large white plank, vertical in the sky. They stopped the car to take a closer look. It then altered its position to horizontal and shot upwards into the sky, and vanished out of sight. A few minutes later, a jet aircraft appeared over where the UFO had been.

(Source: *SCAN* Magazine, *Jan/July 1978* – Leslie Harris)

England: Battleship-size UFO over Lincolnshire

At Whaplode St. Catherine Lincolnshire – (it may have been either summer of 1957 or 1958) – Mr Robinson and his friend sighted:

> *"...an object as big as a battleship, about a mile away. Its colour was like looking into a furnace; rising and travelling South, south- west. Within two or three minutes it had gone."*

According to the South Lincolnshire UFO Study Group, who investigated this matter, the UFO was also seen passing overhead by some people in a local village, five miles away.

18th June – England: Golden UFO seen over Stafford

At 9.15pm on 18th June 1957, Mrs G Pennells and her daughter, June, sighted a cylindrical, silver-gold object with a 'blunt end', about half a mile away, moving across the sky over Stafford. Twenty or thirty minutes later, the object – now more orange in colour – reappeared in the sky – this time moving at the speed of a piston-engine aircraft, before slowing down.

At 9.30pm, a silver, cylindrical, object was seen over Gailey, Staffordshire, by Mr L. Broomhall, following a curved path across the sky, before remaining stationary for a short time, and then proceeding on its journey at a height of between 5-10,000ft and speed of 30-50mph.

At 9.45pm, the same evening, Ann Poulton and her boyfriend were walking along a lane off Bee Lane, close to Bushbury Hill, Wolverhampton, when they saw what looked like:

> *"...a glowing saucer-shaped object, heading in a straight line towards Stafford. We don't think it was a plane. It was oval and orange/red in colour. After a few seconds, it gained height and disappeared towards the North".*

(Source: Wilfred Daniels, British Flying Saucer Bureau)

Is it possible this was the same UFO seen by ex-RAF serviceman Ian Charters, from Glasgow, at the other end of the Country – then a member of the Royal Observer Corps, who, with others, sighted an object *'showing a fiery red 'tail'*, moving over the City, which made a sharp turn near the horizon, before moving out of sight?

19th June – England: Grey rectangular object seen

At 8.30pm on 19th June 1957, a *grey 'rectangle'* was seen for over ten minutes, projecting from the underside of a cloud above the setting sun, over Stafford, by Mrs M. Wilkes – a civil servant.

(Source: Wilfred Daniels, British Flying Saucer Bureau)

20th June – England: Cigar-shaped UFO seen over London

A short, stubby, cigar-shaped object was seen over St. John's Wood, London, on 20th June, heading northward, at great speed, by a number of people – later explained away by the Air Ministry as being

> *"...probably one of the newest meteorological balloons, which, having shed its instruments, got into an air current at great height. These are cigar shaped".*

3pm – Scotland: UFO over East Lothian

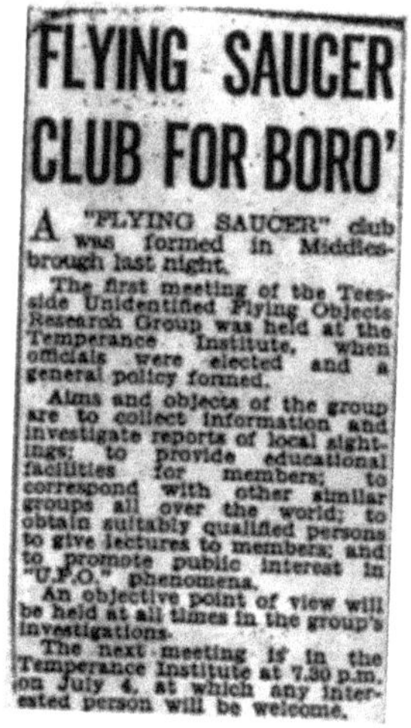
FLYING SAUCER CLUB FOR BORO'

A "FLYING SAUCER" club was formed in Middlesbrough last night.

The first meeting of the Teesside Unidentified Flying Objects Research Group was held at the Temperance Institute, when officials were elected and a general policy formed.

Aims and objects of the group are to collect information and investigate reports of local sightings; to provide educational facilities for members; to correspond with other similar groups all over the world; to obtain suitably qualified persons to give lectures to members; and to promote public interest in "U.F.O." phenomena.

An objective point of view will be held at all times in the group's investigations.

The next meeting is in the Temperance Institute at 7.30 p.m. on July 4, at which any interested person will be welcome.

Was this same object seen at 3pm over Haddington, East Lothian, by Mr J.M. Spark, his wife, and the Reverend J.S. Ritchie?

> *"It had a red top and was motionless in the sky, despite a north-east wind – Seven minutes later it vanished from view."*

10.15pm – Stafford

At 10.15pm, Lorna Horgan of St. Joseph's Convent, Stafford, was looking out into the night sky, after having just watched a TV program on Saturn.

> *"I saw a large bright object in the north-west direction of the sky, which I took to be a planet, until – to my amazement – it moved away, travelling parallel to the horizon towards the direction of Shrewsbury, before disappearing into low cloud."*

(Source: Wilfred Daniels, British Flying Saucer Bureau)

21st June – England: Saucer-shaped object seen above Airliner

At 5.30pm on 21st June 1957, Mr A.N. Haskett of Chiddingfold, Surrey, was resting by the roadside after eating a picnic tea, about four miles from Capel, Surrey (on the Brighton Road) when he spotted a shining pinpoint of light high above him, underneath which a *DC-6* Airliner passed directly underneath, descending towards London Airport (at an estimated height of between 5-7,000 feet).

As soon as the aircraft had passed over, *'the now saucer shaped object'* (believed to be a few thousand feet higher than the aircraft) made an extremely rapid ascent and vanished within seconds.

(Source: *Flying Saucer Review*, Sept/Oct. 1957, Volume 3, No. 5)

25th June – England: Red phenomena sighted in sky

At 9.45pm on 25th June 1957, a *round, red object* was seen in the sky over Wolverhampton, heading southwards, by Mr E. Day, which may well have been the same object sighted by Mrs Bullock of Bilston, who said she had *"never seen anything like it before"*.

(Sources: *Wolverhampton Express and Star*/Wilfred Daniels, British Flying Saucer Bureau)

Summer – England: Mysterious lights seen over Coventry

We thought it was time to remind the reader of the role taken by Coventry Industrialist – Mr Wilfred Grunau, who is also pictured in a *BUFORA* Magazine.

We know, from conversation with Bob Tibbitts that Wilfred disclosed, during a Coventry UFO Research Group meeting attended by UFO contactee – Cathie Connelly – he had seen a saucer-shaped object, while flying a light aircraft in the 1950s.

In addition to this incident he was to construct a large scale model of a UFO, following a sighting that occurred over his factory, many years later. Mr Grunau was a past President of Coventry Round Table and of Coventry North Rotary Club. The Awson Carriage firm created the two huge wooden crosses hanging over the entrance to Coventry Cathedral.

UFO sighting over the factory in 1968

Oddly, Bob – who was former Director of Investigation for CUFORG (Coventry UFO Research Group) – told us about being contacted by the caretaker of the Awson Motor Carriage Company, Coventry – ex Special Police Constable Tommy Gardner – who was checking the factory for flood damage after a recent storm on the morning of 15th August 1968, when he happened to look up into the sky and see:

> *"...a huge circular 'thing' with two orange lights on its side, hovering in the clear blue sky. Ten seconds later, it just disappeared from sight. I told my boss, Wilfred Grunau, who was interested in UFOs. He actually constructed a cardboard model of the UFO, from which he calculated it to be a mile in length."*

In January 1970, he wrote to Bob Tibbitts, the Coventry-based UFO researcher, who currently designs and produces *Haunted Skies* books, about his sightings that took place in the summer of 1957.

Coventry Evening Telegraph, Tuesday, September 24, 1968

Flying saucers not 'a load of tripe'–director

Evening Telegraph Reporter

FLYING SAUCERS were the greatest mystery of our time and should not be dismissed as "a load of tripe" Mr. Wilf Grunau, a believer in U.F.O.s, told Nuneaton Rotary Club.

Mr. Grunau is managing director of the Awson Motor Carriage Company which has works at Coventry and Nuneaton. He is a member of the Coventry North Rotary Club.

Mankind, he said, had been seeing strange things in the sky since the beginning of recorded history but in the last 20 years more strange sights had been recorded than in the previous 20 centuries.

12,000 sightings

The popular name given to U.F.O.s was flying saucers, which was coined in an American newspaper after the reported sightings of nine strange discs in the sky.

Over 12,000 sightings had been reported in the United States in the last 20 years. The U.S. Air Force now had a department to deal with sightings and issued a special comprehensive form which observers were asked to fill in.

This department claimed to have found explanations for all but six per cent. of the sightings.

Mr. Grunau said he had spoken to 13 Rotary clubs on the subject and seven had produced someone who believed he had seen a U.F.O.

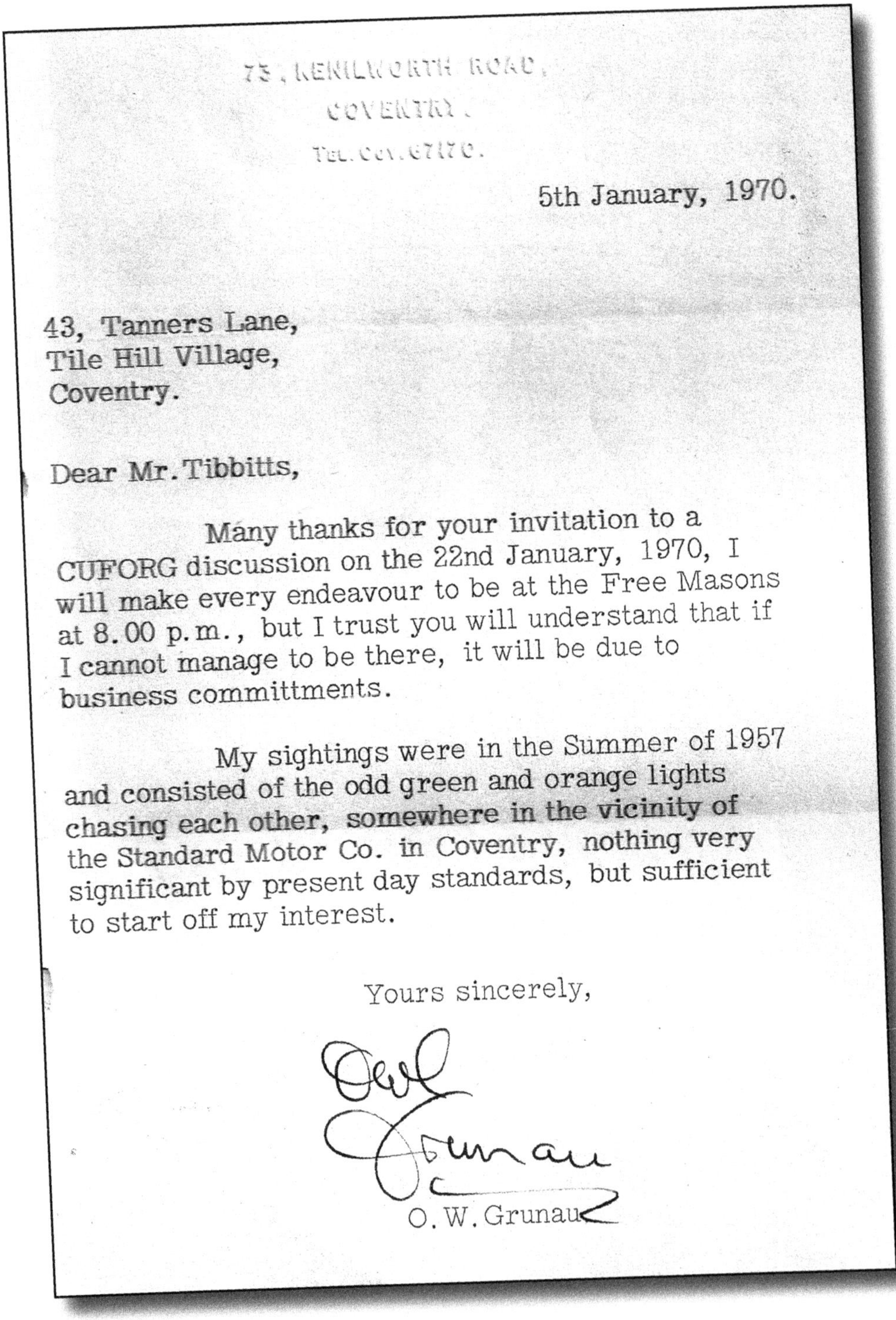

73, KENILWORTH ROAD,
COVENTRY.
TEL. COV. 67170.

5th January, 1970.

43, Tanners Lane,
Tile Hill Village,
Coventry.

Dear Mr. Tibbitts,

Many thanks for your invitation to a CUFORG discussion on the 22nd January, 1970, I will make every endeavour to be at the Free Masons at 8.00 p.m., but I trust you will understand that if I cannot manage to be there, it will be due to business committments.

My sightings were in the Summer of 1957 and consisted of the odd green and orange lights chasing each other, somewhere in the vicinity of the Standard Motor Co. in Coventry, nothing very significant by present day standards, but sufficient to start off my interest.

Yours sincerely,

O. W. Grunau

June – Scotland: Metallic 'disc' seen motionless in the sky

John Spark (then 69 in 1993) of Crichton Road, Rothesay Scotland, would have been the first to have admitted that people would have labelled him as being an eccentric – or worse, crackpot! He was an investigator for *Flying Saucer Review* and founder of the first Scottish UFO research group at Haddington. John also met George Adamski during his visit to Britain in the 1950s.

> *"I have had security following me all over England, while carrying out my investigation into reported UFO activity."*

His interest in the UFO subject was triggered in 1957, while working as a draper in Haddington, next door to the Reverend Joe Ritchie.

> *"The Minister was starting up his car to attend a wedding, when he called me over. We watched this metallic object hovering in the sky above us, for some time. Mr Ritchie appeared on the 6 o'clock news to tell people what we had seen. He believed in it and subsequently preached a sermon in church to the effect that the universe was a big place."*

Encounter with two mysterious men

John Spark claimed an encounter with two aliens, during an investigation into a strange light coming from the direction of the Lammermuir Hills that he and his daughter saw from the family home in West Road.

> *"I phoned the farmer at Kidlaw Farm and asked him to check the hills for a car there, with its lights on. The farmer went out in a jeep but found no sign of the light. We continued to watch it for some hours, through a telescope, before it eventually disappeared."*

Two days later, John and his daughter made their way to the locality, accompanied by other colleagues.

> *"On arrival, I spoke to a fisherman. He told me he had never been there before in his life."*

After making quite a way across the first reservoir, Mr Spark met up with a second man:

> *"He had high cheek bones and a copper complexion; he looked straight into me and never said a word".*

Unsettled after this meeting, Mr Spark made his way to join the rest of the group and then realised that the first man was only in possession of a fishing line which had never been cast. He looked back and discovered both men had completely disappeared from sight! A check of his equipment used to measure radiation revealed radioactivity had been recorded.

(Source: *Midlothian Advertiser*, 6.5.1993 – 'Calling Occupants of Interplanetary Craft – OAP John Spark, above, recalls the day he met two aliens at a reservoir in East Lothian')

10pm – Over Devon

A long, golden cigar-shaped object was seen hovering over the 'Torrs', Ilfracombe, Devon, at 10pm, for a short time, before being seen to head across the English Channel, where it became lost from view in the cloudy haze over the Welsh coast.

(Source: *Flying Saucer Review*, Sept/Oct. 57, Volume 3, No.5)

10.30pm – Over Derby

At 10.30pm Mr Herbert Bennett from Bakewell, near Derby, noticed a bright object in the sky to the west, heading northwards at speed, leaving

> *"one or two purple 'balls' in the air, and a trail of golden light seen to lead up to another bright object in the sky." A few moments later, some smaller bright silver objects descended through the sky, leaving an orange and purple trail, before returning to the larger object".*

At 3pm, the same day, a brilliant spherical silver object was seen in the sky over East Lothian, Scotland, by a number of people, for about seven minutes, before, *'in the blink of an eye'*, it was gone.

(Source: *Flying Saucer Review*, Sept/Oct. 57, Volume 3, No. 5)

11pm – Seen by crew of Aberdeen steam trawler

At 11pm, the Aberdeen steam trawler, *Avondee*, was fishing 36 miles off Aberdeen, when the cook – Mr James Blackball – noticed two orange/red objects, travelling at considerable speed across the sky. At first, they seemed to be moving together, but suddenly one sheared off and disappeared, leaving a luminous trail. By the time the 'skipper' Mr David Jack had come up on deck, all that could be seen was a 'ball of fire' in the sky. **(Source: not validated)**

28th June – England: UFO sighted over London

At 10.15pm, Dr. Bernard E. Finch of 851 Finchley Road, London NW11, was in his garden, watching a BOAC Viscount Airliner pass overhead.

> *"My attention was drawn to a whitish-green circular object, which passed east over the plane. It then veered southwards. The UFO was extremely high and moving at phenomenal speed."*

Other witnesses to this incident included Mr R. Richardson from Wimbledon. He described it as being *"a slightly pear-shaped object, brilliantly lit."* **(Source: *UFOLOG*, Isle of Wight)**

July – England: Cricketer sights UFO over Stroud

Retired Sales Managing Director – Victor Godding, contacted us in August 2006, after reading an appeal from us in the *Cheltenham Echo* Newspaper.

> *"In July, 1957, I was playing cricket at Wycliffe College, Stonehill, near Stroud, one afternoon, when a saucer-shaped object appeared in the sky, towards the south. It resembled two saucers, one on top of each other, light grey in colour. There were four of us that saw it. It's something I've never forgotten, although I don't, as a rule, mention it outside the family."*

July – England: Golden 'cone' seen in the sky

> *At 8.20pm during the same period, on an unknown day (believed July 1957), a woman living a few miles north of* Sheffield was at her home address, when she saw *"a strange 'light' dropping down from the sky, followed by the appearance of a thin golden cone".*

Ten minutes later, people at Firth Park, Sheffield, sighted a similar phenomenon. This was to be just the start of a 'flurry' of UFO reports brought to the attention of the authorities, over the next few days.

7th July – England: Mysterious 'bangs' heard in the sky over London

22nd July – England: Cigar-shaped UFO over Middlesbrough

A bright silver cigar-shaped object was seen over Stokeley, eight miles from Middlesbrough, just after 9.00pm on 22nd July 1957, by Mr D. Rowland, his brother, and a friend – T. Gundry.

(Source: D. Rush)

27th/29th July – USA: Honeycomb UFO seen

During the early morning of the 27th July, a Longmont, Colorado resident – Mr J.L. Siverly, sighted:

> *"...a thick 'disc' – ice blue, with a top like honeycomb (interconnected hexagons) – hovering and rocking below the hilltops, for 10 minutes. The middle band was scalloped, and the bottom showed four kidney-shaped forms".*

At 10.31pm on the 29th – this time over Cleveland, Ohio, *Capital Airlines* Captain R. L. Stimley, and First Officer F. J. Downing, sighted:

> *"...a large, round, yellow-white object in the sky, which dimmed once, and then crossed the bow of the airliner. We gave chase but were unable to catch it and lost sight of it, 8 minutes later."*

England: Brilliant red domed UFO sighted over Lancashire

Miss Blanche Wright was sitting on the railway platform at Barn Station, Bury Old Road, Lancashire, during the same year, when she saw a brilliant 'red light', with a whitish glow at the base, stationary in the sky, that grew dimmer as time passed.

> *"I could see something that looked like portholes, on both sides. Now and then the object performed a funny movement – like the pendulum of a clock – and then it would shoot away in an arc-like movement and return to its original position. I called a station porter, Mr Albert Holt, to come and have a look. He described it as looking like a banana shape, with a dome on top and a bluish light underneath."*

(Source: Mr John Dale – President, Manchester Flying Saucer Research Society)

7th September – England: Earthman travels to distant planet!

An experience best judged was how we would sum up the incredible happenings which befell James Cook from Westfield Road, Runcorn, Cheshire, who described a close encounter with the occupants of a 'flying saucer', which landed at 2.15am on Frodsham Hill, after receiving telepathic messages at 2am on 7th September 1957.

Mr Cook was interviewed by UFO researcher Thelma Roberts, from St. Albans, Hertfordshire – a woman of considerable charm and knowledge,

Thelma Roberts

Gaumont St. Albans
U.F.O. EXHIBITION

Thelma Roberts with a small part of her collection of information on flying saucers.

Flying Saucers

Thelma Seeks Proof For Her Theory

MISS THELMA ROBERTS, of St. Albans, believes there *are* such things as flying saucers.

As Hertfordshire investigator of the IUFOC (International Unidentified Flying Objects Observer Corps) she wants people to help her prove her theory.

At the Gaumont Cinema, St. Albans, she is holding an exhibition hoping to convince people of the existence of aerial phenomena such as flying saucers, fire balls and moving light. The exhibition displays photographs and documentary evidence of the existence of weird flying objects.

The main feature is a model of a flying saucer. It is based on a photograph taken by George Adamski in California, and a photograph taken some hours later of the same object by Stephen Darbyshire, in Coniston, in the Lake District.

IDENTICAL

The two photographs were superimposed by Mr. Leonard Cramp, of Bricket Wood, near St Albans, and the dimensions of the flying saucer were found to be identical in the two photographs.

Miss Roberts has planned the exhibition to try to encourage people to watch out for flying objects and to give her details. She has distributed special forms to the cinemagoers. Any information she collects she sends to the chief investigator of IUFOC, The Hon. Brinsley le Poer Trench.

Mr Cook:

> *"I was instructed to jump onto the rail leading into the spacecraft from the ground – not to step onto it, or I would be hurt. After donning a tight fitting suit I found on board the spacecraft, I was directed to descend from the ship into a larger one below, where I was met by twenty people, tall by Earth standards, who didn't speak but made gestures, placing their left hands over their eyes and their right hands over their hearts. They had no problem reading my mind. I was taken to a planet called 'ZOMDIC', which had a road network – a relic of a bygone age. The inhabitants used small ships, which moved over the ground, operated by the pilot striking what looked like metal strips, protruding like organ stops, producing musical notes.*

In flight

While in flight, the ship is controlled by a small 'ball' on which the pilot's left hand rested. I was taken to meet one of the wise men on the planet and was told:

> *"Inhabitants of your planet will upset the balance if they persist in using force instead of harmony. Warn them of the danger, but they won't listen to me or anyone."*

Returned to planet Earth

Mr Cook was returned home to planet Earth. In the process, he had to remove the tight-fitting suit with a razor blade in his pocket, and arrived home at 10.50pm on Sunday, 8th September. He was met by his mother and four friends – Mr and Mrs W. Hocknell, Mr E. Thomas, and Mrs E. King.

Burn on the hand

Mr Cook showed them a burn on his hand, which had been caused by him forgetting to let go of the rail on the stairs leading off the UFO, and touching the ground with his feet.

The Church of Aquarius formed

After his contact on Frodsham Hill, James Cook started a UFO cult – the Church of Aquarius. It became so popular that a second 'church' was opened, where James Cook 'channelled' information from the Elders of 'Zomdic', for 10 years, before James disappeared from public view in 1969. What happened to him, his 'churches', and parishioners, are unknown from then on.

Thelma Roberts believes, from her interviews conducted with James, that he was a sincere kindly man, devoid of vanity, with a sense of humour. She said:

> *"There was no question of any fabrication at all. He firmly believed what he experienced did actually happen. I seem to remember speaking with the other people, who witnessed his return home. One of them confirmed that he had a burn mark on his hands."*

When we asked Thelma if she had a photograph of James, she told us the only photograph was given to a friend of hers – H. Dudley Wood, clerk to Colney Heath Parish Council, who, while on a trip to the Azures, vanished without trace.

Despite searches made by Authorities, following much concern expressed by his wife and children, the whereabouts of this man remain like the strange events surrounding James Cook and 'Zomdic' – still shrouded in mystery.

25th September – England: Film shown to public about 'Flying saucers'

On 25th September 1957, a film – entitled ***Out of step*** – was shown on *ITV*. It included contributions from Sir Brinsley Le Poer Trench, editor of *Flying Saucer Review,* Gavin Gibbons, and Dr. Percy H. Wilkins. Sir Harold Spencer Jones – former Astronomer Royal – provided the 'opposition'. He suggested that people had seen an electrical phenomenon.

September – England: 'Flying saucer' UFO seen over Luton

Mr Peter Drew from Irwin Road, Luton, Bedfordshire – then owner of a small firm, *Bedford Astronomical Supplies,* specialising in the sale and manufacturer of fine telescopes and astronomical supplies (now living in the Todmorden area, still supplying the public over 50 years later) – forwarded a report on headed notepaper to local Bedford and Luton researcher Peter Davies, with regard to a most unusual sighting, which occurred one evening in September 1957, at 7pm, while in the company of two friends.

Peter:

> *"I suggested, while waiting for it to become dark enough to commence our astronomical observations, that each of us should see who was the first to sight a star appearing in the sky, believing there would be no competition, as I was far more experienced in astronomical observations than my two companions, but was surprised when one of my colleagues told me he had sighted an object, about the brightness of Venus, a little south of due East, at an elevation of approximately 23 degrees."*

The two Beech-hill secondary schoolboys who have confirmed "PICTORIAL" reports of strange objects in outer space. On the left Geoffrey Thompson and (right) Peter Davies, who have submitted reports to the London headquarters of the Unidentified Flying Objects Research Association.

This was a position Peter knew to be not occupied by any known astronomical object.

> *"My first impression was to wonder if it could have been a bright nova, so I turned my telescope on the object – which was out of focus – and peered through it, seeing what looked like an out of focus star. I focused the telescope and was surprised to see a classic 'flying saucer'-shaped object. I told my two friends what I had seen and invited them to look through the eyepiece, which they did, confirming they could see it as well.*
>
> *A check through another telescope revealed the same image. This was kept under observation for seven and-a-half minutes, during which time it failed to appear in the field of the telescope at 640 magnifications.*
>
> *Apart from its shape, the most noticeable feature was a thin 'ray of light', shining downwards from some sort of aperture, about the colour of a welding arc. When it finally moved away, it seemed to disappear in the direction of line of sight – so swiftly that its perspective contracted to zero almost instantly.*
>
> *We decided not to report it to the Press, as much publicity was then being given to bogus sightings of UFOs."*

It was of interest, bearing in mind Bill Dillon's previous UFO sighting, that while Peter placed the position of the object over the vicinity of Cardington Hangers, he knew this was no balloon, as the illustration shows. **(Source: Bill Dillon)**

. R. DREW

Telephone LUTON 411892

Bedford Astronomical Supplies

Specialists in short focus refractors, binocular telescopes, and catadioptric systems.

5B OLD BEDFORD ROAD
LUTON
LU2 7NX

March 27, 1981

22 Park Hill,
Ampthill,
Bedford.

Report of "U.F.O." sighting-September 1957

Definition of U.F.O. in this case is that the object was not identified, was airbourne and therefore presumed flying, and having a well defined form, could qualify as being an object.

Location- 10 Irwin Road, Bedford.

Time- aproximately 1900 hours.

Circumstances of sighting.

The writer and two friends were in the garden with two small telescopes waiting for the sky to become dark enough to start astronomical observation. In order to pass the time I proposed that we competed to be the first to see a star appear to the naked eye. The evening was perfectly clear and the Sun , from memory was either just set or obscured by buildings. As I had far more experience astronomically I was sure that I would pick up a star first, and was most surprised to hear one of my companions claim that he could see one. Sure enough, thre was a stell -ar object about the brightness of Venus when seen against a bright sky. The position was just a little south of due east at an elevation of about 25 degrees, a position which I knew was not occupied by a known astronomical object of that brightness.
My first impression was that it could be a bright nova and accordingly turned my telescope on to the object. The telescope was out of focus as we had earlier been idly looking at nearby terrestrial objects. I located the object which appeared as a star out of focus. To my surprise instead of focussing to a stellar point as expected,the object sharpened up to the classic " flying saucer " shape. I naturally exclaimed to this effect to the disbelief of my friends. I let them both have a look which confirmed my description. I immediately suggested that we each made a sketch of what we had seen. Not only did we agree closely, but we observed the same appearance in the other telescope, thereby eliminating possible optical error. We watched the object telescopically for some 7½ minutes during which time the object did not move in the field of the telescope at 64x magnification. Apart from its shape, the most noticeable feature was a thin ray of light shining downwards from some sort of aperture about the colour of a welding arc. When the object finally moved off it seemed to disappear in the direction of the line of sight so swiftly that its perspective contracted to zero almost instantly.
This sighting was not reported to any authority because quite frankly the popular press was full of bogus sightings at that time.

(cont on page 2

VAT Registration No. 283 7802 33

Page 2

Conclusion

The position of the sighting would have placed the object in the vicinity of Cardington Hangers,an area from which weather balloons and associated equipment are frequently released. However I was very well acquainted with the appearance of these items and could not match the report sighting with any of thse. In any case the fact that the "U.F.O." eventually disappeared suddenly, leads me to believe that the sighting was associated with the area.
In the intervening years I have taken a fringe interest in the U.F.O. phenomina, and, coupled to my current increased experience of unusual objects in the sky, I cannot to this day come up with a satisfactory explanation of what we had seen.

Peter R. Drew

Peter R. Drew.

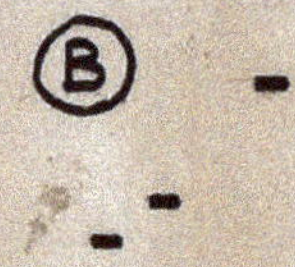

(A) Sketch of object from memory

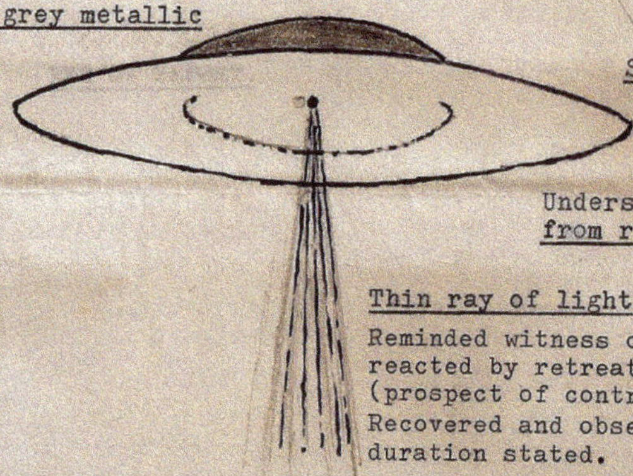

Investigators Notes.

The telescopes being used were both of the astronomical type resulting in an 'inverted image'. Objects'B'. These secondary objects were observed as the result of 'Sky Sweeping' and were located at an approx half passed one position a short distance away from the primary object.

The witness feels certain that the 'thin ray of light' was directed directly downward and, unlike the primary body, was NOT at a slight inclination relative to the observers.

As far as can be established objects 'A' and 'B' both departed at the same moment. The witness still finds the rapid departure most impressive and expressed a sympathetic attitude when I described the often mentioned charactoristic of UFOs seemingly diminishing 'on the spot'.

8th October – USA: UFOs sighted over Washington

At 9.17am, two US Army sergeants, stationed in Washington, saw two flat, round, white objects, flying irregularly, one behind the other in the sky, frequently banking as they did so, before being lost from sight 25-30 seconds later.

October – England: Holidaymaker sights 'silver ball' over Devon

Barbara Moore still ponders what it was she saw in October 1957, while on holiday in Topsham, in Devon, over fifty five years ago.

> *"I was with my landlady, walking along the canal towpath, on a particularly fine day – cold, but with a clear blue sky.*
>
> *All of a sudden, as if from nowhere, a huge 'silver ball' appeared, motionless in the sky above where we were standing.*
>
> *The object defied gravity and was totally silent. Unless you, yourself, have seen something inexplicable, it is difficult to convey the emotions that run through your body when you see*

something as strange as we did. I cannot give any estimate of height, because I didn't know whether this was a small object, low down, or a large object, high up. What I can say is that it was large enough for me to see reasonably clearly, rather than talking about a speck in the sky. We then noticed a number of other similar objects, apparently moving at different heights, heading towards the larger object.

As they approached I could see a glowing, streaky, light behind them, in contrast to the vapour trail of a jet aircraft moving slowly across the sky, at high altitude. One of these 'silver balls' then moved closer, enabling me to see what looked like a clover leaf design on the underneath of the object.

A few minutes later the whole formation, bobbing up and down in the air, moved out of sight. I was so excited I rang the local newspaper and told them what we had seen. Imagine my surprise when, a few days later, I came across details of a number of silver cigar-shaped objects seen over Dartmoor, near Exeter, a few miles away from our sighting."

It may be that this could be connected with what was seen in Cheltenham in the same month, according to Gloucester resident Mr Philip Jones, who is now 70 years of age but was aged ten when the sighting took place.

Philip:

"My mother, sister and I, saw a stationary, cigar-shaped craft in the night sky, facing westwards, at 8pm. It was orange in colour and had portholes along the side. Around the object were a number of smaller light coloured objects, moving instantly to a position in the sky, miles away, before returning to the larger object – which moved away 30 minutes later. We estimated it was about 100 feet high and the length of two to three aircraft carriers – that's how big it was."

Philip said that he later learnt of sightings in the Devon area of the West Country, the same evening.

21st October – England: Pilot sights UFO over atomic bomb base

Although the actual date of Barbara's sighting is unknown, it is intriguing to consider whether there was any connection with these mysterious silver 'globes' and a near mid-air collision, which took place at 9.18pm on 21st October 1957, when the Air Ministry disclosed the following details:

*"The Air Ministry is investigating the sighting, last week, of an unidentified' flying object' over the airfield at *Gaydon, Warwickshire, one of the top RAF's 'V' Bomber stations. It was seen by a night fighter pilot and picked up by ground radar.*

At 9.18pm, last Monday, 21st October 1957, Flying Officer Sweeney – a pilot of considerable experience – was flying a Meteor on a training exercise from RAF Station, North Luffenham,

*Royal Air Force station Gaydon, or more simply RAF Gaydon, is a former Royal Air Force station located 5.2 miles (8.4 km) east of Wellesbourne, Warwickshire and 10.8 miles (17.4 km) north-west of Banbury, Oxfordshire, England.

RAF Gaydon opened in 1942 and is known for its role during the Cold War, when it was under the control of RAF Bomber Command, as it was the first Royal Air Force (RAF) station to receive the Vickers Valiant when No. 138 Squadron RAF reformed here in 1955. In 1978, the site passed into civilian ownership and today contains the Heritage Motor Centre museum, the headquarters and factory of automobile manufacturer Aston Martin, and the Jaguar Land Rover Gaydon Centre.

at 28,000 feet, flying west, when he almost collided with a cigar-shaped object, displaying six lights, moving slowly over Gaydon – then in use as a training base for atomic bomber crews. After taking violent evading action, Flying Officer Sweeney approached the object from the starboard side. Suddenly, its lights extinguished and it vanished from view".

Enquiries made late, revealed the UFO had been plotted on radar, at 28,000 feet over RAF Gaydon, a few minutes before the sighting.

22nd October – England: 'Flying chandelier' UFO

Mrs D.C. Lash of West Worthing, Sussex, was helping her elderly uncle in the garden, at 4.40pm on 22nd October 1957, when she noticed a curious 'cloud' in the clear sky, as the sun was setting.

"It was cigar-shaped, apparently made up of thick pink cloud, hanging there motionless, with the southern end tilted upwards, many miles over the Channel, in the direction of the south-west, at great height. I watched it casually for about 15 minutes, noting that it never changed its position, and was unable to decide whether it was a natural phenomenon or not. After eating tea, uncle asked me to put the lights on while he drew the curtains.

Drawn at 5.45 a.m. on the 27th July 1978. At 8 a.m. confirmed by Mrs. & Mr. Lawrence, with Nos. 13 & 14 added by Mrs. Lawrence (I did not notice these 2 shapes). Mr. & Miss de Negri, 4 days later confirmed each drawing, as exactly what they had also seen.

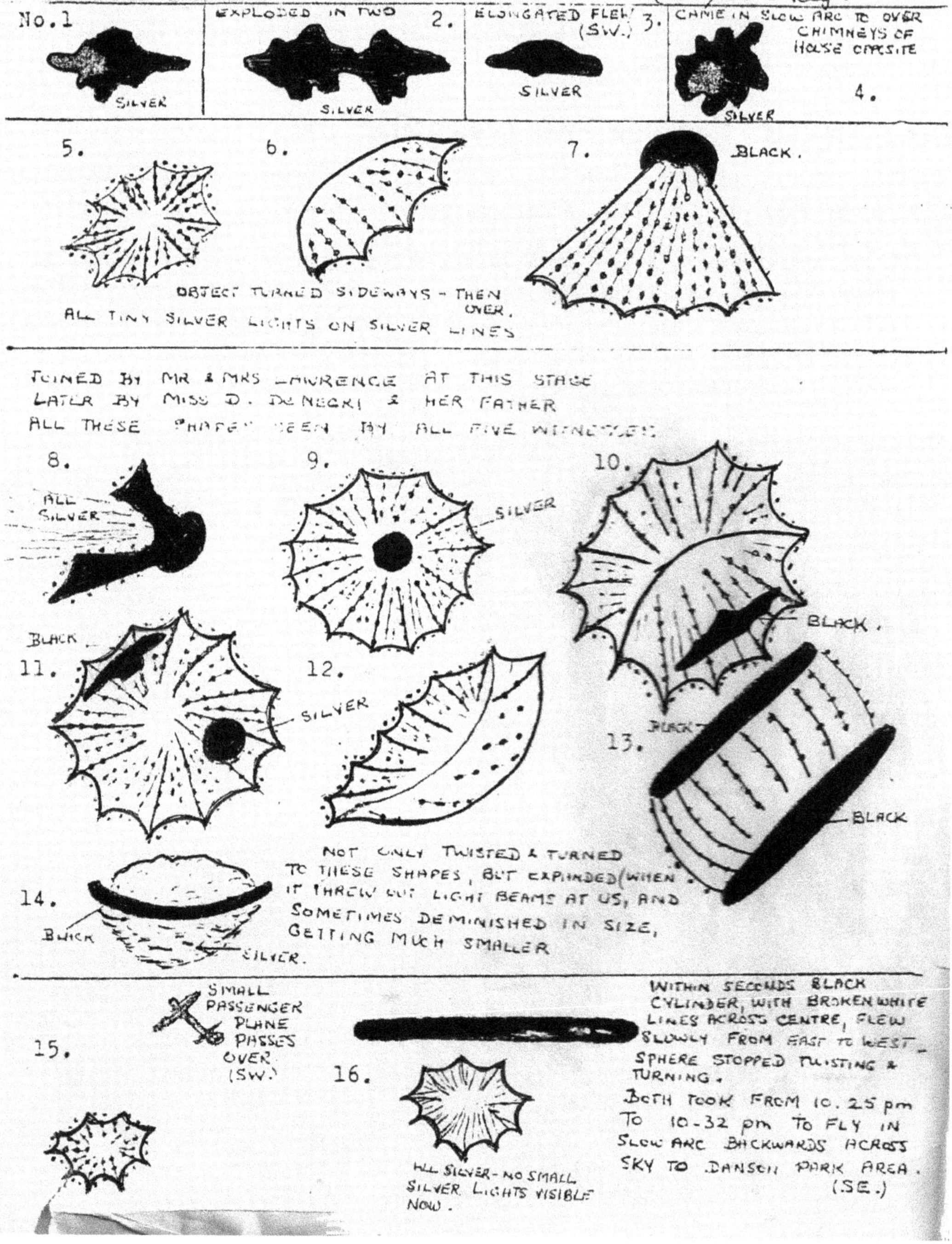

As he did this, I heard him say, 'what in Heaven's name is that thing hanging out there?' I joined him at the window and saw, in exactly the same place in the sky where the 'cloud' had been, a great sparkling object hanging amongst the stars, looking like an enormous chandelier, high in the sky. My uncle fetched a pair of binoculars. Through them, it looked like a cloud, with a double row of lighted portholes, rising to a triple row in the centre, sparkling with red, blue, and golden light. When I arrived home, at 6.10pm, I looked out for the object but it had gone."

(Source: Gordon Creighton)

This was not the first time we were to hear of a UFO looking like a chandelier in the sky. It reminded us of the spectacular sighting over Bexleyheath, Kent, close to the London border, in 1978, witnessed by residents living in the area – including Margaret Fry, whose memorable sighting, in July 1955, has already been outlined. Was this the same UFO seen by the RAF pilot over Gaydon, the previous evening?

October – England: Cigar-shaped UFO over Cheltenham

Mr Philip H. Jones, from Cheltenham, was with his mother and sister, at 8.00pm, in October 1957, when they saw:

"...a brown, cigar-shaped object showing a line of orange portholes along its one side, hovering over the town centre at a height of about 1,000 feet off the ground, one and-a-half miles away. Around the object, smaller light coloured 'craft' were moving from A-B in an instant, to other positions miles away, before returning to the object. I later discovered that sightings of a similar UFO were reported from Devon and other parts of the West Country."

(Source: UFO Evidence website (UFOevidence.org)

2nd November – England: UFO display over football match

At 4pm on 2nd November 1957, Mr I. Andrews of Highlands Road, Andover, was watching a football match at the London Road ground, when he saw a dozen

"circular, disc-shaped objects apparently composed of vapour, resembling dark grey clouds, twisting and turning in the air – like an aircraft performing aerobatics".

(Source: *Echo* newspaper, 4.11.1957)

2nd November – USA: Landed UFO Levelland Texas

At 11pm, Levelland, Texas – Police patrolman Fowler was one of four officers who received the first of fifteen phone calls from people reporting having encountered a landed object in the road. Two men, four miles west of the town, noticed a brilliant object approaching the vehicle. As it passed overhead, the headlights went out and the engine died. After the object moved away, the lights and power were restored. At midnight, the officer received another phone call from a driver on the opposite side of the town. He told of coming across an egg-shaped object, about 200ft long, in the middle of the road, followed by the lights and engine failing.

Explained away as Ball Lightning!

The phenomenon was explained away by *Project Blue Book* as Ball Lightning, which was later dismissed by Dr. Allen Hynek. Further enquiries into the matter revealed that the other police officers involved were Sheriff Weir Clem, and his deputy – Pat McCulloch. One of the sightings involved Pedro Saucedo, who was driving along Highway 116 towards Levelland, with his passenger – Joe Salav, when an immense object, showing blue-green lights swept over the truck. Straightaway, the engine and lights died. Frightened, the men jumped out of the truck and watched, in disbelief, as the object settled onto the highway. Both of them later said they heard what sounded like a faint clanking or hammering, and other noises which they interpreted as voices. The red glare given off by the object was so bright that the men were unable to look directly at it. A few minutes later, the dirigible-shaped object, estimated to be 200ft in length, rose up into the night sky and was soon gone

(Source: *Flying Saucers – Serious Business,* Frank Edwards)

Fiery Object Reported In Wide Area Over Texas

LEVELLAND, Tex., Nov. 4 (AP).—Reports of a mystery object, which one witness said flew around with a "great sound and rush of wind," had officials and the public puzzled today.

Newsmen and authorities had reports of sightings over a wide West Texas area Saturday and yesterday.

Peace officers checking areas where landings were reported were unable to find any trace.

Pedro Saucedo, 30, a farm hand and part-time barber here, told officers and newsmen, "I was driving out to a farm near the Pettit community (west of here, Saturday night) with a friend, Joe Salaz, when we first saw the thing. We first saw a flash of light in a field to our right, and we didn't think much about it at first.

Trucks Lights Go Out

"When it got near, the lights of my truck went out and the motor died. I jumped out of the truck and hit the dirt because I was afraid. I called to Joe, but he didn't get out. The thing passed directly over my truck with a great sound and a rush of wind. It sounded like thunder and my truck rocked from the blast. I felt a lot of heat. Then I got up and watched it go out of sight toward Levelland."

Mr. Saucedo, a Korean War veteran, said it was "torpedo shaped" or like "a rocket," but much larger.

Ronald Martin, 18, a Levelland truck driver, said his truck engine died and the lights went out "when a big ball of fire dropped on the highway" east of here early yesterday. Young Martin said the object changed to a bluish green color when it settled on the highway, then changed to a fireball again when it rose straight up and disappered.

About 15 Reports

Newell Wright, a Texas Tech student from here, reported a similar occurrance also east of Levelland.

Police Patrolman A. J. Fowler said Mr. Saucedo, and about 14 others who called in reports of the object sounded upset and in some cases terrified.

"They seemed to agree that this something was 200 feet long, shaped like an egg and was lit up like it was on fire—but looked more like neon lights," he said.

"They said it was about 200 feet in the air, and when it got close car motors and lights would go off. Everybody that called was very excited," he said.

THE EVENING STAR A-5
Washington, D. C.
MONDAY, NOVEMBER 4, 1957

HEADQUARTERS UNITED STATES AIR FORCE
THE INSPECTOR GENERAL
OFFICE OF SPECIAL INVESTIGATIONS

District Office No. 23 - Carswell Air Force Base
Fort Worth, Texas

23D 24-0-246

UNCLASSIFIED

SUBJECT: (Unclassified)
UNKNOWN SUBJECT(S): Reported Sighting of Unidentified Flying Object in Vicinity of Levelland, Texas, night of 2-3 November 1957.

TO: Director, Special Investigations
Headquarters, USAF
Washington 25, D. C

1. Reference TWX from the Detachment Commander, OSI Detachment 2303, Reese AFB, Texas, subject as above, dated 4 November 1957.

2 At approximately 2300 hours, 2 November 1957, the Provost Marshal's Office, Reese AFB, Texas, advised they had received a report that an airplane had crashed and was burning in the vicinity of Levelland, Texas. Additional reports filtered in to the Provost Marshal's Office by means of civil police radio indicating that an Unidentified Flying Object (UFO) was reported rather than a burning aircraft. Major DANIEL R. KESTER, Reese AFB, Provost Marshal, conducted a preliminary investigation and obtained sufficient information for a TWX report in accordance with AFR 200-2. Such report was transmitted on 3 November 1957 by Captain SAMUEL GOLDSTEIN, Acting Counterintelligence Officer, Reese AFB, Texas.

Rush Of Wind, Motors Stilled, Lights Doused

Mystery Object Puzzles West Texas Areas

3rd November – USA: White Sands UFO sighting

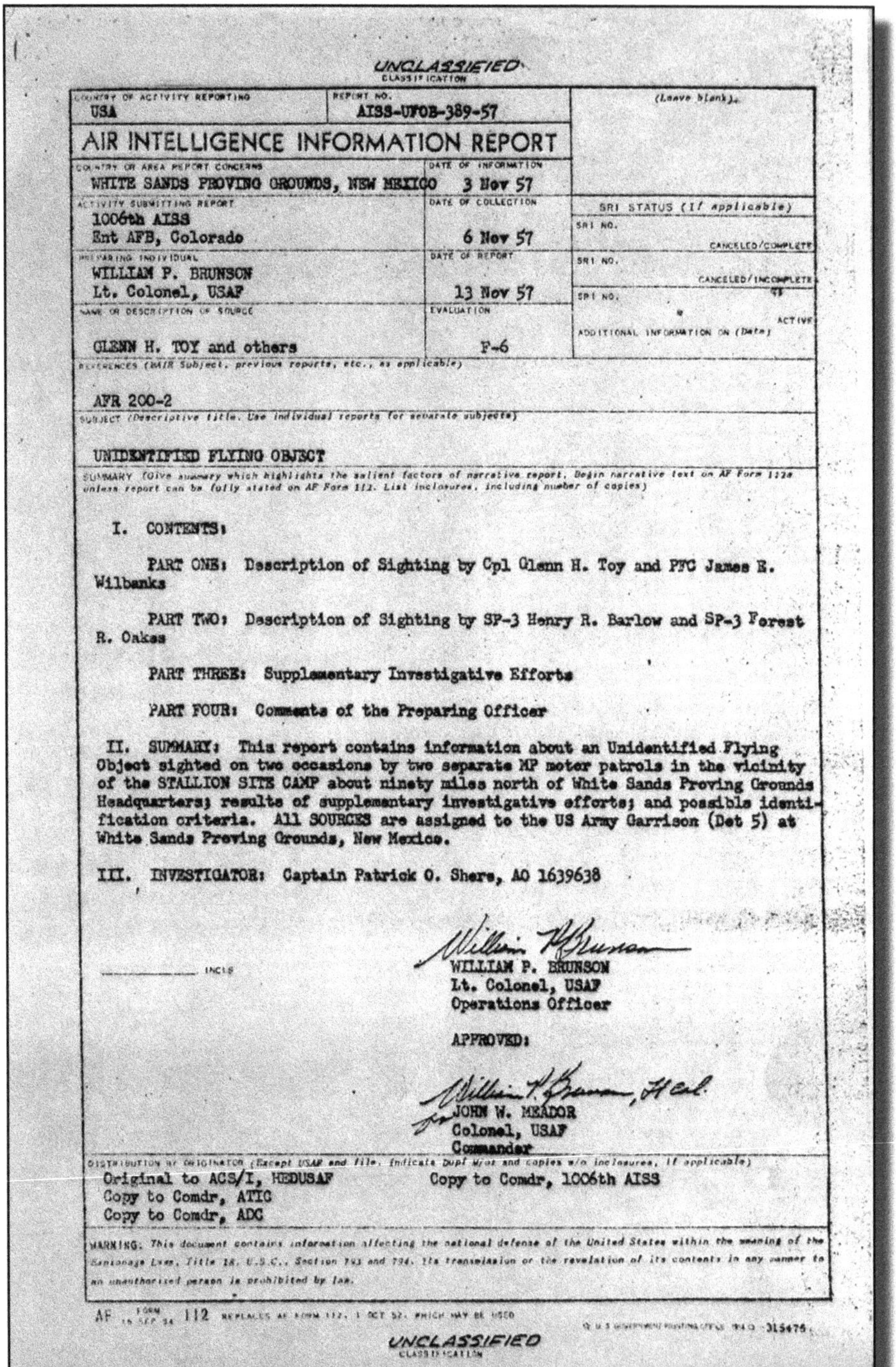

UNCLASSIFIED
CLASSIFICATION

COUNTRY OF ACTIVITY REPORTING: USA
REPORT NO.: AISS-UFOB-389-57
(Leave blank).

AIR INTELLIGENCE INFORMATION REPORT

COUNTRY OR AREA REPORT CONCERNS: WHITE SANDS PROVING GROUNDS, NEW MEXICO
DATE OF INFORMATION: 3 Nov 57

ACTIVITY SUBMITTING REPORT: 1006th AISS Ent AFB, Colorado
DATE OF COLLECTION: 6 Nov 57

PREPARING INDIVIDUAL: WILLIAM P. BRUNSON Lt. Colonel, USAF
DATE OF REPORT: 13 Nov 57

NAME OR DESCRIPTION OF SOURCE: GLENN H. TOY and others
EVALUATION: F-6

SRI STATUS (If applicable)
SRI NO. CANCELED/COMPLETE
SRI NO. CANCELED/INCOMPLETE
SRI NO. ACTIVE
ADDITIONAL INFORMATION ON (Date)

REFERENCES (MAIR Subject, previous reports, etc., as applicable): AFR 200-2

SUBJECT (Descriptive title. Use individual reports for separate subjects): UNIDENTIFIED FLYING OBJECT

SUMMARY (Give summary which highlights the salient factors of narrative report. Begin narrative text on AF Form 112a unless report can be fully stated on AF Form 112. List inclosures, including number of copies)

I. CONTENTS:

PART ONE: Description of Sighting by Cpl Glenn H. Toy and PFC James E. Wilbanks

PART TWO: Description of Sighting by SP-3 Henry R. Barlow and SP-3 Forest R. Oakes

PART THREE: Supplementary Investigative Efforts

PART FOUR: Comments of the Preparing Officer

II. SUMMARY: This report contains information about an Unidentified Flying Object sighted on two occasions by two separate MP motor patrols in the vicinity of the STALLION SITE CAMP about ninety miles north of White Sands Proving Grounds Headquarters; results of supplementary investigative efforts; and possible identification criteria. All SOURCES are assigned to the US Army Garrison (Det 5) at White Sands Proving Grounds, New Mexico.

III. INVESTIGATOR: Captain Patrick O. Shere, AO 1639638

_______ INCLS

William P. Brunson
WILLIAM P. BRUNSON
Lt. Colonel, USAF
Operations Officer

APPROVED:

William P. Brunson, Lt Col
for JOHN W. MEADOR
Colonel, USAF
Commander

DISTRIBUTION BY ORIGINATOR (Except USAF and file. Indicate Dupl Wros and copies w/o inclosures, if applicable)
Original to ACS/I, HEDUSAF
Copy to Comdr, ATIC
Copy to Comdr, ADC
Copy to Comdr, 1006th AISS

WARNING: This document contains information affecting the national defense of the United States within the meaning of the Espionage Laws, Title 18, U.S.C., Section 793 and 794. Its transmission or the revelation of its contents in any manner to an unauthorized person is prohibited by law.

AF FORM 15 SEP 54 112 REPLACES AF FORM 112, 1 OCT 52, WHICH MAY BE USED

U.S. GOVERNMENT PRINTING OFFICE 1954 O - 315475

UNCLASSIFIED
CLASSIFICATION

4th November – USA: UFO flies over Kirtland Air Force Base

A UFO was seen to fly right-to-left along the East-West runway, and then turn south-west toward the tower, where it then halted near the nuclear weapons storage area for about a minute. The object was reported by CAA tower personnel, Mr R.M. Kaser and Mr E.G. Brink, who were reliable observers, with 23 years of airport control tower experience between them. According to them , the lighted object came down steeply at the east end of a runway, left the flight line, crossed runways, taxiways and unpaved areas, at about a 30° angle, and proceeded south-west towards the control tower, at an altitude of less than 100ft.

Egg shaped UFO seen

Through 7x binoculars, the object appeared to be egg-shaped, having no wings, tail, or fuselage, and was elongated vertically. It appeared to be 15-20ft tall, about the size of an automobile, standing on its nose, and had a single white light at its base. After the UFO left the area it was tracked on surveillance radar, where it exhibited some amazing flight characteristics. The object also came back towards Kirtland, until it took up a position behind an Air Force C-46 that had just taken off. It stayed in position behind the C-46, until they both moved out of radar range. There have been several UFO incidents in and around Kirtland Air Force Base through the years.

(Source: Dr. J. Allen Hynek, James McDonald, Francis Ridge, NICAP)

Elliptical UFO disrupts car engine

At about 1.10pm on the same date, James W. Stokes – a high altitude research engineer of the USAF Missile Development Center, near Alamogordo, reported that he saw an elliptical UFO sweep twice across the highway. The car radio and the engine failed. Stokes claimed that ten other drivers were also on the road, and their engines had also failed. Stokes reported a wave of heat and, later, his face appeared sunburned. This case was explained by the Air Force as a hoax.

(Source: *Daily News,* Alamogordo, 8th November 1957)

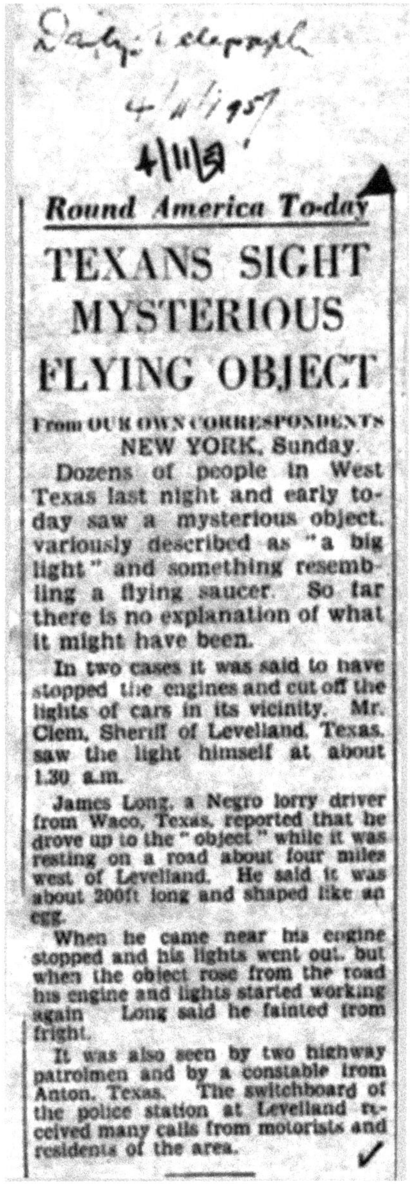

Daily Telegraph
4/11/1957
4/11/57

Round America To-day

TEXANS SIGHT MYSTERIOUS FLYING OBJECT

From OUR OWN CORRESPONDENTS
NEW YORK, Sunday.

Dozens of people in West Texas last night and early today saw a mysterious object, variously described as "a big light" and something resembling a flying saucer. So far there is no explanation of what it might have been.

In two cases it was said to have stopped the engines and cut off the lights of cars in its vicinity. Mr. Clem, Sheriff of Levelland, Texas, saw the light himself at about 1.30 a.m.

James Long, a Negro lorry driver from Waco, Texas, reported that he drove up to the "object" while it was resting on a road about four miles west of Levelland. He said it was about 200ft long and shaped like an egg.

When he came near his engine stopped and his lights went out, but when the object rose from the road his engine and lights started working again. Long said he fainted from fright.

It was also seen by two highway patrolmen and by a constable from Anton, Texas. The switchboard of the police station at Levelland received many calls from motorists and residents of the area.

6th November –USA: Close Encounter with UFO

At 6.30am, Everett Clark (12) – a farm boy of Dante, Texas – got up to let his dog 'Frisky' out. As he did so, he was

'Frankly, I Was Scared,' Says Stokes Of Experience With UFO

By BILLIE HOLDER
Daily News Publisher

"It all happened so fast that I don't know whether I can give you the answers you want or not," was the way that James Stokes, Alamogordo, opened an interview this morning relative to the unidentified flying object he saw yesterday afternoon near Orogrande. "The whole experience is weird, and very frankly I was scared to death, but I'll tell you what I can," he said.

Stokes reported that while driving on Highway 54 about 10 miles south of Orogrande yesterday afternoon, at 1:10, he noticed that his car radio began to fade out, and then the engine of his car slowed, and finally quit.

"There It Was"

"I thought it very strange, but did notice that other cars had pulled off, so I did, too, and the motor of my car quit entirely. I got out of the car and noticed another fellow pointing toward the sky, so I had a good look myself. There it was. Coming in from the northeast was the object. It swooped on toward Orogrande and headed out north. It disappeared quickly. We watched skyward, and it came in once more on the same path, and headed out north once more. We watched it until it disappeared, and that is all there is to it.

"The object was rather egg-shaped, the color of an egg or perhaps 'mother of pearl' color. It was definitely a solid, material thing, but there was no noise, no smoke nor vapor trail."

Extremely High Speed

Stokes, a veteran of 24 years with the U. S. Navy and now retired from Naval service, is employed on a classified experimental project at Holloman. He said that he had lived in Alamogordo and had been employed at AFMDC for the past 18 months, and that this is the first time he had ever had such an experience.

"Judging from the distance the object covered and the extremely short time it took to cover it, I'd judge that it must have been traveling at a rate of Mach 1 or Mach 2," he said. "Again, I must point out that these are purely guesses, and that I was scared, that time was so short, but there were people from six other cars watching the same thing. The object appeared to be about 1,500 to 3,000 feet in altitude. I made this guess based on the heights of the cloud formations that were floating overhead, and that the object flew into now and then. It must have been about 300 to 500 feet long and was of material —would have been something like 100-200 feet in thickness. There were no windows, or observation platforms visible on the object," he continued.

Stokes was reported to have been "sunburned" by the object. He said that he felt the rising of temperature and that his face was "slightly burned." However the burns were not serious and were not painful today. Outside of the heat from the object, Stokes said there was no pain from the burns.

He also pointed out again that there was no noise from the object. "When it changed directions it didn't turn, nor bank. It just went the other way," he said. "We were able to view it only about two or three minutes at the most," Stokes continued.

Stokes made notes on what he had seen, and even made a diagram of its location in relation to the mountains to the east and Highway 54. He said he talked with a Mr. Duncan of Las

See STOKES Page 6

surprised to see a strange glowing object, resting in a field about 300ft from the house. Thinking he may have been dreaming, he went back into the house. A few minutes later he opened the door and called the dog in, and was taken aback to see several other dogs around the oblong object, barking at two men and two women, dressed normally, who were stood next to it. One of the 'men' attempted to grab hold of 'Frisky', but the dog growled and backed away. They were conversing in a language which sounded like German. The 'men' caught one of the other dogs but was forced to let go of it, as the dog snapped at 'him'.

Clark: *"The four 'people' then walked through the wall of the object – like walking through glass."*

Impressions found in the ground

Reporter Carson Brewer, of the *Knoxville News Sentinel,* visited the location and discovered an elongated impression in the ground, 24ft by 5ft.

Alien asked for dog!

Later that night, Farmer John Trasco of Everittstown, New Jersey, went outside to feed his dog, when he saw a glowing egg-shaped object, hovering above the ground near his barn. John claimed that he was approached by,

"...a weird little man, some three and a half feet tall. He had a putty coloured face, with large bulging frog like eyes, dressed in green overalls. He said, 'We are a peaceful people. We don't want any trouble. We just want your dog'. I told him to get the hell out of here. The little man scurried back into the object, which shot off into the evening sky."

UFO Close Encounter, California

During the same evening, at Playa Del Rey, California, three motor vehicles stalled along the Vista del Mar highway. The drivers – Richard Kehoe, Ronald Burke and Joe Thomas – got out and saw an egg-shaped object, surrounded by blue haze, sitting on the ground of a nearby beach. Incredibly, they were approached by two 'men', who spoke to the party in difficult to understand English described as 5ft 5ins tall, dressed in black leather trousers and light coloured jerseys, whose skin appeared to be yellowish-green . The 'entities' asked a number of questions, such as what time was it, and where were the men going? They then left following which power was restored to their vehicles.

Colour changing object seen

Over Radium Springs, New Mexico, a Las Cruces policeman and a Dona Ana County Deputy Sheriff reported seeing a round object, changing from red to green to blue to white, which rose vertically from a nearby mountain top, at 10.50pm – in view for 10 minutes.

7th November – USA: US Coastguard sight UFO

At 5.10am on 7th November 1957, Comander Waring of the Unites States cutter *Sebago* was informed that the ships radar had picked up an object, which was racing around the cutter. On one occasion it halted in mid-air, before darting ahead at speed. Eleven minutes later, at 5.21am, four men on deck – Donald Schafer – Quarter Master, Kenneth Smith – Radioman, Thomas Kirk, and Ensign – Wayne Schottley, were able to obtain a visual image of the circular object, which was described as shiny and moving at speeds beyond the capabilities of known aircraft. The UFO was explained away as being a piston-engine aircraft!

Mississippi sighting – egg-shaped object

Truck driver Malvin Stevens (48) was driving home, near House, at 7.25am when a large egg-shaped object dropped out of the sky and landed on the highway in front of him. Malvin thought it was a weather balloon, at first.

"It had a propeller on either end and on top of the object. I got out and was confronted by three people – two men and a woman – all about four and a half feet tall, with pasty white faces. They were dressed in gray suits. They tried to talk to me but I couldn't understand them; one of then tried to shake my hand. They then got back into the object and flew off."

[On the same date, according to *Project Blue Book,* UFOs were sighted at Boerne, Texas, and Radium Springs, New Mexico]

(Sources: APRO [Aerial Phenomena Research Organization] & *UFOs: Operation Trojan Horse,* John A. Keel)

8th November – USA: Swishing UFO

Merrick, Long Island: a New York housewife sighted a bar-shaped object, three and a half feet long, giving off blue flashes, making a swishing sound as it headed through the sky, at 10.10am.

14th November – England: Red light seen by family out driving

A mysterious orange-red 'light' was seen over Mitcham, Surrey, at 9.15pm on 14th November 1957, by Mr A.B. Martin (who was out driving with his father, between Rose Hill and Mitcham) – which vanished but reappeared, a few minutes later, over Mitcham Common, before disappearing for good. **(Source: *Evening Standard*, 14.11.1957)**

In the same month, Gloucestershire Police Constable Donald Hibbard, from Dursley, was in his back garden in Woodsfield Road, at 8pm, when he saw a round object, sharply defined, brilliant white in colour, moving across the sky under the cloud (which was very low) – only a hundred feet in height. It then circled the locality, about half a mile away, moving at an estimated speed of 500mph.Whatever it was caused some interference to the television set, which was on at the time.

(Source: Mrs Hibbard)

18th November – England: Apparitions appear in Aston, Birmingham

Cynthia Appleton (aged 27), (nee Spencer), was a housewife, living at 87 Fentham Road, Aston, with her husband Ronald Appleton, and two children – Susan (2) and Janet (10). Little is known about her family history, other than she had left the Women's Royal Voluntary Service (WRVS), some years earlier, at the age of 21, after having suffered, it is said, a nervous breakdown.

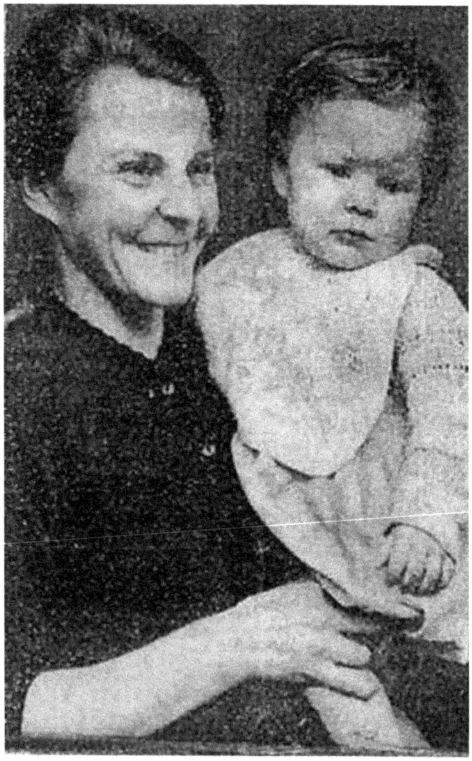

Mrs Cynthia Appleton with 13-month-old son, Mathew

On 18th November 1957, Cynthia's life was to be forever changed, as a result of an incident which took place during the early afternoon (as outlined by the *Birmingham Dispatch* Newspaper).

> *"It was early afternoon. My children were having a rest and I went into the lounge, where the baby was asleep in her pram. There, just a few feet away, stood this slender white-skinned man, with blonde hair, the same as any human being, except that he wore a kind of dome over his head and a tight-fitting all-in-one suit of a grey metallic colour. I was rooted to the spot and terrified until he spoke. He said we were going about space flight the wrong way and those men of his world, which he did not name, would come to Earth before we reached theirs."*

Numerous interviews held with her

Her story was to receive considerable publicity in both local and national newspapers, and lead to a number of visits made to her home address, over the following months, by people such as Gordon Creighton, psychologist, Dr John Dale, from Manchester, the Reverend Tiley, from Powick, near Worcester, Bernard Payne, from the Birmingham Psychic Society, and the Reverend William Cartmel, from Aldridge, Staffordshire – last, but not least, the renowned UFO researcher and brilliant linguist, author of a number of books, including two on UFOs – Shropshire-based, Gavin Gibbons.

Gordon Creighton's investigation following interview

"On November 18th, 1957, Cynthia thought she heard a cry and, on going downstairs to make sure 'baby Janet' was okay, became suddenly conscious of a very real feeling of oppressiveness in the air, similar to that experienced just before a storm.

While standing near the door, there appeared the figure of a man to the left of her fireplace – a blurred image, but then it became clearer – accompanied by a whistling noise, like an old wireless set being tuned in. He was wearing a tight-fitting silver garment, resembling a silvery plastic mackintosh. The sleeves reached to his wrist; the collar part of the garment rose up behind his head, like an Elizabethan collar, and the man's lips were moving but she heard no audible words – communication being telepathically.

Cynthia asked him where he had come from. He replied: 'From another world like yours. It is governed by the sun. We have to visit your world to obtain something of which we are short of. It is at the bottom of the sea'. Cynthia became conscious of a word in her mind. He said, 'You are stripping bark from the wrong tree to line the wrong boat; you are concentrating on the wrong power. You are trying to go up, against the force of gravity. We go like this'. He made sweeping lateral movements with his hands, and there appeared, between his outstretched fingers, what she could only describe, later, as a television screen, in which she could see a spaceship with a half-like transparent dome, with several 'figures' inside looking at her. Cynthia was able to see two of these 'Master Craft', to which the man referred, along with several smaller craft attached to the under part of one of them. He told her, 'We never fight but live in peace and harmony. We will return to see you in January, 1958'."

When her husband arrived home, she explained what had happened and asked him what 'titium' was. He said he didn't know but suggested it could be titanium. Following on from this encounter, Cynthia found she had developed a remarkably increased sense of awareness of other people and that her child, Janet, who had cut her first tooth, the day before, went on to develop a further five by the end of the week. A newspaper on which the 'man' had been standing was found to have been scorched, and was later handed over to a reporter from the *Birmingham Gazette* newspaper.

Doctor John Dale's investigation

His investigation involved interviewing Mrs Appleton on a number of occasions. Sadly, the whereabouts of his 'case notes' pertaining to many visits to the Appleton household have been lost from posterity, although Jenny Randles copied some of them, allowing us to gain further insight into the claims made by Cynthia Appleton.

Events of 16th November 1957

Dr. Dale tells us the events actually began on 16th November, when Cynthia suffered a blackout while doing the housework – caused, according to her visitors, as 'a failed attempt at contact'.

Contact made on the 19th of November

The 19th November contact began when Appleton 'became aware' of an atmosphere, 'like a rosy coloured darkness', which had materialised outside. The light didn't seem to penetrate into the living room. The entity then appeared in the room from nowhere and the light returned to normal. Appleton described how the entity spoke to her in her mind saying, telepathically,

> *'Do not be afraid. I am from another world, but do not want to take you over because the world is so good with you. We wish to live in union but cannot until you stop all wars'.*

The 'visitor' went on to state that he knew space flight experiments *'to get to us'* were taking place, but that the methods being used were fundamentally wrong:

> *"Your scientists are pulling against the greatest force of gravity by going straight up. You should travel with a sideways attitude."*

Shown 'flying saucer' image -with three half spheres underneath

With that, the 'being' slowly opened his arms and a 'TV set' appeared in the space between them, resembling a holographic image – unknown in the 1950s, in three dimensions and full colour. For some reason, Cynthia was more stunned by the colour than anything else about the manifestation. The 'living image', as she called it, showed a classic 'flying saucer', with flat rim and transparent dome. On its underside there were three half spheres. She said:

> *"These spaceships were like nothing I have ever seen in my life before. They seemed to take-off and hover in space for two or three seconds, went off to the left, then they went very quickly to the right."*

Power source also revealed

She was also shown the 'saucer's' power source, which she drew and later showed to Dr Dale, depicting a central hub, with a series of curved arms – like spokes. These, she was told, rotated and collected power from the atmosphere. She was then informed:

> *"Your greatest power is under the sea. It is therein great quantity, just for the taking".*

The entity also revealed he was from 'Gharnasvarn', which Earth people called Venus, and that he would return. The holographic TV set then blinked out and, along with the entity, vanished. Mrs Appleton told Dr. Dale that her visitor

> *"did not seem like a vision, because there was a three-dimensional depth and, although you could not see through him, he did actually seem to be there".*

After he disappeared, Mrs Appleton noticed the entity had been standing on a sheet of discarded newspaper, which now had a scorch mark on it – later shown to Doctor Dale, who noted it looked like the result of a 'lightning strike', or small electrical discharge.

24th November – England: Triangular UFO follows ship

At 9.50am during this month seaman William Anderson was to find himself, once again, in that most bizarre of situations when he witnessed yet another UFO sighting, while on lookout duty on the bridge of the ship he was serving on. What is so frustrating about these sightings is not the fact that we have no reason not to believe him – far from it, but it would be beneficial to know the names of the vessels he served on. Of course, if he was still alive, we are sure he would be most helpful; sadly, time has snatched any chance of that.

> *"I was on the bridge with others when we saw three very large, oval-shaped orange lights, at about 45 degrees to port. They formed a triangular pattern; one at the top and two at the bottom. They appeared to follow the ship for a couple of hours, before just 'blinking out'."*

(Source: Ron West)

26th November – USA: Cigar-shaped UFO sighted by Airbase men

At 10.07am, three control tower operators, stationed at Robins Air Force Base, Georgia, were on duty, along with a weather observer and four others, when they saw a silver, cigar-shaped, object in the sky, which suddenly vanished after eight minutes of observation.

27th November – England: UFO over Southampton Water

A most peculiar object was seen at 4pm on the 27th November 1957, high over Southampton Water, drifting towards the direction of Hythe, before disappearing from view. A number of people who saw the object described it as a 'stubby, rigid cross', with solid looking appendages hanging from it. Enquiries with the Police, Coastguard, and Southampton Airport, met with no success.

The sighting was even brought to the attention of the Top Secret Aircraft Establishment, at Boscombe Down, who stated:

> *they had no experimental object up and that, if they had, they wouldn't disclose the information to the public!'*

(Source: *Echo* Newspaper, 30.11.1957)

At 9.30pm, John Heard – a full-time worker in the Boy Scouts – was out walking his boxer dog in the Hertfordshire area, when his attention was caught by an object hovering beyond the houses, directly in front of him.

> *"It was a dazzling white 'light', shaped like the tin hats the ARP wardens used during the last war, with shimmering haze around it.*
>
> *It appeared to be over the* River Ivel *in the direction of Holme Mill. Suddenly, within seconds, the 'tin hat' moved away leaving only a vapour trail, and was gone from sight."*

According to Miss Thelma Roberts (who we met some years ago) – the area UFO investigator for Hertfordshire – other witnesses were later found.

(Source: *Flying Saucer Review*, May-June 1958, Vol. 4, No. 3)

29th November – England: Lorry driver sights UFO in Wales

At 2 30am on 29th November 1957, a lorry driver was travelling along the desolate Brecon Beacons, in mid Wales, when he sighted an object with a blue 'nose' and red 'tail' silently crossing the sky. Minutes later, a greenish-blue 'delta'-shaped object was seen by two Police Officers on duty in the Rhonda Valley. It was then seen by people living in the Isle of Man, crossing over the sea, four miles off the coast of Douglas. One man described it as being:

> *"...bluish/white, leaving a sheet of orange flame. There was a boom of an explosion as it vanished from view".*

James Harvey – a Coastguard from Scarlet Point, saw the blue/white object, with a red glow, moving from west to east, '*tapered like a carrot, miles high, going at a terrific speed*'. Any idea that this was some natural phenomenon could be dismissed, perhaps by the nature of the previous reports. After all, there is nothing of any value that indicates this object was a UFO, if it wasn't for the next, even stranger, experience which befell the crew of the Fleetwood fishing trawler, *Ella Hewett*, which was off the north-east of Ireland when boson Hugh Smith saw:

> *"...a massive glow surrounding the ship, accompanied by an eerie feeling; there was no vibration, no explosion – in fact, no sensation at all. The skipper, Fred Sutton, then discovered the white paint on the front of the bridge had vanished, leaving only the red lead undercoat."*

The next day, the ship's owners – Hewett Fishing Company Limited – received another radio trans-mission from ship to say:

> *"...the white paint on the bridge had returned".*

(Source: *Flying Saucer Review*, Jan/Feb. 1958, Volume 4, Number 1/*Daily Express*, 30.11.1957)

NEWS CHRONICLE 30-11-57

A LOW-FLYING mystery object glowing greenish-blue was sighted over South Wales early yesterday.

AT 2.30 a.m. a lorry driver saw it as he drove over the desolate Brecon Beacons. He described it to Mid-Wales police as delta-shaped, "twice the length of his lorry and moving low in flames."

AT 2.35 it was sighted by a police patrol car crew 30 miles away near Cowbridge, Glamorgan.

Two policemen on their beats in the Rhondda Valley saw it moving at high speed.

No air crashes are reported.

Reports of a "ball of fire" were sent to the R.A.F. at Plymouth.

For good measure an object with "a flame tail" crashed with a loud bang off the Isle of Man early yesterday. It is believed to be a meteorite.

30th November – USA: Three UFOs sighted

Three US Coast Guardsmen from New Orleans, Louisiana, were on duty at 2.11pm, when they saw a white, round, object in the sky, which turned gold – then separated into three parts and turned red, over a period of 20 minutes.

7th /14th December – England: Mysterious 'light' over Bedfordshire

John Jordan – a successful local businessman and owner of eight shops in the Bedfordshire area – was on his way home, at 7.30pm, when he saw a 'white light' hovering over his property – Holme Mill.

> *"It looked to be about 12 inches in diameter and reminded me of a landing light of an aircraft. Within seconds it had reached a speed of 100 mph, and was heading towards Sandy on a level course in a northern direction. It then stopped dead in the sky. Oddly, I had seen a similar object hovering over the building on 7th December, while passing over in my private plane."* **(Source: Thelma Roberts)**

15th December – Brazil: Landed UFO with occupant

A BRAZILLIAN FARMERS STORY 1957.

On the 15th December 1957,Adhemar,a young farmer of Ponte Poran Brazil was out ploughing,it was midnight,suddenly Adhemar observed a star like light which approached at great speed from the North,seconds later the light stopped about 300 feet above the field.Adhemar thoroughly alarmed decided to pack up and go home,at that moment the object in the sky swooped down and landed some twenty yards from his tractor.Two "people" emerged from the machine and ran towards him,they grabbed him from behind,as Adhemar struggled,others came from the saucer and finally Adhemar was hustled into the space craft.Inside Adhemar was stripped of his clothes,blood was drawn from his chin by a flexible suction syringe,he was then covered with a plastic material and then moistened all over with a kind of sponge.Adhemar was then left alone for twenty minutes then a girl came into the cabin,she was about 4ft 8ins tall had blonde hair, no eyelashes or eyebrows,she looked "Chinese",she approached Adhemar with open arms,stood near him and waited,perhaps to note his reactions,soon the girl left and Adhemar was given back his clothes,he was then taken outside the saucer,as soon as he was clear of the machine the queer craft suddenly took off in a blinding white light,Adhemar had not been harmed by his encounter.

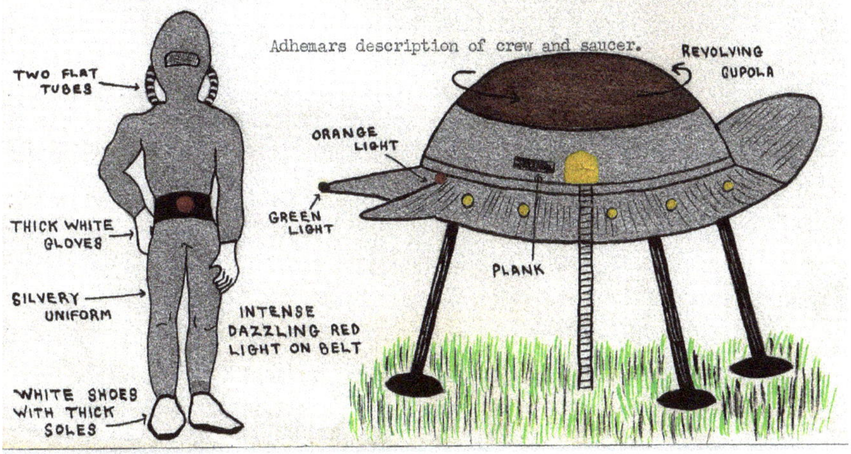

An artistic offering from NICAP UFO researcher Derek Samson, beautifully hand-painted by him.

16th December – USA: Landed UFO, with entities seen

Mrs Mary M. Starr – a resident of Old Saybrook, Connecticut, and a former teacher with a Master's Degree, from Yale – retired to bed, at 10pm, on the night of 15th December. Between 2am and 3am, she was awoken by a 'bright light' and first thought it was an aircraft in trouble. Looking out she saw:

> *"...a cigar-shaped object, brightly lit, with square portholes, hovering just above my clothes-line; I could see men inside".*

The object, no more than ten feet from the north side of Mrs Starr's home, was approximately 20 to 30ft long and dark grey or black in colour. It hovered motionless, about 5ft above the ground, between the house and the tool shed. No wings, fins, or other appendages, were seen. Through the object's lighted windows Mrs Starr saw two figures that passed each other, walking in opposite directions.

> *"I could see that it [the object] was so shallow that the men could not have been more than three and a half or four feet tall. The occupants' right arms were raised but no hands were visible. They wore a kind of jacket that 'flared out' at the base and their heads were unusual – square or rectangular, red-orange in colour, and with a brighter red 'bulb' in the centre. I thought they might possibly be wearing some kind of helmets."*

A third 'being' came into view from the left. Mrs Starr leaned forward to see more clearly, then the portholes faded and the entire shell of the object began glowing brightly. From the top end, closest to her, there arose a kind of six-inch 'antenna' that oscillated and sparkled. After five minutes of glowing steadily, the 'antenna' was retracted and the craft began to move. It retraced its original path, gliding smoothly in the direction from which it had apparently arrived. It then made a very sharp right-angle turn, now appearing oval in shape. The hull had changed to a dull grey-blue, and small circular lights now outlined the entire rim. The UFO dipped and undulated, following the contours of a small depression to the north of the witness' house, then tilted sharply and shot up into the sky, at terrific speed, in total silence.

(Sources: NICAP, Richard Hall & Isabel Davis, Charles Bowen, *Flying Saucer Review*, Jan/Feb.1968, Vol. 14, Page 15-16. 'The Spectre at Winterfold'/ *Woking Review*/SIGAP)

17th December – USA: UFO sighted

Mr F.G. Hickman was near Grand Junction, Colorado, at 7.20pm, when he saw a round object in the sky, which changed from yellow to white, to green and red. Its red tail was twice as long as the body. It then stopped, and shortly afterwards reversed the course taken for up for 45 minutes.

England: Was a UFO photographed over Shrewsbury?

Bill Kerswell from Church Stretton, Shropshire – a former member of the Royal Observer Corps., HQ16 Group, stationed at Shrewsbury, in 1957 – told of a number of occasions when UFOs were tracked on radar. He was out walking, one afternoon, when he noticed what looked like a modern day *Stealth* fighter bomber, moving slowly – enough for him to take a picture of it with a camera that he had at the time. Unfortunately, although he kept the photograph for many years, he has now mislaid it.

> *"The only reason I didn't bring the photo to anybody's attention, at the time, was because of all the excitement in the newspapers about 'flying saucers', knowing that I would be accused of fabricating the photo to fit into other reports of UFOs seen."* **(Source: Personal interview)**

1958

Trevor James Constable

DURING our quest we became influenced by people such as Trevor James Constable (USA), for his research into Etherian Physics, offering us evidence that *"UFOs are either biological organisms, native to the Earth's atmosphere or intelligently controlled craft"*.

We also took into consideration the views held by Trevor (a man we felt privileged to know) with regard to his knowledge on UFOs that can be found in his book *The Cosmic Pulse of Life*, which postulates the existence of *"malevolent fourth dimensional alien forces, who seek to disrupt life on this planet"*.

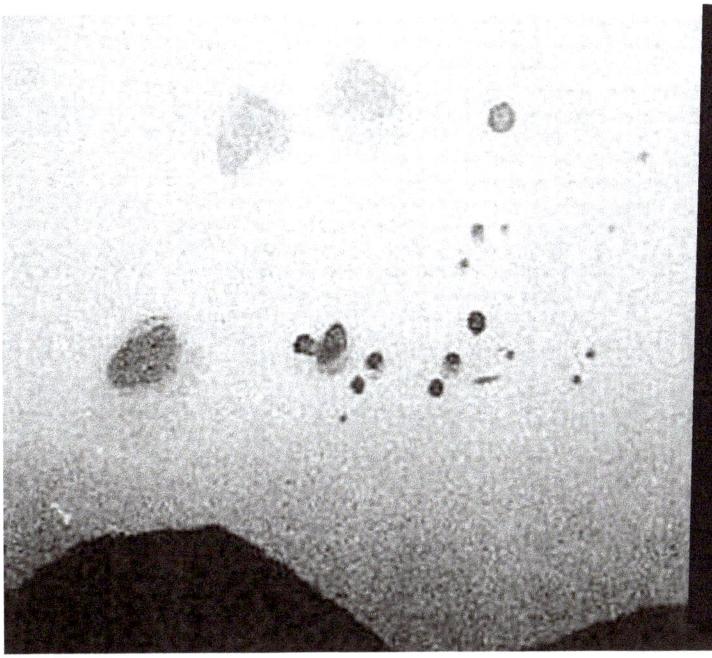

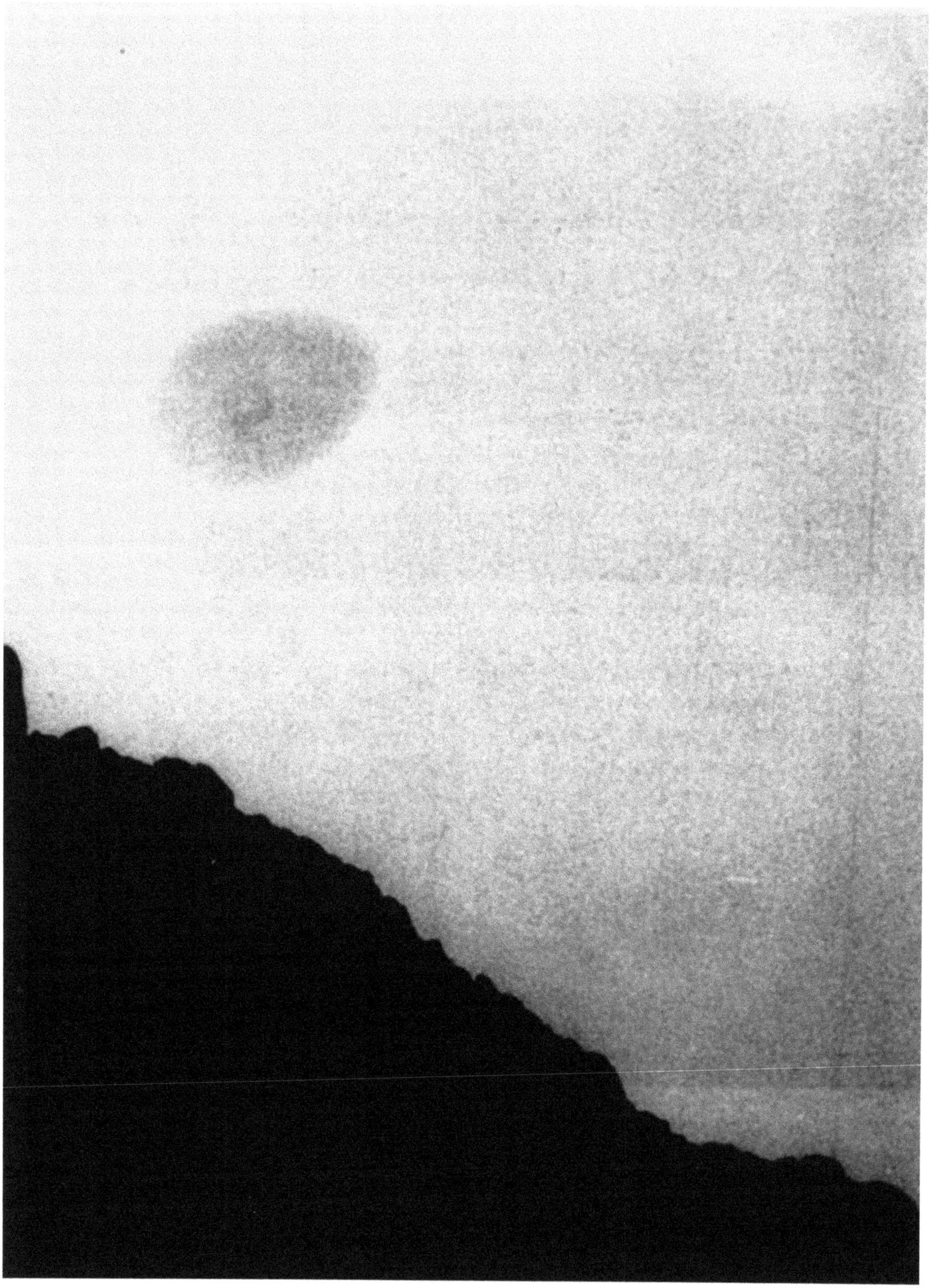

7th January – England: Another encounter for Cynthia Appleton

During the evening of 7th January 1958, Cynthia blacked out, losing consciousness, whilst sitting in front of the fire.

On 'coming around', she felt dazed and bewildered. Fortunately, her husband was present at the time.

8th January – Two 'figures' materialise

At about 2.15pm on 8th January, Cynthia was in the back sitting room, after having put Janet and Susan to sleep, sitting on a pouf with her back resting against the wall, when she heard a whistling sound, followed by the blurred appearance of two 'figures' stood in front of the wall. When the images cleared, she recognised the shorter one as the man seen previously, describing them as wearing close-fitting garments, with low cut collars rising up behind the neck, similar to the 'Elizabethan style'.

The hair of the first 'visitor' was cut 'page-boy' fashion, with the hair straight and falling onto the shoulders, while the second was 'ballerina' style, shorter and curled-up over the ears. The first 'visitor' introduced the other – apparently more senior – addressing Cynthia in a clipped English accent, as a foreigner would speak. He told her:

> *"The blackout you experienced, the day before, was as a result of us trying to contact you, informing you we come from 'Gharnasvarn' – a country on Venus".*

Told that Russians were perfecting a ray gun!

After further conversation relating to her husband's inability to see them, explained away as *'his brain not being able to receive such a transmission'*, she was told the bearers of the 'hammer and sickle', (the Russians), were on the point of perfecting a ray gun.

> *"This could disintegrate matter without firing any shell, such as fired by ordinary artillery, and that in the near future there would be much bloodshed and suffering. Do not be afraid, little one".*

This would be the final visit to her, because of the effects on her health. He then bowed and disappeared – *'like a TV picture fading away'*.

Cynthia appeared on BBC Television

On 13th January 1958, Cynthia appeared on *BBC* Television and told the viewers about her experiences, involving a visit from the 'men from Venus' – an account consistent with what she had told researchers and the Press, previously. Although we were unable to obtain a copy of this film, we know the *BBC* interviewed a man on the same programme, who claimed *'to have met a Martian on a coach going to Leith Hill, Surrey'*, which can hardly be said to have helped her cause!

News Chronicle

The *News Chronicle* (14.1.1958) also featured Mrs Appleton's 'experience'. In an interview conducted with them, she outlined what had happened and, in response to the suggestion made to her that the whole thing was a hoax, replied:

"Oh, no, I have never been interested in this sort of thing before and I'm not a member of a planetary organisation. I felt a little scared, at first, but the 'men' were friendly".

Reverend George Tilley interviews Cynthia and delivers sermon

The Reverend George E. Tilley, Vicar of Powick, Worcestershire, was to also take a keen interest in the affairs of Cynthia and made several visits to the 'Appleton' household, in late 1957 and early 1958.

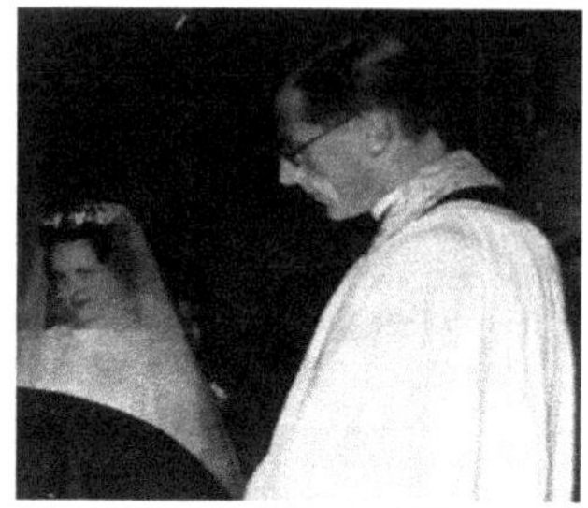

Reverend George Tilley

Sunday Sermon

On 12th January 1958, he made her experiences the focus of his Sunday sermon, the congregation no doubt surprised when he told them:

"If you take the trouble, as I have, to study very deeply, you cannot possibly, if you have an honest, open, sincere mind, review the mass of evidence, from all over the world, that men other than ourselves exist, and refute that evidence. I believe they do exist, for what it's worth, and their visits to this Earth are like the 'Star of Bethlehem'."

The vicar continued:

"I feel very grateful to have had the chance to sit with her in her kitchen and talk about it. A higher hand than mine led me there. These men told this woman that they have overcome war, poverty and disease, and that they had passed through the same stages as we of this world. They came with a message of brotherhood and love. They want to help us."

Healing powers

Our enquiries into the background of the Reverend was to reveal a much loved man, who was believed – according to more than one source of information we spoke to – possess healing powers which did, on a number of occasions, we suspect, save lives. Whether these abilities originated *after* visits to Cynthia Appleton can only be of conjecture, but nevertheless give 'food for thought'.

A glowing testimonial to the healing powers of the Reverend were described to us by Mrs Isobel Brant, from Worcester – aged 18, at the time: (Her wedding day officiated by the Reverend Tilley)

"In 1955 my youngest brother was born. He was 10lbs. in weight, but was very poorly and had problems with his blood clotting. Because of his ill health, he had to be christened straightaway, so we asked the Reverend Tilley to go to the hospital and christen Nicolas Jeremy, after receiving a call from the hospital, who clearly believed the baby was going to die. After christening him he said to my mother, 'With a beautiful name like that, he has got to live'. My brother came home after being in hospital, got better, but then began to experience epileptic fits when aged two. The Reverend came every week to see him and placed his hands on Nicholas's head, praying silently, until the day Nicholas started his first day at school, when he said to my mother, 'Our job is done'.

I believe it was his faith in that child and belief in faith healing which saved the child's life. The Reverend Tilley, who had three children - Fiona, Jonathan and Timothy, left Powick and went to Upton Warren; sadly, his wife later died but he remarried.

His second wife advertised in the newspaper, following his death, appealing for anybody that had been healed by him to contact her."

Addresses the congregation - The golden age of spacemen

In 1957, The Reverend George Tilley preached to his congregation about spaceships and space visitors form other worlds.

"The men who live on Venus and Mars are far in advance of us. They have learned to use everything constructively; they have outlawed war, disease and poverty. In a sense they have began to live the Golden Age. They are so far advanced they would rather be killed than kill."

Reverend Ronald Cartmel

Reverend Ronald Cartmel

Another member of the religious faith, who was to take a keen interest in the affairs of Cynthia Appleton, was Aldridge, Staffordshire-based rector, the Reverend Ronald William Cartmel - member of the Royal Astronomical Society - whose views on UFOs was well-known to many in his parish. On one occasion he published a lengthy account in the parish magazine, outlining his deep-seated overwhelming conviction of the existence of 'flying saucers'.

"It is absurd to think we are the only people in the universe - the Bible teaches us we are not. To deny that these things exist is to shut your eyes to the facts. There are, something like, 20,000 sightings a year. It is always possible for people to make mistakes, but even if only one third are genuine, there is still a tremendous amount of evidence. Throughout the Bible there are stories of angelic messengers. Perhaps today we should call them spacemen."

Whilst Reverend Cartmel saw no conflict between belief in 'flying saucers' and religious faith, and believed the one served to confirm the other, he did not necessarily accept the *'saucer men'* were all benevolent in nature.

Valerie Geary nee Perks

Mrs Valerie Geary (nee Perks), still living in the Aldridge area of Staffordshire (in 2009), contacted us about her knowledge of the Rector who had conducted her marriage ceremony, in 1966.

"I knew him well. He was Rector for over 20 years, and member of a UFO Society. His views on UFOs were well-known. I attended Sunday school, at the Church, and later, Girls Bible Class, which was led by his wife - Mrs Olive Cartmel. He had two daughters - Ann and Elizabeth - but have no idea where they live now."

Bernard Payne, of the 'Birmingham Psychic Society'

Bernard Payne, of the Birmingham Psychic Society, also conducted a lengthy interview with Mrs Appleton and was convinced she believed the truth of her 'story', and planned an experiment in which Mrs Appleton would re-enact her first encounter, repeating exactly the same tasks, at the same time of day, in an effort to recall more details – a technique often used by police in the reconstruction of a crime. Mr Payne commented,

> *"To be on the safe side, a medium would be present as well as a tape-recorder and a super ray machine. We are not sure what will happen, but I think something is bound to occur. We have open minds on the subject at the moment, but I think the visitation will prove to be of a psychic nature".*

We are not informed of the results of this experiment or, indeed, whether it ever took place. Although the 'visitors' told Mrs Appleton on 8th January that this was to be their final visit, it appears this was not the case, as she later reported a number of subsequent visits by the 'visitors', *'who arrived in a large black car with tinted windows'* – now wearing *'black business suits and Homburg hats'!*

While it would be easy to believe she had become confused and mixed them up with the visits made by the many researchers to her house (as this seems a rational explanation) was it possible they could have been 'visits' from the mysterious 'Men in black', whose role in UFO folklore is well-known to all of us? However, Cynthia – as far as we know – never claimed to have been threatened, or intimidated.

We also considered the implications of the tinted widows, but discovered tinted windows were fitted into some cars from 1952.

On another occasion, Cynthia was told their 'saucer' was waiting for them in the vicinity of Edinburgh. On each of the six or so visits Appleton received, during 1958, her 'Venusian confidants' revealed further information about themselves and their beliefs.

Jenny Randles

Jenny Randles, working from Dr. Dale's notes, writes:

> *"She was advised time did not exist. It was a philosophical invention, by mankind, who failed to understand all life was connected at some deep inner level, not separate as we assumed. Detailed scientific facts about the nature of atoms were then conveyed to her.*
>
> *She was told this was the basis to understand how to cure cancer and a complex cure was explained to her, which involved changing the vibration rate of atoms at a subatomic level, but Cynthia struggled to remember the terms used when she tried to describe this to Dr. Dale. Nuclear physics and the subatomic world clearly held a special fascination for the Venusians and many conversations revolved around the subject. To the Venusians, science and religion appeared to be synonymous and they were keen to share their version of the secret of the universe, telling Cynthia: 'The deity itself dwells at the heart and core of the atoms.' Cynthia told them it was pointless revealing this type of detailed technical and philosophical knowledge to her, because she simply didn't understand".*

Patrick Kent of the 'Sunday People'

Patrick Kent – a reporter for the *Sunday People*, asked Cynthia's four year-old daughter – Susan – if she remembered any of the 'Venusians" visits:

"Yes, I remember mummy bathing the hand of a man with funny long hair and a fur collar."

Cynthia may have had the support of the Church of England, the Birmingham Psychic Society, and UFO researchers, but unfortunately, many of her friends deserted her following the publication of the newspaper articles.

"Some people are saying I'm a crank, some that I am loose-headed, and others that I have been working too hard, but I know what I saw."

Brinsley Le Poer Trench (Lord Clancarty)

Editor of *Flying Saucer Review* was certain Mrs Appleton's claims were genuine:

"The woman's story ties up, in many respects, with what we have learned in the last 10 years from others who have had contact with men from other worlds. Throughout the 1950s, US contactees had been telling their tales of meeting, talking to, and even taking flight with spacemen from planets within our solar system, often Venus and Mars. Like Cynthia's visitors, they were tall, humanoid, communicated by telepathy, and travelled in classic, dome-shaped, 'flying saucers', and espoused a philosophy similar to that explained to Cynthia Appleton. These 'Venusian' values were essentially socialist in nature, tinged with elements now familiar from many New Age philosophies – beliefs quite at odds with the 'You've never had it so good' capitalism of the 1950s.

Contactees were repeatedly told by their mentors that, to save Earth from certain disaster, mankind should stop tampering with nuclear forces and live in peace and harmony. Only then would we be included in the Intergalactic Parliament, taking our rightful place among the stars with other highly evolved civilizations. The 'space brothers' often illustrated their concerns by showing contactees visions of nuclear and ecological disasters. Cynthia Appleton was shown a vision of two asteroids colliding and causing widespread panic and devastation on Earth. This she was told was going to happen soon."

George Adamski lectures to a crowd of 1,000 people in Birmingham

In April 1959, George Adamski visited Britain, as part of a world lecture tour, and spoke at the Birmingham Midland Institute. Unsurprisingly excited, Cynthia Appleton was one of a reported audience of over 1,000 people who attended Adamski's lecture. Afterwards she was asked:

"What do you think of Mr Adamski? Reply: *"When I had my first visit, I thought I must be going mad. I'm scatty. I should like to be the first to know about it, but so much of what Mr Adamski says tallies with my own experiences that I feel much happier now. My daughter, aged four, has seen the visitor too, for she asks me when he is going to come back."*

Sunday People – Baby from Venus!

On 10th May 1959, the *Sunday People* newspaper headlines screamed: 'I'm going to have a baby from Venus', says Mrs Cynthia Appleton, of 87 Fentham Road, Aston Birmingham. The sub-heading read: *'This is the biggest crackpot statement a woman has ever made'*. The *Sunday People* reporter 'cut straight to the chase' and suggested she might have been imagining things, to which Mrs Appleton retorted, *"But it's true, and my husband believes it to"*.

She explained how the man from Venus had given her other predictions and instructions about her, as yet, undiagnosed pregnancy. It transpired the 'Venusians' had called again in September, 1958, informing Cynthia she was in the state of 'being with child'. It was news to her but he was adamant, telling her she would give birth in late May, 1959. The child would be a boy and would weigh exactly 7lbs. 3oz. He would be a leader of men at the age of 14 and must be called Mathew.

Shortly after the Venusians' visit on 2nd June 1958, Cynthia was found to be pregnant. On 2nd June1959, Cynthia Appleton gave birth to a boy whom she named Mathew, with blonde hair, at two minutes after midnight, weighing in at just a little over 7lbs. – almost exactly as the Venusians had predicted. Not long after the birth, Cynthia received a telepathic message, giving her advance warning that her Venusian friend was going to call again soon – this time with a friend from the planet Uranus.

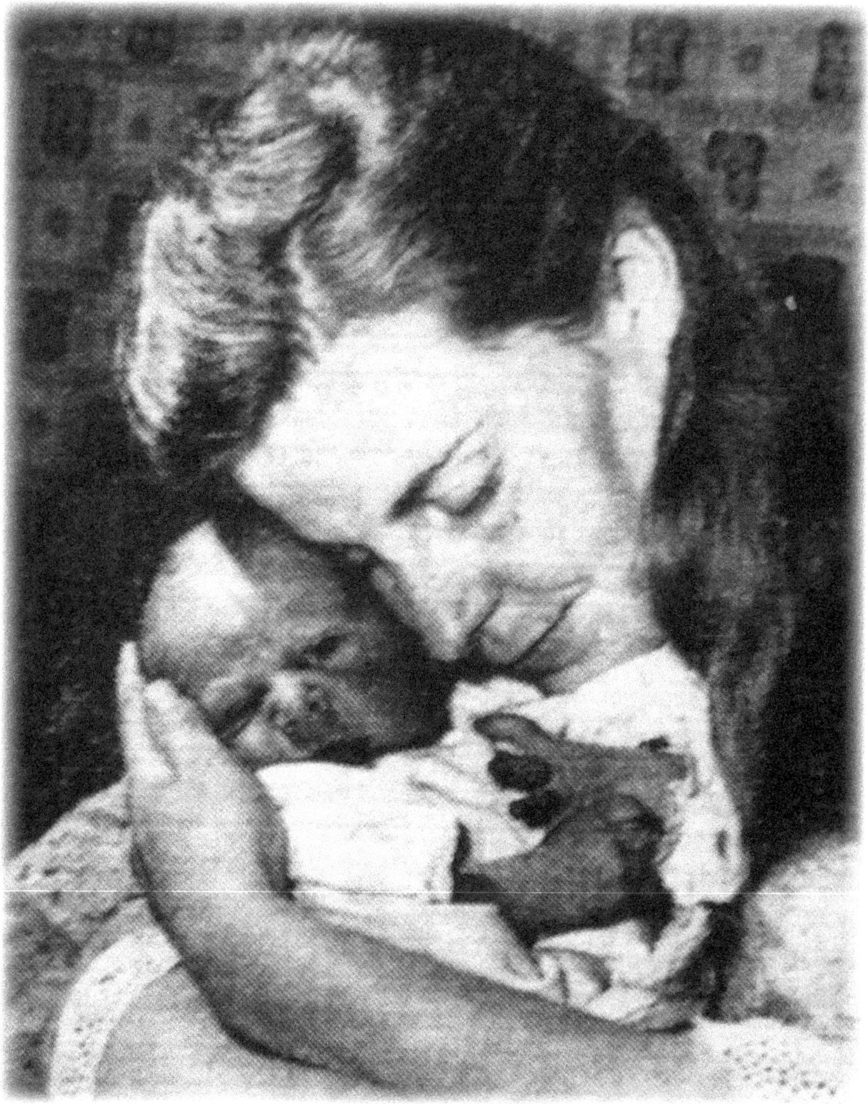

Venus baby is just as the spaceman prophesied

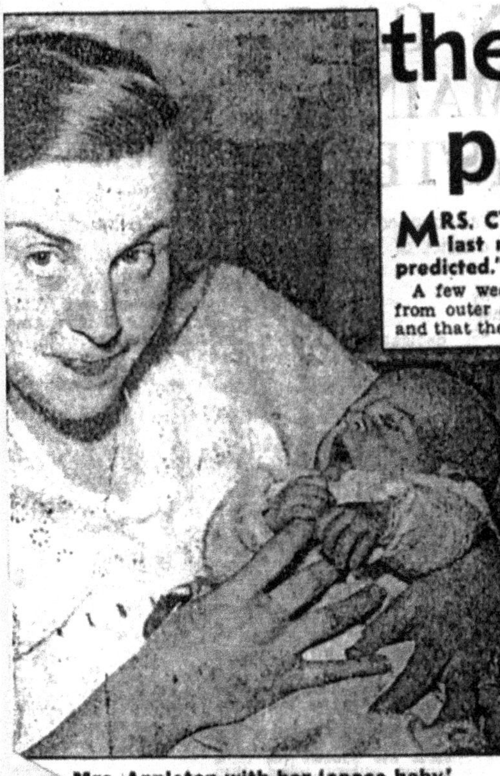

Mrs. Appleton with her 'space baby'

PEOPLE 14-6-59

MRS. CYNTHIA APPLETON looked at her new baby last night and said: "Just as the man from Venus predicted." Well, almost.

A few weeks ago, she told in a "People" interview of a visitor from outer space who declared that she was going to have a baby and that the child would—

Be a boy—he is;
Have fair hair—right;
Weigh 7 lb. 3 oz.—7 lb. 2 oz.; and
Arrive late in May—he came a week later.

"Of course, my husband, Ron, is the father, but really the baby will spiritually belong to a race who live on Venus," said Mrs. Appleton a few days before the first "space child" entered the earth's orbit in the front room of the Appleton's terrace house in Fentham Road, Aston, Birmingham.

And, as directed by the Man from Venus, the newest Appleton will be named Matthew.

"I know my story sounded fantastic," Mrs. Appleton admitted. "People were bound to be sceptical.

"Maybe now, they'll think twice. My other children (Susan 4, Janice 2) both weighed less than 6 lb. at birth and were premature babies."

What does husband Ron, a 35-year-old welder, think of the baby who, according to Mrs. Appleton, "has the delicate features of his spiritual race."

Mr. Appleton has not seen the spaceman. Each of his eight visits—by flying saucer, based on Edinburgh—has been made in the day-time when Ron was at work, says Mrs. Appleton.

The funny man

But young Susan remembers "the funny man with long hair who sat down while Mummy bathed his hand."

That was when Mr. Venus said he had burned his hand on the exhaust of his flying saucer.

"I believe everything Cynthia has told me," said Mr. Appleton, "but I would love to have a yarn with him. I told her to suggest he leaves a couple of quid a week to help feed Matthew.

"But he said on his last visit that they didn't bother about money on Venus.

"Since Matthew was born he has sent a telepathic message to Cynthia saying he was bringing along a mate from Uranus.

"If he shows up I'm going to tell him I'm Matthew's father. If he doesn't give me the right answers I'll crack his 'delicate features' with a crowbar.

"His mate from Uranus will get the same."

Still wanting confirmation: The spaceman's forecast of a major collision in outer space

Ron Appleton threatens the visitors

Ron Appleton once again stood by his wife, but issued a stern warning to the visitor from Venus:

> *"I believe everything Cynthia has told me, but I would love to have a yarn with him. If he shows up I'm going to tell him I'm Mathew's father. If he doesn't give me the right answers, I will crack his delicate features with a crowbar; his mate from Uranus will get the same."*

Empire News

In 1960, the *Empire News* reported that 13 month-old Mathew was doing well, although Mrs Appleton was still at a loss to know what to make of it all. As yet, there was no sign of Mathew becoming 'a leader of men', but Mrs Appleton was keeping a close eye on him and said:

PAGE 6 THE PEOPLE, SUNDAY, MAY 10, 1959

THIS IS THE BIGGEST CRACKPOT STATEMENT HAS EVER MADE . . .

'I'm goi have a from V

says Mrs. Cynthia Appleton, of 8 Aston, Bi

MRS. CYNTHIA APPLETON could be anyone's next-door neighbour. She lives an ordinary life in an ordinary street.

But there was nothing ordinary about the fantastic claim Mrs. Appleton made to me last week. She said: "I'm going to have the world's first SPACE CHILD."

She stroked her long blonde hair, tied up in a ponytail, and went on: "Of course, my husband is the baby's father —but really the child will belong to a race who live on the planet Venus."

And to that crackpot statement Mrs. Appleton added: "A man from Venus called one day while I was doing the washing and told me so."

No, don't laugh yet . . . read on.

I suggested to Mrs. Appleton that perhaps she was imagining things. "But it's TRUE," she said. "And my husband believes it too."

Twenty-nine-year-old Mrs. Appleton lives at 87, Fentham Road, Aston, Birmingham.

She and her husband, Ro[illegible], a welder, have two children, Susan, 4, and Janice, 2.

Their third baby—the one with supposed links with outer space—is expected to be born this week. And Mrs. Appleton is convinced that it will be a boy. Why?

The Man from Venus told her.

According to Mrs. Appleton he knocked at her back door one day last September, raised his black homburg and told her she was "in the state of being with child."

Nonsense? Not to Mrs. Appleton. "He wasn't just a stranger," she said. "He'd been here to see me several times before."

Well, after the Man from Venus had delivered his astonishing news, Mrs. Appleton went straight off to the doctor to see about a down-to-earth medical opinion.

For she had no idea she was pregnant. .

Imagine her astonishment

Mrs. Cynthia Appleton and her husband. SHE says her baby is going to be the world's first space child. HE says: "I believe her completely."

Vicky Hanson (John Hanson's daughter) in Fentham Road, Aston

OT STATEMENT A WOMAN

'I'm going to have a baby from Venus'

s. Cynthia Appleton, of 87, Fentham Road, Aston, Birmingham

her back door
ptember, raised
g and told her
state of being

to Mrs. Apple-
: just a stran-
He'd been here
times before."
ne Man from

husband.

Venus had delivered his astonishing news, Mrs. Appleton went straight off to the doctor to see about a down-to-earth medical opinion.

For she had no idea she was pregnant.

Imagine her astonishment, then, when the doctor confirmed it. She WAS pregnant.

But that is only part of her story. For in the course of his 20-minute wash-day chat, the Man from Venus also had this to say about the child expected this week:

It would be a boy.

He would weigh exactly 7 lb. 3 oz.

He would be a leader of men at 14.

He must be called Matthew.

Mrs. Appleton has accepted all this as fact. So has her husband Ron—although he has never seen the gentleman caller from outer space. He always seems to call when Mr. A. is at work.

Mrs. Appleton showed me her baby clothes. They are all blue—for a boy, of course.

In all, the Man from Venus has visited Mrs. Appleton eight times in 18 months, she says.

On the first two visits he [illegible] goldfish bowl.

But on subsequent visits he has looked less out of this world in a smart camel-coloured short overcoat, with beaver lamb collar, a homburg hat, tweed trousers and casual shoes.

'WE TALK'

Mrs. Appleton says he is tall and slim, with fair hair down to his shoulders. "We sit and talk," she says.

Not talk as you and I understand it. "We use thought transference," said Mrs. Appleton.

What do they talk about? "Oh, religion, politics, conditions in outer space, racial differences."

One day when the man called, said Mrs. Appleton, he told her he had burned his hand. He asked her to bathe it for him in boiling water.

The man went and Mrs. Appleton poured the water down the sink. It was then, she says, that she noticed something in the bottom of the glass bowl. It was a piece of skin as big as the sole of a woman's shoe.

She showed it to her husband when he came home. I saw a small piece of it at the Appletons' home.

There is only a little bit left now because Mrs. Appleton sent a piece away to Birmingham University for examination.

They found after three weeks that the skin could not be identified in any way because it was too small.

[illegible]

The man hasn't been around in any form since January 17.

But Mrs. Appleton isn't worrying. She feels sure he will pay another visit shortly after the birth of the baby.

When I asked four-year-old Susan about her mother's strange visitor, she told me after a moment's thought: "Yes, I remember Mummy bathing the hand of a man with funny long hair and a fur collar."

But she couldn't remember anything else about the visits. Neither could her little sister Janice.

So there you have all the details of the Man from Venus. Mrs. Appleton says he told her he was on his second visit to Earth, that he travelled by flying saucer and was "stationed near Edinburgh."

All that remains is to mention something of Mrs. Appleton's character. She says herself she is extremely sensitive.

'THE BEST'

To me she seemed natural and sincere. Though she did say that she was released from the Women's Royal Army Corps when she was 21 after a nervous breakdown.

Today Mrs. Appleton seems fine and well. She has a loving husband and a happy family.

What does Mr. Appleton think about this? He told me with a shrug of his shoulders: "Cynthia is the best wife any man could have and of course I BELIEVE HER COMPLETELY.

"I'm only sorry I haven't been around to meet our friend too.

"I'm not worried about being the father of a child inspired by a man from space."

My hope is that the Appletons' new baby won't grow up with [illegible] head in the clouds, too!

—Patrick Kent

> *"I don't know what to expect, but I haven't noticed the slightest thing that could be taken as a sign'.*

She spoke of being concerned that,

> *"... since Matthew's birth, contact with the Venusians had been somewhat sparse. He used to pop in quite regularly every seven or eight weeks. When he left, after forecasting Mathew's birth, he said he would be looking in again soon, but he never returned. I just can't make it out."*

In July 1960, the trail goes cold. Newspapers never again mentioned Mrs Appleton or her 'Venus' baby, and there was no major collision between two asteroids, which the 'spacemen' had predicted. Matthew would have turned 14 on the 1st June 1973 – the year when he was prophesied to become 'a leader of men'. History shows that, as yet, he appears not to have taken up this challenge and would now be nearing 50 years of age.

Since the early 1960s, UFO publications have often repeated the Appleton 'star child' story, but added nothing of relevance to the narrative, despite many attempts made to trace Cynthia and Ron Appleton, and their offspring, by Dr. David Clarke, Andy Roberts, and ourselves.

Their current whereabouts still remain unknown.

When we read about this incident, our first reaction was of stark disbelief. Surely we could not really be expected to believe any of this to have happened? The very idea that men from Venus and Uranus had contrived to enter into communication with this Birmingham housewife, rather than cultivating a relationship with a politician or scientist, seems laughable – until you examine all of the facts surrounding not only this case but of the people involved, when you realise the likelihood that something extraordinary happened at Fentham Road, Aston, rather than any fabrication involving a series of manifestations more in keeping with psychic behaviour than visits by alien beings from Venus and Uranus.

(Source: Andy Roberts, Dr. David Clarke, and Jenny Randles)

9th January – England: Ex Radar officer sights two UFOs

Mr J.D. Hole-Gale – a former lecturer on aircraft recognition to the Territorial Army in Dorset, and ex-radar Officer with the Air Ministry – was walking behind a group of friends in Savile Park Crescent, at 11.39pm, when he saw two luminous 'discs', hovering overhead in the clear night sky.

> *"One was in the vertical plane – the other, horizontal. I shouted to a photographer in the group; by the time he and the others turned around they had moved away at great speed, southwards, heading in a straight trajectory. I was sceptical before, but now I do not know what my attitude is. To me, this seems to be confirmation of other reports I have read."*

Mr Hole-Gale stated he could recognise 400 types of aircraft and was sure this was neither of them, or a balloon, the moon, or reflections.

(Source: *Flying Saucer Review*, Volume 3, No. 1, Jan/Feb 1957)

10th January – England: Cigar-shaped UFO over Stafford

At 4.30pm (our now friend) Jessie Roestenberg, from Staffordshire, sighted a glowing, orange cigar-shaped object, high over Stafford. She immediately alerted her two sons and then called her next door neighbour – Mrs D. Osborn. Other witnesses to the phenomena were researcher Wilfred Daniels and a Mrs Ina Sangster, who also saw its passage through the sky.

Jessie:

> *"It left an orange trail, about twice the size of the object. It was heading in a south-west direction, very high, about 20,000 feet. From the ground the size of the object was 18 inches long* [approximately a mile long]. *A jet aircraft approached the object, which then ascended vertically and vanished into the sky."* **(Source: Personal interview)**

25th January – England: 'Man' from Venus calls at the family home

During the early hours, Mrs Mary King – mother of the chairman of the Aetherius Society, run by her son George, then living in North Devon – was awoken by an insistent ring from her front door on what was a bitterly cold night.

> *"I opened the door and in front of me was what I first took to be a man, but then realised, from his face, that this was no Earth man.*
>
> *He was slim, about 6 feet 4 inches tall, with white hair that shone like silk. He had very bright eyes and hands that were very long.*
>
> *He was wearing an all-in-one piece suit of brown material."*

Mrs Mary King

The 'being' told her he was:

> *"...from the world you call Venus. They are now helping you, because we are all brothers – one Creator, one father, one family."*

After further conversation, Mrs King said goodbye and took him to the door. She said:

> *"I closed the door for a fraction of a second, as I was impressed to do this. When I opened the door again, he was gone."*

As there had been a fall of light snow, she fetched a torch and went outside onto the main road but was unable to see any sign of footprints or marks in the snow made by her unearthly visitor, although she did find one or two footprints between the porch and the font gate. These ended, she claimed, with two footprints together on the spot on which she had last seen her visitor.

George King – voice of the Interplanetary Parliament

George King was born on 23rd January 1919, in Wellington, Shropshire, England, and brought up in a Christian family with strong occult interests. Before founding the Aetherius Society, King had

George King, founder of the Aetherius Society

been deeply involved in spiritual healing and had joined various theosophical-based metaphysical groups in London that were a marginal part of the religious scene.

In 1944 he took up yoga, allegedly mastering bhakti, gnani (see jnana) and kundalini yogas and attaining the state of 'Samadhi' and, according to the Aetherius Society, developed psychic powers that allowed him to learn many of the secrets of the universe.

King claimed that in 1954, a voice told him, *"Prepare yourself! You are to become the voice of Interplanetary Parliament."*

A week later, an unnamed but supposedly world-famous swami was reported to have entered King's locked apartment. King claims that the swami instructed him to form a group dedicated to helping the planet, and that the swami further taught him in yoga, prayer, and meditation. According to King, this training enabled him to receive telepathic messages from Venus, the first coming from Aetherius. King rented space in Caxton Hall, in London, in which he allegedly channelled Cosmic Masters and recorded their messages. Based on his experiences and these messages, King founded the Aetherius Society. It appears that immediately prior to founding the Society, King was earning his living as a London taxi driver.

10th February – England: RAF jet and UFO seen over Worcestershire

On l0th February 1958, an RAF Jet was seen passing over Ipsley, Worcestershire, during broad daylight, being followed by a silver 'disc' – to the surprise of the witness. Later, the same afternoon, three similar objects were seen flying over Studley, Warwickshire – a few miles away.

(Source: UFOSIS, Birmingham)

17th February – England: Woman sights flaming object over London

One week later, on the 17th February 1958, Antoinette Cooper was sat on a bench in Regent's Park, London, when she saw a silver/ aluminum coloured oval object, with a greenish rim of light around it, trailing a spurt of red flame, moving over the Capital at tremendous height. Seconds later, it was out of view.

Miss Cooper contacted the Air Ministry and explained what had happened, as a result of which she received a visit by an investigator from their Department. When she telephoned their office to ask if it was all right to fill in a sighting report for *Flying Saucer Review*, who wrote to her about the incident, the Ministry official expressed annoyance that she had been interviewed personally by an MOD investigator, pointing out to her, quote: *'Flying saucers were either hallucinations or, alternatively, reflections from something on Earth'.*

(Source: Gordon Creighton, *Flying Saucer Review*, 1958, Volume 4, No. 5)

13th March – England: Silver-grey 'disc' seen over Newcastle-on-Tyne

On 13th March 1958, at 3.30pm, Mr F. Fawcett of Gosforth, Newcastle-on-Tyne, was in St. Nicholas Avenue, when he sighted:

> *"...a silver-grey coloured 'disc', edge-on with its outer edge revolving, tilting towards the east. It then headed southwards, tilting towards the west, allowing me to see what looked like a conning tower."* **(Source: UFOLOG)**

14th March – USA: Black object touches ground

At 8.45am, Healdsburg, California couple - Mr and Mrs W.F. Cummings – and one other person, sighted a three feet round, black object, which descended through the air, touched the ground, and then took off two minutes later.

March – England: Seven heart-shaped objects seen over Nottingham

Towards the end of March 1958, during the Easter holidays, Mr E. Rogers decided to visit Nottingham Castle. While strolling around the grounds, he saw seven heart-shaped objects travelling across the sky, heading west to east. After they had moved out of sight, a few seconds later, nine RAF Jets, in formation, thundered across the sky at a lower altitude. **(Source: Mr James Gaynor)**

March – England: UFO over Portsmouth –did RAF jets respond?

Ernie Sears – a long-standing veteran of the UFO subject and previously a member of the Southampton Group (SUFOG), run by Steven Gerrard, was out walking, in March, 1958, when he noticed a cigar-shaped UFO, hovering over the experimental Radar Base, on Portsdown Hill, Portsmouth.

> *"It was a blustery morning. I watched the object for a full minute, assuming it was an aircraft fuselage caught in the sun. Approximately thirty minutes later, two RAF Fighter jets raced over the town at low altitude. As an ex-RAF man, I knew their actions were very unusual. I watched as they climbed in a gradual curve, towards the gleaming 'cigar'. As*

they closed in, it slowly turned on end and vanished, leaving the aircraft circling the area. I rushed to a telephone box and rang the control tower, at Thorney Island Airbase (where the 'Meteor' jets were based) and asked the official what the object was which the 'Meteor' jets were chasing? He replied, 'You didn't see any jets!'." **(Source: Personal interview)**

Ernie passed away aged 83 in October 2009

The Daily Echo covered his death on the 18th October 2009 – Quote:

'UFO 'abductee' Ernie Sears dies of heart attack'

'His fascinating tales of alien abductions, little grey men, and UFOs flying through the night sky, caught the imagination of fellow believers and sceptics across Hampshire. It will be those stories that will be the lasting legacy of UFO believer Ernie Sears, who has died at his home in Netley. The 83-year-old, who claimed he had been abducted by aliens eight times during his lifetime, passed away after suffering a heart attack. Ernie, a member of the now defunct Southampton UFO Group, had claimed to have had close encounters with the third kind, beginning in the 1960s. From hovering objects over Gosport, to being abducted from his Southampton garden where he met little grey men, the dad of one said he had seen it all.'

Speaking about his experiences in 2006, he said:

"I remember little grey aliens. They were very short, less than five feet. They have smaller ones that I have only encountered once. They are blue; one in uniform, very dwarf-like. I remember going up towards this triangular object floating in the sky and I remember going through a jelly-like door. They do talk to me in English but it is all in your mind. They don't have mouths or ears as such, but they put things in your mind and you understand it perfectly."

Ernie Sears

Early years – Acker Bilk and Kenny Ball

Although Ernie dedicated his later years trying to convince non-believers of extraterrestrial activity, his first true love was jazz music.

During the 1960s and '70s Ernie opened many jazz clubs, bringing big names such as Acker Bilk and Kenny Ball to his stages across Hampshire. It was through his work at his club in Fareham, *Rendezvous* that brought him together with cabaret artist Sandra Lane, who he married in 1973. The couple graced the front page of the *Daily Echo* in the 1970s when they starred in the Wurzel Gummidge Christmas Special that was filmed in Lymington. Despite the pair divorcing in 1982, Sandra (now 60) and Ernie remained good friends. She said:

> *"UFOs were his hobby in his latter years, but jazz was his first love and his work in the entertainment business is what brought us together. He was a very happy and kind man, who would do anything to help anyone. His sudden death has come as quite a shock."*

14th April – USA: Rectangular object sighted by pilot

At 1pm, USAF Major D.G. Tilley was flying a *C-47* transport plane, when he saw a grey-black rectangular object, rotating very slowly on its horizontal axis in the sky over Lynchburg, Virginia. A few seconds later it was gone from view.

19th April – England: RAF fighter jets scrambled to intercept UFO

On 19th April 1958, aircraft from RAF Lakenheath were scrambled to intercept UFOs plotted on the station's radar, ten miles away from the Airbase – later explained away as being due to freak weather conditions.

23rd April – England: Two UFOs seen approaching each other

At 10.20pm, two buff or yellow circular objects were sighted moving in opposite directions across the sky, over Kilkenny, near Andoversford, Gloucestershire, by Sheila James of Hewlett Road, Cheltenham. They then moved towards each other and became brighter and more oval in shape. As they approached each other, they promptly disappeared from sight.

(Source: David Jones, Saucer Forum/*LUFORO Bulletin*, Volume 11, July/August 1961)

May – England: Silver UFO seen over Newmarket Racecourse

Eric Apter from Newmarket, Suffolk, with over forty years experience of working with horses outside, still remembers, vividly, a day in May 1958, while exercising a horse along the main track at Newmarket Racecourse, along with twenty other riders, when they saw:

> *"...a silver UFO, darting in and out of small clouds in the sky above us – almost 'as if playing a bizarre game of tag'.*
>
> *We watched it for about 20 minutes, until it left. The strangest thing is that none of us seemed to think it was out of the ordinary".*

Questions in the House about UFOs – mundane explanations offered

On 10th June 1958, the under-secretary of State for Air, Mr Charles Orr-Ewing, was asked:

> *"How many instances of unidentified flying objects had been reported during the last 12 months, and what steps were taken to co-ordinate such observations?"*

AN INTERSTING BRAZILIAN SIGHTING 1958.

One day in April 1958,a Brazilian jeweller named Senhor Wilson Lustosa was travelling along the beach from, the port of Maceio to Parapueira,Wilson was driving along the beautiful beaches of white sand which streatch for miles,as he neared a spot called Saude Wilson noticed several fishermen looking at something that was in the sky above them. Wilson asked the men what they were watching?they said that they had seen a flying saucer,he could see nothing at first,then he heard a humming noise which grew louder and louder,and then he saw something which seemed to fall out of the sky towards him.It was a machine of some sort,about 15 to 20 metres in height, Wilson described the width as "travelling circus"it seemed to be made up of three parts,the upper half was like aluminium,like an inverted bowl,on the top was a small dome which shone as bright as an electric welding arc.The lower part was also a bowl,but dark in colour, around the centre was a band with square portholes,as the machine moved over the water it made a humming sound and the water seemed to boil.

He replied:

> *"Reports of 54 unidentified flying objects have been received in the last 12 months. Such co-ordination as is necessary is undertaken by the Air Ministry. Most of the objects turn out to be meteors, balloons, or aircraft. Satellites have also accounted for a number of reports."*

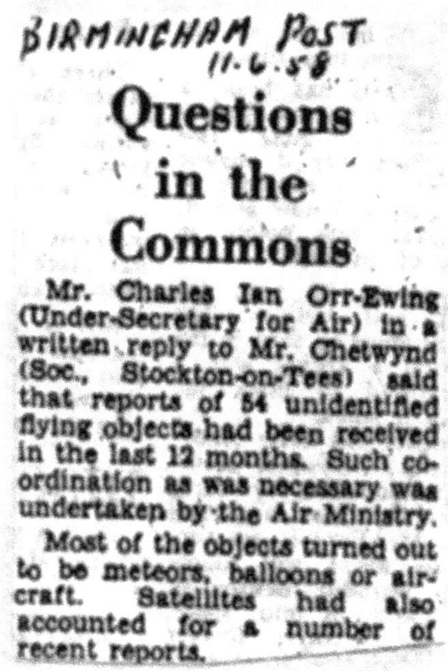

BIRMINGHAM POST 11.6.58

Questions in the Commons

Mr. Charles Ian Orr-Ewing (Under-Secretary for Air) in a written reply to Mr. Chetwynd (Soc., Stockton-on-Tees) said that reports of 54 unidentified flying objects had been received in the last 12 months. Such co-ordination as was necessary was undertaken by the Air Ministry.

Most of the objects turned out to be meteors, balloons or aircraft. Satellites had also accounted for a number of recent reports.

June/July – England: Was this a lightning strike?

During an investigation made into reported UFO activity on the 7th March 1963, in the Epping area, BUFORA member – Paul Webb, spoke to a Major Frank Collins, who told him about a strange incident that took place approximately 150 yards away, in June or July 1958.

> *"I was in my garden during daylight hours when I heard a tearing, rendering, screaming, sound – like a jet out of control, accompanied by a green light that outlined objects against the white wall of my sitting room (my back was to the window).*
>
> *A crash followed and I saw bushes were alight and smoldering some way off. I made my way to the scene, followed by other residents who wanted to know what was going on. Later, the Police and Fire Brigade arrived and examined the area, which was black and smouldering for about 35 yards.*
>
> *The Police began probing a hole in the centre, which was some seven inches in diameter and fourteen inches deep. When they had gone, I used a knife to scrape around the wall of the hole. I retrieved pieces of silvery material resembling fused plastic. A neighbour – Mrs Hutton, took some photographs of these fragments."*

(Source: *BUFORA Journal*, Volume 1, Number 1, summer 1964)

14th June – USA: Silver Saturn-shaped UFO sighted

At 10.46am over Pueblo, Colorado, Airport weather observer – Mr O.R. Foster (using a theodolite) tracked a silver object, shaped like Saturn, minus the bottom part, which flew overhead for five minutes.

20th June – USA: Silver UFO seen

At 11.05pm over Fort Bragg, North Carolina, Battalion Communication Chief Parsley sighted a silver, circular object, its lower portion seen through a green haze, which hovered in the sky and then oscillated slightly, before moving away at great speed 10 minutes later.

16th July – England: Schoolchildren sight UFO in the sky

On 16th July 1958, a few minutes before 4pm, Peter Smith (then aged 13) – a pupil of Rickmansworth Grammar School, Hertfordshire, which is situated on a hill close to electric power generators and main railway line – was looking out of the window at an overcast sky, as dark storm clouds gathered.

In an interview, later conducted with local UFO researcher Thelma Roberts – a member of the International Unidentified Flying Objects Observer Corps – he told her:

> *"Suddenly, a bright white glowing hat-shaped object appeared in the sky and performed a number of movements, slowing slightly on the downward 'runs', travelling faster than a jet and disappeared out of sight behind trees."*

Other pupils in the same class spoke of seeing a yellow band around the centre, with a blurred top and sharply defined base.

In October 2009, we again spoke to Thelma Roberts about this matter. She told us, after some thought, she believed it was, in fact, Gordon Creighton who had carried out an interview, as her interviews were recorded on a 'Grundig' tape-recorder.

(Source: Personal interview)

17th July – England: Two Silvery 'discs' seen behind airliner

At 4pm on 17th July 1958, ex-RAF Air gunner – Mr F. Harding (then 35) of Devenish Road, Winchester, was watching, through a pair of binoculars, a four-engine airliner, flying in a north-west direction, when he was surprised to see two silvery 'tilted' 'flying discs', one behind the other, above and beyond the aircraft, moving at an estimated speed of 800-1,000 mph.

Enquiries later made into the incident revealed another witness – Mr Rogers of Brassey Road, Winchester.

Dr. Cleary-Baker:

> *"One of the witnesses is well-known to me personally and I am satisfied, after my investigations, that the plane was 'buzzed' by two unknown objects."*

(Source: Dr. John Cleary-Baker/*LUFORO Bulletin*, July/August 1961, Vol. 11, No's. 7/8)

England: Grey 'flying disc' sighted over Sutton Moor, West Yorkshire

One Saturday afternoon in the same year, Mr Thomas Austin – then living at 7, Sutton Fields, near Keighley, West Yorkshire, was stood outside, talking to the local policeman.

> *"We saw a large, grey, 'disc'-shaped object, heading across the sky through patchy cloud, eastwards, at the top of Sutton Moor.*
>
> *The Policeman told me he didn't want to get involved with the sighting."*

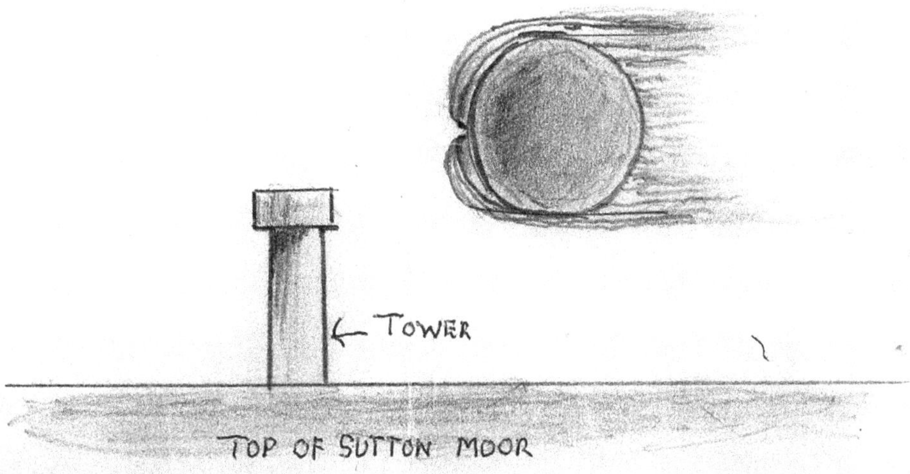

U.F.O. seen at 7 Sutton fields near keighley West Yorkshire where I was living at the year of the sighting in 1958.

Talking to a police man out side the house one saturday afternoon we saw a large gray looking disc moving across the sky through patchy cloud, moving in a easterly direction at the top of sutton moor.

The police man did not wont to get involved with the sighting

July 1958 – England: Burn marks found in field at Worcestershire

Charles Morris – a retired farm worker, living near the village of Wolverley, just outside Kidderminster – contacted us after deciding to tell someone about the strange marks he discovered in sugar beet crop, on land at the time owned by Lea Castle Farm (now known as Brown Westhead Park), originally the site of a United States Air Force Hospital but then in use by the British Army Pay Corps.

> *"I was employed as a foreman, in July 1958. One of the workers told me he had come across what he thought was aphid damage, caused to part of the sugar beet crop. I visited the area concerned and noticed, straightaway, an elliptically-shaped patch of burnt crop, situated roughly in the middle by four strange slot-like impressions. I measured these and found them to be 22 inches square, 22 feet equal distance between the 'slots', and two inches deep. There was nothing left of the crop inside the square, although I found one withered sugar beet plant in the middle of the top right-hand slot. Intrigued as to what could have caused*

this, I made an examination of the affected area and noticed one of the 'slot' marks had an adjacent impression in the soil, an inch or so from it, suggesting whoever or whatever was responsible had slipped, due to the soil being soft. I have no idea what could have caused the marks in the ground. It certainly wasn't likely to be farm machinery. I decided to keep quiet about it, knowing what people would say if I made it public knowledge."

0/5

WOLVERLEY
KIDDERMINSTER
WORC'S,
DY11 5TF

26/7/00

Dear MR HANSON,

I read in the KIDDERMINSTER SHUTTLE that you are trying to trace a MRS HILL with regard to a reported object seen in BEWDLEY in 1977, I'm afraid I cannot help you find MRS HILL but I have some information you may find interesting.

In 1958 I was foreman on a farm, (and until someone convinces me different) I saw where a object I believe to be a U.F.O. landed, it was in a large field of sugar beet during the last week of JULY 1958, the marks left by the legs were clearly visible and the heat from the power unit burnt the sugar beet inside the area covered by the four legs to leave only scorched earth.

Summer – England: Pearl-grey object seen in sky over Brightstone

In 1958, Mr William Davis, now aged 81 – a retired RAF pilot and navigator, well-trained in aircraft recognition, (see previous sighting over Gimli, Canada), was on holiday with his wife, and son (aged seven), on the beach at Marsh Chine, east of Grange Farm, south of Brightstone.

"One late morning, my wife, who was lying down, sun bathing, shouted out, 'what's that up there?' We all gazed upwards and saw what looked like a luminous, circular raindrop, with a pearl grey exterior, vibrating in the sky south of St. Catherine's Point.

I had a feeling we were being watched, in some way. The next thing is that it shot off at high speed and was gone."

A few minutes later, a RAF jet appeared from the north-north-east and circled the area where the object had been hovering, before flying back inland.

William told us the incident was to leave a lasting impression on his son, who still remembers the incident clearly, and made a personal visit to the location last summer – now nearly 50 years later.

4th August – England: Five separate UFOs seen over Coventry

On 4th August 1958, five separate UFOs were seen passing over Coventry, Warwickshire, between 10.45pm and 11.02pm. **(Source: Bob Tibbitts, Coventry UFO Research Group)**

17th August – USA: Bell-shaped UFO

At 7.05pm, Warren, Michigan resident – Mr A.D. Chisholm, saw:

"...an extremely bright object – shaped first like a bell, then like a saucer – hovering in the sky, for 5 minutes. It then flipped over and sped away to the west-south-west, 6-10 minutes later".

20th August – England: UFO over West Sussex

On or about the 20th August 1958, Gilbert Wilkinson – (then aged 12 at the time), living in Crawley, West Sussex – was out roller skating at the back of his house, just after the sun had set, when he happened to glance into the sky to his left, and see a huge 'disc' shaped object flash across his field of vision between the houses in the close.

"I probably had it in view for no more than two seconds, because of the tremendous speed. It was golden-yellow in colour, and travelling on its edge – like viewing a bicycle wheel from its side – showing a small flame flowing from the bottom of its circumference. It was larger than a full moon in size, completely silent, showing no condensation trail or sonic boom, etc. Unfortunately, there was no-one else with me at the time.

I rushed in to tell my parents, but they did not report it to the police. I knew straightaway this was a UFO, as the only man-made object in the skies at the time was the Russian Sputnik. The course the object was flying on would have brought it right across the western end of Gatwick Airport – surely someone must have seen it? The sighting was truly awesome. I wasn't frightened, but completely taken aback by the marvellous beauty of what I saw."

England: RAF serviceman tells of UFO tracked on Radar

In the same year, Eric Trodd – a trainee RAF Radar operator, was on duty at 4am. His attention was caught by a particular echo, somewhere over the middle of England (possibly the Derbyshire area).

When he aimed his height equipment at the echo, he was amazed to see it was flying at 60,000 feet – far too high to have been an aircraft – and not moving in any aggressive, or hostile, action. Fascinated, he kept it under observation for about 30 minutes,

> *"...by which time it had descended slowly to about 15-20,000 feet. It then began to rise upwards to 90,000 feet (covered 17 miles above the Earth) and onto the un-calibrated part of the radar, at the top, and out-of-sight."*

When Eric was relieved by the next person on duty, he asked the NCO in charge what he thought it was. The man failed to be drawn into any conversation about the matter, but added, *"Don't worry, we see these sometimes"*.

23rd August 1958

The Aetherius Society staged a demonstration in Trafalgar Square, London, against Government silence of 'flying saucers'.

31st August – England: Spinning 'discs' over Coventry

On the 31st August 1958, William McGregor from Addison Road, Coventry – who had seen service in the Royal Navy as a meteorologist – was returning home after walking his dog, at Bilton, Coventry, when he noticed a silver coloured object moving in circles across the sky and alerted his wife, daughter Carole (aged 16) and neighbours – Mr and Mrs Harkness, who came outside to watch the object.

> *"I looked at the object through a pair of powerful binoculars when I saw an object rotating on its axis, at a height of some 30,000 feet, surrounded by half-a-dozen smaller spinning 'discs'. I watched the object as it moved northwards, but then lost sight of it."*

(Source: Bob Tibbitts, *Syntonic*, November/December 1971/*Coventry Evening Telegraph*, 31.8.1959)

August – England: Silvery-white sphere seen over London

Mr Alfred Glider from Addlestone, Surrey, was working in his garden, 8 miles north of London Airport, when he noticed a Boeing *Stratocruiser* climbing slowly, after having taken-off at a height of between 1,000 to 1,500 feet, approximately half-a-mile away.

> *"Behind it appeared a delicate silvery-white sphere, with a hint of translucent blue, apparently moving on the same course.*
>
> *Suddenly the sphere, in one swift movement, closed the distance between itself and the aircraft and paused in the sky, just above the fin of the plane, then moved again – now towards the rear of the flight deck, before rising vertically upwards at speed.*
>
> *Some years later, 1 attended a BOAC Meeting, held at London Airport. The lecturer asked the audience if they had any questions.*
>
> *I explained what I had seen. He suggested it must have been a meteorological balloon."*

What he didn't know was that Alfred had joined the RAF as an apprentice, aged 15, and spent 27 years in the Service as an aircraft fitter and German interpreter. He then went on to serve as an aircraft Production Inspector on the *Hawker Hunter* jet, followed by a number of years with BEA/BA as an Engineering Instructor and Senior Development Engineer. Obviously, Alfred is more than suitably qualified to know the difference between a meteorological balloon, which only moves vertically, not horizontally, and a UFO. **(Source: Personal interview)**

9th September – England: 'Flying saucer' over Canterbury

"Although it happened many years ago, it is as clear as yesterday", was how May Gentry described what she and her sisters – Edna, Ellen and Margaret – saw, while picking apples from a field in Petham, a few miles from Canterbury, at 9pm on 9th September 1958, after having finished work as hop pickers.

> *"Edna shouted, 'Look at that shooting star!'*

I looked up and saw what I took to be a 'shooting star' moving rather slowly in the sky. We stood watching as it moved around in circles, descending, bathing us in its glowing light, accompanied by a swishing noise, reminding me of an electric saw.

Ellen shouted, 'It's a flying saucer!', and began to run. We followed her.

When we arrived back at the huts where we were staying, some boys were talking around the campfire. One mentioned he had seen a cigar-shaped object in the sky. The others told him it must have been an airplane, but we knew this wasn't the explanation."

(Source: Personal interview)

September – England: Flying saucer seen over Southampton

Ron Lucas spoke to us on a number of occasions about what he saw in the same year, over Southampton.

"I was chatting to a young apprentice at work about, of all things, UFOs. Rather foolishly, I told him we should go outside and have a look, never imagining, in my widest dreams, that we would see anything. We were astounded to see a saucer shaped object moving across the sky, under cloud cover, at a height I estimated to be 20,000 ft.."

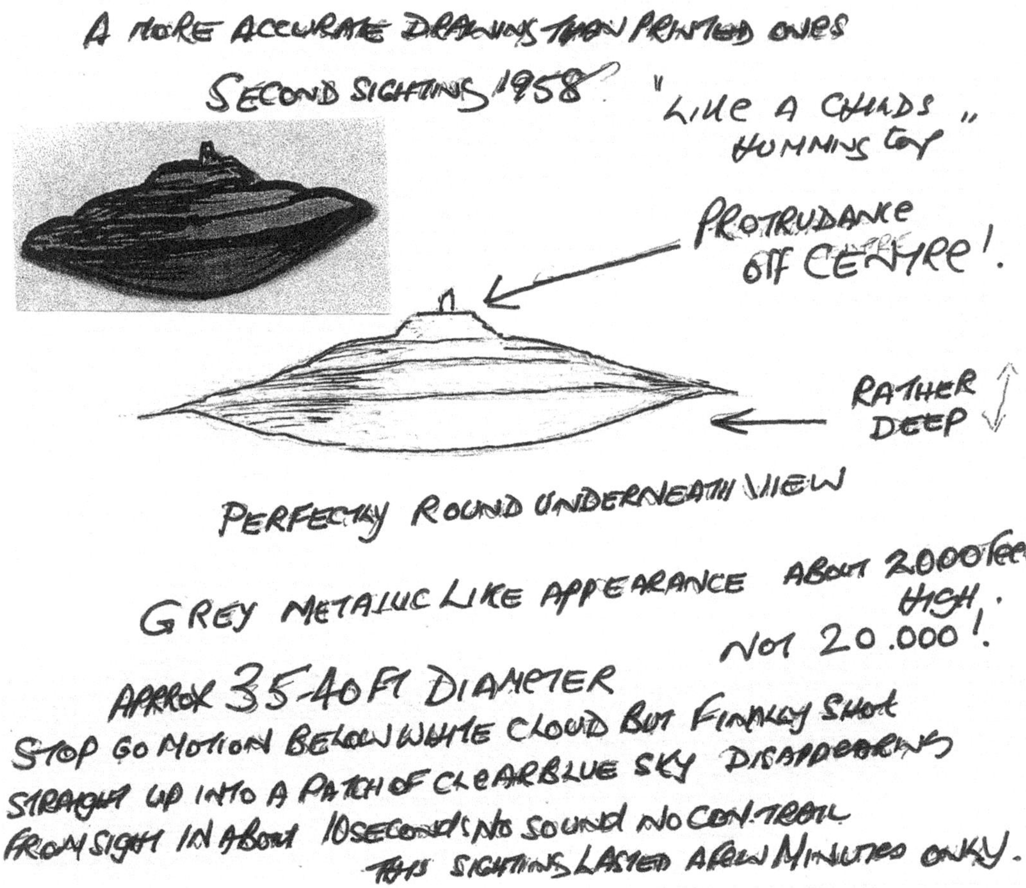

George Hunt Williamson lectures in England

On 18th September 1958 *Dr. H. Williamson came to England and spoke at many venues, including Caxton Hall, in London, where an audience of 500 people heard him talk, after being introduced by the Honorable Brinsley le Poer Trench – editor of *Flying Saucer Review*. He was also invited to talk on the *BBC* programme, 'Tonight' (unprecedented, one would have thought!)

The following evening, he spoke at the Tunbridge Wells Flying Saucer Club with Lord Dowding in the chair. According to *The Tunbridge Wells Advertiser*, he spoke uninterrupted for more than two hours – something around 40,000 words. This lecture (involving the showing of many coloured slides) was repeated on five successive

*George Hunt Williamson (December 9, 1926 – January 1986), aka *Michael d'Obrenovic* and *Brother Philip*, was an American 'flying saucer' contactee, channel and metaphysical author who came to prominence in the 1950s.

nights at Bristol, Nottingham, Manchester, Birmingham, Stoke-on-Trent, Edinburgh and Ballater. Sadly, while he was over here, he learned that his wife Betty had passed away. In addition, he was interviewed by Peter Lee and appeared on a Gaumont Newsreel, shown in London on the 13th October. He stressed that:

> *"People should look up and try to see a 'saucer' at regular times. At the same time they should try to establish mental contact".*

The film also showed shots of photos, published in *Flying Saucer Review.*

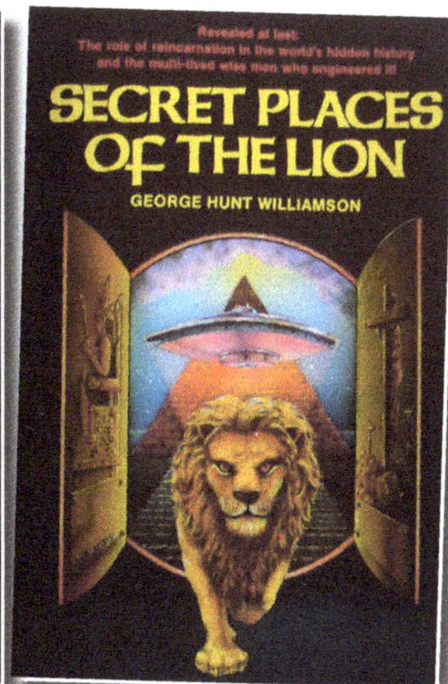

William Dudley Pelley's book *Star Guests* (1950)

Having read William Dudley Pelley's book *Star Guests* (1950), Williamson worked for a while for Pelley's cult organisation, helping to put out its monthly publication *Valor*. Pelley had generated huge quantities of communications with 'advanced intelligences' via automatic writing and very clearly was an immediate inspiration to Williamson, who combined his fascination with the occult and with 'flying saucers' by trying to contact 'flying saucer' crews with a home-made Ouija board. After hearing about the 'flying saucer'-based religious cult of George Adamski, perhaps through Pelley, Williamson and his wife, and fellow 'saucer' believers, Alfred and Betty Bailey became regular visitors to Adamski's commune at Palomar Gardens and eventually members of Adamski's Theosophy-spinoff cult. They witnessed Adamski 'telepathically' channelling and tape-recording messages from the friendly humanoid Space Brothers who inhabited every solar planet.

A handsome blond man from Venus!

The Willamsons, the Baileys and two other Adamski disciples became the 'witnesses' to Adamski's supposed meeting with Orthon – a handsome blond man from Venus, near Desert Center, California on 18th November 1952. In fact, the 'witnesses' experienced nothing more than Adamski telling them to wait and stay put while he walked over a hill, then came back into view an hour later, with a preliminary story of his experiences – a story subsequently greatly changed for book publication in *Flying Saucers Have Landed* (1953), as Williamson himself later pointed out.

The initial publication of Adamski's tale in an Arizona newspaper on 24th November 1952 triggered an explosive growth in the membership of Adamski's cult. The Williamsons' and Baileys continued their Ouija board sessions, getting their own personal revelations from the Space Brothers, which led to a drastic falling-out with Adamski.

Book – *The Saucers Speak*

In 1954, Williamson and Bailey published *The Saucers Speak* which emphasized supposed short-wave radio communications with friendly 'saucer' pilots, but in fact depended for almost all its contents on the Ouija board sessions Bailey and Williamson held regularly from 1952 onward. They heard from Actar of Mercury, Adu of Hatonn in Andromeda, Agfa Affa from Uranus (presumably not the same Affa who was the exclusive contact of Frances Swan), Ankar-22 of Jupiter, Artok of Pluto, Awa from Outer Space, Garr from Pluto, Kadar Lacu from Saturn, Karas the Space Brother, Lomec of Venus, Nah-9 from Neptune, Noro of the Saucer Fleet, Oara of Saturn, Ponnar of Hatoon (presumably not the same Ponnar who was the exclusive contact of Frances Swan), Regga of Mars, Ro of Torresoton, Sedat of Hatonn, Suttku of Saturn, Terra of Venus, Wan-4 of the Safanian planets, Zago of Mars and Zo of Neptune. The 'board' contacts were in good if uninformative English, but the few reported radio contacts, in International Morse Code, left a little to be desired. Sample: "AFFA FROM THE P. RA RRR OK K5 K5 FROM THE PLA CHANT RRT IT". Perhaps influenced by the Shaver Mystery, Williamson also reveals that while most space aliens are helpful and good, there are some very bad ones hanging out near Orion and headed for Earth in force, bent on conquest.

Williamson became a more obscure competitor to Adamski, eventually combining his own channel-ling and the beliefs of a small contactee cult, known as the Brotherhood of the Seven Rays, led by Marion Dorothy Martin, to produce a series of books about the secret, ancient history of mankind: *Other Tongues – Other Flesh* (1957), *Secret Places Of The Lion* (1958), *UFOs Confidential* with John McCoy (1958), *Road In The Sky* (1959) and *Secret Of The Andes* (1961). These books, when not rewriting the Old and New Testaments to depict every important person as a reincarnation of one of only six or eight different 'entities', expanded on the usual late 19th Century Theosophical teachings (borrowed without credit from Thomas Lake Harris) that friendly Space Brothers in the distant past had taught the human race the rudiments of civilization and, according to Williamson, spacemen had also helped materially in the founding of the Jewish and Christian religions, impersonating 'gods' and providing 'miracles' when needed. Williamson spiced his books with additional Ouija-revelations to the effect that some South, Central and North American ancient civilizations actually began as colonies of human-appearing extraterrestrials. Williamson can be considered a more mystically-inclined forerunner of Erich von Däniken; *Secret Places Of The Lion* also displays the clear and explicit influence of Immanuel Velikovsky, like his role-model Adamski.

Professor Williamson

Williamson enjoyed referring to himself as 'professor', and claimed an extensive academic background, which in fact was completely non-existent. In the late 1950s he withdrew from the contactee scene and even changed his name, concocting a new fictitious academic and family background to go along with the new name, while continuing to live in California. His 1961 book was published under a still different pen name. Little is known about his life between 1961 and his reported death in 1986, other than that at one time he became a priest of the Nestorian Church, actually the Assyrian Church of the East. **(Source: Wikipedia 2016)**

September/October – Caribbean: *USS Franklin D. Roosevelt*

While we accept, generally, that the majority of UFO sightings brought to the attention of the reader have taken place over English soil, common sense dictates the geographic importance of outlining other sightings which may, or may not, be connected with what was seen a few hours, or days ago, because of their importance in UFO Social History.

On other occasions we will, and have, introduced for the readers' attention, UFO incidents that have happened overseas – involving British service personnel, who appear to have been followed by these objects.

What Chester witnessed

One such incident involved the sighting of a UFO, with apparent occupants, according to Chester Grusinski – a member of crew aboard the Aircraft Carrier *USS Franklin D. Roosevelt* – who found himself; once again, witnessing further examples of UFO activity, while en-route from New York to Cuba, in the Caribbean, during September/October, 1958.

"I was below decks at the time, one evening, when a group of excited men came running up from the engine room, followed by another group a few minutes later. Curious, I made my way onto the flight deck and noticed that they were watching a small 'light', apparently

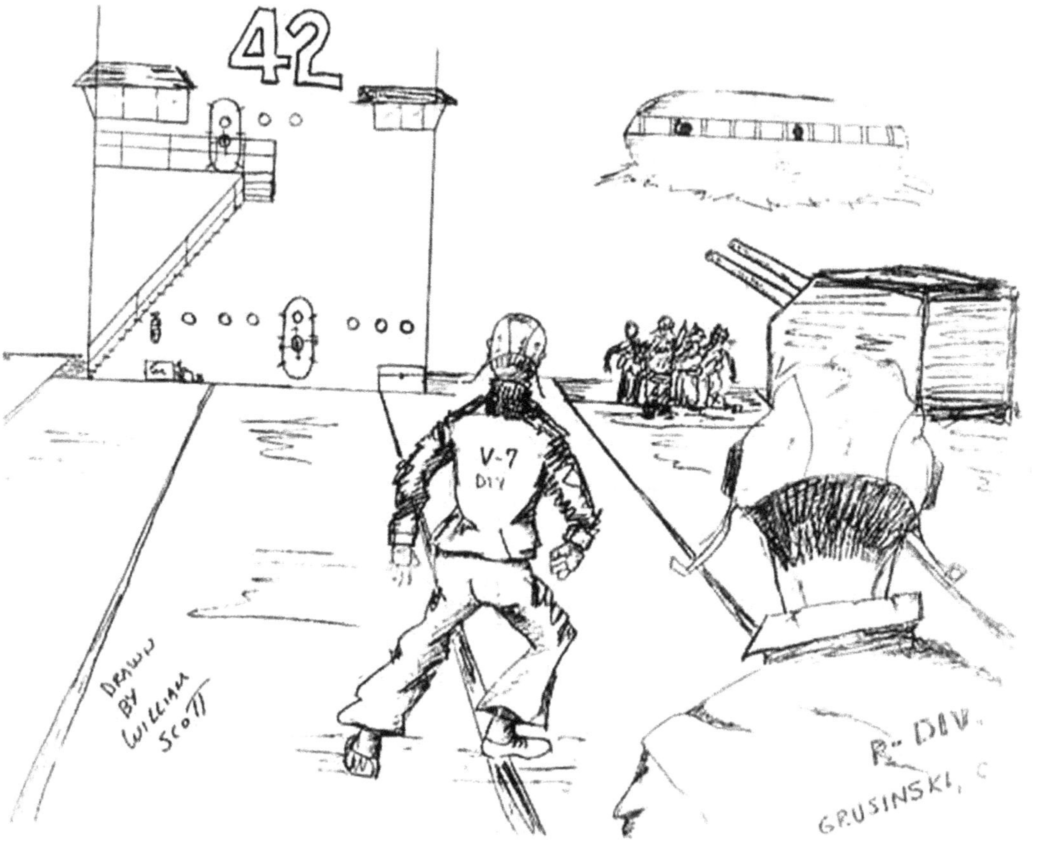

following the ship. As it approached closer, I saw it had a row of windows along its side, with what appeared to be alien figures, rather than humans, looking out. While all of this was going on, the bridge watch was screaming on the ship's intercom for the Officer of the Deck to 'get up, on the double'. It took off so quickly, I could feel the heat of it passing on my skin."

(Source: Personal interview)

2nd October - USA: Erratic UFO sighted

At 2.30pm, Stroudsburg, Pennsylvania naturalist *Ivan Sanderson reported having sighted:

"...a dull-grey object, shaped like a pickle with a flat base, flying erratically through the sky, making loops for 15 seconds".

*Ivan Terence Sanderson (January 30, 1911 - February 19, 1973) was a biologist and writer born in Edinburgh, Scotland, who became a naturalized citizen of the United States. Sanderson is remembered for his nature writing and his interest in cryptozoology and paranormal subjects. He also wrote fiction under the name Terence Roberts.

During World War II, Sanderson worked for British Naval Intelligence, in charge of counter-espionage against the Germans in the Caribbean, then for British Security Coordination, finally finishing out the war as a press agent in New York City. Afterwards, Sanderson made New York his home and became a naturalized U.S. citizen. In the 1960s Sanderson lived in Knowlton Township in northwestern New Jersey, before moving to Manhattan. He died in 1973. **(Source: Wikipedia)**

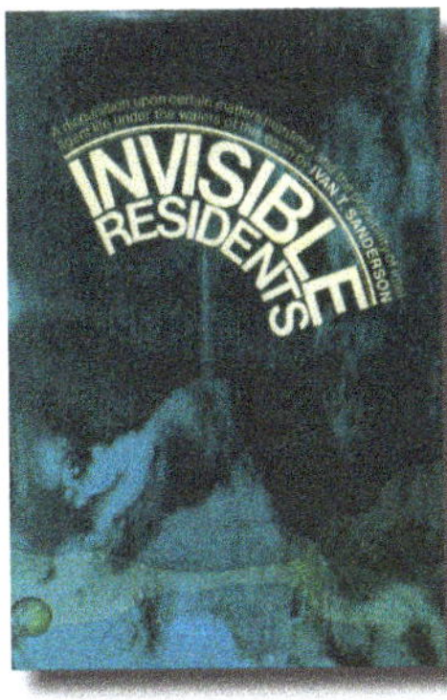

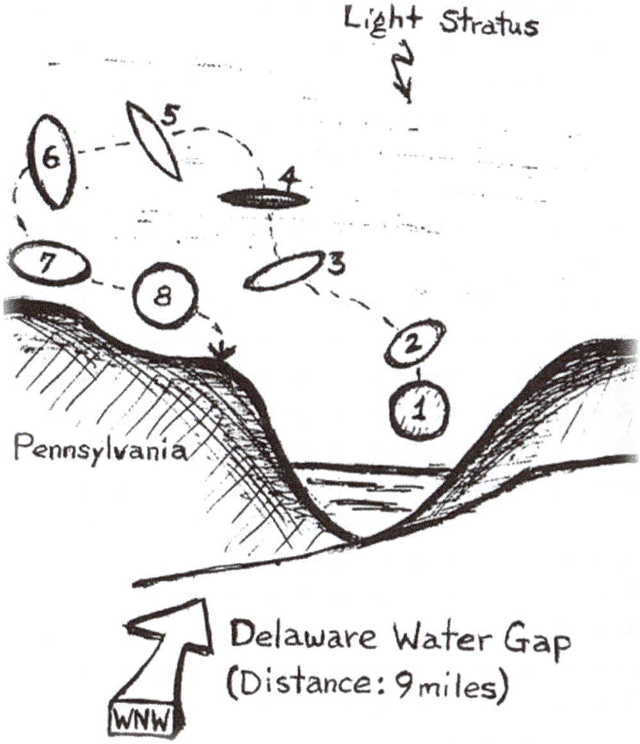

Ivan Sanderson's Story

"Some of my ancestors were fishermen on the West Coast of Scotland back in the 18th Century," Ivan said. "They'd go out in winter in tiny boats across the Atlantic to fish on the Newfoundland Banks. Big schooners used to come out from England to bring them water and food and to pick up their cod. These fish were then dried and salted and shipped back to be sold to the American colonies.

Fishermen Made Whisky

"But when these fishermen had nothing else to do they made whisky out of barley and burne (brook) water. This water was the color of fine sherry because it was colored by the peat bogs over which it ran.

"This whisky, manufactured only for home consumption, was kept in big vats made of the timbers of old sailing ships which had carried fish. Well, the bacteria of the dead cod had inpregnated the wood. It was this, plus the peat water, which gave Scotch its original and distinctive flavor.

"Now, at this time in Scotland, only the poor people drank whisky. The wealthy confined themselves to fine wines and brandies imported from France.

From Poor to Rich

"So these fishermen, who took plentiful supplies of whisky on their long journeys, eventually asked themselves: 'Instead of getting our food from the English schooners, why don't we buy it in the colonies?'

"And that's exactly what they did. Often they exchanged their whisky for food and other supplies in New England, whose inhabitants were able to buy the potent stuff for a penny a mug. Of course, eventually Scotch became the drink of the rich.

"My ancestors, incidentally, were the first to bottle whisky and my family once owned the company which made Vat 69. But," Ivan added with a spirited sigh, "not today."

(What about those fantastic creatures, the Abominable Snowmen? And what of color TV in 1918? Ivan Sanderson will tell you here in next week's SUNDAY NEWS.)

3rd October – USA: Train crew sight four lights

At 3.10am, Cecil Bridge, fireman, and engineer Harry Eckman, aboard a southbound freight train on the Monon Railroad in Clinton County, Indiana, sighted four odd lights crossing the track in front of them. The lights then turned and approached the train, dropping down to 2-300ft, before crossing the length of the train and heading eastwards, in formation. The men alerted the rest of the crew about the incident. Conductor Edward Robinson shone a torch at the objects, which flew away but returned. After manoeuvring around the train for 1hr and 10mins, they headed north-west and disappeared from view. **(Source: NICAP)**

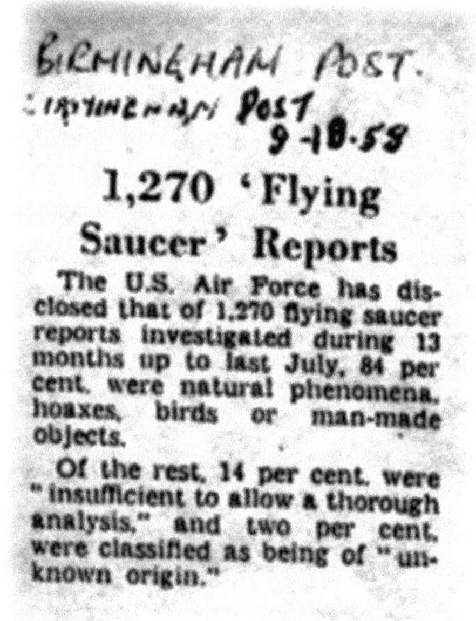
BIRMINGHAM POST.
Birmingham Post 9-10-58

1,270 'Flying Saucer' Reports

The U.S. Air Force has disclosed that of 1,270 flying saucer reports investigated during 13 months up to last July, 84 per cent. were natural phenomena, hoaxes, birds or man-made objects.

Of the rest, 14 per cent. were "insufficient to allow a thorough analysis," and two per cent. were classified as being of "unknown origin."

1st November – England: Mysterious flashes over England

A vivid green-blue flash lit up the sky over the western end of the English Channel, attracting the attention of several newspapers.

November – England: UFO seen hovering over Oxford

In November 1958, Stephen Skolimowski, from Headington, near Oxford, was out playing with a friend near Shotover Hill, when they noticed a dull white, luminous object (not quite saucer-shaped) hovering over a pine wood, about three miles away.

As they stood watching, a third of the glowing object detached itself and began to slowly circle the area before merging into one and accelerating upwards into the sky.

(Source: *Magic Saucer*, Crystal Hogben)

1958 – Letters to the Air Ministry

Illustrating the way in which little has changed with regard to the attitude of the Air Ministry/MOD, to enquiries received from the public on the subject of UFOs, can be seen in letters of personal correspondence written to Mr A.D.J. West, at the Air Ministry, during 1958, by Winchester-based UFO enthusiast, Dr. John Cleary-Baker, Ph.D., who was to later take up the role of evaluation officer on the newly formed BUFORA group, in 1964. (With its member societies that included the Anglo-Polish Research Group, British Flying Saucer Bureau, Cambridge University Group, Cheltenham Flying Saucer Group, Croydon UFO Research and Investigation Society, Direct Investigations Group on Aerial Phenomena, Isle of Wight UFO Investigation Society, Merseyside UFO Research Group, Oxford University UFO Study Group, Scottish UFO Research Society, and UFOSIS [Birmingham]).

In a letter of reply, received by Dr. John Cleary-Baker, dated 4th September 1958, from the Air Ministry, in response to a letter dated the 29th August we learn:

> *"There have been quite a number of statements in the House of Commons about unidentified flying objects, the most recent being in reply to Parliament Questions by Mr Chetwynd, on 10th June 1958 & 30th July1958. As these statements make clear, the Air Ministry view is that there are no unidentified flying objects in the sense of a class of phenomena of extraterrestrial origin, though there are a good many things which people see which, for one reason or another, they are unable to identify.*
>
> *Yours sincerely,*
> *Signed, A.D.J West"*

Reply letter to Air Ministry, dated 10th September, from Dr. J. Cleary-Baker:

> *"As long as any flying objects remain unidentified the possibility that some of them may be of extraterrestrial origin is present. I find the Air Ministry's attitude on UFOs illogical for this reason.*
>
> *The Ministry seems to reject the extraterrestrial on prior grounds and there is no valid justification for such an arbitrary attitude.*
>
> *I have written a little on the UFO problem and hope to write more, since I wish to get the official Air Ministry attitude quite clear and to be fair on the subject as possible. May 1 ask you to clean up the following points please?Is the Ministry aware that many UFO reports by persons trained in such observations, such as pilots and scientists, describe manoeuvres UFOs such as abrupt turns, dives, ascents, and so on, which could not possibly be ascribed to the play of natural forces upon controlled objects?*
>
> *[UFO reports available to public?]*
>
> *Is it the view of the Ministry that all reports of such controlled motion of UFOs is due to the observers having either lied, or been, in some way, hallucinated? If there is nothing more to UFO reports than misidentification of known objects and phenomena, why is there too much secrecy maintained in respect of investigations which have been conducted into UFOs by the RAF and Air Ministry? Are UFO reports available to the public on request? If not, since there is supposed to be nothing in them beyond bad observation of ordinary objects and phenomena, why not?*
>
> *Yours sincerely,*
> *Signed, John Cleary-Baker"*

Reply from Mr A.D.J. West:

> *"I am afraid it is not possible even to accept that there is any basis for asking the first two questions in the third paragraph of your letter. I can only reply to them, therefore, by restating that when the Air Ministry has investigated reports that people have seen things which they have not been able to identify, it has found either that an explanation impossible*

in terms of known phenomena, or that the information available is inadequate to enable any conclusion to be drawn. On this is based the view given in my letter of the 4th September. As regards your third and fourth questions, the reticence of Government departments about the conduct of their business may be irritating at times, but no other policy's really possible. Quite apart from such military security requirements as may exist, these would of course, extend both to facts and the absence of facts which were not assembled with any thought of immediate publication. Such reports contain statements and expressions of view from members of the public, Crown servants, and other public officials, such as the Police, all made on the assumption that no breach of confidence was contemplated.

Yours sincerely,
Signed, A D J .West"

Reply letter to Air Ministry, dated 27th September, from Dr. J. Cleary-Baker:

Reply from Dr. J. Cleary-Baker, 27th September, sent to Mr West at the Air Ministry, London SW1.

"Dear Mr West,

Your reference 8F.2178/56

Thank you for your letter of the 15th instant and for patience and courtesy you have shown in dealing with my enquiry. You can do no more than advance the official views on UFOs and it is not your fault, (those views fail to make sense in the light of the facts). I am, of course, aware that some 90% of UFO sightings cannot be evaluated through lack of data, or resolve them when evaluated into reports of misidentified known objects, or natural phenomena. There are a certain number of sightings, however, in which profusion of data is available but which, on evaluation, cannot be related to anything known. To mention two of many, the report by the crew and some of the passengers of the BOAC 'Stratocruiser', over Goose Bay, on 29th June 1954, and the report by Flight Lieutenant J.R. Salandin, from North Weald, on October 14th this year, all the relevant data in these sightings, as in many others, and competent observers, with no motives for fabrication – yet impossible to explain in everyday terms. The official reasons for denying UFO data to competent students are not very convincing either. It is possible to issue a personal report without either giving the names of the observer, or their personal views on what they saw.

The US Air Force has sometimes done this at any rate, with sightings explicable in ordinary ways.

As for the military security angle, the few UFO reports attributable to aircraft, or missiles on the secret list, could easily be kept from the public view or, if already reported in the Press, covered by a few non-committal 'blanket phrases'. So far as I know, the evidence for the interplanetary origin of certain UFOs is still circumstantial. While that remains so, the Ministry and the RAF may be justified in not committing themselves to an unqualified endorsement of the extraterrestrial view.

Nevertheless, since the circumstantial evidence is very strong, they should stop making a mystery of the entire subject and invite the co-operation of independent researchers. A study of sightings of genuine UFOs where and when they appear and what they do, while under observation, may provide valuable clues to enable us to solve the problems they raise. The Ministry is in possession of data which active researchers find hard to come by. He may have to waste much time and effort before he can, in a given case, eliminate the possibility that the UFO he is studying may be one of the 90% which ought to be discarded. If UFOs are extraterrestrial constructions, a spate of sightings, or some new manifestations of alien activity in our skies, it may at anytime blow the lid off the official policy of reticence.

With the public totally unprepared for the advent of interplanetary denizens, this could precipitate an ugly panic. My personal opinion is that something of the kind may well happen within the course of the next decade.

The RAF and Air Ministry seem to believe that an ostrich policy is desirable – hide our

From:- Mr. D.A.J. West.

Tel. No.
TRAFALGAR 8811, Ext. 6332

AIR MINISTRY,
WHITEHALL GARDENS,
LONDON, S.W.1.

BF 2178/56

4th September, 1958.

Dear Dr. Cleary-Baker,

Thank you for your letter of 29th August, 1958.

There have been quite a number of statements in the House of Commons about unidentified flying objects, the most recent being in reply to Parliamentary Questions by Mr. Chetwynd on 10th June 1958 and 30th July 1958 (Official Report Col.10 (written) and Col.1343/4). As these statements make clear, the Air Ministry view is that there are no "Unidentified Flying Objects" in the sense of a class of phenomena of extra-terrestrial origin though there are a good many things which people see which for one reason or another they are unable to identify.

Yours sincerely,

J. Cleary-Baker Esq., Ph.D.
3, Devenish Road.,
Weeke,
Winchester,
Hants.

From:- Mr. C.W. Ralph

Tel. No.
TRAFALGAR 8811, Ext. ~~6555~~ 6981.

AIR MINISTRY, (S.6)
WHITEHALL GARDENS,
LONDON, S.W.I.

BF.2178/S.6.

1st October, 1958.

Dear Dr. Cleary-Baker,

Thank you for your letter of 27th September addressed to West who is on leave.

I notice that his letter to you of 15th September explains in some detail why your request cannot be met. I regret that there is nothing more I can say without repeating what you have already been told.

Yours sincerely,

C.W. Ralph.

Dr. J. Cleary-Baker, Ph.D.,
3 Devenish Road,
Weeke,
Winchester,
Hants.

heads in the sand and hope the UFOs will go away – only perhaps they won't. If I submit a list of UFO sightings to the Ministry, 1 cannot believe that the National security will be impaired if that list be returned to me with the official explanation in each case added, 'balloon', 'ice', meteor', or whatever it may be, and in the small percentage of cases, when the tag applies, 'unknown', so long as the conclusions stated are honest and reasonable ones, I certainly would be content and would not ask for more.

[Events of 29th April 1957]

There are, as you know, cases in which officialdom has come out with findings which are a little queer. I have in mind April 29th, 1957, and the two 'Hawker Hunter' aircraft, which RAF radar tracked, flying westward along the Channel, near Dover, at more than 900 miles per hour. The official attitude on the UFOs is shifty and not in the public interest. If it be maintained, I consider that everyone in possession of the facts is justified in taking all the possible steps to bring about a radical revision of the policies responsible for it.

Yours sincerely,

John Cleary-Baker"

Dr. Cleary-Baker received a reply on the 1st of October, 1958, from Mr C.W. Ralph, Air Ministry(S.6), Whitehall Gardens, London SW1Reference BF2178/S.6 Dear Mr Cleary-Baker,

Nick Pope, 2016

"While the MOD's UFO project dates from 1953 (with some ad hoc research and investigation having been done even before that), very few documents from the early years have survived. This is because – in common with MOD records on a number of subjects -UFO files were generally only kept for five years before being destroyed. It was only in 1967 that Defence Ministers made a policy decision that UFO files should be retained permanently, in view of the public interest in the subject and the historical significance of the documents. While the loss of these documents is a tragedy in terms of trying to piece together an official history of the government's handling of the subject, there was nothing sinister about it. Files on many subjects were treated in exactly the same way, to avoid the MOD sinking in a sea of paper."

November – Scotland: Alien beings seen during Army exercise

The Territorial Army was on a weekend exercise, just outside of Tarland, between Braemar and Ballatar (some 60 miles from Aberdeen) in 1958. Two of the young TA men were assigned the duty of guarding a hilltop and dug a trench to lie in. The duty should have lasted only a few hours. As dawn was breaking, the men heard a *"strange gurgling"* sound, a few hundred yards away, behind some trees. Because the noise continued, the men decided to investigate.

Two large 'figures' approach men

Leaving their position, the men moved in the direction of the noise when two 'large figures' came stumbling toward them. The young men were paralysed with fear; the two 'figures' were at least 2.10-2.40 metres [7-8 feet] tall; they were dressed in rather unusual clothing that seemed to make it difficult for them walking across the rough ground; the guttural sounds appeared to be them talking to each other.

The young men now turned and fled down the hill to the main Tarland Road. As they ran along the road, one of the men looked back as they heard a 'swishing' sound. A huge, 'disc'-shaped and glowing object was behind them and only a few feet above the ground –the two ran faster. The object then swooped up above them and disappeared quickly from sight, leaving a trail of sparks behind.

A temporary Post Office engineers hut was the first sign of normality the men encountered – several engineers were within. The men banged on the door, begging to be let in. Opening the door, the engineers let the men in and, because of the state they were in, made them rest a while.

Terry Hooper-Scharf

We discussed this incident with Terry Hooper-Scharf, in 2015, puzzled, like him, as to why somebody hadn't conducted an investigation into what was, after all, a claim of a landed UFO and an encounter with its perceived alien occupants.

Terry:

> *"When I initially read this, I assumed that someone from the* Flying Saucer Review *[FSR, May-June, 1959] must have followed this account up, because it was, potentially, one of the best close encounters which had taken place in the UK.*
>
> *In the 1970s, Charles Bowen – then editor of* Flying Saucer Review *– told me he had checked: no-one had investigated – but he did have the news item. It was suggested I try UFO groups from that time."*

According to this 'write-up' in *The Humanoids,* edited by Charles Bowen, the names of the two soldiers were known but not identified. It's a shame, as there is so little about any follow-up investigations or interviews conducted with the other witnesses.

(Source: *Flying Saucer Review: The Humanoids*)

Tarland (Gaelic: *Turlann*) is a village in Aberdeenshire, Scotland, and is located five miles north-west of Aboyne, and 30 miles west of Aberdeen. Population 540 (2004).Tarland is home to the Culsh Earth House, an Iron Age below-ground dwelling that is otherwise known as a Souterrain. Souterrains were used to store food and the Culsh Earth House probably served as a community cellar. Tomnaverie Stone Circle just south of Tarland is the Tomnaverie Stone Circle, a 4000-year-old recumbent stone circle. The land is owned by the MacRobert Trust and in the care of Historic Scotland. The circle was recently restored with help from a donation by the trust. Melgum Lodge near Tarland was originally built as a hunting lodge for the physician to Queen Victoria who frequently stayed in the vicinity at Balmoral Castle. Tarland Church (Scottish Gaelic: *Cill Mo Luaig*) commemorates *Mo Luag,* a saint more often associated with the west coast. .According to legend, a wizard once lived in the area. It was said that he once came to Tarland Fair and cut open a cheese, which produced a swarm of bees. **(Source: Wikipedia)**

1959

January – England: UFO Landing, Stratford-upon-Avon

IN January 1959, Leonard Hewins from Tredington, near Shipston-on-Stour – employed by Stratford-upon-Avon Council – was walking home towards the rear of the car park, in Arden Street, to collect his cycle, at 5.15pm, when he noticed a fiery red object – the size of the setting sun – approaching his position from out of the darkness.

> *"It then came to a stop above the ground, about a hundred yards away from where I was stood, next to the fence of a nearby tennis court. As the glare dimmed, I was able to make out what looked like three human figures inside a blue haze, twelve feet or so off the ground. In a clumsy, bulky movement, one of the figures lifted itself and sat down again, joined by a fourth occupant – now seated two behind each other, in what looked like an invisible 'craft'. At this stage, I became very frightened and found I was unable to move any of my limbs. The object then rose swiftly upwards, increasing in luminously to that when first seen, leaving a trail of multicoloured stars, accompanied by the sound of rushing water."*

This was not to be the first or last time we were to hear of such sound associated with the movement of UFOs. **(See Jessie Roestenberg UFO sighting, 21st October 1954)**

Mr John Dennis Llewellyn carried out an investigation into this incident. He learned that Leonard had seen a similar object in 1930 when aged 14. In 1953 he had witnessed the passage of three objects across the sky.

Sadly, we were to learn, during conversation with Mrs Anne Smith (passed away in 2007) (her mother, Violet, was Len's sister), that Mr Hewins had died in an accident, while cutting the hedge in Bordon Hill, Evesham Road, after being hit by a bus skidding across the road, some years later. **(Source: John 'Dennis' Llewellyn, BUFORA)**

10th January – England: UFO seen following USAF *B-52* Bomber

At 11.35am on 10th January 1959, Mr J. P. Roddam of Roundway, Grimsby – a clerk with the Royal Observer Corps sighted a white fuzzy sphere over the town, about 70 degrees of the horizon, apparently following a USAF *B-52* bomber – until out of sight, towards the east-north-east direction.

In an interview conducted with members of the Isle of Wight UFO Society, some years later, Mr Roddam told them:

> *"It was about the size of the B-52s fuselage, some 4 metres in diameter – the distance from me was, overall, miles away. It was in motion all the time and gyrated around the plane fairly fast, except when it shot off into a cloud bank in seconds, in an erratic motion."*

Was this an example of what became known as a Foo-fighter – a phenomenon which was reported by Allied and Axis servicemen, during World War Two – or was there another explanation?

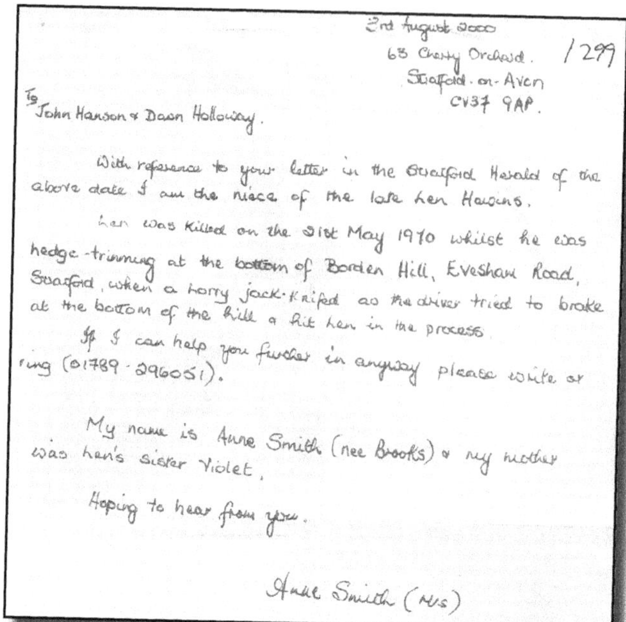

2nd August 2000
63 Cherry Orchard. /299
Stratford-on-Avon
CV37 9AP.

To John Hanson & Dawn Holloway.

With reference to your letter in the Stratford Herald of the above date I am the niece of the late Len Hawkins.

Len was killed on the 21st May 1970 whilst he was hedge-trimming at the bottom of Borden Hill, Evesham Road, Stratford, when a lorry jack-knifed as the driver tried to brake at the bottom of the hill & hit Len in the process.

If I can help you further in anyway please write or ring (01789-296051).

My name is Anne Smith (nee Brooks) & my mother was Len's sister Violet.

Hoping to hear from you.

Anne Smith (Mrs)

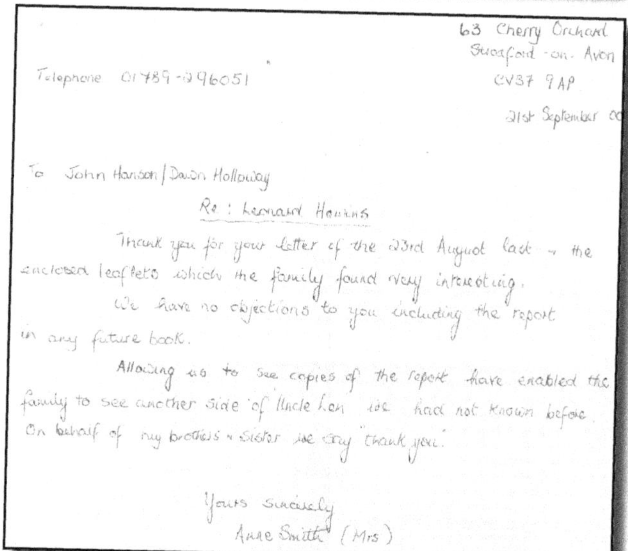

63 Cherry Orchard
Stratford-on-Avon
CV37 9AP
Telephone 01789-296051
21st September 00

To John Hanson / Dawn Holloway

Re: Leonard Hawkins

Thank you for your letter of the 23rd August last & the enclosed leaflets which the family found very interesting.

We have no objections to you including the report in any future book.

Allowing us to see copies of the report have enabled the family to see another side of Uncle Len we had not known before.

On behalf of my brothers & sister we say "thank you".

Yours sincerely
Anne Smith (Mrs)

1959 – England: Metallic sphere appears over sea at Skegness

Retired Nottinghamshire Police Officer – Philip Holmes – told of a very strange occurrence which happened to him, in 1959, while attending St. John's Ambulance training course, at Skegness Minors holiday home, Lincoln.

> *"One morning, when the camp was surrounded by a heavy fog, known locally as the Haar, I decided to sneak out and have a cigarette. I was stood looking out to sea, close to the*

waves, when a silver 'sphere', or 'ball', about a metre in diameter, with four metallic prongs, appeared about 20 feet away from where I was standing. A few seconds later, a bright blue flash of light shot out of the bottom prong – then it rose rapidly upwards, and headed out over the sea, where 1 soon lost sight of it." **(Source: Personal interview)**

23rd February – England: 'Flying saucer' over Sheffield

At 6.40pm on 23rd February 1959, Mr George Wild from Honeysuckle Road, Sheffield, was one of a number of people who sighted a 'flying saucer' hovering 200 feet off the ground over the City, after experiencing unusual interference on the television set. The sighting was later explained away by the Commanding Officer, at RAF Norton, who suggested they had seen the Fairy Rotodyne – the World's first vertical take-off Airliner – although this appears unlikely, as the object seen was totally silent. **(Sources: *Sheffield Star/Sheffield Telegraph*, 25.2.1959)**

24th February – USA: Three objects pace airliner

During the last stage of flight, Captain Peter Killian and his 35 passengers, aboard a *DC-6* from Newark to Detroit, sighted three objects pacing the aircraft. The USAF suggested, after the incident was made public, that they had seen three stars in Orion's Belt! Later this was changed to three *B-47s* being refuelled in the air by a *KC-97 Tanker.*

Peter:

> *"If the Air Force wants to believe that it can, but I know what a B-47 looks like and I know what a KC-97 Tanker looks like in operation at night. There are 14 lights on the belly of a tanker and none of them are orange hued or the size of those objects I saw. They were triple the size of any bomber or tanker. The Air Force had intimated that I had been drinking. I never had a drink before or during a flight, and there wasn't cloud in the sky. These explanations come from Washington people and not from the Air Force men who interviewed me to hear my story first-hand."*

AFTERMATH
The day following the sighting the Detroit Times reported in banner headlines:

Detroit Times
WEDNESDAY, FEBRUARY 25, 1959 — 7 CENTS

MYSTERY DISCS TRAIL PLANE HERE

FLYING SAUCERS
" Plane Was Followed "

Three shining "saucers" accompanied their plane for 45 minutes last night, the pilot and passengers of an airliner flying from Newark, New Jersey, to Detroit, reported. Capt. Peter Killian, a pilot for 15 years, said: "One would move in at intervals, fall back again and change its place in the formation while keeping abreast of the ship.

Mr. N. D. Puscas, an aircraft firm manager and one of the passengers, said: "There was not a cloud in the sky when I saw the objects in precision formation."

26th February – England: UFO over Airport – RAF scrambled

Between 7.25pm and 7.45pm, a yellow 'disc' was sighted hovering over London Airport, by four trustworthy witnesses; one was the Air Traffic Controller, who studied it through binoculars after failing to find any trace of it on the radar screens.

RAF Fighter Command at Stanmore, Middlesex, issued this description of it:

"…bright yellow light, varying in intensity, some 300 feet off the ground; it stayed in that position for about 20 minutes – then climbed away at high speed."

Explanation by the Air Ministry: The nose-cone light of a civilian aircraft. **(Source: *Birmingham Post*)**

THE air force is clamming up on information about flying saucers, men from Mars, and the like, complains America's dedicated band of saucer-seekers today.

Reports from all over the U.S. on "unidentified flying objects" are collected by two agencies.

One is the National Investigation Committee on Aerial Phenomena in Washington, the other the Civilian Saucer Intelligence in New York.

This sample of the "evidence" they sift and tabulate came from retired schoolteacher Mrs. Mary Starr:—

"I was awakened about two in the morning at my home on Long Island Sound by a bright light shining in from the garden.

I saw a cigar-shaped object, brightly lit with square portholes, hovering above my clothes line. I could see three men inside.

The men could not have been more than four feet tall. For about five minutes the thing hovered without sound, then it glided upwards and disappeared."

Richard Hall, one of the organisers of the committee, smacked out at the air force today with these charges:—

It fails to investigate all the reports;

It holds back publication of details which do not fit in with known facts.

"We want a full dress Congressional inquiry," he told me.

But the official reaction in Washington is cold and, I fear, Mr. Hall is not going to get his inquiry until Mrs. Starr's flying saucer comes down in a Congressman's backyard.

DAILY EXPRESS 28-4-59

DT 7/3/59

'FLYING SAUCER' VENUS AND PLANE

LIGHTS CONFUSED

Daily Telegraph Reporter

A combination of the planet Venus and the nose light of a civilian aircraft led to reports 10 days ago of a yellow disc hovering over London Airport for 20 minutes and then moving rapidly. The Air Ministry classed it as an "unidentified flying object."

A Ministry spokesman said yesterday that this did not mean it was thought to be something weird from outer space but simply "a flying object we could not identify." Investigation had shown an aircraft was flying with its nose light on, and the stationary light was probably Venus, which is extremely bright at the moment.

A Ministry of Civil Aviation official said: "It seems fairly obvious that the incident was caused by two different lights."

DT 6/3/5-

DISC IN SKY A MYSTERY

LONDON AIRPORT

The Air Ministry has officially recorded as an "unidentified flying object" a yellow disc which, observers say, hovered for 20 minutes over London Airport a week ago before climbing rapidly away. At least four reliable witnesses saw it.

An air traffic control officer studied it for several seconds through binoculars before checking with radar operators. They found no image on their screens.

One witness last night described the phenomenon as "like the reflection of a light such as that made by a searchlight on clouds. But there were no clouds." An airport official said no weather balloons had been launched.

March – England: Object seen over Cheltenham

In March 1959, people living in the Woodmancote are of Cheltenham sighted a dazzling object, hovering above Cleeve Hill on the outskirts of Cheltenham.

(Source: David Jones/ *The Chronicle*, March 1959, 'Cleeve Flying Saucer Mystery …. What were strange objects?')

1st April – USA: *May Day* -Did a UFO bring aircraft down?

At 8.19pm, the pilot of an Air Force *C-118* transport plane, from McChord Air Force Base, with a crew of four was over Orting, Washington, when he radioed: *"We have hit something or something has hit us… May Day"*

The pilot then said he was returning to Base, at which point his last words were, *"This is it"*.

The aircraft was torn to

shreds in a tremendous explosion when it crashed into mountains over the Rhodes Lake area. Two officers and two enlisted men died. Barricades were then set-up around the vicinity. Newsmen, police officers, and the public, were banned from going anywhere near the area. Colonel Robert E. Booth – Commander of the 1705th Air Transport Group – only disclosed a mid-air collision had taken place, but refused to give any further details. An enquiry into the matter by Robert Gribble – then director of the Aerial Phenomena Research Group – revealed through conversations held with some of those witnesses at the scene that the aircraft was found smashed to pieces.

Two bodies were recovered from deep in the ground following impact by the aircraft, which was seen to come to earth while in a horizontal position. The fourth body was never found. It was also ascertained that prior to the accident, a number of mystery explosions had shaken the North Seattle area.

At 7.20pm another aerial explosion occurred, causing some damage. At 7.45pm mysterious 'lights' were seen in the sky and a brilliant glow sighted near the crash area, followed by flashes of light. Mr Gribble learnt, from other witnesses, that none of the four engines of the plane had been running as it passed over their homes.

Parachute-like objects seen

Other witnesses spoke of seeing what resembled two glowing parachute-like objects following the aircraft, and that part of the tail assembly was missing.

At 10pm, further explosions rattled windows over the Seattle area. An anonymous telephone call was made to Mr Gribble, the day after the crash, informing him that UFOs had been tracked on radar. Unfortunately, for whatever reason, the Air Force then decided not to enter into any further discussion about the matter.

The Air Accident report, later published, attributed the crash to the aircraft being too low and its right wing struck several treetops, causing the wing to burst into flame. The plane lost altitude and flew for another six and three quarters miles before final impact in the Rhoade Lake area, 12 miles east of McChord Air Force Base, Washington. It appears that this might have been the case.

(Sources: *Flying Saucers are Hostile,* Brad Steiger & Joan Whritenour, & T. Scott Crain Jr., *Flying Saucer Review,* Volume 32, No. 3, 1987)

May – England: Glider pilot sights UFO over radio transmitter

In May 1959, Anthony Vincent French (then aged 18) from Nottingham – a glider pilot with the Nottingham 412 ATC Squadron, was at his cousin's house in Sutton Coldfield, close to the Sutton Coldfield transmitter, at 11.45pm, when they saw:

> *"...a brightly lit object, hovering near the mast. It then slowly moved downwards and eventually vanished over some nearby houses. Whatever I saw was no aircraft or helicopter".*

(Source: Personal interview)

1st May – England: Brinsley Le Poer Trench writes to Frank Marshall

FLYING SAUCER REVIEW

A FLYING SAUCER SERVICE LTD. PUBLICATION

1 DOUGHTY STREET
LONDON, W.C.1
ENGLAND
Telephone CHAncery 3192

1st May, 1959.

F. E. Marshall Esq.,
8 Reap Lane,
Weston,
Portland,
Dorset.

Dear Mr. Marshall:

Thank you for your letter of April 19th and for your kind enquiry about International Flying Saucer Contact Week-end.

In recent years Flying Saucer Review has organised special International flying saucer sighting days. Space-ships from other worlds are, of course, reported every day from some place on this planet, judging from the reports that reach us from the news agencies, our own Observer Corps, our readers and other research groups. This year it has been decided to go a step further and so we are having an International Flying Saucer Contact Weekend. This will take place over Whitsun Holiday, May 16-18 inclusive. Overseas groups all over the world are taking part and they have been advised to use whatever methods they consider best to establish contact with our visitors. For example (1) the electro-magnetic spectrum, ~~thoughts~~ i.e. by radio or light waves and (2) telepathy, are possible ways to attract the visitors.

Amateur wireless operators (radio "hams") are invited to join us in this world-wide contact attempt. In the U.S.A several saucer groups have their own ham net-works, one is the Interplanetary ~~Special~~ Space Patrol operating from W5AAO (620 Cedar Street, Abilene, Texas). This group meets every Monday night at 8.30 p.m. (local time) on 3933 kc.s. If you are permitted to do so you could try transmitting messages which may be picked up by our visitors. However, I am not sure of your regulations - you will know all about these - but, as this will be a very large world wide attempt to connect with the visitors and many of the groups participating will be using telepathy it may be that the visitors will respond to this mass call, therefore they may contact us either physically (i.e. landing in a space-craft to a certain group) or they may contact us by some other method of communication or for example through radio waves. Therefore all you may need to do is to listen on your sets and connect with colleagues on your net-work when you pick something up.

Contd......

Directors:
E. Lewis Barton (Managing), The Hon. Brinsley le Poer Trench (Editor), Derek D. Dempster, Reginald Dutta, Waveney Girvan

It may be that you yourself, knowing more about radio procedure, now that you have a brief outline of the operation will be able to advise how best to utilise your own stations for this event.

Another method of connection that we are suggesting some people may care to use is "light-beam". As you know light-beam radio equipment was developed for service use in the last war to provide secret connection between two visible points. It does not suffer from interference and cannot be picked up by ordinary radio. The range of ground to air is considerable and the light-beam itself may not be visible if an infra red filter is used. The principle is simply that, in place of the transmitted carrier wave as used in radio, a narrow light-beam is varied in its intensity by subjecting voltages that are super-imposed upon it from a microphone circuit. At the receiving end this moderate beam is picked up by a photo tube (or light-sensitive cells). The different pitch of each is passed through a simple amplifier and converted back into speech. One does not need a transmitting license to operate such gear and it is possible to obtain light-sensitive cells equivalent to an RCA 923 photo tube in Britain. In the U.S.A. many people are experimenting in this way, some with reported success.

All these activities could be tried out over Whitsun week-end. Telepathy is now pretty well established in scientific circles as a result of intensive research work carried out by Dr. J. B. Rhine of Duke University in the U.S.A. and of Dr. Soal of Cambridge University, England. Those groups who decide to try telepathy - there is no reason why all groups should not use this method in addition to any others - are advised to send out friendly thoughts to the occupants of the space-ships at a set time every 24 hours for a period of 7 days immediately prior to Whitsun week-end and thereby establish a rhythm. They should also deliberately ask for the contact. If it is true that the visitors belong to an incredibly ancient and evolved civilization they may well wish not to actively intervene in our affairs without being invited to do so. This may well be in accordance with universal law, but if hundreds of sincere groups send out a friendly telepathic invitation to make contact, then the space people may well respond to such a call.

During the actual three days of the week-end whatever other methods members of groups may use they are asked to try and keep their

will give you some idea of the various means we are adopting to try and attract our visitors. We have been promised support from all over the world, from Iceland, U.S.A., Australia, South America and in fact everyone wants to be in on this attempt. It will be the greatest world-wide mass telepathic experiment in history and the biggest invitation yet to the inhabitants of other worlds to land among us on the planet earth.

Thank you for your interest.

Yours sincerely,

Brinsley le Poer Trench

Brinsley le Poer Trench,
EDITOR

5th May – England: Mysterious 'ring angels' picked up on radar

The *Sunday Express,* in its article entitled: 'Angels over Britain, seen by Radar men', said 'mystery ripples' had been plotted in the control room at London Airport, Canterbury, Reading, Hertford and Chelmsford. Since 5th May 1959, they had been observed at the rate of three a week.

Angus Macpherson – air correspondent for the *London News Chronicle,* in an issue of the newspaper dated the 21st July 1959 – told that radar scientists at the Marconi Research Station at Great Baddow, near Chelmsford, were testing out new equipment and watching their screens.

Points of light appear

Just before dawn, a strange 'point of light' appeared, which spread outwards in the shape of a ring, before fading and vanishing. Then with an interval of two and-a-half minutes, another, and another appeared, making eighteen in all – like ripples on a pond, some extending as far as 20 miles. They had been photographed with a cine camera and a special radar device had estimated the height of the ripples as being 2,000 feet. The first [of these] picked up occurred over Tunbridge Wells.

Ipswich sustained five incidents

The phenomena were christened 'ring angels', as since the war any unexplained apparition on a radar screen has been referred to as an 'angel'. Macpherson stated that about seventy 'ring angel' centres have been found all over south-east England, adding that nothing on the ground, or for that matter in the air, has been found to correspond with them or give any clue why these strange 'rings' should form at the 70 'angel' centres and nowhere else? It was also revealed that the phenomenon could be as much as 30 miles in diameter, and tended to recur near particular places; Ipswich having had five incidents during the period from approximately the end of 1958 to June 1959.

Pondered if birds could be responsible

Dr E. Eastwood, director of the research laboratories, pondered whether birds could be a likely explanation – then dismissed this idea, after admitting the 'rings' sometimes moved at speeds of 50 mph. Apart from that, if they were birds, roosting, why didn't they show up on radar every night?

(Source: As above/Arthur Constance, writing in *Orbit,* Volume 2, No. 4, December/January 1961)

18th May – England: Four 'silver discs' fly over Warwickshire

At Bascote, Warwickshire, a housewife and her ten year-old daughter were lying down on the grass, gazing up at the sky on what was a beautiful day, when a silvery 'disc'-shaped object flew silently low, in a north-west to south-east direction.

> *"The underside seemed to be revolving. It was in view for a minute, and when it had gone out of sight a second, similar, object flew along the same course. In all, within a minute, four identical 'discs' were sighted."*

(Source: John 'Dennis' Llewellyn)

Juliana sees saucer man

News Chronicle Reporter

THE HAGUE, Monday.

QUEEN JULIANA and Prince Bernhard of the Netherlands today received the self-styled Californian flying saucer expert, George Adamski.

The audience lasted over an hour, and was meant to give the queen and the prince a chance "to get acquainted with Mr. Adamski and his views," said a court spokesman.

Others at the audience included the Chief of Staff of the Royal Dutch Air Force, Lt.-Gen. Heye Schaper; the medical aeronautic professor, Jacob Jongbloed, of the Utrecht University, Prof. Dr. Maarten Rooy, specialist in Press matters, from Amsterdam University; and Dr. C. Kolff, president of the Royal Dutch Association for Air Traffic.

Moon trip

Mr. Adamski, who is 68, claims to have met inhabitants of the planet Venus and to have travelled round the moon.

He says he has had several rides in flying saucers.

Adamski's private visit to Queen Juliana has been strongly criticised in some Dutch newspapers.

The Roman Catholic morning paper De Volkskrant said:

"We have no objection whatsoever against a court jester who, on Whit Monday, contributes his items on the lawns of the Soestdijk Palace, but we do not like his being considered an astronomic philosopher.

NEWS CHRONICLE.

19th May – Netherlands: George Adamski meets Queen Juliana

21st May – England: George King appears on *BBC* TV

DAILY TELEGRAPH 22-5-59

VENUS MESSAGE CLAIM ON TV

MAN IN TRANCE

By A Radio Correspondent

A man who claims to receive messages from people living on the planets, Mr. George King, 40, ex-taxi driver, appeared in B.B.C. television's "Lifeline" last night. He was seen by a consultant psychiatrist, and his remarks were discussed by a psychologist and a scientist.

Mr. King said he had met a man from Saturn, that he had seen 20 flying saucers, and that his mother had been for a flight in one. A tape recording, said to be his mother's impressions of her ride, was played.

On being invited to go into a trance and receive a message from outer space, he put on dark goggles, and his head slumped forwards and backwards. In a few moments he delivered a message purporting to come from a Venusian. It contained a warning about the danger of atomic experiments on earth and an exhortation for men to return to their religions.

In his summing up, the psychiatrist said he could not doubt Mr. King's sincerity. A dozen viewers telephoned the B.B.C. complaining of Mr. King's remarks, and saying that the programme was ill advised.

5th June – England: 'Pear drop'-shaped UFO seen

At 8pm on 5th June 1959, a pink-red coloured object was seen moving over the town of Pwllheli, Caernarvonshire, by a large number of people, who gathered to watch. Through binoculars it looked like a 'pear drop' – at times, brilliantly lit.

Local coastguard – Mr Ken Curtis – confirmed they had received several calls about the sighting, although he had not seen it for himself. However, he did say the Meteorological Office, at RAF Valley, could see it but were unable make out what it was.

(Was it a weather balloon?) **(Source: *Cork Examiner,* 6.6.1959)**

18th June – England: House of Lords deride UFO subject

See opposite page.

FLYING SAUCER REVIEW

Vol.5.No.4. Strike Issue July-August, 1959

Edited by the Hon. Brinsley le Poer Trench

BEYOND OUR CONTROL

Britain and 'Flying Saucer Review' have been hit by a strike in the printing trade. Consequently, this issue is not in its usual format. We apologise for not having our customary glamorous appearance and hope that the printing dispute will soon be resolved, so that once again we can present your favourite magazine in its proper garb.

PEER ASKS ABOUT LIFE ON PLANETS AND HOUSE OF LORDS ROCKS WITH LAUGHTER

London, June 18 - The House of Lords had a hilarious 15 minutes today - at least the noble lords apparently considered the question of Lord Fraser of Lonsdale (formerly Sir Ian Fraser, the blind M.P.) and the Government answer from Viscount Hailsham.

Lord Fraser asked whether the Government had sought or received any advice "as to the possibility or probability that sentient creatures live in other worlds, and whether any attempts at communication have been considered or foreshadowed

Lord Hailsham replied that "The Government does not include communications with any possible inhabitants of other worlds among the objects of the United Kingdom space research programme....Certainly, the Government has not sought or received any advice as to whether sentient creatures live in other worlds". (Laughter)

U.S. AIR FORCE CHIEF ON COMMUNICATION WITH ADVANCED SPACE RACES

Washington, April 14 (UPI)- Major General Donald J.Keirn Chief of US AF nuclear-engine programme stressed prospect of communicating with other worlds as important reason for establishing a moon base or space station. He said AF had no proof that intelligent beings existed elsewhere, but the UFO reports had "emphasized our innate curiosity." He went on, "it is entirely possible that some of them may have passed through our stage of evolution, and may have already achieved a higher level of social and technological culture than our own".

Dr. Harlow Shapley, former director, Harvard Observatory: "We must now accept it as inevitable....there are other worlds with thinking beings."

·1.

30th June – USA: Golden UFO seen

At 8.23pm, a gold, oblate-shaped object – nine times as wide as thick, metallic in appearance, showing sharp edges – was seen flying through the sky over *Patuxent River*, Maryland, by USN Commander D. Connolly, before moving out of sight 20-30 seconds later.

1st July – England: Flashes of light – four cigar-shaped objects seen

Mr and Mrs Grant from Wokingham, about 6 miles south-east of Reading, in Berkshire, were attracted by a bright flash in the sky.

On going to have a look they saw the flashes were emanating from the tail-end of four cigar-shaped objects, which each showed a bright light at the front (nose end); they watched the spectacle for about an hour. Unfortunately, no time was given.

(Source: *Flying Saucer Review,* Volume 5, No. 6, November/December 1959)

NEWS CHRONICLE 21-7-59

ANGUS MACPHERSON, our Air Correspondent, investigates . . .

The mystery of the morning angels

WHAT does the early bird do before it settles down to eat its worm? Shake itself, flap its wings and then flutter down to start pulling its breakfast out of the ground?

Not a bit of it, apparently. It may go on a 10- to 15-mile circular flight at a brisk 20 m.p.h. before it decides that it's hungry.

Radar scientists have asked the bird men: Is this the way birds go on?

The ornithologists have scratched their heads and replied: Well, it's possible, but it's surprising.

And so the latest, and biggest radar mystery remains unsolved.

It started nearly a year ago.

Radar scientists at the Marconi research station at Great Baddow, near Chelmsford, Essex, were watching their screen an hour or so before dawn.

STRANGE LIGHT

A STRANGE point of light appeared. It spread outwards in the shape of a ring, faded and vanished.

Another followed to take its place, and another, spreading outwards like the ripples on a pond.

The same thing happened a few mornings later — from another place.

The Marconi scientists christened them "ring angels" —since the war an unexplained apparition on a radar screen has been irreverently christened an "angel"—and got down to investigate them seriously.

ANGEL WATCH

EVER since there has been an "angel watch" at Great Baddow once a week. And about 70 "ring angel" centres have been found all over South-East England.

On the radar screen these are definite familiar points, recurring again and again.

But nothing on the ground, or for that matter in the air, has been found to correspond with them or give any clue why these strange rings should form there and nowhere else.

Some are near big towns—Ipswich, Reading, Canterbury, Tunbridge Wells, etc. Others are in open country.

The rings form in all kinds of weather, including fog.

"At the moment, the odds are on the birds," Dr. E. Eastwood, director of the research laboratories says.

"But it is far from obvious why the birds should behave in this way."

After a "ring angel" centre had been several times noted just west of Canterbury, a local bird expert identified a well-known roost for starlings in that area.

But there are some serious snags to the bird theory. The biggest is speed. At times the rings move at a sedate 20 m.p.h.—a possible speed for a starling.

At others, however, the rings may move as fast as 50 m.p.h. —which is surprisingly high for a bird of this kind.

DIFFERENT ROOSTS

"ANOTHER problem," says Dr. Eastwood, "is that if these *are* bird roosts, the birds don't use them every night.

"Our once-a-week observations don't show the same centres each time by any means."

Any other theories? Yes; the runner-up to the birds is air itself, which arranges itself in different layers at sunrise, and which could produce "ripples" moving at exactly that speed range—20 to 50 m.p.h.

PURE SCIENCE

"THIS makes it a very attractive theory," said Dr Eastwood, "except that no one has satisfactorily explained why the air should produce a radar echo."

The ripples last for anything between two and a half minutes and six minutes—not long enough to interfere with the practical use of a radar set.

So the Marconi "bird watch"—if it is a bird-watch—is in the interests of pure science alone.

But the radar scientists would like to know just what it is they get up so early in the morning to watch—and suggestions are still welcome. . . .

25th July – USA: Crescent moon-shaped UFO

At 1pm, a thin crescent moon-shaped object, with a small white dome in its centre, was seen moving at tremendous speed – visible for 5-10 seconds, over New York, by technical illustrator, Mr W.D. Neva.

29th July – Scotland: Silvery object seen in the sky

Hundreds of people living in the Ayre area reported a white or silvery object, high in the clear blue western sky, just under the crescent moon, at about lunchtime. One of the witnesses was William McClymont (38), a stamp worker at Caledonia Road.

> *"It was a bright, silvery object. I stood watching it for more than an hour, and aw it start to circle the moon."*

The authorities were unable to explain it away. There were some suggestions it miht have been a meteorological balloon, but none had been launched.
(Source: *The Glasgow Daily Record,* 30.7.1959)

14th August – Scotland: Fin tailed object seen over golf coue

On 14th August, Mrs G.E Williams and Mrs A Lovie, from Huntley Cottages, accomanied by Mrs G Buchan of Post Office House, Aboyne, were walking across the golf course, just afte.45pm, when they noticed a strange object heading at leisurely speed across the sky, in an east-wesdirection.

> *"It was rounded, with a kind of fin or tail on the front, and had a dull light emanatg from it – unlike any aeroplane."* **(Source: *Aberdeen Express,* 14.8.1959)**

6th September – England: *Viscount* Airliner crew sight UFO

According to *Flying Saucer Viewpoint,* written by veteran UFO Researcher – Rex Dutt (published by Pelham Books, many years ago), we learnt of a spectacular incident, witnessed bythe crew of a *Viscount* Airliner, who were flying near Amiens, France, on 6th September 1959, when a vivid flash lit up the sky, together with a noise – 'like the breaking of the sound barrier', follwed by the appearance of a 'flying saucer', out of which tumbled a number of smaller objects.

> *"The 'saucers' then headed towards the English coast where, over Northumberlad, it launched smaller objects which swooped down to sea level, sparking off a number of alerts as lifeboats put out to sea, believing a vessel or aircraft to be in trouble."*

'Flying saucers' then headed towards London

Even stranger, Rex tells us that the 'saucers' headed towards London, where they was seenswooping up and down through the sky all over the City, and parts of Essex – before 'dropping a large piece of something' reported to have fallen into a farm at Basildon.' The matter was later explained away to thousands of people, who telephoned the Authorities, as being a meteor – despite an unsuccessful search of farmland, near Basildon, by the police.

September – Scotland: Schoolgirls' close encounter at Dunnon

Schoolgirls Linda McCulloch and Patricia Murchison (both aged 14) were out taking a walk near Sandbank, about two miles from Dunnon, when they sighted two UFOs in the sky. Terrified, they ran home in a near hysterical condition. The parents then telephoned the police, who came to interview them. The girls described the UFOs as being:

> *"...round in shape, black and white in appearance, tapering to a point at the bottom. We were so scared we ran into a field at Ardnadam Farm, and tried to hide, but they came down – until they were above the telegraph poles. We got up and moved, but they followed us. We went into a ditch to hide and they hovered above us. We tried to stop cars on the road but nobody would stop".*

Eventually one did, driven by Mr Henry English of Paisley, who was on holiday with his wife at a nearby caravan site. The girls asked him to look up into the sky, which he did, and then became scared after seeing: "*...the two things floating about; it wasn't a mirage, they were flying saucers.*"

(Source: Robert Chapman, *Unidentified Flying Objects*)

13th September – USA: Jet aircraft attempts intercept with UFO

At 1.05am, a round yellow light with eight blue lights inset, accompanied by five larger red lights, was seen moving vertically through the sky over Gills Rock, Wisconsin, by Mr R.H Daubner, making a pulsating jet noise – out of sight 10 minutes later.

On the same day – this time at 4pm over Bunker Hill Air Force Base, Indiana – at least two control tower operators, and the pilot of a *Mooney* private airplane, observed a metallic, pear-shaped object – white and cream in colour, showing a trail under it. The object showed little movement during 3 hours, and an attempted intercept by a USAF *T-33* jet trainer failed.

UFO hovers over Stella Power Station, Newcastle-on-Tyne

In the same month, Mrs Ruth Pine, from Hexham, saw something strange hovering over Stella Power Station, Blaydon, Newcastle-upon-Tyne.

> *"It was circular, with a dome on top; you could see the portholes in it. After a few minutes, it banked steeply and soared at high speed – until it disappeared in the sky, accompanied by another object, shaped like a pencil."*

24th September – USA: 'Flying disc' seen – Jets scrambled

City Policeman Robert Dickerson was on patrol at the edge of town, when he saw a glowing disc like object drop down out of the sky and hover some 200ft off the ground. A few minutes later the object climbed upwards and headed past Redmond Airport, where it once again stopped in mid-air – now hovering in a north-east direction.

Robert contacted Flight Specialist Laverne Wertz at the airport. He and other Federal aviation men went outside to see the object, which had 'tongues of flame' around the rim. Wertz telexed the Air Force Traffic Control, at Seattle, who told him Air Force jets from Portland were being scrambled and that Air Force Radar at Klamath Falls, Oregon, was tracking the UFO.

At Redmond, the ground observers were still watching the UFO when they heard the roar of jets.

As the planes dived towards the UFO, the flames emanating from it vanished. A fiery exhaust blasted from the bottom of the 'disc' and it accelerated upwards, at terrific speed – close enough to cause one pilot to frantically move out of its path. Another struggled to control the plane, after being struck by the object's exhaust. Three planes headed-off in pursuit, but were quickly left behind. When the pilots landed, they were ordered not to discus the incident. The Air Force explained it away as being a routine checkup, following a false radar return. It is claimed that Laverne Wertz checked one of the aircraft with a Geiger counter but that the results of the examination were never released, although it is believed it was no normal reading. The explanation then put forward was that it had been a weather balloon. Unknown to them, copies of the F.A.A logs had been handed to NICAP. When they pressed for further information, they were told it had been Venus!

(Source: *Aliens From Space... The Real Story Of Unidentified Flying Objects,* Major Donald E. Keyhoe)

29th September 1959 – Flight 542 crashes – Was it a UFO?

At 10.37pm, Flight 542 – a *Braniff Lockheed* turbo prop airliner – took off from Houston, Texas, en route to New York, with a crew of six and 28 passengers. A short time later the aircraft approached Buffalo, cruising at 15,000ft, at 275 knots.

Major R.O. Braswell was piloting a *C-47,* at 6,500ft, between Shreveport, Louisiana, and Lufkin, north-east of Buffalo, when he saw:

> *"...a thing coloured like a large red fire; it looked like an atomic cloud. It was massive, about 5° above my plane. The base was at an altitude of 12-15,000ft; the top was at 16,000ft."*

Billie Guyton of Centreville, Texas, saw an object emerge from the 'glow'. Teacher Jackie Cox (39), who was driving towards Buffalo, heard:

> *"...the noise of a plane, which sounded louder than normal. I then saw a bright light in the sky that spread to cover the entire sky, as if phosphorous or magnesium was burning."*

They were not the only ones. Mr William S. Webb, of Buffalo, had just gone to bed. He happened to look outside and see:

> *"...a 'ball of fire' that looked like a star shooting across the sky – then I heard a noise like something falling from the sky; it was a whooshing, shrill sound."*

Farmer Richard White, and his wife, had just retired for the night. Richard decided to sleep outside, as it was so hot. He lay down, watching the late summer stars, when he noticed:

> *"...a brilliant light, high in the southern sky. The whole sky seemed to be lit-up like a giant fireball passing overhead, only to be followed by a tremendous explosion, so violent it seemed to shake the ground."*

Seconds later, the night was filled with shrill whistles as debris fell through the sky. The airliner had been torn into thousands of fragments. Brannif vice-president of operations – Mr R.V. Carleton – told newspaper reporters:

> *"Airplane crashes usually leave twenty or thirty major pieces on the ground. I've investigated lots of crashes but never seen one where the plane was so thoroughly demolished, wreckage so widely scattered, and people so horribly mangled. There was nothing which would indicate a fire or bomb aboard the plane."*

[The bodies were torn into fragments. Chunks of bloody pulp were barely recognizable; some parts of bodies were plastered into tree limbs]

Investigation into accident

An investigation into the crash revealed that there had been no fire or explosion aboard the plane while in flight, or after it had crashed. Scorch marks were found on glass window ports; the rear of the fuselage showing signs of having been exposed to tremendous exterior heat. The force which had caused the explosion had not come from the inside of the aircraft. Moments after the fireball had disengaged itself from the red cloud, it is said every dog within miles of the Buffalo area began to howl. Whether the accident was caused by a weapon discharged by the UFO or structural failure of the left wing as a result of an un-dampened propeller whirl mode as put forward by the Air Accident Investigators is something we shall never know

(Source: *Flying Saucers Are Hostile,* Brad Steiger and Joan Whritenour)

Autumn – Scotland: Golfers sight saucer-shaped object

In autumn of the same year, golfers out playing at Ravenglass sighted a well-defined cloud above their heads, followed by the appearance of a saucer-shaped object, with cupola, at 3.30pm. A beam of apparent 'solid' light – like a searchlight – projected down from the object, onto the green, some distance away, followed by another beam of light. The men continued to watch it for a short time, until it disappeared from sight. **(Source: *UFOLOG*/BUFORA)**

6th October – USA: White-yellow 'light' observed

At 8.15pm, Lt. Colonel L. Liggett (Selective Service), and his wife, were in Lincoln, Nebraska, when they saw a round, white-yellow 'light' in the sky, which was seen to make several abrupt turns in flight over the two minutes' observation.

12th October – England: Newspaper tells of holes found in fields

The *Portsmouth Evening News* – 'Mysterious holes discovered' (12.10.1959), told of a number of mysterious holes in the ground, discovered in fields in Kent, Hampshire and Berkshire, attracting the attention of the Bomb Squad. The holes, which varied between six inches to three feet in diameter, were, at first, thought to be due to an unexploded bomb – much to the consternation of the Bomb Disposal Squad, based at Horsham, who alleged to 'having received 30-40 calls a day, from members of the public, who had come across these strange marks in the ground'. If this was the case, without becoming too heavily involved in the research of such phenomenon, then these 'anomalies' were, in fact, far more widespread than we initially believed.

19th October – England: Three lights over Lincolnshire

Brian Paine – then a reporter for the *Gainsborough News* – witnessed something unusual, while out walking, near Thonock Woods, close to the coast, at 10.30 pm on *19th October 1959.

Brian:

> *"At that time, Gainsborough was surrounded by oil derricks, drilling for crude oil. At night, these rigs were floodlit and bore a remarkable resemblance, from a distance, to a rocket launching pad. This particular evening, I was walking along a footpath, which passes by a*

*A Russian rocket nears Earth at 10.30pm, same night.

field in which one of these derricks was placed. I happened to glance over towards Thonock Woods and noticed an orange/yellow 'dot of light' moving over the trees. As it approached closer, I saw two 'lights' close together – like cat's eyes – then there were three 'lights'. I wondered if it was a 'shooting star', but when does a 'shooting star' gain height? It glided across the sky in a north to south direction, until almost above me, at 10.30pm."

Now five egg-shaped lights

"It was not an airplane, because there were now five orange, egg-shaped, 'lights'. The object then turned silently, caught in the light of the moon, as it turned in a wide arc, south-east towards the Lincoln area. I noticed a glow from its rear, showing three 'dots of light', visible in a triangular shape – the light glowing bright and then dim every few seconds; I lost sight of it over the trees. I looked at my watch; it was 10.40pm – ten minutes after I had first seen the speck of light in the sky. When I look back on that eerie night, I sometimes wonder whether 'it' was looking at me as it hovered above – but there could be a more reasonable answer – perhaps the object was more interested in the oil rig."

As a result of publicity given to this incident, nineteen other people contacted the newspaper.

(Source: Bob Tibbitts, CUFORG & *The Retford, Worksop and Gainsborough News*, 23.10.1959)

19th October – USA: UFO swoops at aircraft

At 9.25pm, Captain F.A. Henney – an engineering instructor at a USAF Academy – was flying a *T-33* jet trainer over Plaiville, Kansas, when a bright yellowish 'light' headed towards the aircraft. The pilot avoided it and the 'light' dimmed; 30 seconds later it was gone.

19th October – USA: Youths fire at UFO!

At 6.15pm, Mark Muza (15), and Harold Moore (14), sighted a circular object – about 4ft in diameter, making a whirring noise – hovering above the ground in a desolate area known as the Big Marsh, at Poquson, Virginia. The object, apparently metallic, was seen to have a dark centre, surrounded by a 6ins wide silvery rim. On seeing the object descend, Muza, who was in possession of a 12ins gauge shotgun, fired three times – the last shot ringing on the 'metal' when about 50ft above him. The object then went straight upwards, like a spinning top, making noise like a tornado.

(Source: *Newport Daily Press*, 21st October 1959) USA: Oregon, 23rd October 1959 – Boys fire at Creature!

October – England: Bright 'disc' over Essex

In the same month, civil aviation pilot Gerald Newman, from Southend, was waiting at a bus stop in Southend, Essex, at 7.45pm, when he saw a bright orange 'disc' hovering overhead, but without a point of reference he was unable to say whether it was a small object at 1,500 feet, or a large one at 15,000 feet.

"After a couple of minutes, it began to move – then shot away, at terrific velocity. Just before

> *it went out of sight, without slowing down, it turned at a sharp angle – that's what I found astonishing."*

27th October – USA: Egg-shaped UFO seen in the sky

Phillip Small and Alvin Cohen were driving near Lock Raven Dam, Maryland, at 10.30pm, when they saw a large, flat, egg-shaped object in the sky, which affected the car's electrical system and caused a burning sensation to one of them. The object vanished a minute later.

30th October – Scotland: Builders sight 'flying saucer'

On 30th October 1959, builder Jerry Kearns was with three others, working on top of a 15 storey tower block at Blackhall, Paisley, when they sighted a 'flying saucer' travelling towards the direction of Greenock:

> *"We were right on top of the scaffolding when James McBride, from Barrhead Barriers, shouted, 'Look at that queer thing'. I looked up and saw this object (it is hard to say how high it was) speeding through the air, shaped like a sphere. We thought it was a plane – until we noticed there were no wings. Within four minutes it had gone out of sight."*

(Source: *Dundee Evening Telegraph*, 30.10.1959)

1st November – England: *Evening News* reports on UFO sighting

The *Eastern Evening News*, Norwich, (2.11.1959) told of being contacted by Mr I. M. Love, Mr T. Bradshaw and Miss Jean Richards, who spoke of sighting a vivid blue streak in the sky, over Norwich, at 11.40pm on 1st November 1959.

> *"It seemed as if it had hit something. The whole streamer seemed to take on a round shape, like a doughnut with a hole in the middle, and then it started to move slowly in the sky in different directions, slowly breaking up. Ten minutes later, no trace of it remained."*

Mr Ridley Larwood – a farmer – was outside his house that evening, tending to his cows, when he saw an object in the sky – like a round of white smoke in the black sky – positioned between the Plough and the North Star ... *"I have never seen anything like it before, or afterwards, in my life."*

5th November – England: UFO sighted over Coventry

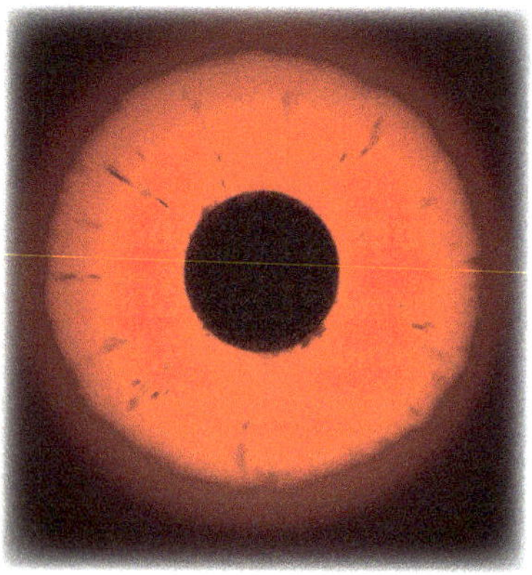

A few days later, on 5th November 1959, Bob Tibbitts – who was to become Head of the Coventry UFO Research Group, (CUFORG) over ten years later – was out watching fireworks, when he and his companion were surprised to see the appearance of a glowing, ruby-red coloured light in the sky.

Bob:

> *"This was no firework. It looked like a glowing, ruby-red coloured Chinese lantern, divided into segments, with a*

large black central hole in it. It seemed to float above our heads, silently and in size about that of a half-penny piece, held at arm's length. It didn't appear to be moving either . . . it was just 'there'! None of us remember the object leaving . . . it was just 'not there anymore', but my friend's father said he had seen something similar, while serving aboard an aircraft carrier in World War Two. An object which he said was similar to this had shot out of the sea near to the ship and flew off into the sky."

November – England: UFO over Merseyside

Another incident, involving a peculiar object, happened at Norris Green, Merseyside, when Kenneth Doyle (then aged 8) was watching fireworks, a couple of hundred yards away from him. He noticed a silver coloured, gleaming object, crossing the sky – which became lost from view as it entered cloud cover, but reappeared 'looking like an upside-down saucer, with what appeared to be blacked out windows, and a brighter glow of white underneath'.

Kenneth ran home and told his mother what he had seen, who refused to believe him – insisting it was some sort of firework.

In disgust, he ran back out of the house. As he reached the front gate, there was a flash of light and he became enveloped in a blue glow, which lasted for several seconds. Frightened, he sought the safety of the house. **(Source: Bryan Hartley, NUFON)**

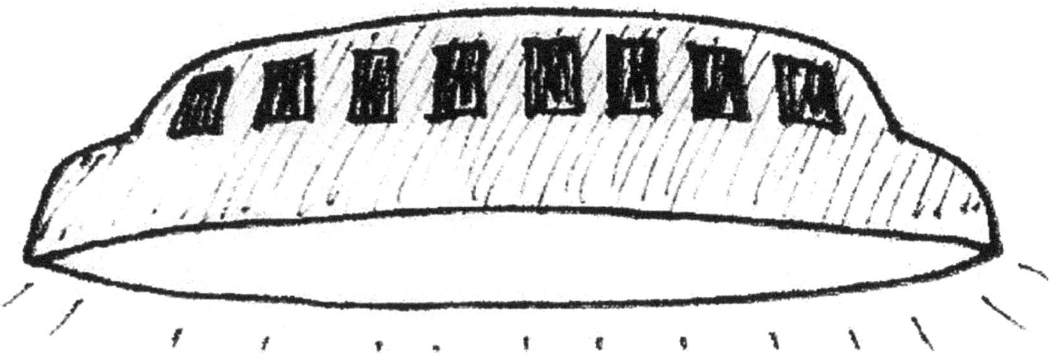

Kenneth Doyle's sketch of the object

24th November – England: 'Bowler hat' UFO sighted

During the early morning of 24th November 1959, Mrs Sperring from New Ferry, Wirral, Cheshire, was hanging out the washing when she noticed

> *"a silver object with a top part resembling an orange Bowler hat, travelling over the River Mersey at a height of about 200 feet. It then banked and moved away".*

(Source: Tyneside UFO Society, 1963)

RECONSTRUCTED SIGHTINGS

from LUFORO files

MRS.SPERRING of NEW FERRY,CHESHIRE

24 NOVEMBER 1959

"I thought it was just another plane- we see plenty here as Liverpool airport is just across the river from where I live.

I thought there was something odd about this one - so I stopped what I was doing and stepped into the centre of the garden to get a better look at it.

It was an oval-shaped object with an outer rim spinning around a domed yellow centre."

3rd December – USA: Bright green UFO

At 2.01pm, M/Sgt. William R. Butler – a medic by occupation – from Minot, North Dakota, sighted:

> *"...a bright green object, shaped like a 10 cent piece, accompanied by a smaller, silver round object. The first object exploded – then the second object moved toward the location of the first, at high speed, out of view one minute later."*

8th December – England: Sighting of UFOs

Philip Luce told of an incident witnessed by him and his father, while driving along Victoria Avenue, St. Ouen, in Jersey.

> *"I'm not sure of the date, but it was when the reservoirs went dry. We saw a red, luminous, object flying over the bay, some miles out, travelling faster than an aircraft but much slower than a meteor – similar to the one reported having been seen the previous Saturday night, by Mr Fitzgerald. It looked like a planet – about half the size of the moon – moving from town towards St. Brelade, trailing what looked fire behind it (east to west) and was not very high up.*

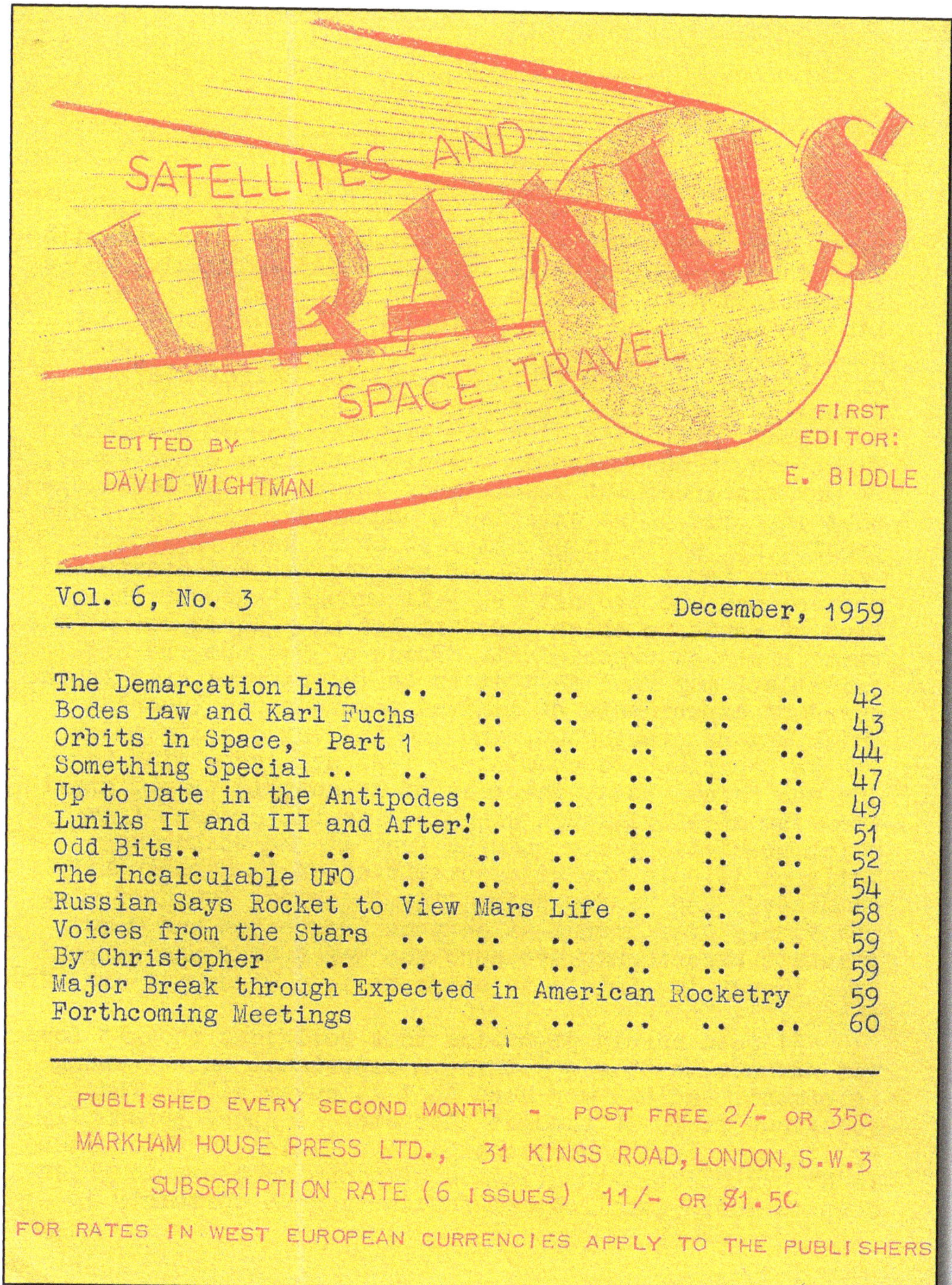

SATELLITES AND

URANUS

SPACE TRAVEL

EDITED BY
DAVID WIGHTMAN

FIRST EDITOR:
E. BIDDLE

Vol. 6, No. 3 December, 1959

PUBLISHED EVERY SECOND MONTH - POST FREE 2/- OR 35c
MARKHAM HOUSE PRESS LTD., 31 KINGS ROAD, LONDON, S.W.3
SUBSCRIPTION RATE (6 ISSUES) 11/- OR $1.50
FOR RATES IN WEST EUROPEAN CURRENCIES APPLY TO THE PUBLISHERS

> *I also want to tell you about two UFOs I saw moving from South to North, at 6.52pm, on the evening of 8th December 1959, which happened after watching a programme on the BBC about the Echo 2 satellite – which was definitely not what I saw."*

(Source: Fred Smith, Isle of Wight UFO Society)

England: UFO attempts to land on RAF runway

Former RAF employee, Brian Stafford – now living in Lincolnshire, who spent many years working at RAF Binbrook – contacted us with regard to the following incident, brought to his attention by an airman on duty in the radar caravan at the end of the airfield, some time in 1959.

> *"Although aircraft from Binbrook were stood down it was decided to man the radar caravan, because of a number of USAF planes taking part in a NATO Night Exercise, should an emergency arise. At about 2.30am, one of the airmen decided to stretch his legs outside, when he casually glanced along the runway and saw, with great alarm, what he took to be the landing light of an aircraft on final approach. He dashed back inside and ran over to the radar scope. Nothing showed. All four men then went outside and watched an object, resembling a car headlight, motionless in the sky, a few hundred feet off the ground."*

Witnesses warned of restrictions of Official Secrets Act

> *"The men telephoned the Station Commander, who confirmed a visual on the UFO, which suddenly dropped downwards and sped along the runway about ten feet off the ground, before shooting vertically upwards into the sky and vanishing from view.*
>
> *The Station Commander instructed all witnesses to the event that they were not to speak to anybody about what they had seen, reminding them of the Official Secrets Act. The matter was reported to the Air Ministry, who sent some officials down to the airbase to interview the men concerned."*

England: Young girl sights strange lights in a field, Gloucestershire

Meg Bryant was then aged 10 and living in Alvington, Lydney, in Gloucestershire.

> *"I saw a bright light appear at the end of the field, about 400 yards away. It stopped and was joined by four others. I ran outside; my mother and father came out to have a look. They alerted the neighbours, who joined us. A couple of minutes later the objects had gone."*

(Source: Personal interview)

LATE ADDITIONS

In May 2016 as this book was finally nearing completion UFO researcher Ananda Sirisena contacted us with an important update to the Shuttlewood UFO sighting – (see page 23 …) He had found the original letters sent to him by Mr Thomas Hills Harrison along with letters from Phil Klass.

Diary Describes UFO Seen In 1808

BY HAL STOKES

Back in 1808 in Camden, Maine, there certainly were no weather balloons or Air Force jets to be confused with flying saucers. George Washington's soldiers had barely gotten back home to their farms.

But something odd happened one summer night that year which was recorded in the diary of a Potsdam man's great-great grandmother.

Today the passage is interpreted by his wife, an historian who is studying the diary, as a first-hand account of a UFO sighting in the early 19th century.

"I thought she was describing a UFO when I first read it," said Dr. Judith Becker Ranlett, an historian who teaches at the State University College at Potsdam. "If she had seen something normal, she would have atempted to explain it as a natural phenomenon," according to Dr. Ranlett, who is using the diary as the basis for scholarly research on women's history.

The diary was written by Cynthia Everett, a Massachusetts-born school teacher who taught in Maine during the early 1800s. Born in Rutland, Mass., in 1785, she moved to Maine in 1804 with her family and kept the diary between 1804 and 1815, the year she married. The diary remained in the family.

The past year, Dr. Ranlett undertook the task of transcribing the manuscript into 600 typewritten pages. It was then that she first read the passage that she believes describes a UFO sighting.

The account is written in a firm hand on yellowing rag paper that is in remarkably good condition. The entry begins as a new paragraph to her recollections of the events of July 22, 1808; it is quite unrelated to the passage that preceeds it.

"About 10 o'clock I saw a very strange appearance. It was a light which proceeded from the East. At the first sight, I thought it was a Metier, but from its motion I soon perceived it was not. I(t) seem to dart at first as quickly as light; and appeared to be in the Atmosphere, but lowered toward the ground and kept on at an equal distance sometimes ascending and sometimes descending. It moved round in the then visable Horison. (it was not very light) and then returned back again, nor did we view it till it was extinguished."

That is the only passage in the entire diary that mentions the sighting, according to Dr. Ranlett. She finds it significant that Cynthia Everett did not explain what she witnessed as a natural phenomenon, since she was well-educated and had first-hand knowledge about the night sky. "She was the kind of person who would have explained it as a natural phenomenon, if she could have," said Dr. Ranlett. "In fact she did, her first thought was that it was a meteor."

Cynthia Everett was a woman who was well aware of the occurrences of nature according to Dr. Ranlett. In her diary she recorded earthquakes and the appearance of a comet. Her son became the captain of a clipper ship and navigated by the stars on a ship out of Thomaston, Maine.

Dr. Ranlett is quick to point out that she herself is personally not a fan of the extraterrestrial. "I have no feelings one way or the other on UFOs," she said.

The sighting must have been at night, Dr. Ranlett reasoned, because Cynthia would have been teaching school at 10 a.m. and besides she always made her entries in the diary just before she went to bed. Dr. Ranlett said she determined that the sighting was in Camden through the various people that are referred to on that day.

Cynthia was 24 years old when she wrote about seeing the strange light. She was single but was living, as teachers did, with a family in the area of the school. She changed her lodgings about once a week, according to Dr. Ranlett.

The schoolteacher had a good education for the period, Dr. Ranlett said. She had attended Leicester Academy at Leicester, Mass., one of the few truly coeducational schools where women went to class with men.

The diary was written until Cynthia was in her 30th year. Entries cease three days after her marriage to John Ranlett, a widower with six children. He later died, but she remarried and the diary went to her son, who kept it in the family. Her grandson, who became a lawyer, did some work transcribing it about 1880. The manuscript was bound in a handmade cover made of cloth backed with newspaper.

The diary belongs to Dr. Ranlette's father-in-law, who loaned it to her. She said that she is not nearly as interested in the passage about the strange light as she is about the revelations of the woman earning her own living in the early 19th century.

"At the first sight, I thought it was a Metier, but from its motion I soon perceived it was not."

Ananda L. Sirisena – Addendum to the Shuttlewood sighting

"After I had written up the report about 'The Light at Shuttlewood', which was eventually published in Flying Saucer Review, I sent copies of the intriguing story to both Philip Klass and Dr. J. Allen Hynek.

I felt that this report was very detailed, unusual, and worthy of scientific scrutiny. Also, I realised that it had happened just one night before the birth of a famous British contactee, during a period when UFO reports were very scant indeed. The responses from both of them are quite interesting; in one case a trifle amusing. I first wrote to Philip J. Klass – well-known sceptic – about the UFO phenomenon, on the 29th October 1976. To my delectation, Klass replied on 20th November 1976. This was his reply, verbatim":

FSR Publications Limited,
~~21 Cecil Court,~~
~~Charing Cross Road,~~
~~London WC2N 4HB~~
Telephone 01-639 0784

FSR PUBLICATIONS LTD.,
PO BOX 25,
BARNET,
HERTS. EN5 2NR

Mr. Ananda Sirisena,
[redacted]

20th April, 1975

Dear Mr. Sirisena,

Thank you for your letter of 11th April. We regret very much the errors which appeared in the article on "Shuttlewood". Unfortunately, we do not receive proofs of drawings and pictures, only the actual text. Also the printers were very hard pressed to get the job done by the deadline we gave them and probably rushed the job of lettering the diagram without bothering to check with the text. This often happens, I'm afraid. Most of our misprints happen in captions and wording on diagrams, simply because we never see them. I must say I nearly hit the roof when I noticed the mistakes in your article, but I am probably to blame for not noticing "forty" when it should have read "four" in the text. I too am under extreme pressure to get the work turned round as quickly as possible to make up for lost time at the printers.

I trust that you have received the copies you ordered from the subscription department. If not please let us know and I will see that they are sent to you.

Yours sincerely,

E Buckle

Eileen Buckle (Miss)
Assistant Editor

EST. 1922

PHONE: BOLSOVER 2119

T. H. Harrison

PROPRIETOR: A. G. HARRISON

WATCHMAKERS AND JEWELLERS

26 Town End,
Bolsover,
Near Chesterfield

Amanda Sirisend Esq.
[redacted]

9th October 1973

Dear Mr Sirisend

I thank you for your interest in the Ball of Light I saw at Shuttlewood. I am writing to explain that so far I have made some notes on the incident which cover three pages of an old exercise book, the incident happened so long ago I have to jog my memory for some of the smaller details, but in the end I want to send you a full report and I can see it will take some time probably three to four weeks, my son Ian will be with us from the U.S. from the 12th and also I have never been so busy with antique clock restoration as I am just now. If of course you would like to come over I would take an hour or two off to show you just where the light was although I see no point in this as I shall be sending you a map of the district and also a plan of the land where it all happened. If there is anything specially important that you would like to know please drop me a line.

Shuttlewood is about three miles from here.

Yours sincerely
T.H. Harrison

EST. 1922 PHONE : BOLSOVER 2119

T. H. Harrison

PROPRIETOR: A. G. HARRISON

WATCHMAKERS AND JEWELLERS

26 Town End,
Bolsover,
Near Chesterfield

15 High Street,
Tel. Bolsover 2461

Ananda Sirisena
[redacted] S.W. 19.

17th November 1973

Dear Mr Sirisena

Your interest in the Ball of Light I encounted Jan 22nd 1919 at Shuttlewood is greatly appreciated & as promised I enclose for your research a complete write up of my experience, if you would care to have this typed in some letter form with your own wording etc. & let me have it to check I will then return it duly signed but please use it only for research.

Sorry I have kept you waiting so long & please excuse note paper it has been done in haste as I am so busy being hounded by antique clock enthusiasts.

With best wishes

Yours faithfully

T H Harrison Sen

Thomas Willis Harrison

EST. 1922 PHONE : BOLSOVER 2119

T. H. Harrison

PROPRIETOR: A. G. HARRISON

WATCHMAKERS AND JEWELLERS

26 Town End,
Bolsover,
Near Chesterfield

23rd Aug. 73

Dear Mrs Townsend

[For your research only]

In answer to your letter of the 18th August.
I will be glad to let you have a detailed account of my experience with regard to the light I saw on January 22 or 23rd 1919 together with a sketch showing the path of the ~~light~~ object etc, in return for a Photostat or otherwise copy of what is set out in Arthur Shuttlewood's book about the incident. I was not informed that my letter would be included in the book & I would like to know just how it has been set out, if anything has been added or left out, because of this and after seeing Mr Shuttlewood being interviewed on television, I have no intension of buying the book.

Your questions to date:-

Size of ball, 2 inches dia.
Distance from me 3 feet when still (10 minutes to 15 mins)
moved away 100 feet or more then came back & was still again for 10 minutes or so.
Time ~~20 past ten~~ 10.20 to 10.45 P.M.
Altitude 5 feet when still & on the move until it had to negotiate a hedge & some buildings & 6ft wire netting.
Names of witnesses, William Harrison, (now dec.)
Robinson an aunt of our neighbours (now dec.)
Mrs Newman my sister.

Yours truly
T.H. Harrison Sen.

EST. 1922

PHONE: BOLSOVER 2119

T. H. Harrison

PROPRIETOR: A. G. HARRISON

WATCHMAKERS AND JEWELLERS

26 Town End,
Bolsover,
Near Chesterfield

Ananda Sirisena Esq.
[redacted]

15 High Street
Bolsover

23rd November 1973

Dear Mr Sirisena

Further to my letter with reference to the "Light" at Shuttlewood in 1919. I would suggest that you condense the writeup of my experience and pick out only what is applicable to your research work. I included the dream also the coincidence because you asked for these kind of details in your last letter.

I would be glad to answer any further questions on the subject if it will help you in any way.

Yours truly

T H Harrison
Sen

EST. 1922 PHONE: BOLSOVER 2119

T. H. Harrison

PROPRIETOR: A. G. HARRISON

WATCHMAKERS AND JEWELLERS

26 Town End,
Bolsover,
Near Chesterfield

Home address
15 High Street,
Bolsover
Tel. 2461

26th September 1973

Dear Mrs Sirisena

I find your letter waiting on my return from holiday & note your remarks also the questions you ask. I must confess that I hate letter writing & as I have a son Dr. I.T. Harrison who is a research chemist in California U.S.A. I realise you will want the most precise details and described with the correct wording. for instance I have been calling the ~~noise~~ sound I heard when the white light changed to orange (Sizzling) when it should be Searing. I find that I am writing then checking with my memory which is quite clear on this matter although it is so long ago, then re writing another proplem with me I am not too good at spelling & this worries me so a letter takes longer time for me to write. therefore I propose to start from the beginning with a set of notes and sketches and if you come over here. Write down as many questions as you can possibly think of as these seem to help me recall the situation on the night of January the 22. I have been able to check with my sister who saw the light

EST. 1922 PHONE : BOLSOVER 2119

T. H. Harrison

PROPRIETOR: A. G. HARRISON

WATCHMAKERS AND JEWELLERS

26 Town End,
Bolsover,
Near Chesterfield

2/

from about 20 yards. she tells me the light went through the wire netting, I only noticed it seemed to be confused when it reached it as I turned away to go round the fence to be able to chase it but changed my mind, a second thought struck me that the fense must be down & I went back to see it coming back & over the top towards me. I will try & include all this in my notes, As you see it will take some time, I am also very busy helping my son Alan who has taken over the business so I hope you will excuse the delay. The date by the way was the 22 Jan. for sure. for my age at the time (I was born Jan 24th/1902). you need not bother with the reprint from Shuttlewoods book also you may include my sighting in your write-up.
The light at first was what we now call fluorescent white & it had the power of a storm lantern although it did not dazzle. I stared at it all the time, the change to orange must have been very gradual as I only noticed it had changed when it began to move slowly away. Well I am writing this on the work bench with jobs all round me so must close now and to end please note I wish to help you all I can as you seem to be the only person who is really interested, others seem to think I am half way round the bend when I talk about the light & this includes my wife. Yours sincerely

P.S. see over

T.H.Harrison Sen.

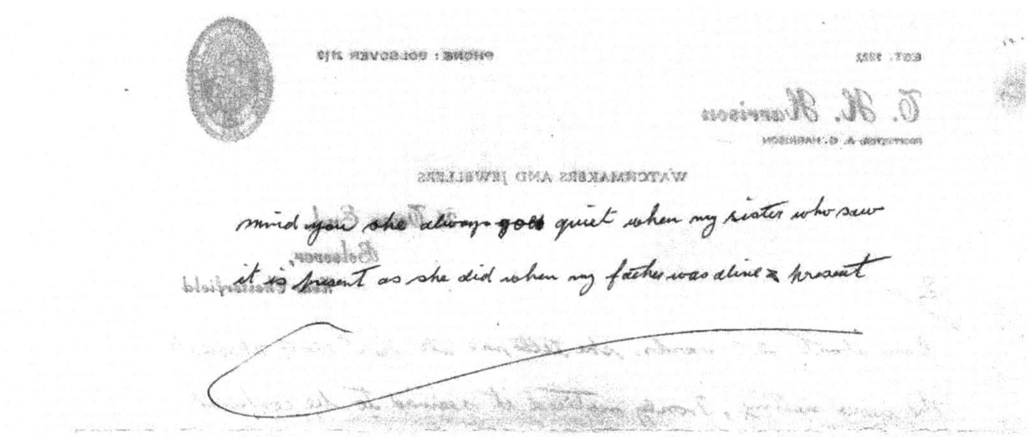

mind you she always goes quiet when my sister who saw it is present as she did when my father was alive & present

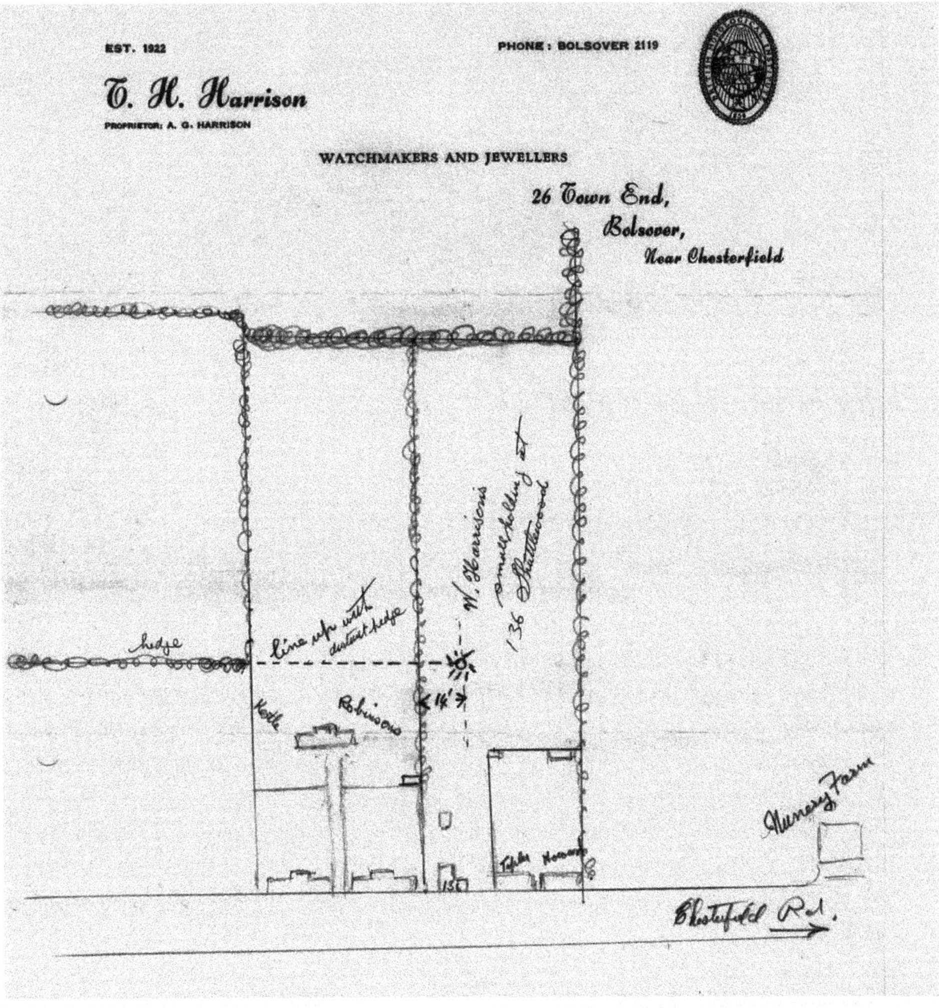

EST. 1922

PHONE: BOLSOVER 2119

T. H. Harrison

PROPRIETOR: A. G. HARRISON

WATCHMAKERS AND JEWELLERS

26 Town End,
Bolsover,
Near Chesterfield

Thomas Hills Harrison, seen with his daughter

Philip Julian Klass replies

"Dear Ananda,

Several weeks ago I received a letter from England from a 'UFO believer' who had read my book and was much less polite than you – so his letter is waiting until my busy schedule provides much time, while I shall respond to yours promptly because of your courteous tone.

Let me tell you of my reactions as I read your account. First, noting the date (1919), the year in which I was born, I realized that the incident had occurred nearly 60 years earlier, and so a 'caution flag' went up in my mind because human memory is not very accurate for details of an incident that occurred so long ago – and we all, humanly, tend to embellish an exciting incident. As I began to read of the glowing light and its characteristics, I immediately thought of 'ball lightning', an atmospheric electrical freak (which I treat quite extensively in my first book, 'UFOs – Identified', as a possible explanation for some UFO reports. The sort of vaporous, luminescent illumination, the seemingly capricious behavior – all reminded me of 'ball lightning'.

But as I read on about the duration of the incident, more than 10 minutes, I found it hard to believe it might be ball lightning, which seldom lasts for more than a minute or two at most. Then, when you recounted Mr Harrison's 'remarkable dream' – the pieces began to fall into place. An encounter with ball lightning is so striking – and quite rare – that it would or might prompt a person to dream about the incident. And in our dreams, our mind adds embellishments from our subconscious. Now I began to suspect that a brief encounter with ball lightning might have occurred, prompting dreams which embellished the incident – dreams so vivid that with the passage of time the dream began to assume reality – naturally since it was based on a real experience. Ball lightning is reported to make a buzzing 'Tesla coil' like sound.

When Harrison thinks he recalls the 'real incident' and that 'he could not see the ground when he looked down, etc. etc.' these are the sort of frustrations characteristic of a dream. The fact that the sister's recollection does not fully check his adds support for this hypothesis.

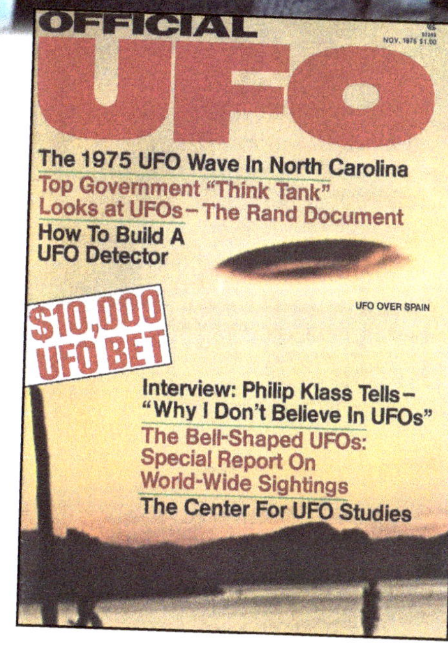

In summary, then, I'm inclined to believe (1) that a real incident was involved, (2) that what he saw was 'ball lightning' – most frequently seen before, during or after a rain, snow or sandstorm – and that (3) the long duration and embellishments were added during the dreams. Obviously there is no way of proving this hypothesis. If you have access to my book 'UFOs – IDENTIFIED' in a library, you will find many fascinating, similar types of incidents therein.

I hope your dreams for UFOs come true – but caution you that I am quite certain you will go to the grave disappointed.

Cordially, signed Philip J. Klass" – (20th November 1976)

Ananda writes back to Philip

Since Thomas Hills Harrison had been very careful to separate the dream that he had that night from the actual close encounter with the 'globe of light', Ananda felt a strong compulsion to respond to Philip Klass. Harrison had sent him many pages of hand-written notes and colour diagrams which detailed both the real experience and the vivid dream, and was clear that he was not confusing the two. Could this have been a case of 'extreme' duration ball lightning? Could ball lightning display intelligent behaviour, or was all of this, as Klass had suggested, simply been 'capricious' movement? Ananda wrote to Klass again on 11th December 1976, as follows:

> *"Dear Philip,*
>
> *I hope you have no objection to my addressing you, a person much older than me, by your first name and thank you for your quick reply.*
>
> *I was highly intrigued by the last line in your letter: I hope your dreams for UFOs come true--but caution you that I am quite certain you will go to the grave disappointed. Frankly, I am already disappointed – at your explanation of Mr Harrison's experience of 1919. I had considered the ball lightning theory but rejected it, for more than one reason, not least the 'capricious' behaviour. Indeed, such behaviour can reasonably be deemed the result of intelligence, animal if not human.*
>
> *Another reason was that four different people saw it, during which time it must have traversed quite a distance and therefore been in existence for more than two minutes. Considering that the median duration of ball lightning is four seconds, I think this is being more than cautious. The final run by the light of about one-tenth of a mile, prior to circling the group of houses absolutely rules out ball lightning.*
>
> *All the above mentioned manoeuvres were witnessed by others and thus there is no question of subconscious exaggeration on the part of Harrison.*
>
> *I agree that the dream was an entirely different affair and may have been the result of a rare and traumatic experience. In fact, this could be one of the reasons for Harrison's clear memory. We do remember unusual and worrying events very well, even 60 years! The fact that his sister could not see him, although she could see the light only proves that the light was in the hencote and adds another facet of strangeness to the story, rather than support your hypothesis.*
>
> *Your explanation hinges around the 'real-dream-confusion' supposition; how would you have dealt with it if Harrison had not mentioned the dream? Indeed, your 'caution' to me suggests that you feel all UFOs will be explained in the future through advancing scientific knowledge. Does this mean that Harrison's report would have been unsolvable prior to our understanding of ball lightning?*
>
> *In fairness, I think you have failed to account for the entire report and although I am prepared to concede that my conclusion may be out of this world, I feel yours is utterly improbable in this instance.*

As for my UFO dreams – they are very simple. I will accept whatever the UFOs are honestly, objectively and scientifically shown to be – whether 'natural' phenomena, or some exotic atmospheric animals, or 'ultra-terrestrial' visitors, or even more 'natural' extraterrestrial life-forms. I have no inner fear about space people existing. If such powerful interplanetary or interstellar races exist, then they have every right to visit our skies in whatever form and way they wish and humanity would just have to come to sensible terms with them.

Best wishes for Christmas and a happy New Year.

Ananda L. Sirisena" – (11th December 1976)

A second reply to Ananada

Ananda did not really expect a reply to his candid letter but was mildly surprised when an airmail envelope arrived, for which he had to pay extra postage, with his name and address clearly printed in the top left-hand corner. His 'tongue-in-cheek' response was dated 16th December 1976:

"Dear Ananda,

Your willingness to put great credence in the fading memory of people for events that occurred many decades ago reflects a tragic ignorance of how little credence can be put in the accuracy even of people for recent events. See for example the article on the unreliability of eyewitnesses in the Dec. 1974 edition of Scientific American. I can understand why you reject the possible ball lightning explanation on the grounds that the median duration of ball lightning is four seconds. It is on the same grounds that I am positive today that I saw an extraterrestrial creature walking down the street. The reason is that the median height for American males is 5 ft. 10 in., and this human-like creature was easily 6 ft. 6 in. -- clearly he must have been extraterrestrial. May I suggest some other possible explanations for your sighting incident:

(1) Evil/Good spirits. (No one has ever proved that spirits don't exist and the famous Sir Arthur Conan Doyle believed in spirits.)

(2) Fairies. These are tiny human-like creatures, in which Sir Arthur also believed. He accepted as authentic a number of photos purporting to show English girls sitting alongside miniature fairie-like creatures.

(3) God. Obviously God can manifest himself or herself in any form he/she wishes.

(4) Leprechauns: Although I have never seen one, I have some Irish friends who swear they have--especially following a long drinking party. Now you might conclude that my friends were drunk. I choose to believe that Leprechauns choose to reveal themselves only to persons who have relaxed with a bit of alcohol.

I fear that it will not be possible for me to continue this correspondence. Your mind is made up, as is mine--after 10 years of investigating the most famous UFO cases in the U.S.

I am currently working 7 days/week, 18-20 hours per day and my schedule just will not permit wasteful enterprises. Have enjoyed our communications and hope for your sake that someday, somewhere is found physical evidence of an extraterrestrial visitation, or of Leprechauns, or Fairies, or Evil Spirits. But please don't hold your breath until such evidence shows up. Happy holidays.

Signed:
Philip J. Klass" – (16th December 1976)

Further letter sent to Philip

Ananda, certain that he would receive no further communications from Philip Klass but nevertheless feeling that his letter suggesting alternative explanations for 'The Light At Shuttlewood' needed a prompt reply, wrote to him again in a light-hearted vein on the 8th January 1977.

"Dear Philip,

I respect your wish not to continue corresponding with me and so, whilst hoping that I do not receive a further reply from you, I would like to correct a false impression you have acquired. I did not settle on the extraterrestrial theory for Harrison's light of 1919 simply because the median duration of ball lightning is four seconds. On the contrary, my conclusion was based on the overall dynamic, luminescent and apparently intelligent behaviour of this globe of light. I merely rejected the ball lightning theory from my list of probable explanations because of the extended duration.

I notice that although you chide me for putting credence in the memory of people for events of many decades ago, you depend on this selfsame memory (no doubt slightly manipulated to suit your theory better) to conclude that it was Kugelblitz. I am pleased that you did offer alternative suggestions in your letter dated December 16th, 1976. I agree that it may have been a spirit and concur that no-one has ever proved spirits don't exist. Neither has anyone proved that extraterrestrial life forms (physical or spirit-nature) don't exist. As for your second hypothesis, all I can say is that it must have been some Fairy! The light was obviously a manifestation of God in the sense that God is all and therefore everything is part of God.

I have enjoyed our brief exchange of ideas but I cannot understand why you feel that physical evidence is so important. For example, there is no physical evidence of 'abstract thought', yet we accept this in principle as the basic requisite of all works of imagination, art and science.

May the Leprechauns sit ever by your wine bottles – You never know, for no-one has proved that one has to be Irish to see them.

With best wishes,

Signed:
Ananda Sirisena." – (8th January 1977)

No further letters were received from Philip J. Klass.

Ananda points out, for the information of the reader, that Harrison's encounter had taken place literally some hours before the birth (23.1.1919) of England's most famous contactee; namely George King (who had founded 'The Aetherius Society', after he claimed a first contact in May, 1954).

In 1976, Philip J. Klass helped to found the Committee for the Scientific Investigation of Claims of the Paranormal (CSICOP), and has served on its Executive Council since the outset. He also chaired CSICOP's UFO Subcommittee, and contributed numerous articles on UFOs to CSICOP's journal, *Skeptical Inquirer.* In March of 1999, with a little help from his friends, the International Astronomical Union formally changed the name of asteroid 1983 RM2/7277 to "Klass." [Late note: CSICOP has subsequently been renamed Committee for Skeptical Inquiry (CSI).]

Klass has written six books on UFOs, including one for young readers. His one non-UFO book, *Secret Sentries in Space* (1971), was the first to deal with spy satellite technology. He is also proud of having written the first article on secret inertial guidance technology (1956), the first on infrared missile guidance and detection (1957), and the first on the coming age of microelectronics (1957) in which he predicted – without benefit of "psychic" power – that the then-embryonic technology would revolutionize electronics.

Philip, who has a younger sister, was born in Des Moines and raised in Cedar Rapids, Iowa. He dedicated his first book to his father, whom he credits with imparting to him "*the crusader's zeal for what seems 'right' regardless of whether it brings popular acclaim.*"

His mother had the honor/duty of proofreading his second book, *UFOs Explained,* which is still widely regarded as the best ever written on the subject. Although he has no children of his own, Phillip has been married for nearly 20 years to Nadya, who, after escaping from communist Bulgaria with her son in 1973, joined the Voice of America as a news editor for its Bulgarian service.

(Source: Gary P Posner)

Klass died of cancer in Cocoa, Florida, on August 9, 2005, after moving to Merritt Island, Florida, in 2003.

Professor J. Allen Hynek

Ananda:

> *"I had already sent a copy of 'The Light at Shuttlewood', with some other reports, to Professor J. Allen Hynek on 22nd January 1974. As Hynek had been the astronomical consultant to the US Air Force on the subject of UFOs, I thought he might be interested in Harrison's report; Hynek replied to me from the Department of Astronomy at the Lindheimer Astronomical Research Center, based at Northwestern University in Evanston, Illinois."*
>
> *"Dear Mr Sirisena,*
>
> *Thank you for your most interesting reports, particularly your most recent one. Though it is very old, it is useful in a statistical manner.*

> *You may be interested in the Center for UFO Studies - an association of scientists and professionals in various fields, involved in the serious study of the UFO problem. I enclose some preliminary information.*
>
> *Sincerely,*
>
> *J. Allen Hynek" - (12th February 1974)*

Ananda Sirisena:

> *"At least Hynek found Thomas Harrison's report useful, even if Klass did not." - (April 2016)*

1910 – UFO over Cambridge

1910 – Mrs F. Ryder, of 42 Ward Road, Cambridge (a young married woman) – accompanied by her father and husband – was walking over the railway bridge in Mill Road, heading towards the town, at 8pm.

> *"We saw a cigar-shaped 'light' – its edges well-defined, showing what looked like square windows in the side – heading silently through the sky. Inside was a flickering light. One end was tapered with flames coming from the base. (It reminded her of a V1 'flying bomb', which missed their house in the Second World War.) It looked about 6-8 feet in length and was moving in a north-east to south-west direction." Mrs Ryder was interviewed in 1966 about this matter by, it is believed, members of the Isle of Wight UFO Society.*

1932 – Runner's Close encounter with strange 'light'

Ananda Sirisena also told us about another incident brought to his attention, involving Harry White (then aged seventeen), who was a keep-fit fanatic. Harry often went for a three-mile run at night. It was during such an exercise, in October 1932, that he tangled with a 'light' which expressed a curious interest in him. White was on a minor road that leads from Bolsover to Sandhills, in the county of Derbyshire, approaching the junction with the main road to Rotherham. It was a clear evening, with the moon casting a subdued glow.

When approximately a 120 yards from the intersection he noticed a bright 'light' playing 'tag' with him, at about 8pm. He stopped still. The 'light' also stopped still! It was hovering three yards away from him, on the far side of the hedgerow which lined his route. Fascinated by this intelligent response, he remained calm at this stage of the experience and coolly scanned the entire area looking for a logical explanation. Finding none, he resumed his run.

> *"The 'light' then also started up, maintaining a level pace with me, at a height of three feet above the ground. For the next fifty yards or so, this silent race between me and the 'light' continued until the 'light' suddenly moved towards me. Not so fast as to be a blur, but a calculated move which I could easily follow with my eye, the object left the hedgerow and suddenly moved towards and around my legs and in between my feet as I ran. I felt it had come to investigate and had become aggressive. But this could have been a nervous reaction on my part. It was, however, very real and not an illusion. I began to kick out at the thing, really scared and now in a panic."*

Seemingly undamaged by this vigorous retaliation, it remained close to Harry, evading his kicking, and easily moved around him without making physical contact.

Upon reaching the road junction, the 'light' left him and returned to its position behind the hedgerow. For another hundred yards it kept pace with his now fast run. Then it just disappeared.

He estimates the 'light' to have been a perfect sphere, twelve inches in diameter. This is somewhat puzzling: how could a 'light', that size, have passed between a pair of running legs? It would have to be endowed with a keen sense of timing and lightning-like reflexes not to have touched his legs.

Ananda:

> *"Mr White was adamant that the 'light' did not touch him. He felt no warmth or pain when it moved around his legs. It made no sound and emitted no smell. It did not change in size; there were no markings on it – only a uniform non-dazzling glow. It left no trail in the night sky and did not vary in brightness. Harry was a schoolmaster by profession. He was a captain in the infantry during World War II and saw many horrors and felt intense fear on many occasions – these are now dim memories but the 'light' is still a vivid memory.*
>
> *The Sandhills is not a marshy area, so the whole range of swamp gas explanations can be discounted. The night was dry and there was not a rain or snow storm later, making the ball lightning proposition weak but not entirely untenable as the duration of the sighting was at least three minutes. Harry White himself offers no explanation except to say that he witnessed something very unusual, and comments, 'All I know is what I experienced and I have not embroidered the account in any way'."*

When he arrived home after his eventful run, his grandfather (sitting in his chair by the fireside) remarked, *"You look scared to death."* Upon recounting his story, his grandfather propounded a simple explanation: the area where Harry had seen the 'light' was the traditional burying place of suicides, and one must expect to see the occasional tormented soul in such nether regions.

[In June 1932, a similar 'light' was seen on a farm 18 miles south of Erie, Pennsylvania. Its reported manoeuvres and size – fourteen inches in diameter – make a noteworthy comparison. The 'light' seen at Shuttlewood, on 22nd January 1919, was only a few miles from Sandhills.]

(Sources: Ananda Sirisena/*Mysteries of the Skies: UFOs In Perspective,* by Gordon Lore & Harold Deneault, published by Prentice-Hall, 1968)

1941 – Alison Richards' close encounter

On page 64, we outlined a close encounter by Kidderminster woman – Alison Richards. Sadly, she passed away some years ago.

We have now recovered some photos of Alison and the author John Hanson, taken during a visit to her house. One of the photos shows the mysterious marks that were discovered on her leg, which she claims are associated with what happened to her. Whatever you believe, one thing is certain – her integrity is not in question and similar marks have been brought to our attention, over the years.

Author, John Hanson with Alison Richards. Below: The strange scoop marks on Alison's leg.

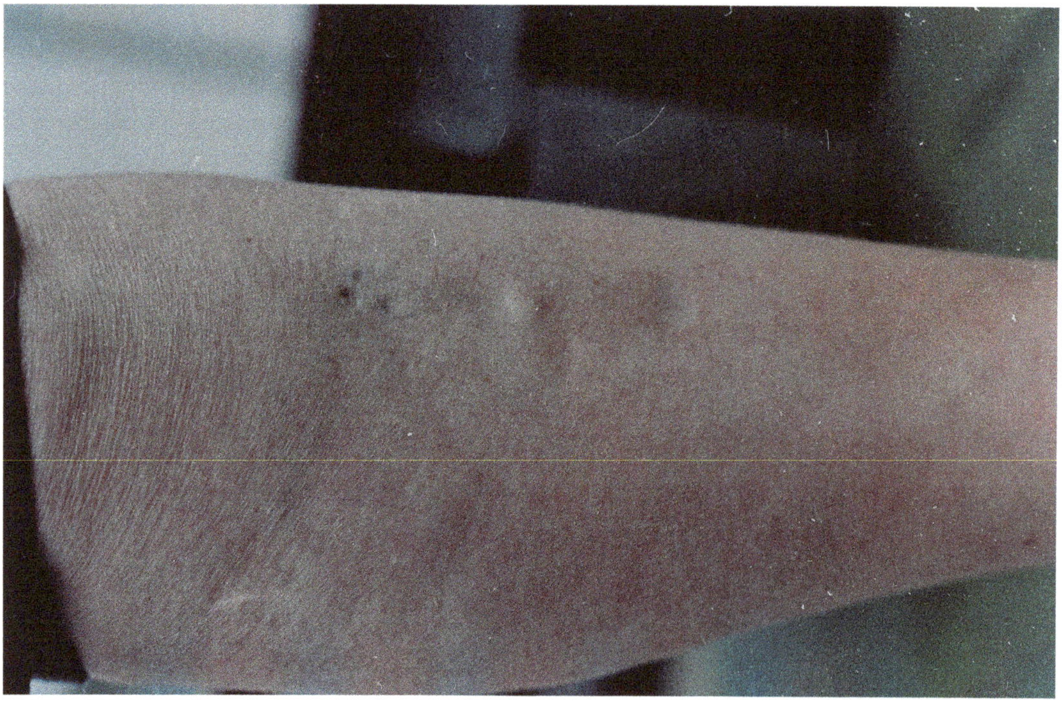

1951 – UFO close encounter with UFO

Mrs A.Y. Lees of Clinton Avenue, Welling, Kent, contacted Mark Stenhoff and C. David Oakley-Hill of *Gemini* Magazine, in 1972, wishing to bring his attention to what she saw in 1951 (aged 14).

> *"At the time I was living at Wester Cally Farm, half a mile from Ballintuim Village, Blairgowrie Town, Perthshire.*
>
> *One bright morning in the summer of 1951, my sister and I were travelling at the rear of a trailer being driven by my father. We were climbing a fairly steep hill, rather slowly, when this bright golden-orange object suddenly appeared extremely close and directly behind us. We drew our father's attention to the object, which then hovered momentarily when it first came over the fenced track along which the tractor was driving, before starting to follow us.*
>
> *It was silent and in view for about a minute and a half. It was apparently solid with a sharp outline and shaped like two shallow bowls, joined together, with a rim running around it. I estimated it to be 14 feet wide at its largest diameter, with a thickness of 19 feet, some 60 feet up in the air, and about 30 yards away from us; the tractor was moving at about 5 miles per hour. It was a clear, dry, warm, day and the object was lost from view as it headed away towards the east-north-east."*

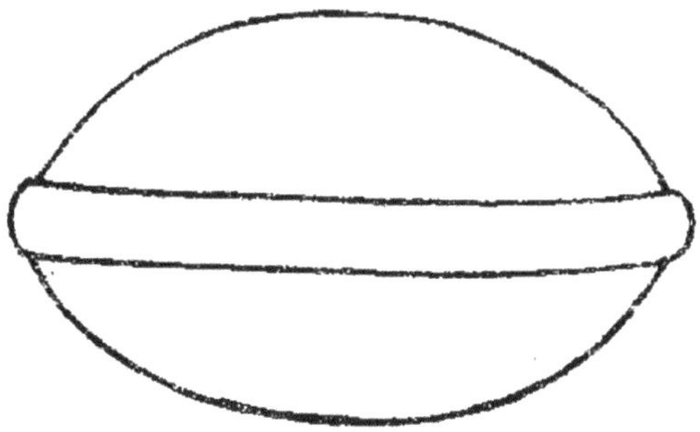

1957 – RAF Hawker Hunter jets chase UFO over London

Another report from the files of Ananda Sirisena:

During the week in June or July 1957, three Royal Air Force Jets were seen heading in a NNW direction, pursuing a large 'flying disc', estimated to be 50-60 feet in diameter over south-west London, by a schoolboy (aged 12) returning home along Atherton Road, Barnes, London SW13.

He recognised the aircraft as three Hawker Hunters, being familiar with all RAF planes then in service, and observed them for five seconds chasing a 'flying disc', which was much larger than a Hawker Hunter. The sighting was at an elevation of 80 degrees above the horizon and he observed the pursuit until some houses obscured his view. It was enough time for him to roughly estimate the altitude to be between 5,000 and 8,000 feet and based on his civil aviation experience, the speed of the craft to be no more than 400 miles per hour.

If we assume that the 'disc' was 50 feet in diameter, a calculation tells us that if the craft were at an altitude of 5,000 feet, then the 'flying saucer' would have subtended an angle in the sky such that it appeared about one-seventh the size of a full moon. An interesting feature of the three RAF Hunters was that the jet in the centre was behind the other two jets, i.e. they were in an inverted 'V' formation.

The witness, who was alone at the time, cannot recall seeing any other reports in the newspapers.

He wrote:

> *"In general, I was not a particularly imaginative child at that age and had no apparent reason (from memory) in conjuring up such a vision. I can only assume it occurred as I remember it. As you can imagine, it left quite an impression."*

(Source: Ananda Sirisena – personal interview with witness)

INDEX

A

B

C

D

E

F

G

H

I

J

K

L

M

N

O

P

R

S

T

U

V

W

Y

CREDITS

Front Cover – © 'Modo'
Inside cover – © David Sankey
Page 3/4 – www.Internet, 2016
Page 5 – © Photo, Peter Leek
Page 8 – © Photo, John Hanson
Page 8 – © UFO image, David Sankey
Page 11 – © Photo, John Hanson
Page 12 – © Photo, Gordon www.Internet
Page 12 – © Photo, Mirror Pix
Page 12 – © Photo, Christine Smith
Page 13 – © Painting, 'Modo'
Page 14 – © Artwork, 'Modo'
Page 15 – © Derek Samson
Page 16 – © Sketch, Julian Sampson
Page 19 – © UFO sketch, David Sankey
Page 19 – © www.Internet
Page 21 – © Railway Hotel
Page 21 – © Sketch/Photos, Agnes Whiteland
Page 22 – © John Hanson
Pages 23/24 – © Dennis Hanna
Page 25 – © Thomas Hills Harrison
Page 26 – © Susan Harrison
Page 28 – © Dennis Hanna
Page 28 – © Ananda Sirisena
Page 30 – © John Hanson
Page 31 – © Jose Steadman
Page 32 – © www.Interet
Page 33 – © Sketch, William Anderson
Page 34 – © www.Internet
Page 35 – © Sketch, Mark Brown
Page 36 – © Photos, John Hanson
Pages 38-46 – © Bob Tibbitts
Page 48 – © Photo, John Hanson
Page 48 (lower) – © David Sankey
Page 49 – © David Sankey
Page 53 – © Artwork, *'Gemini'* C. David Oakley Hill
Pages 54-58 – © Ken Rogers
Page 59 – © Illustration, William Green
Pages 60/61 – © Photo/Letter, Emily Crewe
Page 63 – © Letter, Arthur Long
Page 64 – © Email, John Hanson
Pages 65/67 – © David Sankey
Page 69 – © Ron West
Pages 71/74 – © David Sankey
Page 75 – © www.Internet
Page 76 – © John Warren
Page 76 – © Audrey Church
Page 77 – © David Sankey
Page 78 – ©Audrey Church
Page 78 – © John Hanson
Page 80 – © www.Internet
Page 81 – © David Sankey
Page 82 – © George Bernard Dye
Page 83 – © Mr Howard John Sandall, RAF Historian
Page 84 – © John Hanson
Page 87 (top) – © Steven Franklin
Pages 87/88 – © 'Modo'
Page 90-95 – © Ronald Claridge
Page 95 (lower) – © David Sankey
Pages 96-98 – © Ronald Claridge
Page 101 – © www.Internet
Page 102 – © www.Internet
Page 103 – © William David
Page 104 – © Wayne Mason
Page 105 – © www.Internet
Page 106 – © L. Bucknell
Page 107 – © Vernon Wilkes, DFC
Page 107 (left) – © John Hanson
Page 108 – © Vernon Wilkes, DFC
Page 109 – © William Anderson
Page 110 – © 'Modo'
Page 112 – © David Sankey
Page 113 – © Julian/Derek Sampson
Page 115 – © William Anderson
Page 115 (lower) – © www.Internet
Pages 116/117 – © www.Internet
Page 119 – © Mollie Tilley
Page 120 – © www.Internet
Pages 122-125 – © Andrew Bryce Cherry
Page 126 – © Illustration, David Sankey
Page 126 – © Photo, John Hanson
Page 127 – © www.Internet
Pages 128/129/131 – © www.Internet
Page 132 – © Ron West
Pages 133-136 – © www.Internet
Page 139 – © www.Internet
Page 141 – © Richard Thompson
Page 142 – © *Project Blue Book*
Page 143 – © www.Internet
Page 148 – © Steven Franklin
Pages 149/154 – © www.Internet

Page 156 – © John Hanson
Pages 157-160 – © Dennis Maycroft
Page 161 – © www.Internet
Page 163 – © Steven Franklin
Pages 164/5 – © Stanley Hubbard
Page 166 – © Bernard Green
Page 169 – © Arthur Bearne
Page 174 – © 'Modo'
Pages 176/77 – © Kath Smith
Page 178 – © www.Internet
Page 181 – © Len Burrell
Page 182 – © David Sankey
Page 184 – © Andrew Collins
Pages 184/5 – © David Sankey
Page 188 – © David Sankey –
Page 193 – © Robin Gibbons
Pages 195-206 – © www.Internet
Pages 207/8 – © www.Internet
Page 213 – © Source not identified
Page 215 – © *Sunday Dispatch*
Page 216 – © *Yorkshire Evening Press*
Page 219 – © Not known
Page 220 – © Mrs Wilson-Sharp
Page 221 – © David Sankey
Page 223 – © Nick/Frank Redfern
Page 225 – © Steven Franklin
Pages 227/229 – © Sir Peter Horsley
Page 228 – © Michael Swiney
Page 229 – Prince Philip © Paul France
Pages 230/32 – © Michael Swiney
Page 233 – © David Crofts
Pages 236/237/238/239 – © www.Internet
Page 249 – © Dawn Gould
Pages 251/252 – © Ron West
Page 253 – © David Sankey
Page 255 – © *Daily Mail* (11.2.1954)
Pages 256/257 – © www.Internet
Page 261 – © National Library of Australia
Pages 263-266 – © Geofrey Smythe
Page 267 – © Margaret Walker
Pages 268/269 – © www.Internet
Page 272 – © Wayne Mason
Page 273 – © Janet & Colin Bord
Page 274 – © David Sankey
Page 274 – © John Hanson
Page 275 – © Ivan Bunn
Page 277 – © www.Internet
Page 278 – © Steven Franklin
Page 280 – © John Hanson
Page 284 – © www.Internet
Pages 285-287 – © www.Internet
Page 289 – © Omar Fowler
Page 291 – © John Hanson
Pages 294/295 – © Arthur Constance
Page 296 – © www.Internet
Page 298 – © Denis Plunkett
Page 299 – © John Hanson
Page 301 – © *Derby Telegraph* (13.5.1954)
Page 302 – © John Hanson
Page 305 – © Jill Clarby
Page 306 – © David Sankey
Page 306 – © John Hanson
Pages 316/317/318 – © Harold Hill
Pages 319/324 – © David Sankey
Page 326 – © George Hartropp
Pages331/332/336/337 – © James Salandin
Pages 333/334 – © Steven Franklin
Page 334 – © John Hanson
Pages 338/339/340 – © Derek Dempster
Page 342 – © John Hanson
Pages 343/344/345 – © Jesse Roestenberg
Page 346 – © Gavin Gibbons
Page 348 – © John Hanson and Denette France
Page 350 – © John Hanson and Jessie Roestenberg
Page 351 – © Wolverhampton *Express & Star*, (25.10.54)
Page 352 – © Gavin Gibbons/ Robin Gibbons
Page 353 – © Not determined
Page 355 – © Jessie Roestenberg
Pages 364/365/366 – © Doris Jacques/ Pam Rossitter
Pages 366/367 – © Margaret Fry
Page 368 – © David Sankey
Page 368 – © *News Shopper* (4.9.2006)
Page 370 – © *Kentish Times*
Page 371 – © Rodney Maynard
Page 372 – © John Hanson
Page 373 – © David Sankey
Page 374 – © Jim Streek
Page 375 – © Unidentified source
Page 377 – © John Hanson
Page 378 – © David Sankey
Page 379 – © www.Internet
Page 381 – © Leonard Ferriday
Page 382 – © David Sankey
Page 382 – © Ernest Suddards
Page 386 – © David Sankey
Pages 389/90 – © Wayne Mason
Page 391 – © www.Internet
Page 401 – © *Flying Saucer Review*
Page 402 – © www.Internet
Page 406 – © 'Modo'
Page 409 – © www.Internet
Page 410 – © Fred Jones
Page 411 – © David Jones
Page 414 – © John Hanson
Pages 416/417 – © Freddie Wimbledon/ John Hanson
Pages 419-421 – © Ivan Logan
Pages 422/423 – © John Brady/ John Hanson
Page 439 – © John Hanney
Page 442 – © www.Internet
Page 443 – © John Gregory
Page 452 – © John Hanson
Page 453 – © David Sankey
Page 453 – © Sylvia Payne
Page 458 – © Frank Marshall
Page 458 – © John Hanson
Pages 459/460 – © Milton Torres
Page 461 – © Steven Franklin
Pages 462/465 – © Milton Torres/ John Hanson
Page 464 – © David Cayton
Page 465 – © Peter Leek
Pages 466/467 – © Bill Dillon

Page 468 – © Barry Deamer
Page 469 – © David Sankey
Page 469 – © Stephen Clarke
Pages 470-477 – © Bill Dillon
Pages 478/479 – © Ivor McNish/ John Hanson
Page 484 – © Wilfred Grunau
Page 486 – © Bob Tibbitts
Pages 490/491 – © Thelma Roberts
Pages 495/496 – © Peter Drew
Page 497 – © David Sankey
Page 499 – © Steven Franklin
Page 500 – © Margaret Fry
Page 504 – © www.Internet
Page 508 – © *Birmingham Dispatch*
Page 513 – © Derek Samson
Pages 515/516 – © Trevor James Constable
Page 518 – © Isobel Brant
Page 519 – © Valerie Geary (nee Perks)
Page 524 – © John Hanson
Page 527 – © Source declined to be named
Page 528 – © www.Internet
Page 530 – © Ernie Sears
Page 532 – © Derek Samson
Page 535 – © Thomas Austin
Pages 536/537 – © Charles Morris
Page 539 – © David Sankey
Page 541 – © David Sankey
Page 542 – © Ron Lucas
Page 545 – © William Scott
Page 546 – © www.Internet
Pages 551/552 – © John Cleary Baker
Page 555 – © Ruby Llewellyn
Page 556 – © Anne Smith
Page 557 – © David Sankey
Pages 561/562 – © Frank Marshall
Page 572 – © Bob Tibbitts
Page 573 – © Kenneth Doyle
Page 574 – © Mrs Sperring
Page 578-583 – © Ananda Sirisena
Page 586 – © Susan Hills Harrison
Page 587 – © www.Internet
Page 594 – © John Hanson
Page 596 – © Steven Franklin

REVIEWS

Volume 1 Reviews - Amazon (In the main 5 stars)

By *The Guardian* - 19th September, 2010

"This book is volume one of a planned four-volume history of the UFO phenomenon as observed and recorded in and over the UK, the first time such a major undertaking has been seriously attempted. The authors, police officer John Hanson and his partner Dawn Holloway, have done a pretty good job of recording and detailing the history and seem to be meticulous at sorting the wheat from the chaff. The brief foreword is penned by Timothy Good.The years covered in this volume are 1940-1959. To many readers the earlier accounts will be the most revealing - i.e. before the "flying saucer" issue burst into the public domain through the mainstream media post-1947. Early contactee and abduction accounts from 1940-1941 (such as that from Alison Richards in 1941) do demonstrate that the abduction phenomenon was experienced way back then and was in all essentials identical to the more numerous reports decades later. A great many encounters with strange aerial objects were reported by RAF aircrew in world war two, particularly from bomber crews who operated in large fleets of aircraft at night and through the twilight hours. At just over 300 pages this large-format paperback adopts a magazine-type layout with some good illustrations (by David Sankey) of cases either rarely or never previously published. Probably thousands of sightings and encounters have been missed, simply because only what has been reported can be investigated: it is suspected that 90% of sightings/encounters are never "officially" reported, and some not even to friends and family. The text is well-written and edited and virtually free of typos; the authors seem to be intelligent, agenda-free and thorough in their research. Good job guys and best of luck with the rest of the project. My guess is that having put out volume one, you're going to receive a few phone calls from people with later sightings and are going to have your work cut out."

By Hothouse - 28.11.2010 – *"As a newcomer to the UFO subject, I found this book to be very informative and was fascinated by the events that people had witnessed, which would not have come to my attention without reading this book."*

"Awesome book I am going to start on reading all of them in the series."

By ZP - 5th August, 2010 – *"For the authors' first publication I found it to be a quirky, well researched and interesting read. Certainly makes you think after reading all the documented sightings! Even if you're uncertain on this subject or a tad sceptical - I would highly recommend this, 10 out of 10."*

By PP - 10th August, 2010 – *"This book was a exhilarating from start to finish it has a no nonsense approach to separating the UFO non-fiction from fiction. It is informative and precise in detail. The authors' approach to the subject matter comes across in an easy digest manner making it an excellent read. Looking forward to the next chapter fascinating"*

By Alfred – 15th October, 2010 – *"John and Dawn have obviously put a lot of research into this project that has involved many hours of hard work. This book captures the atmosphere of those times and is a book that any newcomer to the subject would do well to read. I particularly liked the illustrations by David Sankey which gives freshness to the reports, and the very comprehensive index, an absorbing book, difficult to put down. I look forward to the next volume with anticipation.* ***Five stars*** *without reservation."*

By David Bryant – 28th August, 2010 – *"This book fills a gap in the library of any serious UFOlogy student: it provides a complete chronology of the phenomenon in the UK with a wealth of well-researched first-hand accounts. The illustrations, maps and tables are first class, and the paintings are almost photographic in quality! I cannot wait for the next volume to become available!*

By D L Taylor – *"I first met John Hanson about 15 years ago when he had plans to write a book. Since those early days John has gone far – becoming a well known and respected UFOlogist. This is an impressive and mammoth task to undertake – a four volume set of books that deals with the history of British UFO sightings. This first volume deals with the years 1940-1959.*

In these pages John and Dawn give a broad selection of UFO reports from the various years. Many of them will not be known to readers as they come from the author's own investigations. The book is better for this approach I feel, as it saves going over the same old ground of well known cases. There is also a broad geographical spread for all the cases, although I found myself being drawn to those from the Midlands. And there are some classic cases here – alien contact case from Kidderminster in the 1940's, not to mention the famous Cynthia Appleton case from Birmingham in the 1950's.

My only minor quibble with this first volume was the inclusion of a case from (again) Kidderminster that involved `burn' marks in a field. There were no accompanying reports of UFOs or other anomalies. So why the mention in the book? As this is a history of British UFO reports, I would have liked to have seen more historical sociological context for reports, which are very much `of their time'. But this aside, this is a great book that deserves to be read by all serious researchers. Bring on Volume Two!"

By J Fest – 1st May, 2011 – *"A fascinating compendium of cases which runs the gamut from the decidedly flaky to the highly impressive. The landing of a saucer in a suburban street in Kent in 1955 is a particularly stunning case, apparently being witnessed by dozens of people. If only someone managed to get a photograph during the few minutes it was present, it would leave sceptics in a difficult position. This series of books, well illustrated by David Sankey and Wayne Mason, brings to light many little-known encounters in UK airspace and deserves to be a big success."*

By Will Moore – 6th August, 2011 – *"This is an outstanding piece of work, the authors have compiled an authoritative record of reports on the UFO phenomena while keeping themselves in the background with little commentary to push readers one way or the other. The illustrations add real other worldliness to the book that enhances the read very well indeed."*

By J. H. Davies – 5th February, 2011 – *"I purchased this book based upon the good reviews that have been written by the best Ufologists on the subject; they are not wrong. This is an important book on Ufology and a chronicle into this cultural phenomenon, it is a treasure. The authors have obviously worked very hard as this amount of research detail does not come easy. The only gripe I have is that it is not hard bound, this would have increased the cost but I would gladly pay £25-£30 for a book of this quality, I only want it hard bound as I love it so much. Thank you Dawn Holloway and John Hanson for top notch work."*

Volume 2 Reviews – Amazon

The Guardian – 7th August, 2011

"This is the second volume of a planned multi-volume history focusing on UFO-related phenomena from the British Isles, the first serious and organized attempt at this major undertaking. This volume covers the period 1960-64, and there's a lot of material. The authors/compilers of the series are police officer John Hanson and his partner Dawn Holloway, with many other researchers credited as contributors of material. The introduction this time is penned by Jenny Randles, with a brief note from the late, delightfully straight-talking (some would say curmudgeonly) Admiral of the Fleet Lord Hill Norton, once head of NATO, about the UFO issue and its impact on officialdom. As with the first volume the authors have done an excellent job of detailing cases, meticulously sorting wheat from chaff.

The large-format paperback with magazine-style layout is carried over from the first volume, and this one comes in at just over 290 pages. David Sankey again supplies illustrations where relevant and useful. One interesting revelation is that large black triangular craft, with a light near each point of the triangle and one in the centre, were reported as far back as 1964 in British skies and this distinctive shape did not originate with the wave of sightings of identically described phenomena over Belgium in 1990. Again thousands of sightings and encounters have probably been excluded because only what has been reported can be investigated and recorded. As with the first volume the text is literate, free of typos and obviously edited to a professional standard (why can't all works in this field be so good in this area?). Let's look forward to volume three."

By D. Bryant – 27.3.2011 – *"John & Dawn continue their methodical and meticulous task of cataloguing UK UFO reports. There are no other books that cover the subject with such rigour: a 'must-have' for all SERIOUS researchers: I can't wait for the next volume!"*

By J. H. Davies – 27th February, 2011 – *"This is the second of a four part series of books on British UFO sightings, this one detailing the period 1960-1965. The authors have mined great depths to pull out newspaper cuttings and accounts from the swinging 60's, many of the accounts have been buried for years i.e. black triangles almost identical to those accounted in modern times and another forgotten incident in Rendlesham Forest/Woodbridge in 1961. I cannot wait for the next instalment; if the authors are reading please let me know when it will be published so I can get in a pre-order! Bravo!"*

By numanoid – 14th September, 2011 – *"This book is amazing. You will not find another as detailed, articulate and in depth like this. Unique is the word. The authors have tried to put in as much information about each UFO case as possible. The amount of research and time spent on these volumes is incredible. The authors are a credit to the UFO subject. You will not be disappointed."*

Volume 3 Reviews – Amazon

The Guardian – January 8th, 2012

"This third volume of a planned multi-volume history of UFO-related phenomena from the British Isles focuses on a busy 24-month period between January 1966 and December 1967. Once again police officer John Hanson and his partner Dawn Holloway, together with other collaborators, have produced an impressive catalogue of sightings spiced with photos, illustrations and relevant documents. The chosen presentation is 'magazine format' with the text and images mixed on each page. Veteran researcher

and author Nick Redfern writes the foreword to this edition. As with the first two volumes in the series, the authors have done an excellent job of studiously sorting wheat from chaff and presenting dozens of professional case studies. With a 25cm x 19cm page size, these illustrated soft-cover books are quite large. There is a lot of stuff here, filling the now standard 300 pages. One feature of this period was the 'flying cross' objects reported from a variety of UK locations, apparently not reported in subsequent years. Some of the famous photos from the 'Warminster wave' are also reproduced.

An interesting exchange on the subject of UFOs between Merlyn Rees, the then Home Secretary, and Sir John Langford-Holt MP in Parliament on June 22nd 1966 is reproduced in full. As with previous volumes the text is literate, free of typos and edited to a professional standard. Why all published works in this field don't seem to reach even this basic publication standard remains a mystery. Thousands of sightings and encounters have probably been excluded for the usual reason: only what has been reported can be recorded. In summary: a good work of reference."

By Will Moore –13th January, 2012 –*"As noted by the other reviewers this is the 3rd in the series, the series is a must have for folks with a real interest in the field. The narrative is clear and uncluttered its "just the facts" and no wild speculation. The reports are seen as they were originally reported with some updates and the illustrations produced from the reports giving the illustrations some merit. Interesting to note that the same descriptions and "types" of UFO have a good degree of consistency from the first in the series through to this edition suggestive that the same type of "craft" if I may use that term are seen by each generation of witnesses."*

By David P. Bryant - 6th November, 2011 - *"A third in the series of 'must have' UK UFO archives. Any serious researcher cannot really afford to omit this volume from their collection!* **I had the pleasure to present a copy to Moonwalker, Dr Ed Mitchell, recently: he expressed his admiration for the book and acknowledged the work that had gone into its production.** *Well done John & Dawn!"*

Volume 4 Reviews - Amazon

The Guardian - June 9th, 2012

This is the fourth volume of the chronological history of UFO-related phenomena from the British Isles compiled by police officer John Hanson and his partner Dawn Holloway. The chronicle has now reached 1968-71. Again, the catalog of sightings is liberally spiced up with photos, drawings, facsimiles of documents and letters from the period, laid out in the publishers' chosen magazine format with text and imagery on each page. This edition is dedicated to the memory of New York City based abduction researcher Budd Hopkins, who died on 21st August 2011 aged 80 after a years-long battle with cancer. Pages 4-6 are given over to a brief biopic of Budd outlining his truly revolutionary contribution to the research field, with photos of him with Dawn and with Peter Robbins, who also contributes to the biopic by recounting his long partnership and association with Hopkins' Intruders Foundation. The foreword to this volume is then penned by veteran researcher Philip Mantle, followed by a 2-page introduction by the authors and a full page of acknowledgements. If you have read or scanned the first three volumes in the series then you will know what to expect from the contents of volume four, and are unlikely to be disappointed. The authors present their data in a lively and readable format and steer clear of speculation in deference to factual reporting. A lot of valuable research work is documented here, and this series is becoming something of a benchmark for any serious overview of incidents reported in the British Isles in the modern era. As usual the text is literate, virtually typo-free and edited to a professional standard."

By David P. Bryant - 5th March, 2012 - *"John & Dawn's books just keep getting better! This, the latest volume in the series, is superb: it is detailed, complete, authoritative and totally free from the usual hype and bull excrement!I'm looking forward to the next instalment!"*

By Majors - 17th November, 2013 - *"Even if only one person did see something that cannot be explained then surely there must be a case to say 'We are not alone'!"*

Volume 5 Reviews - Amazon

The Guardian - October 13th, 2012

"This is the fifth volume of the chronological history of UFO-related phenomena from the British Isles, compiled by police officer John Hanson and his partner Dawn Holloway. This book covers the years 1972-74. It seems remarkable that only three years' worth of sightings in one geographical area of the globe can take up an entire book, but such is the wealth of strangeness reported throughout the British Isles during this period. The narrative is spiced with photos, drawings, facsimiles of documents and letters. The page-layout follows the usual magazine-format with text and imagery mixed, and uses different fonts both italicised and plain to emphasize the separate sections. The foreword to this volume is by Matt Lyons, which follows brief tributes to the late Margaret Fry, Margaret Westwood and ex-US Air Force career-pilot Wendelle Stevens.If you have seen previous volumes in the series then you will know what to expect from the content and are unlikely to be disappointed. The authors present their data in a lively and readable style and report factually, with the wild speculations so often evident in this genre absent from the text.As usual the text is literate, typo-free and edited to a good standard. Obviously such a work can never be comprehensive as only what is reported and investigated can be recorded, but it's nevertheless a fine work of reference."

Volume 6 Reviews - Amazon

By dolittlee - 8th October, 2013 - *"Having got Vol 3, Vol 4, Vol 5 and Vol 7 thought would get Vol 6; it is just as good as others, and no stories repeated."*

By Cazz - 21st February, 2015 - *"A splendid read. Spent some lovely afternoons reading this fascinating book with many a cup tea and a slice of cake. I feel if I purchase the other volumes I may end up the size of a house from over indulgence of Victoria sponge ho ho ho."*

Volume 7 Reviews - Amazon

Matt Lyons - 1.8.2013 - Five Stars

"Please do treat yourself to a copy of 'Haunted Skies' Volume 7; there is an account in there of a highly respected pilot who saw impossible manoeuvres by UFO in proximity, in 1978. Here's my review of the volume and it will add to your knowledge of this incident as a vital precursor to Volume 8, soon to be published: REVIEW - 'Haunted Skies' Volume Seven: By John Hanson and Dawn Holloway. In this volume, there is impressive diversity in the huge age range of accounts and cases with many accounts by more than one witness. This latest instalment in the best and most comprehensive account of UFO cases also feature some of the key moments for the subject as an additional accompaniment to the largest edition of this

series to date. There are contributions from highly respected researchers and presenters such as Malcolm Robinson and Jenny Randles and once again, we can see John and Dawn methodically and carefully review cases, returning wherever possible to not only interview witnesses but also the original investigators where ever possible. This includes the debate to recognise the international awareness of UFOs, with the United Nations council meeting to debate the subject and set policy. This involved leading authors of the time such as Dr. Jacques Vallee and Dr. Allen Hynek, who brought an abundance of analytical and new classification category proposals to this global discussion. We don't just have pilot accounts, as Gordon Cooper, the Apollo mission astronaut, also joined the ranks of witnesses, investigators and researchers whether at sea, in the air, from outer space or dry land."

David Bryant - February 24th, 2013 - *"If, like me, you have an interest in the UFO phenomenon and already possess Volumes 1 - 6, then this, the latest in the series is a must-have! The book is packed with photographs, illustrations and first-hand accounts and has absolutely none of the too-frequently encountered over-credulity. John & Dawn are doing us all a service with their meticulous logging of the UK UFO phenomenon!"*

By Philip Laskey - 22nd June, 2013 - *"This hefty tome collects a huge number and variety of UFO cases from these two years, from the intriguingly baffling to the outright comical. It generally refrains from drawing groan-inducing conclusions - otherwise I wouldn't have bought it! Collecting all these volumes is a daunting prospect so I just settled for this one. The computer generated art is pleasing - the cover especially so - but should be considered more decorative than anything else. The reproductions of newspaper clippings are generally poor - it would be nice to be able to read them - and there are some typographic errors. The layout is sometimes a bit messy. Other than this, I say to UFO fans, especially sceptics, buy one of these volumes, it will give you plenty to think about!"*

By Stephen Graham - 18th June, 2013 - *"Ongoing and as detailed as ever this is a great series of books on the UFO phenomenon and a regular release too!"*

By Majors - 26th August, 2013 - *"Once again an in depth view of UFO's through the years. A must buy for anyone interested in the subject."*

Volume 8 Reviews - Amazon

Matt Lyons, former Chairman BUFORA - 10th December, 2013 - Now in colour! *"We reach 1980 in this instalment of the 'Haunted Skies' series. This edition is the first to go into full colour production, with the addition of being at least an extra two thirds in page content. Volume 8 does include a huge segment dedicated to the Rendlesham incident but it is not a 'Rendlesham special' in the sense of detracting from the large number of cases covered outside of this famous incident. In fact, the other events in that year add up to the same relative size of the preceding volumes in this series. A fighter plane UFO chase in Volume 7 leads us to many strange events that fall outside of that key December 1980 date, for example, Base Captain Lori Rehfeldt gives a description of a strange UFO sighted over the twin bases in Suffolk before the more famous events occur in December that year.*

There is a close encounter in an area that was to become famous for its sightings, including a Vehicle Interference case in the Todmorden area. We find accounts from sightings where children have been interviewed again by the authors as adults, amongst many other cases across the whole U.K. Each case is reviewed and original witnesses traced. You will read accounts by multiple witnesses from all of the public service professions, from police officers to a depot of railway staff. UFO shapes and sizes abound and remind us that the real UFOs are very often anything other than saucer shapes, which include silver orbs and moving craft of cylindrical, triangular and side-on wing shaped objects with no conventional aerodynamic attribute to staying in the air at all. There is a reminder of the physical effects experienced by witnesses, with photographic evidence of skin blisters that bear no relation to everyday irritation or burns after being proximity to a sighting. Entities encountered include beings with solid appearance and yet barely humanoid in form and many encounters describing craft occupants far beyond the 'alien grey' icons of the mass media.

There are police officers of various ranks on and off duty, motorway drivers taken aback by the seemingly impossible sighted whilst driving on long journeys. A wide selection of different cases from different UFO groups in the U.K. and independent researchers show that there were hundreds of cases this year, including Hilary Porter's encounter and a police officer who attends a mysterious death near a railway line, only to also have a vivid close encounter case occur whilst on patrol himself which bore no direct relation to the railway line Adamski case. Incidents focus on missing time and multiple accounts of occupants leaving a landed craft and in addition to many press clippings, there are early accounts beckoning to a massive rise in the fascination and reporting of the crop circle phenomena.

The Rendlesham sequences in this book have new accounts of high strangeness inside and outside the base perimeters by both military and civilian workers and the local villagers in the districts around the near and wider proximity to the twin airbases. Leading researchers and key witnesses of the December 1980 events are interviewed and also forthcoming with new material, including the behaviour and reactions of senior staff ranks and departments in the higher command structures of the United States Air Force and the U.K. Ministry of Defence. Radar operators, control tower staff, security police, flight maintenance, farmers, local workers, forestry and gamekeepers, local villages and houses bordering the bases with all ages and professions have stories to tell of very strange lights and closer encounters. Key authors are highlighted and their quest for information in the compiling of their profiles of the case. 'Haunted Skies' also looks at the leading investigators that brought this particular case to the fore and the progressive appearance of key witness accounts not exclusively at the airbase but in the wider local population too.

Finally, we are reminded of what a strange place the forest is, with events that have occurred before and after the famous event up to the present day. New cases bought to attention, excellent reviews of unfamiliar cases and new accounts added to well known cases. This whole series continues to set a benchmark in the chronology of UFO events and how people, often with no previous interest in the whole subject, have been subject to various encounters with the unexplained. These are their stories and the 'Haunted Skies' relays them to you without bias, so you can draw your own conclusions and take your own curiosity further."

David Bryant- 1.12.2013 – *"Just stunning a perfect supplement to Georgina, Brenda & Larry's books: bang up to date, copiously illustrated in colour, page after page of intriguing, well-researched data...This is the latest (and IMHO, the best!) in John & Dawn's magnum opus: – their great relationship with Col. Halt makes this THE definitive account of events at Rendleham Forest!"*

By Derek Savory – 18th December, 2013 – *"Excellent book. Well put together. Its crammed full of witness statements pictures newspaper cuttings etc. – these guys really have put some work into this. As books go this is one of the best books I have read – a must read for newcomers and us old school that remember most of the cases presented. I would highly recommend this book."*

By the reader – 12th February, 2014 – *"These books are great – all the dates and places of sightings in Britain – just wished they had photos but still worth buying."*

By Majors – 7th January, 2014 – *"Once again John and Dawn have surpassed themselves with this edition. Very well researched with colour pictures also included for the first time. UFO's not real? Yeah right. Too much evidence by too many respected people. Recommended."*

By Philip Kinsella – 27th November, 2013 – *"This is a most comprehensive piece of work with regards to the Rendlesham UFO mystery. John Hanson and Dawn Holloway have done it again! I would urge anyone remotely interested in the case to purchase this book and make up their own minds about what they think really happened in Suffolk, England in 1980. Considered England's Roswell, this book deserves to stand as one of the most detailed accounts with regards to the case. An excellent read and very well written book. It's 5 stars from me. The 'TRUTH' is out there!!!!!"*

By Martin Marshall – 23rd May, 2015 – *"This surely has been the best read I've had so far since beginning my 'quest' to find out more and more as to what happened in the forest in 1980. So glad John and Dawn and Brenda continue to inform and record what is really happening out there ! Thank You. Thank You"*

Volume 9 Reviews – Amazon

By dolittlee – 7th April, 2014 – *"A lot thicker than previous editions in this series, bough for as present so can't comment on it, but my husband loved it."*

By Walkswithwolves – 27th May, 2014 – *"Anyone with a serious interest in ufology should read these books, because rather than go over old ground or do a rehash of something we already know or have read, John & Dawn have spent many years putting in the footwork , doing the research and travelling all over to personally interview witnesses and the result is the fantastic 'Haunted Skies' series which is a new and fresh read that you'll want re-read or use as a reference guide from time to time. Cannot wait for Vol 10."*

By Derek Savory – 17th January, 2014 – *"Excellent book for the people new to the subject and those of us who have been involved for years. Crammed full of reports, pictures, information. Very well put together with a lot of research. A must read for everyone."*

By fireground monkey – 9th March, 2014 – *"John Hanson has compiled a fantastic catalogue of UFO information and is of great value to anyone studying this subject."*

Volume 10 Reviews – Amazon

By David P. Bryant – 27th October, 2014 – *"This, the latest in an impressive series, is a vast collection of carefully-researched data about the global UFO phenomenon. Each new volume shows improved standards of graphics and collation and the switch to a new publisher was a wise move. Whether you read the book from cover to cover or just dip in to research a particular event, this is a 'must have' for students of the subject."*

By Derek Savory – 24th September, 2014 – *"Excellent book, as are all the volumes. This is crammed full of people's accounts. My own encounter is in this and the author took the trouble to actually come to see me at Rendlesham Forest on several occasions and visit the site of my encounter. A must have for anyone interested in this subject."*

By Majors – 2nd December, 2014 – *"Once again 'The UFO Team' deliver all the facts in a clear and concise manner. Recommended to all – even the sceptics. 10/10"*

Volume 11 Reviews – Amazon

By Martin Marshall – 17th June, 2015 – *"Looked forward to receiving this wonderful record of John Hanson and Dawn Holloway and Brenda Butler's passion and dedication to the haunted skies we live under. Thank you so much will treasure this."*

Mike Blake – 6th August, 2015 – *"Wow! Visually stunning, I must have flipped through the book as much as read it. I loved it. The sources are all newspapers or sighting reports, many filled out in the witnesses own handwriting. This book presents cases unknown here in the United States. I loved this book. It would rank top 20 or so in all-time UFO books I have read. I have read over 4,000."*

By K. Turley – 4th January, 2016 – *"I bought this as I have an interest in the period covered as I had a sighting a year later (which I hope will be covered in Vol 12 ??). I just took delivery of this and have been blown away by the quality and effort of the production. Absolutely packed with contemporary news articles, photos, witness diagrams, etc etc. This is a stunning production and I take my hat off to the authors. If you have an interest in the UFO subject from whatever period I would suggest you pick up a volume or two – you wont be disappointed. More than outdid my expectations. Highly recommended."*

Volumes 1 to 6 *not* currently available – Being Revised and Updated

Volume 1 of *Haunted Skies* 1940-1959 *(Foreword by Timothy Good)*

We present sightings from the Second Word War. They include many reports from allied pilots, who describe seeing unidentified flying objects, while on bombing missions over Germany. Some pilots we interviewed told of being ordered to intercept a UFO; one pilot was even ordered to open fire! In addition to these are reports of early close encounters, involving allegations of abduction experiences.

Another report tells of strange 'beings' seen outside an RAF Base. We also outline a spectacular sighting, in 1957, that took place in Bedfordshire, which appears identical to that seen over Oregon by employees of the Ames Research Laboratory, San Francisco. There are also numerous reports of 'saucer', 'diamond' and 'cigar-shaped' objects seen during these years.

Volume 2 of *Haunted Skies* 1960-1965 *(Foreword by Jenny Randles)*

We re-investigated what may well be one of the earliest events, involving mysterious crop circles discovered in June 1960, at Poplar Farm, Evenlode. A 'V'-shaped UFO over Gloucestershire, and an example of a early 'Flying Triangle' over Tyneside in early September 1960. This type of object attracted much media interest in the early 1980s, following attempts by the Belgium Air Force to intercept what became labelled as 'Triangular' UFOs. This book contains many reports of saucer-shaped objects, and their occasional effect on motor vehicles. We also, wherever possible, include numerous personal letters and interviews with some of the researchers. We should not forget the early magazines, such as UFOLOG, produced by members of the (now defunct) Isle of Wight UFO Society.

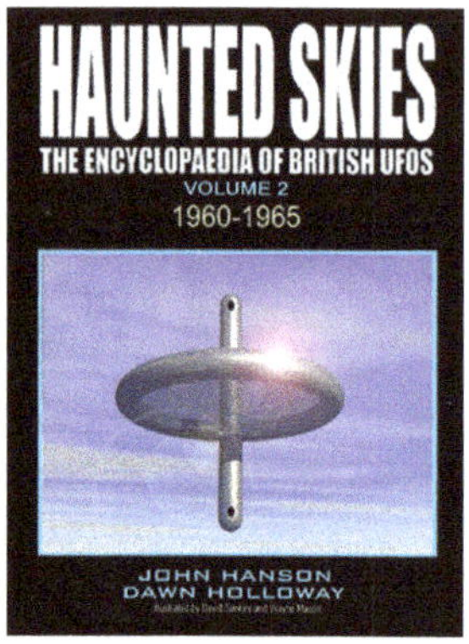

Volume 3 of *Haunted Skies* 1966-1967 *(Foreword by Nick Redfern)*

This was two years before manned landings took place on the Moon. In October 1967, there was a veritable 'wave' of UFO sightings which took place in the UK, involving cross-shaped objects, reported from Northumberland to the South Coast, with additional reports from Ireland and the Channel islands. (The police in the USA also reported sightings of 'Flying Crosses'). The sightings took place at various times, mostly during the evening or early morning hours, and involved an object which was manoeuvrable, silent – and at times – apparently flying at a low altitude. Attempts were made by the police and various authorities to explain away the sightings as Venus, based on the fact that the planet was bright in the sky during this period, which is clearly, in the majority of sightings, not the answer.

Volume 4 of *Haunted Skies* 1968-1971 *(Foreword by Philip Mantle)*

This book begins with a personal reference to Budd Hopkins, by USA researcher – Peter Robbins.

We outline a close encounter from Crediton, in Devon, which was brought to the attention of the police. Further police sightings of UFOs have been tracked down from Derbyshire, and a police chase through Kent. Multiple UFO sightings occur over the Staffordshire area, which are brought to the attention of the MOD. UFO researchers – Tony Pace and Roger Stanway – travel to London to discuss the incidents with the MOD. Close encounters at Warminster are also covered. A domed object at Bristol and further UFO landings are covered. They include a chilling account from a schoolteacher, living near Stratford-upon-Avon, and a 'flying triangle' seen over Birmingham.

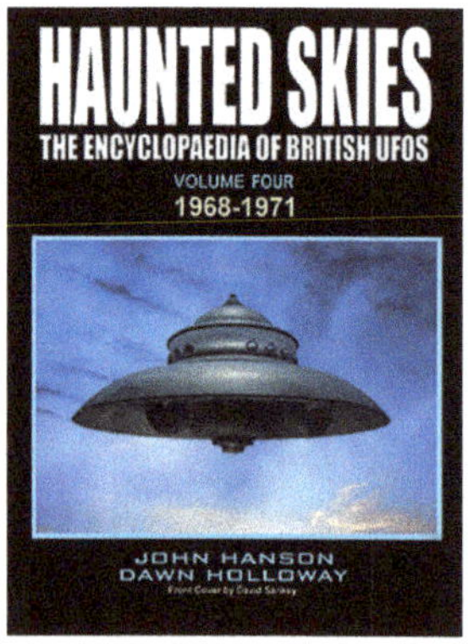

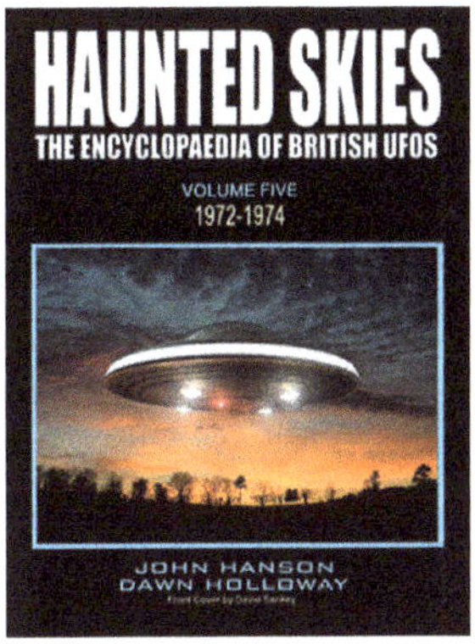

Volume 5 of *Haunted Skies* 1972-1975 *(Foreword by Matt Lyons, Chairman of BUFORA)*

Further examples of UFO activity at Warminster, involving classic 'sky watches' from such locations as Cradle Hill, was the focus of worldwide attention during this period. In addition to this are reports of mysterious footsteps heard. A visit from the 'Men in Black', and other amazing stories, form just a tiny part of some amazing material collected by us, over the years, during personal interviews with the people concerned. UFO fleets are seen over Reading, and a landed saucer-shaped object is seen at Lancashire.

A UFO, containing aliens, is seen at close range over Worcestershire. A local councillor also described seeing what he believes was an alien spaceship, with occupants. There is also an investigation into the famous Berwyn Mountain incident, when it was alleged, by some, that a 'craft' had landed.

Volume 6 of *Haunted Skies* 1976-1977 Jubilee edition *(Foreword by Kevin Goodman)*

Strange globes of light, seen moving in formations of three (often referred to as triangular in overall shape). Warminster, Wiltshire – reports of mysterious black shadows, flying globes of light and a triangular-shaped UFO seen over Cleeve Hill, near Cheltenham by police officers. There is also an investigation into a number of reported landings of alien craft around the Dyfed area, in February 1977. We present some original illustrations, drawn by children at the local school (which will be reproduced in colour, in a later edition of Haunted Skies). A triangular UFO is seen over Stoke-on-Trent. Comprehensive details were also obtained, regarding Winchester woman, Joyce Bowles – who was to report many encounters with UFOs and their alien occupants.

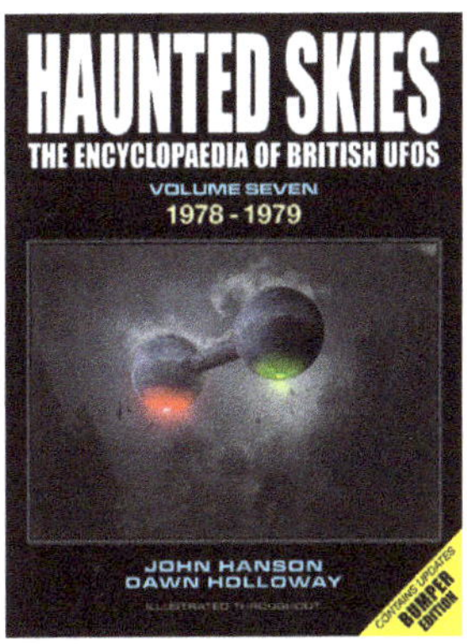

Volume 7 of *Haunted Skies* 1978-1979 *(Foreword by David Bryant)*

The famous debate into UFOs, held at the United Nations, is covered. A UFO landing at Rowley Regis, West Midlands – involving housewife Jean Hingley – labelled by the Press as the 'Mince Pie Martian' case. Many original sketches and additional information supporting her claims are offered. Another classic UFO sighting is re-investigated, following interviews held with Elsie Oakensen – a housewife from the Daventry area – who sighted a dumb-bell shaped UFO while on the way home from work. Thanks to Dan Goring, editor of EarthLink we were able to include a large number of previously unpublished sighting reports from Essex and London. We also include a close encounter from Didsbury, Manchester involving Lynda Jones, who is known personally to us.

Volume 8 of *Haunted Skies* 1980 *(Foreword by Philip Mantle)*

This book covers the period of just one year and is now, for the first time in the *Haunted Skies* series of books, published in colour. Unfortunately, due to the increase in pagination and the use of colour, the price has been raised, but still represents extremely good value. The first part of the book covers the period from January to November 1980. This includes numerous reports of UFO sightings and encounters. In addition to this, we outline our investigation into the Zigmund Adamski death, and the UFO sighting involving Todmorden Police Constable Alan Godfrey. In the second part, which covers December 1980, we present a comprehensive overview of the events that took place in Rendlesham Forest, thanks to the assistance of retired Colonel Charles Halt and long-standing UFO researcher, Brenda Butler.

Volume 9 of *Haunted Skies* 1981-1986 *(Foreword by Nick Redfern)*
Over 450 pages, many in colour

The authors point out that the majority of the information contained within the *Haunted Skies* series of books will not be found in declassified UFO files, catalogued in the Public Records Office, Kew, London.

This book contains:

UFO sightings over RAF Woodbridge, Suffolk – the scene of much interest during the previous month; a landed UFO at South Yorkshire; UFOs seen over Kent – harrowing close encounters between UFOs and motorists are outlined. These include a report from three women, driving home along the A5 in rural Shropshire (UK), which can be contrasted with a similar allegation made by three women from Kentucky, USA. A close encounter over the M50 Motorway, Gloucestershire; a couple from Hampshire tell of their roadside encounter – which left the husband with some strange marks on his body; a man out fishing, in Aldershot – who was approached by aliens; mysterious apports of stones that occurred, over a number of years, at Birmingham, West Midlands, involving the police – who staked out the locality in a bid to catch the offender. In addition to this, falls of coins and stones in other parts of the world are also outlined.

Although primarily covering British UFO sightings – wherever space permits (always in short supply) – we now include other forgotten worldwide cases of interest, brought to the attention of the reader. One such incident tells of a triangular UFO, seen over Arizona; another of a UFO sighted by a Russian astronaut.

A bizarre story involving David Daniels, who approached a number of prominent worldwide UFO researchers during the early 1980s – he alleged he was from the Pleiades and claimed to be able to metamorphosise from a human body to a reptilian. While it is difficult to believe rationally that this could be true, the authors tell of visits made to influential people, such as the head of the MOD, and The Lord Hill-Norton. Fact is stranger than fiction!

Volume 10 of *Haunted Skies* 1987-1988 *(Foreword by Nick Pope)*
632 pages, many in colour

Includes a focus on UFO cases reported from USA, Australia and New Zealand, 1940-1962.

Volume 10 of *Haunted Skies* catalogues the results of over 20 years research into reported UFO activity by the authors. The majority of those sightings and personal experiences will not be found in any declassified MOD files. Despite promises by their department to release specific individual files from 1971 (which we brought to their notice), the situation remains unchanged.

This volume covers the period of 1987-1988; which documents not only British UFO activity but also UFO activity from New Zealand, Australia and the United States, and forms an ongoing process by the authors to document such matters. In addition, a number of historical UFO cases between the periods 1940 and 1962 is also presented.

The book contains over 600 pages – many in colour – including numerous original illustrations relating to increased UFO activity over the Essex area. In addition to this, the authors outline a mysterious incident in 1987, involving claims of a UFO crash-landing in Nottinghamshire, and a spectacular sighting of goblin-like creatures that invaded a farm in Kentucky. A number of thought-provoking images, captured on camera, are shown from locations such as Cumbria, Rendlesham Forest and the Sedona area of the United States.

Volume 11 of *Haunted Skies* 1989-1990 *(Foreword by Charles I. Halt, USAF Col. Ret.)*
756 pages, many in colour

Includes a focus on UFO cases reported from UK, USA, Australia and New Zealand, 1963-1964.

Volume 11 contains over 750 pages with a foreword written by retired USAF Colonel Charles Halt – then the Deputy Base Commander of RAF Woodbridge – during the now famous UFO incident that has attracted worldwide attention, which took place in late December 1980. In this Volume the the authors continue their examination of further chronological reports of UFO activity over Great Britain, USA, Australia, New Zealand and Tasmania, for the period 1989-1990.

They also include previously unpublished material from the late Essex UFO researcher Ron West, which shows that the Essex area, like its Belgium and European counterparts, was the source of much UFO activity involving sightings of the Flying Triangle .

There is also an examination of historical UFO reports covering the period of 1963-1964, which includes sightings from the archives of Project Blue Book for the first time. In addition, the Volume outlines the valuable commitment made by the researchers themselves and their efforts to preserve what forms part of our important social history, rather than relying on other dubious sources of information.
The authors point out that very few of the UFO sighting reports published in the *Haunted Skies* books will be found in any declassified MOD files.

The Halt Perspective *(Foreword by Nick Pope)*
Over 780 pages, many in colour

Over three nights running, in December 1980, a series of UFO encounters occurred at RAF Bentwaters and United States Air Force Woodbridge – twin bases, in Suffolk.

"As the Deputy Base Commander in a senior management position, I knew most of the main witnesses to the reported sightings, and was involved in investigating these incidents. Additionally, as many of the readers will know, I was a witness myself to UFO activity taking place in the nearby forest. I wasn't sure what to make of what I and the other airmen saw. Other than briefly reading a book as a teenager, I never gave any thought to UFOs, although I had read one or two out of interest.

I asked UK retired Police Officer, John Hanson, to assist me with the publication of this book in order to set the record straight, instead of relying on the continuing rumours about what did or didn't take place. Ironically, when initially confronted with the unexplained, I did everything in my power to keep the events quiet. Over the years there has been so much rubbish and sensational accounts given in the media surrounding the allegations made, who talk of missing time, alien beings meeting with the base commander, and so forth – more in keeping with science fiction than reality! I decided it was time to let people know exactly what took place and then make up their own minds, rather than trusting assessments made by people who weren't there and continuing publication of so much misinformation over the last 36 years. My own personal perspective on what took place needs to be told for posterity's sake." **Colonel Charles I. Halt USAF Retired**

RECOMMENDED READING

OUR FORBIDDEN MOON

David Bryant's book *'Our Forbidden Moon'* has taken fifteen years of meticulous planning and research to write. During meetings with over thirty astronauts and cosmonauts, including seven of the twelve alleged Moonwalkers, the author gradually became aware of a number of major inconsistencies in their recollections of the Apollo program. Furthermore, in occasional unguarded moments, several space travellers have revealed personal experiences of the UFO phenomenon and hinted at even more dramatic encounters.*'Our Forbidden Moon'* examines these revelations and considers whether there might be a link between UFOs, extraterrestrial races and mankind's forty-year failure to travel beyond low Earth orbit. The author uses his knowledge gained during forty years as a teacher, lecturer and respected authority on spaceflight and meteoritics to ask controversial questions and provide convincing solutions.

UFOS OVER POLAND – The land of high strangeness

(Paperback and Kindle) Publishers Phil Mantle of Flying Disk Press (2016) – Author: Piotr Cielebiaś-on sale on Amazon

A unique history of UFO sightings and close encounters from Poland published in English for the very first time. Fully illustrated with 10 black & white photos and illustrations.

UFOS OVER POLAND is no ordinary book and certainly is not just another book about Flying Saucers. It is, instead, quite extraordinary.

For those who thought that the UFO phenomenon was only reported in the West then think again. This book covers, in extraordinary detail, UFO close encounters, military pilot's sightings, observations by police officers, UFO crash accounts and encounters with other-worldly beings that are the stuff of nightmares. It comes fully illustrated and is published in English for the very first time.

DISCLAIMER

Should we have inadvertently missed anybody, we unreservedly apologise and will credit the copyright in *Haunted Skies,* Volume 12.

Special thanks go to Philip Mantle, 'Modo', Steven Franklin, David Sankey, David Boardman and Wayne Mason for their assistance – and Dawn Holloway for editing/proof-reading the book.

Also thanks to many others that have contributed over the years including the typesetter/UFO Consultant, Bob Tibbitts – now a personal friend and long-time UFO researcher.

All statements made by the people in the book involved are opinions expressed by them and should be treated as such.

These books have cost us a great deal of money to produce, but we strongly believe that this information forms part of our social history and rightful heritage. It should therefore be preserved, despite the ridicule still aimed at the subject by the media.

If anyone is willing to assist us with the preparation of any illustrations, it would be much appreciated. We can be contacted by letter at **31, Red Lion St, Alvechurch, Worcestershire B48 7LG**, by telephone **0121 445 0340**, or email: **johndawn1@sky.com** • Website: **www.hauntedskies.co.uk**

Lightning Source UK Ltd.
Milton Keynes UK
UKHW050750061120
372914UK00001BA/1

9 780995 642805